THE LOEB CLASSICAL LIBRARY

FOUNDED BY JAMES LOEB

EDITED BY

G. P. GOOLD

DIO CHRYSOSTOM

III

LCL 358

DIO CHRYSOSTOM

DISCOURSES 31–36

WITH AN ENGLISH TRANSLATION BY

J. W. COHOON

AND

H. LAMAR CROSBY

HARVARD UNIVERSITY PRESS
CAMBRIDGE, MASSACHUSETTS
LONDON, ENGLAND

First published 1940
Reprinted 1951, 1961, 1979, 1995

ISBN 0-674-99395-0

Printed in Great Britain by St Edmundsbury Press Ltd,
Bury St Edmunds, Suffolk, on acid-free paper.
Bound by Hunter & Foulis Ltd, Edinburgh, Scotland.

CONTENTS

PREFACE

The first Oration in this volume, addressed to the Rhodians, is the work of Professor J. W. Cohoon, as were the first two volumes of Dio Chrysostom in the Loeb Classical Library. Unfortunately Professor Cohoon was obliged to relinquish further work upon this author and Professor H. Lamar Crosby is responsible for Orations XXXII–XXXVI in this volume and for the remaining two volumes.

THE EDITORS.

DIO CHRYSOSTOM

THE THIRTY-FIRST DISCOURSE:
THE RHODIAN ORATION

Some information about the island of Rhodes and its capital city of the same name may contribute to an appreciation of this Discourse.

The island, which has an area of approximately 424 square miles, lies in the extreme eastern part of the Aegean Sea and is about ten miles south of Cape Alypo, the ancient Cynossema Promontorium, on the coast of Asia Minor. From it one can see to the north the elevated coast of Asia Minor and in the south-east Mount Ida of Crete. It is still noted for its delightful climate and its fertile soil.

There is a legend that the earliest inhabitants of Rhodes were the Telchines, skilled workers in metal, and the Children of the Sun, who were bold navigators; yet, whatever the racial affinity of these people may have been, in historic times the population was Dorian.

In the fifth century before Christ its three cities of Lindus, Ialysus, and Camirus were enrolled in the Delian League, but in 412 B.C. they revolted from Athens. Then in 408 they united to form the new city of Rhodes on the north-east tip of the island. This city presented a very impressive appearance, laid out as it was by the architect Hippodamus in the form of an amphitheatre on a gentle slope running down to the sea.

After the founding of this city the prosperity and political importance of the island steadily increased. It threw off the yoke of Athens in the Social War, 357–354, and although it submitted first to Mausolus of Caria and then later to Alexander the Great, it reasserted its independence after the latter's death, greatly expanded its trade, and became

more powerful than before, so that its standard of coinage and its code of maritime law became widely accepted in the Mediterranean. In 305–4 the city successfully withstood a siege by the redoubtable Demetrius Poliorcetes, who by means of his formidable fleet and artillery attempted to force the city into an active alliance with King Antigonus. On raising the siege Demetrius presented the Rhodians with his mighty siege-engines, from the sale of which they realized enough to pay for the Colossus, the celebrated statue of the Sun-god, one hundred and five feet high, which was executed by Chares of Lindus and stood at the entrance of the harbour.

In 227 Rhodes suffered from a severe earthquake, the damages of which the other states helped to restore because they could not endure to see the state ruined. Chiefly by her fleet Rhodes supported Rome in her wars against Philip V. of Macedon, Antiochus III., and Mithridates, who besieged the city unsuccessfully in 88. It assisted Pompey against the pirates and at first against Julius Caesar; but in 42 that Caius Cassius who formed the conspiracy against Caesar's life captured and ruthlessly plundered the city for refusing to submit to his exactions; and although befriended by Mark Antony after this, it never fully recovered from the blow. In the year 44 of our era, in the reign of Claudius, it lost its freedom temporarily, but recovered it at the intercession of Nero, who throughout his life remained very friendly to Rhodes. Then at the beginning of the reign of Vespasian it was reduced to a Roman province. This has been considered the end of Rhodes' freedom. Von Arnim, however (*Leben und Werke*, 217–218), gives good reason for believing that Rhodes was given its freedom again for a short time under Titus. This view is accepted by Van Gelder (*Geschichte der alten Rhodier*, 175), who suggests that this may have occurred somewhat later under Nerva or Trajan, by Hiller von Gaertringen in his article on Rhodes in Pauly-Wissowa, Suppl. V., col. 810, and by Lemarchand in his *Dion de Pruse*, 84.

Rhodes was noted for its paintings and its sculpture. In Dio's time the city is said to have had 3000 statues. (See Pliny the Elder 34. 7. 36 and cf. § 146 of this Discourse.) Then too it was the birthplace of the philosopher Panaetius, whose pupil, the philosopher and historian Poseidonius, had his school there; Apollonius Rhodius also spent part of his

3

THE THIRTY-FIRST DISCOURSE

life there; and in this city both Cicero and Caesar in their youth studied rhetoric under Apollonius Molo.

This Rhodian oration, by far the longest of Dio's extant Discourses, purports to have been delivered by Dio before the Rhodian Assembly. In it Dio urges the Rhodians by all possible arguments to give up their bad habit of not actually having the statue of a man made and set up when one was decreed him as an honour, but of simply having his name engraved on some statue already standing, after first chiselling out the name, if any was there, which was already on the statue.

This Discourse throws an interesting light upon the time in which Dio lived. Then it was thought one of the highest honours for a man to have a statue of himself which was erected by public decree in a city like Rhodes, so that even Romans sought this honour. No doubt it was because so many Romans whom Rhodes could not afford to offend brought pressure to bear in order to secure the honour of a statue, that this practice of ' switching inscriptions ' developed. The city already had some 3000 statues in its temples and streets, and yet many others were anxious for the honour of a statue. This was all the vogue at that time. Lemarchand (op. cit., 58) quotes from Cicero, Plutarch, Philo, Favorinus, Pausanias, Pliny the Elder, and Dio Cassius to show that the practice was not unknown elsewhere. Yet perhaps it had well-nigh ceased by Dio's time, for in §§ 105–106, 123 he says that the Rhodians alone are guilty of it.

Von Arnim thinks that this address was not actually delivered, that it was merely written. The Rhodians, he says, met in Assembly to deal with matters of state, would not have been willing to listen to such a " long-winded expectoration " on a subject not on the order of the day. He points also to the unusually careful avoidance of hiatus. Lemarchand, on the other hand, who believes that we have here at least two addresses by Dio on the same subject, which were later made into one by some editor (perhaps by Dio himself, who then carefully removed cases of hiatus), thinks that at least the first address was actually delivered. He feels that the speech is not a unit on account of the numerous repetitions and contradictions in it which he lists, and on account of two different styles and tones, the one dry and dull, the other vigorous and at times impassioned.

4

THE RHODIAN ORATION

Von Arnim, in attempting to date this Discourse, takes into account three factors: Rhodes is a free city (see for example §§ 111–113), Nero is dead (as may be inferred from §§ 148–150), and the Discourse shows Dio as a sophist, yet not hostile to philosophy, as he was in early life according to Synesius. To be sure Rhodes was free until 70 or 71 of our era, but he feels that even then Dio, who would have been about twenty-four years old, he says (about thirty would be nearer the truth if Dio was born about A.D. 40), would still have been too immature to compose such a speech as this. Therefore he would put this speech in the reign of Titus, when, as he attempts to show, Rhodes regained its freedom for a time.

Lemarchand, on the other hand, with his theory of two speeches, at least, combined into one, would place the first speech in the early years of Vespasian's reign, when Rhodes had just lost its freedom. For in this first speech Dio does not once refer to the freedom of Rhodes and sections 45–46 imply that it is not free, he says. The second speech, where Rhodes is spoken of as free, he would put in the reign of Titus; and he would accept von Arnim's contention that Rhodes then regained its freedom for a short time.

ΔΙΩΝ ΧΡΥΣΟΣΤΟΜΟΣ

31. ΡΟΔΙΑΚΟΣ

1   Εἰκὸς μέν ἐστιν, ὦ ἄνδρες Ῥόδιοι, τοὺς πολλοὺς ὑμῶν ἐμὲ νομίζειν ὑπὲρ ἰδίου τινὸς πράγματος ἐντευξόμενον ὑμῖν ἀφῖχθαι· ὥστε ἐπειδὰν αἴσθησθε τῶν ὑμετέρων τι κοινῶν ἐγχειροῦντα ἐπανορθοῦν, δυσχερανεῖτε ἴσως, εἰ μήτε πολίτης ὢν μήτε κληθεὶς ὑφ᾿ ὑμῶν, ἔπειτα ἀξιῶ συμβουλεύειν, καὶ ταῦτα ὑπὲρ οὐδενὸς ὧν σκεψόμενοι συνελη-
2 λύθατε. ἐγὼ δὲ ἂν μὲν ὑμῖν ἀκούσασιν ἢ μηδὲν τῶν δεόντων ἢ περί τινος τῶν μὴ πάνυ ἀναγκαίων φανῶ λέγων, δικαίως ἂν ἀμφότερά φημι δόξειν, ἅμα εὐήθης καὶ περίεργος· ἐὰν δ᾿ ὡς οἷόν τε καὶ περὶ μεγίστου πράγματος, καὶ τούτου σφόδρα φαύλως ἔχοντος, ὥστε δημοσίᾳ τὴν πόλιν ἀπ᾿ αὐτοῦ διαβεβλῆσθαι καὶ πάντας ὑμᾶς ἐπὶ πᾶσι τοῖς ἄλλοις εὐδοκιμοῦντας καθ᾿ ἓν τοῦτο δόξης οὐ προσηκούσης τυγχάνειν, εἰκότως ἂν μοι χάριν ἔχοιτε καὶ νομίζοιτε εὔνουν ἑαυτοῖς. δῆλον γὰρ ὡς εἰ καὶ [1] μὴ πάνυ τις ὑμᾶς ἀγαπᾷ, τοῖς

---

[1] καὶ added by Cohoon.

---

[1] The application is obviously to Dio himself.

DIO CHRYSOSTOM

THE THIRTY-FIRST DISCOURSE:
THE RHODIAN ORATION

It is reasonable to suppose, men of Rhodes, that the majority of you are thinking that I have come to talk to you about some private matter; consequently, when you perceive that I am attempting to set right a matter which concerns your own general interests, you will perhaps be vexed that I, who am neither a citizen nor have been invited to come here, yet venture to offer advice, and that too concerning no one of the subjects for the consideration of which you have assembled. But for my part, if after hearing me you find that the topic on which I am speaking is either inappropriate or not altogether urgent, I say that I shall be rightly regarded as both foolish and officious. But if you find that my topic is really of the greatest possible importance, and, furthermore, that the situation of which I speak is very bad indeed, so that the state as such is in evil repute on that account, and that you yourselves, one and all, though you bear a good reputation in everything else, in this one matter do not enjoy the general esteem to which you are entitled, you would have good reason to be grateful to me and to regard me as a true friend of yours. For it is evident that even if any person [1] is not altogether content with you, the

7

γε ἄλλοις οὐθὲν μέλει δήπου τῶν ὑμῖν τινα φερόν-
3 των αἰσχύνην ἢ βλάβην. οὐκοῦν ἄτοπον, εἰ
μὲν ἀργύριόν τις ὑμῖν ἐχαρίζετο ἀφ' ἑαυτοῦ,
ξένος ἢ μέτοικος, τοῦτον μὲν οὐκ ἂν ἡγεῖσθε
περίεργον, ὅτι, μηδὲν προσήκειν δοκῶν, ἐφιλοτι-
μεῖτο μηδ' ὑμῶν ἀπαιτούντων, συμβουλεύοντος
δέ τι τῶν χρησίμων δυσχερέστερον ἀκούσεσθε,
ὃς ἂν μὴ τύχῃ κληθεὶς ἢ μὴ πολίτης ὑπάρχῃ;
καίτοι χρημάτων μὲν οὔθ' ὑμεῖς σφόδρα ἴσως ἐν
τῷ παρόντι δεῖσθε, καὶ μυρίους ἔστιν εὑρεῖν,
οἷς μᾶλλον ἂν[1] ἀφελέσθαι[2] τῶν ὄντων συνέφερε·
γνώμης δὲ ἀγαθῆς οὐκ ἔστιν οὐδεὶς ὁ μὴ δεόμενος
ἐν παντὶ καιρῷ καὶ πρὸς ἅπαντα τὸν βίον, οὐδ'
ὁ κάλλιστα πράττειν δοκῶν.

4 Εἰ μὲν οὖν περί τινος τῶν προκειμένων ἔλεγον,
οὐθὲν ἂν[3] ὑπ' ἐμοῦ τηλικοῦτον ὠφελεῖσθε· εἰκὸς
γὰρ ἦν καὶ καθ' αὑτοὺς ὑμᾶς τὸ δέον εὑρεῖν σκο-
ποῦντάς γε ἅπαξ· ἐπεὶ δὲ ὑπὲρ οὗ μηδὲ ζητεῖτε τὴν ἀρχὴν ὅπως ποτὲ ἔχει,[4] τοῦτό φημι
δείξειν αἴσχιστα γιγνόμενον, πῶς οὐκ ἂν εἴην
παντελῶς ὑμῖν χρήσιμον πρᾶγμα πεποιηκώς,
ἐὰν ἄρα μὴ φανῶ ψευδόμενος; νομίζω δ'
ἔγωγε πάντα μὲν προσήκειν ἀποδέχεσθαι τῶν δι'
εὔνοιαν ὁτιοῦν λεγόντων καὶ μηδένα ὀχληρὸν

---

[1] ἂν added by Emperius, Geel.
[2] ἀφελέσθαι Cohoon, ἀφειδοῦσι Weil, Naber, Schwartz.
ἀποβαλοῦσι Geel: ἀφελοῦσι.
[3] ἂν added by Reiske.
[4] ἔχει Reiske: ἔξει BM, ἔξῃ U.

8

world at large, as you presumably know, cares not at all about those matters which may bring upon you some shame or injury. Is it not, therefore, very strange that, whereas if a man, a foreigner or a resident alien, were offering you a gift of money out of his own means, you would not consider him officious just because, although under no apparent obligation to do so, he was zealous on your behalf even though you did not demand it, and yet, if a man offers you useful advice, just because he happens not to have been invited to do so or is not a citizen you are going to listen with considerable vexation to whatever he has to say? And yet as for money, perhaps you are in no pressing need of it at the moment, and, besides, thousands can be found to whom it would be a greater benefit to have taken away from them some of the money they have; but as for good advice, there is no one who does not stand in need of it at every moment and for every circumstance of life, even the man who is regarded as most successful.

Now if I were speaking about one of the questions which are before you, you would not be so greatly benefited by me, for you would be reasonably sure to arrive at the proper conclusion by yourselves if you were once to consider the problem. But since, in discussing a matter concerning which you are not even making any attempt at all to ascertain what the situation is, I assert that I shall prove that it is being most disgracefully managed, shall I not have done you an altogether useful service—that is, if I shall, indeed, prove not to be misrepresenting the facts? And what I think myself is, that it is right to welcome any man who, moved by a spirit of friendliness, has anything whatever to say, and to regard no such one

ποιεῖσθαι τῶν τοιούτων, μάλιστα δὲ ὑμᾶς, ἄνδρες
Ῥόδιοι. δῆλον γὰρ ὅτι τούτου χάριν σύνιτε
βουλευόμενοι καθ᾽ ἡμέραν, καὶ οὐ καθάπερ
ἄλλοι δυσκόλως καὶ διὰ χρόνου καὶ τῶν ἐλευθέρων
τινὲς εἶναι δοκούντων, ὅπως ὑμῖν ᾖ σχολὴ περὶ
πάντων ἀκούειν καὶ μηδὲν ἀνεξέταστον παρα-
λίπητε.

5   Ταυτὶ μὲν οὖν ἦν ἀναγκαῖον προειπεῖν, ὥστε
τὴν ἀρχὴν ὑμᾶς ἐπὶ τοῦ πράγματος γενέσθαι·
νυνὶ δὲ ἐπ᾽ αὐτὸ βαδιοῦμαι, τοσοῦτον ὑπειπών,
ὅτι μοι προσήκειν δοκεῖ πάντα μὲν πράττειν
δικαίως καὶ καλῶς τὰ κατὰ τὸν βίον, ἄλλως τε
τοὺς δημοσίᾳ ποιοῦντας ὁτιοῦν, οὐ μόνον ἐπειδὴ
τὰ κοινὰ ὑπάρχει φανερώτερα, ὧν ἂν ἕκαστος
ἰδίᾳ πράττῃ μὴ δέον, ἀλλὰ καὶ δι᾽ ἐκεῖνο ὅτι τὰ
μὲν τῶν ἰδιωτῶν ἁμαρτήματα οὐκ εὐθὺς ἀποφαίνει
τὴν πόλιν φαύλην, ἐκ δὲ τῶν δημοσίᾳ γιγνομένων
οὐχ ὃν προσήκει τρόπον ἀνάγκη δοκεῖν καὶ τοὺς
6   καθ᾽ ἕνα μοχθηρούς. ὁποῖοι γὰρ ἂν ὦσιν οἱ
πλείους ἐν δημοκρατίᾳ, τοιοῦτο φαίνεται καὶ τὸ
κοινὸν ἦθος· τὰ γὰρ τούτοις ἀρέσκοντα ἰσχύει
δήπουθεν, οὐχ ἕτερα. μάλιστα δ᾽ ἂν φαίην
ἔγωγε τοῖς καλλίστοις καὶ σεμνοτάτοις οἰκεῖον
εἶναι χρῆσθαι προσέχοντας· παρ᾽ οἷς γὰρ τὰ
τοιαῦτα ἀμελεῖται, καὶ κακίαν τινὰ ἐμφαίνει τῆς
πόλεως τῶν τε ἄλλων οὐδὲν οἷόν τε ἐπιτηδείως
7   πράττεσθαι. καὶ μὴν ὅτι γε τῶν πρὸς τοὺς θεοὺς
ἐξῃρημένων, ἃ δεῖ μέγιστα ἡγεῖσθαι, τῶν λοιπῶν
οὐδέν ἐστι κάλλιον οὐδὲ δικαιότερον ἢ τιμᾶν
τοὺς ἀγαθοὺς ἄνδρας καὶ τῶν εὖ ποιησάντων

10

as a nuisance, and especially, that you, men of Rhodes, should do so. For evidently the reason that you come together to deliberate every day and not, as other people do, reluctantly and at intervals and with only a few of you who are regarded as free-born being present, is that you may have leisure to hear about all matters and may leave nothing unexamined.

So much it was necessary to say by way of preface in order that you might understand the situation at the very beginning; and now I shall proceed to the subject itself, after simply adding that I think it is our duty to conduct all the affairs of life justly and honourably, and especially is it the duty of those who do anything in the name of the people; not only because official acts are more readily observed than private misdeeds, but also because, while the mistakes of persons in private station do not at once put the city in a bad light, improper action in public affairs inevitably causes every individual citizen to be looked upon as a knave. For in a democracy the character of the majority is obviously the character of the state, since it is their will, surely, and no one's else, that prevails. And I myself would venture to say that it is especially fitting that the majority should scrupulously observe the noblest and most sacred obligations; for in the state where such considerations are neglected, such neglect even reveals a sort of vicious defect in the body politic and no other matter can be properly administered. Furthermore, if we except the honours which we owe the gods, which we must regard as first in importance, of all other actions there is nothing nobler or more just than to show honour to our good men and to keep in remembrance those who have served us well—

μεμνῆσθαι νομίζω μηδὲ λόγου δεῖσθαι· καίτοι
καὶ τὸ συμφέρον οὐχ ἥκιστα ἐν τούτῳ τις ἂν
ἴδοι. τοὺς γὰρ σπουδαίους ὄντας περὶ τοὺς
εὐεργέτας καὶ τοῖς ἠγαπηκόσι δικαίως χρωμένους
πάντες ἡγοῦνται χάριτος ἀξίους καὶ βούλοιτ᾽
ἂν ἕκαστος ὠφελεῖν κατὰ τὴν ἑαυτοῦ δύναμιν·
ἐκ δὲ τοῦ[1] πολλοὺς ἔχειν τοὺς εὐνοοῦντας καὶ
συμπράττοντας, ὅταν ᾖ καιρός, καὶ πόλις πᾶσα
καὶ ἰδιώτης ἀσφαλέστερον διάγει.

8 Ταῦτα τοίνυν ἡγεῖσθε, ἄνδρες Ῥόδιοι, πάνυ
φαύλως παρ᾽ ὑμῖν ἔχοντα καὶ τῆς πόλεως οὐκ
ἀξίως, τὰ περὶ τοὺς εὐεργέτας λέγω καὶ τὰς
τιμὰς τῶν ἀγαθῶν ἀνδρῶν, οὐκ ἀρχῆθεν ὑμῶν
οὕτω τῷ πράγματι χρωμένων—πόθεν; τοὐναντίον γάρ, ὥσπερ ἄλλο τι τῶν ὑμετέρων διαφερόντως
ἂν τις ἀποδέξαιτο καὶ θαυμάσειεν, οὕτω μοι
δοκεῖτε καὶ τιμῆς μάλιστα προνοῆσαι· γνοίη δ᾽
ἄν τις εἰς τὸ τῶν εἰκόνων πλῆθος ἀπιδών—μοχθηροῦ
δὲ ἄλλως κατεσχηκότος ἔθους ἔκ τινος χρόνου,
καὶ μήτε τιμωμένου λοιπὸν παρ᾽ ὑμῖν μηδενός,
εἰ βούλεσθε τἀληθὲς εἰδέναι, τῶν τε πρότερον
γενναίων ἀνδρῶν καὶ περὶ τὴν πόλιν προθύμων,
οὐκ ἰδιωτῶν μόνον, ἀλλὰ καὶ βασιλέων καί τινων
δήμων ὑβριζομένων καὶ τὰς τιμὰς ἀποστερου-
9 μένων. ὅταν γὰρ ψηφίσησθε ἀνδριάντα τινί· ῥᾳδίως
δὲ ὑμῖν ἔπεισι τοῦτο νῦν ὡς ἂν ἄφθονον ὑπάρχον·

[1] ἐκ δὲ τοῦ Emperius : ἑκάστου Μ, ἑκάστους καὶ UB.

[1] For this practice elsewhere cf. Cicero, *Ad Atticum* 6. 1.
26, Equidem valde ipsas Athenas amo. volo esse aliquod
monumentum. *odi falsas inscriptiones statuarum alienarum.*
See also Plutarch, *Life of Antony* 60; Favorinus in Dio 37. 40;
Pausanias 2. 17. 3; Dio Cassius 59. 28; 63. 11; Philo, *Legatio
in Gaium* 20; Pliny the Elder *H.N.* 35. 2. 4.

that is my opinion and needs no argument; and yet one may most clearly see in the principle also a practical advantage. For those who take seriously their obligations toward their benefactors and mete out just treatment to those who have loved them, all men regard as worthy of their favour, and without exception each would wish to benefit them to the best of his ability; and as a result of having many who are well-disposed and who give assistance whenever there is occasion, not only the state as a whole, but also the citizen in private stations lives in greater security.

It is in regard to these matters, men of Rhodes, that I ask you to believe that the situation here among you is very bad and unworthy of your state, your treatment, I mean, of your benefactors and of the honours given to your good men, although originally you did not handle the matter thus—most assuredly not! Why, on the contrary, just as a person might very emphatically approve and admire any other practice of yours, so it is my opinion that you once gave very especial attention to bestowing honours, and one might recognize this to be so by looking at the great number of your statues—but it is only that a habit in another way bad has prevailed here for some time, and that nobody any longer receives honour among you, if you care to know the truth, and that the noble men of former times who were zealous for your state, not alone those in private station, but also kings and, in certain cases, peoples, are being insulted and robbed of the honours which they had received.[1] For whenever you vote a statue to anyone—and the idea of doing this comes to you now quite readily because you have an

ἐκεῖνο μὲν οὐκ ἂν αἰτιασαίμην, τὸ χρόνον τινὰ καὶ
διατριβὴν προσεῖναι· τοὐναντίον γὰρ εὐθὺς ἕστηκεν
ὃν ἂν εἴπητε, μᾶλλον δὲ καὶ πρότερον ἢ ψηφίσασθαι.
συμβαίνει δὲ πρᾶγμα ἀτοπώτατον· ὁ γὰρ στρατηγὸς ὃν ἂν αὐτῷ φανῇ τῶν ἀνακειμένων τούτων
ἀνδριάντων ἀποδείκνυσιν· εἶτα τῆς μὲν πρότερον
οὔσης ἐπιγραφῆς ἀναιρεθείσης, ἑτέρου δ' ὀνόματος ἐγχαραχθέντος, πέρας ἔχει τὸ τῆς τιμῆς,
καὶ λοιπὸν τέτευχε τῆς εἰκόνος ὁ δόξας ὑμῖν
ἄξιος, πάνυ ῥᾳδίως, οἶμαι, καὶ λυσιτελῶς οὑτωσὶ
σκοπουμένοις, ὥστε θαυμαστὴν εἶναι τὴν εὐπορίαν
καὶ τὸ πρᾶγμα εὐχῆς ἄξιον, εἰ μόνοις ὑμῖν ἔστιν
ὃν ἂν βούλησθε ἱστάναι χαλκοῦν δίχα ἀναλώματος
καὶ μηδεμίαν δραχμὴν μήτε ὑμῶν καταβαλόντων
10 μήτε τῶν τιμωμένων. τίς γὰρ οὐκ ἂν οὕτως
ἀγασθείη τῆς σοφίας τὴν πόλιν;

'Αλλ', οἶμαι, πολλὰ τῶν ἐν τῷ βίῳ γιγνομένων
καὶ [1] μετὰ πόνου πλείονος καὶ δαπάνης οὐ σμικρᾶς
ἔστι προῖκα καὶ πάνυ ῥᾳδίως ποιεῖν, εἴ τις ἀμελεῖ
τοῦ προσήκοντος καὶ τοῦ πράττειν ἀληθῶς. οἷον
εὐθὺς τὰς θυσίας, ἃς ἑκάστοτε τελοῦμεν τοῖς
θεοῖς, ἔστι μὴ θύσαντας φάσκειν τεθυκέναι, μόνον,
ἂν δοκῇ, στεφανωσαμένους καὶ τῷ βωμῷ προσ-
ελθόντας καὶ τῶν οὐλῶν [2] θιγγάνοντας καὶ τἆλλα
ποιοῦντας ὡς ἐφ' ἱερουργίας. τί δ'; οὐχὶ

---

[1] καὶ deleted by Arnim.
[2] οὐλῶν Valesius : οὐδῶν UB, ὁδῶν M.

abundant supply of statues on hand—though for one thing I could not possibly criticise you, I mean for letting a little time elapse and delaying action; for, on the contrary, as soon as any person is proposed for the honour by you—presto! there he stands on a pedestal, or rather, even before the vote is taken! But what occurs is quite absurd: your chief magistrate, namely, merely points his finger at the first statue that meets his eyes of those which have already been dedicated, and then, after the inscription which was previously on it has been removed and another name engraved, the business of honouring is finished; and there you are! The man whom you have decreed to be worthy of the honour has already got his statue, and quite easily, it seems to me, and at a good bargain, when you look at the matter from this point of view—that the abundance of supply is wonderful and your business a thing to envy, if you are the only people in the world who can set up in bronze any man you wish without incurring any expense, and in fact, without either yourselves or those whom you honour putting up a single drachma. Who, pray, from this point of view, could help admiring the cleverness of your city?

But I imagine that many things in life which require both special effort and no little expense can be done without cost and quite easily, if one disregards propriety and sincerity. Take, for instance, the sacrifices which we duly offer to the gods : it is possible simply to say they have been offered without offering them, merely, if you please, putting on our wreaths and approaching the altar, and then touching the barley groats and performing all the other rites as we do in an act of worship. And here is an idea! We

ταὐτὸ ἱερεῖον ἅπασιν ἐν κύκλῳ τοῖς ἀγάλμασι
προσάγοντας, τῷ τοῦ Διός, τῷ τοῦ Ἡλίου, τῷ
τῆς Ἀθηνᾶς, καὶ πανταχῇ κατασπείσαντας πᾶσιν
11 οἴεσθαι τεθυκέναι τοῖς θεοῖς οὐ ῥᾴδιον; τίς δ'
ὁ κωλύσων; ἐὰν δὲ δὴ βωμὸν ἢ ναὸν νῦν τινος
ἱδρύσασθαι θελήσωμεν· καὶ γὰρ εἰ πάντων εἰσὶ
παρ' ὑμῖν τῶν θεῶν, οὐκ ἀδύνατον οἶμαι καὶ
κρείττω κατασκευάσαι τοῦ πρότερον καὶ διὰ
πλειόνων τιμᾶν προελέσθαι τὸν αὐτόν· ἆρ' οὐχ
ἕτοιμον ἐξοικίσαι τινὰ τῶν ἄλλων θεῶν ἢ μετενεγκεῖν τι τῶν ἤδη καθιερωμένων; ἢ καὶ τὴν
ἐπιγραφὴν ἀλλάξαι μόνον, ὃ νῦν ποιοῦμεν; καίτοι
τὸν μὲν Ἀπόλλω καὶ τὸν Ἥλιον καὶ τὸν Διόνυσον
ἔνιοί φασιν εἶναι τὸν αὐτόν, καὶ ὑμεῖς οὕτω
νομίζετε, πολλοὶ δὲ καὶ ἁπλῶς τοὺς θεοὺς πάντας
εἰς μίαν τινὰ ἰσχὺν καὶ δύναμιν συνάγουσιν,
ὥστε μηδὲν διαφέρειν τὸ τοῦτον ἢ ἐκεῖνον τιμᾶν.
ἐπὶ δὲ τῶν ἀνθρώπων οὐθέν ἐστι τοιοῦτον· ἀλλ'
ὁ διδοὺς τὰ τοῦδε ἑτέρῳ τοῦτον ἀφῄρηται τῶν
ἑαυτοῦ.

12 Νὴ Δία, ἀλλ' οὐχ ὅμοιον τὸ παραβαίνειν τὰ
πρὸς τοὺς θεοὺς καὶ [1] τὰ πρὸς τοὺς ἀνθρώπους.

Οὐδ' ἐγώ φημι. παραβαίνειν δὲ ὅμως ἔστι καὶ
τὰ [2] πρὸς τούτους, ὅταν τις αὐτοῖς μὴ ὑγιῶς
προσφέρηται, μηδὲ τοὺς μὲν εἰληφότας ἐᾶν ἔχειν
ἅ γε δικαίως ἔλαβον, τοῖς δὲ ἀξίοις [3] δόξασι τῶν
αὐτῶν ὅ φησιν ὄντως διδούς, ἀλλὰ τοὺς μὲν
ἀποστερῶν τῆς δωρεᾶς, τοὺς δὲ ὥσπερ ἐνεδρεύων

[1] καὶ Cobet: ἤ.   [2] ἔστι καὶ τὰ Emperius: ἔστιν ἕκαστα.
[3] ἀξίοις Reiske: αἰτίοις.

---

[1] For this view see Antisthenes Φυσικός, Frag. 1, Winkelmann.

might lead the same sacrificial victim up to all the statues in turn: to that of Zeus, to that of Helius, to Athena's, and after pouring libations at each one, make believe that we have sacrificed to all the gods —would not that be easy? Who is going to prevent our doing this? And if we wish now to set up an altar or a temple to some god—for even though altars of all the gods are to be found among you, I take it that it is not impossible both to build a better altar than the last one you built and also deliberately to honour the same god by a greater number of them—is it not quite feasible to dispossess one of the other gods, or to shift one that has been already consecrated? Or else simply to alter the inscription—exactly as we are now doing? Indeed, some do maintain that Apollo, Helius, and Dionysus are one and the same, and this is your view, and many people even go so far as to combine all the gods and make of them one single force and power,[1] so that it makes no difference at all whether you are honouring this one or that one. But where men are concerned the situation is not at all like that; on the contrary, whoever gives A's goods to B robs A of what is rightfully his.

" Yes, by Zeus," someone says, " but there is no similarity between violating our obligation towards the gods and that toward men."

Neither do I say there is. But still it is possible to violate one's obligation towards men also, when one does not deal honestly with them, when one does not even permit those who have received anything to keep what they have justly acquired, or actually gives what the giver asserts he is giving to those who have been considered worthy of the same reward, but deprives the one class of their gift and deceives and

DIO CHRYSOSTOM

13 καὶ παραλογιζόμενος. ἡ μὲν οὖν φύσις τοῦ
πράγματος ὁμοία καὶ τὸ ποιεῖν ὁτιοῦν μετὰ
ἀπάτης καὶ φενακισμοῦ καὶ τῆς ἐσχάτης μικρολο-
γίας ταὐτό· διαφέρει δ᾽, ὅτι τὰ μὲν περὶ τοὺς
θεοὺς γιγνόμενα μὴ δεόντως ἀσεβήματα καλεῖται,
τὰ δὲ πρὸς ἀλλήλους τοῖς ἀνθρώποις ἀδικήματα.
τούτων τὴν μὲν ἀσέβειαν ἔστω μὴ προσεῖναι
τῷ νῦν ἐξεταζομένῳ πράγματι· τὸ λοιπὸν δέ,
14 εἰ μὴ δοκεῖ φυλακῆς ὑμῖν ἄξιον, ἀφείσθω. καίτοι
καὶ τὴν ἀσέβειαν εὕροι τις ἂν ἴσως τῷ τοιούτῳ
προσοῦσαν· λέγω δὲ οὐ περὶ ὑμῶν οὐδὲ περὶ τῆς
πόλεως· οὔτε γὰρ ὑμῖν ποτε ἔδοξεν οὔτε δημοσίᾳ
γέγονεν· ἀλλ᾽ αὐτὸ σκοπῶν κατ᾽ ἰδίαν τὸ πρᾶγμα·
τὰ γὰρ περὶ τοὺς κατοιχομένους γιγνόμενα οὐκ
ὀρθῶς ἀσεβήματα κέκληται καὶ τῆς προσηγορίας
ταύτης τυγχάνει παρὰ τοῖς νόμοις,[1] εἰς οὓς ἄν
ποτε ᾖ; τὸ δ᾽ εἰς ἄνδρας ἀγαθοὺς καὶ τῆς πόλεως
εὐεργέτας ὑβρίζειν καὶ τὰς τιμὰς αὐτῶν καταλύειν
καὶ τὴν μνήμην ἀναιρεῖν ἐγὼ μὲν οὐχ ὁρῶ πῶς
ἂν ἄλλως ὀνομάζοιτο· ἐπεὶ καὶ τοὺς ζῶντας
εὐεργέτας οἱ ἀδικοῦντες οὐκ ἂν εὐλόγως εἶεν
15 ἀπηλλαγμένοι τοῦδε τοῦ ὀνείδους. οἱ γοῦν περὶ
τοὺς γονεῖς ἐξαμαρτάνοντες, ὅτι τῆς πρώτης
καὶ μεγίστης ὑπῆρξαν εὐεργεσίας εἰς ἡμᾶς,
εἰκότως ἀσεβεῖν δοκοῦσιν. καὶ τὸ μὲν τῶν
θεῶν ἴστε δήπουθεν, ὅτι κἂν σπείσῃ τις αὐτοῖς
κἂν θυμιάσῃ μόνον κἂν προσάψηται, μεθ᾽ ἧς
μέντοι προσήκει διανοίας, οὐθὲν ἔλαττον πεποίη-

[1] For παρὰ τοῖς νόμοις Wilamowitz conjectured παρὰ τοῖς πολλοῖς.

18

hoodwinks the other. Now the essential nature of the act is the same,[1] and doing anything whatever with deceit and trickery and the extreme of niggardliness amounts to the same thing; but there is this difference, that unseemly actions in what concerns the gods are called impiety, whereas such conduct when done by men to one another is called injustice. Of these two terms let it be conceded that impiety does not attach to the practice under examination; and henceforth, unless it seems to you worth guarding against, let this matter be dropped. And yet even impiety might perhaps be found to attach to such conduct—I am not speaking about you nor about your city, for you never formally approved nor has the practice ever been officially sanctioned; I am considering the act in and of itself from the private point of view—for is it not true that wrong treatment of those who have passed away is rightly called impiety and is given this designation in our laws, no matter who those are against whom such acts are committed? But to commit an outrage against good men who have been the benefactors of the state, to annul the honours given them and to blot out their remembrance, I for my part do not see how that could be otherwise termed. Why, even those who wrong living benefactors cannot reasonably be clear of this reproach. At any rate those who wrong their parents, because these were the authors of the first and greatest benefaction to us, are quite fairly held guilty of impiety. And as for the gods, you know, I presume, that whether a person makes a libation to them or merely offers incense or approaches them, so long as his spirit is right, he has done his full

---

[1] i.e. whether it affects gods or men.

κεν· οὐδὲ γὰρ δεῖται τῶν τοιούτων οὐθενὸς ἴσως
ὁ θεὸς οἷον ἀγαλμάτων ἢ θυσιῶν· ἄλλως δὲ οὐ
μάτην γίγνεται ταῦτα, τὴν προθυμίαν ἡμῶν καὶ
16 τὴν διάθεσιν ἐμφαινόντων πρὸς αὐτούς. οἱ δὲ
ἄνθρωποι δέονται καὶ στεφάνου καὶ εἰκόνος καὶ
προεδρίας καὶ τοῦ μνημονεύεσθαι. καὶ πολλοὶ καὶ διὰ ταῦτα ἤδη τεθνήκασιν, ὅπως ἀνδριάντος
τύχωσι καὶ κηρύγματος ἢ τιμῆς ἑτέρας καὶ τοῖς
αὖθις καταλίπωσι δόξαν τινὰ ἐπιεικῆ καὶ μνήμην
ἑαυτῶν. εἰ γοῦν τις ὑμῶν πύθοιτο, ἁπάντων
τῶν τοιούτων ἀνηρημένων καὶ μηδεμιᾶς εἰς
ὕστερον μνήμης ἀπολειπομένης μηδὲ ἐπαίνου
τῶν εὖ πραχθέντων, εἰ καὶ [1] πολλοστὸν ἡγεῖσθε
μέρος ἂν γεγονέναι τῶν θαυμαζομένων παρὰ
πᾶσιν ἀνδρῶν ἢ τῶν ἐν πολέμῳ ποτὲ προθύμως
ἠγωνισμένων ἢ τῶν τυράννους καθῃρηκότων ἢ
τῶν ἑαυτοὺς ἢ τέκνα προειμένων [2] ἕνεκα [3] κοινῆς
σωτηρίας ἢ τῶν πόνους μεγάλους πονησάντων
ὑπὲρ τῆς ἀρετῆς, ὥσπερ Ἡρακλέα φασὶ καὶ
Θησέα καὶ τοὺς ἄλλους ἡμιθέους ποτὲ ἥρωας,
17 οὐκ ἂν οὐθένα εἰπεῖν οἶμαι. τὸ γὰρ προκαλού-
μενον ἕκαστον καὶ κινδύνων καταφρονεῖν καὶ
πόνους ὑπομένειν καὶ τὸν μεθ᾽ ἡδονῆς καὶ
ῥᾳθυμίας ὑπερορᾶν βίον οὐκ ἂν ἄλλο τις εὕροι
παρά γε τοῖς πλείοσι. τοῦτό ἐστι τὸ ποιοῦν ἐν

---

[1] καὶ added by Reiske.
[2] προειμένων Dindorf; προῃρημένων UB, προειρημένων M,
προεμένων T.
[3] ἕνεκα Dindorf : οὕνεκα.

---

[1] For the same thought cf. Seneca, De Beneficiis 1. 6. 3;
Poseidonius in Cicero, De Natura Deorum 2. 28. 71; Xenophon,

duty; for perhaps God requires no such thing as images or sacrifices at all.[1] But in any event these acts are not ineffectual, because we thereby show our zeal and our disposition towards the gods. But when we come to men, they require crowns, images, the right of precedence, and being kept in remembrance; and many in times past have even given up their lives just in order that they might get a statue and have their name announced by the herald or receive some other honour and leave to succeeding generations a fair name and remembrance of themselves. At any rate, if anyone should inquire of you, all things such as these having been taken away and no remembrance being left for future times nor commendation given for deeds well done, whether you think there would have been even the smallest fraction of men who are admired by all the world either because they had fought zealously in some war, or had slain tyrants, or had sacrificed themselves or their children in behalf of the common weal, or had undergone great labours for virtue's sake, as they say Heracles[2] did, and Theseus and the other semi-divine heroes of the past, no man here among you, I think, would answer yes. For you will find that there is nothing else, at least in the case of the great majority, that incites every man to despise danger, to endure toils, and to scorn the life of pleasure and ease. This is the reason why brave men are

Memorabilia 1. 3. 3; *Agesilaüs* 11. 2; Epictetus, *Encheiridion* 31; Dio Chrysostom 3. 52; 4. 76; 13. 35; 33. 28; Horace, *Odes*, 3. 23; *The Old Testament*, Isaiah 1. 11 ff.; *Psalm* 51. 16–17.

[2] Heracles, the pattern of the Cynics, according to them pursued virtue for its own sake, and Dio usually so represents him.

ταῖς μάχαις τοὺς ἀγαθοὺς ἄνδρας ἔμπροσθεν
εὑρίσκεσθαι τετρωμένους καὶ μὴ μεταστραφέντας
οἴχεσθαι, πολλάκις ἑτοίμου τῆς σωτηρίας ἀποκει-
μένης. διὰ τοῦτό φησιν ὁ ποιητὴς τὸν Ἀχιλλέα
μὴ θελῆσαι γηράσαντα ἀποθανεῖν οἴκοι, καὶ τὸν
Ἕκτορα μόνον στῆναι πρὸ τῆς πόλεως, εἰ δέοι,
18 πᾶσι μαχούμενον. τοῦτο ἦν τὸ ποιῆσαν Λακεδαιμονίων τινὰς ἐν τοῖς στενοῖς ἀντιτάξασθαι
πρὸς τοσαύτας Περσῶν μυριάδας. τοῦτο ἐποίησε
τοὺς ὑμετέρους προγόνους ἅπασαν γῆν καὶ
θάλατταν ἐμπλῆσαι τροπαίων καὶ τῆς λοιπῆς
Ἑλλάδος τρόπον τινὰ ἐσβεσμένης μόνους ἐφ᾽
αὑτοῖς[1] διαφυλάξαι τὸ κοινὸν ἀξίωμα τῶν
Ἑλλήνων εἰς τὸν νῦν παρόντα χρόνον. ὅθεν
εἰκότως μοι δοκεῖτε μεῖζον ἁπάντων ἐκείνων
19 φρονεῖν. οἱ μὲν γὰρ ἐν ἀρχῇ τὰ πρὸς τοὺς βαρβάρους εὐτυχήσαντες καὶ λαμπροὶ φανέντες τὰ
λοιπὰ ἐξήμαρτον, φθόνου μᾶλλον καὶ ἀνοίας
καὶ φιλονικίας ἤπερ ἀρετῆς ἐπίδειξιν ποιούμενοι,
μέχρι μηδενὸς ἔξωθεν ἐνοχλοῦντος αὐτοὶ παρ-
είθησαν καὶ πάντα ἤδη τὸν βουλόμενον εἶναι
δεσπότην ἐκάλουν. ὑμεῖς δὲ τοσούτους πολέμους
κατωρθωκότες ἅπαντας οὐχ ἧττον καλῶς
20 διελύσασθε[2] ἢ γενναίως ἐπολεμήσατε· πλὴν ἐκεῖνό
γε δῆλόν ἐστιν, ὅτι μήτε ὑμεῖς μήτε ἄλλοι τινές,
οἳ δοκοῦσιν Ἑλλήνων ἢ βαρβάρων μεγάλοι

---

[1] αὑτοῖς Reiske : αὐτοὺς UM, ἑαυτοὺς B.
[2] διελύσασθε Arnim : ἀνείλεσθε. Cf. Isocrates *Panegyric*
172 : " For we do not settle our wars, but only postpone
them "—οὐ γὰρ διαλυόμεθα τοὺς πολέμους ἀλλ᾽ ἀναβαλλόμεθα.

found on the battlefield wounded in front instead of having turned and fled, though safety was often ready at hand. This is what the poet gives as Achilles' reason for refusing to grow old and die at home,[1] and for Hector's standing alone in defence of his city, ready if need be to fight against the entire host. This is what made a mere handful of Spartans stand in the narrow pass against so many myriads of Persians.[2] It was this which made your ancestors fill every land and sea with their monuments of victory, and when the rest of Hellas in a sense had been blotted out, to guard the national honour of the Hellenes by their unaided efforts up to the present time.[3] For this reason I think that you are justified in feeling greater pride than all the rest of them taken together. For whereas the others at the beginning did win successes against the barbarians and made themselves a brilliant name, for the rest they failed by giving a display of jealousy, folly, and quarrelsomeness rather than of virtue, until, although no foreign power was troubling them, they deteriorated of themselves and finally invited anyone who wished to be their master. But you Rhodians, who have won so many wars, have settled them all no less honourably than you have gallantly waged them. However, this much is clear, that neither you nor any others, whether Greeks or barbarians, who are thought to

---

[1] Achilles' mother, Thetis, told him that it was his fate either to gain glory and die young, or to live a long but inglorious life. Achilles chose the former.

[2] Leonidas with his three hundred Spartans was slain in 480 B.C. while trying to hold the western end of the pass of Thermopylae against the vast army of Xerxes. See Herodotus 7. 209–233.

[3] Cf. Demosthenes 20 (*Against Leptines*) 64 f.

γενέσθαι, δι' ἄλλο τι προῆλθον εἰς δόξαν καὶ δύναμιν ἢ τῶν κατὰ μέρος φιλοτίμων [1] τυχόντες καὶ
περὶ πλείονος τοῦ ζῆν ἡγουμένων τὴν ὕστερον
εὐφημίαν. ἡ γὰρ στήλη καὶ τὸ ἐπίγραμμα καὶ
τὸ χαλκοῦν ἑστάναι μέγα δοκεῖ τοῖς γενναίοις
ἀνδράσι, καὶ μισθὸς οὗτος ἄξιος τῆς ἀρετῆς τὸ
μὴ μετὰ τοῦ σώματος ἀνῃρῆσθαι τὸ ὄνομα μηδ'
εἰς ἴσον καταστῆναι τοῖς μὴ γενομένοις, ἀλλὰ
ἴχνος τι λιπέσθαι καὶ σημεῖον, ὡς ἂν εἴποι τις,
τῆς ἀνδραγαθίας.

21   Τοὺς ἀγωνιστὰς τούτους ὁρᾶτε ὅσα πάσχουσι
γυμναζόμενοι, δαπανῶντες, τὸ τελευταῖον ἀποθνῄ-
σκειν αἱρούμενοι πολλάκις ἐν αὐτοῖς τοῖς ἄθλοις.
τί οὖν; εἴ τις ἀνέλοι τὸν στέφανον, οὗ χάριν
φιλοτιμοῦνται, καὶ τὴν ἐπιγραφὴν τὴν ἐσομένην
Ὀλυμπίασιν ἢ Πυθοῖ τῆς νίκης, ἆρ' οἴεσθε
μίαν ἡμέραν αὐτοὺς ἀνέξεσθαι τὸν ἥλιον μόνον,
οὐχ ὅπως τὰ ἄλλα ὅσα τῷ πράγματι πρόσεστιν
ἀηδῆ καὶ χαλεπά; τί δ'; ἐὰν γένηται δῆλον αὐτοῖς
ὅτι τὴν εἰκόνα, ἣν ἂν στήσωσιν, ἕτερος αὐτοῦ
ποιήσεται, τὸ μὲν τοῦ θέντος ὄνομα ἀνελών,
αὑτὸν δὲ ἐπιγράψας, ἔτι θεασόμενον ἡγεῖσθε
ἐλθεῖν ἄν τινα ἐκεῖσε, οὐχ ὅπως ἀγωνιούμενον;
ὅθεν, οἶμαι, καὶ βασιλεῖς ἐπιδικάζονται τῆς τοιαύτης
22   μαρτυρίας. ἅπασι γάρ ἐστι περὶ πολλοῦ τὰ
τῆς ἀρετῆς σύμβολα, καὶ οὐδεὶς αἱρεῖται τῶν
πολλῶν, ὅ τι ἂν οἴηται καλὸν εἶναι, μόνον αὑτῷ
πεπρᾶχθαι, μηδένα δὲ εἰδέναι.

        [1] φιλοτίμων Reiske : φιλοτιμῶν.

    [1] For the thought of §§ 16–22 cf. Demosthenes *In Lept.*
64 ; 23. 136 ; Aeschines *In Ctes.* 245 f. ; Lycurgus, *In Leocr.*
46 ; Cicero, *Pro Archia* 11. 26.
    [2] Cf. Demosthenes *In Lept.* 41.

have become great, advanced to glory and power for any other reason than because fortune gave to each in succession men who were jealous of honour and regarded their fame in after times as more precious than life. For the pillar, the inscription, and being set up in bronze are regarded as a high honour by noble men, and they deem it a reward worthy of their virtue not to have their name destroyed along with their body and to be brought level with those who have never lived at all, but rather to leave an imprint and a token, so to speak, of their manly prowess.[1]

You see what hardships these athletic competitors endure while training, spending money, and finally often even choosing to die in the very midst of the games. Why is it? If we were to abolish the crown for the sake of which they strive, and the inscription which will commemorate their victory at the Olympian or the Pythian games, do you think that they would endure for even one day the heat of the sun, not to mention all the other unpleasant and arduous things which attach to their occupation? Well then, if it becomes clear to them that any statue of them which their countrymen may set up another man is going to appropriate, first removing the name of the victor who dedicated it and then putting his own name there, do you think that anyone will go there any longer even to witness the games, to say nothing of competing? It is for this reason, I think, that kings, too, claim such testimony as this.[2] For all men set great store by the outward tokens of high achievement, and not one man in a thousand is willing to agree that what he regards as a noble deed shall have been done for himself alone and that no other man shall have knowledge of it.

Πρὸς τοῦ Διός, ἆρα ἀγνοεῖτε τοῦτο τὸ ἔργον οὐκ ἐκείνους μόνον ἀτίμους ποιοῦν, ἀλλὰ καὶ τὴν πόλιν ἔρημον τῶν εὐνοησόντων καὶ προθυμησομένων ὑπὲρ αὐτῆς; μηδὲ γὰρ ἐκεῖνο εἰσέλθῃ μηδένα ὑμῶν ὅτι εἴπερ ἄρα μίαν τιμὴν καταλύσετε τὴν τῶν εἰκόνων, αἱ λοιπαὶ δή εἰσιν ἀναφαίρετοι. πρῶτον μὲν γὰρ οἱ τὴν μεγίστην ἀναιροῦντες καὶ ἧς μάλιστα ἕκαστος ἐπιθυμεῖ τυγχάνειν, ὁμολογοῦσι δήπουθεν ἐκ τοῦ πλείονος μέρους τὴν πόλιν βλάπτειν, εἴ γέ φασι βλαβερὸν εἶναι τὸ πάσας αὐτὰς καταλελύσθαι.

23 Πρὸς τούτῳ δὲ κἀκεῖνό ἐστιν, ὅτι παρ' οἷς ἂν ἕν τι κινηθῇ, παρ' ἐκείνοις κεκίνηται πάντα ὁμοίως καὶ τῶν παραπλησίων βέβαιον οὐθέν ἐστιν. οἱ γὰρ τὴν αἰτίαν παραβάντες, καθ' ἣν οὐκ ἂν ἐδόκει τι συμβῆναι, καὶ ταύτην παρ' οὐδὲν ἡγησάμενοι, πάντα λελύκασιν ἃ τὴν αὐτὴν εἶχε πρόφασιν τοῦ μένειν βέβαια. οἷον εἴ τις μίαν λύσαι τῶν τιμωριῶν ἡντιναοῦν, οὐδὲ τῶν 24 ἄλλων οὐδεμίαν ἰσχυρὰν καταλέλοιπεν. εἰ δέ γέ τις τὴν μεγίστην ἀνέλοι, φυγὴν ἢ θάνατον, τά γε ἐλάττω τῶν ἐπιτιμίων λοιπὸν ἀνάγκη μηδὲ γεγράφθαι δοκεῖν. ὥσπερ οὖν οἱ παραχαράτ-

---

[1] Cf. Demosthenes, *In Lept.* 22 : "And no one will be willing to do us a service if he sees that those who did so in the past have been wronged "; also *ibid.* 7. 17, 50, 155.

[2] The ' principle ' in this case being that all citizens should have all possible incentives for serving the state and enhancing its glory, and the ' certain thing ' (evidently undesirable since it was to be prevented from happening) being the annulling of the chief incentive, the public bestowal of honours like statues.

In Heaven's name, do you fail to recognize that this action of yours not only deprives those men of honour, but also leaves the city destitute of men who will be well-disposed and strenuous in her behalf?[1] For let not the thought enter the mind of any of you, that even if you do abolish that one honour, the honour of the grant of a statue, the other honours, nevertheless, cannot be taken away. For, in the first place, those who annul the greatest honour and that which every man is most anxious to gain, admit, I presume, that they are doing injury to the state in the greatest degree, since they concede that it would be injurious that *all* honours should have been abolished.

Moreover, there is this also to be considered—that wherever one part of an institution has been changed, there all parts alike have suffered change and no similar institution is secure. For those who have infringed the principle by observing which it was believed that a certain undesirable thing[2] would not happen, and because they thought the principle was of no importance, have thereby undermined every institution whose stability rested upon the same premises.[3] For instance, if a person should do away with any one whatsoever of the penalties of the law, he has not left any of the others secure either. And if a man were to do away with the greatest of your punishments, banishment or death, it would necessarily be thought in the future that the lesser penalties also were not even on the statute books. Therefore, just as

---

[3] Cf. Demosthenes, *In Lept.* 120: "Whenever you take away any of the gifts which you once gave to anybody, you will destroy the confidence which the recipients have had in all your other gifts."

τοντες τὸ νόμισμα, κἂν μέρος λυμήνωνται, τὸ
σύμπαν διεφθαρκέναι δοκοῦσιν ὕποπτον[1] ποιήσαντες, ὁμοίως οἱ τῶν τιμῶν τινας ἢ τῶν τιμωριῶν
ἀναιροῦντες ὅλον τὸ πρᾶγμα καταλύουσι καὶ
25 τοῦ μηδενὸς ἄξιον δεικνύουσι. καὶ μὴν εἴ τίς
με ἔροιτο, τὴν μεγίστην ὡς οἷόν τε ἑκατέρων
βλάβην φερόντων, τοῦ τε τὰς τιμὰς ἀπίστως
ἔχειν καὶ τοῦ τὰς τιμωρίας ἀσθενῶς, εἰ μὴ δυνατὸν
ἀμφότερα εὐλαβηθῆναι, πότερον αὐτῶν ἐπιεικέστερον κρίνω καὶ μετριωτέρων ἀνθρώπων, οὐκ ἂν
διστάσας τὸ περὶ τὰς τιμωρίας εἴποιμι· εἴ γε
τοῦτο μὲν ἔστιν ἀνενεγκεῖν εἰς φιλανθρωπίαν,
εἰς ἔλεον, εἰς ἄλλα τοιαῦτα, ἅπερ ἐστὶν οἰκεῖα τοῖς
χρηστοῖς· τὸ δὲ τῶν ἀρίστων ἀνδρῶν ἐπιλανθά-
νεσθαι καὶ τὰ τῆς ἀρετῆς ἆθλα ἀποστερεῖν οὐκ
ἔνι τυγχάνειν οὐδεμιᾶς εὐπρεποῦς προφάσεως,
ἀλλ' ἀχαριστίᾳ, φθόνῳ,[2] μικρολογίᾳ, πᾶσι τοῖς
αἰσχίστοις ἀνάγκη προσήκειν. ἔτι δὲ οἱ μὲν
τοὺς ὄντως[3] πονηροὺς ἧττον κατείργουσι, τὰς
κολάσεις ἀνιέντες· οἱ δὲ αὐτοὶ τὰ μέγιστα
ἐξαμαρτάνουσι περὶ τοὺς εὐεργέτας. τοσούτῳ
δὲ τοῦτο ἐκείνου κάκιον ὅσῳ τὸ αὐτὸν ἀδικεῖν τοῦ
μὴ σφόδρα κωλύειν ἕτερον.
26   Οὐ τοίνυν οὐδὲ ἐκεῖνο ἔστιν εἰπεῖν, ὅτι μὴ τοῦτο
ὑπάρχει μέγιστον τῶν δεδομένων τισί· δίχα γὰρ
τοῦ πᾶσιν εἶναι φανερὸν ἑαυτοῖς ἐναντία ἐροῦσιν
οἱ λέγοντες. φασὶ γὰρ ἀνάγκην εἶναι πολλοὺς

---

[1] ὕποπτον Capps : ὑπαίτιον.
[2] φθόνῳ Reiske : φθόνος UB, φθόνως M.
[3] ὄντως Capps : ὄντας.

---

[1] Cf. Demosthenes In Lept. 154; In. Tim. 215.
[2] Cf. Demosthenes In Lept. 5 ff.; 39.

men who falsely stamp the currency, even if they injure only a part, are regarded as having ruined the whole by making it suspect, in like manner those who annul any of the honours or the punishments are doing away with the whole system and showing that it is worth nothing whatever. Moreover, if anyone were to put this question to me: Admitted that each of the two things causes the greatest possible harm, namely, that there should be no confidence in the honours which a city bestows and that the punishments it inflicts should be ineffectual, if it is not possible to guard against both, which of them I consider more conducive to justice and characteristic of more respectable men, I should unhesitatingly say in reply, "That its punishments should be ineffectual," since this can be credited to humanity, to pity, and to other sentiments of that nature, the very qualities that characterize good men. But to let the memory of the noblest men be forgotten and to deprive them of the rewards of virtue cannot find any plausible excuse, but must be ascribed to ingratitude, envy, meanness and all the basest motives.[1] Again, whereas the former, when they relax their punishments, merely slacken their constraint upon those who are really bad, the latter are themselves committing the greatest sins against their benefactors. This is just as much worse than the other as committing a wrong yourself is worse than failing rigorously to prevent another man from committing a wrong.[2]

So, then, it cannot be said, either, that this is not the greatest of the gifts that have been given to any persons, since, apart from the fact that the truth is patent to everyone, those who deny it will be contradicting themselves. For they protest that it is

ἐν τῷ παρόντι τιμᾶν τῶν ἡγουμένων, οἷς ἅπασιν
εἰκόνας εἰ δεήσει κατασκευάζεσθαι, μεγάλην τινὰ
ἔσεσθαι τὴν δαπάνην, ὡς τάς γε ἄλλας τιμὰς οὐκ
οὔσας κατ᾽ αὐτοὺς οὐδὲ ἀποδεξομένων αὐτῶν ὡς
27 πολὺ ἐλάττους. τὸ μὲν δὴ τῆς δαπάνης οἷόν ἐστιν
ὄψεσθε μετὰ μικρόν· τὸ δὲ μεγίστην εἶναι τῶν
τιμῶν, ἣν ἀφαιροῦνται τοὺς εἰληφότας πρότερον,
ἐκ τούτων ὡμολόγηται.

Καὶ μὴν ἀτόπου γε ὄντος τοῦ τινα παρεῖναι
τῶν ἀξίων τιμῆς καὶ μηδεμίαν παρασχεῖν ἀμοιβὴν
τῆς εὐεργεσίας, ὡς πάντων μάλιστα ἀνάγκη τούτοις
ὁμολογεῖν, οἳ καὶ τὸ μετριώτερον τιμῆσαί τινα τῆς
ἀξίας δεινὸν οἴονται, τὸ τιμήσαντας, ἔπειτα δ᾽
οὐδὲν αἰτιωμένους ἀφαιρεῖσθαι τὰ δοθέντα πῶς
οὐχ ὑπερβολὴν ἀδικίας ἔχει; τὸ μὲν γὰρ ἀχαριστεῖν
ἐστι τοῖς εὐεργέταις, τὸ δὲ ὑβρίζειν εἰς αὐτούς,
τὸ μέν ἐστι μὴ τιμᾶν τοὺς ἀγαθοὺς ἄνδρας, τὸ
28 δὲ ἀτιμάζειν. οἱ μὲν γὰρ ἃ δοκοῦσι τοῖς ἐπιεικέσιν ὀφείλειν οὐ παρέχουσιν, οἱ δὲ ἃ σύνηθές ἐστι
γίγνεσθαι κατὰ τῶν ἄκρως πονηρῶν, ταῦτα πράττουσι κατ᾽ αὐτῶν. εἰ γοῦν τις τῶν ποτε νομισ-
θέντων μετρίων αὖθις ἀνήκεστον ἁμάρτοι τι
καὶ χαλεπόν, οἷον εἰ προδοσίαν βουλεύσειεν ἢ
τυραννίδα, τῶν τοιούτων ἔθος ἐστὶ τὰς τιμὰς
ἀναιρεῖσθαι, κἂν ἐπιγραφῇς τινος πρότερον
ὦσι τετυχότες. εἶτ᾽ οὐκ αἰσχρὸν τῶν αὐτῶν
ἀξιοῦν ὑμᾶς τοὺς ὁμολογουμένως ἀρίστους,

---

[1] For the view that the honour should be left see Favorinus
in Dio 37. 31.

necessary to honour many of the leading men at the present time, and that if it proves necessary to get statues made for them all, enormous expense will be incurred, since the other honours are not in keeping with their position, and the men themselves would not accept them, as being far too inadequate. As to the matter of expense, you will see in a short time what there is in that plea. But that this is the greatest of your honours which they are taking away from the former recipients, is by this protest conceded.

Again, since it is preposterous to pass over any one of those who are worthy of honour and to offer no recompense for his benefaction, as those men above all others must admit who think it a terrible thing even to bestow a lesser honour than a person deserves; is it not an excess of wrong-doing to honour men and then, though having no fault to find with them, to deprive them of what has been given them? The one act, namely, means being ungrateful to your benefactors, but the other means insulting them; the one is a case of not honouring the good men, the other, of dishonouring them. For whereas in the one case you merely fail to grant to men of excellent character what you believe is their due, in the other case you give them the treatment which is customarily accorded to men who are utterly base. If, for instance, any man who formerly was thought respectable should afterwards commit any unpardonable and grievous sin, such as plotting treason or a tyranny, the practice is to revoke this man's honours, even if previously he had received the honour of an inscription.[1] Then is it not a disgrace for you to consider that men who are admittedly the noblest deserve the same treatment as that which the laws command to be

ὧν τοὺς ἀσεβεῖς καὶ τοὺς ἀνοσίους τυγχάνειν οἱ
νόμοι κελεύουσιν, οἷς οὐδὲ ταφῆς μέτεστιν;
29 ὥστε μοι δοκοῦσιν, ὅσην παρ' ἑτέροις ἔχουσι
τοῦ τιμᾶσθαι πάντες ἐπιθυμίαν, τοσαύτην ἢ
καὶ πλείονα ἕξειν παρ' ὑμῖν, ὅπως μηδέποτε
τεύξονται τῶν τοιούτων μηδενός· ὅσῳ τὴν ὕβριν
ἕκαστος καὶ τὸ προπηλακισθῆναι μεῖζον ἡγεῖται
κακὸν ἢ τὴν τιμὴν ἀγαθὸν νενόμικεν. εἰ γοῦν
τινα καλοῖτε εἰς προεδρίαν ἢ πολίτην ἀναγράφοιτε,
μέλλοντες ὕστερον ἀναστήσειν ἢ τὴν πολιτείαν
ἀφελεῖσθαι, πολλὰ ἂν ἱκετεύσειεν ὑμᾶς ἐᾶν αὐτόν.
τοὺς γοῦν τυράννους ἢ τοὺς βασιλέας, ὧν αὖθις οἱ
βιαίως ἀρχθέντες καὶ παρανόμως τὰς εἰκόνας
ἀνεῖλον καὶ τὰ ὀνόματα ἠφάνισαν, ὅπερ, οἶμαι, καὶ
ἐφ' ὑμῶν συμβέβηκε, διατεινάμενος εἴποιμ' ἄν,
εἰ προῄδεισαν τοῦτο ἐσόμενον, μήτ' ἂν εἰκόνας
ἑαυτῶν ἐᾶσαί τινα στῆσαι μήτε ὀνόματα ἐγγράψαι.
30 Καίτοι τοῦτο οὐ μόνον ἐκείνους ἀδικουμένους
καὶ δεινὰ πάσχοντας, ἀλλὰ καὶ τὴν πρόφασιν
δείκνυσι κενήν, δι' ἣν ἴσως ὑμᾶς τινες ἀξιώσουσι
τοῦτο ποιεῖν, μᾶλλον δὲ κατὰ τοῦ πράγματος
οὖσαν. εἰ γὰρ ἀναγκαῖον ἅμα καὶ συμφέρον
φήσουσιν εἶναι καὶ ὑστέρους[1] τιμᾶν, πῶς οὐχ
ὑπεναντίον ἐστὶ τούτῳ τοὺς πρότερον οὕτω
τετιμημένους ὑβρίζειν; ὃ γὰρ τῶν πρότερόν τις
οὐκ ἂν εἵλετο λαβεῖν, εἰδὼς τοῦτο ἐσόμενον, πῶς

---

[1] εἶναι καὶ ὑστέρους Capps, νεωτέρους Schwartz, εἶναι τὸ
ἑτέρους καὶ ἑτέρους Sonny : εἶναι τὸ ἑτέρους or νέον αἴ τι ἑτέρους.

---

[1] On the thought of §§ 27–28 cf. Demosthenes In Lept. 97
and 117.

imposed on the impious and unholy, men who have not even a claim to burial?[1] Consequently, I think that, great as is the desire which all men have to receive honour among other peoples, they will have just as great a desire, or even a greater, that they may never receive any such honour among you; inasmuch as everyone considers the insult and contumely to be a greater evil than he has regarded the honour a good. If, for instance, you were to invite anyone to take a seat of honour or should enroll him as a citizen with the intention of afterwards unseating him or depriving him of his citizenship, he would earnestly implore you to leave him alone. · Take tyrants, for instance, or those kings whose statues were destroyed afterwards and whose names were blotted out by those who had been governed with violence and in defiance of law—the very thing, I am inclined to think, that has happened in your time also—I should emphatically say that, if they had foreseen that this was going to take place, they would not have permitted any city either to set up statues of themselves or to inscribe their names upon them.

And yet this argument shows, not only that these men are suffering injustice and outrageous treatment, but also that the argument by which some will perhaps urge that you shall continue your present practice is only an empty subterfuge, or rather, that it argues against the practice. I mean, if they shall say that it is both necessary and expedient to honour men of a later time also, is it not the very reverse of this to insult the men who in the past have received these honours? For what any man of former times would not have chosen to accept if he had known that this was going to happen, is it at all

εἰκός ἐστι τῶν νῦν τινα ἡδέως λαμβάνειν ὁρῶντα τὸ
γιγνόμενον; ὥστ' εἰ μὴ καὶ δι' ἐκείνους τοὺς
θᾶττον εὐεργέτας, ἀλλὰ τούτους γε οὓς νῦν τιμῶ-
31 μεν, εἰκὸς ἦν φυλάξασθαι τὸ πρᾶγμα. πάντες μὲν
γὰρ ὑπόπτως ἔχουσι πρὸς τὰ ὑπὸ τούτων διδόμενα
οὓς ἴσασι τῶν πρότερόν τινα[1] ἐπαινεθέντων καὶ
δοξάντων φίλων οὕτως ἀμελοῦντας, μάλιστα δὲ
οἱ τῶν αὐτῶν τυγχάνοντες, ὧν τοὺς εἰληφότας
ὁρῶσιν ἀπεστερημένους. εἰ δὲ δὴ καὶ ὅπως
αὐτοὶ· λάβωσι τοῦτο γίγνοιτο, μᾶλλον δὲ ὅπως
δοκῶσιν εἰληφέναι, παντελῶς ἤδη τὸ πρᾶγμα
εἰρωνείαν καὶ χλεύην νομίζουσιν. πολὺ δὲ βέλτιον
ἦν λέγειν τοῖς βουλομένοις ποιῆσαι[2] μικρὰ φροντίζειν
ὑμᾶς τῶν τάχιον τετιμημένων, ὅτι μηκέτι μηδεμία
χρεία τοῦ τιμᾶν τινά ἐστιν, ἢ τοὐναντίον οὐ
τὴν μεγίστην φασὶν εἶναι τῇ πόλει χρείαν καὶ
πρὸς πλείονας νῦν ἢ πρότερον, τοῦτο διαβάλλειν.
32 Καίτοι μὰ τὸν Δία καὶ τοὺς θεοὺς οὐδ' εἰ τὴν
ἀνωτάτην χάριν ὑμῖν ἕξειν ἔμελλον οἱ δοκοῦντες
νῦν τῶν εἰκόνων τυγχάνειν καὶ σφόδρα ἐπαινέσειν
τὸν δῆμον, οὐδ' οὕτως ἐχρῆν αὐτὸ γίγνεσθαι.
τὸ γὰρ μόνον ζητεῖν ἐξ ὧν ἄν τις ἀρέσαι τινὰ
ποιήσας καὶ προσαγάγοιτο, εἰ δ' ἄλλον ὃν οὐ
προσῆκεν ἀδικήσει τοῦτο ποιῶν ἢ καθόλου τι

---

[1] τινα deleted by Emperius.
[2] Arnim deleted ποιῆσαι.

reasonable to suppose that any man of the present day is glad to accept when he sees what is being done? Consequently, even if not on account of those former benefactors, yet at any rate on account of these whom we are now honouring, it stands to reason that you should guard against the practice. For all men look with suspicion on gifts which are proffered by those who to their knowledge disregard in this manner any person who formerly received public commendation and was regarded as a friend; but those men are especially suspicious who are getting the very honours of which they see that the previous recipients have been deprived. But if your motive should be that they were to receive this honour themselves, or, rather, be thought to have received it, they must at once look upon the action as downright pretence and a mockery. It would be much better to tell those who prefer to have you give yourselves very little concern about those who have previously been honoured, that there is no longer any need for honouring anybody at all, rather than, on the contrary, to bring into disrepute that practice which men say your city has the greatest need of and with respect to a greater number of persons now than ever before.

And yet, by Zeus and the gods, even if those who think they are now getting statues were going to feel the warmest gratitude towards you and to praise your democracy to the skies, not even so should this thing have been done. For merely to seek how one can please a person in what one does and how win his good will, and not to consider whether one will be wronging another person whom one should not wrong by so doing, or

μὴ δέον πράξει, μὴ σκοπεῖν, οὔτε μὰ τοὺς θεοὺς
ἐλευθέρων ἐστὶν ἀνθρώπων οὔτε μετρίων τὸ
ἦθος. οὐδεὶς γὰρ οὐδὲ τῶν πάνυ πονηρῶν προ-
αιρεῖταί τι φαῦλον, ὃ μὴ συμφέρειν ἑαυτῷ νομίζει
πρὸς τὸ παρόν, ἀλλ' ἔστιν αὐτὸ τοῦτο ἢ μοχθηρία
τὸ κέρδους ἕνεκα καὶ χρείας μηδενὸς αἰσχροῦ μηδὲ
ἀδίκου πράγματος ἀποστρέφεσθαι [1] μηδὲ φροντίζειν
ποῖον τὸ γιγνόμενον, ἀλλὰ μόνον εἰ λυσιτελές.
33 οὐκοῦν ὁ τὸν μὲν παρόντα θεραπεύων, ὀλιγωρῶν
δὲ τοῦ θᾶττον φίλου, καὶ τῆς μὲν γεγενημένης
χρείας ἐπιλελησμένος, τὴν δ' ἐλπιζομένην ὠφέλειαν
περὶ πλείστου ποιούμενος, ἆρ' οὐκ ἴστε ἧστινος
τυγχάνει προσηγορίας; οὐ κόλαξ ὁ τοιοῦτος
ὀνομάζεται παρὰ πᾶσιν; οὐκ ἀγεννής, οὐκ ἄπι-
στος δοκεῖ; νῦν τοίνυν οὐδὲ τοῦτο περιγίγνεται
τῇ πόλει, τὸ θεραπεύεσθαί τινας ὑπὸ αὐτῆς καὶ
μεγάλου τινὸς οἴεσθαι τυγχάνειν ὧν ἂν τὰ ὀνόματα ἐπιγράφηται. τοὐναντίον γὰρ δυσχεραί-
νουσι καὶ μέμφονται παρ' αὑτοῖς, εἰ καὶ σιωπῶσιν
ἄλλως, προσκρούειν οὐ θέλοντες. ἢ νόμισμα μὲν
εἴ τῳ χαρίζοισθε [2] κίβδηλον, οὐδεὶς ἂν ἑκὼν
λάβοι, μᾶλλον δὲ ὕβριν ἡγοῖτο ἢ δωρεὰν τὸ
γιγνόμενον· τιμὴν δὲ κίβδηλον καὶ μηδὲν ἔχουσαν
ὑγιὲς νομίζετε δέχεσθαι τοὺς νοῦν ἔχοντας;
34 ἀλλ' ἐὰν μὲν οἰκέτην τις ἀλλότριον ἢ σκεῦος
ἀποδῶται ψευσάμενος ὡς ἑαυτοῦ, σφόδρα ἕκαστος
ἀγανακτεῖ τῶν ἠπατημένων, καὶ θαυμάζοιμ' ἄν,
εἰ μὴ κἂν [3] θανάτῳ ἐζημιοῦτε τοῦτον ὑμεῖς· εἰ δ'

[1] ἀποστρέφεσθαι Cohoon : ἐπιστρέφεσθαι.
[2] χαρίζοισθε Reiske : χαρίζεσθε EM, χαρίζεσθαι B.
[3] κἂν added by Schwartz.

will be doing anything at all that one should not—by the gods I declare this befits neither liberal-minded men nor men of decent character. For no one, even the most wicked, chooses any base action which he does not think is to his own advantage at the time, but the essence of wickedness consists in being led by the desire for gain and profit to shrink from no base or unjust action and not to care about the nature of the act, but only whether it is profitable. Therefore, the man who courts the person who is present but slights his former friend, and having forgotten the service this friend has rendered, places the highest importance upon the hoped-for benefit from the other—do you not know the term that is applied to him? Is such a man not called a toady everywhere? Is he not considered ignoble, a man not to be trusted? As the case now stands, therefore, the city does not even get the advantage that sundry men are courted by her and so think they are getting a grand thing when their names are put into an inscription. For in fact the opposite is the case: they are annoyed and find fault when by themselves, even if on other occasions they are silent because they do not wish to give offence. Or if you should offer a man a counterfeit coin as a present, there is nobody who would ever willingly take it but would consider the offer an insult rather than a gift, and yet do you imagine that a counterfeit honour, a thing utterly worthless, is ever accepted by persons who have any sense? Yet if any one sells another man's slave, or chattel, falsely claiming that it is his own, the man who is deceived is without exception very indignant, and it would surprise me if you would not even punish the offence with death; but if

ἀλλοτρίαν τις εἰκόνα καὶ μηδὲν αὐτῷ προσήκουσαν
ἐξαπατηθεὶς λάβοι παρὰ τῶν μὴ κυρίων· ὃ γὰρ
ἂν ἄλλῳ δῷ τις, τούτου κύριος οὐκέτ' ἐστὶν
ἑτέρῳ διδόναι· χάριν αὐτὸν οἴεσθε τοῖς παρακρουσα-
35 μένοις ἔχειν; δέομαι δέ, ἂν οἱ λόγοι φαίνωνται
πικρότεροι, μηθὲν ἐμοὶ δυσχεραίνειν· οὐδὲ γὰρ ὑμᾶς
φημι τοῦτο ποιεῖν, τρόπον δέ τινα ἀκούσῃς τῆς
πόλεως αὐτὸ γίγνεσθαι. τὸ δὲ[1] πρᾶγμα εἰ
τοιοῦτόν ἐστιν ὥστε πάναισχρον δοκεῖν ἐξεταζό-
μενον, τοσούτῳ προθυμότερον ὑμᾶς ἀκούειν
δεῖ τοῦ λέγοντος, ὥστε ἀπηλλάχθαι τὸ λοιπὸν
τῆς αἰσχύνης. οὐδὲ γὰρ τὰ ἐν τοῖς σώμασι
δυσχερῆ χωρὶς ὀδύνης ἔστιν ἰάσασθαι, πολλάκις
δὲ αὐτὸ τοῦτο σημεῖον ὑπάρχει τοῦ σφόδρα
ἐπείγειν τὴν θεραπείαν, τὸ σφόδρα ἀλγεῖν τὸ
θεραπευόμενον.

36   Ὁ τοίνυν ἀρχόμενος εἶπον, οὐδ' ἂν νῦν ὀκνήσαιμι
εἰπεῖν, ὅτι πανταχοῦ μὲν οἰκεῖόν ἐστι φαίνεσθαι
τοὺς ἀγαθοὺς ἄνδρας ὑγιεῖς καὶ μηδὲν παλίμβολον
ἔχοντας μηδὲ δυσχερές, ἀλλὰ πλεῖστον ἀπάτης
καὶ πονηρίας ἀπηλλαγμένους· λέγω δὲ τοὺς ὑμῖν
ὁμοίους· μάλιστα δέ, οἶμαι, περὶ τὸ τιμᾶν καὶ
τὰς δωρεάς. τὸ γὰρ αἰσχύνην τινὰ προσάπτειν
τοῖς καλοῖς καὶ τὸ ἀδίκως ποιεῖν τὸ πάντων
δικαιότατον οὐδ' αἰσθανομένων ἐστὶν ἀνθρώπων
τῆς ἑκάστου φύσεως. ὥσπερ οὖν οἱ παρανομοῦν-
τες εἰς τὰ ἱερὰ τῶν εἰς ἄλλ' ὁτιοῦν ἁμαρτανόν-
των χείρους εἰσίν, οὕτως οἱ περὶ ταῦτα ἄδικοι
37 καὶ πονηροὶ φαινόμενοι. τί γάρ ἐστιν ἱερώτερον

---

[1] δὲ Morel : τε.

a person should be tricked into taking another man's statue to which he has no right from those who have no authority to give it—for what a person gives to another, he no longer has the authority to give to yet another—do you think that he is grateful to those who have duped him? But I ask you, if my words seem rather bitter, not to be at all vexed at me; for I am by no means saying that it is you who do this, but that it happens, in a manner of speaking, against the wish of your city. Still, if the practice is of such a nature that it seems utterly shameful when subjected to examination, the more eagerly ought you to listen to the speaker, so as to be free from the shame of it for the future. For neither can our bodily troubles be healed without pain; and often the very presence of marked pain in the part treated is itself an indication that the treatment is making marked progress.

So what I said at the beginning I would not hesitate to say at this point also—that in every situation it is proper that good men should show themselves to be morally sound and to have in their character no equivocal or hateful trait, but, on the contrary, should be utterly free from deceit and baseness—I mean men who are like yourselves— and I think this applies especially to conferring honour and the giving of gifts. For to put any shame upon a noble practice, and to carry out unjustly that which is the most just thing in the world, is the mark of men who have no delicate sense of the nature of each act. Hence just as those who commit sacrilege are worse than those who err in respect to anything else, so too are those who prove unjust and wicked in the matter under discussion. For what is more

τιμῆς ἢ χάριτος; οὐκ ἴστε ὅτι καὶ θεὰς νομίζουσιν
οἱ πλεῖστοι τῶν ἀνθρώπων τὰς Χάριτας; ἐὰν
οὖν τὰ ἀγάλματα αὐτῶν περικόπτῃ τις ἢ τοὺς
βωμοὺς ἀνατρέπῃ, τοῦτον ἡγεῖσθε ἀσεβεῖν· ἐὰν
δὲ αὐτὸ λυμήνηται καὶ διαφθείρῃ τὸ πρᾶγμα,
ἀφ' οὗ καὶ τὰς θεὰς ὠνομάσθαι συμβέβηκε, μὴ
ὃν δεῖ τρόπον χαριζόμενος, ἀλλ' ἀγεννῶς καὶ
ἀνελευθέρως καὶ μετὰ τέχνης τοῖς εὐεργέταις
ἀχαριστῶν,[1] αὐτὸν φρονεῖν φήσομεν καὶ τῶν
ἄλλων εἶναι συνετώτερον; ἀλλὰ τοὺς μὲν καπήλους
τοὺς ἐν τοῖς μέτροις κακουργοῦντας, οἷς ὁ βίος
ἐστὶν αὐτόθεν ἀπὸ αἰσχροκερδείας, μισεῖτε καὶ
κολάζετε· τὴν δὲ πόλιν, εἰ δόξει περὶ τοὺς ἐπαίνους
τῶν ἀγαθῶν ἀνδρῶν πανουργεῖν καὶ τὰς δωρεὰς
καπηλεύειν, οὐκ αἰσχυνεῖσθε,[2] παλίμβολα καὶ
38 παλίμπρατα ποιοῦσαν τὰ σεμνά; καὶ οὐδὲ ἐκεῖνο
ἐνθυμεῖσθε ὅτι μηδὲ τοῖς καπήλοις μηδεὶς ἔτι
ῥᾳδίως πρόσεισι, παρ' οἷς ἂν πονηρὰ ᾖ τὰ μέτρα;

Καὶ μὴν ὅτι φύσει τὸ πρᾶγμα τοιοῦτόν ἐστιν,
οὐχ ὁ λόγος αὐτὸ ἐξονειδίζει, θεάσασθε οὕτως·
εἰ γάρ τις πύθοιτο ὑμῶν πότερα βούλεσθε τοὺς
τιμωμένους ὑφ' ὑμῶν, οἷς οἴεσθε διδόναι τὰς εἰκόνας, ἐπίστασθαι τἀληθὲς καὶ τὸ γιγνόμενον οἷον

---

[1] ἀχαριστῶν Reiske : ἀχαρίστως BM, καὶ ἀχαρίστως E.
[2] αἰσχυνεῖσθε Cobet : αἰσχύνεσθε.

---

[1] The Graces were usually described as the daughters of
Zeus and as being three in number. To the Greek they were
the personification of all the qualities expressed by χάρις, of
which ' gratitude ' was one and ' grace ' another. Here
follows a play upon these two meanings of the word χάρις.
Cf. Plato, Laws 11, 912 b–c. This allegorizing theory is said to

sacred than honour or gratitude? Do you not know that the majority of men regard the Graces as indeed goddesses?[1] Therefore, if anyone mutilates their statues or overturns their altars, you hold this man guilty of impiety; but if injury or ruin is done to that very *grace* (*charis*) from which these goddesses have derived their name (*Charites*) by anyone's performing a *gracious* act in a way that is not right, but in an ignoble, illiberal, and crafty manner showing rank ingratitude to his benefactors, can we say that such a man has sense and is more intelligent than his fellows? Nay, tradesmen who cheat in their measures, men whose livelihood from the very nature of the business depends upon base gain, you hate and punish; but if your city shall gain the reputation of playing the knave in connection with her commendations of good men and of making a traffic of her gifts, will you feel no shame that she makes her sacred awards equivocal and subject to repeated sale?[2] And do you give not even a thought to this truth—that nobody will ever again willingly have dealings with those tradesmen whose measures are dishonest?

And besides, that the practice is in essence such as I have shown, and that it is not my speech which casts reproach upon it, I ask you to see from the following consideration: If anyone were to inquire of you whether you prefer, in the case of those who receive honours from you and on whom you think you are bestowing the statues, that they should know

come from the Stoic Chrysippus. Cf. Seneca, *De Beneficiis* 1. 44 and see Charly Clerc, *Les Théories relatives au Culte des Images*, page 197, note 3.

[2] For this sentence cf. Demosthenes *In Lept.* 9.

ἐστιν ἢ λανθάνειν αὐτούς, οὐκ ἄδηλόν ἐστιν ὃ
ἂν εἴποιτε εὖ φρονοῦντες. τί γὰρ ἐκώλυεν εὐθὺς
ἐν τῷ ψηφίσματι γράφειν ὥσπερ τἆλλα καὶ τοῦτο,
εἶναὶ δὲ τὴν εἰκόνα αὐτοῖς μίαν τῶν ἀνακειμένων
ἢ τὴν τοῦ δεῖνος, εἰ κἀκείνους ἐβούλεσθε γιγνώσκειν; ἀλλ᾽ οὐδέποτε, οἶμαι, τοῦτο ἐγγράψατε.[1]
39 οὐκοῦν ὅτι μὲν τὰ γιγνόμενα ὀρθῶς καὶ μηθὲν
ἔχοντα ἄτοπον οὐδεὶς περιστέλλει, δῆλόν ἐστιν.
ὅτι δὲ ἥκιστ᾽ ἄν τις φυλάξαιτο τοὺς εὖ πάσχοντας
εἰδέναι τίνα τρόπον τῆς χάριτος τυγχάνουσι καὶ
τῶν γιγνομένων περὶ τὴν τιμὴν ὁτιοῦν, εἴ γέ τις
ἁπλῶς αὐτὸ πράττοι καὶ δικαίως, ἔτι [2] μοι δοκεῖ
τοῦ πρώτου φανερώτερον· ὥστε ἀνάγκη τὸ συμβαῖνον εἶναι πανταχῆ φαῦλον καὶ μηδενὶ μηδὲ
ἰδιώτῃ πρέπον. ὁ γὰρ ἐν αὐτοῖς οἷς τινας εὖ
ποιεῖ, ἢ [3] παθὼν πρότερος ἢ νὴ Δία κατάρχων
καὶ προκαλούμενος εἰς φιλίαν, παρακρουόμενος
καὶ φενακίζων, τί ἂν οὗτος ἄλλως ποιήσειεν;

Ἐπίστασθε τοίνυν ὅτι μηδένα λανθάνει τὸ
γιγνόμενον, ἀλλ᾽ ἔστι διαβόητον καὶ τῶν παρὰ
πᾶσι θρυλουμένων, οὐ μόνον ἐπειδὴ λίαν κατακόρως
καὶ ἀνέδην [4] αὐτῷ κέχρηνταί τινες, ἀλλὰ ὅτι καὶ [5]
40 παρ᾽ ὑμῖν πράττεται. τὸ γὰρ ἀξίωμα τῆς πόλεως

---

[1] So BMJ, ἐγράψετε E; Arnim ἐγγράφετε.
[2] ἔτι Aldine edition : ἔστι.
[3] ἢ added by Capps.
[4] ἀνέδην Davis : ἀναίδην.
[5] ἀλλ᾽ ὅτι καὶ] ἀλλὰ καὶ ὅτι Emperius.

the truth and what sort of transaction it is, or that they should be kept in ignorance, it is perfectly clear what you would say if you are in your right senses. For what was there to prevent your writing explicitly in the decree to begin with, just like its other provisions, this also: that 'their statue shall be one of those already erected' or 'shall be So-and-so's', if you really wanted the recipients also to understand? But you will never put this in your decrees, I warrant! Well, it is perfectly clear that no one tries to disguise things that are done in a straightforward fashion and have nothing irregular about them. And I think it is even more obvious that nobody would be in the least inclined to take precautions to prevent men who are receiving favours at their hands from knowing in just what manner they were getting them and anything whatsoever that was being done in connection with the honour, at least if the action taken were done in a sincere and honourable way. So what is now happening must necessarily be contemptible in every way and ill-befitting for even a man in private station. For the man who, in the very act of doing a kindness to others either because he has previously received a kindness from them, or because he is actually taking the initiative and inviting them to be his friends, then deceives and cheats—what would such a man do in an honest fashion?

So, then, you do know that no one is unaware of what is going on, nay, it is notorious and on everybody's tongue, not only now that certain cities have followed this practice to great excess and with utter lack of restraint, but because it is being done even among you. For the high standing of your city and

καὶ τὸ μέγεθος οὐδὲν ἄγνωστον ἐᾷ τῶν ἐν αὐτῇ,
καὶ τὸ σεμνότερον ὑμᾶς ἁπάντων ἐν τοῖς ἄλλοις
ἑαυτοὺς ἄγειν, ἔτι δέ, οἶμαι, τὸ πράττειν ἄριστα
τῶν Ἑλλήνων φθόνον κινεῖ καὶ ζηλοτυπίαν,
ὥστε πολλοὺς εἶναι τοὺς ἐξετάζοντας, ἐάν τι
δοκῆτε ἁμαρτάνειν.   οὐκοῦν οἱ μὲν ὅλως ὅ τι[1]
πράττουσιν ἀγνοεῖσθαι μᾶλλον ἐθέλοντες κακίας
τοῦτο σημεῖον ἐκφέρουσιν, οἱ[2] δ' ἃ μηδεὶς ἀγνοεῖ[3]
λανθάνειν νομίζοντες, εὐηθείας· οἷς ἀμφοτέροις
οὐκ ἂν ἕλοισθε ἔνοχον εἶναι τὴν πόλιν.

41   Νὴ Δία, ἀλλὰ δαπανήσομεν, εἰ μὴ τοῖς οὖσι
χρησόμεθα, καὶ πόσων δεήσει χρημάτων, ἐὰν πᾶσι
κατασκευάζωμεν ἀνδριάντας ὅσοις ψηφιζόμεθα;

Καὶ πόσῳ κρεῖττον ἐλάττοσι διδόναι τὴν δωρεὰν
ἢ πλείους ἐξαπατᾶν, μέλλοντάς γε[4] ὑπὸ πλειόνων
καταγιγνώσκεσθαι καὶ μισεῖσθαι, σαφῶς εἰδότων ὃ
ποιεῖτε;

Καὶ γὰρ εἰ μὲν οὐ σφόδρα ἐπιεικεῖς εἰσιν, οὓς
ὁπωσδήποτε ἵστατε νῦν, ὃ μηδαμῇ φρονοῦντες
εἴποιτ' ἄν, ὁρᾶτε τὸ γιγνόμενον· διὰ γὰρ τοὺς
φαύλους ἀδικεῖτε τοὺς χρηστούς. ὅτι γὰρ ὑμῶν
οἱ πρόγονοι μὴ ἐθαύμαζον εἰκῆ μηδὲ ἀνάξιόν
τινα, ἐγὼ διαβεβαιωσαίμην ἄν. εἰ δὲ ἀγαθοὺς
τιμᾶτε, τούς γε τοιούτους εἰκὸς ἄχθεσθαι τῷ πράγ-
42 ματι. τίς γὰρ ἂν μέτριος ἄνθρωπος βούλοιτο
ἕτερον κακῶς πάσχειν καὶ τῶν δικαίως δεδομένων
ἀποστερεῖσθαι δι' αὐτόν; ἢ πῶς οὐκ ἂν ὀργίζοι-

---

[1] ὅλως ὅ τι Arnim: ὅπως ὅ τι MSS, ὅπως deleted by cor-
rector in E.
[2] οἱ Casaubon: εἰ.
[3] ἀγνοεῖ Casaubon: ἀεὶ EB, ἀκούει M.   [4] γε Reiske: τε.

---

[1] Cf. Demosthenes In Lept. 39 and 47.

her greatness allow nothing that goes on here to remain unknown; and the greater decorum of your conduct as compared with that of any other city; and, besides, I presume, your being the most prosperous of the Greeks, all arouse dislike and jealousy, so that there are many who watch to see if you appear to be at fault in any matter. Therefore those who prefer that what they do shall remain utterly unknown thereby reveal a sign of baseness, while those who think that what nobody is ignorant of goes unnoticed show their simplicity; and you would not care to have your city held guilty of both these faults!

" Oh yes! " you say, " but we shall be put to expense if we do not use those we already have! And what sums will be required if we are to have new statues made for all those to whom we vote them! "

And how much better it would be to make the gift to fewer persons rather than to deceive a larger number, since you will be condemned and hated by a larger number, for they know well what you are doing!

Again, if they are not very distinctly superior men whose memorials you are now setting up in some fashion or other—and if you are wise, you will by no means say that they are—see what takes place: on account of the inferior you are wronging the excellent; for your ancestors, I dare assert, did not bestow their admiration at random or upon any undeserving person.[1] On the other hand, if you are honouring good men, then these have good reason to be indignant at your action. For what fair-minded man would wish another to be ill-treated on *his* account and deprived of what had been justly given? How could he help being angry at such

τὸ ἐπὶ τούτῳ γιγνομένῳ μᾶλλον ἤπερ εἰδείη
χάριν; ἢ γυναῖκα μὲν οὐδεὶς ἂν ὑπομείνειε χρηστὸς
ὢν διὰ μοιχείαν λαβεῖν, ὅτι τὸν πρότερον ἔχοντα
ἠδίκησε· μᾶλλον δὲ οὐδ' ἂν ὅλως λάβοι¹ τις
ἡδέως παρὰ ἀνδρὸς ἑτέρου· καίτοι πολλάκις
γίγνεται τοῦτο οὐ μετὰ πονηρᾶς αἰτίας· τιμὴν
δέ, ἣν οὐκ ἔστι δικαίως ἀπ' ἄλλου λαβεῖν οὐδὲ
χωρὶς ὕβρεως τῆς εἰς ἐκεῖνον, ἀγαπᾶν τινα
οἴεσθε, καὶ ταῦτα μηδ' αὐτὸν ἐλπίζοντα ὡς
οὐθὲν ἂν πάθοι τοιοῦτον; ἀλλ' ἀνδράποδον μέν
τις ὠνούμενος εἴ ποτε ἀπέδρα σκοπεῖ καὶ εἰ μὴ
παρέμενε τῷ πρώτῳ δεσπότῃ· δωρεὰν δὲ καὶ
χάριν ἣν ἄπιστον ἡγεῖται καὶ σαφῶς οἶδε μηδὲν
ἔχουσαν βέβαιον, ἑκὼν ἂν πρόσοιτο;

43   Ῥωμαῖοι γάρ εἰσιν οἱ πλείους αὐτῶν, καὶ τίς
ἂν τούτων ἅψαιτο; οἱ δέ γε παρεστῶτες αὐτοῖς
Μακεδόνες, οἰδὶ δὲ Λακεδαιμόνιοι· καὶ νὴ Δία²
τούτων ἁπτόμεθα.

Καίτοι τοὺς μὲν πρότερον κειμένους πάντας
ἢ τούς γε πλείστους δι' εὐεργεσίαν φήσετε τεθῆναι,
τῶν δὲ νῦν τιμωμένων πολλοὺς δι' ἰσχὺν θεραπεύ-
εσθαι. τὸ μὲν δὴ ποτέρους αὐτῶν δικαιότερόν
ἐστι ποιεῖσθαι περὶ πλείονος, ἐάσω· τὸ δέ, εἰ μὴ
πᾶσι τὰ δοθέντα δικαίως ὑπάρξει, ποτέρους μᾶλλον

---

¹ λάβοι Emperius : λάβῃ.
² νὴ Δία Emperius : διὰ τί.

---

¹ On the principle involved cf. § 64 and § 94 ad fin.
² Among other uses ὕβρις was a legal term. Aristotle
(*Rhetoric* II. 2. 5, 1378b) defines it as " doing or saying anything to cause the complainant shame." At Athens an
indictment could be brought before the thesmothetes against
anyone guilty of this. See Demosthenes *In Mid.* 47. The

treatment, instead of feeling grateful? To take another case: no man, if he were honourable, would consent to get a wife through having committed adultery with her, because by that act he had done an injury to her former husband;[1] or rather, a man would not willingly take any woman at all away from another, her husband, although this is often done without any base motive. But an honour, which it is not possible justly to take away from another person or without inflicting an injury [2] on him—do you think that anyone cares to have, even though he is not expecting to be subjected to any such treatment himself? Nay, a man who is buying a slave inquires if he ever ran away, and if he would not stay with his first master; but a gift or a favour which a man believes was not given in good faith and which he knows well enough has no permanence in it at all—would he willingly accept that?

" Yes," you say, " for the majority of them are Romans and who would think of touching [3] them? But those who stand beside them here are Macedonians, while these over here are Spartans, and by heavens, it is these we touch."

And yet all that stood here formerly, or the most of them at any rate, you will admit were erected in acknowledgement of a benefaction, whereas of those now receiving honour many are being courted owing to their political power. Now the question which of the two classes has the greater right to be held in higher regard I will pass over; but this further question, which of the two classes—assuming

punishment was a fine or imprisonment. Taking a man's statue from him would cause him shame.

[3] This is, of giving their statues to others.

εἰκὸς ἐπ᾽ ἀδήλῳ λαμβάνειν, οὐδ᾽ αὐτοὺς τούτους
λανθάνει.   πάντες γὰρ οἴδασιν ὅσῳ βεβαιότερόν
ἐστιν εὐεργεσία δυνάμεως. ἰσχὺν μὲν γὰρ οὐκ
ἔστιν ἥντινα οὐκ ἀναιρεῖ χρόνος, εὐεργεσίαν δὲ
44 οὐδεμίαν. ἵν᾽ οὖν τὴν ὑπερβολὴν ἐκείνην ἀφῇ
τις, ἀληθῆ τρόπον τινὰ οὖσαν, τὸ πρὸς τὴν πόλιν
ἀηδέστερον ἔχειν τοὺς οὕτω [1] τιμᾶσθαι ζητοῦντας
καὶ τὸ συμβαῖνον εἰς ὕβριν λαμβάνειν καὶ κατα-
φρόνησιν ἑαυτῶν· ἀλλὰ τοῦτό γε εἰδέναι φημὶ
βεβαίως ὅτι μηδὲ χάριν ὑμῖν μηδεμίαν οἴδασι
μηδ᾽ οἴονται τυγχάνειν μηδενός, τὸ γιγνόμενον
εἰδότες καὶ τὴν ῥᾳδιουργίαν τὴν ἐν αὐτῷ· πρὸς τοῦ
Διός, εἶθ᾽ ἃ καὶ τούτων δεχομένων οὐκ εἰκὸς ἦν
ἀφαιρεῖσθαι τοὺς ἔμπροσθεν εἰληφότας, ταῦτα
ἀφαιρώμεθα τοὺς ἔχοντας οὐδὲ ἑτέροις διδόντες;
45 Καὶ μὴν εἴ γε ἐν οἷς ἡ πόλις δοκεῖ τινος δεῖσθαι,
τὴν δαπάνην μόνον ὀψόμεθα καὶ τὸ πῶς ἂν εὐ-
χερέστατα γένοιτο,[2] μηθὲν ἄλλο ἐξετάζοντες, τί
κωλύει μὴ μόνον ταύτην ὑπάρχειν ἐν ἑτοίμῳ
τὴν δωρεάν, ἀλλὰ κἂν ἄλλο τι θέλητε χαρίσασθαί
τινι, γῆν, ἀργύριον, οἰκίαν, τοὺς ἔχοντας ἀφαιρουμένους; ἢ τί δεῖ πόρους ζητεῖν καὶ τὰ κοινὰ
ἀναλίσκειν, ὅταν ᾖ καιρὸς ἢ τεῖχος ἐπισκευά-
ζειν ἢ ναῦς, ἀλλὰ μὴ τὰ τοῦ δεῖνος λαβεῖν ἢ

---

[1] τοὺς οὕτω Reiske : τοσούτῳ.
[2] γένοιτο Emperius : γένηται.

that the honours granted are not to belong rightfully to all—can more reasonably be expected to take them on the basis of so uncertain a title, this question, I say, even these men themselves know well how to answer. For all know how much more permanent a benefaction is than power, for there is no strength which time does not destroy, but it destroys no benefaction. Assuming, therefore, that we may reject that extreme view, which in a sense is true, that those who are seeking to be honoured in this way are quite displeased with your city and take what is done as an insult and affront to themselves, yet at least I assert positively that they feel no gratitude whatever to you and do not think that they are getting anything, knowing as they do what is taking place and the unscrupulousness displayed in it. In heaven's name, when even if the men in question do accept from us honours which we should have no right to take away from their former recipients, are we, then, to take them away from whoever possesses them, even though we do not really 'give' them to another set of men?

Furthermore, if in cases where the city is thought to need anything, we shall consider the expense alone and how the thing can be done most easily, examining into no other aspects of the matter, what is to prevent our having not only this gift ready at hand, but any other favour you may wish to bestow upon any one, such as land, money, or a house, by simply taking them away from those who have them? Or what need is there to seek ways and means and to expend the public money when occasion arises to repair either a wall or ships, instead of merely taking So-and-so's property, either that of some citizen or

τὰ τῶν πολιτῶν τινος ἢ τῶν ἐνοικούντων παρ᾽
ὑμῖν;

Ἀλλὰ νὴ Δία βοήσονται καὶ δεινὰ φήσουσι
πάσχειν.

46 Οὐκοῦν ἐξέσται δήπουθεν μὴ προσέχειν αὐτοῖς.
καὶ γὰρ εἰ νῦν εἰσιν ἐφ᾽ οὓς ἂν ἔλθοιεν ὑμῶν ταῦτα
ποιούντων, πρότερόν γε οὐκ ἦν ἕτερος οὐδεὶς τοῦ
δήμου κυριώτερος.

Ἆρ᾽ οὖν οἱ τότε ὄντες οὕτω προσεφέροντο τοῖς
κατὰ μέρος;

Πόθεν; οἳ τοῦτο πάντων ἡγοῦντο χαλεπώ-
τατον, καὶ τοῖς θεοῖς ἐπεύχοντο μηδέποτε συμβῆναι τοιοῦτον καιρὸν ἐν ᾧ δεήσει κατ᾽ ἄνδρα
ἕκαστον ἀπὸ τῶν ἰδίων εἰσενεγκεῖν· καὶ τὸ
τοιοῦτον [1] σπανίως ποτὲ παρ᾽ ὑμῖν γενέσθαι
φασίν, οὐδὲ ἐν ἅπασι τοῖς πολέμοις, ἀλλ᾽ εἴ ποτε
ἐσχάτως ἡ πόλις ἐκινδύνευσεν.

47 Ἴσως οὖν ἐρεῖ τις ὡς οἵ γε ἀνδριάντες τῆς
πόλεώς εἰσιν. καὶ γὰρ ἡ χώρα τῆς πόλεως,
ἀλλ᾽ οὐθὲν ἧττον τῶν κεκτημένων ἕκαστος κύριός
ἐστι τῶν ἑαυτοῦ. καὶ κοινῇ μὲν ἐὰν πυνθάνηταί
τις τίνος ἐστὶν ἡ νῆσος ἢ τίνος ἡ Καρία, φήσουσι
Ῥοδίων. ἐὰν δὲ ἄλλως ἐρωτᾷς, τουτὶ τὸ χωρίον
ἢ τὸν ἀγρόν, δῆλον ὅτι πεύσῃ τοῦ δεσπότου
τὸ ὄνομα. καὶ τὰς εἰκόνας ἁπλῶς μὲν πάσας

---

[1] καὶ τὸ τοιοῦτον Emperius: καίτοι τοῦτο.

---

[1] Apparently he means the Romans.
[2] Greek cities as a rule had no regular direct taxation. At
Athens a special levy was made in emergencies. For cases
see Demosthenes 18. 66; 20. 10; 22. 76. In 428 such a
special tax was levied to enable Athens to continue the war

of one of the strangers who are sojourning among you?

" Never, by Zeus," you say, " they will raise an outcry and say that it is an outrage."

Then it will be possible, presumably, to pay no attention to them. For even if there are now those[1] to whom they can appeal when you act this way, in the old days, at any rate, there was no person who had greater authority than the people.

" Can it be that the men of that time treated individuals in that way? "

What nonsense! Why, they considered it to be the worst thing imaginable, and prayed the gods that the time might never come in which it would be necessary that each individual citizen should ever be obliged to pay a tax out of his own private means; and it is said that so extreme a measure has only rarely been taken among you in spite of all your wars, except at a time when your city was in extreme peril.[2]

Now perhaps some one will say that the statues belong to the city. Yes, and the land also belongs to the city, but none the less every one who possesses any has full authority over what is his own. Speaking in a political sense, if anyone inquires who owns the Island[3] or who owns Caria, he will be told that the Rhodians own it. But if you ask in a different sense about this specific estate here or this field, it is clear that you will learn the name of the private owner. So also with the statues; in a general

against Sparta, when all except the reserve funds had been exhausted by the siege of Potidaea. Those with a capital of less than one-sixth of a talent were exempt.

[3] He means the island of Rhodes, upon the north-eastern tip of which the city of Rhodes was situated.

Ῥοδίων εἶναι λέγουσιν, ἰδίᾳ δὲ ἑκάστην τοῦ δεῖνος, ἢ τοῦ δεῖνος, ᾧ ἄν ποτε ᾖ δεδομένη. καίτοι τὰ μὲν χωρία καὶ τὰς οἰκίας καὶ τἄλλα κτήματα οὐκ ἂν εἰδείης ὧν ἐστιν, εἰ μὴ πυθόμενος· ἡ δὲ εἰκὼν ἐπιγέγραπται, καὶ οὐ μόνον τὸ ὄνομα, ἀλλὰ καὶ τὸν χαρακτῆρα σῴζει τοῦ λαβόντος, ὥστ᾽ εὐθὺς εἶναι προσελθόντα εἰδέναι τίνος ἐστίν. λέγω δὲ ἐφ᾽ ὧν ἔτι μένει τἀληθές.

48 Καὶ μὴν τό γε ἐν κοινῷ κεῖσθαι γελοιότατόν ἐστιν, εἴ τις ἄρα σημεῖον ἡγεῖται τοῦ μὴ τῶν εἰληφότων αὐτὰς ὑπάρχειν, ἀλλὰ τῆς πόλεως. οὕτω μὲν γὰρ ἐξέσται λέγειν καὶ τὰ ἐν μέσῳ τῆς ἀγορᾶς πιπρασκόμενα τοῦ δήμου, καὶ τὰ πλοῖα δήπουθεν οὐχὶ τῶν κεκτημένων, ἀλλὰ τῆς πόλεως, ἐπείπερ ἐν τοῖς λιμέσιν ἔστηκεν.

Ὁ τοίνυν ἤκουσά τινος ὑπὲρ τούτου λέγοντος ὡς ἰσχυρότατον, οὐκ ἂν ἀποκρυψαίμην, ὅτι δημοσίᾳ τοὺς ἀνδριάντας ἀπεγράψασθε ὑμεῖς. τί οὖν τοῦτό ἐστιν; καὶ γὰρ τὴν ἄντικρυς χώραν καὶ Κάρπαθον ταύτην καὶ τὴν¹ ἤπειρον, ἑτέρας νήσους καὶ καθόλου πολλὰ ἔστιν εὑρεῖν, ἃ κοινῇ μὲν ἀπεγράψατο ἡ πόλις, διῄρηται δὲ εἰς τοὺς κατὰ

49 μέρος. ὅλως δὲ οὐκ εἰ μὴ τοῦτον τὸν τρόπον

¹ τὴν added by Capps.

---

¹ That is, those on which the inscription still matches the person represented.

² He means the tongue of land jutting out towards Rhodes from Caria. Its promontory was about ten miles distant from the city of Rhodes. Hence ἤπειρον is not objectionable, as some have thought.

³ Carpathos, the modern Scarpanto, is an island about thirty-five miles south-west of Rhodes and half-way between it and Crete.

sense men say that they belong to the people of Rhodes, but in the particular or special sense they say that this or that statue belongs to So-and-so or to So-and-so, naming whatever man it has been given to. And yet, whereas in the case of estates, houses, and other possessions, you cannot learn who owns them unless you inquire, the statue has an inscription on it and preserves not only the name but also the lineaments of the man to whom it was first given, so that it is possible to step near and at once know whose it is. I refer to those on which the truth is still given.[1]

Moreover, the plea that they stand on public property is most absurd, if this is really held to be an indication that they do not belong to those who received them, but to the city. Why, if that be true, it will be possible to say that also the things which are on sale in the centre of the market-place belong to the commonwealth, and that the boats, no doubt, do belong, not to their possessors, but to the city, just because they are lying in the harbours.

Then, too, an argument which I heard a man advance, as a very strong one in support of that position, I am not disposed to conceal from you: he said that you have made an official list of your statues. What, pray, is the significance of that? Why, the country lying opposite us,[2] Carpathos yonder,[3] the mainland,[4] the other islands, and in general many possessions can be found which the city has listed in its public records, but they have been parcelled out among individuals. And in fine,

[4] As a reward for assisting the Romans in the war against Antiochus, Rhodes was given control of South Caria, where the Rhodians had had settlements from an early period.

ἕκαστος τὴν εἰκόνα ἔχει τῶν τιμηθέντων, καθάπερ
ἂν ἄλλο τι κτησάμενος, διὰ τοῦτο ἂν ἔλαττον
αὐτῷ προσήκειν λέγοιτο ἢ μηδὲν ἀδικεῖσθαι διδόν-
των ὑμῶν ἑτέρῳ τὴν ἐκείνου. μυρίους γὰρ εὑρήσετε τρόπους, καθ' οὓς ἑκάστου τί φαμεν εἶναι,
καὶ πλεῖστον διαφέροντας, οἷον ἱερωσύνην, ἀρχήν,
γάμον, πολιτείαν· ὧν οὔτε ἀποδόσθαι τι ἔξεστι
τοῖς ἔχουσιν οὔτε ὅπως ἂν τις ἐθέλῃ χρῆσθαι.
50 κοινὸν δ' οὖν ἐπὶ πᾶσιν ὥρισται δίκαιον, τὸ
πάνθ' ὅσα δικαίως τις ἔλαβεν, ἄν τε καθάπαξ
τύχῃ λαβών, ἄν τε εἴς τινα χρόνον, καθάπερ, οἶμαι,
τὰς ἀρχάς, βεβαίως ἔχειν καὶ μηδένα ἀφαιρεῖσθαι.
πῶς οὖν δικαιότερον ἔστιν ὁτιοῦν ἔχειν ἢ εἴ τις
ἀνὴρ ἀγαθὸς γενόμενος καὶ χάριτος ἄξιος ἀντὶ
πολλῶν καὶ καλῶν τύχοι τιμῆς; ἢ παρὰ τίνος
κυριωτέρου καὶ μείζονος ἢ παρὰ τοῦ ῾Ροδίων
δήμου καὶ τῆς ὑμετέρας πόλεως; καὶ γὰρ τοῦτο
οὐ σμικρόν ἐστι, τὸ μὴ Καλυμνίους εἶναι τοὺς
δεδωκότας ἢ τοὺς κακοβούλους τούτους Καυνίους·
ὥσπερ ἐπὶ τῶν ἰδιωτικῶν, ὅσῳ τις ἂν κρείττω
καὶ πιστότερον δεικνύῃ, παρ' οὗ τυγχάνει τι
κτησάμενος, τοσούτῳ κρατεῖ καὶ οὐδεὶς ἂν
ἀμφισβητήσειεν αὐτῷ. καίτοι πᾶσα πόλις, ἣν

---

[1] i.e., in perpetuity.

[2] Calymna, a small island near Cos and about 65 miles
north-west of Rhodes. It was a colony of Epidaurus.

[3] Caunus was a city on the coast of Caria and north-east of
Rhodes. See § 124, where it is coupled with Myndus, and
§ 125, where it is said to be doubly enslaved.

Probably the Caunians are here called foolish because in
88 B.C. they helped carry out, and with especial fury, Mithridates' orders to massacre all Italians in Asia Minor (see

even if each man who has been honoured does not in this sense 'possess' his statue as he would possess anything else he has acquired, it cannot for that reason be said that it belongs to him any the less or that he suffers no wrong when you give his statue to another. For you will find countless senses in which we say that a thing 'belongs' to an individual and very different senses too, for instance, a priesthood, a public office, a wife, citizenship, none of which their possessors are at liberty either to sell or to use in any way they like. But certainly a common principle of justice is laid down in regard to them all, to the effect that anything whatsoever which any one has received justly—whether he happens to have got it once for all[1] or for a specified time, just as, for instance, he obtains public offices—that is his secure possession and nobody can deprive him of it. How, then, is it possible to have anything more justly, than when a man who has proved himself good and worthy of gratitude receives honour in return for many noble deeds? Or from whom could he receive it that has fuller authority and is greater than the democracy of Rhodes and your city? For it is no trifling consideration that it was not the Calymnians[2] who gave it, or those ill-advised Caunians;[3] just as in private business the better and more trustworthy you prove the man to be from whom you obtain any possession, the stronger your title to it is, and by so much more no one can dispute it. Yet any

Appian 23). As a punishment for this Sulla made them once more subject to the Rhodians, from whom the Romans had freed them. Cicero (ad Quintum fratrem 1. 1. 11. 33) refers to this and says that they appealed to the Roman senate— probably in vain—to be freed once more. See p. 130, note 1.

ἂν εἴπῃ τις, ἑνὸς ἀνδρὸς ἰδιώτου, κἂν ὁ σεμνότατος
ᾖ, πιστοτέρα τῷ παντὶ καὶ κρείττων, καὶ τὰ
κοινῇ γιγνόμενα τῶν κατ' ἰδίαν πραττομένων
ἰσχυρότερα.

51 Σκοπεῖτε δὲ ὅτι πάντες ἡγοῦνται κυριώτερα
ταῦτα ἔχειν, ὅσα ἂν δημοσίᾳ συμβάλωσι διὰ τῶν
τῆς πόλεως γραμμάτων· καὶ οὐκ ἔνι λυθῆναι τῶν
οὕτω διῳκημένων οὐδέν, οὔτ' εἴ τις ὠνήσαιτο
παρά του χωρίον ἢ πλοῖον ἢ ἀνδράποδον, οὔτ'
εἴ τῳ δανείσειεν, οὔτ' ἂν οἰκέτην ἀφῇ τις ἐλεύθερον
οὔτ' ἂν δῷ τινι [1] δωρεάν. τί δήποτ' οὖν συμβέβηκε
ταῦτ' εἶναι βεβαιότερα τῶν ἄλλων; ὅτι τὴν πόλιν
μάρτυρα ἐποιήσατο τοῦ πράγματος ὁ τοῦτον τὸν
52 τρόπον οἰκονομήσας τι τῶν ἑαυτοῦ. πρὸς τοῦ
Διός, εἶθ' ὧν μὲν ἄν τις παρ' ἰδιώτου τύχῃ διὰ
τῆς πόλεως, οὐκ ἔστιν ὅπως ἀφαιρεθήσεται
τούτων· ἃ δέ τις εἴληφεν οὐ δημοσίᾳ μόνον,
ἀλλὰ καὶ τοῦ δήμου δεδωκότος, οὐκ ἔσται βέβαια;
καὶ τὸ μὲν ὑπ' ἄλλων γενόμενον τοῦτον τὸν
τρόπον οὐ λυθήσεται διὰ τὴν πόλιν, ἃ δ' ἡ πόλις
αὐτὴ πεποίηκε, ῥᾳδίως οὕτως ἀνελεῖ; καὶ ταῦτα
οὐχ ὡς ἔδωκεν, ὁμοίως ἀφαιρουμένη κατὰ κοινόν,
ἀλλ' ἑνὸς ἀνδρός, ἂν τύχῃ στρατηγοῦν, ἐξουσίαν
53 ἔχοντος τοῦτο ποιεῖν; καὶ μὴν καὶ γράμματά
ἐστιν ἐν κοινῷ περὶ τούτων, ὑπὲρ ὧν ἔφην· τὰ
γὰρ ψηφίσματα γέγραπται δήπουθεν τὰ τῶν

---

[1] τινι Cohoon : τινα.

---

[1] For the thought see Demosthenes *In Lept.* 15 and 36.
[2] Cf. Discourse 38. 29 at the end and Dem. *ibid.* 136.
[3] στρατηγός was the general title of the chief magistrate of
independent or semi-independent Greek communities and
leagues under Roman domination.

city which one might mention is in every way better and more trustworthy than one private citizen, even if he has the highest standing,[1] and arrangements made by the state are more binding than those which are negotiated privately.

Then consider, further, that all men regard those agreements as having greater validity which are made with the sanction of the state and are entered in the city's records; and it is impossible for anything thus administered to be annulled, either in case one buys a piece of land from another, a boat or a slave, or if a man makes a loan to another, or frees a slave, or makes a gift to any one. How in the world, then, has it come to pass that these transactions carry a greater security than any other? It is because the man who has handled any affair of his in this way has made the city a witness to the transaction. In heaven's name, will it then be true that, while anything a person may get from a private citizen by acting through the state cannot possibly be taken from him, yet what one has received, not only by a state decree, but also as a gift of the people, shall not be inalienable?[2] And whereas an action taken in this way by anybody else will never be annulled by the authority of the state, yet shall the state, in the offhand way we observe here, cancel what it has itself done?—and that too, not by taking it away in the same manner in which it was originally given, that is, by the commonwealth officially, but by letting one man, if he happens to be your chief magistrate,[3] have the power to do so? And besides, there are official records of those transactions of which I have spoken; for the decrees by which honours are given are recorded, I take it, and

τιμῶν καὶ δημοσίᾳ μένει τὸν ἅπαντα χρόνον. τὸ
μὲν γὰρ ἀποδοῦναι χάριν οὕτως ἀκριβῶς γίγνεται
παρ' ὑμῖν, τὸ δ' ἀφελέσθαι τοὺς εἰληφότας πάνυ
ῥᾳδίως. εἶτα τὸ μὲν οὐχ οἷόν τε γενέσθαι δίχα
ψηφίσματος, ἁπάντων ὑμῶν πεισθέντων, τὸ δὲ
ἔθει τινὶ συμβαίνει, κἂν ἑνὶ δόξῃ μόνον· πλὴν ὅ
γε ἔφην ὅτι δημοσίᾳ ταῦτα ἀναγέγραπται, καὶ
οὐ μόνον ἐν τοῖς ψηφίσμασιν, ἀλλὰ καὶ ἐπ' αὐτῶν
τῶν εἰκόνων, τό τε ὄνομα τοῦ τιμηθέντος καὶ τὸ
δεδωκέναι τὸν δῆμον, καὶ τούτων πάλιν ἐν τῷ
δημοσίῳ κειμένων.

54   Ὅτι τοίνυν οὐθέν ἐστι τὸ τῆς ἀπογραφῆς οὐδὲ
τὸ ἐν κοινῷ κεῖσθαι πρὸς τὸ μὴ τῶν εἰληφότων
εἶναι τοὺς ἀνδριάντας, πάλαι μὲν ἴσως ὑπάρχει
δῆλον· ἀλλ' ὥστε μηδ' ἐπιχειρῆσαι μηδένα
ἀντειπεῖν, ἐκεῖνο ὑμῖν ἐρῶ. ἴστε που τοὺς
Ἐφεσίους, ὅτι πολλὰ χρήματα παρ' αὐτοῖς ἐστι,
τὰ μὲν ἰδιωτῶν, ἀποκείμενα ἐν τῷ νεῷ τῆς
Ἀρτέμιδος, οὐκ Ἐφεσίων μόνον, ἀλλὰ καὶ ξένων
καὶ τῶν ὁπόθεν δήποτε [1] ἀνθρώπων, τὰ δὲ καὶ
δήμων καὶ βασιλέων, ἃ τιθέασι πάντες οἱ
τιθέντες ἀσφαλείας χάριν, οὐδενὸς οὐδεπώποτε
τολμήσαντος ἀδικῆσαι τὸν τόπον, καίτοι καὶ
πολέμων ἤδη μυρίων γεγονότων καὶ πολλάκις
ἁλούσης τῆς πόλεως. οὐκοῦν ὅτι [2] μὲν ἐν κοινῷ
κεῖται τὰ χρήματα, δῆλόν ἐστιν· ἀλλὰ καὶ δημοσίᾳ
κατὰ τὰς ἀπογραφὰς ἔθος αὐτὰ τοῖς Ἐφεσίοις

---

[1] δήποτε Emperius : δήποθεν BM.
[2] ὡς before ὅτι deleted by Pflugk.

remain on public record for all time. For though re-
paying a favour is so strictly guarded among you, yet
taking it back from the recipients is practised with
no formality at all. Then, while the one action
cannot be taken except by a decree passed by you
as a body, yet the other comes to pass by a sort of
custom, even though it is the will of only one
person. Note, however, that, as I said, these
matters have been recorded officially, not only in
the decrees, but also upon the statues themselves, on which we find both the name of the
man who received the honour and the statement
that the assembly has bestowed it, and, again,
that these statues are set up on public property.

Well then, that there is nothing in the official list,[1]
or in the fact that these memorials stand on public
property, which tends to show that they do not belong
to those who have received them, has perhaps long
been evident; but in order that nobody may even
attempt to dispute it, let me mention this: You know
about the Ephesians, of course, and that large sums
of money are in their hands, some of it belonging to
private citizens and deposited in the temple of Artemis, not alone money of the Ephesians but also of
aliens and of persons from all parts of the world, and in
some cases of commonwealths and kings, money which
all deposit there in order that it may be safe, since no
one has ever yet dared to violate that place, although
countless wars have occurred in the past and the
city has often been captured. Well, that the money
is deposited on state property is indeed evident,
but it also is evident, as the lists show, that it is the
custom of the Ephesians to have these deposits

---

[1] Of statues; cf. §§ 48 and 53.

55 ἀπογράφεσθαι. τί οὖν; ἆρά γε καὶ λαμβάνουσιν
ἐξ αὐτῶν, ὅταν ᾖ χρεία τις, ἢ δανείζονται γοῦν,
ὃ τάχα δόξει μηδὲν εἶναι δεινόν; ἀλλ᾽, οἶμαι,
πρότερον ἂν περιέλοιεν τὸν κόσμον τῆς θεοῦ πρὶν
ἢ τούτων ἅψασθαι. καίτοι τοὺς Ἐφεσίους οὐκ
ἂν εἴποιτε εὐπορωτέρους αὐτῶν. τοὐναντίον γὰρ
ὑμεῖς μὲν καὶ πρότερον ἦτε πλουσιώτατοι τῶν
Ἑλλήνων καὶ νῦν ἔτι μᾶλλόν ἐστε· ἐκείνους δὲ
πολλῶν ἔστιν ἰδεῖν καταδεέστερον πράττοντας.

56 Μὴ τοίνυν εἴπητε,[1] ἐκεῖνα μὲν ἔστιν ἀνελέ-
σθαι τοῖς θεῖσι, τῆς εἰκόνος δὲ οὐθεὶς οὕτως ἐστὶ
τῆς ἑαυτοῦ κύριος, καὶ μὴ τὸ πρᾶγμα ἀνόμοιον
ἡγήσησθε· τὸ γὰρ μὴ πάντ᾽ εὐθὺς τῆς πόλεως
εἶναι τὰ ἐν κοινῷ κείμενα καὶ δημοσίας ἀπογραφῆς
τυχόντα δεῖξαι βουλόμενος ὡς τύπῳ[2] κατὰ
τοῦτο ἐχρησάμην. τὸ μέντοι μηθένα πρὸς ἄλλο
τι τὴν εἰκόνα ἔχειν ἢ τὸ ἑστάναι παρ᾽ ὑμῖν, ᾧ
μόνῳ διαφέρουσιν οὗτοι τῶν ἐκεῖ τὰ χρήματα
τιθέντων, ἔτι μᾶλλον ὑπὲρ αὐτῶν ἐστιν. ἃ
γὰρ μηδὲ τοῖς λαβοῦσιν ἔξεστιν ἀνελεῖν, ἦπου
γε τοῖς δεδωκόσιν ἐξεῖναι προσήκει.

57 Καθόλου δὲ ἄλλως ἔγωγε φιλονεικεῖν ἔοικα
πρὸς τὸν εἰπόντα δὴ ὡς τῆς πόλεως πάντες εἰσὶν
οἱ ἀνδριάντες. ἐπεὶ τοῦτό γε οὐθέν ἐστι σημεῖον

---

[1] εἴπητε Cohoon, εἰ Casaubon and most editors: ἤ.
[2] ὡς τύπῳ Emperius: τούτῳ EB, ὃς τούτῳ M.

---

[1] From this passage, taken together with others such as
CIG II, No. 2953b; Plautus, *Bacchides* 312; Caesar, *Civil
War* 3. 33, we conclude that in the temple of Artemis at
Ephesus there was a treasure-house or bank under official
control. According to Nicolaus of Damascus, *fragment* 65,
money was lent. Aristides (Oration 42. 522) calls Ephesus

officially recorded.[1] Well then, do they go on and take any of these monies when any need arises, or do they ' borrow ' them at any rate—an act which, perhaps, will not seem at all shocking?[2] No; on the contrary, they would sooner, I imagine, strip off the adornment of the goddess than touch this money. Yet you would not say that the Ephesians are wealthier than yourselves. The very opposite is the case, for not only were you the richest of the Greeks in former times, but now you are still richer; whereas the Ephesians, one can see, are less prosperous than many.

Pray do not say to this : " The people who deposited that money have the privilege of withdrawing it, but no one has in this way the disposal of his own statue," and do not consider the cases dissimilar. For in my desire to show that not all things deposited in a public place and recorded officially belong forthwith to the city, I used this case as an illustration. The fact, however, that no one has a statue for any other purpose than to stand in your midst—the one respect in which these men differ from those who deposit their money there [3]—speaks still more in their behalf. For when it is not lawful for even the recipients of gifts to annul them, can it possibly be right that the donors should have the power to do so ?

However, I seem to be arguing quite needlessly against the man who asserts that all the statues belong to the city; for this is no indication that

---

'the common treasury and the refuge for necessity ': ταμιεῖον κοινὸν καὶ χρείας καταφυγή. See p. 70, note.

[2] Athens borrowed from her own temple-treasuries during the Peloponnesian War, and paid interest.

[3] At Ephesus; see § 54.

ὡς οὐκ ἔστιν ἄτοπον τὸ γιγνόμενον. τὰ γοῦν ἐν
τοῖς ἱεροῖς ἀναθήματα, ἃ κατασκευάσασα ἡ
πόλις ἐκ τῶν ἰδίων ἀνατέθεικεν, οὐκ ἂν οὐδεὶς
ἀμφισβητήσειεν ὡς οὐ δημόσιά ἐστιν. ἆρ᾽ οὖν
οὐχὶ δεινόν, εἰ καταχρησόμεθα τούτοις πρὸς
ἄλλο τι;

Νὴ Δία, ταῦτα γάρ ἐστιν ἀναθήματα, αἱ δ᾽
εἰκόνες τιμαί· κἀκεῖνα δέδοται τοῖς θεοῖς, ταῦτα
δὲ τοῖς ἀγαθοῖς ἀνδράσιν, οἵπερ εἰσὶν ἔγγιστα
αὐτῶν.

58 Καίτοι καὶ θεοφιλεῖς ἅπαντες οἱ χρηστοὶ
λέγονται καὶ εἰσίν. εἶτα ἡμᾶς μὲν οὐχ ὁ τῶν
κτημάτων τι τῶν ἡμετέρων ἀφαιρούμενος, ἀλλὰ
κἂν¹ τοὺς φίλους βλάπτῃ τις² τοὺς ἡμετέρους,
ἀδικεῖ τῷ παντὶ πλέον· τοὺς δέ γε θεοὺς φήσομεν,
ὡς ἔοικε, τῶν φίλων μᾶλλον ὀλιγωρεῖν ἢ τῶν
κτημάτων;

Ἀλλὰ πάντα μὲν προσήκει βεβαίως ἔχειν τοὺς
κτησαμένους, καὶ ταῦτα ἐν δημοκρατίᾳ καὶ παρ᾽
ὑμῖν, οἳ μέγιστον φρονεῖτε ἐπὶ τῷ νομίμως καὶ
δικαίως διοικεῖν τὰ παρ᾽ ἑαυτοῖς, μάλιστα δέ,
οἶμαι, τὰς τιμὰς καὶ τὰς χάριτας· οὐ μόνον
ἐπειδὴ τὰ μὲν ἄλλα καὶ φαῦλος ὧν τις ἂν ἔχοι,
χρήματα, οἰκίας, ἀνδράποδα, χώρας, ταῦτα δὲ
μόνοις ὑπάρχει τοῖς ἐπιεικέσιν· ἀλλὰ καὶ δι᾽
ἐκεῖνο, ὅτι ταῦτα μὲν ἔστι κεκτῆσθαι καὶ δι᾽
ἑτέρου τρόπου, κληρονομήσαντα ἢ πριάμενον·

¹ ἀλλὰ κἂν] ἀλλ᾽ ἂν Arnim, ἀλλ᾽ ὃς ἂν Cohoon.
² τις most MSS, τι M.

---

¹ That God loves the good is a Stoic idea. Cf. Discourses
1. 16; 3. 51, 53; 33. 28; 39. 2 and see H. Binder, *Dio Chrysostom and Poseidonius*, pp. 81, 83.

what is being done is not an outrage. For instance, consider the votive offerings in the sacred places: the city made them at its own expense and dedicated them. No one would dispute that they are the property of the people. Then will it not be an outrage if we misappropriate them for some other purpose?

"Yes, by heaven," you rejoin, "for these are dedications, but the statues are marks of honour; the former have been given to the gods, the latter to good men, who, to be sure, are nearest of kin to them."

"And yet," I reply, "all men of highest virtue are both said to be and in fact are beloved of the gods.[1] Can it be, then, that while not he who deprives *us* of any of our possessions, but whoever does an injury to our friends, is guilty of an altogether greater wrong, yet we are to say of the gods, as it seems we are doing, that they are more inclined to slight their friends than they are their possessions?

Nay, on the contrary, it is right that in regard to all sorts of possessions those who have acquired them should be secure in their tenure, especially in a democracy and among a people like yourselves, who take the greatest pride in having matters in your state handled in accordance with law and justice, and above all, I should imagine, your honours and expressions of gratitude; not only because even a man of no account might have all other things, such as money, houses, slaves, lands, whereas those two are possessions enjoyed by virtuous men alone, but also for the reason that these things can be acquired through some other means, such as inheritance or purchase, whereas such things

τῶν δὲ τοιούτων διὰ μόνης ἀρετῆς ἐστιν ἡ
κτῆσις.

59 Καὶ μὴν ὧν γέ τις τὴν τιμὴν κατέβαλε τοῖς
κυρίοις, οὐδ' ἀμφισβητεῖ δήπουθεν οὐδεὶς ὡς
οὐ δίκαιόν ἐστιν ἐὰν ἔχειν αὐτόν, τοσούτῳ μᾶλλον
ὅσῳπερ ἂν πλείονα ἢ δεδωκώς. οὐκοῦν ἅπαντες
οὗτοι δεδώκασι τιμὴν ἕκαστος τῆς εἰκόνος τῆς
ἑαυτοῦ, καὶ ταύτην οὐδὲ μετρίαν, οἱ μὲν στρατη-
γίας λαμπρὰς ὑπὲρ τῆς πόλεως, οἱ δὲ πρεσβείας,
οἱ δὲ καὶ τρόπαια ἀπὸ τῶν πολεμίων, οἱ δέ τινες
καὶ χρήματα ἴσως, οὐ μὰ Δία χιλίας δραχμὰς
οὐδὲ πεντακοσίας, ὅσων ἔστιν εἰκόνας [1] ἀναστῆσαι.

60 Τί οὖν; οὐχὶ νενόμισται παρά γε τοῖς μὴ παντάπασιν ἀδίκοις τὸν ἀποστερούμενόν τινος κτή-
ματος ὃ γοῦν κατατέθεικε κομίζεσθαι παρὰ τῶν
εἰληφότων; ἆρ' οὖν ἐθέλοιτ' ἂν ἀποδοῦναι
τὰς χάριτας, ἀνθ' ὧν ἐψηφίσασθε ἐκείνοις τοὺς
ἀνδριάντας; λυσιτελεῖ γοῦν ὑμῖν ἐκτίνουσιν,
ἐπειδὴ τὸ λυσιτελὲς οἴονται δεῖν τινες ὁρᾶν ἐξ

61 ἅπαντος. ἐὰν οὖν ἢ πόλεμον ᾖ τις κατωρθωκώς,
ὃν εἰ μὴ συνέβη κατορθῶσαι τοῖς τότε, ἡμεῖς
οἱ νῦν οὐκ ἂν εἴχομεν τὴν πόλιν, ἢ τὴν ἐλευθερίαν
ἡμῖν κεκομισμένος ἢ τῶν οἰκιστῶν ὑπάρχῃ τις·
οὐ γὰρ ἔχομεν σαφῶς εἰπεῖν τίνες εἰσὶν οἷς

---

[1] For εἰκόνας Wilamowitz conjectured εἰκόνα.

---

[1] Cf. Sophocles, Ant. 312: οὐκ ἐξ ἅπαντος δεῖ τὸ κερδαίνειν
φιλεῖν.
[2] See also § 77. οἰκιστής, like κτίστης (' restorer,' or
primarily, ' founder,' was evidently an honorary title at
Rhodes. It seems about equivalent to the Latin ' pater
patriae,' applied to Cicero after he suppressed the Catilinarian
conspiracy. Plutarch (Life of Cicero 22. 3) uses the expres-

as honours and grateful recognition are acquired through virtue alone.

Furthermore, those things for which a man has paid the price to their owners nobody even thinks of maintaining, I presume, that he cannot justly be permitted to keep for himself, and the more so, the greater the price he has paid. Well, each and every one of these men *has* paid a price for his statue and no moderate price either; some of them brilliant service as generals in defence of the city, others as ambassadors, while others have given trophies won from the enemy, and certain others money as well, perhaps—not, by heavens, a mere matter of a thousand or five hundred drachmas, sums for which it is possible to erect statues.

Well, what then? Is it not the established usage, at any rate among men who are not utterly lacking in sense of justice, that whoever is dispossessed of any piece of property should recover at least what he paid from those who have seized it? Would you, then, be willing to give back the favours in return for which you voted those honoured men their statues? It is to your advantage, at any rate, to make payment—since there are those who think a man ought to look out for his own advantage from whatever source.[1] Therefore, if a man has carried through a war successfully, a war so threatening that, had he not had the good fortune to win it for the people of his day, we who now live would not have our city, or if he has won back our freedom for us, or is one of the Restorers [2] of our city—for we cannot state specifically what persons have enjoyed

sion, "Saviour and Restorer of his Country," σωτῆρα καὶ κτίστην τῆς πατρίδος, as its Greek equivalent.

συμβέβηκεν ἢ συμβήσεται, τοῦ πράγματος εἰκῇ
γιγνομένου καὶ μόνον ἔθει τινί· μὴ δυσχερὲς
εἰπεῖν ᾗ τὸ μετὰ ταῦτα, ὅτι καὶ τῆς πόλεως αὐτῆς
ἀποστῆναι δεήσει βουλομένους[1] γε τὰ δίκαια
ποιεῖν. εἰ δὲ δή τις εἴη τι τοιοῦτον δεδωκὼς
ὃ μηδὲ βουληθέντας ἀποδοῦναι δυνατόν· μύριοι
δ᾽ εἰσὶν οἱ τὰς ψυχὰς προειμένοι ἑαυτῶν ὑπὲρ τῆς
πόλεως καὶ τοῦ ζῆν ἐωνημένοι τὴν εἰκόνα καὶ τὴν
ἐπιγραφήν, καθάπερ εἶπον καὶ πρότερον, ἆρ᾽ οὐ
δεινὰ πάσχουσιν;

62   Οὐ τοίνυν οὐδὲ ἐκεῖνο ἔστιν εἰπεῖν, ὅτι οὐχὶ
ἡμεῖς ἐσμεν οἱ ταῦτ᾽ εἰληφότες. πρῶτον μὲν
γὰρ ἅπαντα ὀφείλουσι τὰ τῶν προγόνων οὐχ
ἧττον αὐτῶν ἐκεῖνοι[2] εἰς οὓς ἄν ποτε καθήκῃ
τὸ γένος. οὐ γὰρ ἀφίστασθαί γε φήσετε τῆς
διαδοχῆς. εἶτα πάνθ᾽ ὅσα ἐξ ὧν τότε ἐκείνους
τινὲς εὐηργετήκασι καὶ προυθυμοῦντο πάσχοντες
ἢ δρῶντες ὑπὲρ αὐτῶν συνήχθη[3] χρήσιμα καὶ
μεγάλα, ὑμῖν ἔστι νῦν· ἡ δόξα τῆς πόλεως, τὸ
μέγεθος, τὸ χωρὶς μιᾶς αὐτὴν πασῶν τῶν ἄλλων
63   ὑπερέχειν. εἰ τοίνυν, ὅτι μὴ παρ᾽ ὑμῶν εἰλήφασι
διὰ τοῦτο ἔλαττον ἀδικεῖν οἴεσθε, ἢ εἴ τι τῶν
ἄλλως[4] ὑπαρχόντων τινὸς ἀφαιρεῖσθε, τῶν ἄγαν
τι φανερῶν ἀγνοεῖτε· πρῶτον μὲν ὅτι πάντες οἳ
τινα ἀποστεροῦντες ὁτιοῦν κἀκεῖνον ἀδικοῦσιν
οὐχ ἧττον, παρ᾽ οὗ ποτ᾽ ἂν τοῦτο εἰληφὼς τύχῃ·

---

[1] βουλομένους Emperius : βουλομένοις EB, μὴ βουλομένου M.
[2] αὐτῶν ἐκεῖνοι Cohoon, αὐτοὶ ἐκεῖνοι Schwartz: αὐτῶν
ἐκείνων. αὐτῶν ἐκείνων εἰς ὅσους Capps.
[3] συνήχθη Reiske : συνήθη.   [4] ἄλλως Arnim : ἄλλων.

---

[1] Rome,

this good fortune, or will enjoy it, since that comes as it will and only by caprice, so to speak—I am afraid the conclusion may be unpleasant to state, namely, that if we wish to do the right thing, we shall actually have to cede to him the city herself! But if there should be any man who has indeed made such a splendid offering that even with the best of intentions we are unable to repay him—and countless are those who have sacrificed their lives on behalf of the city and at the price of life itself have bought their statue and the inscription—are they not, as I asked before, being treated shamefully?

And what is more, we cannot say that it is not ourselves who have received these benefits. For, in the first place, all the obligations incurred by our ancestors are debts which are owed, no less than they were owed by the ancestors themselves, by all those to whom their blood has descended. For you will not say that you withdraw from the succession! In the second place, all the benefits, valuable and great as they are, which have accrued from the services which certain men rendered to your ancestors in their time, and from what they gladly suffered or did in their behalf, are now yours: the glory of your city, its greatness, its pre-eminence over all other cities save one.[1] If, therefore, simply because these benefactors did not receive their gifts from you directly, you think you are committing a lesser wrong than if you take away from a man a piece of property that came into his hands in some other way, you are blind to truths most patent: first, that all those who deprive anybody of anything whatsoever do just as great a wrong to the man from whom he once happens to have received it; for instance,

οἷον οἱ τῶν δημοσίων τι καταλύοντες οἰκοδομημά
των, ὅ τις τῶν καθ᾽ ἕνα ἐποίησε χαριζόμενος
ὑμῖν, μᾶλλον ἂν δόξειαν[1] τὸν ποιήσαντα ἀδι
κεῖν ἢ τὴν πόλιν. οὐκοῦν ὁ αὐτὸς λόγος κἂν[2]
ἡ πόλις ᾖ τι τῶν ἰδιωτῶν τινι δεδωκυῖα πρὸς τὸν
ἀφαιρούμενον τοῦτο. τοιγαροῦν[3] ὑμεῖς πρὸς
ἐκείνοις, ὧν τὰς εἰκόνας ἀνεστήσατε, καὶ τὴν
πόλιν, οἶμαι, τὴν δεδωκυῖαν ἀδικεῖτε, τοῦτ᾽ ἔστιν
64 ἑαυτούς. ἀλλ᾽ ὁ μὲν εἰς ἄλλον ἁμαρτὼν ὥστε
ἑαυτὸν ὠφελῆσαι κακίᾳ μόνον ἐστὶν ἔνοχος ἐν[4]
τοῖς πολλοῖς· ὁ δ᾽ ἑαυτὸν ἀδικῶν ἐν οἷς ἕτερον,
τῆς μὲν πονηρίας ὑπερβολήν τινα ἔδειξεν, ἐκ
περιττοῦ δὲ ἀνόητος δοκεῖ.

Πρὸς τούτῳ δ᾽ ἂν ἴδοι τις καὶ ἕτερον· ὁ μὲν
ἀφαιρούμενος ἁπλῶς ὅ τις ἔχει δικαίως, ὅτῳ δήποτε
τρόπῳ κτησάμενος, κατ᾽ αὐτὸ τὸ πρᾶγμα ἁμαρτά
νει, φύσει τι ποιῶν ἄτοπον· ὁ δὲ τῶν ὑφ᾽ ἑαυτοῦ
δεδομένων ἐν μέρει τιμῆς καὶ χάριτός τινα ἀποστε
ρῶν οὐ μόνον τὸ κοινὸν τοῦτο παραβαίνει, καθ᾽
ὃ προσήκει μηδένα βλάπτειν, ἀλλὰ καὶ χρηστὸν
ἄνδρα ἀδικεῖ, καὶ τοῦτον ὃν ἥκιστα αὐτῷ προσῆκεν.
οὐδαμῇ γὰρ ἰδεῖν ἔστι τοῖς φαύλοις τὰς τιμὰς
διδομένας οὐδὲ ὑφ᾽ ὧν μηδὲν εὖ πεπόνθασιν.
65 ὅσῳ δὴ χεῖρον τὸ τοὺς ἀγαθοὺς ἀφαιρεῖσθαι τιμὰς
ἢ τὸ τοὺς ἄλλους, καὶ τὸ τοὺς εὐεργέτας βλάπτειν
τοῦ τὸν τυχόντα ἀδικεῖν, οὐδένα λανθάνει.

Καὶ τοίνυν καὶ τοὺς Ἐφεσίους, εἴ τις ἀφέλοι

---

[1] δόξειαν Dindorf : δόξειε EB, δείξαιεν M.
[2] κἂν Jacobs: καὶ εἰ EB, καὶ M.
[3] τοιγαροῦν Emperius : ἀρ᾽ οὖν EB, ἄρα M.
[4] ἐν added by Weil.

those who demolish any public building which some individual benefactor built as an expression of his gratitude to you, would seem to wrong the builder more than the city. Therefore, when it is the city that has given something to one of its own citizens, the same argument applies to the man who would deprive him of this. For this reason, in addition to wronging the persons whose statues you have set up, you are also, in my opinion, wronging the city which gave them, that is, your own selves. But whereas he who sins against another man and thereby benefits himself is guilty of wrongdoing only, in the eyes of the majority, he who wrongs his own self while wronging another man shows an exceeding measure of depravity and is looked upon as needlessly a fool also.

Besides this, one might consider another point also. The man who simply takes away from any one that which is justly in his possession, no matter how he got it, errs in this very act, since he is doing a thing which is by its very nature unseemly; but the man who deprives any one of what he himself has given in the way of honour and gratitude, not only violates that universal principle which says that we should injure no one, but also does wrong to a good man, and that, too, the man whom he ought least of all to wrong. For in no case do you see honours being given to worthless men or to those from whom no benefit has been received. How very much worse it is to rob good men of honours bestowed than to rob anybody else, and to injure your benefactors than to injure any chance person, is something that nobody fails to see.

Moreover, let us take the case of the Ephesians:

τὸ [1] πρὸς τὴν θεόν, κατ' αὐτὸ τοῦτο φαίη τις
ἂν ἁμαρτάνειν, λαβόντας ἀπ' ἐκείνων τῶν χρη-
μάτων· τοὺς δὲ [2] οὕτω προσφερομένους ταῖς
εἰκόσιν, οὐ μόνον διὰ τὰ νῦν εἰρημένα δήπουθεν,
ὅτι μηδὲν προσήκοντας ἀνθρώπους ἔμελλον ἀδικεῖν,
ὧν τοὺς πολλοὺς οὐδὲ ἔγνωσαν, ἀλλὰ καὶ διὰ
τὴν ἀπὸ τοῦ πράγματος αἰτίαν. τοῖς μὲν γὰρ
παρακαταθήκην τινὰ μὴ φυλάξασιν οὐδεὶς ἂν
οὐδὲν ἔτι τῶν ἑαυτοῦ πιστεύσειεν· τοὺς δὲ ὑβρί-
ζοντας εἰς τοὺς εὐεργέτας οὐδεὶς κρινεῖ χάριτος
ἀξίους. ὥσθ' ὁ κίνδυνος ὑμῖν μὲν ἐν τῷ μηκέτ'
εὖ πάσχειν ὑπὸ μηδενός, ἐκείνοις δὲ ἐν τῷ μηκέτι
φυλάττειν τὰ ἀλλότρια.

66   Βούλομαι τοίνυν ὑμέτερόν τι ἔργον εἰπεῖν οὐ πάλαι
μὲν γεγονός, εὐδοκιμοῦν δὲ παρὰ πᾶσιν οὐχ
ἧττον τῶν πάνυ παλαιῶν,[3] ἵν' εἰδῆτε παραθέντες
εἰ καθόλου τοὺς τοιούτους ἄξιόν [4] ἐστι τοιοῦτόν
τι ποιεῖν. μετὰ γὰρ τὸν συνεχῆ καὶ μακρὸν
ἐκεῖνον Ῥωμαίων πόλεμον, ὃν πρὸς ἀλλήλους
ἐπολέμησαν, ὅτε ὑμῖν ἀτυχῆσαι συνέβη διὰ τὴν

---

[1] ἀφέλοι τὸ Emperius: ἀφέλοι τι τῶν EB, ἀφέλοιτο M.
[2] δὲ added by Selden.
[3] παλαιῶν Casaubon: χαλεπῶν.
[4] ἄξιόν Morel: ἄξιος.

---

[1] In the plain outside the walls of Ephesus was the famous
temple of Artemis, or Diana, which was regarded as one of the
wonders of the world. It contained an image of the goddess
which was believed to have fallen down from Zeus. See *Acts
of the Apostles* 19. 23–28 and 35, and § 54 *supra*.

Leaving aside scruples having to do with the goddess,[1] one would say that they commit a misdeed if they take from the deposits to which I have referred, so far as the act itself is concerned;[2] but that people who treat the statues in this way do an injustice, not merely, to be sure, for the reasons already given—that they would be wronging persons in no wise related to themselves, the majority of whom they did not even know—but also on account of the ill repute which arises from their act. For to those who have not taken good care of a deposit entrusted to them nobody would thereafter entrust any of his own property; but those who insult their benefactors will by nobody be esteemed to deserve a favour. Consequently, the danger for you is that you will no longer receive benefactions at the hands of anybody at all, while the danger to the Ephesians is merely that they will no longer have other persons' property to take care of.

I wish, moreover, to mention a deed of yours which took place not very long ago, and yet is commended by everyone no less than are the deeds of the men of old, in order that you may know by making comparison whether on principle it is seemly for people like you to be guilty of such behaviour as this. After that continuous and protracted civil war among the Romans,[3] during which it was your misfortune to suffer a reverse on account of your

[2] Even if the acts were not a sacrilege, a sin against the goddess, cf. §§ 54 ff.
[3] He refers to the battles between the leaders of the aristocratic and the popular party at Rome which began with the fighting between Marius and Sulla and ended with the victory of Augustus over Mark Antony at Actium in 31 B.C.

πρὸς τὸν δῆμον εὔνοιαν, ἐπειδὴ πέρας εἶχε τὰ
δεινὰ καὶ πάντες ᾤοντο σεσῶσθαι, καθάπερ ἐν
ταῖς μεγάλαις νόσοις πολλάκις δεινοῦ τινος
ἐδέησε βοηθήματος, καὶ τότε ἔδοξε τὰ πράγματα
ζητεῖν τοιαύτην ἐπανόρθωσιν. ὅθεν πᾶσιν ἐδόθη
67 τοῖς ἔξωθεν χρεῶν ἄφεσις. ἀσμένως δὲ αὐτῶν
προσεμένων καὶ τὸ πρᾶγμα δωρεὰν ἡγησαμένων,
μόνοι τῶν ἄλλων ὑμεῖς οὐκ ἐδέξασθε, καίτοι τῆς
ἁλώσεως ὑμῖν, ὅπερ ἔφην, ἄρτι γεγενημένης καὶ
τῶν πολεμίων ἐν τῇ πόλει τὰς οἰκίας μόνον
εἰακότων· ἀλλ' ὅμως δεινὸν ὑμῖν ἔδοξε τὸ ἐν
ὁποίῳ δήποτε καιρῷ παραβῆναί τι τῶν δικαίων
καὶ διὰ τὰς συμφορὰς τὰς καταλαβούσας ἔτι
καὶ τὴν πίστιν ἀνελεῖν τὴν παρ' αὐτοῖς· καὶ τἆλλα
πάντα Ῥωμαίοις παραχωροῦντες οὐκ ἠξιώσατε
καθ' ἓν τοῦτο παραχωρῆσαι, τὸ μηδὲν αἰσχρὸν
68 αἱρεῖσθαι κέρδους ἕνεκα. ὧν γάρ, οἶμαι, τὴν
ἐκείνων πόλιν ἑωρᾶτε [1] μὴ δεηθεῖσαν δι᾿ ἀρετὴν
ἅμα καὶ εὐτυχίαν, τούτων [2] τὴν ὑμετέραν ἀπεφή-
νατε μὴ δεομένην διὰ μόνην τὴν ἀρετήν. οὐ τοίνυν
φήσετε ἔλαττον, ὦ ἄνδρες Ῥόδιοι, τὴν χάριν
ὀφείλεσθαι τοῖς εὖ πεποιηκόσιν ἢ τοῖς συμ-
βάλλουσι [3] τὸ χρέος.

Εἶτα τὸ μὲν μὴ ἑκόντας ἐκτίνειν τὰ ὀφειλόμενα
δεινὸν ὑμῖν ἔδοξε, τὸ δὲ ἀποδόντας ἀφαιρεῖσθαι

---

[1] ἑωρᾶτε Morel : εὕρετε EB, εὕρατε M.
[2] τούτων Cohoon : τούτου.
[3] συμβάλλουσι] συμβαλοῦσι Reiske.

---

[1] Rhodes espoused the cause of Julius Caesar, in punishment for which Cassius captured and plundered the city in
42 B.C. See page 3, and page 106, note 1.

sympathy with the democracy,[1] when, finally, the
terrible scenes came to an end, and all felt they
were safe at last, just as in a severe illness there
is often need of some heroic remedy, so then, too,
the situation seemed to require a similar corrective
measure. Consequently all the provinces were
granted a remission of their debts.[2] Now the others
accepted it gladly, and saw in the measure a welcome
gift ; but you Rhodians alone of all rejected it,
although the capture of your city had recently
occurred, as I have said, and the enemy had spared
nothing in the city except your dwellings. But
nevertheless, you thought it would be a shame to
violate any principle of justice in any crisis whatsoever and on account of the disasters that had befallen
you to destroy your credit to boot ; and while deferring
to the Romans in everything else, you did not think
it right to yield to them in this one respect—of choosing a dishonourable course for the sake of gain.[3]
For the things, methinks, which you saw that Rome
did not lack because of its high character at
once and of its good fortune, these you demonstrated
that your city did not lack, because of its high
character alone. Certainly you will not say, men
of Rhodes, that gratitude is owing less to those who
have done a service than to those who were ready
to contribute the amount of your debt.[4]

After that, though you thought it a scandal not
to pay your debts willingly, yet is it an equitable

[2] Perhaps he refers to the relief which Augustus afforded the
various provinces on his visits to them.

[3] In 30 B.C. Augustus allowed the cities of Asia Minor,
which was ruined financially, to declare bankruptcy, but, as
we read here, Rhodes refused to avail herself of this concession.

[4] Cf. Demosthenes *In Lept.* 12.

μέτριον; οὐ γὰρ δὴ τὸ μετὰ πάντων ἀσχημονεῖν
τοῦ μόνους αἴσχιον ὑπειλήφατε. καίτοι τοσαύτης
μεταβολῆς καθ᾽ ὃν εἴρηκα καιρὸν γενομένης καὶ
περὶ πάντα συγχύσεως, τά γε [1] δοθέντα ὑπῆρχε
βεβαίως ἔχειν τοῖς προειληφόσι, καὶ οὐδεὶς ἐτόλ-
μησεν εἰσπράττειν τοὺς ἤδη τι κεκομισμένους.
ὑμεῖς δὲ νῦν οὐδὲ ἃ ἔφθητε διαλῦσαι τοῖς εὐεργέταις
ἐᾶτε, ἀλλ᾽ οἱ μηδὲ τῶν αὐτῶν μηδὲν ὑπομείναντες
τότε τοῖς ἄλλοις, καὶ ταῦτα ἐπταικότες, νῦν εὐ-
τυχοῦντες πράττετε ὃ μηδὲ ἐκείνων τότε μηδὲ εἷς.

69   Καίτοι τὸ μὲν περὶ [2] τῶν χρεῶν γεγονὸς εὕροι τις
ἂν καὶ ἐν ἄλλῳ χρόνῳ καὶ Σόλωνα λέγεται παρὰ
Ἀθηναίοις ποτὲ ποιῆσαι. δίχα γὰρ τοῦ πολλάκις ἀναγκαίως αὐτὸ συμβαίνειν ἐκ τῆς ἀπορίας
τῶν δεδανεισμένων, ἔσθ᾽ ὅτε οὐδὲ ἀδίκως γίγνεται
διὰ τὸ μέγεθος τῶν τόκων, ὅταν τινὲς πολλαπλασίως [3] ὦσιν ἐν τούτοις τὰ ἀρχαῖα κεκομισμένοι.
τὸ δὲ τὰς χάριτας τὰς ἀντὶ τῶν εὐεργεσιῶν ἀποστερεῖσθαι τοὺς εἰληφότας οὔτε ἀφορμὴν οὐδεμίαν
δύναται παρασχεῖν εὔλογον οὔτε εἰσηγήσατο
οὐδεὶς πώποτε, ἀλλὰ μόνου τούτου σχεδὸν ἁπάντων
οὐδέποτε καιρὸς γέγονε.

---

[1] γε Emperius : τε.   [2] περὶ added by Capps.
[3] πολλαπλασίως Capps : πολλάκις.

---

[1] Cf. Demosthenes *In Lept.* 12.
[2] There seems to be no reference to any particular event in
this passage; at any rate no light is thrown by anything that
is known from other sources upon just what τὰ δοθέντα in line 4
of the text means. But the words would seem to refer to
'gifts' of some sort rather than, for instance, to advances or
loans of money.
[3] Solon relieved Athenian debtors of a part of their debts,
chiefly by a depreciation of the coinage. This disburdening
measure was called the σεισάχθεια or 'shaking off of burdens.'

act, having discharged an obligation, then to rob the recipient of his requital?[1] For surely you have not supposed that it is more shameful to act dishonourably in common with all the world than to be alone in so doing! And yet when that great revolution occurred at the time I have mentioned and there was repudiation of every kind, the gifts which had been made remained undisturbed in the possession of those who had received them previously, and no one was so bold as to try to exact a return from those who already had anything.[2] You, however, are at this present time not leaving undisturbed even what you were so prompt to pay to your benefactors, but although at that time you would not consent to follow in any respect the same course as all the others took, and that too, in spite of the reverses you had suffered, now when you are prosperous you do what not a single one of the peoples in that crisis did!

And yet the action taken in regard to the debts you will find was taken at other times as well; Solon, for instance, is said to have taken it once at Athens.[3] For apart from the fact that this measure often becomes necessary in view of the insolvency of those who have contracted loans, there are times also when it is even justifiable on account of the high rate of interest, on occasions when lenders have got back in interest their principal many times over. But to deprive the recipients of the tokens of gratitude which they have received in return for their benefactions can find no plausible excuse, nor has anyone ever yet formally proposed the adoption of this procedure; no, this is almost the only thing in the world for which there has never yet been found any occasion.

75

70 Καὶ μὴν δύο ταῦτα ὁμοίως τῆς μεγίστης[1] φυλακῆς ἐν τοῖς νόμοις ἠξίωται καὶ ἀρᾶς καὶ ἐπιτιμίων τῶν ἐσχάτων, ἐάν τις εἰσάγῃ χρεῶν ἀποκοπὰς ἢ ὡς τὴν γῆν ἀναδάσασθαι προσήκει. τούτων τοίνυν τὸ μὲν παρ' ὑμῖν οὐ γέγονε· τὸ δὲ λοιπόν, ὃ μηδ' ὅλως ἴσμεν εἴ ποτε συνέβη, σκέψασθε παραθέντες τῷ νῦν ἐξεταζομένῳ πράγματι. τῆς μέν γε χώρας ἄνωθεν διαιρουμένης, τοῦτο ἂν εἴη δεινότατον τὸ ἐξ ἴσου γίγνεσθαι τὸν ἔχοντα πρότερον τῷ μὴ κεκτημένῳ· τῆς δὲ εἰκόνος ἑτέρῳ δοθείσης οὐδαμῶς ἴσος ἐστὶν ὁ ἀφαιρεθεὶς τῷ λαβόντι. ὁ μὲν γὰρ τέτευχεν, εἴπερ ἄρα, τῆς τιμῆς, τῷ δὲ οὐθὲν περίεστι.

71 Φέρε τοίνυν, εἴ τις ἔροιτο τὸν στρατηγὸν ὑμῶν ἐφεστῶτα καὶ κελεύοντα ἐκχαράττειν τὴν ἐπιγραφήν, ἕτερον δ' ἐγγράφειν, τί ἐστι τὸ γιγνόμενον; ἢ νὴ Δία πέφηνέ τι δεινὸν εἰργασμένος τὴν πόλιν τοσούτοις ἔτεσιν ὕστερον οὗτος ἀνήρ; πρὸς τοῦ Διὸς οὐκ ἂν ὑμῖν δοκεῖ[2] διατραπῆναι, καὶ ταῦτα ἐὰν ᾖ μέτριος; ἐγὼ μὲν γὰρ οἶμαι καὶ τὸν τεχνίτην ἐρυθριάσειν. εἰ δὲ δὴ παῖδες ἢ συγγενεῖς τινες παρατύχοιεν τἀνδρὸς ἐκείνου, πόσα οἴεσθε ἀφήσειν αὐτοὺς δάκρυα, ἐπειδὰν ἄρξηταί τις ἀφανίζειν τὸ ὄνομα; οὐμενοῦν·

72 ἀλλὰ ἐνστήσονται πάντες εἰς ὑμᾶς παριόντες,

---

[1] μεγίστης Reiske : μεγάλης.
[2] δοκεῖ Casaubon : δοκῇ.

Furthermore, the following two practices have alike been considered worthy of being most carefully guarded against in our laws and as deserving of execration and the most extreme penalties, namely, a proposal that debts be cancelled, or that the land ought to be redistributed. Well, of these two measures, the former has never been adopted in your city; the latter, however, of which we have not the slightest knowledge that it ever has been taken, please consider by comparing it with the practice now under examination. If the land were being parcelled out anew, the very worst consequence would be that the original holder should be put on an equality with the man who possessed no land at all; but where a man's statue has been given to another, the one who has been robbed is by no means on an equality with the man who received it. For the latter has gained the honour, if you can really call it such, whereas the other has nothing left.

Come, then, if any one were to question the magistrate who is set over you, who commands that the inscription be erased and another man's name engraved in its place, asking: "What does this mean? Ye gods, has this man been found guilty of having done the city some terrible wrong so many years after the deed?" In heaven's name, do you not think that he would be deterred, surely if he is a man of common decency? For my part I think that even the mason will blush for shame. And then if children or kinsmen of the great man should happen to appear, what floods of tears do you think they will shed when some one begins to obliterate the name? No, not they merely, but everybody will protest, coming before you, in your assembly, creating

εἰς τὸν δῆμον, βοῶντες. ἆρ᾽ οὖν, οὐδ᾽ ἂν τοιοῦτο
συμβῇ, κωλύσετε οὐδὲ ἐπιστραφήσεσθε; ἐγὼ
μέν οὐδὲν ἂν τοιοῦτον περὶ ὑμῶν ὑπολάβοιμι,
μᾶλλον δὲ καὶ νῦν φημι λανθάνειν αὐτὸ γιγνόμενον, ἀλλ᾽ οὐκ ἐάσετε γνόντες· οὐκοῦν νῦν γε
ἐπίστασθε δήπουθεν τὸ πρᾶγμα ὅλον, ὥστε καθάπαξ κωλῦσαι προσήκει.

Νὴ Δία, ἀλλ᾽ οὐχ ὅμοιόν ἐστι, πολλῶν ὄντων
οἷς μηδεὶς προσήκει, καὶ τοῦ πράγματος συμβαί-
νοντος ἐπ᾽ οὐδενὶ τῶν γνωρίμων.

73   Ἐγὼ δ᾽ ὅτι μὲν οὐκ εἴ τινες ἀγνοοῦσι προσήκοντας ἑαυτοῖς ἐνίους τούτων, ὅπερ εἰκός, διὰ
τοῦτο ἔλαττον ἀδικοῦνται τῶν προγόνων ἀτιμαζο-
μένων, ἀφίημι· χαλεπώτερον δὲ ἄλλως εἶναί μοι
δοκεῖ τὸ γιγνόμενον εἰς ἐκείνους, οἷς μηδὲ ἔστιν
οἰκεῖος μηδὲ εἷς ἔτι. καὶ γὰρ τῶν ζώντων
δοκεῖ δεινότερον εἶναι τούτους ἀδικεῖν οἷς μηδὲ
εἷς ἔστιν ὁ βοηθῶν ἔτι. ἐπεὶ κατά γε τοῦτο
λεγέτωσαν μηδὲν εἶναι χαλεπὸν μηδὲ τὸ τοὺς
ὀρφανοὺς βλάπτειν τοὺς παντάπασιν ἐρήμους, οἳ
μήτε ἑαυτοῖς ἀμύνειν δύνανται μήτε ἄλλον ἔχουσι
τὸν κηδόμενον. ἀλλὰ ὑμεῖς τοὐναντίον καὶ μᾶλλον
ἐπὶ τούτοις ἀγανακτεῖτε καὶ δημοσίᾳ καθίστασθε
ἐπιτρόπους, ὅπως μηδὲν ἀδικῶνται.

74   Καθόλου δὲ πάντων ὧν μέλλουσιν ἐρεῖν λόγων
οὐδενὸς ἔχοντος ἐπιεικὲς οὐδέν, ὁ τοιοῦτός ἐστιν

an uproar. Let me ask you, then: Even if such a demonstration does occur, will you refrain from trying to prevent the deed, and take no notice at all? I for my part cannot conceive of your taking such a course, but rather maintain that even now you do not know that this is going on, but that you will not permit it, now that you have learned of it; anyhow you know it all now at any rate, I imagine, so that it is your duty to put a stop to the practice once for all.

"Oh! but assuredly your illustration is not apposite," someone may object, "since many of them are persons who have no surviving relative and the practice is not followed in the case of any person who is well known."

Well, for my part, I will pass over the point that even if some are unaware, as is likely, that some of these honoured men are related to them, yet none the less on this account they suffer an injustice if their ancestors are dishonoured. But far more grievous at all events, it seems to me, is the wrong done to those honoured men who have not one single surviving relative. For in the case of the living it seems a greater indignity to wrong those who have not even one person left to help them. For on that principle you might as well say that it is not cruel to injure orphans either, children utterly alone in the world, who cannot protect themselves and have no one else to care for them. But you, on the contrary, look upon such conduct with even greater displeasure, and through the state appoint guardians to protect them from any possible wrong.

But, speaking in general terms, while none of the pleas that these people intend to urge has any

DIO CHRYSOSTOM

ἀτοπώτατος, ὡς ἄρα οὐδενὸς ἅπτονται τῶν
γνωρίμων ἀνδριάντων οὐδὲ οὓς ἐπίσταταί τις ὧν
εἰσιν, ἀλλὰ ἀσήμοις τισὶ καὶ σφόδρα παλαιοῖς
καταχρῶνται. καθάπερ εἴ τις λέγοι μηδένα τῶν
ἐπιφανῶν ἀδικεῖν πολιτῶν, ἀλλὰ τοὺς δημοτικοὺς
καὶ οὓς μηδεὶς οἶδεν. καίτοι μὰ τὸν Δία οὐχ
ὅμοιον. ἐν μὲν γὰρ τοῖς ζῶσι καὶ δι' εὐγένειαν
καὶ δι' ἀρετὴν ἄλλος ἄλλου φανερώτερός ἐστι,
καὶ διὰ πλοῦτον τοῦτο συμβαίνει καὶ δι' ἑτέρας
προφάσεις ἀξιολόγους· ἐπὶ δὲ τῶν εἰκόνων μὴ
τοὐναντίον λέγοι τις ἂν ὡς εἰσιν αὗται βελτιόνων
ἀνδρῶν. οὐ γὰρ δι' ἀγένειαν ἢ κακίαν τινὰ
οὐκ ἐπιστάμεθα αὐτούς, οἵ γε τῶν αὐτῶν τοῖς
λαμπροτάτοις τετεύχασιν, ἀλλὰ διὰ μῆκος χρόνου
τοῦτο γέγονεν.

75   Ὅσῳ τοίνυν τοὺς πρότερον ἀεὶ τῶν ἐπιγιγνο-
μένων πάντες ἡγοῦνται φύσει κρείττους, καὶ
πάλαι τὸ[1] τυχεῖν τινας τούτου σπανιώτερον
ὑπῆρχε, τοσούτῳ περὶ ἀμείνους ἄνδρας καὶ μειζόνων ἀγαθῶν αἰτίους ὁμολογοῦσιν ἁμαρτάνειν.
ὅτι δ' ἀληθῆ ταῦτα ἀμφότερα, δῆλον. τούς τε
γὰρ σφόδρα ἀρχαίους ἡμιθέους ὄντας ἐπιστάμεθα
καὶ τοὺς μετ' αὐτοὺς οὐ πολὺ ἐκείνων χείρονας·

---

[1] πάλαι τὸ Arnim : τὸ πάλαι.

---

[1] Cf. §§ 80, 124, 126, 163; Discourse 21. 1 ff. and Discourse
15. This is a Stoic doctrine said to be due to Chrysippus.
Cf. Lucian, *Rhetorum Praeceptor* 9; Themistius, Oration 22,
p. 281 A; Plato, *Laws* 10, p. 886 C; Lucretius, 2. 1157 ff.;
Seneca, *Epistle* 90. 44 : " Still I cannot deny that in the past
there existed men of lofty spirit and, if I may say so, fresh from
the gods. For there is no doubt whatever that the world,

equitable basis whatever, the most absurd plea of all is to say that after all they are not molesting any of the statues of well-known persons, nor those whose owners any one knows, but that they take liberties with sundry insignificant and very ancient ones. It is as if a person should say that he did not wrong any prominent citizen, but only those of the common crowd, persons whom nobody knows! And yet, by heavens, I maintain that the two cases are not alike. For in the case of the living one person is more prominent than another owing to his good birth or his good character, and it may also be on account of his wealth or for other good reasons; but in the case of the statues, on the contrary, one cannot point to one group and say 'These are statues of better men.' For it is not due to their humble birth or any baseness that we do not know them, seeing that they have received the same honours as the most famous men, but our ignorance has come about through lapse of time.

Moreover, insofar as the men of the past were, as all believe, always superior by nature to those of the succeeding generations,[1] and as in ancient times it was a rarer thing for any men to receive this honour, just in so far were those better men and the authors of greater blessings against whom it is acknowledged we are sinning. And that both these statements are true is clear, for we know that the exceedingly ancient men were demi-gods and that those who followed them were not much inferior to them; in

before it was worn out, produced better things."—Non tamen negaverim fuisse alti spiritus viros et, ut ita dicam, a dis recentes. neque enim dubium est quin meliora mundus nondum effetus ediderit.

ἔπειτα τοὺς ἐφεξῆς ἐλάττονας ἀεὶ κατὰ τὸν χρόνον,
καὶ τέλος τοὺς νῦν ὁποίους ἡμᾶς αὐτοὺς οἴδαμεν.
καὶ πρότερον μὲν οὐδὲ τοῖς ἀποθνήσκουσι πᾶσιν
ὑπὲρ τῆς πόλεως ἦν ἑστάναι χαλκοῖς, ἀλλ' εἰ
μή τις ὑπερφυᾶ καὶ θαυμαστὰ πράξειε· νῦν δὲ
τοὺς καταπλέοντας τιμῶμεν, ὥστ' εἴπερ ἄρα, τοὺς
ὕστερον μᾶλλον καὶ τοὺς ἔγγιστα τοῦ [1] νῦν ἀνακει-
76 μένους μεταποιητέον. οὐδὲ γὰρ ἐκεῖνο ἀγνοεῖτε
δήπουθεν ὅτι πάντες οἱ νοῦν ἔχοντες τοὺς παλαιοὺς
τῶν φίλων μᾶλλον ἀγαπῶσι καὶ περὶ πλείονος
ποιοῦνται τῶν δι' ὀλίγου γεγονότων, καὶ τούς γε
πατρικοὺς τῷ παντὶ πλέον ἢ τοὺς ὑφ' αὐτῶν
ἐγνωσμένους. οἱ μὲν γὰρ τὰ πρὸς τούτους
παραβαίνοντες μόνους αὐτοὺς ἀδικοῦσιν· οἱ δὲ
τῶν πρὸς ἐκείνους τι λύοντες καὶ τῶν κτησαμένων
77 αὐτοὺς ὀλιγωροῦσιν. καθόλου δέ, ὥσπερ ὅταν
τῶν ζώντων τις ἐξετάζηται παρ' ὑμῖν, ὃν αὐτοὶ
μὴ σφόδρα οἴδατε ἢ παντάπασιν ἀγνοεῖτε, τοῖς
ἐπισταμένοις αὐτὸν [2] προσέχετε καὶ τίθεσθε τὴν
ψῆφον κατὰ τοὺς μάρτυρας, ἄλλως τε ἂν ὦσιν
οὗτοι μὴ πονηροί, ταὐτὸ καὶ νῦν ποιήσατε·
ἐπεὶ καὶ περὶ ἀνδρῶν ὁ λόγος ἐστίν, οὓς φατι
μηδένα εἰδέναι τῶν ζώντων, παρὰ τῶν ἐγνωκότων
αὐτοὺς μάθετε. οἱ τοίνυν τότε ὄντες καὶ σαφέστατα ἐκείνους εἰδότες εὐεργέτας ἡγοῦντο τῆς πόλεως

---

[1] τοῦ added by Arnim.   [2] αὐτὸν Capps : αὐτούς.

---

[1] For instance, in the Athens of Demosthenes in this class
were the statues of only Solon, Harmodius, Aristogeiton,
Conon, Iphicrates, and Chabrias. See Wenkebach, *Quaestiones
Dioneae*, p. 59.

[2] See Friedländer, *Sittengeschichte Roms*, Vol. 3, pp. 226 and
230.

[3] That is, their own forefathers.

the second place, we understand that their successors steadily deteriorated in the course of time, and finally, we know that the men of to-day are no better than ourselves. Indeed formerly even those who gave their lives for the state were not in all cases set up in bronze,[1] but only the occasional man who performed extraordinary and wonderful exploits; but now we honour those that land at our ports,[2] so that we should transfer to new owners, if transfer we must, rather the later statues and those which have been set up nearest to the present time. For you are not unaware, I presume, that all persons of good sense love their old friends more and esteem them more highly than those who have become friends but recently, and that they honour their ancestral family friends altogether more than they do those whose acquaintance they themselves have made. For any who transgress the rights of these latter wrong *them* alone, but those who annul any of the rights of the former must also despise the men who acquire their friendship.[3] And, to state a general principle, just as when any man now living whom you do not know very well personally or not at all is being subjected to a judicial examination in your courts, you listen to those who do know him and cast your vote according to what the witnesses say, especially if they are not knaves; so do the same thing now also. Since we too are speaking concerning men whom they say that no one now alive knows anything about,[4] learn from those who did know them.[5] Well then, those who lived in their time, who knew them perfectly, regarded them as benefactors of the city and considered them worthy

---

[4] Cf. § 131.   [5] Cf. § 61.

DIO CHRYSOSTOM

καὶ τῶν μεγίστων ἠξίουν. οἷς οὐ θεμιτὸν ὑμᾶς
ἀπιστεῖν, ὑμετέροις γε οὖσι προγόνοις, οὐδὲ
φῆσαι πονηρούς.

78 Οὐ τοίνυν οὐδὲ τοιοῦτον οὐδέν ἐστιν εἰπεῖν,
ὡς κατὰ πολὺν χρόνον ἐσχήκασι τὰς τιμάς·
οὐ γὰρ ἔσθ᾽ ὅπως δείξουσι πλείονα ἐκείνους
χρόνον τιμωμένους ὑπὸ τῆς πόλεως ἢ τὴν πόλιν
ὑπ᾽ αὐτῶν εὖ πεπονθυῖαν. ὥσπερ οὖν ὁ χρέος
πάλαι μὲν ὀφείλων, πάλαι δὲ ἀποδούς, οὐθὲν πλέον
τι πεποίηκε τοῦ νῦν ἀποδιδόντος ὃ ἄρτι [1] εἴληφεν,
ὁμοίως οὐδ᾽ εἴ τις πάνυ πρὸ πολλοῦ τινα ἠμείψατο
79 τότε εὖ παθών. ἄλλως δέ,[2] εἰ μὲν ἀτέλειαν ἢ
χρήματα ἢ γῆν ἢ τοιοῦτόν τι δεδωκότες ἀφῃρεῖσθε,[3]
μᾶλλον ἂν ἴσως ἠδικοῦντο οἱ μετὰ ταῦτα
εἰληφότες· ὁ γὰρ χρόνον τινὰ κατασχὼν τὰ
τοιαῦτα ὠφέληταί τι καὶ προείληφεν. ἐπὶ δὲ
τῆς τιμῆς οὐδέν ἐστι τοιοῦτον. οἱ μὲν γάρ
εἰσιν εὐπορώτεροι καὶ τὸν ἄλλον χρόνον· ἃ γὰρ
ἐκτήσαντο, ἀπὸ τούτων ἔχουσιν· τοῖς δὲ τοὐναντίον
ἀτιμοτέροις ὑπάρχει γεγονέναι. ὅπου μὲν γὰρ
ἐλάττων ἡ ζημία τοῖς πολὺν χρόνον καρπωσαμένοις,
ὅπου δὲ ἡ ἀτιμία μείζων τοῖς σφόδρα παλαιᾶς
τιμῆς ἀφαιρουμένοις.

[1] ὃ ἄρτι Capps : ὅ τι Arnim : ὅτε.
[2] δὲ Cohoon : τε.
[3] ἀφῃρεῖσθε Casaubon : ἀφαιρεῖσθε EB, ἀφαιρεῖσθαι Mv.

---

[1] Cf. Demosthenes In Lept. 47 and 119.

of the highest honours. These are witnesses whom you have no right to disbelieve, being indeed your own forefathers—nor yet to declare that they were knaves.[1]

Furthermore, you cannot advance any such argument, either, as to say that those who were honoured long ago have held their honours for a long time. For it will not be possible for you to prove that those men have been honoured for a longer time by the city than the city has been the recipient of their benefactions. Hence, just as a man who incurred a debt long ago and long ago repaid it has done not a whit more than the man who pays back now what he has just received, so does a similar statement apply if it was very long ago indeed that a man requited another for a benefit received from him at that time. But the case would be different if you had given exemption from taxes, money, land, or some other such thing and were now taking it away—then perhaps those who would have received such an exemption afterwards *would* indeed suffer a greater wrong; for the man who has held such things for any length of time has received benefit and advantage therefrom already. But in the case of an honour conferred there is nothing like this. For whereas the former are better off for the future as well, since what they acquired then is the source of wealth which they enjoy now; the others, on the contrary, find that they have suffered an actual diminution of their honours. For in the one case the loss is less because the men have enjoyed the usufruct for a long time, but in the other case the dishonour is greater, since the victims are being deprived of a very ancient honour.

80 Ὅτι τοίνυν οὐδὲ ἀσεβείας ἀπήλλακται τὸ
γιγνόμενον, μάλιστα ὃν οὗτοί φασι τρόπον
δείξω,[1] κἂν ὑπερβολῆς ἕνεκα δόξω τισί λέγειν,
οὐχ, ὡς πρότερον εἶπον, ὅτι πάντα ἁπλῶς ἀσεβή-
ματά ἐστι τὰ περὶ τοὺς τεθνεῶτας γιγνόμενα,
ἀλλὰ ὅτι καὶ πάντες ἥρωας νομίζουσι τοὺς σφόδρα
παλαιοὺς ἄνδρας, κἂν[2] μηδὲν ἐξαίρετον ἔχωσι,
δι' αὐτόν, οἶμαι, τὸν χρόνον. τοὺς δὲ δὴ σεμνοὺς
οὕτως καὶ τῶν μεγίστων ἠξιωμένους, ὧν ἔνιοι
καὶ τὰς τελετὰς ἐσχήκασιν ἡρώων, τοὺς τοσαῦτα
ἔτη κειμένους, ὥστε καὶ τὴν μνήμην ἐπιλελοιπέναι,
πῶς ἔνι τῆς αὐτῆς τυγχάνειν προσηγορίας ἧς οἱ
τεθνηκότες ἐφ' ἡμῶν ἢ μικρὸν ἔμπροσθεν, ἄλλως
81 τε μηδενὸς ἄξιοι φανέντες; καὶ μὴν τά γε εἰς
τοὺς ἥρωας ἀσεβήματα οὐδ' ἂν ἀμφισβητήσειεν
οὐδεὶς ὡς οὐχὶ τὴν αὐτὴν ἔχει τάξιν, ἣν τὰ περὶ τοὺς
θεούς. τί οὖν; οὐκ ἀδίκημά ἐστι τὸ τὴν μνήμην ἀναιρεῖν; τὸ τὴν τιμὴν ἀφαιρεῖσθαι; τὸ
ἐκκόπτειν τὸ ὄνομα; δεινόν γε καὶ σχέτλιον,
82 ὦ Ζεῦ. ἀλλ' ἐὰν μὲν στέφανόν τις ἀφέλῃ τὸν
μίαν ἴσως ἢ δευτέραν μενοῦντα ἡμέραν, ἢ κηλῖδά
τινα τῷ χαλκῷ προσβάλῃ, τοῦτον ἡγήσεσθε
ἀσεβεῖν, τὸν δὲ ὅλως ἀφανίζοντα καὶ μετατιθέν-
τα καὶ καταλύοντα τὴν δόξαν οὐδὲν ποιεῖν
ἄτοπον; ἀλλ' ἐὰν μὲν δοράτιον ἐξέλῃ τις ἐκ τῆς
χειρὸς ἢ κράνους ἀπορρήξῃ τὸν λόφον ἢ τὴν
ἀσπίδα τοῦ βραχίονος ἢ χαλινὸν ἵππου, τῷ δημοσίῳ
τοῦτον εὐθὺς παραδώσετε, καὶ τὴν αὐτὴν ὑπομενεῖ

---

[1] δείξω added by Capps; Arnim indicates a lacuna.
[2] κἂν Geel : ἐὰν.

---

[1] Cf. § 75.   [2] As heroes.

And that the present practice is not free from impiety either, especially in view of the way these men describe it, I shall now prove, even if some will think that I speak with intent to exaggerate—not, as I said before,[1] because offences committed with reference to the dead are all without exception acts of impiety, but also because it is generally believed that the men of very ancient times were semi-divine, even if they have no exceptional attribute, simply, I presume, on account of their remoteness in time. And those who are so highly revered and have been held worthy of the highest honours, some of whom actually enjoy the mystic rites given to heroes, men who have lain buried so many years that even the memory of them has disappeared—how can they possibly be designated in the same way [2] as those who have died in our own time or only a little earlier, especially when these latter have not shown themselves worthy of any honour? And assuredly, acts of impiety toward the heroes everyone would agree without demur should be put in the same class as impiety toward the gods. Well then, is it not a wrongful act to blot out their memory? To take away their honour? To chisel out their names? Yes, it is a shame and an outrage, by Zeus. But if anyone removes a crown that will last perhaps one or two days, or if one puts a stain on the bronze, you will regard this man guilty of impiety; and yet will you think that the man who utterly blots out and changes and destroys another's glory is doing nothing out of the way? Why, if anyone takes a spear out of a statue's hand, or breaks the crest off his helmet, or the shield off his arm or a bridle off his horse, you will straightway hand this man over to the executioner, and he

τιμωρίαν τοῖς ἱεροσύλοις, ὥσπερ ἀμέλει καὶ πολλοὶ
τεθνήκασι διὰ τοιαύτας αἰτίας, καὶ πλέον οὐδὲν
λέγουσιν αὐτοῖς ὅτι τῶν ἀνωνύμων τινὰ καὶ σφόδρα
παλαιῶν ἐλωβήσαντο εἰκόνων· δημοσίᾳ δὲ ἡ
πόλις τῷ παντὶ χείρων καὶ φαυλοτέρα φανεῖται
περὶ τοὺς ἥρωκας;

83 Καὶ τοίνυν ἐὰν εἴπῃ τις εἰσελθὼν ὅτι πεφώραταί
τις ξένος ἢ καὶ πολίτης ἢ χεῖρα ἢ δάκτυλον ἀφαιρῶν
ἀνδριάντος, βοήσεσθε καὶ παραχρῆμα ἐπιθεῖναι
κελεύσετε ἐπὶ τὸν τροχόν. καίτοι χειρὸς μὲν
ἀφαιρεθείσης ἢ δόρατος ἢ φιάλης, ἐὰν τύχῃ κρατῶν,
ἡ τιμὴ μένει καὶ τὸ σύμβολον ἔχει τῆς ἀρετῆς
ὁ τιμηθείς, ὁ δὲ χαλκὸς μόνος ἐλάττων γέγονεν·
τῆς δὲ ἐπιγραφῆς ἀναιρουμένης ἀνῄρηται δήπουθεν
καὶ[1] ἡ μαρτυρία τοῦ[2] δοκεῖν ἄξιον ἐπαίνου γεγονέναι
τὸν ἄνθρωπον.

84 Βούλομαι τοίνυν, ὅπερ Ἀθήνησι μὲν οἶδα γιγνόμενον, οἶμαι δὲ κἀνταῦθα γίγνεσθαι κατὰ νόμον
πάνυ καλῶς ἔχοντα, εἰπεῖν πρὸς ὑμᾶς. ἐκεῖ γὰρ
ὅταν δημοσίᾳ τινὰ δέῃ τῶν πολιτῶν ἀποθανεῖν ἐπ᾽
ἀδικήματι, πρότερον αὐτοῦ τὸ ὄνομα ἐξαλείφεται.
τίνος ἕνεκα; ἑνὸς μέν, ὅπως μηκέτι δοκῶν πολίτης
εἶναι πάσχῃ τι τοιοῦτον, ἀλλ᾽ ὡς δυνατὸν ἀλλότριος
85 γεγονώς· εἶτ᾽, οἶμαι, καὶ τῆς τιμωρίας αὐτῆς τοῦτο
μέρος οὐκ ἐλάχιστον δοκεῖ, τὸ μηδὲ τὴν προσ-
ηγορίαν ἔτι φαίνεσθαι τοῦ προελθόντος εἰς τοῦτο
κακίας, ἀλλ᾽ ἠφανίσθαι παντελῶς, καθάπερ, οἶμαι,
τὸ μὴ θάπτεσθαι τοὺς προδότας, ὅπως μηδὲν

---

[1] καὶ ἡ μαρτυρία Cohoon: ἡ μαρτυρία καί.   [2] τοῦ Capps: τό.

[1] From the list of citizens; cf. Xeonophon, *Hellenica*, 2.51.
[2] The full form of the appellation would give the man's
name and the country of his origin, e.g. 'Solon of Athens.'

will suffer the same punishment as temple-robbers—
just as many undoubtedly have already been put to
death for such reasons—and they give them no more
consideration because it is one of the nameless and
very old statues they have mutilated.   Then shall the
city in its official capacity prove altogether worse and
more contemptible in the treatment of its heroes?

Again, if a person comes in and says that some
stranger or even citizen has stolen either a hand or a
finger that he has taken from a statue, you will raise
an outcry and bid him be put to the torture forthwith.   Yet, even though the statue has been deprived
of a hand or a spear, or a goblet if it happens to be
holding one, the honour remains and the man who
received the honour retains the symbol of his merits;
it is the bronze alone that has suffered a loss.   But
when the inscription is destroyed, obviously its
testimony has also been destroyed that the person
in question is " considered to have shown himself
worthy of approbation."

And so I now wish to tell you of a practice which
I know is followed at Athens, and here too, I imagine,
in accordance with a most excellent law.   In Athens,
for instance, whenever any citizen has to suffer death
at the hands of the state for a crime, his name is
erased [1] first.   Why is this done?   One reason is that
he may no longer be considered a citizen when he
undergoes such a punishment but, so far as that is
possible, as having become an alien.   Then, too,
I presume that it is looked upon as not the least
part of the punishment itself, that even the appellation [2] should no longer be seen of the man who had
gone so far in wickedness, but should be utterly
blotted out, just as, I believe, traitors are denied

ἢ σημεῖον εἰς αὖθις ἀνδρὸς πονηροῦ. φέρε οὖν,
ἐὰν εἴπῃ τις ἐπὶ τοῖς εὐεργέταις τοῦτο γίγνεσθαι
παρ' ὑμῖν, ὃ παρὰ πολλοῖς ἔθος ἐστὶν ἐπὶ τοῖς
κακούργοις, ἆρ' οὐ σφόδρα ἀλγήσετε; μὴ τοίνυν
ἀχθεσθῆτε τῷ νῦν αὐτὸ δοκοῦντι εἰρηκέναι· τοῦ
γὰρ μηκέτι μηδ' ἀεὶ λέγεσθαι γένοιτ' ἂν ὑμῖν
αἴτιος.

86   Καὶ μὴν ἐάν τις ἓν μόνον ἐκχαράξῃ ῥῆμα
ἀπὸ στήλης τινός, ἀποκτενεῖτε αὐτόν, οὐκέτι
ἐξετάσαντες ὅ τι ἦν ἢ περὶ τίνος, καὶ εἰ δή τις
ἐλθὼν οὗ τὰ δημόσια ὑμῖν γράμματά ἐστι, κεραίαν
νόμου τινὸς ἢ ψηφίσματος μίαν μόνην συλλαβὴν
ἐξαλείψειεν, οὕτως ἕξετε ὥσπερ ἂν εἴ τις ἀπὸ
τοῦ ἅρματός τι καθέλοι. οὐκοῦν ὁ τὴν ἐπιγραφὴν ἀναιρῶν εἰκόνος τινὸς ἧττόν τι ποιεῖ τοῦ
τὴν στήλην ἀποχαράττοντος; καὶ μὴν ὅλον γε
ἐξαλείφει τὸ ψήφισμα, καθ' ὃ τὴν τιμὴν ἐκεῖνος
ἔλαβε, μᾶλλον δὲ ἄκυρον ποιεῖ τὸ [1] γεγραμμένον.
ἀλλ' εἴ τις καταδικασθεὶς ὑπὲρ ὅτου δήποτε
ἐπὶ [2] ζημίαν τινὰ λαθὼν ἢ διαπραξάμενος ἐξαλείψειεν ἑαυτόν, καταλύειν δόξει [3] τὴν πολιτείαν·
ὥστε δεινότερον ὑμῖν δοκεῖ τὸ ζημίας τινὰ ἀπαλλάττειν αὐτὸν τοῦ τιμῆς ἀποστερεῖν ἄλλον.

---

[1] τὸ added by Capps. [2] ἐπὶ Cohoon : καὶ.
[3] δόξει Pflugk : ἐδόκει.

---

[1] This probably refers to a work of sculpture by Lysippus
which represented the Sun-god standing in a four-horse chariot.
The people of Rhodes, who highly honoured the Sun-god, were
very proud of this sculpture. See also note on Helius in § 93,
and cf. Dio Cassius (47. 33) : " Cassius appropriated their

burial, so that in the future there may be no trace whatever of a wicked man. Come, therefore, if anyone says that in the case of benefactors the same course is followed in your city as is customary among many peoples in the case of evil-doers, will you not be exceedingly offended? Then do not be vexed at the man who seems to have given expression to this criticism on the present occasion, for you may find that he is to be thanked for its not being said again in the future or even always.

Again, if any one chisels out only one word from any official tablet, you will put him to death without stopping to investigate what the word was or to what it referred; and if anyone should go to the building where your public records are kept and erase one jot of any law, or one single syllable of a decree of the people, you will treat this man just as you would any person who should remove a part of the Chariot.[1] Well then, does the man who erases the inscription on a statue commit a less serious offence than the man who chisels something off the official tablet? Indeed the fact is that he erases the entire decree by virtue of which that man received his honour, or rather he annuls the record of it. But if anyone who for any offence whatever is condemned to some punishment erases his own name secretly or by intrigue, he will be thought to be destroying the constitution. Accordingly, you think it a more serious matter for a person to free himself from punishment than to deprive another man of his honour!

ships, their money, and their sacred treasures except the chariot of the Sun "—τὰς δὲ ναῦς καὶ τὰ χρήματα καὶ τὰ ἱερὰ πλὴν ντο ἅρματος τοῦ Ἡλίου παρεσπάσατο ⟨ὁ Κάσσιος⟩.

DIO CHRYSOSTOM

87 Οὐ τοίνυν οὐδὲ ἐκεῖνό ἐστιν ἀφετέον, ἐπείπερ
τοὺς λόγους ὡς ἐπ' ἀσεβήματι ἐποιησάμην.
ἐπίστασθε γὰρ σαφῶς ὅτι ἅπασα μὲν ἡ πόλις ἐστὶν
ἱερά, τῶν δὲ ἀνδριάντων πολλοὺς ἂν εὕροιτε τῶν
ἐν αὐτοῖς τοῖς ἱεροῖς ἑστηκότων τοῦτο πεπονθότας.
καὶ γὰρ ἀρχαιοτάτους συμβέβηκε τούτους εἶναι,
καὶ τῶν στρατηγῶν ὃν ἂν ἕκαστος ἐθέλῃ θεραπεύειν,
ὡς ὑμῶν τιμώντων, φιλοτιμεῖται τοῦτον ὡς
κάλλιστα ἑστάναι. καὶ τί δεῖ λόγων; οἶμαι
γὰρ μηθένα [1] ἂν ἀντειπεῖν [2] ὅτι καὶ τῶν οὕτως
κειμένων, εἰ καὶ μὴ [3] καθάπερ ἐγὼ νῦν ἔλεγον,
οἱ πλείους εἰσὶ μετωνομασμένοι, τινὲς δ', οἶμαι,
88 καὶ σφόδρα ἐγγὺς παρεστῶτες τοῖς θεοῖς. εἶθ'
ὅποι μηδὲ τοὺς κακὸν δράσαντας ἐάνπερ καταφύγω-
σιν ἔθος ἐστὶν ἀδικεῖν, τοὺς εὐεργέτας οὐ δεινὸν
ἐὰν φαινώμεθα ἀδικοῦντες; καὶ τὴν ἀσυλίαν
ἣν παρέχουσι τοῖς φαύλοις οἱ τοιοῦτοι τόποι, μόνοις,
ὡς ἔοικε, τοῖς ἀγαθοῖς οὐ δυνήσονται παρέχειν;
ἀλλ' ἐὰν μὲν θυμιατήριόν τις ἀλλάξῃ τῶν ἔνδον
ἀνακειμένων [4] ἢ φιάλην, ἱερόσυλος οὐχ ἧττον
89 νομισθήσεται τῶν ὑφαιρουμένων· ἐὰν δὲ εἰκόνα
ἀλλάξῃ καὶ τιμήν, οὐθὲν ἄτοπον ποιεῖ; καίτοι καὶ
τοὺς ἀνδριάντας οὐχ ἧττον ἀναθήματα εἴποι τις
ἂν εἶναι τῶν θεῶν τοὺς ἐν τοῖς ἱεροῖς· καὶ πολλοὺς

---

[1] μηθένα Reiske : μηθὲν UM, μηδὲν B.
[2] ἂν ἀντειπεῖν Reiske : ἀντειπεῖν M, ἄν τι ποιεῖν UB.
[3] καὶ μὴ Wilamowitz : μὴ καὶ M, μὴ UB.
[4] ἀνακειμένων Capps : κειμένων.

---

[1] And hence share somewhat in their sanctity.

THE THIRTY-FIRST DISCOURSE

Neither can I, furthermore, pass over another thing, inasmuch as I have based my argument on the assumption of an act of impiety. For you Rhodians are perfectly aware that, while the whole city is sacred, yet you will find that many of the statues which stand within your very sanctuaries have been subjected to this indignity. For it so happened that these are very ancient; and whenever one of your chief magistrates wants to flatter any person, he is always eager, carrying out the idea that you are giving the honour, to have him set up in bronze in the finest possible place. What need is there of words? For I suppose that no one would deny that even of the statues so placed, even though the facts do not exactly accord with the statement I made a moment ago, the greater number *have* had the names on them changed, and some, I believe, that stand very close indeed to the statues of the gods.[1] What then? Is it not outrageous if we shall be found to be wronging our benefactors in the very place where it is not the custom to wrong even those who have committed some evil deed, if they flee there for refuge? And are such places to be unable, as seems to be the case, to afford to good men alone the sanctuary they afford to worthless men? Nay, if anyone merely shifts from its position a censer or a goblet belonging to the treasures dedicated inside a temple, he will be regarded as guilty of sacrilege just as much as those who filch those sacred things; but if it is a statue and an honour that he shifts, does he do nothing out of the way? And yet any of us could say that the statues too are just as much votive offerings belonging to the gods, that is, the statues which stand in gods' sanctuaries; and one may see

93

ἰδεῖν ἔστιν οὕτως ἐπιγεγραμμένους, οἷον, ὁ δεῖνα
ἑαυτὸν ἀνέθηκεν ἢ τὸν πατέρα ἢ τὸν υἱὸν ὅτῳ
δήποτε τῶν θεῶν. ἐὰν οὖν ἀπὸ τῶν ἄλλων
ἀναθημάτων ἀφελών τις τοῦ θέντος τὸ ὄνομα
ἄλλον ἐπιγράψῃ, μόνον τοῦτον οὐκ ἀσεβεῖν φήσομεν; ὁ δέ τοι Ἀπόλλων οὐκ εἴα δήπουθεν
ἐκ τοῦ περιβόλου τοὺς νεοττ ὺς ἀναιρεῖσθαι τὸν
Κυμαῖον, ἱκέτας ἑαυτοῦ λέγων.

90   Δι' ὧν τοίνυν πειράσονταί τινες τὸ πρᾶγμα
ἀποφαίνειν ἐπιεικέστερον, τῷ παντὶ χεῖρον ἀποδεί-
ξουσιν ἰον ὅταν λέγωσι τοῖς σφόδρα ἀρχαίοις
καταχρῆσθαι καί τινας εἶναι καὶ ἀνεπιγράφους.
εἰ γὰρ δοίη τις αὐτοῖς οὕτως τοῦτο ἔχειν, οὐκ
ἂν εἴποιμι τὸ πρόχειρον ὡς ἄρα ἐγὼ νῦν ὑπὲρ
τῶν ἐπιγεγραμμένων ποιοῦμαι τὸν λόγον, ἀλλ'
οὐδὲ ἐκείνων φημὶ δεῖν ἅπτεσθαι. σκοπεῖτε γάρ,
ἄνδρες Ῥόδιοι, τὴν αἰτίαν, δι' ἣν εἰκὸς τεθῆναί
τινας οὕτως. οὐ γὰρ ἐκλαθέσθαι γε οὐδὲ ὀκνῆσαι
τὸν ἱστάντα εἰκὸς οὐδὲ φείσασθαι τῆς εἰς τοῦτο
91 δαπάνης· οὐ γὰρ ἦν οὐδεμία. λοιπὸν οὖν τῶν
δύο θάτερον, ἢ τῷ σφόδρα εἶναί τινας μεγάλους
καὶ κατ' ἀλήθειαν ἥρωας οὐκ ᾤοντο δεῖν ἐπιγράφειν, ὡς ἂν ἅπασι γνωρίμους ὄντας, ἡγούμενοι

---

[1] Arnim suspected a lacuna after ἐπιγράψῃ.

---

[1] I.e., the private ones as contrasted with those set up by
the state.

[2] On the coast of Asia Minor north-west of Smyrna. The
man of Cymê was Aristodicus, the nestlings were sparrows;
cf. Herodotus 1. 159.

many of them inscribed to that effect; for instance, " So-and-so set up a statue of himself (or of his father, or of his son) as dedicate to a god " (whatever god it might be). Hence, if one removes the name of the person so honoured from any of the other dedications [1] and inscribes the name of a different person, are we to say that the person now in question is alone not guilty of impiety? Apollo would not allow, as you know, the man of Cymê [2] to remove the nestlings from his precinct, saying that they were his suppliants.

Moreover, the arguments by which some persons will attempt to make the practice appear more consistent with honour will prove it to be in every way less creditable: for instance, when they say that it it is the very old statues that they misuse and that some of them also bear no inscriptions. Well, if one were inclined to concede to them that this is the case, I should not make the obvious retort, that, after all, I am at present speaking about those which do bear inscriptions; on the contrary, I maintain that they have no right to touch those others either. As for my reasons, just consider, men of Rhodes, what the motive was which in all probability led in certain cases to the statues being set up uninscribed. For it is not reasonable to suppose that the man who set them up merely overlooked this matter, or hesitated to inscribe the names, or wanted to save the expense of an inscription; for there was no expense. There remains, consequently, one of two possible reasons: in the case of some, since they were very great men indeed and in very truth heroes, it was considered unnecessary to add an inscription, in the thought that the statues would be recognized by everybody and because it was believed that, on

διὰ τὴν ὑπερβολὴν τῆς τότε οὔσης δόξης εἰς
ἅπαντα καὶ τὸν αὖθις χρόνον παραμενεῖν τὸ ὄνομα·
ἢ τῷ [1] τινων ἡμιθέων ἢ καὶ θεῶν ὄντας ὕστερον ἀγνοη-
θῆναι διὰ τὸν χρόνον. τοὺς γὰρ θεοὺς ἐπιγράφειν
οὐκ ἔστιν ἔθος· ὡς ἔγωγε οὐκ ἀπελπίζω καὶ τῶν
92 ἄλλων τινὰς εἶναι τοιούτους. ἐν γοῦν Θήβαις
᾿Αλκαῖος ἀνάκειταί τις, ὃν ῾Ηρακλέα φασὶν
εἶναι, πρότερον οὕτω καλούμενον· καὶ παρ᾽
᾿Αθηναίοις ᾿Ελευσινίου μύστου παιδὸς εἰκὼν οὐκ
ἔχουσα ἐπιγραφήν· κἀκεῖνον εἶναι λέγουσιν ῾Ηρα-
κλέα. καὶ παρ᾽ ἑτέροις οἶδα πολλούς, τοὺς μὲν
ἡμιθέων, τοὺς δὲ ἡρώων, ἀνδριάντας, οἷον ᾿Αχιλ-
λέως, Σαρπηδόνος, Θησέως, διὰ τοῦτο ἀρχῆθεν
οὐκ ἐπιγραφέντας καὶ Μέμνονος ἐν Αἰγύπτῳ
κολοσσὸν εἶναι τοιοῦτον [2] λέγουσιν. ἀλλ᾽ ἐπ᾽
ἐνίων μὲν ἡ δόξα παρέμεινε καὶ διεφύλαξε τὴν
φήμην ὁ χρόνος· οὐ μὴν ἐπὶ πάντων συνηνέχθη
93 δι᾽ ἣν δήποτ᾽ οὖν αἰτίαν. οὐκοῦν καὶ παρ᾽ ὑμῖν
οὐκ ἀδύνατον εἶναί τινας τοιούτους. οἷον οὖν
ἔστιν ῾Ηρακλέους ἢ Τληπολέμου φέρ᾽ εἰπεῖν ἢ
τῶν ῾Ηλίου παίδων τινὸς ἀνδριάντα διδόναι τῷ
δεῖνι, χρηστῷ μὲν ἀνδρὶ καὶ τιμῆς ἀξίῳ· πάντες
γὰρ ἔστωσαν, οὓς ἡ πόλις θεραπεύει, τοιοῦτοι,

---

[1] τῷ added by Cohoon.
[2] τοιοῦτον added by Capps.

---

[1] That is, at the time when the statues were set up.
[2] Perhaps the Heracles–Alcaeus of Diodorus Siculus, 1, 14.
[3] See Vol. II, page 371, note 1.
[4] Pausanias (1. 42. 3) refers to it. He says that at Thebes
in Egypt there was a seated statue which most people called a
Memnon, but the Thebans themselves maintained that it
represented Phamenophes, a Theban. Others said it repre-

account of the surpassing glory then [1] attaching to
these men, their names would remain for all future
time; or else because the persons honoured, being the
sons of certain demi-gods or even of gods, had later
through lapse of time been forgotten. For it is not the
custom to put inscriptions on the statues of the gods,
so that I rather expect that some of the others, too,
are in this class. In Thebes, for example, a certain
Alcaeus [2] has a statue which they say is a Heracles
and was formerly so called; and among the Athenians
there is an image of a boy who was an initiate in the
mysteries at Eleusis and it bears no inscription; he,
too, they say, is a Heracles. And in various other
places I know of many statues, some of which represent demi-gods and others heroes, as, for example,
Achilles, Sarpedon,[3] Theseus, which for this reason
had not been inscribed from the first; and they say
there is in Egypt a colossal statue of Memnon
similarly uninscribed.[4] But in the case of some of
them their glory has remained and time has guarded
their fame; but for some reason this did not happen
in the case of all of them. Therefore, among you
also it is not impossible that there are some like these.
So you might, for instance, be giving a statue of
Heracles, or, let us say, of Tlepolemus,[5] or of one of the
children of Helius,[6] to So-and-so, no doubt an excellent
man and deserving of honour. For even supposing
all are such whose favour the city seeks to win—and

sented Sesostris. After Cambyses cut the statue in two, the
lower part, which remained on its base, emitted a musical sound
at sunrise.

[5] Son of Heracles and King of Argos. Slain by Sarpedon.
[6] The Sun-god, the son of Hyperion and Thea, worshipped
in many parts of Greece and especially in Rhodes; see
§ 86, note 1. One of his sons was Phaethon.

καὶ δεῖ γε εὔχεσθαι πάντας εἶναι χρηστούς, μάλιστα
δὲ¹ τοὺς ἡγουμένους· ἀλλ' οὐκ ἐκείνοις ὅμοιοι·
πόθεν; οὐδ' ἂν αὐτοὶ φήσαιεν ὀλίγον αὐτῶν
ἐλάττους ὑπάρχειν, ἀλλὰ κἂν φοβηθεῖεν εἰπεῖν
τι τοιοῦτον. ἆρ' ὑμῖν ἐκ τῶν εἰρημένων δοκεῖ
μᾶλλον ἀπὸ τούτων ἀρχομένους, λέγω δὲ τῶν
οὐκ ἐχόντων τὰς ἐπιγραφάς, τὸ πρᾶγμα ἐπὶ πάντας
μεταφέρειν, ἢ σφόδρα εἶναι τῶν τοιούτων φειστέον;

94 Καίτοι τὸ τῆς ἀγνοίας καὶ τὸ τῆς ἀρχαιότητος
ὅμοιόν ἐστιν ὥσπερ ἂν εἴ τις λέγοι μηδὲ τοὺς τυμ-
βωρυχοῦντας τοὺς σφόδρα παλαιοὺς τάφους μηδὲν
ἁμαρτάνειν, ὅτι μηδεὶς αὐτοῖς προσήκει μηδὲ
ἴσμεν οἵτινές εἰσιν. ὁ μὲν οὖν τάφος οὐκ ἔστι
σημεῖον ἀρετῆς, ἀλλ' εὐπορίας, οὐδὲ ἔχομεν εἰπεῖν
τοὺς ἐν τοῖς μνήμασι κειμένους ὡς ἦσαν ἀγαθοί,
πλὴν εἰ μή γε δημοσίᾳ τις φαίνοιτο τεθαμμένος,
ὅπερ, οἶμαι, τρόπον τινὰ τούτοις συμβέβηκεν.
ἡ δὲ εἰκὼν δι' ἀνδραγαθίαν δίδοται καὶ διὰ τὸ²
δόξαι τινὰ πρότερον γενναῖον· ὅτι γὰρ οὐδεὶς
ἐστάθη τούτων ἁλοὺς κλέπτων οὐδὲ μοιχεύων,
οὐκ ἄδηλόν ἐστιν· οὐδέ γε ἐπὶ τοῖς τυχοῦσιν, ἀλλ'
ὡς οἷόν τε ἐπὶ τοῖς μεγίστοις.

95 Ὅτι τοίνυν καὶ θείας τινὸς δυνάμεως καὶ προνοίας,
ὡς ἂν εἴποι τις, οἱ τοιοῦτοι μετέχουσιν, ἐπ'

¹ δὲ added by Reiske.
² διὰ τὸ Casaubon : δεῖ M, δὴ τῷ UB.

---

¹ For example, in Athens graves which lay in a circumscribed
portion of the Outer Ceramicus could be assumed to hold the
bones of soldiers who had died in war or of statesmen who had

we may well pray that they may all be good men, and especially your rulers—yet they are not the equals of those great men of the past. How could they be? Not even the men themselves would maintain that they are only a little inferior to them; nay, they would actually be afraid to make any such claim. Does it seem to you from the arguments which have been advanced that you should choose to begin with those statues—I mean with those which have no inscription—and extend the practice to all, or that you should very decidedly spare all of that kind?

And yet, after all, this plea of ignorance and of antiquity is about the same as if a person should say that those who rifle the very old tombs do no wrong, on the ground that no one of the dead is related to them and we do not even know who they are. No, the tomb is rather an indication, not of its occupant's excellence, but of his affluence; nor can we say of those who rest in sepulchres that they were good men, except where there is evidence in a particular case that the person had received burial by the state,[1] just as I suppose happened to those men in a sense. But the statue is given for distinguished achievement and because a man was in his day regarded as noble. For that no one of these men was given a statue who had been convicted of theft or adultery is perfectly clear; nor was the award made for ordinary performances, but for the very greatest possible deeds.

Again, because men such as these also share in a sort of divine power and purpose, one might say, I wish to tell of an incident that happened in the case

been honoured by the state; cf. Thucydides 2. 34. 5 and Judeich, *Topographie von Athen*,[2] pages 400 ff.

ἀνδριάντος τι βούλομαι γεγονὸς εἰπεῖν. Θεαγένης
ἦν Θάσιος ἀθλητής· οὗτος ἐδόκει ῥώμῃ διενεγκεῖν
τοὺς καθ᾿ αὑτόν, καὶ δὴ σὺν ἑτέροις πολλοῖς καὶ
τὸν Ὀλυμπίασι τρὶς εἰλήφει στέφανον. ὡς δ᾿
ἐπαύσατο καὶ ἧκεν εἰς τὴν πατρίδα, λοιπὸν τοῦ
σώματος παρακμάσαντος ἦν ἀνὴρ οὐδενὸς χείρων
περὶ τὰ κοινά, ἀλλὰ ὡς οἷόν τε ἄριστος. ἐντεῦθεν,
ὅπερ εἰκός, εἰς ἔχθραν τινὶ προῆλθε τῶν πολιτευο-
96 μένων. ὁ δὲ ζῶντι μὲν ἐφθόνει μόνον, τελευτή-
σαντος δὲ πρᾶγμα πάντων ἀνοητότατον καὶ
ἀσεβέστατον ἐποίει· τὸν γὰρ ἀνδριάντα αὐτοῦ
τὸν ἑστῶτα ἐν μέσῃ τῇ πόλει νύκτωρ ἐμαστίγου.
τοιγαροῦν εἴτε ἀπὸ τύχης εἴτε δαιμονίου τινὸς
νεμεσήσαντος αὐτῷ κινηθεὶς ποτε ἐκ τῆς βάσεως
ἠκολούθησεν ἅμα τῇ μάστιγι καὶ κτείνει τὸν
ἄνδρα. νόμου δὲ ὄντος καταποντίζειν κρίναντας,[1]
ἐάν τι τῶν ἀψύχων ἐμπεσὸν ἀποκτείνῃ τινά, οἱ
τοῦ τεθνεῶτος προσήκοντες αἱροῦσι δίκῃ τὸν
97 ἀνδριάντα καὶ κατεπόντωσαν. λοιμοῦ δὲ συμ-
βάντος, ὥς φασι, χαλεπωτάτου, καὶ τῶν Θασίων
οὐδενὶ τρόπῳ λῆξαι δυναμένων τῆς νόσου, καὶ
τελευταῖον χρωμένων, τοὺς φυγάδας αὐτοῖς ἀνεῖπε

---

[1] κρίναντας Selden : κρίνοντας M, κρίνοντος UB.

---

[1] Pausanias (6. 11) says that Theagenes showed quite
unusual strength even as a boy, for when he was only nine
years old, on his way home from school one day he took the
bronze statue of one of the gods which was standing in the
market-place and carried it home on his shoulder. As an
athlete he was said to have won 1,400 crowns in all.

of a statue. Theagenes was a Thasian athlete.[1]
He was thought to surpass in physical strength the
men of his own day, and in addition to many other
triumphs had won the victor's crown three times at
Olympia. And when he gave up competing and
returned to his native city, thenceforth, though his
body was past its prime, he was a man inferior to
none in the affairs of his country, but was, so far as
a man may be, a most excellent citizen. For that
reason, probably, he incurred the enmity of one of
the politicians. And although while he lived, the
other man merely envied him, yet after the death
of Theagenes the other committed a most senseless
and impious act; for under cover of night he would
scourge the man's statue, which had been erected in
the centre of the city. Consequently, whether by
accident [2] or because some divinity was incensed at
him, the statue at one time moved from its base
and, following the lash back, slew the man. And
since there was a law which required, in case any
inanimate object should fall upon a person and cause
his death, that they should first give it a trial and
then sink it in the sea,[3] the relatives of the dead man
got judgment against the statue and sank it in the
sea. And then, when a most grievous pestilence
broke out, so they say, and the people of Thasos,
being unable in any way to get rid of the plague,
finally consulted the oracle, the god announced to

[2] Apparently the lash became entwined about the statue so
that when the man jerked to free it, he pulled the statue over.

[3] Like Draco's law in Athens, according to Pausanias, *l.c.* Cf.
Eusebius (*Praeparatio Evangelica* 5. 34) who quotes the exact
words from Oenomaus, who probably got them from Calli-
machus' Περὶ ἀγώνων (*On Contests*); Favorinus in Dio 37.
20 ff.; Lucian, *Assembly of the Gods* 12.

κατάγειν ὁ θεός. ὡς δὲ πλέον οὐδὲν ἦν ἁπάντων
κατεληλυθότων,[1] χρωμένοις αὖθις λέγεται τὴν
Πυθίαν οὕτως ἀνειπεῖν·

Θεαγένους δ' ἐλάθεσθε ἐνὶ ψαμάθοισι πεσόντος·
κεῖθ' ὑμῖν ὁ πρὶν μυριάεθλος ἀνήρ.

ᾧ καὶ δῆλον ὅτι καὶ τὸ πρῶτον οὐχὶ τῶν φυγάδων
ἕνεκ', ἀλλὰ τούτου[2], ἐχρήσθη καὶ τὸ συμβὰν οὐ
δι' ἄλλην τινὰ αἰτίαν ἐγένετο.

98   Καὶ μηδεὶς ἐκεῖνο ὑπολάβῃ·

Τί οὖν; ἡμεῖς τοὺς ἀνδριάντας ἀφανίζομεν ἢ
ῥιπτοῦμεν;

'Αλλ' ἀτιμάζετε ἐκείνους ὧν εἰσι, καὶ ἀφαιρεῖσθε
τοὺς ἔχοντας, ὅπερ καὶ τότε ἔδοξε τῷ θεῷ, ἐπεὶ
τοῦ χαλκοῦ οὐκ εἰκὸς ἦν φροντίσαι αὐτόν. μὴ
τοίνυν τοῦ Θασίου μὲν ἡγεῖσθε ὑβρισθέντος οὕτως
ἀγανακτῆσαι τὸ δαιμόνιον, τῶν δὲ παρ' ὑμῖν
τετιμημένων μηδένα θεοφιλῆ εἶναι μηδὲ ἥρωα.

99   Οὐ τοίνυν οὐδὲ τοῦτο ἔστιν εἰπεῖν ὅπως οὐκ
ἂν καὶ πρὸς ἔχθραν ὑπ' ἐνίων τοῦτο γένοιτο,
ἐὰν ἄρα τύχῃ τις τῶν στρατηγούντων μισῶν τινα
τῶν πρὸ αὐτοῦ. τὸ γοῦν τοῦ Θεαγένους ἀκηκόατε
ὡς συνέβη διὰ τὸν φθόνον καὶ τὴν ζηλοτυπίαν
τὴν ἐκ τῆς πολιτείας. καὶ γὰρ εἰ νῦν ἐπὶ μόνοις

---

[1] κατεληλυθότων Cobet : ἐληλυθότων.
[2] ἕνεκ', ἀλλὰ τούτου Cohoon : ἕνεκα τοῦτο.

---

[1] See Pausanias 6. 11. 8, where only the following verse is
credited to the oracle,

" Ye have cast out forgotten Theagenes, your great one."
   Θεαγένην δ' ἄμνηστον ἀφήκατε τὸν μέγαν ὑμέων.

Pausanias goes on to say that certain fishermen caught the
statue in their net while fishing.

them that they should " restore the exiles." When all who were in exile had returned and no improvement came, and the Thasians consulted the god again, the story is that the Pythian priestess gave them the following reply:

" Him that did fall in the ocean's deep sands you
    now have forgotten,
Even Theagenes staunch, victor in myriad games." [1]

These lines make it evident both that the oracle was not delivered in the first place for the exiles' sake but for Theagenes', and also that what afterwards happened [2] had been due to no other cause.

And let no one interrupt and say:
" What of it? Do *we* make away with our statues or throw them aside? "

No, but you are dishonouring the men whose statues they are and you are robbing their rightful owners, just as the god felt on the occasion to which we refer, since it is not reasonable to suppose that it was the image of bronze about which he was troubled. Do not, therefore, think that, although the god was so indignant at the insult shown to the Thasian, no one of those who have been honoured in your city is dear to Heaven or that none is a hero.

Neither can we be so sure, moreover, that such treatment might not be brought about by some persons through hatred, I mean if it so happens that one of your chief magistrates has a grudge against any of his predecessors. You have heard how the Theagenes incident, at any rate, grew out of political envy and jealousy. For even if they urge that now they

---

[2] The outbreak of the plague.

τοῖς παλαιοῖς αὐτό φασι ποιεῖν, χρόνου γε προϊόν-
τος, ὥσπερ ἐπὶ πάντων ἀεὶ συμβαίνει τῶν φαύλων
ἐθῶν, ἀνάγκη καὶ τοῦτ' ἐπὶ πλέον προελθεῖν.
οὐδὲ γὰρ οὐδ' αἰτιάσασθαι οἷόν τε, ἐπ' αὐτῷ γε
ὅλου τοῦ πράγματος ὄντος.

Νὴ Δί', ἀλλὰ κωλύσουσιν οἱ προσήκοντες.

Ἐὰν οὖν ἀπόντες ἢ ἀγνοήσαντες τύχωσιν,
ὅταν γνῶσι, τί ποιήσομεν; ἆρά γε δεήσει τοῦτον
ἐκχαράττειν πάλιν, ὃν ἂν φθάνῃ τις ἐπιγράψας;

100   Πάνυ τοίνυν ὄντος ἀτόπου τοῦ γιγνομένου, μᾶλλον
δὲ ἀσεβοῦς, ἧττον ἂν δεινὸν ἦν, εἰ μὴ διὰ τοιαύτην
πρόφασιν συνέβαινε, δι' οἵαν τινές φασιν, ὡς
ἀπολογούμενοι περὶ τῆς πόλεως. τὸ γὰρ δι'
ἀργύριον πράττειν ὁτιοῦν τῶν ἄλλως αἰσχρῶν
ἅπαντες αἴσχιον ἡγοῦνται τοῦ καθ' ἑτέραν τινὰ
αἰτίαν. ὅταν οὖν προβαλλόμενοι τὴν δαπάνην καὶ
τὸ δεῖν ἀναλίσκειν εἰ ποιήσεσθε [1] ἑτέρους ἀνδριάντας, ἀξιῶσι παραπέμπειν τὸ πρᾶγμα, δῆλον ὅτι
μεῖζον τὸ ὄνειδος κατασκευάζουσιν, εἰ χρημάτων
ἕνεκα δόξετε [2] ἀδικεῖν, καὶ ταῦτα πλουτοῦντες,
ὡς οὐδένες ἄλλοι τῶν Ἑλλήνων.

101   Καίτοι τί δήποτε ἐπὶ μὲν τῶν προγόνων ὑμῶν
οὐθὲν ἐγίγνετο τοιοῦτον, οὐχ ἐχόντων αὐτῶν πλείονα
ἢ νῦν ἔχετε ὑμεῖς; ὅτι γὰρ ὑθ' ἡ νῆσος χείρων
γέγονε καὶ τὴν Καρίαν καρποῦσθε καὶ μέρος τι
τῆς Λυκίας καὶ πόλεις ὑποφόρους κέκτησθε, καὶ

---

[1] εἰ ποιήσεσθε Wilamowitz : ἢ ποιήσασθαι.
[2] δόξετε Arnim : δόξουσι.

---

[1] Cf. §§ 140–142.
[2] That is, of the στρατηγός; cf. § 133.

follow this practice only in the case of the old statues, yet as time goes on, just as ever happens in the case of all bad habits, this one too will of necessity grow worse and worse.[1] The reason is that it is utterly impossible to call the culprit to account because the whole business from first to last lies in his[2] hands.

" Yes, by heavens," you say, " but the kinsmen will certainly put a stop to it."

Well then, if the kinsmen happen to be absent or to have had no knowledge of the matter, what do we propose to do when they do learn of it? Will it be necessary to chisel out again the man's name which someone has been in a hurry to insert?

Again, since this practice is quite improper, or impious rather, it would be less of an outrage if it were not done under the pretext which some offer by way of excusing the city. For everybody considers it a greater disgrace to do for money anything whatsoever that is in other respects disgraceful, than to do it for any other reason. So when they put forward as a plea the cost and the necessity of going to heavy expense if you shall ever undertake to make another lot of statues, and thus seek to condone the practice, it is clear that they make the reproach all the worse, since men are going to think that you are doing a wrong thing for the sake of money, and that too although you are rich, richer than the people of any other Hellenic state.

And yet why, pray, did not something like this happen in the time of your ancestors, seeing that they had no more wealth than you now possess? For you must not suppose that anyone is unaware that your island has not deteriorated, that you draw revenue from Caria and a part of Lycia and possess

χρήματα ἀεὶ πολλὰ ὑπὸ πολλῶν ἀνατίθεται[1] τῷ
δήμῳ καὶ τῶν πρότερον οὐδεὶς ἀφῄρηται, μηθένα
νομίζετε ἀγνοεῖν.

102   Καὶ μὴν οὐδὲ δαπανᾶν φήσετε τῶν[2] τότε μᾶλλον·
τότε μὲν γὰρ εἰς πάνθ' ὅσα καὶ νῦν ἀνηλίσκετο,
πανηγύρεις, πομπάς, ἱερουργίας, εἰς τὰ τείχη,
τοῖς δικάζουσι, τῇ βουλῇ. νῦν δὲ οὐκ ἔστι τὰ
μέγιστα τῶν πρότερον. τὰς γὰρ εἰς τὸν πόλεμον
δαπάνας σχεδόν τι συνεχῶς αὐτῶν πολεμούντων
καὶ σπάνιον, εἴ ποτε, ἀναπαυομένων, οὐκ ἔνι
συμβάλλειν, οἶμαι, τοῖς ἐν εἰρήνῃ γιγνομένοις
103 ἀναλώμασιν. οὐ γὰρ ὅμοιον ἑκατὸν νεῶν ἢ καὶ
πλειόνων στόλον ἀποστεῖλαι καὶ πάλιν ἑβδομήκοντα
καὶ τριάκοντα ἑτέρων, καὶ τοῦτον ἔσθ' ὅτε μὴ
καταλύειν τριῶν ἢ τεττάρων ἐτῶν· οὐδὲ συνεχῶς
τριήρεις πλεῖν, οὐ μέχρι Κύπρου καὶ Κιλικίας,
ἀλλ' ὁτὲ μὲν εἰς Αἴγυπτον, ὁτὲ δὲ εἰς τὸν Εὔξεινον,
τὸ δὲ τελευταῖον ἐν αὐτῷ τῷ Ὠκεανῷ· οὐδὲ ξένους
στρατιώτας τρέφειν τὰ φρούρια καὶ τὴν χώραν
φυλάττοντας, καὶ ὃ νῦν ἐφ' ἡμῶν ἰδεῖν ἔστι, μιᾷ
καθ' ἕκαστον ἐνιαυτὸν ἢ δυσὶν ἀφράκτοις ἀπαντᾶν
104 εἰς Κόρινθον. καὶ λέγω ταῦτα οὐκ ὀνειδίζων
οὐδὲ τῶν προγόνων ὑμᾶς χείρονας ποιῶν· οὐ
γὰρ ὅτι μὴ δύνασθε ταῦτα πράττειν ἐκείνοις,

----

[1] ἀνατίθεται Dindorf : ἀνατίθενται.
[2] τῶν added by Wilamowitz.

----

[1] According to Kromayer (*Philologus* N.F., X, p. 479 f.)
the first two numbers are too high. In the year 42 B.C. the
Rhodians could find only 33 ships with which to meet Cassius'

tribute-paying cities, that large sums of money are continually being entrusted to your commonwealth by many men, and that none of the earlier depositors has withdrawn anything.

Furthermore, you will not claim that you have heavier expenses than had the men of those earlier times, since in that period there were expenditures for every purpose for which they are made now—for their national assemblies, sacred processions, religious rites, fortifications, jury service, and for the council. But in these days the heaviest outlays of those borne in earlier times do not exist. For instance, their expenditures for war, seeing that they were almost continually at war and rarely, if ever, had a respite, are, in my opinion, not to be brought into comparison with those which are made in times of peace. Indeed, it was not the same thing at all to send out an expedition of one hundred ships or even more, and again, one of seventy and then a third of thirty others,[1] and then sometimes not to disband this expedition for three or four years; or for warships to sail continuously, not merely across to Cyprus and Cilicia, but sometimes to Egypt and at other times to the Black Sea and finally on the Ocean itself, or to keep mercenary soldiers to garrison the forts and the country—it is not possible to compare all that with what may now be seen in our time, when you appear with merely one or two undecked ships every year at Corinth. I say all this, not by way of reproaching you, nor to show that you are inferior to your ancestors; for it is not because you are unable to match their deeds, but because the

80. He says that they never sent more than 20 ships to help the Romans. See also § 113.

ἀλλ' ὅτι καιρὸς οὐκ ἔστι τῶν τοιούτων, ἐν εἰρήνῃ
διάγετε. δῆλον γὰρ ὡς κἀκεῖνοι [1] μᾶλλον ἐβούλοντο μὴ κινδυνεύειν, καὶ διὰ τοῦτο ἐπόνουν,
ἵνα καταστῇ ποτε τὰ πράγματα· πλὴν ὅτι γε
οὐκ ἴσα ὑμῖν ἀνήλισκον. ἵνα γὰρ τἄλλα ἀφῇ τις,
τὸ τῶν νεωρίων, τὸ τῶν ὅπλων, τὸ τῶν μηχανη-
μάτων, ὃ [2] νῦν εἶπον, αὐτὸ δήπου τὸ τῶν τειχῶν
οὐκ ἔστιν ὅμοιον, ὡς ἐφ' ὑμῶν ἐπισκευάζεται.
καὶ γὰρ ἂν τὰ τῆς ἐπιμελείας θῇ τις μὴ διαφέρειν, ἀλλά τοι σχολῇ γίγνεται καὶ κατ' ὀλίγον
καὶ ὁπηνίκα τις βούλεται· τότε δὲ οὐκ ἦν αὐτὰ
μὴ ἑστάναι. καὶ νῦν μὲν ὑφ' ὑμῶν δοκιμασθησό-
μενα οἰκοδομεῖται, τότε δὲ ὑπὸ τῶν πολεμίων.
105 εἶεν· οὐ τοίνυν οὐδὲ τοῦτο ἔστιν εἰπεῖν ὡς πλείονας
τιμᾶτε· τὸ γὰρ πλῆθος αὐτὸ δηλοῖ τῶν ἐξ ἐκείνου
τοῦ χρόνου κειμένων ἀνδριάντων. χωρὶς δὲ
τούτου τίς ἂν εἴποι πλείους εἶναι τοὺς νῦν φιλοτιμουμένους περὶ τὴν πόλιν;

Νὴ Δία, ἀνάγκην γὰρ ἡμεῖς ἔχομεν τοὺς ἡγεμόνας τιμᾶν ἅπαντας.

Τί δ'; οὐχὶ καὶ Ἀθηναῖοι καὶ Λακεδαιμόνιοι
καὶ Βυζάντιοι καὶ Μυτιληναῖοι τοὺς αὐτοὺς
τούτους θεραπεύουσιν; ἀλλ' ὅμως ὅταν δόξῃ
τινὰ στῆσαι χαλκοῦν, ἱστᾶσι καὶ τῆς εἰς τοῦτο
106 δαπάνης εὐποροῦσιν. καὶ μὴν ἤδη τινὸς ἤκουσα
Ῥοδίου λέγοντος· οὐχ ὅμοια τὰ ἐκείνων καὶ τὰ
ἡμέτερα. τοῖς μὲν γὰρ μόνον ὑπάρχειν τὴν

---

[1] κἀκεῖνοι Pflugk : ἐκεῖνοι.
[2] ὃ Reiske : ἅ.

---

[1] The Roman provincial governors.

occasion for such things is past, that you live in uninterrupted peace. For it is clear that they too would have preferred to keep out of danger, and that their object in exerting themselves was in order to win security in the end. The point I am making, however, is that their scale of expenditures was not on as low a level as yours. To pass over the other items, such as your shipyards, the arms and armour, the war engines, the mere upkeep of the walls, to which I just made reference, as they are now kept up in your time, is assuredly not comparable. For if one does suppose that there is no difference in the care given to them, yet, you see, they are kept in shape in a leisurely fashion, a little at a time, and whenever a magistrate so desires; but in former times they had to be kept standing. And while now they are built to be tested by yourselves, then they were to be tested by the enemy. So much for that. Well then, neither can it be said that the persons you honour are more numerous; for the mere number of the statues standing which date from that time reveals the truth. And apart from that, who would say that those who are zealous to serve the state are now more numerous than then?

Oh yes! you may say, "but we simply *must* honour the commanders [1] who rule over us, one and all."

What of it? Do not also the Athenians, Spartans, Byzantines, and Mytilenaeans pay court to these same? But nevertheless, whenever they decide to set up in bronze one of these, they do so, and they manage to find the cost. Indeed I once heard a certain Rhodian remark—"The position of those people is not comparable to ours. For all that they,

ἐλευθερίαν δίχα Ἀθηναίων, καὶ τούτους δὲ μηδὲν
μέγα κεκτῆσθαι· τὴν δὲ ἡμετέραν πόλιν ἐπίφθονον
εἶναι παρὰ πᾶσιν, ὡς ἄριστα πράττουσαν· διόπερ
αὐτῇ πλειόνων δεῖν τῶν εὐνοούντων. ἔτι δὲ
μηδένα τῶν Ῥωμαίων διαφέρεσθαι παρὰ τοῖσδε
ἑστάναι, τῆς δέ γε ἐνθάδε τιμῆς οὐκ ἀμελεῖν.

107   Ταῦτα δέ ἐστι μὲν ἀληθῆ, μᾶλλον δὲ ὀφείλετε
ἀποστῆναι δι᾽ αὐτὰ τοῦ πράγματος. τούς τε
γὰρ λόγον ἔχοντας ταύτης τῆς παρ᾽ ὑμῖν τιμῆς[1]
εἰκός ἐστι μὴ παραπέμπειν μηδὲ τὸ[2] πῶς αὐτῆς
τυγχάνουσιν, ἀλλ᾽ ἅμα καὶ τὴν διάνοιαν τὴν ὑμετέραν
σκοπεῖν· τούς τε ἐπίφθονον εἶναι τὴν εὐπορίαν
τῆς πόλεως ὁμολογοῦντας οὐκ εἰκὸς ἦν ὑπολογί-
ζεσθαι τὸ τῆς δαπάνης. οὐ γάρ τοι τοσούτῳ διὰ
τοῦτο πλείους τιμᾶτε τῶν ἄλλων ὅσῳ πλείονα
κἀκείνων κέκτησθε.

Καὶ μὴν τῶν γε αὐτοκρατόρων καὶ νῦν ποιεῖσθε
εἰκόνας, καὶ τῶν ἄλλων δὲ τῶν ἐπ᾽ ἀξιώματος.
οὐδὲ γὰρ ὑμᾶς λέληθεν ὡς οὐδέν ἐστι τὸ τοῦτον
ἵστασθαι τὸν τρόπον. ἵν᾽ οὖν τίνας τιμήσητε
λοιπόν, οὕτως αἰσχρὸν καὶ ἀνάξιον ὑμῶν αὐτῶν
108 ἔργον διαπράττεσθε; εἰ μὲν γὰρ ἅπασιν ὁμοίως
προσεφέρεσθε δίχα τῶν αὐτοκρατόρων, οὐκ ἂν
οὕτως ἠλέγχεσθε. νῦν δ᾽ εἰσὶν οὓς αὐτοὺς[3]
ἵστατε· ὥστε τοῖς ἄλλοις εἶναι φανερὸν ἐκ τούτων

---

[1] ταύτης and τιμῆς added by Capps, cf. schol. in U συνεξα-
κουστέον τιμῆς, and superscript in T τιμῆς δηλονότι. εἰκόνος
Wilamowitz.
[2] τὸ Reiske : τοῦ.
[3] αὐτοὺς Selden : αὐτοῦ.

---

[1] That is, to the really important Romans whom the
Rhodians wish to honour.

the Athenians excepted, possess is liberty and the Athenians have no great possessions either; but our city is the envy of all because it is the most prosperous, and consequently it needs a greater number of loyal friends. Furthermore, none of the Romans particularly cares to have a statue among those peoples, but they do not despise that honour here."

All this is true, and that is all the more reason why you should give up that practice. For we may reasonably assume that those who put any value upon having this honour in your city do not overlook the manner in which they get it, but at the same time take into consideration also the spirit in which you give it; and on the other hand, it would not be reasonable to assume that those who acknowledge that the wealth of their city arouses envy should take into account the matter of the expense. For assuredly you do not because of that consideration honour a greater number than do the other states in proportion to the relatively greater wealth which you possess.

And besides, even at this moment you are having statues made of the emperors and of other men also who are of high rank. For even you must have noticed that to be set up in your present way means nothing![1] Whom, then, do you think of honouring in the future that you continue a practice so shameful and so unworthy of your own selves? I ask this because, if you were treating everybody alike with the exception of the emperors, you would not be shown up as you are being at present. But as it is, there are persons for whom you do set up statues of themselves; consequently from these cases you make it evident to all the others that you are not really

DIO CHRYSOSTOM

ὅτι οὐ τιμᾶτε αὐτούς. εἰ δὲ τῶν πολλῶν καὶ τῶν μηδὲν ἂν[1] ὠφελησάντων εἰσὶν οὗτοι, τίνος χάριν ἀσχημονεῖτε; ἢ τί βουλόμενοι τούτους θεραπεύετε, καὶ ταῦτα ἐνὸν ὑμῖν ἄλλως ἐπιμελεῖσθαι; καὶ γὰρ ξένια πλείω καὶ τὸ τῆς ὑποδοχῆς ἐλευθέριον τοῖς πολλοῖς ἱκανόν, κἂν βελτίων ᾖ τις, ἔτι καὶ ψήφισμα ἤρκεσεν ἁπλοῦν, εἶτ᾽ οὖν[2] εἰς τὸ πρυτανεῖον ἢ[3] εἰς προεδρίαν ἐκλήθη. νυνὶ μὲν γὰρ δοκεῖτε, ὥσπερ οἱ σφόδρα γέμοντες τῶν ναυκλήρων καὶ χειμαζόμενοι διὰ τοῦτο, ἐκβολὴν ποιεῖσθαι τῶν ἀνδριάντων.

109 Καίτοι φέρε, εἴ τις ὑμῖν ἔλεγεν ὡς ἄρα ἀποδόσθαι προσήκει τοὺς πολλοὺς αὐτῶν, ἵνα εὐπορήσητε χρημάτων, οὐκ ἔστιν ὅπως οὐκ ἂν[4] ἀνδράποδον ἡγήσασθε εἶναι τὸν λέγοντα. νῦν τοίνυν αὐτὸ τοῦτο ποιεῖτε· ὅσου γὰρ ἀνδριὰς γένοιτ᾽ ἄν, τοσοῦτον ἐφ᾽ ἑκάστῳ κερδαίνετε·[5] πλὴν ὅτι γε αὐτοῖς ἀποδίδοσθε αὐτοὺς καὶ οὐκ ἐπ᾽ ἐξαγωγῇ, καθάπερ, οἶμαι, τὰ σφόδρα πονηρὰ ἀνδράποδα. καθόλου δὲ εὖ ἴστε ὅτι μηδέν ἐστι τῶν τοιούτων μέγα μηδὲ τίμιον ἄλλως, εἰ μὴ παρὰ τοὺς διδόντας, ἐὰν διδῶσιν ὡς τοιοῦτον ὄν[6]. εἰ δὲ τῶν ὄντων ὅ τι ἂν θέλῃ τις ῥᾳδίως καὶ τῷ τυχόντι παρέχοιεν,[7]

110 ταχὺ δόξει τοῦ μηδενὸς ἄξιον. διὰ τοῦτο σεμνότερόν ἐστι τὸ παρ᾽ ὑμῖν κληθῆναι[8] εἰς προεδρίαν ἅπαξ τῆς παρ᾽ ἑτέροις εἰκόνος. καὶ τὸ μὲν

---

[1] μηδὲν ἂν Post : μηδένα.
[2] εἶτ᾽ οὖν added by Post, ᾧ by Selden.
[3] ἢ Casaubon : εἰ UB, om. M.   [4] ἂν added by Pflugk.
[5] κερδαίνετε Casaubon : κερδανεῖτε UBT, κερδανεῖται M.
[6] ὄν added by Capps, as in § 142. Cohoon would add δεῖ after ὡς.   [7] παρέχοιεν Pflugk : παρέχειν.
[8] παρ᾽ ὑμῖν κληθῆναι Emperius : κληθῆναι παρ᾽ ἑτέροις.

honouring them. And if these persons are commoners and could have rendered no service at
all, what motive have you for this unseemly conduct? What is your object in courting the favour
of those persons, and that too when it is possible for
you to show your solicitude for them in other ways?
For the fact is that for the commoners several
gifts of friendship and lavish entertainment were
sufficient; and if a person is of higher rank a simple
decree in addition was enough, whether indeed he
was invited to dine in the city hall or to take a seat of
honour. For as things are, you give the impression
that you are doing what ship-captains do whose
vessels are heavily laden and consequently in danger
of foundering—jettisoning your statues!

But come, consider: if anyone told you that it was
better after all to sell the most of them in order to
be well supplied with funds, you could not possibly
help considering the speaker a base slavish sort of man.
Yet this is just what you are doing now; for what
a statue would cost to make is just so much gain
for you; except that you are selling them to yourselves and not for export, just as you deport to
foreign parts, I presume, your vilest slaves. But
in general, you well know that there is nothing
great or valuable in such gifts anyhow, except as it
is in the givers—if they give it for what it is. But
if a man makes a present from his own property
of whatever any person wants, giving it carelessly and to any person that comes along, soon the
gift will be looked upon as utterly valueless. For
this reason it is a matter of greater pride to the
recipient to be invited to a seat of honour just once
in your city than to get a statue elsewhere. And a

ὑμᾶς καθημένους ἐπαινέσαι λαμπρόν· ἄλλοι δὲ
οὐδὲ ἂν διαρραγῶσι κεκραγότες οὐ δοκοῦσιν
ἱκανῶς τιμᾶν.

Τὸν Ὀλυμπίασι στέφανον ἴστε δήπουθεν ἐλάϊνον
ὄντα, καὶ τοῦτον πολλοὶ προτετιμήκασι τοῦ
ζῆν, οὐχὶ τῆς ἐκεῖ φυομένης ἐλαίας ἐχούσης τι
θαυμαστόν, ἀλλ' ὅτι μὴ ῥᾳδίως μηδ' ἐπὶ μικρῷ
δίδοται. τοιγαροῦν ἔγγιστα, ἐφ' ἡμῶν, ὡς ἐπίστασθε, τῶν αὐτοκρατόρων τις οὕτω σφόδρα
ἡττήθη τοῦ πράγματος καὶ ἐπεθύμησε τῆς ἐκεῖ
νίκης ὥστε καὶ ἀγωνίσασθαι παρ' Ἠλείοις, καὶ
τοῦτον ὅρον ἡγήσασθαι τῆς εὐδαιμονίας. εἰ δέ
γε πάντας ἐστεφάνουν τοὺς ἐπὶ τὴν θέαν ἀφικνου-
μένους τῶν ἡγουμένων, τίνα ἂν [1] ζῆλον ἢ ποίαν
ἔτι δόξαν ἔσχεν ὁ στέφανος; ἀλλὰ ἐκείνους γέ
111 φασι μηδὲ τὰς ἐπιστολὰς λύειν, ἃς ἂν γράψωσι
τῶν ἀθλητῶν τινα συνιστάντες, πρὶν ἢ ἀγωνίσηται.
καὶ τοῦτο οὐδένα πώποτε αὐτοῖς ἤνεγκε κίνδυνον,
ἀλλὰ τοὐναντίον τιμὴν καὶ ἔπαινον τῷ δοκεῖν
ἀξίους εἶναι βραβεύειν τὸν ἀγῶνα. μὴ γὰρ
οἴεσθε Ῥωμαίους οὕτως εἶναι σκαιοὺς καὶ
ἀμαθεῖς ὥστε μηδέν [2] αἱρεῖσθαι τῶν ὑφ' αὑτοῖς
ἐλευθέριον εἶναι μηδὲ καλόν, ἀλλὰ βούλεσθαι
μᾶλλον ἀνδραπόδων κρατεῖν.
112 Εἶτα Ἠλεῖοι μὲν οὕτως ἀξιοῦσι τὰ ἑαυτῶν,
οὐδενὸς Πελοποννησίων κατά γε τἄλλα ἀμείνους
ὄντες· ὑμεῖς δὲ τοὺς παριόντας δεδοίκατε,

[1] ἂν added by Arnim.
[2] μηδέν' Budé : μηδὲν UM, μηδένα B.

---

[1] This emperor was Nero. See Dio Cassius 63. 14; Suetonius, Life of Nero 24.

resolution of commendation voted by you from your seats in the assembly is a splendid distinction; but other peoples, even if they burst their lungs with cheering, seem not to show honour enough.

You doubtless know that the Olympian crown is of olive leaves, and yet this honour many people have preferred to life itself, not because there is anything wonderful about the olive that grows there, but because it is not given carelessly or for slight achievement. This explains why very recently, in our own time, one of the emperors, as you know, was so taken with this practice and was so eager to win the victory there that he actually competed at the Elean festival and considered this the height of happiness.[1] But if it had been their custom to crown all the potentates that came to the spectacle, what emulation would the crown any longer have aroused and what sort of glory would it have won? On the contrary, they say that the Eleans do not even open the letters written by those who would recommend a particular athlete,[2] until he has competed. And this has never brought upon them any risk of harm, but, on the contrary, honour and applause, because they are considered worthy to supervise the games. For you must not suppose that the Romans are so stupid and ignorant as to choose that none of their subjects should be independent or honourable but would rather rule over slaves.

Then again, whereas the Eleans, who are not superior in other respects to any of the other Peloponnesians, put so high a value upon their own position, are you Rhodians so afraid of all your

---

[2] Casaubon thinks that some of the emperors would at times recommend an athlete, while Reiske thinks that other Romans in high position also did it.

κἂν ἕνα τινὰ μὴ στήσητε χαλκοῦν, τὴν ἐλευθερίαν
οἴεσθε ἀποβαλεῖν;[1] ἀλλ᾽ εἴ γε οὕτω σφόδρα
ἐπισφαλής ἐστιν ὥστε ἐκ τῆς τυχούσης προφάσεως
περιαιρεθῆναι, δουλεύειν ὑμῖν τῷ παντὶ βέλτιον
ἤδη. καὶ γὰρ τοῖς τὸ σῶμα οὕτως ἐπικινδύνως
ἔχουσιν ὥστε μηκέτ᾽ ἀνενεγκεῖν τεθνάναι κρεῖττον
113 ἢ ζῆν. εἰ γὰρ ὑμῖν ἡ μὲν ἐκ τοσούτου χρόνου
πίστις καὶ πρὸς τὸν δῆμον εὔνοια τὸν ἐκείνων
καὶ κοινωνία πάσης τύχης οὐ δύναται βεβαιοῦν
τὴν πολιτείαν, οὐδὲ Μιθριδάτης καθαιρεθεὶς οὐδ᾽
Ἀντίοχος, οὐδ᾽ ἡ τῆς θαλάττης ἀρχὴ παραδοθεῖσα
διὰ πολλῶν κινδύνων καὶ πόνων, οὐδ᾽ οἱ πρὸ τοσούτων ἐτῶν ὅρκοι τῆς φιλίας, οὐδ᾽ αἱ παρ᾽ αὐτὸν
τὸν Δία στῆλαι κείμεναι μέχρι νῦν, οὐδ᾽ ἡ μέχρι
Ὠκεανοῦ συγκινδυνεύσασα δύναμις, οὐδ᾽ ἡ τὸ
τελευταῖον ὑπὲρ αὐτῶν ἁλοῦσα πόλις, ἀλλ᾽ εἰ
μὴ τὸν δεῖνα καὶ τὸν δεῖνα κολακεύσετε ἀγεννῶς,
πάντα ταῦτα ἀνατέτραπται, ὡς ἀεὶ προσδοκᾶν
ὀργήν τινα ἢ μῖσος, σφόδρα ὑμῖν φαύλως τὰ πράγματα ἔχει καὶ ἐπ᾽ οὐδενὸς ἵδρυσθε ἰσχυροῦ. καὶ
ἔγωγε φαίην ἄν, εἰ καὶ χαλεπῶς ἀκούσεσθε,
κρεῖττον ὑμῶν ἀπαλλάττειν τοὺς ἐν Φρυγίᾳ μέσῃ
114 δουλεύοντας ἢ τοὺς ἐν Αἰγύπτῳ καὶ Λιβύῃ. τὸ

---

[4] ἀποβαλεῖν Selden : ἀποβάλλειν.

---

[1] At the time when Dio was speaking, whenever that was,
Rhodes seems to have been a *civitas libera et foederata*, but in
danger of losing that position.

[2] *I. G.* xii, No. 58, says that Hermagoras, son of
Phaenippus, as a prytanist gave expression to the εὔνοια

casual visitors that you think if you fail to set up some one person in bronze, you will lose your freedom?[1] But if your freedom is in so precarious a state that it can be stripped from you on any petty pretext, it would in every way be better for you to be slaves forthwith. So too when men's bodies are so dangerously ill that there is no longer hope for their recovery, death is better than life. Why, if your long-standing loyalty and good will[2] toward that people, and your having shared with them every fortune, are unable to give your state security, nor yet the subjugation of Mithridates or of Antiochus, nor the command of the sea which you have delivered over to them at the cost of so many dangers and hardships, nor the vows of friendship taken so many years ago, nor the tablets[3] which up to the present time have stood at the very side of your statue of Zeus, nor your mighty[4] fleet, which has shared in their battles as far as the Ocean's edge, nor finally, the capture of your city[5] endured for their sake, yet if you omit to flatter ignobly this man and that man, all these things have come to naught—if this is your condition, so that you are always expecting some outburst of wrath or hatred, then your position is extremely wretched and rests upon no firm foundation. And I, for my part, would say, even at the risk of angering you, that slaves in the interior of Phrygia, and those in Egypt and Libya, fare better than yourselves. For it is less

(good will) and πίστις (loyalty) of the state of Rhodes to Titus and his house, and to the senate and Roman people.

[3] On these the treaty between Rome and Rhodes would be recorded.

[4] See § 103 and note.

[5] By Cassius in 42 B.C. See note on the Chariot § 86.

γὰρ ἀγνοούμενον καὶ μὴ δοκοῦντα μηδενὸς ἄξιον ποιεῖν ὁτιοῦν ἔλαττον αἰσχρόν· τὸ δὲ οὕτως ὄντας ἐπισήμους καὶ θαυμαζομένους παρὰ πᾶσιν ἀνάγκην ἔχειν ὥσπερ τοὺς ἀγεννεῖς κύνας σαίνειν τὸν παριόντα δεινόν.

Φέρε τοίνυν, εἰ δὲ καὶ πάντας δέοι τιμᾶν οὕτως [1] καὶ τὴν ἐσχάτην ἀπορίαν θείη τις εἶναι περὶ τὴν πόλιν, πόσῳ κρεῖττον αὐτὸ τὸ ψήφισμα προσπέμψαι τὸ τῆς εἰκόνος, ἵν᾿, ἐὰν βούληται, στήσῃ παρ᾿ ἑαυτοῦ;

115   Νὴ Δί᾿, ἀλλ᾿ αἰσχρόν, εἰ τοσαύτην στενοχωρίαν ὁμολογήσομεν, καὶ Ῥοδίων οὐκ ἄξιον.

Καίτοι [2] τίς οὐκ ἂν εὖ φρονῶν ἕλοιτο πένης δοκεῖν μᾶλλον ἢ πονηρός; ἢ τὸ νυνὶ γιγνόμενον ἧττον ὑμῖν δοκεῖ τινος αἰσχρὸν εἶναι, τὸ τοὺς ἀνδριάντας ὑμῶν δύνασθαί τινα διηγεῖσθαι, καθά-περ τὰς οἰκίας, ὅτι πρότερον μὲν ἦν αὕτη τοῦ δεῖνος, νῦν δὲ τοῦ δεῖνος γέγονεν, ἂν δ᾿ οὗτος τελευτήσῃ, πάλιν ἔσται τοῦ κληρονομήσαντος ἢ τοῦ πριαμένου; καίτοι τὴν εἰκόνα οὐκ ἔστιν οὐδενὶ δικαίῳ μεταθεῖναι, καθάπερ τὴν οἰκίαν.

116   Ἤδη τοίνυν ἤκουσά τι [3] καὶ τοιοῦτόν τινος ἀποσχεδιάζοντος, ὅτι καὶ παρ᾿ ἑτέροις ἰδεῖν ἔστι τοῦτο γιγνόμενον· πάλιν δὲ ἑτέρου, ὡς καὶ παρ᾿ Ἀθηναίοις πολλὰ πράττεται νῦν, οἷς οὐκ

---

[1] οὕτως Wilamowitz : ὅπως.
[2] καίτοι Capps : καὶ.
[3] ἤκουσά τι Valesius : ἠκούσατε.

shameful that a man who is unknown and thought to be utterly without desert should resort to any and every expedient; but that a people so distinguished as yourselves and so admired throughout the world should be constrained like low-bred curs to fawn upon every passer-by, is scandalous.

Come then, tell me this: Suppose that it should be necessary to honour all the world in this fashion and that we should assume the city to be in desperate financial straits, how much better it would be to send the simple decree in which the statue is voted to each man so honoured, in order that, if he chooses, he may set it up at his own expense!

" Good heavens ! " you exclaim, " but it would be a disgrace if we are to admit such straightened circumstances, and beneath the dignity of the people of Rhodes ! "

And yet what person in his right mind would not prefer to be thought poor rather than unprincipled? Or does the present situation seem to you in a less degree disgraceful than any other—that a person is able to describe your statues in the same way as your houses, saying that this one *used* to belong to So-and-so but that now it has come into the hands of So-and-so; and when the present owner dies it will in turn belong to whoever has inherited it—or who buys it? And yet it is not possible for any right-minded man to transfer the ownership of a statue as he does that of a house.

Well, I once heard a man make an off-hand remark to the effect that there are other peoples also where one can see this practice being carried on; and again, another man, who said that even in Athens many things are done now which any one, not without

ἀπεικότως ἄν τις ἐπιπλήξειεν, οὐ περὶ τὰ ἄλλα
μόνον, ἀλλὰ καὶ περὶ τὰς τιμάς· οἵ γε τὸν δεῖνα
μὲν 'Ολύμπιον κεκλήκασιν οὐδὲ φύσει πολίτην
ἑαυτῶν, Φοίνικα δὲ ἄνθρωπον οὐκ ἀπὸ Τύρου καὶ
Σιδῶνος, ἀλλ' ἀπὸ κώμης τινὸς ἢ τῆς ἠπείρου, καὶ
ταῦτα πιττούμενον τοὺς βραχίονας καὶ περιδήματα
φοροῦντα· τὸν δεῖνα δὲ τὸν εὐχερῆ λίαν ποιητήν,
ὃς καὶ παρ' ὑμῖν ποτε κἀνθάδε ἐπεδείξατο, οὐ
μόνον χαλκοῦν ἑστάκασιν, ἀλλὰ καὶ παρὰ Μέναν-
δρον. λέγειν δὲ εἰώθασιν οἱ διασύροντες τὴν
πόλιν καὶ τὸ ἐπίγραμμα τὸ ἐπὶ τῆς Νικάνορος
εἰκόνος, ὡς [1] αὐτοῖς καὶ τὴν Σαλαμῖνα ἐωνήσατο.
117 ἐγὼ δ' εἰ μέν τις ἢ τοῖς 'Αθηναίοις ἐπιτιμῶν
λέγει ταῦτα, καὶ δεικνὺς οὐκ ὄντας ἀξίους τοὺς
ἐνοικοῦντας τῆς πόλεως οὐδὲ τῆς δόξης, ἣν οἱ
πρότερον γενόμενοι κατέλιπον, ἢ καθόλου τὴν
'Ελλάδα ἐλεῶν εἰς ὃ πέπτωκεν, ὅταν τοιαῦτα
πράττωσιν οἱ χρόνον τινὰ δόξαντες αὐτῆς προεστάναι, καλῶς αὐτὸν ἡγοῦμαι λέγειν· εἰ δ' ὅτι προσήκει μηδ' ὑμᾶς μηδὲν μέγα φρονεῖν μηδ' ἐκείνων

---

[1] ὡς Post: ὅς.

[1] Cf. Philostratus, *Life of Apollonius of Tyana* 8. 7 : τοὺς
'Ολυμπίους καὶ τὰς τοιάσδε ἐπωνυμίας ἔθεντο ('Αθηναῖοι).

[2] On this meaning of εὐχερής, the opposite of δυσχερὴς
' finical ', ' fastidious ', ' particular ', see Shorey *Classical
Philology* XV (1917), p. 308, and cf. Arist. *Eth. Eud.* 1221 b 2
and *Hist. Anim.* 595 a 18 : ὗς εὐχερέστατον πρὸς πᾶσαν τροφὴν
ἐστιν. The glutton and the pig are typical of this quality,
and Dio obviously so characterizes this poet.

[3] Pausanias (1. 21. 1) says : "The Athenians have statues
of their writers of Tragedy and of Comedy set up in their
theatre, mostly mediocrities, for except Menander, there is
no writer of Comedy of outstanding ability." The inscribed
basis of Menander's statue, found in the theatre, is extant :

justice, could censure, these being not confined to ordinary matters, but having to do even with the conferring of honours. " Why, they have conferred the title of ' Olympian [1],' " he alleged, upon a certain person he named, " though he was not an Athenian by birth, but a Phoenician fellow who came, not from Tyre or Sidon, but from some obscure village or from the interior, a man, what is more, who has his arms depilated and wears stays " ; and he added that another, whom he also named, that very slovenly [2] poet, who once gave a recital here in Rhodes too, they not only have set up in bronze, but even placed his statue next to that of Menander.[3] Those who disparage their city and the inscription on the statue of Nicanor are accustomed to say that it actually bought Salamis for them.[4] But I, for my part, if any one makes these statements either to reproach the Athenians and to show that its present inhabitants are not worthy of it or of the glory which the Athenians of old bequeathed to them, or to express in a general way a feeling of commiseration for Hellas, that she has fallen to so low an estate, when such acts are committed by a people who for a time were regarded as the foremost of the race, I believe he is right ; but if it is his thought that you also should be lacking in pride

I.G. II², 3777.   Friedländer (*Sittengeschichte Roms*, Vol. 3, p. 224) says that this poet may have been Q. Pompeius Capito, who also appeared as an improvisator.

[4] Pausanias (2. 8. 6) says that Aratus of Sicyon (not Nicanor) persuaded Diogenes, Macedonian commandant of the Peiraeus, Munychia, Salamis, and Sunium, to surrender them for 150 talents, and that of this sum he himself contributed one sixth for the Athenians.   Nicanor of Stageira, a friend of Cassander, captured the Peiraeus in 319 B.C.

κρεῖττον, οὐκ ἔχω τὴν ὑπερβολὴν τῆς ἀναισθη-
118 σίας εἰπεῖν τοῦ ταῦτα λέγοντος. οὐ γὰρ ὃν
τρόπον τὰ καλῶς παρ' ἑτέροις γιγνόμενα πᾶσιν
ἔθος ἐστὶ λέγειν ζήλου καὶ προτροπῆς ἕνεκεν,
ὁμοίως κἂν φαῦλόν τι πράττηται παρ' ἄλλοις,
δεῖ τοῦτο μνημονεύειν, ὥστε μιμεῖσθαι, τοὐναντίον
δὲ ὑπὲρ τοῦ φυλάξασθαι καὶ μὴ λαθεῖν εἴς τι
τοιοῦτον ἐμπεσόντας. καὶ γὰρ εἰ μὲν ἐπαινῶν
τις ἐκείνους ταῦτα ἔλεγε καὶ μηδὲν χείρονος
δόξης ἀποφαίνων ἐπιτυγχάνοντας, ἦν μὲν ἂν
δήπουθεν εὐήθης, μᾶλλον δὲ ἀναιδής· πλὴν κατά
γε τὴν ἑαυτοῦ γνώμην οὐ ¹ παρεῖχέ τινα ἀφορμὴν
τοῖς ἁμαρτάνειν βουλομένοις. εἰ δ' ὡς αἰσχρὰ
καὶ ὀνείδη πάντες αὐτὰ προφέρουσι καὶ οὐθεὶς
ἂν εἴποι τῶν ἐγκωμιαζόντων τὴν πόλιν τοιοῦτον
οὐδέν, ἀλλ' ἤτοι βλασφημῶν τις ἢ καθαπτόμενος
ἄλλως καὶ ἐπιπλήττων, παντελῶς εὐήθης ὁ ²
διὰ τῶν τοιούτων ὑμᾶς προτρέπειν δοκῶν ὥστε
119 ἀμελεῖν τῶν παρ' αὑτοῖς· καθάπερ εἴ τις
ἀθλητὴν πείθων ἀπειπεῖν καὶ προέσθαι τὸν στέφανον ἀργυρίου λέγοι πρὸς αὐτόν· Οὐχ ὁρᾷς
ἐκεῖνον τὸν παραχωρήσαντα πρὸ σοῦ μαστι-
γούμενον; ἢ νὴ Δία εἴ τις τῶν ὑποκριτῶν τινι ³
δεικνὺς τοὺς ἐκπίπτοντας ⁴ καὶ συριττομένους

---

¹ οὐ added by Capps.
² ὁ added by Reiske.
³ τινι added by Arnim.
⁴ ἐκπίπτοντας Reiske : ἐκεῖ πίπτοντας.

---

¹ Referring again to Athens.
² It's scourging for you too if you drop out.

and should be no better than they, then I am unable to characterize the utter lack of fine feeling shown by the speaker. For as it is the custom of all men to recount the admirable institutions and practices which are found among other peoples for the purpose of encouraging eager emulation of them, we should not in the same way mention any bad practice that is current elsewhere for the sake of encouraging imitation of it, but, on the contrary, only in order that one's people may be on their guard against it and may not fall unawares into that sort of thing. Indeed if a man were in fact reciting any such things by way of praising that other people and of showing that they enjoyed a reputation no whit worse on that account, he must surely be reckoned a simple, or rather a reckless, person ; but yet according to his own opinion he was not offering any incentive to those wishing to do wrong. But if all men cite these practices as a shame and a reproach and not one of those who eulogize the city[1] would mention any such thing, but only a person who wanted either to slander or in some other way to criticize and assail it, that man is an utter simpleton who thinks that by such means he could induce you to abandon your own customs. It is just as if a person, in trying to persuade an athlete to give up and forego the crown for the price of a piece of silver, should say to him : " Do you not see yonder man, the one who is being scourged, just in front of you, because he dropped out of the contest ? "[2] Or, by heavens, just as if a man should point out to one of the actors several who were being hissed off the stage, and should offer this sort of encouragement : " See to it that you also pay no

τοιαῦτα παραμυθοῖτο· Ὅπως μηδὲ σὺ προσέξεις,
ἀλλ' ὁμοίως ἀγωνιεῖ. Καὶ νῦν ὑμῖν σχεδὸν ἐκεῖνοι
λέγουσιν· Οὐχ ὁρᾶτε τοὺς Ἀθηναίους ὡς ἀσχη-
μονοῦσιν, ὡς κακῶς ἀκούουσιν, ὡς παράδειγμα[1]
πᾶσίν εἰσι τῆς ἀγεννείας καὶ τῆς ὕβρεως ἣν
ὑβρίζουσιν εἰς τὴν πατρίδα;

120   Καίτοι πότερον θῇ τις αὐτοὺς ἀνταγωνιστὰς
ὑμῶν, ὥσπερ ἀξιοῦσιν, ἢ μᾶλλον, ὃ τῷ παντὶ
βέλτιον καὶ δικαιότερον, καὶ τούτους καὶ τοὺς
Λακεδαιμονίους καὶ πάντας τοὺς ὁμοίους μερίτας
ὑμετέρους[2] ἢ ὑμᾶς ἐκείνων; ἀλλ' οὔτε τοὺς
ἀνταγωνιστὰς ἁμαρτάνοντας εὔλογόν ἐστι μιμεῖσθαι, τοὐναντίον δὲ τοσούτῳ μᾶλλον κατορθοῦν,
ἵνα τῷ παντὶ φαίνησθε προέχοντες αὐτῶν, καὶ μὴ
μόνον διὰ τὴν ἐκείνων κακίαν, ἀλλὰ καὶ διὰ τὴν
αὐτῶν ἀρετὴν εὐδοκιμῆτε· οὔτε τοὺς οἰκείους καὶ
προσήκοντας, ἀλλὰ μάλιστα μὲν κωλύειν, εἰ δ'
οὖν,[3] αὐτούς γε πειρᾶσθαι τοῖς ἑαυτῶν ἔργοις τὰ
ἁμαρτήματα ἐκείνων ἐλάττω ποιεῖν.

121   Ἔτι δ' εἰ μὲν ἐν τοῖς ἄλλοις μηδὲν αὐτῶν
διεφέρετε, οὐδὲν ἴσως ἔδει[4] καθ' ἓν τοῦτο φιλοτιμεῖσθαι καὶ σκοπεῖν ὅπως κρείττους δόξετε.
νῦν δὲ οὐθέν ἐστιν ἐφ' ὅτῳ τῶν ἐκεῖ γιγνομένων
οὐκ ἂν αἰσχυνθείη τις. οἷον εὐθὺς τὰ περὶ τοὺς
μονομάχους οὕτω σφόδρα ἐζηλώκασι Κορινθίους,

---

[1] παράδειγμα Emperius : παραδείγματα.
[2] μερίτας ὑμετέρους Capps, cf. Pollux 8. 136, and Ditten-
berger, Sylloge² 134, 1. 8 and note : μέρος ὑμέτερον.
[3] εἰ δ' οὖν Wyttenbach : εἰ γοῦν M, ἤγουν B, ἢγ' οὖν U.

attention to your part, but go through the performance the way they did." And now those whom we
have just described are to all intents and purposes
saying to you: " Do you not see how the Athenians
are disgracing themselves, how they are getting a
bad name, how they are an example to all the
world of baseness and of the kind of insolence with
which they outrage their own country ? "

And yet, let me ask, shall anyone class the
Athenians as your rivals, as these persons demand,
or rather—and this is in every way better and fairer—
hold both them and the Spartans and all others
like them to be your co-partners, or you theirs?
But it is not sensible to imitate your rivals when they
err, but on the contrary to endeavour so much the
more to do right yourselves, in order that you may
be found superior to them in every respect and ever
win credit, not only on account of their demerits,
but also on account of your own virtue; nor should
you copy your friends and relatives, but should try
to check them if possible, or, if you *do* copy them,
should by the merit of your own conduct try to
minimize their shortcomings.

Moreover, if you were no whit superior to the Athenians in other respects, perhaps you would not find
it necessary to feel any jealousy of them in this one
matter and to consider how you might have a reputation better than theirs. But as matters now stand,
there is no practice current in Athens which would
not cause any man to feel ashamed. For instance,
in regard to the gladiatorial shows the Athenians
have so zealously emulated the Corinthians, or rather,

---

⁴ ἔδει Reiske : δεῖ.

μᾶλλον δ' ὑπερβεβλήκασι τῇ κακοδαιμονίᾳ κἀκείνους καὶ τοὺς ἄλλους ἅπαντας, ὥστε οἱ Κορίνθιοι
μὲν ἔξω τῆς πόλεως θεωροῦσιν ἐν χαράδρᾳ τινί,
πλῆθος μὲν δυναμένῳ δέξασθαι τόπῳ, ῥυπαρῷ δὲ
ἄλλως καὶ ὅπου μηδεὶς ἂν μηδὲ θάψειε μηδένα
τῶν ἐλευθέρων, Ἀθηναῖοι δὲ ἐν τῷ θεάτρῳ θεῶν-
ται τὴν καλὴν ταύτην θέαν ὑπ' αὐτὴν τὴν ἀκρόπολιν,
οὗ τὸν Διόνυσον ἐπὶ τὴν ὀρχήστραν τιθέασιν·
ὥστε πολλάκις ἐν αὐτοῖς τινα σφάττεσθαι τοῖς
θρόνοις, οὗ τὸν ἱεροφάντην καὶ τοὺς ἄλλους ἱερεῖς
122 ἀνάγκη καθίζειν. καὶ τὸν εἰπόντα περὶ τούτου
φιλόσοφον καὶ νουθετήσαντα αὐτοὺς οὐκ ἀπ-
εδέξαντο οὐδὲ ἐπήνεσαν, ἀλλ' οὕτως ἐδυσχέραναν,
ὥστε ἐκεῖνον γένει μὲν ὄντα [1] Ῥωμαίων μηδενὸς
ὕστερον, δόξαν δὲ τηλικαύτην ἔχοντα ἡλίκης
οὐδεὶς ἐκ πάνυ πολλοῦ τετύχηκεν, ὁμολογού-
μενον δὲ μόνον μάλιστα μετὰ τοὺς ἀρχαίους
ἀκολούθως βεβιωκέναι τοῖς λόγοις, καταλιπεῖν
τὴν πόλιν καὶ μᾶλλον ἑλέσθαι διατρίβειν ἀλλα-
χόσε τῆς Ἑλλάδος. ἀλλ' οὐκ ἂν ὑμεῖς, ἄνδρες
Ῥόδιοι, τοιοῦτον οὐθὲν ὑπομείναιτε, παρ' οἷς

---

[1] γένει μὲν ὄντα Capps, ὄντα μὲν γένει Emperius. μεν ὄντα
γένει.

---

[1] According to Curtius (*Peloponnesus* 2. 527) Dio is here
referring to a rocky depression at the foot of a hill east of the
new town. This depression was enlarged by the Corinthians
to form an amphitheatre, which one could not see until he came
to the very crest. Friedländer, however, thinks that Dio
refers here to the natural depression before it was made into
an amphitheatre. Otherwise he would have described it
differently because it is called a splendid structure in the 4th
century A.D. See Harold North Fowler, Vol. I of the American
School at Athens *Corinth* series, chapter "Topography".

have so surpassed both them and all others in their
mad infatuation, that whereas the Corinthians watch
these combats outside the city in a glen, a place
that is able to hold a crowd but otherwise is dirty
and such that no one would even bury there any
freeborn citizen,[1] the Athenians look on at this
fine spectacle in their theatre under the very walls
of the Acropolis, in the place where they bring their
Dionysus into the orchestra and stand him up,[2] so
that often a fighter is slaughtered among the very
seats in which the Hierophant and the other priests
must sit. And the philosopher[3] who spoke about
this matter and rebuked them they refused to obey
and did not even applaud; on the contrary, they were
so incensed that, although in blood he was inferior
to no Roman, but enjoyed a reputation greater than
any one man has attained for generations, and was
admittedly the only man who since the time of the
ancients had lived most nearly in conformity with
reason, this man was forced to leave the city and preferred to go and live somewhere else in Greece. But
you, O men of Rhodes, would not tolerate any such
thing as that, since among you there is a law which

---

[2] At the City Dionysia a statue of the god was escorted by
the ἔφηβοι from the Dipylon Gate and placed in the orchestra
of the theatre. See I.G.II², l. 11.

[3] In a note on Philostratus, *op. cit.* 4. 32, where Apollonius
is represented as saying σὺ δέ, Διόνυσε, μετὰ τοιοῦτον αἷμα ἐς τὸ
θέατρον φοιτᾷς; Valesius offered reasons for believing that
the philosopher here referred to was Apollonius of Tyana.
The description given above fits Apollonius except that he
appears to be a Roman. Consequently it is now generally
believed that this philosopher was Musonius Rufus, whom Dio,
owing to his admiration of the man whom he knew personally,
praised so highly. Did not Musonius Rufus convert Dio to a
belief in philosophy?

νόμος ἐστὶ τὸν δημόσιον μηδέποτε εἰσελθεῖν εἰς τὴν πόλιν.

123 Τίνος οὖν ἕνεκα ἐπεμνήσθην;[1] οὐ μὰ τὸν Δία λοιδορῆσαι βουλόμενος τοὺς Ἀθηναίους· τοὐναντίον γὰρ πᾶσιν ἐλεεῖν αὐτοὺς ἐπέρχεται τοῖς μετρίοις· ἀλλ᾽ ὅπως εἰδῆθ᾽ ὅτι λοιπὸν ὑμῖν οὐ πρὸς ἐκείνους ἐστὶν ὁ λόγος, ἀλλὰ πρὸς ὑμᾶς αὐτοὺς καὶ τῶν ἄλλων εἴ τις σωφρονεῖ. καίτοι πάντα ὅσα ἂν εἴποι τις κατὰ Ἀθηναίων ἢ κατὰ Λακεδαι- μονίων ἢ καθ᾽ ὧν δήποτε, παρ᾽ οἷς ἄλλα τινὰ φαύλως ἔχει καὶ σφόδρα ὀλιγώρως, ἐμοὶ συναγω- νιεῖται· τὸ γὰρ τῶν εἰκόνων οὐκ ἔστι παρ᾽ αὐτοῖς ἰδεῖν οὕτω γιγνόμενον· ὥσθ᾽ ὅ γε μηδὲ παρ᾽ ἐκείνοις ἁμαρτάνεται τοῖς ἐσχάτως ἀπολωλόσι, πῶς οὐκ ἂν ὑπερβολήν τινα ἔχοι τῆς ἀτοπίας;

124 Ἔτι δὲ μᾶλλον αὐτὰ τὰ περὶ τὰς τιμάς τινα[2] παρατεθέντα ἀποδείκνυσι τοῦτο. εἰ γὰρ τὸ τῶν νῦν τινα παραστῆσαι τῶν ἀρχαίων τινὶ δοκεῖ δεινόν, πόσῳ δεινότερον τὸ οὕτως ἀφελέσθαι τινὰ ἐκείνων τῆς τιμῆς, ὥστε ἑτέρῳ δοῦναι; καὶ εἰ τὸ ὄνομα ἐπιγράψαι τινὸς ἄλλῳ τῳ πολὺ ἐλάττονι τηλικαύτην κατάγνωσιν φέρει, τὸ ἐξαλεῖψαι καὶ ἀνελεῖν τὸ τοῦ κρείττονος, ἐὰν οὕτω τύχῃ, ποῖόν τι φαίνεσθαι νομίζετε;

---

[1] ἐπεμνήσθην Emperius : ὑπεμνήσθην.
[2] τινα added by Capps, αὐτῶν ἁμαρτήματα Arnim.

prescribes that the executioner must never enter the city.

What, then, was my object in mentioning this? Not, I assure you, any desire to abuse the Athenians; for, on the contrary, all decent men instinctively feel pity for them; it was rather in order that you might know that from this time on your reckoning is not with them but with your own selves and with all others who are sober-minded. And yet everything that might be said in criticism of the Athenians or of the Spartans or any other peoples among whom are found other practices which are bad and due to gross carelessness, will reinforce my argument; for in the matter of statues you can find no such abuse among them as prevails here; must we not, therefore, of necessity conclude that this particular form of wrongdoing, which is not practiced even among those we have mentioned who are utterly lost to shame, is beyond all exaggeration monstrous? [1]

And this characterization becomes still more convincing if some few details of what happens in connection with the honours you grant are brought into comparison by themselves. If, for instance, it is considered an outrage to place any man of the present day beside any of the ancients, how much more of an outrage is it to deprive, as you are doing, an ancient of his honour for the purpose of bestowing it upon another? And if the inscribing of one person's name over that of another and a much inferior person brings so great condemnation, completely to erase and remove the name of the better man, if it so happens—in what sort of light do you think this act appears?

[1] Cf. § 75 and note.

DIO CHRYSOSTOM

Καὶ μὴν εἴ τις ὑμᾶς Καυνίοις ἢ Μυνδίοις ὁμοίους
εἶναι λέγοι, σφόδρα ὀργιεῖσθε καὶ βλασφημεῖν
αὐτὸν ἡγήσεσθε κατὰ τῆς πόλεως· πῶς ἂν οὖν
ἔθ' ὑμῖν ἀπολογίαν τινὰ φέροι περί τινος τῶν παρ'
125 ὑμῖν τὸ καὶ παρ' ἐκείνοις αὐτὸ γίγνεσθαι; καθάπερ εἰ καὶ τὰ τείχη τις οἴοιτο δεῖν λῦσαι τὰ παρ'
ὑμῖν ἢ καὶ καταπίπτοντα ἐᾶν, ὅτι καὶ παρ'
ἑτέροις πέπτωκε, μᾶλλον δὲ πᾶσι τοῖς ἄλλοις
σχεδόν. καίτοι τὰ μὲν τείχη διὰ τὴν εἰρήνην
καὶ τὴν δουλείαν ἐᾶται παρ' αὐτοῖς, ὧν τὸ μὲν
ἅπαντες εὔχονται, τὴν εἰρήνην, τὸ δὲ λοιπὸν οὐκ
ἔστι κακίας σημεῖον· τὸ δὲ τοῖς παλαιοῖς τῶν
εὐεργετῶν οὕτω προσφέρεσθαι δι' ἀχαριστίαν
γίγνεται. φαίην δ' ἂν ἔγωγε παρὰ τούτοις μηδὲ
εὐεργέτας ἀδικεῖσθαι· τίς γὰρ παρὰ Καυνίοις
γέγονε γενναῖος ἀνήρ; ἢ τίς πώποτε ἐκείνους
ἀγαθόν τι πεποίηκεν; οἵ γε δουλεύουσιν οὐχ
ὑμῖν μόνοις, ἀλλὰ καὶ Ῥωμαίοις, δι' ὑπερβολὴν
ἀνοίας καὶ μοχθηρίας διπλῆν αὐτοῖς τὴν δουλείαν
κατασκευάσαντες. ταῦτα δὲ καὶ περὶ ἄλλων
τις ἂν εἴποι τῶν ὁμοδόξων.
126 Ἐγὼ δὲ καὶ καθόλου τοὺς [1] τηλικοῦτον ἐφ'
αὐτοῖς [2] φρονοῦντας ἡλίκον ὑμεῖς δικαίως οὐ
πρὸς ἑτέρους ἀποβλέπειν οἴομαι δεῖν ἐν οἷς

---

[1] τοὺς Emperius : καίτοι.
[2] ἐφ' αὑτοῖς Reiske : ἐπ' αὐτοῖς.

---

[1] At some period between 70 and 60 B.C. the Caunians, who
had been made tributary to Rhodes by Sulla in punishment
for their part in the massacre of Italians in Asia Minor in 88
on orders by Mithridates, appealed to the Roman senate to be
allowed to pay tribute to Rome rather than to Rhodes; see
Cicero, *Ad Quintum fratrem* 1. 1. 11. 33. This passage in Dio

Moreover, if anyone says that you are no better than the Caunians [1] or Myndians,[2] you will be very angry and think that he is slandering your city; how, then, could any man any longer bring forward before you in defence of any practice prevalent among you the argument that that very thing is done by those other peoples also? It is just as if a person thought that you ought to demolish your own walls, or let them lie when they fall, simply because they lie fallen in the other cities, or rather, in practically all the others. Yet with them the walls are neglected because of their condition of peace and servitude, one of which everybody welcomes, to wit, peace, whereas the other is no longer a sign of baseness; but when people treat in this way their benefactors of long ago, the reason is ingratitude. But I for my part venture to assert that even among your neighbours yonder wrong is not done to benefactors! For who among the Caunians has ever proved himself a noble man? [3] Or who has ever conferred any benefaction upon them? Why, they are in a state of abject slavery, not alone to you but also to the Romans, on account of their excessive folly and wickedness having made their slavery a double one. And this one might also say about others who have the same reputation.

But, speaking generally, I think that a people who take such pride in themselves as you justly do should not, in shaping their conduct, keep their eyes on these

leads us to infer that their petition was rejected and that they were required to pay tribute to both Rhodes and Rome. See also page 54, note 3

[2] Myndus was a city of Caria near Halicarnassus.

[3] And hence entitled to a mark of honour by some state.

DIO CHRYSOSTOM

πράττουσιν, ἄλλως τε τοὺς τοσοῦτον χείρονας, ἀλλὰ πρὸς τὴν ἑαυτῶν δόξαν καὶ τὸ τῆς πόλεως ἀξίωμα. γελοῖον γὰρ ἂν ἦν, εἰ τῶν ὑμετέρων τις πολιτῶν, Δωριεὺς ἐκεῖνος ἢ Λεωνίδας, οὓς τοσαυτάκις φασὶν Ὀλυμπίασι νικῆσαι, πρὸς ἄλλον τινὰ ὁρῶν ἐγυμνάζετο, καὶ ταῦτά γε μηδέποτε στεφανωθέντα. τοῖς μέντοι Λακεδαιμονίοις ἢ τοῖς Ἀθηναίοις εἰ βούλεσθε ἀντεξετάζεσθαι, συγχωρῶ τοῖς τότε οὖσιν, ὅτε αὐτοῖς εἰκότως ἄν τις τῶν
127 ὁμοίων ὑμῖν συνεκρίνετο. καὶ γὰρ τὸν ἀθλητὴν τὸν φιλοτιμούμενον ἔτι καὶ μηδέπω παραχωροῦντα τῆς ἰσχύος οὐ τοὺς νοσοῦντας εὔλογόν ἐστι προκαλεῖσθαι τῶν καθ' αὑτὸν ἐνδόξων οὐδὲ τοὺς τεθνεῶτας, ἀλλ' εἰ μὲν εἶέν τινες ἐρρωμένοι, πρὸς ἐκείνους ἀγωνίζεσθαι περὶ τῆς νίκης· εἰ δὲ μή, τοιοῦτόν τι πρᾶξαι ζητεῖν, ὃ μηδενὸς αὐτὸν ἀσθενέστερον δείξει τῶν πρότερον. ὁ μὲν οὖν ὑγιὴς οὗτός ἐστι περὶ τῶν τοιούτων λόγος. εἰ δὲ ἄρα παρεῖναί τι δεῖ, μήτε πρὸς τοὺς τότε, οἳ ἦσαν κράτιστοι, παραβάλλοντες ἐξετάζετε τὸ πρᾶγμα, μήτε πρὸς τοὺς νῦν οἳ μηδενὸς τῶν φαυλοτάτων διαφέρουσιν, ἀλλὰ πρὸς τοὺς μέσους αὐτῶν ἢ καὶ τοὺς ἔτι τούτων ἐλάττονας.

---

[1] Cf. Demosthenes 20. 10, 142, 165; 22. 76.

[2] The Rhodian athlete Diagoras had three sons, all athletes, of whom Dorieus was the youngest and most famous. He was victor in the pancratium at three successive Olympiads. The second of these victories is mentioned in Thucydides 3. 8. He also had eight victories in the Isthmian games and seven in the Nemean, while he is said to have won in the Pythian games without a contest. Cf. Pindar *Ol.* 7.

[3] Leonidas, also a Rhodian, was twelve times victor in the foot-race. See Pausanias 6. 13. 4.

others, especially on those who are so much their inferiors, but rather upon their own reputation and the proud position of their city.[1] It would have been absurd if one of your own citizens, that famous Dorieus,[2] or Leonidas,[3] men who are said to have won so many victories at Olympia, had done his training with his eye on some other athlete, and him a man who had never been crowned. However, if you wish to measure yourselves against the Spartans or the Athenians, I concede the point in regard to the Athenians of the olden days,[4] when any people similar to yourselves might with good reason have tried to be comparable to them. Take, for instance, the athlete: If he is still eager for honours and is not yet declining in bodily vigour, it is not sensible for him to challenge the famous prize-winners of his own time who are sick, nor yet the dead, nay rather, if there are any who are at the top of their strength, he should select these and strive with them for the victory ; but if none such are available, he should aim to achieve an exploit of such a kind as will show that he is no whit inferior in strength to any athlete of former times.[5] That is sound reasoning about such matters. But if after all it is necessary to make some concession, do not test the question by making a comparison with the peoples who in former times were the strongest, nor yet with those of the present day who are no better than any people of the most worthless sort, but measure yourselves against those who are in between, or against those who are still lower in the scale than they.

[4] Cf. § 117.
[5] Cf. for a similar sentiment Demosthenes 18. 319, Aeschines 3. 189.

128 Παρὰ τοίνυν τοῖς Ἀθηναίοις κατὰ Φίλιππον,
μάλιστα δ' ὅτε τῆς ἡγεμονίας παρακεχωρήκεσαν,
τῆς δ' ἐλευθερίας μόνης λοιπὸν ἀντείχοντο,
Λεπτίνης τις εἰσήνεγκε νόμον ὡς χρὴ [1] τὰς ἀτελείας
ἀφελέσθαι τοὺς ἔχοντας παρὰ τοῦ δήμου, δίχα
τῶν ἀφ' Ἁρμοδίου καὶ Ἀριστογείτονος, καὶ
μηκέτι τὸ λοιπὸν ἐξεῖναι διδόναι μηδενὶ τὴν
δωρεὰν ταύτην. τί οὖν; ἔσθ' ὅπως παρεδέξαντο
129 τὸν νόμον; οὐμενοῦν, ἀλλ' ἑάλω γραφῆς. φέρε
τοίνυν συμβάλετε τοῦτο τὸ ἔθος ἐκείνῳ τῷ νόμῳ,
κἂν μὲν ὑμῖν κατά τι βέλτιον [2] φαίνηται, φυλά-
ξατε αὐτὸ καὶ ποιήσατε ἰσχυρότερον πρὸς τὸ
λοιπόν· ὅπερ ἐξ ἀνάγκης γένοιτ' ἄν, εἰ μὴ λυθήσεται νῦν· ἐὰν δὲ πανταχῇ σκοπούμενοι χεῖρον
εὑρίσκητε,[3] μιμήσασθε τοὺς κατ' ἐκεῖνον τὸν
χρόνον Ἀθηναίους καὶ τὸ μᾶλλον ἄτοπον τοῦ τότε
λυθέντος ὑπ' ἐκείνων καὶ ὑμεῖς νῦν λύσατε.

130 Τὸ μὲν οὖν ψευδῆ τὴν πόλιν δεικνύναι καὶ περὶ
τὰς δωρεὰς ἄπιστον καὶ τὸ τοὺς εὐεργέτας ἀδικεῖν, ἀφαιρουμένους [4] αὐτῶν τὰς ἀμοιβάς, κατὰ [5]
πάντα τὰ τοιαῦτα ἐπ' ἴσης κοινὰ ἀμφοτέροις
πρόσεστιν· ἀλλ' ἐκεῖ μὲν οὐκ ἦν μηδὲν ὠφελῆσθαι [6]
τοὺς τὴν ἀτέλειαν ἐσχηκότας· ἃ γὰρ ἐκτήσαντο

[1] χρὴ Arnim : χρῆν.
[2] βέλτιον added by Arnim, ἄμεινον by Selden.
[3] εὑρίσκητε Reiske : εὑρίσκηται.
[4] ἀφαιρουμένους Arnim : ἀφαιρουμένην.
[5] κατὰ Capps : καὶ.
[6] ὠφελῆσθαι Emperius : ὠφελῆσαι.

Well then, among the Athenians of the time of Philip, and at very near the time when they had given up the primacy among the Greeks and their liberty was the only thing to which they still clung, there was a certain Leptines who proposed a law to the effect that all should be deprived of the privileges of exemption from public duties [1] who had received it from the people, with the exception of the descendants of Harmodius and Aristogeiton, and that for the future it should be no longer permissible to grant to any one this gift. Well, what happened? Did they by any chance accept that law? They did not, but the law's proposer was convicted on an indictment for introducing an illegal measure. Come then, compare this custom with that law, and if it seems to you in any way better, retain it and make it stronger for the future—which is bound to happen if it is not abolished now—but if after considering it on all sides you find it to be inferior, then imitate the Athenians of that early period and abolish now that practice which is more monstrous than the one abolished formerly by them.

However, as to any attempt to show that the city is insincere, is faithless in its gifts, and that it wrongs its benefactors by robbing them of their rewards—such reproaches apply in all respects equally to both Athens and Rhodes. But whereas at Athens those who had formerly received exemption from public burdens could not possibly have received no benefit at all—for whatever they had previously acquired

---

[1] This was in 356 B.C., and the speech of Demosthenes *Against Leptines* was delivered in 355 in an action challenging the legality (γραφὴ παρανόμων) of the proposal. The present passage is the only direct testimony that Leptines lost his case. On the λειτουργίαι see Vol. II, page 276, note 2.

ἐκ τῆς ἀφέσεως εἰς ἅπαν αὐτοῖς ἔμεινε ὡς καὶ[1]
τὸν ἄλλον χρόνον, καὶ ἔμελλον εὐπορώτεροι δι᾽
αὐτὴν ἔσεσθαι· τοῖς δέ γε τῆς εἰκόνος ἀφαιρεθεῖσιν
ἐκ τοῦ τετιμῆσθαι πρότερον οὐδ᾽ ὁτιοῦν περίεστι
131 δίχα γε τῆς ὕβρεως καὶ τῆς ἀτιμίας. πρὸς
τούτῳ δὲ ὁ μὲν τιθεὶς τότε τὸν νόμον ἔστιν ὧν
κατηγόρει τῶν εἰληφότων τὴν ἀτέλειαν καὶ
πονηροὺς ἀπέφαινε τοὺς πλείους, οὐ μόνον ἀνα-
ξίους χάριτος· ὥστε τοῦτ᾽ εἶναι τὸ δεινὸν ὅτι
μὴ πᾶσιν ἐγκαλῶν πάντας ἀπεστέρει τὰς δωρεάς.
ἐνθάδε δὲ οὐδ᾽ ἔνεστι[2] τοῖς ἀφελομένοις εἰπεῖν
τι κατ᾽ ἐκείνων· οὓς γὰρ μηδ᾽ ἴσασι, ὥς[3] φασιν,
132 πῶς αὐτοὺς αἰτιᾶσθαι δυνατόν; ἔτι δὲ ὁ μὲν
νόμος ἐξαιρέτους τινὰς ἐποίει τοὺς τὰ μέγιστα
δοκοῦντας εὐεργετηκέναι τὴν πόλιν, τοὺς ἀφ᾽
Ἁρμοδίου καὶ Ἀριστογείτονος· ἐνθάδε δὲ οὐδέν
ἐστιν ἐξαίρετον. τῷ γὰρ ἀγράφως τὸ πρᾶγμα
γίγνεσθαι καὶ μήτε κατὰ νόμον μήτε κατὰ ψήφισμα
περὶ οὐδενὸς ὅλως ἀπείρηται, καὶ ἐπὶ παντὶ
συμβῆναι δυνατόν ἐστιν, ἐφ᾽ ὅτῳ ποτὲ ἂν δόξῃ
133 τῷ στρατηγῷ. καὶ μὴν ὅ γε νόμος δεινὸν ἐδόκει
ποιεῖν ἀφαιρούμενος τοῦ δήμου τὴν ἐξουσίαν,
ὥστε μηδὲ τὸ λοιπὸν ἐξεῖναι ψηφίσασθαι τὴν

---

[1] ὡς καὶ Budé omits with UBT; Wilamowitz and Arnim
deleted ὡς.

[2] οὐδ᾽ ἔνεστι Emperius : οὐδέν ἐστι.

[3] ὡς added by Capps; φασίν deleted by Jacobs, Arnim,
Budé : ἴσασί φασιν (or φασι) BTU, εἴσαί φασι M.

from the immunity remained theirs in every respect for the future as for the past, and they could not fail to be better off on account of it; those, on the other hand, who have had their statues taken away from them have nothing left over from the honour they had formerly enjoyed—except the insult and the dishonour. And, in addition, the Athenian who, on the occasion I have mentioned, proposed the law attacked a considerable number of those who had received exemption from public duties and tried to show that the majority of them were knaves, not merely unworthy of any favour, so that the unfairness of it was that, while not accusing all, he was proposing to deprive all of their gifts. But in Rhodes here it is utterly impossible for those who have deprived men of their statues to say anything against them; for when they do not even know who the original recipients were, as they admit,[1] how is it possible to bring a charge against them? Furthermore, that law proposed to make an exception in favour of those who were regarded as having conferred the greatest benefactions upon the city, to wit, the descendants of Harmodius and Aristogeiton, but here no exception is made. For since the practice is carried on without any record being kept and is not regulated by either law or decree, absolutely no concession is made for anyone, and this indignity may happen to anyone at the pleasure of the chief magistrate at any time. Again, the Athenian law was thought to be committing an outrage in depriving the people of their authority in the matter, so that not even in the future would it be possible for them to vote

[1] Cf. *supra* § 77.

δωρεὰν ταύτην. καὶ πόσῳ κρεῖττον τὴν ἀρχὴν
κωλῦσαί τι διδόναι τὸν δῆμον, εἰ μὴ συνέφερε
τῇ πόλει, ἢ[1] καταλιπόντα τὸ χαρίζεσθαι, τὸ
ἀφαιρεῖσθαι ταῦτα ἐφ' ἑνὶ ποιήσασθαι; αἰσχροῦ
γὰρ ὄντος, ὡς οὐδ' ἂν εἷς ἀντείποι, τοῦ ἀφαιρεῖσθαι τοὺς λαβόντας τι, κατὰ μὲν τὸν νόμον τοῦτο
ἅπαξ ἐγίγνετο, κατὰ δὲ τὸ ἔθος ἀεὶ συμβαίνει.

134   Καὶ μὴν εἰ δοκεῖ δυσχερὲς τὸ ἀφαιρεῖσθαί
τινος ἐξουσίας τὴν πόλιν, καὶ ὑμεῖς ἀφαιρεῖσθε τὴν
ἐξουσίαν τοῦ φυλάττειν βέβαια τὰ δοθέντα τοῖς
λαβοῦσιν. ὅτῳ γὰρ ἂν ὑμεῖς δῶτε τὴν τιμήν,
οὐκέτ' ἔστ' ἐφ' ὑμῖν τὸ ἐᾶν ἔχειν αὐτόν· ἀλλ'
εἷς ἀνὴρ ἀεὶ τούτου κύριος, ὁ στρατηγῶν. καίτοι χεῖρόν ἐστι τὸ ἔθει μὴ ἐφ' ὑμῖν εἶναι τοῦ κατὰ
νόμον κεκωλῦσθαι.[2] οἱ μὲν γὰρ οὐκ ἀφήρηνται
τὴν ἐξουσίαν τούτου τρόπον τινά, ὃ πράττειν
ἑαυτοὺς νόμῳ κεκωλύκασιν, ἀλλ' ἀπέστησαν
135 ἑκόντες διὰ τὸ συμφέρον· ἐπὶ δὲ τοῦ ἔθους οὐδὲ
τοῦτο ἔστιν εἰπεῖν ὅτι αὐτούς, εἴπερ[3] ἄρα,
ἀφήρηνται τοῦθ' ὑπὲρ οὗ μήτε ἔκριναν μήτε
ἐβουλεύσαντο.

Καὶ μὴν ἐκεῖ γε παραμυθίαν τινὰ ἔσχον τὸ
τοῦ πράγματος ἴσον καὶ κοινόν, ἁπάντων ὁμοίως
ἀφαιρουμένων τὰς ἀτελείας, παρ' ὑμῖν δὲ ὃς
ἂν τύχῃ τῆς εἰκόνος ἀφήρηται καὶ πολλάκις

---

[1] ἢ added by Selden.
[2] κεκωλῦσθαι Reiske : κεκωλυμένου.
[3] αὐτούς, εἴπερ Pflugk : αὐτούς περ UM, αὐτούς περ B.

---

[1] This is Demosthenes' chief argument against the proposal
of Leptines, in § 4 he asks : " Shall we, then, make a law that
hereafter neither Council nor Assembly shall be permitted to
deliberate or to vote on a similar subject ? "

this gift.[1] Yet how much better to prevent the people from granting any honour or any privilege at all if it were not of advantage to the city to do so, than, while leaving the right to confer a favour, to place the power of taking it away in the hands of one man! For while it is disgraceful, as no man would deny, to take any gift away from those who have received it, according to that Athenian law this was happening just once, but according to this Rhodian custom it takes place all the time!

Besides, if it appears vexatious that your city should be deprived of any power, it is you your own selves who are depriving it of the power to guarantee for the recipients the security of its gifts. For whenever *you* confer this honour upon a man, it is no longer in *your* power to allow him to keep it; on the contrary, one official always has this in his control, namely, the chief magistrate. And yet, it is worse for you to lack this power owing to custom than to be estopped by law. For in the one case men in a certain sense have not been deprived of the control of that which they have by law estopped themselves from doing, but they have renounced their right willingly because of the advantage thereby gained. But when we have to deal with a custom, one cannot even say that men have deprived themselves—if deprived they have been—of a thing on which they have neither passed judgment nor deliberated.

And although in Athens the people had some consolation—in that the measure was impartial and general, since all alike were being deprived of their exemption from public burdens—here it is only the recipient of the statue who has been deprived of it,

ὁ[1] βελτίων. ἔτι δὲ ἐκεῖ μὲν οὐχ ἵνα ἄλλος
λάβῃ, τὸν ἔχοντα ἀφῃρεῖτο ὁ νόμος· παρ' ὑμῖν
δὲ τούτου χάριν γίγνεται, ὃ τῷ παντὶ λυπρό-
136 τερόν ἐστι τοῦ μόνον ἀποστερεῖσθαι. καὶ μὴν
ἐκεῖνό γε οὐδεὶς ἀγνοεῖ δήπουθεν, ὅσῳ δοκεῖ
χαλεπώτερον τὸ δι' ἄλλον τι πάσχειν τοῦ δι'
αὐτόν. οὐκοῦν ἐκ μὲν τοῦ νόμου συνέβαινεν,
ἵνα μή τινες ἔχωσι τὰς ἀτελείας, περὶ ὧν ὡς
ἀναξίων ἔλεγεν, ἀποδῦσαι[2] τοὺς λοιπούς· ἐκ
δὲ τοῦ παρ' ὑμῖν ἔθους, ἵν' ἄλλοι λάβωσι, τοὺς
137 ἔχοντας ἀποστερεῖσθαι γίγνεται. τῷ παντὶ δὲ
τοῦτο τοῖς πάσχουσι βαρύτερον.[3]

Εἰ τοίνυν ἐφ' ὧν μάλιστα ἀνήκεστόν[4] ἐστιν,
ἐπὶ τούτων βούλοιτό τις ἰδεῖν, τίνας ἀδικεῖ τοῦτο
τὸ ἔθος καὶ τίνας ἔμελλε λυπήσειν ἐκεῖνος ὁ νόμος,
ἀφελὼν μὴ μόνον τοὺς[5] ἔχοντας ἀτέλειαν, ἀλλὰ
καὶ τοὺς[6] εἰκόνος τετυχηκότας, οὕτω σκοπείτω
τοὺς λοιποὺς ἑκατέρων. οὗτοι μὲν γὰρ τρόπον
τινὰ οὐδὲ ἔπασχον οὐδέν, ὃ γὰρ εἰλήφεσαν ἂν[7]
ἐν προσθήκης μέρει, τοῦτο ἀπώλλυον, τῆς μεί-

---

[1] ὁ added by Pflugk.
[2] ἀποδῦσαι Cohoon, ἀπολλύναι Wilamowitz: ἀποδοῦναι.
[3] Arnim deleted § 136 καὶ μὴν . . . through βαρύτερον § 137.
[4] ἀνήκεστον Capps: ἀναγκαῖον.
[5] μὴ μόνον τοὺς Cohoon: τοὺς μὴ μόνον.
[6] τοὺς instead of τῆς UBT, M in margin; Budé retains
τῆς.
[7] ἂν added by Capps.

and often he is the better man. Moreover, in Athens it was not in order that another person might receive the exemption that the law proposed to take it away from the possessor, but in your city that is precisely why it is done, a thing that is altogether more distressing than merely to be dispossessed. Furthermore, no one, I presume, is unaware how much more grievous it seems to suffer any harsh treatment on account of another than it is to suffer it on your own account. So, whereas it was the intention of the Athenian law to divest all others of their privilege of exemption in order to prevent certain men, whom it designated as undeserving, from retaining theirs, the result of your custom is that the owners of statues are robbed of them in order that others may receive them; and this treatment is altogether more grievous to those affected.

If, further, any one wishes, confining his consideration of the matter strictly to those cases in which the loss suffered is most nearly irreparable, to ask who are being wronged by this custom of yours and who were bound to be hurt by that Athenian law, let him disregard, not only those who were enjoying exemption from public burdens there, but also those who have received a statue here, and then let him consider those who are not in either class.[1] Since those who had been honoured at Athens were in a sense not suffering any loss at all, for it was only what they would have received

---

[1] That is, (1) those who had not had the tax-exemption privilege at Athens and (2) those who have not been honoured with a statue in Rhodes.

ζονος δωρεᾶς αὐτοῖς τηρουμένης· ἐπὶ δὲ τῶν
ἄλλων ἴσος[1] ἂν γένοιτο ὁ λόγος. ἀλλ' ἔστι
μὲν δῆλον καὶ αὐτόθεν, οἶμαι, τὸ πρᾶγμα· ὅσῳ
γὰρ τὸ τῆς εἰκόνος μεῖζον ἢ[2] τὸ τῆς ἀτελείας,
τοσούτῳ κρείττονες οἱ τούτου τυχόντες. ἔτι
δ' ἂν οὕτω γένοιτό γε ὁ λόγος[3] φανερώτερος·[4]

138 ἡ μὲν γὰρ ἀτέλεια τοὺς λαβόντας εὐπορωτέρους
ποιεῖ, καὶ οὗτοι μάλιστα ἐπιθυμοῦσιν αὐτῆς οἵτινες
ἂν ὦσι περὶ χρήματα ἐσπουδακότες, ἡ δὲ εἰκὼν
τὸ σεμνὸν μόνον ἔχει καὶ τὸ τῆς τιμῆς· ὅσῳ δὴ
πάντες εἴποιμεν ἂν κρείττους τοὺς προῖκα καὶ
δόξης μᾶλλον ἕνεκεν αἱρουμένους εὖ τινας ποιεῖν
τῶν ἐπ' ἀργυρίῳ καὶ διὰ κέρδος, τοσούτῳ φαίην
ἂν ἔγωγε οὐ μόνον ἀμείνους ἀνθρώπους ἀδικεῖν
τοῦτο τὸ ἔθος, ἀλλὰ καὶ ὑπὸ βελτιόνων ὑμᾶς
κωλύειν εὖ πάσχειν ἤπερ ἐκείνους ὁ νόμος.

139 Ἀλλ' ἔγωγε ἀπορῶ τί δήποτε οὐχὶ καὶ νόμον
τίθεσθε ἐπὶ τούτῳ, καθ' ὃν ἔσται[5] τὸ λοιπόν,
εἴπερ ὑμῖν ἀρέσκει.

Νὴ Δί', αἰσχύνην γὰρ οὐ μικρὰν ἔχει νόμος
τοιοῦτος ἐν τῇ πόλει κείμενος.

Εἶτα ὃ γράφειν αἰσχρὸν ἡγεῖσθε, τοῦτο ποιεῖν οὐκ

---

[1] ἴσος Emperius: ἴσως.
[2] ἢ Casaubon: καί.
[3] After λόγος the MSS. have ἀλλ' ἔστι μὲν δῆλον καὶ αὐτόθεν
οἶμαι τὸ πρᾶγμα, which Reiske deleted.
[4] φανερώτερος Reiske: φανερώτερον.
[5] For ἔσται Herwerden proposed ἔξεσται.

---

[1] He means that the law would have deprived them of the continued benefit of the exemption (the 'supplement'), but would
have taken from them neither the material benefits they had
already enjoyed nor the honour conferred by the original grant.
This honour he calls 'the greater gift,' as the sequel shows.
[2] 'The other gifts' being such honours as the front-sea

by way of a supplement [1] that they were losing, whereas the greater gift continued to be theirs; but as regards the other gifts, the reckoning would come out the same for both classes.[2] But, I think, the case is quite self-evident: For in proportion as the grant of a statue is a greater honour than the exemption, in just that degree those who receive the former are superior men. The argument can be made still clearer, though, if stated thus: Whereas the exemption from public burdens makes the recipients of it wealthier, and those men are especially eager for it who are interested in money-making, the statue implies only dignity and honour; so just in proportion as those are superior men, as we would all agree, who choose to confer benefits upon others without remuneration and rather for reputation's sake than those who set a price upon it and are moved by desire for gain, by just so much, as I at least would assert, are not only they better men whom this custom of yours wrongs, but also by just so much are those persons whom you are preventing from conferring benefits upon yourselves superior to those whom the Athenian law prevented from benefitting the Athenians.

But for my part I am at a loss to understand why on earth you do not pass a law on this matter to regulate it for the future, if such is your pleasure.

"Good heavens!" you exclaim, "Why, the existence of a law like that in a city brings no little shame."

And so it is not disgraceful to do what you

privilege (*proedria*), dinner in the *prytaneion*, a golden crown, and the like. Those who had lost the tax-exemption at Athens and those who had never been honoured by a statue at Rhodes were on a parity as regards the other, the prospective, honours.

DIO CHRYSOSTOM

αἰσχρόν ἐστι; καίτοι[1] πόσῳ κρεῖττον μὴ χρῆσθαί
τισι τῶν φαύλως γεγραμμένων ἢ φαῦλα[2] ποιεῖν;
ἢ ποτέρους ἂν εἴποιτε βελτίους, τοὺς οὕτως
ἔχοντας πρὸς τὰ ἄτοπα, ὥστε ἀπέχεσθαι καὶ
δεδομένων, ἢ τοὺς οὐ συγκεχωρημένα πράττοντας;
140 ἀλλ' ἔγωγε φαίην ἄν, ὁμολογουμένου τοῦ μηδαμῶς
δεῖν μηδὲν ἄδικον πράττειν μηδὲ ἀπρεπές, παρ'
οἷς ἂν νόμῳ γίγνηται τὸ τοιοῦτον, ἥττονα ἂν[3]
ἔχειν κατηγορίαν ἢ παρ' οἷς ἂν κατὰ ἔθος. πρῶτον
μὲν γὰρ ὁ νόμος ῥητός ἐστι, καὶ οὐκ ἄν ποτε
γένοιτο χείρων, οὐ γὰρ ἔστιν οὔτε ἀφελεῖν οὔτε
προσθεῖναι τοῖς γεγραμμένοις· τὸ δέ γε ἔθος, ἂν
ᾖ φαῦλον, ἀνάγκη καὶ φαυλότερον ἀεὶ γίγνεσθαι
141 τῷ μὴ κατειλῆφθαι μηδὲ ὡρίσθαι. λέγω δ'
οἷον εὐθὺς τοῦτό φασι τὴν ἀρχὴν λαβεῖν ἀπὸ
τῶν συντετριμμένων καὶ οὐδὲ ἐφεστώτων ἐπὶ[4]
ταῖς βάσεσι· τούτοις γὰρ ἀποχρῆσθαι τοὺς στρα-
τηγοὺς ἐπισκευάζοντας καὶ τρόπον τινὰ ἐξ
ἀρχῆς ποιοῦντας ἑτέρους· εἶθ', ὅπερ λοιπόν,
τοὺς ὑγιεῖς μέν, οὐκ ἔχοντας δὲ ἐπιγραφάς,
ἐπιγράφεσθαι· καὶ τὸ λοιπὸν ἤδη καὶ τῶν ἐπιγεγραμμένων τινὰς τῶν σφόδρα παλαιῶν· ἔστω
γὰρ ὃ λέγουσιν ἀληθές· εἰς ὕστερον ἀνάγκη
μηδεμίαν εἶναι διάκρισιν· καὶ γὰρ ἐπὶ τῶν ἄλλων
142 οὕτως ἔχει, δαπάνης, ἀκοσμίας, τρυφῆς· οὐδέποτε
τῶν χειρόνων ἐθῶν οὐθὲν εὑρήσετε ἱστάμενον οὐδὲ

---

[1] καίτοι Arnim : καὶ.
[2] φαῦλα supplied in lacuna by Capps, μηδὲ γράψαντας by
Arnim, μὴ γεγραμμένων by Herwerden.
[3] Wilamowitz followed by Arnim would delete ἄν.
[4] Reiske followed by Arnim would change ἐπὶ to ἔτι.

---

[1] Cf. page 105, § 99.

think it is disgraceful to enact in writing? And yet how much better it is to refrain from following any written laws which are badly conceived than to do bad things! Or which class of men would you call the better, those who are so disposed toward improper things that they refrain from doing them even when they are authorized, or those who do them even though they are not allowed? But as for me, I would say that, while it is agreed that one should by no means do any unjust or unseemly act, yet among peoples where such acts are under the control of law there would be less cause for reproach than among people where they are regulated by custom. For, in the first place, the law is explicit and can never become worse, since it is not possible either to take away from or add to its written terms; whereas the custom, if it is a bad one, must necessarily become steadily worse because it is not clearly apprehended or defined.[1] I mean, for instance, the case we now have before us: they tell us that this practice began with the statues that were broken and not even standing on their pedestals; it was these that the chief magistrates used after repairing them and in a way making them altogether different; then the next step was that those which were well preserved but bore no inscriptions were inscribed; and at last came the taking of some statues which did have inscriptions on them, provided they were very old. Well, let us assume that their statement of the case is true. In the future there will necessarily be no distinction made at all—for this is the way it is with all other evils, such as extravagance, disorderly conduct, luxury—you will never find any really bad custom halting or remaining stationary until it

διαμένον,[1] ἕως ἂν παντάπασι κωλυθῇ. διὰ γὰρ τὸ δέχεσθαι πρόσθεσιν ἀεὶ καὶ τὸ παρὰ μικρὸν ἀνεξέλεγκτον εἶναι καὶ μηδενὶ φαίνεσθαι ῥᾳδίως, ὅσῳ τοῦτο ἐκείνου κάκιον, ἐπὶ πᾶν πρόεισιν, ὥσπερ, οἶμαι, καὶ τῶν ἑλκῶν τινα καὶ τῶν νοσημάτων ὅσα ἐξ ἀνάγκης[2] αὔξεσθαι φύσιν ἔχει.

Πρὸς τούτῳ δὲ κἀκεῖνό ἐστιν· οἱ μὲν νόμῳ τι πράττοντες πονηρὸν οὐχ ὡς τοιοῦτον ὂν[3] αὐτὸ πράττουσιν, ἀλλὰ ἐξηπατημένοι· τοὺς δὲ ἔθει φαῦλα ποιοῦντας ἅπαντες ἂν φαῖεν εἰδότας ἁμαρτάνειν, ἅ γε μηδ᾽ αὐτοῖς ἐπιτήδεια εἶναι γεγράφθαι δοκεῖ.

143 Μὴ τοίνυν εἰ πρότερον ἤρξατο καὶ χρόνος πλέων γέγονε, διὰ τοῦτο ἔλαττον ὑμῖν νομίζετε προσήκειν αὐτὸ ἀνελεῖν·[4] οὐδὲν γὰρ ἥττονα αἰσχύνην ὄφλουσιν οἱ φυλάττοντες τὰ τοιαῦτα τῶν παραδεξαμένων, ἀλλὰ τοὐναντίον μᾶλλον ὑπόκεινται τοῖς βουλομένοις αἰτιᾶσθαι. τὸ μέν γε πρῶτον γιγνόμενον οὐδὲ λαθεῖν ἀδύνατον τοὺς τότε, καὶ ταῦτα φυλαττομένων ἔτι τῶν ποιούντων· τὸ δὲ ἐκ πολλοῦ συμβαῖνον ἀνάγκη μηδένα ἀγνοεῖν, ἄλλως τε παντελῶς ἀνηρημένης ὑμῖν[5] τῆς προφάσεως ταύτης, οἵ γε περὶ αὐτοῦ τούτου κάθησθε κρίνοντες. ὥσπερ οὖν εἰ ἄρξασθαί τινος ἔδει τῶν καλῶν ὑμᾶς, οὐκ ἂν ὠκνεῖτε διὰ τοῦτο,

---

[1] For διαμένον UM have διδόμενον.
[2] ἀνάγκης Capps exempli gratia; "non intellego" Arnim: ἅπαντος.
[3] ὂν added by Capps cf. § 109.
[4] αὐτὸ ἀνελεῖν Pflugk: αὐτὸν ἀνελεῖν M, αὐτῶν ἀμελεῖν UBT.
[5] ὑμῖν Selden: ὑμῶν.

is utterly suppressed. For because it continually receives some accretion and because a gradual process is almost impossible to detect and does not readily become perceptible to anyone, inasmuch as the present state is worse than the former it goes on to extremes as, I believe, is the case with some ulcers and all those diseases whose nature it is inevitably to get worse.[1]

Then there is this further consideration—that those who do anything which the law makes wrong, do it, not as being such, but under a misconception, whereas with those who do things which custom regards as base, would one and all admit that they sin deliberately, those acts being of such a kind that even the perpetrators themselves think they are not fit to be forbidden by an enactment.

Moreover, just because the practice began some while ago and considerable time has elapsed, do not for this reason consider that it is any the less your duty to get rid of it; for those people who perpetuate such practices as this incur no less disgrace than those who first allowed them; nay, on the contrary, they are more exposed to the attack of any who wish to censure. When the thing was done first, it may well have even escaped the notice of the people of that time, particularly as those who practised it were still cautious about it; but when a thing has been going on for a long time, nobody can be unaware of it; and, besides, that excuse has been completely taken away from you, because you are sitting here passing judgment on this very matter. Therefore, just as if you felt it to be necessary to initiate some honourable usage, you would not hesitate on *that*

[1] The text here has caused considerable trouble to editors, but with the changes suggested in the critical notes it yields at least a logical sense.

ὁμοίως εὐλόγως ἔχει, κἂν λῦσαί τι τῶν φαύλων
144 δέῃ. μὴ τοίνυν ὁ χρόνος ὠφελείτω τὸ ἔθος,
εἴπερ ἐστὶ μοχθηρόν, ὡς πάλαι νομίζω πεποιη-
κέναι φανερόν. οὐ γὰρ εἰ πολὺν χρόνον ἔβλαψεν
ὑμᾶς, διὰ τοῦτο οἶμαι προσήκειν αὐτὸ μηδέποτε
παύσασθαι βλάπτον. οὐδὲ γὰρ ἄνδρα μοχθηρὸν
ἐκ πολλοῦ λαβόντες ἀφήσετε τοῦ χρόνου χάριν
οὗ διῆλθε πονηρὸς ὤν. οὐδέ γε εἴ τις νόσον
ἰάσασθαι δύναιτο ἐνοχλοῦσαν πάλαι, φείδοιτ᾽ ἂν
145 ἐξ ἀρχῆς ὑγιαίνειν.[1] οἶμαι δ᾽ ὑμᾶς, εἴ τις θεῶν
φανερὸν ὑμῖν ποιήσειε τὸ μέλλον αὖθίς ποτε
λυπήσειν τὴν πόλιν, πάντως φυλάξεσθαι τοῦτο,
ἐν ὑμῖν γε ὄν· εἶτα τοῦ μὲν ἑτέρους βλάψοντος
οὐκ ἀμελήσετε, ἐπειδὴ μετὰ ταῦτα ἔσται,[2] τὸ
δὲ ὑμᾶς αὐτοὺς τὰ μέγιστα ἀδικοῦν ἐάσετε,
εἰ[3] πρότερον ἤρξατο; τουτὶ μὲν οὖν παντελῶς
εὔηθες, εἴ τις οἴεται μηδέποτε δεῖν κωλῦσαι τὸ
συνήθως μέν, ἀτόπως δὲ γιγνόμενον.
146 Ἀξιῶ δ᾽ ὑμᾶς ἐκεῖνο ἐνθυμηθῆναι μᾶλλον,
ὅτι πολλῶν ὄντων κατὰ τὴν πόλιν, ἐφ᾽ οἷς ἅπασιν
εὐλόγως σεμνύνεσθε, πρῶτον μὲν τῶν νόμων
καὶ τῆς εὐταξίας τῆς περὶ τὴν πολιτείαν, ἐφ᾽
οἷς καὶ μάλιστα φιλοτιμεῖσθε, ἔπειτα, οἶμαι, καὶ
τῶν τοιούτων, ἱερῶν, θεάτρων, νεωρίων, τειχῶν,
λιμένων, ὧν[4] τὰ μὲν πλοῦτον ἐμφαίνει καὶ μεγα-

---

[1] For φείδοιτ᾽ . . . ὑγιαίνειν Arnim suggests φοβοῖτ᾽ ἂν τὸ
ἐξ ἀρχῆς πάλιν ὑγιαίνειν.
[2] ἔσται Reiske : ἐστιν M, ἐστι UB.
[3] For εἰ Wilamowitz, Arnim read ὅτι.
[4] ὧν added by Selden.

---

[1] That is, because of its being an innovation.

account,[1] so you have every reason now to act with equal readiness if it is desirable to abolish some unworthy practice. Therefore, do not let its antiquity support the custom if it is really a vicious one, as I think I have long since made clear. For I do not think that just because a thing has injured you for a long time it ought never to cease injuring you. For instance, if you take into custody a man who has been wicked for a long time, you will not release him on account of the length of time which he has spent in being a bad man. Nor yet if a person should be able to cure a disease that had long been harassing him, would he count the cost of enjoying good health all over again. And you, in my opinion, if some god should reveal to you a thing that your city was sure to regret some time in the future, would by all means take measures to prevent it, if it lay in your power to do so. Then, while you will of course not neglect guarding against anything that will harm others simply because the injury will be in the future, are you going to give free rein to that which is now doing the greatest injury to yourselves, because it originated in the past? Nay, it is utterly foolish for a man to think that he should never check a practice which, while customary, is nevertheless shocking.

I ask you to bear in mind, rather, that, although there are many things about your city on all of which you have a good right to pride yourselves—your laws in the first place, and the orderliness of your government (things of which you are wont to boast most), and, in the second place, I imagine, such things also as temples, theatres, shipyards, fortifications, and harbours, some of which give evidence of your wealth and high aspirations and the greatness

λοψυχίαν καὶ τὸ μέγεθος τῆς πρότερον δυνάμεως,
τὰ δὲ καὶ τὴν πρὸς τοὺς θεοὺς εὐσέβειαν, οὐθενὸς
ἧττον ἤδεσθε ἐπὶ τῷ πλήθει τῶν ἀνδριάντων,
147 εἰκότως· οὐ γὰρ μόνον κόσμον φέρει τὸ τοιοῦτον,
ὥσπερ ἄλλο τι τῶν ἀναθημάτων, ἀλλὰ καὶ τὴν
ἰσχὺν τῆς πόλεως οὐχ ἥκιστα ἐπιδείκνυσι καὶ τὸ
ἦθος. οὔτε γὰρ εὖ πάσχουσιν ὑπὸ πολλῶν οἱ
τυχόντες οὔτε θέλουσιν οὔτε ἴσως δύνανται
πολλοὺς τιμᾶν. ἔτι δὲ κἀκεῖνό ἐστιν· οὐ γὰρ
μόνον διὰ τὸ[1] πλείστους εἶναι παρ' ὑμῖν ἀνδριάντας
τοῦτο[2] συμβέβηκεν, ἀλλ', οἶμαι, καὶ διὰ τὸ Ῥωμαίους πολλάκις πανταχόθεν εἰληφότας κατασκευὴν
ἱερῶν καὶ βασιλείων μηδέποτε κινῆσαι τῶν παρ'
148 ὑμῖν μηδέν· ὅπου καὶ Νέρων, τοσαύτην[3] ἐπιθυμίαν
καὶ σπουδὴν περὶ τοῦτο ἔχων, ὥστε μηδὲ τῶν
ἐξ Ὀλυμπίας ἀποσχέσθαι μηδὲ τῶν ἐκ Δελφῶν,
καίτοι πάντων μάλιστα τιμήσας ταῦτα τὰ[4] ἱερά,
ἔτι δὲ τοὺς πλείστους τῶν ἐκ τῆς ἀκροπόλεως
Ἀθήνηθεν μετενεγκεῖν καὶ τῶν ἐκ Περγάμου
πολλούς, αὐτῷ προσήκοντος ἐκείνου τοῦ τεμένους·
περὶ μὲν γὰρ τῶν παρ' ἄλλοις τί δεῖ λέγειν·
τοὺς παρὰ μόνοις ὑμῖν εἴασε, καὶ τοσαύτην ἐπεδείξατο εὔνοιαν καὶ τιμὴν ἅμα πρὸς ὑμᾶς, ὥστε
τὴν πόλιν ἅπασαν ἱερωτέραν κρῖναι τῶν πρώτων

---

[1] For διὰ τὸ Wilamowitz, Arnim read διὰ τοῦτο.
[2] Arnim deletes τοῦτο.
[3] τοσαύτην Reiske : τοιαύτην.
[4] ταῦτα τὰ Reiske : ταῦτα πάντα τά.

---

[1] Cf. Demosthenes 24. 210; Lycurgus, *Against Leocrates*
75, 17, 150; Lysias 12. 99.

of your former power, others of your piety toward the gods [1]—you rejoice no less in the multitude of your statues,[2] and rightly; for not only do such things do you credit just as any of your other dedicated monuments do, but they also more than anything reveal the strength of your city and its character. For it is no ordinary people that receives benefactions from many or that wishes or perhaps has the means to honour many. And note this also—that it is not only because the statues you have here are very great in number that the practice in question has arisen, but also, I think, because the Romans, who have often seized from every land the furnishings of sacred places and of palaces, have never disturbed any of those which you possess. Why, even Nero, who had so great a craving and enthusiasm in that business that he did not keep his hands off of even the treasures of Olympia or of Delphi— although he honoured those sanctuaries above all others—but went still farther and removed most [3] of the statues on the Acropolis of Athens and many of those at Pergamum,[4] although that precinct was his very own (for what need is there to speak of those in other places?), left undisturbed only those in your city and showed towards you such signal goodwill and honour that he esteemed your entire city more sacred than the foremost

---

[2] 3000 in number according to Pliny the Elder, 34. 7. 36.

[3] An exaggeration probably. See Pliny the Elder, *N.H.* 34. 7. 36.

[4] Pergamum was famous for its sculptures. Among the most notable was the colossal frieze illustrating the battle of the gods and the giants, now in Berlin. See the Introduction to the Twelfth Discourse.

DIO CHRYSOSTOM

149 ἱερῶν. ἴστε γὰρ Ἄκρατον ἐκεῖνον, ὃς [1] τὴν
οἰκουμένην σχεδὸν ἅπασαν περιελθὼν τούτου
χάριν καὶ μηδὲ κώμην παρεὶς μηδεμίαν, ὡς κἀνθάδε ἧκε. λυπουμένων δ' ὑμῶν, ὅπερ εἰκός,
κατὰ θέαν ἔφη παρεῖναι· μηδὲ γὰρ ἔχειν ἐξουσίαν
μηδενὸς ἅψασθαι τῶν ἐνθάδε. τοιγαροῦν δίχα
τοῦ κοινοῦ τῆς ὄψεως κόσμου καὶ δόξαν ὑμῖν
ἑτέραν περιποιεῖ τὸ τῶν εἰκόνων πλῆθος. τῆς
γὰρ πρὸς τοὺς ἡγουμένους φιλίας καὶ τῆς παρ'
150 ἐκείνων ἐντροπῆς ἀπόδειξις φαίνεται ταῦτα. εἶτα
Ῥωμαῖοι μὲν καὶ Νέρων οὕτω τὰ παρ' ὑμῖν
ἐτήρησαν καὶ σεμνὰ ἔκριναν, ὑμεῖς δὲ οὐ φυλά-
ξετε; καὶ Νέρων μὲν ὁ τῶν βασιλέων σφοδρό-
τατος καὶ πλεῖστον αὐτῷ διδοὺς καὶ πρὸς ἅπασαν
ἐξουσίαν [2] πάντ' ἐλάττω νενομικὼς οὐδενὸς ἀφείλετο
τὴν εἰκόνα τῶν παρὰ μόνοις Ῥοδίοις τιμηθέντων·
αὐτοὶ δ' ὑμεῖς ἀφαιρεῖσθε; καίτοι [3] πόσῳ κρεῖττον
ἦν κἀνθάδε ταὐτὸν γεγονέναι; παρὰ μὲν γὰρ
τοῖς ἄλλοις μένει τὰ τῶν τιμηθέντων ὀνόματα καὶ
τὰς ἐπιγραφὰς οὐδεὶς ἂν ἀπαλείψειεν· ὑμεῖς δ'
ὥσπερ κακόν τι πεπονθότες ὑπ' αὐτῶν ἐκχαράτ-
151 τετε. [4] καίτοι, φαίη τις ἄν, εἰ καὶ παρὰ τῶν
βασιλέων ἀνῃροῦντο, μηδὲν [5] οὕτως ἀδικεῖσθαι

---

[1] Ἄκρατον ἐκεῖνον, ὃς Valesius : ἄκρα τῶν ἐκεῖ μόνος UB, ἁ
κρατῶν ἐκεῖ μόνος M.
[2] Pflugk proposed πλείστην αὐτῷ διδοὺς καὶ πρὸς ἅπαντα
ἐξουσίαν.
[3] καίτοι Capps : καὶ.
[4] Arnim deleted καὶ πόσῳ . . . ἐκχαράττετε.
[5] μηδὲν Emperius : μηδέ.

sanctuaries. You remember the notorious Acratus,[1] who visited practically the whole inhabited world in this quest and passed by no village even [2]—you recall how he came here likewise, and when you were, quite naturally, distressed, he said he had come to see the sights, for he had no authority to touch anything here. Therefore, apart from the beautiful sight which all the world may enjoy, the great number of your statues brings you also a renown of another sort! For these things are manifestly a proof of your friendship for your rulers and of their respect for you. So then, when the Romans and Nero guarded your possessions so scrupulously and esteemed them inviolate, shall you yourselves fail to protect them? Nero, that most immoderate of emperors, who took the most liberties and considered everything subject to his own unlimited power, took away the statue of no one of those who had received honour from the people of Rhodes, and from them only. And do you, your own selves, rob these men? Yet how much better it would have been, had the same thing happened here also! I mean that whereas elsewhere the names of the men who have been honoured are left and no one would think of erasing the inscriptions, you chisel them out just as if the men had done you some wrong. And yet, one might say even if your statues were being carried off by the emperors, the men were not being so grievously wronged as at present; for the emperors were engaged in removing such things, not

---

[1] Freedman of Nero, of unscrupulous character, who in A.D. 64 plundered the art treasures of Greece and Rome at the command of Nero. See Tacitus, *Annals* 15. 45; 16. 23; CIL. 6. 9741.

[2] Cf. Cicero, *Against Verres* 2. 4. 13 for a similar instance.

τοὺς ἄνδρας. οὐ γὰρ ὡς δώσοντες ἑτέροις,
ἀλλὰ κόσμου δεόμενοι μετέφερον, ὥστ' οὐδεὶς
ἂν αὐτῶν ἀφήρει τὸ ὄνομα, οὐδ' αὖ χεῖρον ἀπήλ-
λαττον ἀντὶ Μεγάρων καὶ Ἐπιδαύρου καὶ τῆς
Ἀνδρίων ἢ Μυκονίων [1] ἀγορᾶς ἐν τοῖς Ῥωμαίων
ἱεροῖς ἀνακείμενοι. κἂν ταῦτ' ἀφῇ τις,[2] βέλτιον
ἦν [3] τό γε καθ' ὑμᾶς οὕτως αὐτῶν ἠφανίσθαι τὰς
τιμάς. οὐδὲν γὰρ ὑπῆρχεν ἁμάρτημα ὑμέτερον, οὐδ'
αὐτοὶ τοὺς εὐεργέτας ἂν τοὺς [4] ἑαυτῶν ἠδικεῖτε
καὶ τοὺς ἥρωας, ἀλλ' εἴπερ ἄρα, συνηδικεῖσθε [5]
αὐτοῖς.

152 Καὶ μὴν εἴ τις ὑμῶν πύθοιτο, εἰ καὶ δόξει
γελοιότερον, τί δήποτε οὔθ' ὑμεῖς οὔτ' ἄλλος
οὐδεὶς πηλίνους ποιεῖσθε τὰς εἰκόνας τῶν κριθέν-
των ἀξίων εἶναι τῆς δωρεᾶς ταύτης, εὐχερέστερον
δήπουθεν ὂν καὶ μηδεμίαν ἢ παντελῶς μικρὰν
δαπάνην ἔχον, φαίητ' ἄν, οἶμαι· Οὐ μόνον [6] διὰ
τὸ μὴ ὑβρίζεσθαι, ἀλλὰ καὶ διὰ τὸ διαμένειν,
εἰ δυνατόν, εἰς ἀεὶ τὰς τιμὰς τῶν ἀγαθῶν ἀνδρῶν.
νῦν τοίνυν ἐπίστασθε τοὺς ἀνδριάντας ὑμῖν
ἅπαντας κηρίνων ὄντας ἀσθενεστέρους. οὐ γὰρ
εἰ τὸν ἥλιον φέρουσι, τοῦτο δεῖ σκοπεῖν· ὑπὸ γὰρ
τῆς κολακείας τῆς πρὸς ἑτέρους διαφθείρονται,
κἂν τῷ δεῖνι δόξῃ καὶ τῷ δεῖνι δι' ἡνδήποτ'
153 αἰτίαν, οὐκέτ' εἰσὶν οἱ πρότερον. πολὺ δὲ [7]

[1] Μυκονίων Emperius : μυκηναίων.
[2] κἂν ταῦτ' ἀφῇ τις Emperius : κἀνταῦθα φῇ τις Μ, καὶ ταῦτα
φῇ τις Β, ταῦτα φῆι τις U.
[3] ἦν Arnim : ἦ.
[4] ἂν τοὺς Emperius : αὐτούς.
[5] συνηδικεῖσθε Cobet : συνηδικεῖσθαι Μ, συνηδίκησθε UB.
[6] μόνον added by Emperius.
[7] δὲ Geel : δή.

with the intention of giving them to others, but because they wanted objects of embellishment, so that none of them would think of removing the name, nor would the persons be any the worse off because, instead of being set up as offerings at Megara or Epidaurus or in the market-place of Andros or of Myconos, they were set up in the sacred places of the Romans. But dismissing these considerations, it would have been better, so far as you are concerned, had these men's tokens of honour been thus obliterated. For then there would be no fault on your part, nor would you yourselves be wronging your own benefactors and your heroes, but, if there were any wrong at all, you would be suffering it in common with them.

And further, if anyone should inquire of you, absurd though it may seem, why on earth do neither you nor anyone else make of clay the statues of those who have been adjudged worthy of this gift, since that, no doubt, is easier to manage and involves very little or no expense, you would reply, I suppose: "Not only to avoid giving insult but also in order that the honours which are given to good men may abide forever if that is possible." Yes, but as the case stands, I would have you know that all your statues are less permanent than waxen ones. For it is not a question of whether they can endure the sun, since it is the desire to flatter another group of men which ruins them; and if it seems good to this or that magistrate for any reason whatsoever, the honoured men of former times are no more![1]

[1] Lucian (*Charon*, § 23 f.) represents Hermes as saying that not only the great men of the past but even famous cities and rivers are no more.

DIO CHRYSOSTOM

χείρων ἡ τοιαύτη διαφθορά· τότε μὲν γὰρ ἠλέγ-
χετ᾽ ἂν ἡ τῆς ὕλης ἀσθένεια, νυνὶ δὲ ἡ κακία
τῆς πόλεως φαίνεσθαι δοκεῖ. τοιγαροῦν ὁμοίως
δίδοτε τοὺς ἀνδριάντας, ὥσπερ οἱ τὰς κόρας
ταύτας ὠνούμενοι τοῖς παισίν. καὶ γὰρ ἐκεῖνοι
διδόασιν οὕτως, ὥστε[1] λυπεῖσθαι μετ᾽ ὀλίγον
συντριβέντων.

Ἆρα ἀγνοεῖτε τὴν προσοῦσαν αἰσχύνην τῷ
πράγματι καὶ πόσον γέλωτα ὄφλετε δημοσίᾳ
154 ψευδόμενοι, καὶ ταῦτα φανερῶς οὕτως; ἐν
γοῦν τοῖς ψηφίσμασι γράφετε, στῆσαι δὲ εἰκόνα
τοῦ δεῖνος. Πῶς, εἴποι τις ἂν ὑμῖν, ἄνδρες
Ῥόδιοι, στῆσαι γράφετε τὴν ἑστῶσαν, ἐὰν οὕτω
τύχῃ, πρὸ πεντακοσίων ἐτῶν; εἶτα τῶν μὲν
γυναικῶν τὰς ὑποβαλλομένας παιδία πονηρὰς
κρίνετε καὶ δεινόν τι ποιεῖν ἡγεῖσθε καταψευ-
δομένας· αὐτοὶ δὲ οὐκ αἰσχύνεσθε ταὐτὸ[2] ποιοῦντες ἐπὶ τῶν εἰκόνων, καὶ τοὺς ἀνδριάντας, ὧν
οὐκ εἰσί, τούτων εἶναι λέγοντες, καὶ ταῦτα
οὐκ ὄντες ἀνήκοοι τῶν κατὰ τῆς πόλεως σκωμ-
155 μάτων; φασὶ γοῦν πολλοὶ τοὺς Ῥοδίων ἀνδριάντας ὁμοίους εἶναι τοῖς ὑποκριταῖς. ὥσπερ
γὰρ ἐκείνων ἕκαστον ἄλλοτε ἄλλον εἰσιέναι,[3]
καὶ τοὺς ἀνδριάντας ὑμῖν ἄλλοτε ἄλλα λαμβάνειν
πρόσωπα καὶ μικροῦ δεῖν ὑποκρινομένους ἑστάναι.
τὸν γὰρ αὐτὸν νῦν μὲν εἶναι Ἕλληνα, νῦν δὲ

[1] Reiske added μηδὲν after ὥστε.
[2] ταὐτὸ Arnim : τοῦτο.
[3] εἰσιέναι correction in T, εἰσεῖναι UBM.

---

[1] The dolls are supposed to be of baked clay, and if they
also had jointed limbs they were very fragile.

And this sort of destruction is much worse; for in the old days the fragility of the material would be blamed, but now men think it is the city's moral weakness that is being brought to light. And so you go on handing out your statues very much as parents do who buy for their children these cheap dolls. For they too are so casual about their gifts that very soon there is sorrow—when the gifts have fallen to pieces![1]

Can it be that you are unaware of the shame which attaches to this practice, and how ridiculous you make yourselves by this deception practised by your state, and that too so openly? For instance, in your decrees you propose ' to erect a statue of So-and-so.' "But just how," someone might ask you, "do you propose, men of Rhodes, to ' erect ' the statue that has been erected possibly for the last five hundred years?" After doing that, can you adjudge those women who palm off other women's children as their own [2] to be wicked and regard their deception as a horrible thing, while you yourselves are not ashamed of doing the same thing with your images by saying that the statues belong to those to whom they do not belong, and that too when you cannot help hearing of the jests with which your city is reviled? For instance, many people assert that the statues of the Rhodians are like actors. For just as every actor makes his entrance as one character at one time and at another as another, so likewise your statues assume different rôles at different times and stand almost as if they were acting a part. For instance, one and the same statue, they say, is at

[2] For this practice see Aristophanes, *Thesmophoriazousai* 502 *ff*.

Ῥωμαῖον, πάλιν δ', ἂν οὕτω τύχῃ, Μακεδόνα
ἢ Πέρσην· καὶ ταῦτ' ἐπ' ἐνίων οὕτως ὥστε
τὸν ἰδόντα εὐθὺς εἰδέναι. καὶ γὰρ ἐσθὴς καὶ
ὑπόδεσις καὶ τοιαῦθ' ἕτερα τὸ ψεῦσμα ἐλέγχει.
156 καὶ μυρία ἐῶ τῶν γιγνομένων, οἷον τὸ πολλάκις ἀνδρὸς σφόδρα γέροντος εἰκόνι νέου τινὸς
τὸ ὄνομα ἐπιγράφειν, θαυμαστήν τινα, οἶμαι,
δωρεὰν εὑρηκότων ὑμῶν, εἰ μετά γε τῆς τιμῆς
καὶ τὴν ἡλικίαν δίδοτε· καὶ πάλιν ἀθλητοῦ
τινος ἀνδριάντα ἑστάναι, ὡς ὄντα ἀνθρώπου
παντελῶς ἀσθενοῦς καὶ μετρίου τὸ σῶμα. τὸ
μὲν γὰρ ἱππεύοντα τὸν δεῖνα ὁρᾶσθαι παρ' ὑμῖν
ἢ πολεμίῳ συνεστῶτα ἢ στράτευμα ἐκτάσσοντα
ἄνθρωπον οὐδεπώποτε τῆς γῆς ἁψάμενον τοῖς
αὑτοῦ ποσὶν καὶ ἀπὸ τῶν ὤμων καταβάντα τῶν
φερόντων οὐδὲν ἴσως ἄτοπον· ἀλλ' ὁ δεῖνά γε
ἕστηκε πυκτεύων παρ' ὑμῖν.

157 Καὶ λέγω ταῦτα μὰ τὸν Δία οὐκ ἀπεχθάνεσθαι
βουλόμενος ὑμῖν οὐδὲ διασύρων τὴν πόλιν, ἀλλ'
ὅπως μηδὲν ἀνάξιον ἑαυτῆς μηδὲ ἀλλότριον τῆς
ἄλλης εὐκοσμίας καὶ τῆς πολιτείας φαίνηται
ποιοῦσα. καί μοι δοκεῖ τις ἂν εἰκότως προαχθῆναι
διὰ τὴν πρὸς ἅπαντας εὔνοιαν τοὺς Ἕλληνας,
οὐ μόνον διὰ τὴν πρὸς ὑμᾶς, εἴ τι ἄρα ἐνθάδε

---

¹ Dio seems to be giving examples of especially ridiculous
substitutions of distinguished names placed on statues of
earlier men of a character wholly incongruous with that of the
present owner. By way of a climax he probably, as von Arnim

one time a Greek, at another time a Roman, and later on, if it so happens, a Macedonian or a Persian; and what is more, with some statues the deception is so obvious that the beholder at once is aware of the deceit. For in fact, clothing, foot-gear, and everything else of that kind expose the fraud. And I pass over countless instances of what happens, such as that often the name of some young man is inscribed on the statue of a very old man—a most wonderful gift, methinks, you have discovered, if along with the honour you can also make a present of youth; and again, we hear of a statue of a certain athlete which stands here, that it represents an utter weakling of a man, quite ordinary of body. For while we admit that there is perhaps no incongruity in your having before everybody's eyes in your city the figure of So-and-so mounted upon a horse in the act either of grappling with a foeman or of marshalling an army, even though he was a fellow who never touched the earth with his own feet or descended from the shoulders of the carriers who bore him; but what can one say of So-and-so, who stands in your midst in the pose of a boxer![1]

Now I say all this, I assure you, with no desire to incur your hatred or to disparage your city, but in order to prevent its being found doing anything unworthy of itself or alien to the general decorum of its public life. And it seems to me that anyone would have good reason for being moved, by his good will toward all the Hellenes, and not alone toward you, if in fact there should be any practice here in Rhodes that is not as it should be, to mention it and

thought, used the proper names of the two effeminate persons who in the manuscripts are referred to as ' So-and-so.'

ἔχοι μὴ καλῶς, εἰπεῖν καὶ μηνῦσαι. πρότερον
μὲν γὰρ ἐκ πολλῶν συνειστήκει τὸ κοινὸν ἀξίωμα
καὶ πολλοὶ τὴν Ἑλλάδα ηὖξον, ὑμεῖς, Ἀθηναῖοι,
Λακεδαιμόνιοι, Θηβαῖοι, χρόνον τινὰ Κορίνθιοι,
158 τὸ παλαιὸν Ἀργεῖοι· νυνὶ δὲ τὸ μὲν τῶν ἄλλων
οὐθέν ἐστιν. οἱ μὲν γὰρ αὐτῶν ὅλως ἀνήρηνται
καὶ ἀπολώλασιν, οἱ δὲ ἀσχημονοῦσι πράττοντες
οἷα ἀκούετε καὶ πάντα τρόπον τὴν παλαιὰν δόξαν
ἀφανίζοντες, οἰόμενοι τρυφᾶν οἱ ἀνόητοι καὶ
κέρδος ἀριθμοῦντες τὸ μηθένα κωλύειν αὐτοὺς
ἁμαρτάνοντας. λοιποὶ [1] δὲ ὑμεῖς ἐστε· καὶ γὰρ
μόνοις ὑμῖν ὑπάρχει τὸ δοκεῖν ὄντως τινὰς γεγονέναι καὶ μὴ τελέως καταπεφρονῆσθαι. διὰ
μὲν γὰρ τοὺς οὕτω χρωμένους ταῖς ἑαυτῶν πατρί-
σιν, ὡς ἀληθεύοντες ἔνιοι λέγουσιν, οὐθὲν ἐκώλυε
πάλαι Φρυγῶν πάντας ἢ Θρᾳκῶν ἀτιμοτέρους
159 γεγονέναι τοὺς Ἕλληνας. ὥσπερ οὖν οἰκίας
ἠρημωμένης εὐδαίμονος καὶ μεγάλης, ὅταν εἷς
ἔτι λοιπὸς ᾖ διάδοχος, ἐν ἐκείνῳ πάντα ἐστί,
κἂν οὗτος ἁμαρτάνῃ τι καὶ ἀκούῃ κακῶς, τὴν
ὅλην δόξαν ἀφανίζει τῆς οἰκίας καὶ πάντας κατ-
αισχύνει τοὺς πρότερον, οὕτως τὰ ὑμέτερα νῦν ἔχει
πρὸς τὴν Ἑλλάδα. μὴ γὰρ οἴεσθε πρωτεύειν αὐτῆς,
ἄνδρες Ῥόδιοι, μὴ οἴεσθε. τῶν γὰρ ζώντων ἔτι
καὶ τῶν αἰσθανομένων τιμῆς ἢ ἀδοξίας ἔστι πρώ-
τους εἶναι. τὰ δὲ ἐκείνων οἴχεται καὶ πάντα τρό-

---

[1] λοιποὶ Reiske : λοιπόν.

make it known to you. For in the past, indeed, many elements contributed to the high standing in which we all share, and many peoples exalted Hellas—you, the Athenians, the Spartans, the Thebans, the Corinthians for a while, and in ancient times the Argives; but at the present time all the rest count for naught.[1] For while some of them have been utterly destroyed and have perished, others disgrace themselves by doing the sort of things of which you hear and in every way blotting out their ancient glory, thinking that they are having an easy life, fools that they are, and counting it gain that there is no one to keep them from erring. But you are left, for you alone still are believed to have proved yourselves to be in truth a people of consequence and not utterly despised. In fact, because of those who treat as they do their native countries, there was nothing to prevent the Hellenic race from having become long since—as some men are saying with perfect truth—more despised than the Phrygians or Thracians. Therefore, just as, when a prosperous and great family has been left desolate and only one male descendant survives, everything depends upon him, and if he errs in any way and bears a bad name, he destroys all the glory of his family and puts shame upon all those who preceded him, so too is your position now in respect to Hellas. For you must not take it for granted, Rhodians, that you hold first place in Hellas, nay you must not. For it is only those Hellenes who still live and are sensible of the difference between honour and dishonour of whom it is possible for any to be first. But all the former are past and gone, have perished in an utterly shameful

[1] Cf. Dio 34. 51; 38. 28 ff. and 40.

DIO CHRYSOSTOM

πον αἰσχρῶς καὶ ἐλεεινῶς διέφθαρται· καὶ οὐδὲ
ἐπινοῆσαι λοιπὸν ἔστι τῶν ἄλλων [1] τὴν ὑπεροχὴν καὶ
τὴν λαμπρότητα τῶν πράξεών τε καὶ παθῶν [2] εἴς
160 γε τοὺς νῦν [3] ἄνδρας ὁρῶντα. ἀλλ' οἱ λίθοι μᾶλλον ἐμφαίνουσι τὴν σεμνότητα καὶ τὸ μέγεθος
τῆς Ἑλλάδος καὶ τὰ ἐρείπια τῶν οἰκοδομημάτων·
ἐπεὶ αὐτούς γε τοὺς ἐνοικοῦντας καὶ τοὺς πολιτευο-
μένους οὐκ ἂν εἴποι τις οὐδὲ Μυσῶν ἀπογόνους·
ὥστε ἔμοιγε δοκοῦσι τῶν οὕτως οἰκουμένων αἱ
τελέως ἀνῃρημέναι πόλεις κρεῖττον ἀπαλλάττειν.
ὑγιὴς γὰρ ἡ τούτων μνήμη μένει, καὶ τὸ ὄνομα
δι' οὐθὲν ὑβρίζεται τῶν πρότερον καλῶν· ὥσπερ,
οἶμαι, καὶ τῶν τεθνεώτων τῷ παντὶ βέλτιον τὰ
σώματα ἀνῃρῆσθαι καὶ μηδένα ὁρᾶν ἢ φαίνεσθαι
σηπόμενα.

161 Καὶ ταῦτα μὲν ἴσως πλείω τῶν εἰκότων ἐπῆλθέ
μοι μνησθέντι τῆς ὅλης καταστάσεως, ἐκεῖνο
δ' ὑμῖν ἐβουλόμην ποιῆσαι φανερόν, ὅτι μόνοι
καταλείπεσθε τῶν Ἑλλήνων, οἷς ἂν καὶ παραινέσαι

---

[1] τῶν ἄλλων added by Capps.
[2] πράξεών τε καὶ παθῶν Capps, assuming a lacuna after τῶν :
παθῶν all MSS. Most editors have assumed that παθῶν is
corrupt : πατέρων or πάλαι or παλαιῶν Reiske, πατρίδων
Selden, προγόνων Cobet, πόλεων Pflugk, retained by Arnim.
Emperius and Bude retained the MSS. reading.
[3] νῦν added by Capps.

---

[1] The contrast seems to be between the unworthy Hellenes
who have perished and those of the survivors who have held
fast to principles of honour.
The tone of this passage is that of the Greek panegyrists,
who dwell as much upon the hardships the forefathers endured
(τὰ πάθη) as upon their achievements—e.g. the fate of Leonidas

and pitiable way; and as to the rest,[1] it is no longer possible to form a conception of the pre-eminence and splendour of their deeds and, as well, their sufferings, by looking at the *men* of the present time. Nay, it is rather the stones which reveal the grandeur and the greatness of Hellas, and the ruins of her buildings; her inhabitants themseves and those who conduct her governments would not be called descendants of even the Mysians.[2] So to me, at least, it seems that the cities which have been utterly destroyed have come off better than those which are inhabited as they are now. For the memory of those men remains unimpaired, and the fame of those noble men of the past suffers insult from naught; just as it is true, methinks, with the bodies of the dead—it is in every way better that they should have been utterly destroyed and that no man should see them any more, than that they should rot in the sight of all!

And although these thoughts, which have come to me as I have portrayed the situation as a whole, have perhaps been more numerous than is usual, yet it was my wish to make this point clear to you— that you alone are left of Hellenic peoples to

and his men at Thermopylae, of the Athenians when they left their city, to be burned and sacked by the Persians, etc. The critical notes, however, should be consulted; for the text without supplements is far from satisfactory and no conjectures have a claim to certainty.

[2] The Mysians were regarded with contempt by the Mediterranean peoples, a feeling expressed by the proverb "the lowest of the Mysians" (Μυσῶν τὸν ἔσχατον); cf. Plato *Theaetetus* 209 B, Cicero *Pro Flacco* 27: "Quid in Graeco sermone tam tritum et celebratum quam si quis despicatui ducitur ut 'Mysorum ultimus' esse dicatur?"

τις καὶ περὶ ὧν ἔστιν ἔτι λυπηθῆναι δοκούντων
ἁμαρτάνειν.

Εἰκότως ἂν οὖν πρόσσχοιτε αὐτοῖς καὶ πάντα
τὰ τοιαῦτα ἐξετάζοιτε ἀκριβέστερον τῶν προγόνων.
ἐκείνοις μὲν γὰρ ἐν πολλοῖς ὑπῆρχεν ἑτέροις ἡ
τῆς ἀρετῆς ἐπίδειξις, ἐν τῷ προεστάναι τῶν ἄλλων,
ἐν τῷ βοηθεῖν τοῖς ἀδικουμένοις, ἐν τῷ συμμά-
χους κτᾶσθαι, πόλεις οἰκίζειν, νικᾶν πολεμοῦντας,
ὑμῖν δὲ τοιοῦτον μὲν οὐθὲν πράττειν ἔνεστιν.
162 καταλείπεται δ', οἶμαι, τὸ ἑαυτῶν προεστάναι
καὶ τὴν πόλιν διοικεῖν καὶ τὸ τιμῆσαί τινα καὶ
κροταλίσαι μὴ τοῖς πολλοῖς ὁμοίως καὶ τὸ βουλεύ-
σασθαι καὶ τὸ δικάσαι καὶ τὸ τοῖς θεοῖς θῦσαι
καὶ τὸ ἄγειν ἑορτήν· ἐν οἷς ἅπασιν ἔστι βελτίους
τῶν ἄλλων φαίνεσθαι. τοιγάρτοι καὶ τὰ τοιαῦτα
ὑμῶν ἐπαίνου τυγχάνει (καὶ γιγνώσκεται παρὰ
πᾶσιν οὐχ ὡς μικρά) τὸ βάδισμα, ἡ κουρά, τὸ
μηδένα σοβεῖν διὰ τῆς πόλεως, ἀναγκάζεσθαι
δὲ διὰ τὴν ὑμετέραν συνήθειαν καὶ τοὺς ἐπιδημοῦν-
τας ξένους καθεστώτως[1] πορεύεσθαι· καθάπερ,
οἶμαι, καὶ τοὺς ἀγροίκους ἰδεῖν ἔστιν, ὅταν εἰς
παλαίστραν ἢ γυμνάσιον ἔλθωσιν, ἧττον ἀρρύθ-
163 μως[2] κινουμένους· ἔτι πρὸς τούτοις τῆς ἐσθῆτος
ὁ τρόπος, τὸ ἴσως[3] ἄν τινι γελοῖον φανέν, τῆς
πορφύρας τὸ μέτρον· τὰ φανερώτερα ἤδη, τὸ

---

[1] καθεστώτως Reiske : καθεστῶτας.
[2] ἀρρύθμως Pflugk : ἀρρύθμους B, ἀριθμῶς M, ἀρύθμους U.
[3] τὸ ἴσως Geel : τοῖς ὡς.

---

[1] The hegemony in political matters having passed to the
Romans.
[2] Cf. the advice given to the people of Alexandria in Discourse 32. 74 ff. Cf. also Demosthenes *In Mid.* 158.

whom advice could be offered and regarding whom it is still possible to grieve when they seem to err.

It would, therefore, be reasonable to expect you to give heed to yourselves and to examine all such matters as these more carefully than did your ancestors. For whereas they had many other ways in which to display their virtues—in assuming the leadership over the others, in lending succour to the victims of injustice, in gaining allies, founding cities, winning wars—for you it is not possible to do any of these things.[1] But there is left for you, I think, the privilege of assuming the leadership over yourselves, of administering your city, of honouring and supporting by your cheers a distinguished man in a manner unlike that of the majority, of deliberating in council, of sitting in judgement, of offering sacrifice to the gods, and of holding high festival—in all these matters it is possible for you to show yourselves better than the rest of the world. That indeed is the reason why you are admired for such characteristics as I shall mention—and they are regarded by all the world as no trifling matters—your gait, the way you trim your hair, that no one struts pompously through your city's streets, but that even foreigners sojourning here are forced by your conventional manners to walk sedately;[2] just as, I fancy, one may see even the country clowns, when they enter a wrestling-school or a gymnasium, move their limbs less clumsily than is their wont. Then again, take the mode you affect in dress—which perhaps some appears ridiculous—the width of the purple stripe; we come now to things still more noticeable —your remaining silent as you watch the games,

μεθ' ἡσυχίας θεωρεῖν, ὁ ποππυσμός· πάντα
ταῦτα σεμνὴν τὴν πόλιν ποιεῖ, διὰ ταῦτα πάντα
τῶν ἄλλων διαφέρειν δοκεῖτε, ἐπὶ τούτοις ἅπασι
θαυμάζεσθε, ἀγαπᾶσθε· τῶν λιμένων, τῶν τειχῶν,
τῶν νεωρίων μᾶλλον ὑμᾶς κοσμεῖ τὸ ἐν τοῖς ἔθεσιν
ἀρχαῖον καὶ Ἑλληνικόν, τὸ παρ' ὑμῖν μὲν ὅταν
τις γένηται, εὐθὺς αὐτὸν ἀποβάντα εἰδέναι,
κἂν τύχῃ βάρβαρος ὤν, ὅτι οὐ¹ πάρεστιν εἴς
τινα πόλιν τῆς Συρίας ἢ τῆς Κιλικίας· παρ'
ἄλλοις δέ, ἂν μή τις ἀκούσῃ τοῦ τόπου τὸ ὄνομα,
φέρε εἰπεῖν ὅτι καλεῖται Λύκειον ἢ Ἀκαδήμεια,
μηθὲν διαφέρειν.

164 Τίνος οὖν χάριν ταῦτα παυόμενος ἤδη λέγω καὶ
τί δηλῶσαι βουλόμενος; ὅτι τοσούτῳ μᾶλλον
ὑμᾶς φιλοτιμεῖσθαι δεῖ καὶ μηθὲν παραπέμπειν
τῶν γιγνομένων. κἂν οὕτως ἔχητε ἐν ἅπασιν
οἷς πράττετε, ἴσως οὐθὲν δόξετε κακίους εἶναι
τῶν προγόνων. τὸ γὰρ ἐν τοιαύτῃ καταστάσει
διαφυλάττειν ἑαυτοὺς καὶ μένειν ἐπὶ τοῦ τῆς ἀρετῆς
165 σχήματος θαυμαστὸν ἔμοιγε δοκεῖ· καθάπερ,
οἶμαι, κἀπὶ² τῶν πλεόντων ἰδεῖν ἔστι· χειμῶνος
μὲν ἐπιπεσόντος ἢ σφοδροῦ τοῦ³ πνεύματος μηδὲ
τοὺς ἀσελγεστάτους αὐτῶν αἰσχρόν τι ποιοῦντας,
ἀλλὰ πρὸς μόνῳ τῷ πλεῖν ὄντας, ἐν δὲ τῇ γαλήνῃ
καὶ τῶν ναυτῶν καὶ τῶν ἐπιβατῶν ἐπιπολάζουσαν
τὴν ὕβριν, κἂν μὴ ὦσιν ἀκόλαστοι· τὸν αὐτόν,

¹ οὐ added by Casaubon.   ² κἀπὶ Arnim : καὶ.
³ του Post : τοῦ.

¹ Cf. § 75.
² On this use of archaion, about our "classic," cf. Plutarch, *Pericles* xiii. 3: "each one of them (the buildings of Pericles), in its beauty, was even then and at once antique."

your applauding by making a clucking sound with your lips [1]—all these manners lend your city dignity, they all cause you to be looked upon as superior to the others, for all these customs you are admired, you are loved; more than by your harbours, your fortifications, your shipyards are you honoured by that strain in your customs which is antique [2] and Hellenic, so that when anybody comes among you he recognizes instantly on disembarking, even if he happens to be of barbarian race, that he has not come to some city of Syria or of Cilicia. But in other cities, unless the stranger hears some one mention the name of the place he sees, that it is called, let us say, 'Lyceum' or 'Academy,' they are all alike to him!

What is my object, then, in mentioning these matters when I am about to conclude, and what do I wish to make clear? It is that you ought to be all the more jealous about your city and to be indifferent to nothing that takes place here. And if you have this spirit in everything you do, perhaps men will think that you are no whit worse than your ancestors. For that you do preserve your character in your present situation, and hold fast to your rôle of moral excellence is, in my opinion at least, an admirable thing. An apt illustration is found, I think, in the conduct of men on board a ship at sea: when a storm strikes them or a hurricane, not even the most wanton of them is to be seen doing anything base; but they are all giving undivided attention to the sailing; whereas in fair weather recklessness prevails among both the sailors and the passengers, even if they do not indulge in licentiousness.[3] In

[3] For the same illustration see Xenophon, *Memorabilia* 3. 5. 6.

οἶμαι, τρόπον ὁ μὲν πόλεμος[1] εἴωθε καὶ τοὺς
φαυλοτέρους ἐγείρειν καὶ κρατεῖν, ἐν τοσαύτῃ
δὲ εἰρήνῃ καὶ ῥᾳθυμίᾳ τῶν ἀρίστων ἐστὶν[2]
ἀνδρῶν εἰς μηδεμίαν αἰσχύνην μηδὲ ἀταξίαν
ὑπενεχθῆναι.

[1] ὁ μὲν πόλεμος Emperius : ἐν πολέμοις M, καὶ ἐν πολέμοις
UB.
[2] ἐστὶν added by Arnim.

the same way I believe that war is wont to arouse and to sway even the meaner souls;[1] but in such peaceful and quiet times as these, it is the part of the best men not to drift into any shameful or disorderly practices.

[1] Cf. Plato, *Politicus* 6, p. 488.

THE THIRTY-SECOND DISCOURSE:
TO THE PEOPLE OF ALEXANDRIA

This Discourse was delivered before the people of Alexandria in their great theatre. Public meetings were not infrequently held in Greek theatres. The purpose of this particular meeting is not known, but the great length of Dio's address and the seeming patience with which his audience listened to him lend colour to the supposition that Dio was known to be the bearer of an important message, and the people had assembled especially to receive it. Arnim, who argues with plausibility that the speech was delivered in the reign of Trajan, regards Dio as being, in fact if not in name, the emissary of that emperor. Several passages recall thoughts and phrases found in the four Discourses on Kingship, which are thought to have been addressed to Trajan, and Dio speaks as one who enjoys the friendship of the emperor.

Our Discourse is notable for the frankness with which the speaker attacks the foibles and vices of the populace for which the Alexandria of that day was so notorious. Not all the allusions can be explained with certainty, for the history of the period is none too well documented. The very scarcity of contemporary documents, however, lends especial value to the testimony of Dio. Modern writers have drawn heavily upon his statements.

32. ΠΡΟΣ ΑΛΕΞΑΝΔΡΕΙΣ

1 Ἆρά γε βούλοισθ' ἄν, ὦ ἄνδρες, σπουδάσαι χρόνον σμικρὸν καὶ προσέχειν; ἐπειδὴ παίζοντες ἀεὶ διατελεῖτε καὶ οὐ προσέχοντες καὶ παιδιᾶς μὲν καὶ ἡδονῆς καὶ γέλωτος, ὡς εἰπεῖν, οὐδέποτε ἀπορεῖτε· καὶ γὰρ αὐτοὶ γελοῖοί ἐστε καὶ ἡδεῖς καὶ διακόνους πολλοὺς τούτων ἔχετε· σπουδῆς
2 δὲ ὑμῖν τὴν πᾶσαν ἔνδειαν ὁρῶ οὖσαν. καίτοι τινὲς ἐπαινοῦσιν ὑμᾶς ὡς σοφούς τε καὶ δεινούς, ὅτι τοσαῦται μυριάδες ἀνθρώπων ἅμα καὶ τὰ δέοντα ἐννοεῖτε καὶ ταχὺ φθέγγεσθε ὅ τι ἂν ἐννοήσητε· ἐγὼ δὲ μᾶλλον ἂν ὑμᾶς ἐπῄνουν βραδὺ μὲν φθεγγομένους, ἐγκρατῶς δὲ σιγῶντας, ὀρθῶς δὲ διανοουμένους· ὃ καὶ νῦν ποιήσατε, ἵνα κτήσησθε πρὸς ἐκείνῳ τῷ ἐπαίνῳ καινὸν ἕτερον μεῖζω τε καὶ σεμνότερον, ὅτι τοσοῦτοι ὄντες λόγων χρησίμων γενομένων ἅπαντες ἐσιωπήσατε, καὶ πρὸς τούτῳ ἐδείξατε ὅτι οὐ μόνον ἐστὲ ἱκανοὶ νοήσαντες εἰπεῖν, ἀλλὰ καὶ ἀκούσαντες νοῆσαι. χοροῦ μὲν γὰρ ἔπαινος τὸ ἅμα εἰπεῖν, μᾶλλον δὲ οὐδὲ τούτου· τί γάρ, ἂν κοινῇ πάντες ἀποτυγχά- νωσι τοῦ μέλους; δήμου δὲ τὸ καλῶς ἀκοῦσαι.
3 Νῦν μὲν γὰρ ἁμαρτάνετε τὸ Ἀθηναίων ποτὲ

THE THIRTY-SECOND DISCOURSE: TO THE PEOPLE OF ALEXANDRIA

My friends, would you kindly be serious for a brief while and give heed to my words? For you are forever being frivolous and heedless, and you are practically never at a loss for fun-making and enjoyment and laughter—indeed you yourselves are naturally inclined to laughter and jollity, and you have many who minister to such tendencies—but I find in you a complete lack of seriousness. And yet there are those who praise you for your wisdom and cleverness, asserting that, although you assemble here in thousands, you not only can conceive what is fitting but at the same time are quick to put your conceptions into words. But I for my part should prefer to praise you as being slow to speak, indeed, and self-restrained enough to keep silent, and yet correct of judgement. Pray display these qualities now, in order that you may acquire, in addition to that other praise, new praise of a different nature, both greater and more honourable—for having all become silent in this great throng when useful counsel was being given and, furthermore, for having shown that you can not merely think before you speak but also listen before you formulate your thought. For while it is praising a chorus to say that they all speak the words together in unison—or rather not even a chorus, for what if all in common miss the tune?—the highest praise you can accord a mass-meeting is to say that it listens well.

For nowadays, you know, you make the mistake

173

ἁμάρτημα. τοῦ γὰρ ᾿Απόλλωνος εἰπόντος, εἰ
θέλουσιν ἄνδρας ἀγαθοὺς ἐν τῇ πόλει γενέσθαι,
τὸ κάλλιστον ἐμβάλλειν τοῖς ὠσὶ τῶν παίδων, οἱ
δὲ τρήσαντες τὸ ἕτερον[1] χρυσίον ἐνέβαλον,
οὐ συνέντες τοῦ θεοῦ. τοῦτο μὲν γὰρ κόραις
μᾶλλον ἔπρεπε καὶ παισὶ Λυδῶν ἢ Φρυγῶν·
῾Ελλήνων δὲ παισί, καὶ ταῦτα θεοῦ προστάξαντος,
οὐκ ἄλλο ἥρμοζεν ἢ[2] παιδεία καὶ λόγος, ὧν οἱ
τυχόντες εἰκότως[3] ἄνδρες ἀγαθοὶ γίγνονται καὶ
σωτῆρες τῶν πόλεων.

4 ᾿Εκεῖνοι μὲν οὖν κακῶς ἐχρήσαντο τοῖς ὠσὶ τῶν
παίδων, ὑμεῖς δὲ τοῖς αὑτῶν κάκιον. δήμου γάρ
ἐστιν ἀκοὴ τὸ θέατρον· εἰς τοῦτο δὲ καλὸν μὲν ἢ
τίμιον οὐδὲν ὑμῖν ἢ σπανίως ποτὲ εἰσέρχεται·
κρουμάτων δὲ ἀεὶ μεστόν ἐστι καὶ θορύβου καὶ
βωμολοχίας καὶ σκωμμάτων οὐδὲν ἐοικότων
χρυσῷ. διὰ τοῦτο οὖν ὀρθῶς ἔφην ἀπορεῖν ὑμᾶς
σπουδῆς. οὔτε γὰρ αὐτοὶ σπουδαῖοί ἐστε οὔτε οἱ
ὑμέτεροι συνήθεις καὶ πολλάκις εἰς ὑμᾶς εἰσιόντες,

μῖμοί τ᾽ ὀρχησταί τε χοροιτυπίῃσιν ἄριστοι,
ἵππων τ᾽ ὠκυπόδων ἐπιβήτορες, οἵ κε τάχιστα
ἤγειραν μέγα νεῖκος ἀπαιδεύτοισι θεαταῖς,
νηπιάχοις, ξυνὸν δὲ κακὸν πολέεσσι φέρουσιν.

---

[1] τὸ ἕτερον wrongly suspected by Herwerden.
[2] ἥρμοζεν ἢ Morel: ἥρμοζε or ἥρμοζε δέ.
[3] ἄν after εἰκότως deleted by Emperius.

---

[1] Nowhere else recorded. Men and boys of eastern nations
wore earrings, but for a Greek it was a mark of effeminacy
(Athenaeus 12. 46). Herwerden suspected τὸ ἕτερον, but
Isidorus Hispalensis, *Etymologiarum* 19. 31. 10, s.v. *inaures*,
says: Harum usus in Graecia : puellae utraque aure, pueri
tantum dextra gerebant. A like tradition may be dimly

which the Athenians once made. I mean, when Apollo said that, if they wished to have good men as citizens, they should put that which was best into the ears of their boys, they pierced one of the ears of each and inserted a bit of gold,[1] not understanding what the god intended. In fact such an ornament was suitable rather for girls and for sons of Lydians and Phrygians, whereas for sons of Greeks, especially since a god had given the command, nothing else was suitable but education and reason, for it is natural that those who get these blessings should prove to be good men and saviours of the state.

The Athenians, as we see, made a bad use of the ears of their sons, but you are making a worse use of your own. For the organ of hearing of a people is the theatre, and into your theatre there enters nothing beautiful or honourable, or very rarely; but it is always full of the strumming of the lyre and of uproar, buffoonery, and scurrility, things that bear no resemblance to gold. For that reason, therefore, I was right in saying that you lack seriousness; for neither are you yourselves serious, nor are they serious with whom you are familiar, and who often come before you in the guise of

Both mimes and dancers plying nimble feet,
And men astride swift steeds, most apt to stir
Dire strife amid spectators crude—the fools!—
And bring a general ruin to multitudes.[2]

mirrored in Aristotle's remark (*Problemata* 32. 7) that 'women call the one ear male, the other female.' Possibly some significance may be found also in the observation made by Xenophon (*Anabasis* 3. 1. 31), that the man who had been posing as a Greek was found to have *both* ears pierced.

[2] A cento composed of *Iliad* 24. 261, *Odyssey* 18. 263-4, and *Iliad* 16. 262.

5 τοῦτο γὰρ ἀεὶ ὁρᾶτε καὶ περὶ τοιαῦτά ἐστε, ἀφ' ὧν
νοῦν μὲν ἢ φρόνησιν ἢ δικαίαν διάθεσιν ἢ πρὸς
θεοὺς εὐσέβειαν οὐκ ἔστι κτήσασθαι, ἔριν δὲ
ἀμαθῆ καὶ φιλοτιμίαν ἄμετρον καὶ κενὴν λύπην
καὶ χαρὰν ἀνόητον καὶ λοιδορίαν καὶ δαπάνην.

Λέγω δὲ ταῦτα οὐκ ἀποτρέπων οὐδὲ καταλύειν
κελεύων τὰς τοιαύτας ψυχαγωγίας καὶ ἀπάτας
τῆς πόλεως· μαινοίμην γὰρ ἄν· ἀλλ' ἀξιῶν ὑμᾶς,
ὥσπερ τούτοις ἑτοίμως καὶ συνεχῶς αὐτοὺς
παρέχετε, οὕτω καὶ λόγου χρηστοῦ ποτε ἀκοῦσαι
καὶ τὴν ἐπὶ τῷ συμφέροντι δέξασθαι παρρησίαν·
6 ἐπεὶ καὶ τοὺς Ἀθηναίους, ὧν μικρῷ πρότερον
ἐμνήσθην, οὐ πάντως εὑρήσομεν ἁμαρτάνοντας·
ἀλλὰ τοῦτό γε ἐκεῖνοι καὶ πάνυ καλῶς ἐποίουν, ὅτι
τοῖς ποιηταῖς ἐπέτρεπον μὴ μόνον τοὺς κατ'
ἄνδρα ἐλέγχειν, ἀλλὰ καὶ κοινῇ τὴν πόλιν, εἴ τι [1]
μὴ καλῶς ἔπραττον· ὥστε σὺν πολλοῖς ἑτέροις καὶ
τοιαῦτα ἐν ταῖς κωμῳδίαις λέγεσθαι·

δῆμος πυκνίτης, δύσκολον γερόντιον.
ὑπόκωφον,

καὶ

τί δ' ἔστ' Ἀθηναίοισι [2] πρᾶγμ' ἀπώμοτον; [3]

καὶ ταῦτα ἤκουον ἑορτάζοντες καὶ δὴ [4] δημο-
κρατούμενοι, καὶ οὐ μόνον τῶν σφετέρων πολιτῶν,

---

[1] εἴ τι Pflugk: ἐστὶ or ἐσ ὅτι.
[2] Ἀθηναίοισι Geel: Ἀθηναῖος or Ἀθηναῖος τό.
[3] ἀπώμοτον Suidas: ἀνώμοτον or ἀνώμωτον.
[4] καὶ δὴ Crosby: καί.

---

[1] Horace, *Satires* 1. 4. 1–5, calls attention to this licence
enjoyed by Old Comedy.

That indeed is the nature of what you regularly see, and you are devoted to interests from which it is impossible to gain intelligence or prudence or a proper disposition or reverence toward the gods, but only stupid contention, unbridled ambition, vain grief, senseless joy, and raillery and extravagance.

In saying these things I am not trying to divert you from such entertainments and pastimes of your people or bidding you put an end to them—I should be mad to attempt that—but I am asking, that just as you devote yourselves readily and constantly to that sort of thing, so you should at length listen to an honest speech and welcome a frankness whose aim is your own welfare. Why even the Athenians, to whom I referred a moment ago, we shall find to have been not always in error. On the contrary, at least this custom of theirs was very much to their credit—that they gave their poets licence to take to task, not merely persons individually, but even the state at large, in case the people were doing something unseemly.[1] Accordingly, among many other illustrations that might be cited, we find in their comedies utterances such as these:

> Old Demos of Pnyxtown, testy little old man,
> A bit inclined to deafness,[2]

and

> What deed is there that Athens would abjure?[3]

And, moreover, they listened to these sayings while holding high festival, even during the democratic regime, at a time when they were not only in complete

[2] Aristophanes, *Knights* 42–3. The Athenian assembly met on the Pnyx.
[3] Kock, *Com. Att. Frag.*, Eupolis, frag. 217.

εἴ τινα ἤθελον πρὸς ὀργὴν ἀπολέσαι[1] τῶν ταῦτα
λεγόντων, κύριοι καθεστηκότες, ἀλλὰ καὶ τῶν
ἄλλων Ἑλλήνων ἄρχοντες, καὶ ἐξὸν αὐτοῖς, εἰ
ἐβούλοντο, μηδὲν ἀηδὲς ἀκούειν.

7 Ὑμῖν δὲ οὔτε χορός ἐστι τοιοῦτος οὔτε ποιητὴς
οὔτε ἄλλος οὐδείς, ὃς ὑμῖν ὀνειδιεῖ μετ' εὐνοίας
καὶ φανερὰ ποιήσει τὰ τῆς πόλεως ἀρρωστήματα.
τοιγαροῦν ὅταν ποτὲ φαίνηται τὸ πρᾶγμα, προθύμως δέχεσθαι δεῖ καὶ τότε νομίζειν ἑορτὴν ἄγειν,
ἀλλὰ μὴ βαρύνεσθαι, κἂν ἄρα, δυσωπεῖσθαι[2]
ἐξειπεῖν, ‘ Πηνίκα[3] παύσεται; ’ καὶ ‘ Πότε εἴσεισι
θαυματοποιός; ’ ἢ ‘ Λῆρος ’ ἢ τοιοῦτον ἕτερον;[4]
ἐκεῖνο μὲν γάρ, ὅπερ εἶπον, ἀεὶ ὑμῖν πάρεστι, καὶ
οὐ δέος μήποτε ἐπιλίπῃ· τῶν δὲ τοιούτων λόγων
δι' οὓς ἄνθρωποι εὐδαιμονοῦσι καὶ κρείττους καὶ
σωφρονέστεροι γίγνονται καὶ βέλτιον οἰκεῖν δύνανται τὰς πόλεις, οὐ πολλάκις ἀκηκόατε· οὐ
βούλομαι γὰρ εἰπεῖν, ἀνήκοοί ἐστε.

8 Καὶ τοῦτο ἴσως οὐ δι' ὑμᾶς· δηλώσετε δέ, ἂν
ἀνάσχησθε τήμερον· ἀλλὰ μᾶλλον παρὰ τοὺς
καλουμένους φιλοσόφους. οἱ μὲν γὰρ αὐτῶν
ὅλως εἰς πλῆθος οὐκ ἴασιν οὐδὲ θέλουσι διακιν-
δυνεύειν, ἀπεγνωκότες ἴσως τὸ βελτίους ἂν
ποιῆσαι τοὺς πολλούς· οἱ δ' ἐν τοῖς καλουμένοις

[1] ἀπολέσαι Reiske: ἀπολέσθαι.
[2] δυσωπεῖσθαι Reiske: δυσωπῆσθε.
[3] Πηνίκα Casaubon: ἡνίκα.
[4] ‘ λῆρος ’ ἢ τοιοῦτον ἕτερον Crosby: λῆρος ἢ τοιοῦτος ἕτερος.
Reiske deletes ἢ after λῆρος.

control of their own citizens, in case they desired in a fit of anger to destroy anyone who used such language, but also when they exercised authority over the other Greeks as well, so that they might have avoided listening to anything disagreeable, had they so desired.[1]

But you have no such critic, neither chorus [2] nor poet nor anyone else, to reprove you in all friendliness and to reveal the weaknesses of your city. Therefore, whenever the thing does at last appear, you should receive it gladly and make a festival of the occasion instead of being vexed; and even if vexed, you should be ashamed to call out, " When will the fellow stop?" or " When is a juggler coming on?" or " Rubbish!" or some such thing. For, as I have said, that sort of entertainment you always have in stock and there is no fear that it will ever fail you; but discourses like this of mine, which make men happier and better and more sober and better able to administer effectively the cities in which they dwell, you have not often heard—for I do not care to say that you would not listen to them.

And perhaps this situation is not of your making, but you will show whether it is or not if you bear with me today; the fault may lie rather at the door of those who wear the name of philosopher. For some among that company do not appear in public at all and prefer not to make the venture, possibly because they despair of being able to improve the masses; others exercise their voices in what we call lecture-

[1] Aristophanes, *Acharnians* 377–82, 502–3, 659–60, *Wasps* 1284–91, implies that Cleon tried to curtail the licence of the poet, but without success.

[2] In the parabasis of comedy the chorus was especially outspoken in its criticism of men and affairs.

ἀκροατηρίοις φωνασκοῦσιν,[1] ἐνσπόνδους λαβόντες
9 ἀκροατὰς καὶ χειροήθεις ἑαυτοῖς. τῶν δὲ Κυνι-
κῶν λεγομένων ἔστι μὲν ἐν τῇ πόλει πλῆθος οὐκ
ὀλίγον, καὶ καθάπερ ἄλλου τινὸς πράγματος καὶ
τούτου φορὰ γέγονε, νόθον[2] μέντοι γε καὶ
ἀγεννὲς ἀνθρώπων οὐθέν, ὡς εἰπεῖν, ἐπισταμένων,
ἀλλὰ χρείων τροφῆς· οὗτοι δὲ ἔν τε τριόδοις καὶ
στενωποῖς καὶ πυλῶσιν ἱερῶν ἀγείρουσι καὶ
ἀπατῶσι παιδάρια καὶ ναύτας καὶ τοιοῦτον ὄχλον,
σκώμματα καὶ πολλὴν σπερμολογίαν συνείροντες
καὶ τὰς ἀγοραίους ταύτας ἀποκρίσεις. τοιγαροῦν
ἀγαθὸν μὲν οὐδὲν ἐργάζονται, κακὸν δ᾽ ὡς οἷόν τε
τὸ μέγιστον, καταγελᾶν ἐθίζοντες τοὺς ἀνοήτους
τῶν φιλοσόφων, ὥσπερ ἂν εἰ παῖδάς τις ἐθίζοι
διδασκάλων καταφρονεῖν, καὶ δέον ἐκκόπτειν τὴν
ἀγερωχίαν αὐτῶν οἱ δ᾽ ἔτι αὔξουσιν.

10 Τῶν δὲ εἰς ὑμᾶς παριόντων[3] ὡς πεπαιδευ-
μένων οἱ μὲν ἐπιδεικτικοὺς λόγους καὶ τούτους[4]
ἀμαθεῖς, οἱ δὲ ποιήματα συνθέντες ᾄδουσιν, ὡς
πάνυ φιλῳδῶν ὑμῶν κατεγνωκότες. αὐτοὶ δ᾽ εἰ
μέν εἰσι ποιηταὶ καὶ ῥήτορες, οὐδὲν ἴσως δεινόν·
εἰ δ᾽ ὡς φιλόσοφοι ταῦτα πράττουσι κέρδους
ἕνεκεν καὶ δόξης τῆς ἑαυτῶν, οὐ τῆς ὑμετέρας
ὠφελείας, τοῦτο δ᾽ ἤδη δεινόν. ὅμοιον γὰρ
ὥσπερ εἴ τις ἰατρὸς ἐπὶ κάμνοντας ἀνθρώπους
εἰσιὼν τῆς μὲν σωτηρίας αὐτῶν καὶ τῆς θεραπείας
ἀμελήσειε, στεφάνους δὲ καὶ ἑταίρας καὶ μύρον
αὐτοῖς εἰσφέροι.

---

[1] φωνασκοῦσιν Geel: φωνὰς ἀσκοῦσιν.
[2] γέγονε, νόθον Cobet: γέγονεν οὐθὲν.
[3] παριόντων Cobet: προϊόντων.

halls, having secured as hearers men who are in league with them and tractable. And as for the Cynics, as they are called, it is true that the city contains no small number of that sect, and that, like any other thing, this too has had its crop—persons whose tenets, to be sure, comprise practically nothing spurious or ignoble, yet who must make a living—still these Cynics, posting themselves at street-corners, in alleyways, and at temple-gates, pass round the hat and play upon the credulity of lads and sailors and crowds of that sort, stringing together rough jokes and much tittle-tattle and that low badinage that smacks of the market-place. Accordingly they achieve no good at all, but rather the worst possible harm, for they accustom thoughtless people to deride philosophers in general, just as one might accustom lads to scorn their teachers, and, when they ought to knock the insolence out of their hearers, these Cynics merely increase it.

Those, however, who do come before you as men of culture either declaim speeches intended for display, and stupid ones to boot, or else chant verses of their own composition, as if they had detected in you a weakness for poetry. To be sure, if they themselves are really poets or orators, perhaps there is nothing so shocking in that, but if in the guise of philosophers they do these things with a view to their own profit and reputation, and not to improve you, that indeed is shocking. For it is as if a physician when visiting patients should disregard their treatment and their restoration to health, and should bring them flowers and courtesans and perfume.

---

⁴ καὶ τούτους Arnim, πρὸς τοὺς Reiske: καὶ τοὺς. Geel suspects a lacuna after ἀμαθεῖς.

DIO CHRYSOSTOM

11 Τινὲς δὲ ὀλίγοι παρρησίαν ἀγηόχασι πρὸς
ὑμᾶς, καὶ ταύτην ἐνδεῶς, οὐδ' ὡς ἐμπλῆσαι τὰς
ἀκοὰς ὑμῶν οὐδ' ὥστε διατελέσαι λέγοντες, ἀλλὰ
ἐν ᾗ δύο ῥήματα[1] εἰπόντες, καὶ λοιδορήσαντες
μᾶλλον ἢ διδάξαντες ὑμᾶς, κατὰ σπουδὴν ἀπίασιν,
εὐλαβούμενοι μὴ μεταξὺ θορυβήσητε καὶ παρα-
πέμψητε αὐτούς, ὥσπερ οἱ χειμῶνος ἀποτολμῶν-
τες εἰς τὴν θάλατταν βραχύν τινα καὶ σύντομον
πλοῦν. ἄνδρα δὲ λαβεῖν καθαρῶς καὶ ἀδόλως
παρρησιαζόμενον, καὶ μήτε δόξης χάριν μήτ' ἐπ'
ἀργυρίῳ προσποιούμενον, ἀλλ' ἐπὶ εὐνοίᾳ καὶ
κηδεμονίᾳ τῶν ἄλλων ἕτοιμον, εἰ δέοι, καὶ καταγελᾶσθαι, καὶ ἀταξίαν πλήθους ἐνεγκεῖν καὶ
θόρυβον, οὐ ῥᾴδιον, ἀλλὰ καὶ πάνυ εὐτυχοῦς
πόλεως, ἐν τοσαύτῃ σπάνει γενναίων καὶ ἐλευθέρων
ἀνδρῶν, ἀφθονίᾳ δὲ κολάκων καὶ γοήτων καὶ
σοφιστῶν.

12 Ἐγὼ μὲν γὰρ οὐκ ἀπ' ἐμαυτοῦ μοι δοκῶ προελέσθαι τοῦτο, ἀλλ' ὑπὸ δαιμονίου τινὸς γνώμης.
ὧν γὰρ οἱ θεοὶ προνοοῦσιν, ἐκείνοις παρασκευάζ-
ουσι καὶ συμβούλους ἀγαθοὺς αὐτομάτους καὶ
λόγους ἐπιτηδείους καὶ ξυμφέροντας εἰρῆσθαι.
καὶ τοῦτο ἥκιστα ὑμᾶς ἀπιστεῖν χρή, παρ' οἷς
μάλιστα μὲν τιμᾶται τὸ δαιμόνιον, μάλιστα δὲ
αὐτὸ δείκνυσι τὴν αὐτοῦ δύναμιν καὶ μόνον οὐ
καθ' ἑκάστην ἡμέραν διά τε χρησμῶν καὶ δι'

[1] ῥήματα Casaubon: ῥῆμα.

---

[1] Greek sailors dreaded the winter season. Cf. Hesiod,
Works and Days, 618–30.
[2] Dio may have Socrates in mind, but the *daimonion* of
Socrates served to check, not to impel.

182

But there are only a few who have displayed
frankness in your presence, and that but sparingly,
not in such a way as to fill your ears therewith nor for
any length of time; nay, they merely utter a phrase
or two, and then, after berating rather than enlight-
ening you, they make a hurried exit, anxious
lest before they have finished you may raise an outcry
and send them packing, behaving in very truth
quite like men who in winter muster up courage for a
brief and hurried voyage out to sea.[1] But to find a
man who in plain terms and without guile speaks his
mind with frankness, and neither for the sake of
reputation nor for gain makes false pretensions,
but out of good will and concern for his fellow-men
stands ready, if need be, to submit to ridicule and to
the disorder and the uproar of the mob—to find
such a man as that is not easy, but rather the good
fortune of a very lucky city, so great is the dearth of
noble, independent souls and such the abundance of
toadies, mountebanks, and sophists.

In my own case, for instance, I feel that I have
chosen that rôle, not of my own volition, but by the
will of some deity.[2] For when divine providence is at
work for men, the gods provide, not only good coun-
sellors who need no urging, but also words that are
appropriate and profitable to the listener. And this
statement of mine should be questioned least of all
by you, since here in Alexandria the deity [3] is most
in honour, and to you especially does he display his
power through almost daily oracles and dreams.

[3] Serapis. He had much in common with Asclepius,
with whom he was frequently identified (Tacitus, *Historiae*
4. 84). The cult was widespread, but its most famous centre
was at Alexandria (Pausanias 1. 18. 4).

ὀνειράτων. μὴ οὖν οἴεσθε κοιμωμένων μόνον[1]
ἐπιμελεῖσθαι τὸν θεόν,[2] κατ' ἰδίαν ἑκάστῳ μηνύ-
οντα τὸ συμφέρον, ἐγρηγορότων δὲ ἀμελεῖν καὶ
κοινῇ καὶ ἀθρόοις μηδὲν ἂν δεῖξαι τῶν χρησίμων.
πολλάκις γὰρ ἤδη καὶ ὕπαρ ὤνησε καὶ μεθ'
13 ἡμέραν ἐναργῶς προεῖπεν. ἴστε δήπου τὰς τοῦ
Ἄπιδος φήμας ἐνθάδε ἐν Μέμφει πλησίον ὑμῶν,
ὅτι παῖδες ἀπαγγέλλουσι παίζοντες τὸ δοκοῦν τῷ
θεῷ, καὶ τοῦτο ἀψευδὲς πέφηνεν. ὁ δὲ ὑμέτερος
θεός, οἶμαι, τελειότερος ὤν, δι' ἀνδρῶν ὑμᾶς καὶ
μετὰ σπουδῆς βούλεται ὠφελεῖν, οὐ δι' ὀλίγων
ῥημάτων, ἀλλ' ἰσχυρᾷ καὶ πλήρει κληδόνι καὶ
λόγῳ σαφεῖ, διδάσκοντι περὶ τῶν ἀναγκαιοτάτων,
ἂν ὑπομένητε, μετὰ γνώμης καὶ πειθοῦς.

14 Καὶ πρῶτόν γε ἁπάντων, ἵνα, ὅθενπερ ἐχρῆν,
ἐγγύθεν ἄρξωμαι, τοῦτο πείσθητε βεβαίως, ὅτι
τὰ συμβαίνοντα τοῖς ἀνθρώποις ἐπ' ἀγαθῷ πάνθ'
ὁμοίως ἐστὶ δαιμόνια, κἂν πλέων τις ἐμπείρου
τύχῃ κυβερνήτου, κἂν ἔθνος ἢ πόλις χρηστῶν
ἡγεμόνων, κἂν ἰατρὸς ἐν καιρῷ παραγένηται τῷ
κάμνοντι, καὶ τοῦτον ἡγεῖσθαι χρὴ βοηθὸν ἥκειν
παρὰ θεοῦ, κἂν λόγων τις ἀκούσῃ φρονίμων, ἐκεῖ-
15 θεν ἐπιπεμφθῆναι. καθόλου γὰρ οὐδὲν εὔδαιμον
οὐδ' ὠφέλιμον, ὃ μὴ κατὰ γνώμην καὶ δύναμιν
τῶν θεῶν ἀφικνεῖται πρὸς ἡμᾶς,[3] ἀλλὰ πανταχῇ

---

[1] For μόνον Cobet conjectured μέν.
[2] καὶ after θεόν deleted by Reiske.
[3] ἡμᾶς Reiske : ὑμᾶς.

Think not, therefore, that the god exercises his watchful care only over sleeping men, disclosing to each in private what is for his good, but that he is indifferent toward them when they are awake and would not disclose to them, in public and collectively, anything beneficial; for often in the past he has given aid to men in their waking moments, and also in broad daylight he has clearly foretold the future. You are acquainted no doubt with the prophetic utterances of Apis here, in neighbouring Memphis,[1] and you know that lads at play announce the purpose of the god, and that this form of divination has proved to be free from falsehood. But your deity, methinks, being more potent, wishes to confer his benefits upon you through the agency of men rather than boys, and in serious fashion, not by means of few words, but with strong, full utterance and in clear terms, instructing you regarding most vital matters—if you are patient—with purpose and persuasiveness.

And first of all—to begin, as I ought, with matters close at hand—rest assured of this, that all things which happen to men for their good are without exception of divine origin; not only is this true if a voyager has the luck to find a pilot with experience, or a nation or a city to secure good leaders, but also if a physician arrives in time to save his patient, we must believe that he is a helper come from god, and if one hears words of wisdom, we must believe that they too were sent by god. For, in general, there is no good fortune, no benefit, that does not reach us in accordance with the will and the

---

[1] Pausanias 7. 22. 2–4 tells briefly of this oracle. Apparently the chance utterances of lads playing near the shrine were thought to reveal the god's response.

πάντων ἀγαθῶν αὐτοὶ κρατοῦσι καὶ διανέμουσι
δαψιλῶς τοῖς ἐθέλουσι δέχεσθαι· τὰ κακὰ δὲ
ἀλλαχόθεν, ὡς ἐξ ἑτέρας τινὸς πηγῆς ἔρχεται [1]
πλησίον οὔσης παρ' ἡμῖν, ὥσπερ ἐπὶ τοῦδε τοῦ
ὕδατος τὸ μὲν σῶζον καὶ τρέφον καὶ γόνιμον
ὄντως ἄνωθέν ποθεν ἐκ δαιμονίου τινὸς πηγῆς
κάτεισι, τοὺς ῥυπαροὺς δὲ ὀχετοὺς καὶ δυσώδεις
αὐτοὶ ποιοῦμεν καὶ ἀφ' ἡμῶν οὗτοι ἵστανται.
διὰ γὰρ ἀνθρώπων ἄνοιαν καὶ τρυφὴν καὶ φιλοτιμίαν δυσχερὴς ὁ βίος καὶ μεστὸς ἀπάτης, πονηρίας,
λύπης, μυρίων ἄλλων κακῶν.

16   Τούτων δὲ ἓν ἴαμα καὶ φάρμακον ἐποίησαν οἱ
θεοὶ παιδείαν καὶ λόγον, ᾧ διὰ βίου μέν τις
χρώμενος καὶ συνεχῶς ἦλθέ ποτε πρὸς τέλος
ὑγιὲς καὶ εὔδαιμον· οἱ δὲ σπανίως καὶ διὰ χρόνου
ποτὲ περιτυχόντες

ἄλλοτε μὲν ζώουσ' ἑτερήμεροι, ἄλλοτε δ' αὖτε
τεθνᾶσιν·

ὅμως δὲ ἤδη ποτὲ ἐξαισίων δεινῶν ἐπικειμένων
αὐτοῖς ἀπετράπησαν. οἱ δὲ διὰ παντὸς ἄπειροι
τοῦ φαρμάκου τούτου καὶ μηδέποτε σωφρονίζοντι [2]
λόγῳ τὰς ἀκοὰς ὑπέχοντες ὁλοκλήρως ἄθλιοι
μηδεμίαν σκέπην μηδὲ προβολὴν ἔχοντες ἀπὸ τῶν
παθῶν,

ἀλλ' ἐν ἀκαλύπτῳ καὶ ταλαιπώρῳ βίῳ
χειμαζόμενοι,

---

[1] τῶν after ἔρχεται deleted by Arnim.
[2] σωφρονίζοντι Reiske: σωφρονοῦντι.

power of the gods; on the contrary the gods themselves control all blessings everywhere and apportion lavishly to all who are ready to receive; but evils come from quite a different source, as it were from some other fount close beside us. Take for example the water of Alexandria—that which keeps us alive and nourishes us and is truly the author of our being: it descends from some region up above, from some divine fount; whereas the filthy, evil-smelling canals are our own creation, and it is our fault that such things exist. For it is through man's folly and love of luxury and ambition, that life comes to be vexatious and full of deceit, wickedness, pain, and countless other ills.

However, for these maladies one remedy and cure has been provided by the gods, to wit, education and reason, and the man who throughout life employs that remedy with consistency comes at last to a healthy, happy end; but those who encounter it rarely and only after long intervals,

Alternate live one day, are dead the next.[1]

But, nevertheless, there have been occasions when even such persons have been turned aside when portentous disasters were impending. But those who are wholly unacquainted with the remedy of which I speak, and never give ear to chastening reason, are utterly wretched, having no refuge or defence against their sufferings,

But storm-tossed on the sea of life they drift,
Devoid of shelter and in misery,[2]

---

[1] *Odyssey* 11. 303–4. Homer is speaking of Castor and Polydeuces.
[2] Kock, *Com. Att. Frag.*, Menander, frag. 404. 6–7.

καθάπερ σκάφει σαθρῷ καὶ λελυμένῳ πάντως,
ἐν[1] ἀγνώμονι γνώμῃ καὶ πονηρίᾳ.

17   Συμβαίνει δὲ τοὺς κακίστους καὶ ἀτυχεστάτους
ὡς πορρωτάτω φεύγειν ἀπὸ τοῦ λόγου καὶ μὴ
ἐθέλειν ἀκούειν, μηδ᾽ ἂν βιάζηταί τις, ὥσπερ,
οἶμαι, καὶ τῶν ἑλκῶν τὰ δυσχερῆ λίαν οὐκ ἐᾷ
προσάψασθαι, καὶ τοῦτο αὐτὸ σημεῖόν ἐστι τοῦ
πάνυ πονήρως αὐτὰ ἔχειν. οἱ δὲ τοιοῦτοι παρ᾽
ἑτέρους ἴασιν ἰατροὺς οὐχ ἑκόντες[2] ἰσχυροτέρους.
διττὴ γὰρ θεραπεία κακίας καὶ[3] πρόνοια, καθάπερ
τῶν ἄλλων νόσων· ἡ μὲν ἐοικυῖα διαίτῃ καὶ
φαρμάκοις, ἡ δὲ καύσει καὶ τομῇ, προσήκουσα
μᾶλλον ἄρχουσι καὶ νόμοις καὶ δικασταῖς, οἳ τὸ
περιττὸν δὴ καὶ ἀνίατον ἐξαιροῦσι. βελτίους δὲ
18   εἰσὶν οἱ μὴ ῥᾳδίως αὐτὸ πράττοντες. τὴν δὲ
ἑτέραν ἐπιμέλειαν ἔργον εἶναί φημι τῶν δυναμένων
διὰ πειθοῦς καὶ λόγου ψυχὰς πραΰνειν καὶ μαλάτ-
τειν. οὗτοι δὲ σωτῆρές εἰσι καὶ φύλακες τῶν
οἵων τε σῴζεσθαι, πρὶν ἐλθεῖν εἰς τέλος τὴν
πονηρίαν εἴργοντες καὶ κατέχοντες.

Δεῖ μὲν οὖν ἑκατέρων ταῖς πόλεσι, πολὺ δὲ
ἐπιεικεστέρων[4] τῶν ἐν ταῖς ἐξουσίαις. κολάζειν
μὲν γὰρ προσήκει φειδόμενον, διδάσκειν δὲ μὴ
φειδόμενον· καὶ χρηστοῦ μέν ἐστιν ἡγεμόνος
συγγνώμη, φιλοσόφου δὲ κακοῦ μὴ πικρὸν εἶναι.
τὸ μὲν γὰρ τῆς τιμωρίας σκληρὸν[5] ἀπόλλυσι, τὸ
19   δὲ τοῦ λόγου πικρὸν σῴζειν πέφυκε. κινδυνεύει

---

[1] πάντως, ἐν Reiske, πάντας ἐν Selden, τῇ αὑτῶν or πλανώ-
μενοι Emperius, πλανῶνται ἐν Jacobs: πάντων ἐν.
[2] οὐχ ἑκόντες Selden: οὐκ ἔχοντες.
[3] κακίας καὶ Reiske: καὶ κακίας.
[4] ἐπιεικεστέρων Casaubon: ἐπιεικέστερον.
[5] σκληρὸν Casaubon: πλῆρες.

as if embarked upon a rotten and wholly shattered hulk, amidst a sea of senseless opinion and misery.

And it so happens that it is the most depraved and unfortunate men who flee the farthest from the voice of reason and will not listen to it, not even if you try to force them—just as, I fancy, those sores which are especially distressing shrink from the touch, and that in itself is a sign of their extremely bad condition. But such sufferers will have to visit a different kind of physician, however unwillingly, whose treatment will be more drastic. For there are two systems for the treatment of vice and its prevention, just as there are for maladies in general: the one may be likened to dieting and drugs, and the other resembles cautery and the knife, this being more suitable for the use of magistrates and laws and jurymen, that is, for those whose business it is to remove growths that are abnormal and incurable. But much to be preferred are those who do not lightly resort to removal. The other treatment is, I claim, the proper function of men who have the power through persuasion and reason to calm and soften the soul. These indeed are saviours and guardians of all who can be saved, confining and controlling vice before it reaches its final stage.

It is true, no doubt, that both types of practitioners are required by the state, but the type to be found in public office should be much the milder of the two. For in administering punishment one should be sparing, but not so in imparting instruction; and a good prince is marked by compassion, a bad philosopher by lack of severity. For while the harshness of the one in punishing destroys, the other's severity of speech is by nature salutary. It is likely,

μέντοι πολλή τις εἶναι σπάνις ὑμῖν τῶν τὸ[1]
ὕστερον ἐπισταμένων· οὔτε γὰρ χρήματα αὐτοῖς
οὔτε δύναμις περιγίγνεται διὰ τούτου, ἀλλ'
ἀπέχθεια μᾶλλον καὶ λοιδορία καὶ προπηλακισμός·
ὧν ἴσως οὐκέτι δεῖ[2] φροντίζειν. τοιγαροῦν διὰ τὴν
ἐκείνων ἀναχώρησιν καὶ σιωπὴν ἐρίδων ὑμῖν
φύεται πλῆθος καὶ δικῶν καὶ βοὴ τραχεῖα καὶ
γλῶτται βλαβεραὶ καὶ ἀκόλαστοι, κατήγοροι,
συκοφαντήματα, γραφαί, ῥητόρων ὄχλος, καθάπερ,
οἶμαι, δι' ἔνδειαν ἰατρῶν ἢ δι' ἀπειρίαν πλείους οἱ
θάπτοντες γίγνονται.

20   Καὶ τούτων ἐν ἀρχῇ μὲν ᾐτιασάμην τοὺς μὴ
παριόντας εἰς τὸ πλῆθος μηδὲ τολμῶντας ὑμῖν
διαλέγεσθαι, ἀλλὰ σεμνοὺς μὲν εἶναι βουλομένους,
ἀνωφελεῖς δ' ὁρωμένους καὶ ὁμοίους τοῖς ἀγεννέσι
τῶν ἀθλητῶν, οἳ τὰς παλαίστρας ἐνοχλοῦσι καὶ
τὰ γυμνάσια χειρονομοῦντες καὶ παλαίοντες, εἰς δὲ
τὸ στάδιον οὐκ ἐθέλουσιν ἰέναι, τὸν ἥλιον καὶ τὰς
πληγὰς ὑφορώμενοι. τὸ μέντοι πρᾶγμα δυσχερὲς
ὄντως καὶ δι' ὑμᾶς. οὐ γὰρ ῥᾴδιον ἐνεγκεῖν
τοσοῦδε πλήθους θόρυβον οὐδὲ μυριάσιν ἀνθρώπων[3]
ἀπείροις ἐναντίον βλέψαι χωρὶς ᾠδῆς καὶ κιθάρας.
τοῦτο μὲν γὰρ ἀλεξιφάρμακόν ἐστι πρὸς τὸν
δῆμον ὑμῶν, καθάπερ στέαρ φασὶν ἐνίων ζῴων
ὠφελεῖν πρός τι τῶν χαλεπῶν.[4]

21   Ἐγὼ γοῦν, εἰ ἦν ᾠδικός, οὐκ ἂν δεῦρο εἰσῆλθον

---

[1] τὸ added by Reiske.
[2] οὐκέτι δεῖ] οὐκ ἔδει Reiske.
[3] ἀνθρώπων Reiske : ἀνθρώποις.
[4] ὠφελεῖν πρός τι τῶν χαλεπῶν deleted by Weil, unnecessarily. Arnim believes corrupt and suggests addition of καὶ
ἰοβόλων ἑρπετῶν after χαλεπῶν, apparently unwilling to
construe στέαρ with ἐνίων ζῴων.

however, that you have a great dearth of men who are expert in the latter branch of healing; for its practitioners gain neither wealth nor power thereby, but rather hatred, abuse, and reviling, though perhaps one should pay no more attention to such things. Accordingly, when the philosophers quit the field and are silent, there springs up among you a multitude of quarrels and lawsuits, harsh cries, tongues that are mischievous and unrestrained, accusers, calumnies, writs, a horde of professional pleaders—just as, I suspect, the lack of physicians, or else their incompetence, accounts for the increase in number of the undertakers!

In my opening remarks [1] also I laid the blame for this upon the philosophers who will not appear before the people or even deign to converse with you, but, while wishing to maintain their dignity, are seen to be of no utility, and like those degenerate athletes who are a nuisance to wrestling-schools and gymnasia with their make-believe sparring and wrestling, but refuse to enter the stadium, viewing with suspicion the sun's heat and the blows. However, the trouble becomes truly difficult because of you. For it is not easy to endure the uproar of such a crowd as this, or to face countless thousands of human beings without the support of song and lyre. For music is an antidote in dealing with the populace of your city, just as, we are told, the fat of certain creatures is beneficial in dealing with one of the serious disorders. [2]

I, for instance, had I the gift of song, should not have come here before you without some

---

[1] § 8.
[2] Pliny has much to say on the use of animal fat in the treatment of disease. Cf. *N.H.* 28. 135–144.

δίχα μέλους τινὸς ἢ ᾄσματος. νῦν δὲ τούτου μὲν
ἀπορῶ τοῦ φαρμάκου· θεὸς δ᾽, ὅπερ ἔφην, θαρρῆ-
σαί μοι παρέσχεν,

> ὅς τε καὶ ἄλκιμον ἄνδρα φοβεῖ καὶ ἀφείλετο
> νίκης
> ῥηιδίως, τοτὲ δ᾽ αὐτὸς ἐποτρύνει καὶ ἀνώγει.

εἰ οὖν τὰ τοῦ Ἑρμοῦ ἔπη κἀγὼ λέγοιμι πρὸς ὑμᾶς,
ὡς ἐκεῖνος ἐν Ὀδυσσείᾳ πεποίηται Καλυψοῖ
ἀπολογούμενος ὑπὲρ τῆς ἀγγελίας, ἣν ἀηδῆ
οὖσαν ἐκόμιζε,[1] τάχ᾽ ἂν[2] ληρεῖν με φαίητε, ῥητέα
δ᾽ ὅμως·

> Ζεὺς ἐμέ γ᾽ ἠνώγει δεῦρ᾽ ἐλθέμεν οὐκ ἐθέλοντα·
> τίς δ᾽ ἂν ἑκὼν τοσσόνδε διαδράμοι ἁλμυρὸν ὕδωρ
> ἄσπετον; οὐδέ τις ἄγχι βροτῶν πόλις.

22 Ἐκεῖνος μὲν θεὸς ὢν καὶ πετόμενος δυσχεραίνει
τὰ κύματα καὶ τὸ πέλαγος καὶ τὴν μεταξὺ τῶν
πόλεων καὶ τῶν ἀνθρώπων ἐρημίαν· ἐγὼ δὲ
ἄνθρωπος οὐδεὶς οὐδαμόθεν ἐν τριβωνίῳ φαύλῳ
μήτε ᾄδειν ἡδὺς μήτε μεῖζον ἑτέρου φθεγγόμενος,
οὐκ ἄρα ἔδεισα τὸν ὑμέτερον θροῦν οὐδὲ τὸν
γέλωτα οὐδὲ τὴν ὀργὴν οὐδὲ τοὺς[3] συριγμοὺς
οὐδὲ τὰ σκώμματα, οἷς πάντας ἐκπλήττετε καὶ
πανταχοῦ πάντων ἀεὶ περίεστε καὶ ἰδιωτῶν καὶ
βασιλέων; καὶ ταῦτα ἀκούων Ὁμήρου τε καὶ
τῶν ἄλλων ποιητῶν ὑμνούντων ἀεὶ τὸν ὄχλον ὡς

---

[1] ἐκόμιζε Pflugk : ἐνόμιζε.
[2] τάχ᾽ ἂν Wilamowitz : τάχα.
[3] τοὺς added by Arnim.

tune or lay. But the truth is, I lack that magic spell; yet a god, as I said,[1] has given me courage, the god

> Who routs with ease at times the hero brave
> And robs him of his conquest, then again
> Himself doth urge and cheer to victory.[2]

If, then, in addressing you I were to use the words of Hermes as he is portrayed in the Odyssey, excusing himself to Calypso for the unpleasant message that he bore for her, no doubt you would declare that I was talking nonsense, and yet speak them I must:

> Zeus bade me hither come, though I was loath;
> For who of his own choosing would traverse
> The salty sea so vast, unspeakable?
> Nor is there near a town of mortal men.[3]

If Hermes, a god and a winged god besides, complains of the waves and the sea and the lack of cities and men on the way, was I, a mere mortal, a nobody from nowhere, clad in a mean cloak, with no sweetness of song and a voice no louder than common, not afraid of your noise, your laughter, your anger, your hissing, your rough jokes—the means by which you terrify all men and always dominate men everywhere, both private citizens and princes—and that too, though I hear Homer and the other poets constantly singing of the mob as being cruel and

---

[1] § 12.
[2] *Iliad* 17. 177–8, slightly modified. Hector is justifying his conduct to Glaucus.
[3] *Odyssey* 5. 99–101. The message borne by Hermes is a command to release Odysseus.

χαλεπόν τε καὶ ἀπειθῆ καὶ πρὸς ὕβριν ἕτοιμον,
τοῦ μὲν οὕτω λέγοντος·

23 κινήθη δ' ἀγορή, ὡς κύματα μακρὰ θαλάσσης
πόντου Ἰκαρίοιο, τὰ μέν τ' Εὖρός τε Νότος τε
ὤρορ' ἐπαΐξας πατρὸς Διὸς ἐκ νεφελάων·

ἑτέρου δὲ πάλιν αὖ,

δῆμος ἄστατον κακόν,
καὶ θαλάσσῃ πάνθ' ὅμοιον ὑπ' ἀνέμου ῥιπίζεται.
καὶ γαληνὸς ἦν τύχῃ,[1] πρὸς[2] πνεῦμα βραχὺ
κορύσσεται,
κἄν τις αἰτία γένηται, τὸν πολίτην κατέπιεν.

24 τάχ' ἂν[3] οὖν καὶ ὑμεῖς ἐμὲ τῷ θορύβῳ καταπίοιτε
καὶ τῇ ταραχῇ, βουλόμενον ὑμᾶς ὠφελεῖν. μείν-
αντες δὲ καὶ ἀκούσαντες διὰ τέλους πᾶσι θαυμαστοὶ
δόξετε, καὶ οὐ μόνον κρουμάτων ἔμπειροι καὶ
ὀρχημάτων, ἀλλὰ καὶ λόγων φρονίμων, ἵνα κἀμοὶ
πρὸς τοὺς αἰτιωμένους καὶ καταγιγνώσκοντας,
ὅτι δεῦρο εἰσῆλθον, ᾖ δικαίως ἀπολογεῖσθαι·
αἰτιάσονται γάρ, εὖ ἴστε, καὶ φήσουσι δοξο-
κόπον εἶναι καὶ μαινόμενον, ὅστις ἐμαυτὸν ὄχλῳ
καὶ θορύβῳ παρέβαλον· ὅπως οὖν ἔχω λέγειν
ὅτι οὐ πᾶν πλῆθος ἀσελγές ἐστιν οὐδὲ ἀνήκοον,
οὐδὲ ἀπὸ παντὸς δεῖ τοὺς πεπαιδευμένους φεύγειν.

25 Σαφέστερον δ' ὑμῖν, εἰ βούλεσθε, διελεύσομαι

---

[1] ἦν τύχῃ Kayser: ἐντείχω or ἔντ' ἤχωι or ἔντ' χώρᾳ.
[2] πρὸς Reiske: πᾶν.
[3] τάχ' ἂν Pflugk: τάχ'.

---

[1] Iliad 2. 144–6.
[2] Kock, Com. Att. Frag., Adespota 1324. This bold
simile was paraphrased by Demosthenes, De Falsa Legatione

unruly and prone to violence? This is what Homer has to say:

> Then stirred was the assembly, as the sea
> Sends forth long billows on the Icarian deep,
> Billows the Southeast wind doth raise, with force
> Rushing from out the clouds of Father Zeus;[1]

and here are the words of another:

> Unstable and evil is the populace,
> And wholly like the sea: beneath the gale
> 'Tis fanned to fury; should a calm ensue,
> A little puff doth ruffle it. So let
> Some charge be made, the victim is engulfed.[2]

So you too perhaps might engulf me with your uproar and your turmoil, in spite of my desire to serve you. But if you wait and hear me through, all men will think you wonderful, and will give you credit for acquaintance, not alone with twanging lyres and dancing feet, but with words of wisdom too, that I also may thus have a just defence to offer those who blame and condemn me for coming here; for they will blame me, you may be sure, and will say that I am a notoriety-hunter and a madman to have thus exposed myself to the mob and its hubbub. Let me, then, be able to assert that not every populace is insolent and unwilling to listen, and that not every gathering of the people must be avoided by men of cultivation.

But I will explain to you more clearly, if you wish,

136: ὁ μὲν δῆμός ἐστιν ἀσταθμητότατον πρᾶγμα τῶν πάντων καὶ ἀσυνθετώτατον, ὥσπερ θάλαττ' ἀκατάστατον, ὡς ἂν τύχῃ κινούμενον. The verses have been attributed either to Solon or Archilochus or to some dramatist.

περὶ δήμου φύσεως, τοῦτ᾽ ἔστι περὶ ὑμῶν αὐτῶν.
καὶ γὰρ ἔν τι τῶν χρησίμων ἐστὶ καὶ μᾶλλον ἂν
ὑμᾶς ὠφελήσειεν ἢ περὶ οὐρανοῦ καὶ γῆς εἰ
λέγοιμι. φημὶ δὴ δῆμον ἐοικέναι μάλιστα ἀνδρὶ
δυνάστῃ καὶ σφόδρα ἰσχυρῷ, μεγάλην τινὰ
ἐξουσίαν καὶ ῥώμην ἔχοντι, καὶ τοσούτῳ μείζονι
δυνάστῃ καὶ ἄρχοντι πλεόνων, ὅσῳπερ ἂν αὐτὸς
ᾖ πλείων ὁ δῆμος καὶ πόλεως γενναιοτέρας.
26 ἐκείνων μὲν οὖν εἰσι βασιλεῖς, θεοὶ ἐπὶ σωτηρίᾳ
κοινῇ γεγονότες, κηδεμόνες ὄντως καὶ προστάται
χρηστοὶ καὶ δίκαιοι, τῶν μὲν ἀγαθῶν ἑκούσιοι
ταμίαι, τῶν δὲ χαλεπῶν σπανίως μεταδιδόντες καὶ
κατὰ ἀνάγκην, κόσμῳ πόλεων ἡδόμενοι. οἱ δὲ
τοὐναντίον σκληροὶ καὶ ἄγριοι τύραννοι, χαλεποὶ
μὲν ἀκοῦσαι, χαλεποὶ δὲ συμβαλεῖν· τούτων ἡ
μὲν ὀργὴ πρὸς πάντα ἕτοιμος, ὥσπερ θηρίων
ἀνημέρων, τὰ δὲ ὦτα ἐμπέφρακται, καὶ πάροδος
οὐκ ἔστιν εἰς αὐτὰ λόγοις ἐπιεικέσιν, ἀλλὰ
κολακεία καὶ ἀπάτη κρατεῖ παρ᾽ αὐτοῖς.
27 Ὁμοίως δὲ καὶ δῆμος ὁ μέν τις εὐγνώμων καὶ
πρᾷος καὶ γαληνὸς ὄντως, οἷος γεύσασθαι παρρη-
σίας καὶ μὴ πάντα ἐθέλειν τρυφᾶν, ἐπιεικής,
μεγαλόφρων, αἰδούμενος τοὺς ἀγαθοὺς καὶ ἄνδρας
καὶ λόγους, τοῖς νουθετοῦσι καὶ διδάσκουσι χάριν
εἰδώς· ὃν ἐγὼ τίθημι τῆς θείας καὶ βασιλικῆς
φύσεως, καὶ προσιέναι φημὶ καὶ διαλέγεσθαι

---

[1] We need not suppose that Dio is addressing an official
assembly of the people. The crowd in the theatre is so large
and representative that, like Aristophanes, he identifies it
with the government.

the nature of the demos, in other words, the nature of yourselves.[1]   In fact such an explanation is a useful thing, and it will do you more good than if I were to speak about heaven and earth.   Well then, I claim that the demos most closely resembles a potentate, and a very strong one too, one that has great authority and power, and a more powerful potentate and holding sway over a greater number in proportion as the people itself is more numerous and belongs to a prouder city.   Among these over-lords, then, are included kings, who have been deified for the general safety of their realm, real guardians and good and righteous leaders of the people,[2] gladly dispensing the benefits, but dealing out hardships among their subjects rarely and only as necessity demands,[3] rejoicing when their cities observe order and decorum.   But others, on the contrary, are harsh and savage tyrants, unpleasant to listen to and unpleasant to meet; their rage is prompt to rise at anything, like the rage of savage beasts, and their ears are stopped, affording no entrance to words of fairness, but with them flattery and deception prevail.

In like manner democracy is of two kinds: the one is reasonable and gentle and truly mild, disposed to accept frankness of speech and not to care to be pampered in everything, fair, magnanimous, showing respect for good men and good advice, grateful to those who admonish and instruct; this is the democracy which I regard as partaking of the divine and royal nature, and I deem it fitting that one should

---

[2] The προστάτης was one whose influence determined policy in a democracy.   Aristotle, *Constitution of Athens* 28, calls the roll of such leaders from Solon to Cleophon.

[3] Closely resembles Or. 1. 23–24.

τούτῳ πρέπειν, καθάπερ ἵππον γενναῖον ἐξ ἡνίας
εὐτελοῦς πράως ἄγοντα, οὐδὲν δεόμενον ψαλίων.

28 οἱ δὲ πλείους καὶ[1] θρασεῖς καὶ ὑπερήφανοι,
δυσάρεστοι πρὸς ἅπαντα, ἀψίκοροι, τυράννοις
ὅμοιοι καὶ πολὺ χείρους, οἷα δὴ τῆς κακίας
αὐτῶν οὔσης οὐ μιᾶς οὐδὲ ἁπλῆς, ἀλλὰ συμπεφο-
ρημένης ἐκ μυρίων· ὥστε πάνυ ποικίλον τε καὶ
δεινὸν εἶναι θηρίον, οἷα ποιηταὶ καὶ δημιουργοὶ
πλάττουσι Κενταύρους τε καὶ Σφίγγας καὶ
Χιμαίρας, ἐκ παντοδαπῶν φύσεων εἰς μίαν
μορφὴν εἰδώλου ξυντιθέντες. τῷ δὲ τοιούτῳ
τέρατι ξυμπλέκεσθαι καὶ ὁμόσε ἰέναι μαινομένου
τινὸς ἀληθῶς ἔργον ἢ σφόδρα ἀνδρείου καὶ
πτηνοῦ, Περσέως ἢ Βελλεροφόντου.

29 Τὸν οὖν[2] τῶν Ἀλεξανδρέων δῆμον, τὸν ἄπειρον,
ὥς φασι, τῆς ποίας μερίδος θῶμεν; ἐγὼ μὲν γὰρ
ὡς τῆς βελτίονος οὖσιν ὑμῖν παρέσχηκα ἐμαυτόν·
ἴσως δὲ καὶ ἄλλος προαιρήσεται τῶν ἐμοῦ κρειττόνων.[3] καὶ μὴν οὐδὲν ἂν[4] παρέχοιτε[5] θέαμα
κάλλιον καὶ παραδοξότερον αὐτῶν σωφρονούντων
καὶ προσεχόντων. θεῖον γὰρ δὴ καὶ σεμνὸν
ἀληθῶς καὶ μεγαλοπρεπὲς δήμου πρόσωπον πρᾶον
καὶ καθεστηκὸς καὶ μήτε γέλωτι σφοδρῷ καὶ
ἀκολάστῳ βρασσόμενον μήτε θορύβῳ συνεχεῖ

[1] καὶ Crosby: καὶ οἱ.   Reiske deletes καὶ οἱ.
[2] οὖν Emperius: γοῦν.
[3] Arnim suspects a lacuna here, suggesting the trans-
position of καίτοι . . . ἡσυχάσασιν from § 33 to fill it.
[4] οὐδὲν ἂν Emperius: οὐδέν.
[5] παρέχοιτε Crosby: ἔχοιτε.

[1] Plutarch, *Lives* 858 B, says that Demosthenes thus
apostrophized Athena : Ὦ δέσποινα Πολιάς, τί δὴ τρισὶ τοῖς
χαλεπωτάτοις χαίρεις θηρίοις, γλαυκί, καὶ δράκοντι, καὶ δήμῳ ;
198

approach and address it, just as one directs with gentleness a noble steed by means of simple reins, since it does not need the curb. But the more prevalent kind of democracy is both bold and arrogant, difficult to please in anything, fastidious, resembling tyrants or much worse than they, seeing that its vice is not that of one individual or of one kind but a jumble of the vices of thousands; and so it is a multifarious and dreadful beast,[1] like those which poets and artists invent, Centaurs and Sphinxes and Chimaeras, combining in a single shape of unreal existence attributes borrowed from manifold natures. And to engage at close quarters with that sort of monster is the act of a man who is truly mad or else exceedingly brave and equipped with wings, a Perseus or a Bellerophon.

So, applying our analysis to the populace of Alexandria, the 'unnumbered multitude,' to use the current phrase, in which class shall we put it? I for my part offered you my services on the assumption that you were of the better sort; and perhaps someone else, one of my superiors,[2] will decide to do likewise. And assuredly you Alexandrians could present no more beautiful and surprising spectacle than by being yourselves sober and attentive. For indeed it is a supernatural and truly solemn and impressive sight when the countenance of the assembly[3] is gentle and composed, and neither convulsed with violent and unrestrained laughter nor distorted by continuous and disorderly clamour, but, on the

---

[2] Trajan? Cf. §§ 95 and 96, in which Dio hints at a coming visit of the emperor.

[3] Possibly a reminiscence of Aristophanes, *Knights* 396: καὶ τὸ τοῦ δήμου πρόσωπον μακκοᾷ καθήμενον.

καὶ ἀτάκτῳ τεταραγμένον, ἀλλ' ἀκοὴ μία τοσοῦδε πλήθους.

30 Ἴδετε δὲ αὐτοὺς ἐν τῷ παρόντι καὶ ὅταν τὰ συνήθη θεωρῆτε, οἷοί ἐστε. ἐμοὶ γὰρ νῦν μὲν ἀξιοθέατοι δοκεῖτε εἶναι καὶ ἰδιώταις καὶ βασιλεῦσι, καὶ οὐδείς ἐστιν ὃς οὐκ ἂν εἰσελθὼν καταπλαγείη τε ὑμᾶς καὶ τιμήσειεν· ὥστε, εἰ μηδὲν ἄλλο, τοῦτό γε ὑμῖν ὁ λόγος παρέσχηκεν οὐ μικρόν, μίαν ὥραν σωφρονῆσαι. καὶ γὰρ τοῖς νοσοῦσι μεγάλη ῥοπὴ πρὸς σωτηρίαν μικρὸν ἡσυχάσασιν.[1] ἐν δὲ ταῖς ἄλλαις σπουδαῖς, ὅταν ὑμῖν ἐμπέσῃ τὸ τῆς ἀταξίας πνεῦμα, ὥσπερ ἂν τραχὺς[2] ἄνεμος κινήσῃ θάλατταν ἰλυώδη καὶ ῥυπαράν, ἀτεχνῶς, οἶμαι, καθ' Ὅμηρον ὁρᾶται ἀφρός τε καὶ ἄχνη καὶ φυκίων πλῆθος ἐκχεομένων· ὡσαύτως δὴ καὶ παρ' ὑμῖν σκώμματα, πληγαί, γέλως.

31 Τίς ἂν οὖν τοὺς οὕτω διακειμένους ἐπαινέσειεν; οὐ γὰρ διὰ τοῦτο καὶ τοῖς ἄρχουσιν εὐτελέστεροι φαίνεσθε; καὶ πρότερόν τινα εἰρηκέναι φασί· τὸ δὲ Ἀλεξανδρέων πλῆθος τί ἂν εἴποι τις, οἷς μόνον δεῖ παραβάλλειν τὸν πολὺν ἄρτον[3] καὶ θέαν ἵππων· ὡς τῶν γε ἄλλων οὐδενὸς αὐτοῖς μέλει; οὐ γὰρ ὑμεῖς μέν, ἄν τις ἀσχημονῇ τῶν μειζόνων ἐν τῷ μέσῳ πάντων ὁρώντων, καταφρονήσετε αὐτοῦ καὶ νομιεῖτε οὐδενὸς ἄξιον,

---

[1] ὥστε . . . ἡσυχάσασιν deleted by Geel because of resemblance to § 33.

[2] ἂν τραχὺς Emperius: οὖν ταχύς.

[3] After ἄρτον Friedlaender deletes, as a gloss, οὕτω γὰρ εἰρῆσθαι πολὺ βέλτιον: 'for so to express it is far better.'

---

[1] A medical maxim repeated in § 33.

[2] See *Iliad* 9. 4–7, of which it seems to be a reminiscence.

contrary, listening as with a single pair of ears, though so vast a multitude.

But consider yourselves at this moment and then what you are like when you are watching the performances to which you are accustomed. For, to my mind, you now appear to be a sight worth seeing, for kings as well as for plain citizens, and there is nobody who would not admire and honour you as soon as he came into your presence; and so if this address of mine has accomplished nothing else, it has at any rate rendered you this service, and no small one—one hour of sobriety! As, for instance, it is of critical importance toward the recovery of the sick to have had a brief interval of calm.[1] However, amid the varied activities which occupy your attention, whenever there falls upon you the blast of turbulence, as when a harsh gale stirs up a muddy, slimy sea, as Homer says, we see froth and scum and a mass of seaweed being cast up on the beach,[2] so exactly with you, I fancy, we find jibes and fisticuffs and laughter.

Who, pray, could praise a people with such a disposition? Is not that the reason why even to your own rulers you seem rather contemptible? Someone already, according to report, has expressed his opinion of you in these words: " But of the people of Alexandria what can one say, a folk to whom you need only throw plenty of bread and a ticket to the hippodrome,[3] since they have no interest in anything else?" Why, inasmuch as, in case a leading citizen misbehaves publicly in the sight of all, you will visit him with your contempt and regard him as a worthless fellow, no matter if he has authority a thou-

---

[3] Cf. Juvenal 10. 81 : *panem et circenses.*

κἂν μυριάκις ὑμῶν ἔχῃ τινὰ ἐξουσίαν, αὐτοὶ δὲ
δύνασθε σεμνοὶ δοκεῖν καὶ σπουδαῖοι τοιαῦτα
32 πράττοντες. οὐκ ἴστε ὅτι ὥσπερ ἡγεμὼν καὶ
βασιλεὺς ὅταν προέλθῃ, τότε σαφέστατα ὁρᾶται
καὶ δεῖ μηδὲν ἀγεννὲς μηδὲ αἰσχρὸν ποιεῖν·
παραπλησίως καὶ δῆμος, ὅταν εἰς ταὐτὸ[1] προέλθῃ
καὶ ἀθρόος γένηται; χρὴ μὲν γάρ, οἶμαι, καὶ τὸν
ἄλλον χρόνον σωφρονεῖν ὑμᾶς· ἀλλ᾿ ὅμως ὅ
τι ἂν[2] πράττῃ τις καθ᾿ αὑτόν, οὐ κοινόν ἐστι
τοῦτο οὐδὲ τῆς πόλεως· ἐν τῷ θεάτρῳ δὲ
βλέπεται τὸ δημόσιον ἦθος. ὑμεῖς δὲ μάλιστα
ἐνταῦθα ἀφυλάκτως ἔχετε καὶ προήσεσθε τὴν
δόξαν τῆς πόλεως· ὥσπερ αἱ κακαὶ γυναῖκες,
δέον αὐτάς, κἂν οἴκοι μὴ σωφρονῶσιν, ἔξω γε
προϊέναι κοσμίως, αἱ δὲ μάλιστα ἐν ταῖς ὁδοῖς
πλεῖστα ἁμαρτάνουσιν.

33 Τί οὖν, τάχα ἐρεῖ τις, τοῦτο μόνον ἁμαρτάνομεν, τὸ φαύλως θεωρεῖν; καὶ περὶ τούτου
μόνον λέγεις ἡμῖν, ἄλλο δ᾿ οὐθέν; δέδοικα ἅμα τὸ
περὶ πάντων ἐπεξελθεῖν. καίτοι τάχα φήσει
τις ὡς πολλὰ λέγων οὐδὲν ὑμῖν συμβεβούλευκα
οὐδὲ εἴρηκα σαφῶς, ἐφ᾿ ᾧ μάλιστα ἐπιτιμῶ·
τοῦτο δὲ ἔργον εἶναι τοῦ διδάσκοντος. ἐγὼ δὲ
καὶ νῦν μὲν ἡγοῦμαι πολλὰ καὶ χρήσιμα εἰρηκέναι
τοῖς προσέχουσι καὶ περὶ θεοῦ καὶ περὶ δήμου
φύσεως καὶ περὶ τοῦ δεῖν ἀκούειν, κεἰ μὴ πείθεσθε,[3]
λόγων. τοῦτο γάρ, οἶμαι, καὶ ἀναγκαιότατον

---

[1] ταὐτὸ Reiske: τοῦτο.
[2] ὅ τι ἂν Reiske: ὅταν.
[3] κεἰ μὴ πείθεσθε Emperius: καὶ μὴ πείθεσθαι.

---

[1] See especially §§ 12, 13, and 25-29.

sand times as great as yours, you yourselves cannot succeed in maintaining a reputation for dignity and seriousness so long as you are guilty of like misconduct. Do you not know, that just as a prince or king is most conspicuous when he appears in public and therefore should do nothing ignoble or disgraceful at such a time, the populace also is in like case when it too appears in public and forms a throng? One ought, of course, in my opinion, to behave with sobriety at other times as well; still whatever a man does privately does not concern the general public or the state, but in the theatre the people's character is revealed. But with you it is there above all that you are off your guard and will prove traitors to the good name of your city: you act like women of low repute, who, however wanton they may be at home, should behave with decorum when they go abroad, and yet it is especially in the streets that they are most guilty of misconduct.

"How now," perhaps someone will say, "is that our only fault, our bad behaviour at the theatre? Is that all you have to say to us and nothing more?" I dread the thought of attacking all your failings in one indictment. And yet perhaps someone will claim that, despite my long harangue, I have given you no advice and have not made clear what it is I criticize you for most; and that such is the function of anyone who offers instruction. But for my own part I believe that I have already made many valuable observations—at least for those of you who have been listening—regarding the god, the nature of the demos, and your duty to listen to counsel even though you are not convinced by what is said.[1] For the most urgent need of all, I fancy, was that I should

ἦν, παρασκευάσαι πρῶτον ὑμᾶς ὑπομένοντας
ἀκούειν. ὥστ᾽, εἰ μηδὲν ἄλλο παρέσχηκεν ὑμῖν
μέγα ὁ λόγος, τοῦτο γοῦν ὅτι τοσοῦτον χρόνον
κάθησθε σωφρονοῦντες. καὶ γὰρ τοῖς νοσοῦσι
μεγάλη ῥοπὴ πρὸς σωτηρίαν μικρὸν ἡσυχάσασιν.

34 καὶ μὴν περί γε τῶν ἄλλων τὸ μὲν πάντα ἐπεξελθεῖν, καὶ ταῦτα ἐν ἡμέρᾳ μιᾷ, καὶ τελέως ὑμᾶς
ἀναγκάσαι καταγνῶναι τῆς κακίας καὶ τῶν
ἁμαρτημάτων οὐ δυνατόν·

οὐδ᾽ εἴ μοι δέκα μὲν γλῶσσαι, δέκα δὲ στόματ᾽
εἶεν,
φωνὴ δ᾽ ἄρρηκτος, χάλκεον δέ μοι ἦτορ ἐνείη·
εἰ μὴ Ὀλυμπιάδες Μοῦσαι, Διὸς αἰγιόχοιο
θυγατέρες, μνησαίαθ᾽ ὅση κακότης [1] παρὰ πᾶσιν,

οὐχ ὑμῖν μόνοις.

35 Αὐτὸ δὲ τοῦτο περὶ οὗ λέγειν ἠρξάμην, ὁρᾶτε
ἡλίκον ἐστίν. ὅπως μὲν γὰρ ἑστιᾶσθε καθ᾽
ἑαυτοὺς ἢ κοιμᾶσθε ἢ διοικεῖτε τὴν οἰκίαν ἕκαστος
οὐ πάνυ δῆλός ἐστιν· ὅπως μέντοι θεωρεῖτε καὶ
ποῖοί τινες ἐνθάδε ἐστὲ ἅπαντες Ἕλληνες καὶ
βάρβαροι ἴσασιν. ἡ γὰρ πόλις ὑμῶν τῷ μεγέθει
καὶ τῷ τόπῳ πλεῖστον ὅσον διαφέρει καὶ περι-
φανῶς ἀποδέδεικται δευτέρα τῶν ὑπὸ τὸν ἥλιον.

36 ἥ τε γὰρ Αἴγυπτος [2], τηλικοῦτον ἔθνος, σῶμα
τῆς πόλεώς ἐστι, μᾶλλον δὲ προσθήκη, τοῦ τε [3]
ποταμοῦ τὸ ἴδιον τῆς φύσεως [4] παρὰ τοὺς ἄλλους

[1] So Morel : μνησαίαθ᾽ ὅσοι ὑπὸ Ἴλιον ὅση κακότης.
[2] ὑμῶν after Αἴγυπτος deleted by Reiske.
[3] τοῦ τε Reiske : τοῦ τε γὰρ.
[4] φύσεως Emperius : φύσεως καί.

[1] Cf. § 30.

first put you into a frame of mind to listen patiently. And so, if my address has accomplished nothing else of much importance to you, I have this at least to my credit, that for this space of time you have kept your seats in self-restraint. For, let me remind you, with the sick it is of critical importance toward recovery to have had a brief interval of calm.[1] And, on my word, to examine into all your failings, and that too in one day's time, and to force you to condemn utterly all your vice and your shortcomings, is not within my power,

> E'en though I had ten tongues, as many mouths,
> A voice unyielding, in my breast a heart
> Of bronze; unless the heavenly Muses, sprung
> From Aegis-bearing Zeus, should call to mind
> The varied evils found in all mankind,[2]

and not in you alone.

But to take just that topic which I mentioned in the beginning, see how important it is. For how you dine in private, how you sleep, how you manage your household, these are matters in which as individuals you are not at all conspicuous; on the other hand, how you behave as spectators and what you are like in the theatre are matters of common knowledge among Greeks and barbarians alike. For your city is vastly superior in point of size and situation, and it is admittedly ranked second among all cities beneath the sun.[3] For not only does the mighty nation, Egypt, constitute the framework of your city—or more accurately its appanage—but the peculiar nature of the river, when compared with

---

[2] *Iliad* 2. 489–92, slightly modified by Dio.
[3] Rome of course stood first.

ἅπαντας λόγου μεῖζον, τό τε θαυμαστὸν αὐτοῦ
καὶ τὸ ὠφέλιμον, τήν τε θάλατταν τὴν καθ᾽
ὑμᾶς[1] ἅπασαν ἐκδέχεσθε, κάλλει τε λιμένων καὶ
μεγέθει[2] στόλου καὶ τῶν πανταχοῦ γιγνομένων
ἀφθονίᾳ καὶ διαθέσει, καὶ τὴν ἔξωθεν ὑπερκει-
μένην ἔχετε, τήν τε Ἐρυθρὰν καὶ τὴν Ἰνδικήν,
ἧς πρότερον τοὔνομα ἀκοῦσαι χαλεπὸν ἦν· ὥστε
τὰς ἐμπορίας οὐ νήσων οὐδὲ λιμένων οὐδὲ πορ-
θμῶν τινων καὶ ἰσθμῶν, ἀλλὰ σχεδὸν ἁπάσης
τῆς οἰκουμένης γίγνεσθαι παρ᾽ ὑμῖν. κεῖται γὰρ
ἐν συνδέσμῳ τινὶ τῆς ὅλης γῆς καὶ τῶν πλεῖστον
ἀπῳκισμένων ἐθνῶν, ὥσπερ ἀγορὰ μιᾶς πόλεως
εἰς ταὐτὸ ξυνάγουσα πάντας καὶ δεικνύουσά τε
ἀλλήλοις καὶ καθ᾽ ὅσον οἷόν τε ὁμοφύλους ποιοῦσα.

37 Ἴσως οὖν χαίρετε ἀκούοντες, καὶ νομίζετε
ἐπαινεῖσθαι ταῦτα ἐμοῦ λέγοντος, ὥσπερ ὑπὸ
τῶν ἄλλων τῶν ἀεὶ θωπευόντων ὑμᾶς· ἐγὼ δὲ
ἐπῄνεσα ὕδωρ καὶ γῆν καὶ λιμένας καὶ τόπους καὶ
πάντα μᾶλλον ἢ ὑμᾶς. ποῦ γὰρ εἶπον ὥς ἐστε
φρόνιμοι καὶ σώφρονες καὶ δίκαιοι; οὐχὶ τἀναντία
τούτων; ἔστι γὰρ ἀνθρώπων ἔπαινος εὐταξία,
πρᾳότης, ὁμόνοια, κόσμος πολιτείας, τὸ προσέχειν τοῖς ὀρθῶς λέγουσι, τὸ μὴ πάντοτε ζητεῖν
ἡδονάς. ἀναγωγαὶ δὲ καὶ κατάρσεις[3] καὶ πλήθους ὑπερβολὴ καὶ ὠνίων καὶ νεῶν πανηγύρεως

---

[1] Selden would read ἡμᾶς.
[2] μεγέθει Emperius: μεγέθη.
[3] κατάρσεις Emperius: ἀνακρίσεις.

---

[1] Herodotus had paid high tribute to the Nile. See
especially 2. 14 and 19.
[2] In earlier times it was usual to include both the Red Sea
and the Indian Ocean under the term Ἐρυθρά.

all others, defies description with regard to both
its marvellous habits and its usefulness;[1] and
furthermore, not only have you a monopoly of the
shipping of the entire Mediterranean by reason of
the beauty of your harbours, the magnitude of your
fleet, and the abundance and the marketing of the
products of every land, but also the outer waters
that lie beyond are in your grasp, both the Red Sea
and the Indian Ocean, whose name was rarely
heard in former days.[2] The result is that the trade,
not merely of islands, ports, a few straits and isth-
muses, but of practically the whole world is yours.
For Alexandria is situated, as it were, at the crossroads of the whole world, of even the most remote
nations thereof, as if it were a market serving a
single city, a market which brings together into one
place all manner of men, displaying them to one
another and, as far as possible, making them a
kindred people.[3]

Perhaps these words of mine are pleasing to your
ears and you fancy that you are being praised by
me, as you are by all the rest who are always flattering
you; but I was praising water and soil and harbours
and places and everything except yourselves. For
where have I said that you are sensible and temperate and just? Was it not quite the opposite?
For when we praise human beings, it should be for
their good discipline, gentleness, concord, civic
order, for heeding those who give good counsel,
and for not being always in search of pleasures.
But arrivals and departures of vessels, and superiority
in size of population, in merchandise, and in ships,

[3] Cf. *Cambridge Ancient History*, X., pp. 397–400 and 412,
on Alexandrian commerce.

καὶ λιμένος καὶ ἀγορᾶς ἐστιν ἐγκώμιον, οὐ
38 πόλεως· οὐδέ γε, ἂν ὕδωρ ἐπαινῇ τις, ἀνθρώπων
ἔπαινος οὗτός ἐστιν, ἀλλὰ φρεάτων· οὐδ᾽ ἂν
περὶ εὐκρασίας λέγῃ τις, τοὺς ἀνθρώπους εἶναί
φησιν ἀγαθούς, ἀλλὰ τὴν χώραν· οὐδ᾽ ἂν περὶ
ἰχθύων, τὴν πόλιν ἐπαινεῖ· πόθεν; ἀλλὰ θάλατταν
ἢ λίμνην ἢ ποταμόν. ὑμεῖς δέ, ἂν ἐγκωμιάζῃ
τις τὸν Νεῖλον, ἐπαίρεσθε, ὥσπερ αὐτοὶ ῥέοντες
ἀπὸ Αἰθιοπίας. σχεδὸν δὲ καὶ τῶν ἄλλων οἱ
πλείους ἐπὶ τοῖς τοιούτοις χαίρουσι, καὶ μακαρίους ἑαυτοὺς κρίνουσιν, ἂν οἰκῶσι καθ᾽ Ὅμηρον νῆσον δενδρήεσσαν ἢ βαθεῖαν ἤ τινα ἤπειρον
εὔβοτον, εὔμηλον, ἢ πρὸς ὄρεσι σκιεροῖς ἢ
πηγαῖς διαυγέσιν· ὧν οὐδὲν ἴδιόν ἐστιν ἐκείνων·
ἀρετῆς δὲ οὐδὲ ὄναρ αὐτοῖς μέλει.

39   Ἐγὼ δὲ τούτων ἐμνήσθην οὔτε ὑμᾶς ἐπαίρων
οὔτε τοῖς συνήθως ὑμνοῦσιν αὐτὰ ῥήτορσιν ἢ
ποιηταῖς παραβάλλων ἐμαυτόν. δεινοὶ γὰρ ἐκεῖνοι
καὶ μεγάλοι σοφισταὶ καὶ γόητες· τὰ δ᾽ ἡμέτερα
φαῦλα καὶ πεζὰ ἐν τοῖς λόγοις, οὐ μέντοι περὶ
φαύλων. τὰ μὲν γὰρ λεγόμενα αὐτὰ οὐ μεγάλα,
περὶ μεγίστων δὲ ὡς οἷόν τε.[1] καὶ νῦν εἶπον τὰ
περὶ τῆς πόλεως, δεῖξαι βουλόμενος ὑμῖν ὡς
ὅ τι ἂν ἀσχημονῆτε οὐ κρύφα γίγνεται τοῦτο οὐδ᾽
40 ἐν ὀλίγοις, ἀλλ᾽ ἐν ἅπασιν ἀνθρώποις. ὁρῶ

---

[1] τὰ μὲν . . . οἷόν τε deleted by Emperius.

---

[1] One infers that all these phrases are to be found in Homer;
actually only νῆσον δενδρήεσσαν is so found (Odyssey 1. 51).

are fit subjects for praise in the case of a fair, a harbour, or a market-place, but not of a city; nay, if a man speaks in praise of water, he is not praising men but wells; if he talks of good climate, he does not mean that the people are good but the land; if he speaks of fish, he is not praising the city—how absurd!—but a sea, a lake, or a stream. Yet if someone eulogizes the Nile, you Alexandrians are as elated as if you yourselves were rivers flowing from Ethiopia. Indeed, it is safe to say that most other people also are delighted by such things and count themselves blessed if they dwell, as Homer puts it, ' on a tree-clad isle ' or one that is ' deep-soiled ' or on a mainland ' of abundant pasture, rich in sheep ' or hard by ' shadowy mountains ' or ' fountains of translucent waters,¹ none of which is a personal attribute of those men themselves; however, touching human virtue, they care not at all, not even in their dreams!

But my purpose in mentioning such matters was neither to elate you nor to range myself beside those who habitually sing such strains, whether orators or poets. For they are clever persons, mighty sophists, wonder-workers; but I am quite ordinary and prosaic in my utterance, though not ordinary in my theme. For though the words that I speak are not great in themselves, they treat of topics of the greatest possible moment. And what I said just now about the city was meant to show you that whatever impropriety you commit is committed, not in secrecy or in the presence of just a few, but in the presence of all mankind. For I behold among you, not

εὔβοτον εὔμηλον is applied to an island (*Odyssey* 15. 406) and ὄρεα σκιόεντα, not σκιερά, occurs three times in all.

γὰρ ἔγωγε οὐ μόνον Ἕλληνας παρ' ὑμῖν οὐδ'
Ἰταλοὺς οὐδὲ ἀπὸ τῶν πλησίον Συρίας, Λιβύης,
Κιλικίας, οὐδὲ τοὺς ὑπὲρ ἐκείνους Αἰθίοπας
οὐδὲ Ἄραβας ἀλλὰ καὶ Βακτρίους καὶ Σκύθας
καὶ Πέρσας καὶ Ἰνδῶν τινας, οἳ συνθεῶνται
καὶ πάρεισιν ἑκάστοτε ὑμῖν· ὥστε ὑμεῖς μὲν
ἀκούετε ἑνός, ἂν οὕτω τύχῃ, κιθαρῳδοῦ, καὶ
τούτου [1] συνήθους, ἀκούεσθε δὲ ὑπὸ μυρίων
ἐθνῶν οὐκ ἐπισταμένων ὑμᾶς, καὶ ὁρᾶτε μὲν
τρεῖς ἢ τέτταρας ἡνιόχους, ὁρᾶσθε δὲ ὑπὸ τοσούτων μὲν Ἑλλήνων, τοσούτων δὲ βαρβάρων.

41   Τί οὖν οἴεσθε τούτους ἐπὶ γῆς πέρατα ἐλθόντας
λέγειν; οὐχ ὡς πόλιν εἴδομεν τὰ μὲν ἄλλα
θαυμαστὴν καὶ τῶν ἀνθρωπίνων θεαμάτων πάντων
κρεῖττον θέαμα, κόσμῳ τε ἱερῶν καὶ πλήθει
πολιτῶν καὶ τῶν ἐπιτηδείων περιουσίᾳ, πάντα
ἀκριβῶς διεξιόντας ὡς ἂν δύνωνται τοῖς αὑτῶν,
ἃ καὶ μικρὸν ἔμπροσθεν εἶπον, τὰ τοῦ Νείλου
καὶ τῆς χώρας καὶ τῆς θαλάττης καὶ τὸ μέγιστον
τὴν ἐπιφάνειαν τοῦ θεοῦ· μαινομένην δὲ ὑπὸ
ᾠδῆς καὶ δρόμων ἱππικῶν καὶ μηδὲν ἄξιον
πράττουσαν ἐν τούτοις [2] ἑαυτῆς; οἱ γὰρ ἄνθρωποι
θύοντες μέν εἰσι μέτριοι καὶ βαδίζοντες καθ'
αὑτοὺς καὶ τἆλλα πράττοντες· ὅταν δὲ εἰς τὸ

---

[1] τούτου Reiske: τοῦ.
[2] τούτοις Selden: τοῖς.

merely Greeks and Italians and people from neighbouring Syria, Libya, Cilicia, nor yet Ethiopians and Arabs from more distant regions, but even Bactrians and Scythians and Persians and a few Indians, and all these help to make up the audience in your theatre and sit beside you on each occasion; therefore, while you, perchance, are listening to a single harpist, and that too a man with whom you are well acquainted, you are being listened to by countless peoples who do not know you; and while you are watching three or four charioteers, you yourselves are being watched by countless Greeks and barbarians as well.

What, then, do you suppose those people say when they have returned to their homes at the ends of the earth? Do they not say: "We have seen a city that in most respects is admirable and a spectacle that surpasses all human spectacles, with regard both to beauty of sanctuaries and multitude of inhabitants and abundance of all that man requires," going on to describe to their fellow-citizens as accurately as possible all the things that I myself named a short while ago—all about the Nile, the land, and the sea, and in particular the epiphany of the god;[1] "and yet," they will add, "it is a city that is mad over music and horse-races and in these matters behaves in a manner entirely unworthy of itself. For the Alexandrians are moderate enough when they offer sacrifice or stroll by themselves or engage in their other pursuits; but when they

---

[1] It would seem that Serapis, like Asclepius, with whom he was sometimes identified, showed himself in dreams to those who consulted his shrine (§ 12). Such epiphanies were not infrequent in other cults.

θέατρον εἰσέλθωσιν ἢ τὸ στάδιον, ὥσπερ φαρμάκων αὐτοῖς ἐκεῖ κατορωρυγμένων, οὐδὲν οἴδασι
τῶν προτέρων οὐδὲ αἰσχύνονται λέγειν ἢ ποιεῖν ὅ
42 τι ἂν αὐτοῖς ἐπέλθῃ. τὸ δὲ πάντων χαλεπώτα-
τον, ἐσπουδακότες περὶ τὴν θέαν οὐχ ὁρῶσι καὶ
ἀκούειν ἐθέλοντες οὐκ ἀκούουσι, σαφῶς ἐξ-
εστηκότες καὶ παρανοοῦντες, οὐκ ἄνδρες μόνον,
ἀλλὰ καὶ παῖδες καὶ γύναια. ἐπειδὰν δὲ παύσηται
τὸ δεινὸν καὶ διαλυθῶσι, τὸ μὲν ἀκμαιότερον
ἔσβεσται τῆς ταραχῆς· ἔτι δὲ ἔν τε συνόδοις [1] καὶ
στενωποῖς μένει καὶ δι' ὅλης τῆς πόλεως ἐπὶ
συχνὰς ἡμέρας· καθάπερ ἐμπρησμοῦ μεγάλου
λήξαντος ἰδεῖν ἔστι μέχρι πολλοῦ τήν τε λιγνὺν
43 καὶ μέρη τινὰ φλεγόμενα. καίτοι τάχα ἐρεῖ τις
τῶν Περσῶν ἢ τῶν Βακτρίων, ὡς αὐτοὶ μὲν
ἴσασιν ἱππεύειν καὶ σχεδὸν ἄριστοι δοκοῦσιν
ἱππεῖς· τὸ γὰρ πρᾶγμα ὑπὲρ ἀρχῆς καὶ ἐλευθερίας
ἐπιτηδεύουσιν· ἀλλ' ὅμως οὐδὲν τοιοῦτον οὐδ'
αὖ ὅμοιον [2] πεπόνθασιν· ὑμεῖς δὲ οὐδεπώποτε
αὐτοὶ θιγόντες οὐδ' ἐπιβάντες ἵππων οὐ δύνασθε
κατέχειν αὐτούς, ἀλλ' ἐστὲ ὅμοιοι χωλοῖς ὑπὲρ
δρόμου ἐρίζουσιν. τοιγαροῦν δειλοὶ ὄντες καὶ
ἀστράτευτοι πολλὰς ἤδη νενικήκατε ἱππομαχίας.
44 Σκοπεῖτε δὲ μὴ περὶ ὑμῶν ἀληθέστερον οὗτοι
λέγωσιν [3] ἢ περὶ τῶν Ἑλλήνων Ἀνάχαρσιν τὸν

---

[1] συνόδοις] τριόδοις Cobet, relying on § 9.
[2] οὐδ' αὖ ὅμοιον deleted by Arnim.
[3] λέγωσιν Reiske : λέγουσιν.

---

[1] As we might say, 'the atmosphere was charged with
malign influence.' Rouse suggests that Dio may have had in
mind the practice of burying charms.

enter the theatre or the stadium, just as if drugs that would madden them lay buried there,[1] they lose all consciousness of their former state and are not ashamed to say or do anything that occurs to them. And what is most distressing of all is that, despite their interest in the show, they do not really see, and, though they wish to hear, they do not hear, being evidently out of their senses and deranged—not only men, but even women and children. And when the dreadful exhibition is over and they are dismissed, although the more violent aspect of their disorder has been extinguished, still at street-corners and in alley-ways the malady continues throughout the entire city for several days; just as when a mighty conflagration has died down, you can see for a long time, not only the smoke, but also some portions of the buildings still aflame." Moreover, some Persian or Bactrian is likely to say: " We ourselves know how to ride horses and are held to be just about the best in horsemanship "[2]—for they cultivate that art for the defence of their empire and independence—" but for all that we have never behaved that way or anything like it "; whereas you, who have never handled a horse or mounted one yourselves, are unable to restrain yourselves, but are like lame men squabbling over a foot-race. That may explain why, cowards and slackers though you are, you have won so many cavalry battles in the past![3]

And take heed lest these people prove to have spoken more truthfully about you than Anacharsis

[2] Cf. Herodotus 1. 136 : " Their sons are carefully instructed from their fifth to their twentieth year in three things alone—to ride, to draw the bow, and to speak the truth."

[3] Is Dio hinting that Alexandria depended upon mercenaries, or is he alluding to some recent military reverse?

Σκύθην φασὶν εἰπεῖν· ἐδόκει μὲν γὰρ εἶναι τῶν
σοφῶν· ἧκε δὲ εἰς τὴν Ἑλλάδα θεασόμενος, οἶμαι,
τά τε ἔθη καὶ τοὺς ἀνθρώπους· ἔλεγεν οὖν ὡς
ἔστιν ἐν ἑκάστῃ πόλει τῶν Ἑλλήνων ἀποδεδειγ-
μένον χωρίον, ἐν ᾧ μαίνονται καθ᾽ ἡμέραν,
τὸ γυμνάσιον λέγων· ἐπειδὰν γὰρ ἐλθόντες
ἀποδύσωνται, χρίονται φαρμάκῳ. τοῦτο δὲ ἔφη
κινεῖν αὐτοῖς τὴν μανίαν. εὐθὺς γὰρ οἱ μὲν
τρέχουσιν, οἱ δὲ καταβάλλουσιν ἀλλήλους, οἱ δὲ
τὼ χεῖρε ἀνατείναντες μάχονται πρὸς οὐδένα
ἀνθρώπων, οἱ δὲ παίονται. ταῦτα δὲ ποιήσαντες,
ἀποξυσάμενοι τὸ φάρμακον αὐτίκα σωφρονοῦσι,
καὶ φιλικῶς αὐτοῖς ἤδη ἔχοντες βαδίζουσι κάτω
ὁρῶντες, αἰσχυνόμενοι τοῖς πεπραγμένοις.

45 Ἐκεῖνος μὲν παίζων καὶ καταγελῶν οὐ φαύλου
πράγματος, ὡς ἐγὼ δοκῶ, ταῦτα ἔλεγεν· περὶ δὲ
ὑμῶν τί ἄν τις ἔχοι λέγειν; καὶ γὰρ ὑμεῖς ὅταν
συνέλθητε, πυκτεύετε, βοᾶτε, ῥιπτεῖτε, ὀρχεῖσθε,
ποίῳ χρισάμενοι φαρμάκῳ; δῆλον ὅτι τῷ τῆς
ἀνοίας· ὡς οὐκ ὂν [1] ὑμῖν ἐπιεικῶς αὐτὰ ὁρᾶν.
μὴ γὰρ τοῦτό με [2] οἴεσθε λέγειν ὡς οὐ χρὴ καὶ
τὰ τοιαῦτα γίγνεσθαι ἐν ταῖς πόλεσι· χρὴ γὰρ
ἴσως καὶ ἀναγκαῖόν ἐστι διὰ τὴν τῶν πολλῶν
ἀσθένειαν [3] καὶ σχολήν· ἴσως δὲ καὶ τῶν βελτι-

[1] ὡς οὐκ ὂν Pflugk: ὡς οὐκ ἦν. Arnim suggests either
καίτοι ἐξῆν or τί δέ; οὐκ ἦν.
[2] τοῦτό με Reiske: τοῦτο.
[3] ἀσθένειαν: εὐθένειαν Sonny. If ἀσθένειαν is authentic, it
must have the moral sense.

the Scythian is said to have spoken about the Greeks—for he was held to be one of the sages, and he came to Greece, I suppose, to observe the customs and the people.[1] Anacharsis said that in each city of the Greeks there is a place set apart in which they act insanely day after day—meaning the gymnasium —for when they go there and strip off their clothes, they smear themselves with a drug.[2] "And this," said he, " arouses the madness in them; for immediately some run, others throw each other down, others put up their hands and fight an imaginary foe, and others submit to blows. And when they have behaved in that fashion," said he, " they scrape off the drug and straightway are sane again and, now on friendly terms with one another, they walk with downcast glance, being ashamed at what has occurred."

Anacharsis was jesting and making sport about no trifling matter, it seems to me, when he said these things; but what might a visitor say about yourselves? For as soon as you get together, you set to work to box and shout and hurl and dance— smeared with what drug? Evidently with the drug of folly; as if you could not watch the spectacle sensibly! For I would not have you think I mean that even such performances should not take place in cities; for perhaps they should, and it may be necessary, because of the frailty of the masses and their idle habits; and possibly even among better

---

[1] Herodotus (4. 76) tells of this visit. Lucian tells of it at much greater length and in idealized form in his *Scytha*. Dio's version seems to have been drawn from the source represented by Diogenes Laertius 1. 104.
[2] Olive oil.

ὄνων εἰσὶν οἱ δεόμενοι διατριβῆς τινος καὶ παραμυθίας ἐν τῷ βίῳ· δεῖ δὲ μετὰ κόσμου καὶ
46 σχήματος πρέποντος ἀνθρώποις ἐλευθέροις. οὐ
γὰρ παρὰ τοῦτο οὔτε τῶν ἵππων οὐδεὶς δραμεῖται
βράδιον οὐδὲ χεῖρον ᾄσεταί τις τῶν ᾀδόντων, ἂν
εὐσχημονῆτε ὑμεῖς. νυνὶ δὲ τὸ μὲν τῶν ἡνιόχων
τινὰ ἐκπεσεῖν ἐκ τοῦ δίφρου δεινὸν ἡγεῖσθε καὶ
συμφορὰν πασῶν μεγίστην· αὐτοὶ δὲ ἐκπίπτοντες
ἐκ τοῦ κόσμου τοῦ προσήκοντος καὶ τῆς ἀξίας
τῆς ἑαυτῶν οὐ φροντίζετε. κἂν μὲν ὑμῖν ὁ
κιθαρῳδὸς ἐκμελῶς ᾄδῃ καὶ παρὰ τὸν τόνον,
συνίετε· αὐτοὶ δὲ παντελῶς ἔξω τῆς ἁρμονίας
τῆς κατὰ φύσιν γιγνόμενοι καὶ σφόδρα ἀμούσως
ἔχοντες οὐ διαφέρεσθε.

47   Καίτοι πόσοι διὰ ταῦθ' ὑμῶν ἀπολώλασιν;
ἀδοξοῦσι μέν γε [1] πάντες. αἱ δὲ Σειρῆνες ἄλλο
τι ἐποίουν, ὡς ὁ μῦθός φησιν; οὐκ ἀπώλλυον
τοὺς σφόδρα ἡσθέντας αὐταῖς; ἀλλ' ἐκεῖναι μὲν
ἐν ἐρήμῳ ἦσαν πελάγει καὶ μακρὰν ἀπῳκισμέναι
καθ' αὑτὰς ἐπὶ σκοπέλου τινός, ὅπου μηδεὶς
ῥᾳδίως παρέβαλλε· κἀκεῖ δ' ὁ νοῦν ἔχων ἐσώθη
καὶ μεθ' ἡσυχίας ἤκουσεν. οὗτοι δὲ σχεδὸν ἐν
μέσῳ τῆς οἰκουμένης ἐν τῇ πολυανθρωποτάτῃ
πασῶν πόλει τοιαῦτα ἐργάζονται, μὰ Δί' οὐ δι'
αὑτῶν τινα ἡδονὴν ἢ δύναμιν, ἀλλὰ διὰ τὴν

----

[1] μέν γε Capps : μὲν γὰρ.

----

[1] The underlying meaning of §§ 47–50 is by no means
clear. At first one takes ' destruction ' to mean moral ruin,
but later it seems to mean loss of life, either by decree of the
court or as the result of a duel between rival admirers or

people too there are those who need some diversion and amusement in life, but they should take it with decorum and as befits free men. For it will not cause any of the horses to run more slowly or any of the singers to sing less pleasingly if you preserve a due decorum. But as things are now, if one of the charioteers falls from his chariot, you think it terrible and the greatest of all disasters, whereas when you yourselves fall from the decorum that befits you and from the esteem you should enjoy, you are unconcerned. And if you hear the harpist sing out of tune or off pitch, you are well aware of it, whereas when you yourselves utterly abandon the harmony prescribed by nature and are most discordant, you are quite indifferent.

And yet how many here have met destruction because of these allurements?[1] Loss of reputation, at any rate, everyone has suffered. And did the Sirens do anything else according to the story?[2] Did they not regularly destroy those who took extravagant delight in them? Yet the Sirens dwelt in a lonely sea and far away, all by themselves, on a lofty cliff, where no one could easily approach; and even there the man of sense escaped in safety and heard them with composure. These entertainers of Alexandria, however, ply their trade in what is practically the centre of the civilized world and in the most populous city of all, not, by Zeus, because of any charm or power of their own, but rather because

the suicide of a disgraced and desperate man, or possibly an incident of the rioting of which we hear.

[2] The Sirens appear first in *Odyssey* 12, Odysseus of course being 'the man of sense.' However, Homer places them, not on a lofty cliff, but in a flowery meadow.

ὑμετέραν ἀβελτερίαν. διὰ τί γὰρ ἔξω παραπλησίως ἀκούονται τοῖς ἄλλοις καὶ πολλάκις ἀηδεῖς
ἔδοξαν; μὴ τὰ ὦτα ἐπαλήλιπται τῶν ἐκεῖ;

48   Τί οὖν τοῦτο δείκνυσι; μὰ Δί' οὐ μουσικῆς
ἰσχὺν οὐδ' ὑπερβολὴν τέχνης, ἀλλ' ἀκροατῶν
κουφότητα καὶ πόλεως ἀσθένειαν. φασὶ γοῦν
ἤδη τινὰς τῶν ἀπολωλότων διὰ τὴν τοιαύτην
πρόφασιν νεανιεύσασθαι, μὴ παραιτουμένους τὸν
θάνατον, ἀλλὰ προσλιπαροῦντας, ὅπως ἀκούσωσιν
ἐπὶ πλέον. τοῦτο δ' ἐστὶ θαυμαστὸν ἐπ' ὀνείδει
καὶ καταγέλωτι τῆς πόλεως, εἰ παρὰ μὲν τοῖς
ἄλλοις ἀριστεῖς καὶ τυραννοκτόνοι μνημονεύονται,
σωτηρίας ἕνεκεν τῶν πατρίδων ἐπιδιδόντες αὑτούς·
παρὰ δὲ ὑμῖν ὑπὲρ χορδῆς τοῦτο πάσχουσι καὶ
49 δι' ἡδονὴν μικράν, μᾶλλον δὲ δόξαν κενήν.   οὐ
γὰρ ἡδόμενοι τοσοῦτον ὅσον οἰόμενοι καὶ βουλόμενοι προΐενται σφᾶς αὑτούς.

Τοσαύτη δ' ἐστὶ δυστυχία τῶν ταλαιπώρων,
ὥστε ἀνδρεῖον ἡγοῦνται τὸ πάντων ἀνανδρότατον
καὶ σεμνὸν τὸ αἴσχιστον. ἑλοίμην γὰρ ἂν ἔγωγε
ληστεύων ἀποθανεῖν ἢ διὰ τοιαύτην αἰτίαν. τὸ
μὲν γάρ ἐστιν ἀνδρὸς πονηροῦ θάνατος, τὸ δὲ
ἀνδραπόδου δυστυχοῦς. κἀκεῖνος μὲν ἀδικηθεὶς
ἴσως ἐπὶ τοῦτο ἦλθεν, ὑπὲρ τοὺς νόμους ἀμύνα-
σθαι πειρώμενος [1] καὶ τάχα τι καὶ γενναῖον

---

[1] πειρώμενος Arnim, προθέμενος Casaubon : προέμενος.

of your fatuity. For why is it that outside Alexandria they produce an impression quite like that produced by the usual run of performers, nay, frequently have been thought to be unpleasant? Can it be that the ears of the people in those places have been stopped?

What, then, does their success with you signify? Not, by Zeus, musical power or artistic pre-eminence, but rather the shallowness of you listeners and the weakness of your city. It is said, at any rate, that some who have already met their ruin through such a cause, instead of trying by entreaty to escape their death, with youthful bravado have implored the privilege of listening to their destroyers even more. And here is an amazing thing which brings reproach and ridicule upon the city—that whereas elsewhere nobles and tyrannicides are held in memory because they gave their lives for the salvation of the fatherland, with you it is for a bit of catgut that men meet their fate and because of an enjoyment that is fleeting, or, more properly, a fancy that has no substance. For it is not through real enjoyment so much as through wishful thinking that these men sacrifice their lives.

And so great is the misfortune of the poor wretches, that they regard as manly what is most unmanly of all, and as dignified what is most shameful. Why, I would rather be put to death for robbery than for such a cause. For in the one case it is the death of a bad man but a *man*, in the other of a slave in hard luck. The one possibly came to such a pass because he had been wronged and was striving to get redress over and above the laws, and it may be that he might have achieved something actually noble, had

ἐδύνατο πρᾶξαι,[1] μὴ τοιούτου τυχὼν δαίμονος·
ὁδὶ δὲ κραυγῇ μόνον καὶ ἀνοίᾳ διὰ[2] δυστυχῆ
φθόγγον καὶ κακὴν ἔγκλισιν καὶ τὰς ἐκμελεῖς
καμπὰς καὶ λήρους καὶ κυνισμοὺς καὶ ὀλέθρους
ἀκλεῶς ἀπολλύμενος. ἔστι δὲ ὁ τοιοῦτος μυίας
θάνατος. καὶ γὰρ ἐκείναις ὅ τι ἂν γευσαμέναις
50 γλυκὺ φανῇ, πρὸς αὐτῷ[3] διαφθείρονται. τί οὖν
τοῦτο λαμπρόν, ὦ κακοδαίμονες; ὑπὲρ μὲν γὰρ
δικαιοσύνης καὶ ἀρετῆς καὶ πατρῴων γερῶν καὶ
νόμων καὶ χρηστοῦ βασιλέως, εἰ δέοι, πονεῖν καὶ
ἀποθνήσκειν ἀγαθῆς ἐστι καὶ οὐ φιλοζῴου ψυχῆς·
ὑπὲρ δὲ τῆς ψαλτρίας ἀπάγχεσθαι, καθάρματος
ἀγεννοῦς καὶ ζῆν οὐκ ἀξίου, πόσης αἰσχύνης;

Καὶ τούτους μὲν ἐάσωμεν, ἀλλ' ἐν αὐτῇ τῇ
θέᾳ τὰ γιγνόμενα οὐκ αἰσχρὰ καὶ μεστὰ πάσης
ὕβρεως, τὸ[4] ἀνατετάσθαι καὶ ἀποβλέπειν, μόνον
οὐκ ἐπὶ τοῖς χείλεσι τὰς ψυχὰς ἔχοντας,[5] καθάπερ,
οἶμαι, διὰ τῶν ὤτων τὴν εὐδαιμονίαν δεχομένους,
σωτῆρα καὶ θεὸν καλοῦντας[6] ἄνθρωπον ἄθλιον;
πόσον τινὰ γέλωτα τοὺς θεοὺς ὑμῶν καταγελᾶν
οἴεσθε, ὅταν πάλιν ἐκείνους προσκυνοῦντες ταὐτὰ
προσφέρησθε[7] καὶ διὰ τῶν αὐτῶν ἀναγκάζησθε
τιμᾶν τὸ δαιμόνιον; ἀλλ' ἔστιν εὐγνώμων ὁ θεός,
ὡς θεός, οἶμαι, καὶ φέρει πρᾴως τὴν τῶν πολλῶν
51 ἄνοιαν. τοιγαροῦν ὡς παισὶν ὑμῖν παιδαγωγοὺς
δέδωκε τοὺς φρονιμωτέρους τῆς πόλεως, μεθ' ὧν

---

[1] πρᾶξαι Reiske: πράξας.
[2] διὰ δυστυχῆ Reiske: δυστυχῇ.
[3] πρὸς αὐτῷ M, πρὸς αὐτὸ UB.
[4] τὸ added by Reiske.
[5] ἔχοντας Reiske: ἔχοντες.
[6] καλοῦντας Reiske: καλοῦντες.
[7] προσφέρησθε Emperius: προσφέρεσθε or προσφέρεσθαι.

he not encountered such an evil genius; but the other
came to his inglorious end merely through shouting
and a frenzy caused by an ill-starred voice and a
wicked nod of the head, by dissonant variations and
nonsense and a cynical, pestilential behaviour. But
such is the death of a fly! For whatever tastes sweet
to the fly is the thing at which it meets destruction.
What distinction, then, can your conduct bring you,
you luckless creatures? For whereas in the cause of
justice and virtue and ancestral rights and laws and
for a good king, a noble soul, one that does not cling
to life, will, if need be, suffer and even die; yet if a man
hangs himself for the sake of his chorus-girl, a low-born
outcast, not fit to live, what depths of disgrace does
that betoken!

And now let us say no more about these poor
unfortunates; but, directing our attention to the
spectacle itself, is the conduct of the spectators not
disgraceful and replete with every variety of wantonness?—I mean the intensity of their gaze, their souls
all but hanging on their lips—as if, one would
think, it were through the ear that men receive
felicity—and applying the terms 'saviour' and
'god' to a pitiful human being! With what bound-
less laughter, think you, must the gods laugh you to
scorn, when next in your worship of them you conduct
yourselves in the same fashion and find yourselves
compelled to use those same terms in honouring the
deity? However, god is indulgent, I suppose, since
he is god, and he treats lightly the folly of the masses.
Accordingly to you as his children has he given as
guardians and guides those who are more prudent
than you Alexandrians, and by their companionship,
not only at the theatre but elsewhere too, your

καὶ θεωρεῖτε καὶ τἆλλα ἄμεινον πράττετε. ἐπεὶ
πῶς ἂν ἀπείχεσθε ἀλλήλων;

Καίτοι ποίους τινὰς ἂν ὑμεῖς ἡγοῖσθε ἀνθρώπους, οἷς ἐλευθερία μὴ συμφέρει; νὴ Δία, τὸ γὰρ
πρᾶγμά ἐστι φύσει τοιοῦτον. οὐ γὰρ καὶ ἐν
ἄλλαις πόλεσιν ᾄδουσι καὶ νὴ Δία αὐλοῦσι καὶ
τρέχουσι καὶ πάνθ᾽ ὅσα γίγνεται καὶ¹ παρ᾽
ἡμῖν² καὶ παρ᾽ ἑτέροις τισίν; ἀλλ᾽ οὐδαμοῦ
τοιοῦτος ἔρως ἐστὶ τοῦ πράγματος οὐδὲ οἶστρος.
52 ἴστε Ῥοδίους ἐγγὺς οὕτως ὑμῶν ζῶντας ἐν
ἐλευθερίᾳ καὶ μετὰ πάσης ἀδείας· ἀλλὰ παρ᾽
ἐκείνοις οὐδὲ τὸ δραμεῖν ἐν τῇ πόλει δοκεῖ
μέτριον, ἀλλὰ καὶ τῶν ξένων ἐπιπλήττουσι τοῖς
εἰκῇ βαδίζουσι. τοιγαροῦν εἰκότως εὐδοκιμοῦσι
καὶ πάσης τιμῆς τυγχάνουσιν. αἰδούμενοι γὰρ
αὐτοὺς πρῶτοι καὶ μηδὲν ἀνόητον ποιοῦντες
εἰκότως, οἶμαι, παρά τε³ τῶν ἄλλων καὶ τῶν
ἡγουμένων αἰδοῦς τυγχάνουσιν.

Ἐπεὶ καὶ τῶν ἄλλων εὑρήσομεν τὰ πλεῖστα
ταὐτὰ πράττοντας τοῖς ἀνοήτοις τοὺς σώφρονας,
οἷον ἐσθίοντας, βαδίζοντας, παίζοντας, θεωροῦντας·
53 ἡ γὰρ φύσις ἀναγκάζει πολλῶν ὁμοίων δεῖσθαι·
διαφέρουσι μέντοι περὶ ταῦτα πάντα. αὐτίκα
ἐστιώμενοι πρῶτον οἱ μὲν οὔτε ἀμαθῶς οὔτε
ἀπρεπῶς διάγουσιν, ἀλλ᾽ εὐσχημόνως ἅμα καὶ

---

¹ καὶ deleted by Arnim.   ² ἡμῖν Crosby : ὑμῖν.
³ παρά τε Reiske : παρά γε.

---

¹ A grim joke referring to the presence of Roman troops in
Alexandria. See § 71 and Arnim, *Dio von Prusa*, p. 438. The
point of the joke—which must have been plain enough to the
audience—is made plainer for the modern reader by the em-
phasis on freedom in what follows.

conduct is improved.[1] For otherwise how could you keep your hands off one another?

And yet what kind of human beings do you think they are for whom freedom is not advantageous? "None, by Zeus," someone says, "for freedom is by nature advantageous. For do not other cities also have singing, aye, by Zeus, and flute-playing and foot-racing and all those other entertainments that are found, not only here in Alexandria, but among certain other people too?" Aye, but nowhere is there such a passion for that sort of thing, such a mad desire, as with yourselves. For example, you know that the Rhodians, your near neighbours, enjoy freedom and complete independence of action; however, in Rhodes even running within the city limits is held not to be respectable, but, on the contrary, they even reprove strangers for being careless in their walk.[2] So it is with good reason that the Rhodians should enjoy fair renown and universal honour. For since they are the first to show respect to themselves and to refrain from any foolish act, it is with good reason, I believe, that they have the respect of men in general and of their leaders as well.

The fact is, we shall find that in most other matters too the wise engage in the same activities as the foolish, such as eating, walking, playing, attending the theatre and the games. For nature compels them to have many needs in common with the foolish; there are, however, differences of behaviour in all these matters. Take feasting as the first instance: whereas the wise behave neither boorishly nor regardless of decorum, but with elegance combined with courtesy, as men

---

[2] See Or. 31. 162.

προσηνῶς, εὐωχίας, οὐ παροινίας, ἄρχοντες,
φιλοφρονούμενοι τοὺς συνόντας, οὐ θρασυνόμενοι
πρὸς αὐτούς· οἱ δὲ ἀπηνῶς καὶ ἀκολάστως,
μετὰ βοῆς καὶ ἀταξίας ὀργιζόμενοι καὶ γελῶντες,
πλεονεκτοῦντες ἀλλήλους, οὐ παρακαλοῦντες,[1]
τελευτῶντες ἅπασι κακόν τι τοῖς συμπόταις
δόντες ἢ παρ' ἐκείνων λαβόντες· οἵαν ποτὲ
γενέσθαι φασὶ Κενταύρων συνουσίαν.

54   Καίτοι[2] τί δεῖ τἄλλα ἐπεξιέναι καθ' ἕκαστον;
ἀλλὰ τὸ βαδίζειν, ὃ κοινόν ἐστι καὶ ἁπλοῦν
δήπουθεν, τοῦ μὲν ἐμφαίνει τὴν ἡσυχίαν τοῦ τρόπου
καὶ τὸ προσέχειν ἑαυτῷ, τοῦ δὲ ταραχὴν καὶ[3]
ἀναίδειαν· σπουδῇ πρόσεισι, φθέγγεται βαδίζων,
ἢ εἰσπεσών[4] τινα ἔωσε, μάχεται πρὸς ἕτερον.
ὁμοίως καὶ περὶ τὰς θέας οἱ μέν εἰσιν ἄπληστοι
καὶ λίχνοι καὶ περὶ πάντα ὁμοίως ἐπτοημένοι
τὰ τυχόντα, οἱ δὲ κοσμίως καὶ μετ' εἰρήνης
55   μετέχουσιν. ἀλλ' οὐχ ὑμεῖς, ἀλλ' ἐκπεπληγμένοι
κάθησθε, ἀναπηδᾶτε τῶν ὀρχηστῶν μᾶλλον,
συντείνεσθε ὑπὸ τῶν ᾀσμάτων· τοὺς μὲν γὰρ
ἄλλους ἀνθρώπους ἡ μέθη πρὸς ᾠδὴν τρέπει καὶ
ὄρχησιν· παρ' ὑμῖν δὲ τοὐναντίον ἐστίν. ἡ
γὰρ ᾠδὴ μέθην ἐμποιεῖ καὶ παράνοιαν. οἴνου
μὲν οὖν τοιαύτη φύσις, τὸ μὴ δύνασθαι σωφρονεῖν,

---

[1] οὐ παρακαλοῦντες] καὶ προκαλοῦντες Herwerden, καὶ
παροινοῦντες Arnim.
[2] Καίτοι Capps: καὶ.
[3] καὶ added by Wilamowitz.
[4] ἢ εἰσπεσών Capps, ἐμπεσών Emperius, πεσών Arnim: ἢ
πεσών.

---

[1] The famous wedding party of Peirithoüs and Hippo-
dameia. The fight that ensued between Lapiths and Centaurs
was a favourite subject with the Greek artist.

beginning a joyous feast and not a drunken debauch, being gracious toward their companions, not subjecting them to effrontery; the foolish, on the other hand, behave disgustingly and without restraint, giving vent to anger or to laughter with shouts and disorder, trying to get more than their companions, not inviting them to partake, and finally, before leaving for home, either they have done some damage to their fellow banqueters or received damage themselves, as we are told was the case at the party once held by the Centaurs.[1]

And yet why run through all the other differences one by one? But just take walking, for example, an activity common to all men and surely a simple one. One man's gait reveals the composure of his nature and the attention he gives to his conduct, while that of another reveals his confusion of mind and his shamelessness: he is hurried as he approaches, talks as he walks, or bursts in and jostles someone, comes to blows with someone else.[2] Similarly also with reference to the theatre: some persons are insatiate and greedy and all aflutter over everything alike, however commonplace, but others participate in the spectacle decorously and in peace. But not so with you; on the contrary, you sit dumbfounded, you leap up more violently than the hired dancers, you are made tense with excitement by the songs: for while other people are moved to song and dance by drink, with you the opposite is true—song is the occasion of drunkenness and frenzy. So while wine's natural effect is as we have seen, producing inability to pre-

[2] See Demosthenes 37. 52, 55; 45. 77 for the conventional Greek attitude regarding men's gait and general comportment.

ἀλλὰ πολλὰ δυσχερῆ πράττειν ἀναγκάζεσθαι
τοὺς σκαιῶς αὐτῷ καὶ ἀμέτρως χρωμένους·
ὑπὸ δὲ ᾠδῆς σφαλλομένους καὶ πολὺ κάκιον
ἔχοντας τῶν παροινούντων εὐθὺς ἀπὸ τῆς ἀρχῆς,
οὐχ ὥσπερ ἐν τῷ πότῳ προϊόντας, οὐκ ἔστιν
56 ἄλλους ἰδεῖν. παρὰ μὲν γὰρ ἐνίοις τῶν βαρβάρων
μέθην φασὶ γίγνεσθαι πραεῖαν δι' ἀτμοῦ θυμιω-
μένων[1] τινῶν· ἔπειτα χαίρουσι καὶ ἀνίστανται
γελῶντες καὶ πάντα ποιοῦσιν ὅσα ἄνθρωποι
πεπωκότες, οὐ μέντοι κακὸν οὐδὲν ἀλλήλους
ἐργάζονται· τῶν δὲ Ἑλλήνων ὑμεῖς μόνοι δι'
ὤτων καὶ φωνῆς αὐτὸ πάσχετε, μᾶλλον δὲ
ληρεῖτε ἐκείνων καὶ κάκιον[2] παραφέρεσθε καὶ
μᾶλλον ἐοίκατε κραιπαλῶσιν.

Καίτοι τὰ τῶν Μουσῶν καὶ τὰ τοῦ Ἀπόλλωνος
ἤπια δῶρα καὶ προσηνῆ. τὸν μὲν γὰρ Παιήονα
καὶ Ἀλεξίκακον προσαγορεύουσιν, ὡς ἀποτρέπον-
τα τῶν κακῶν καὶ ὑγίειαν ἐμποιοῦντα ταῖς
ψυχαῖς καὶ σώμασιν, οὐ νόσον οὐδὲ μανίαν · τὰς δὲ
παρθένους, ὡς ἂν αἰδουμένας τε καὶ σώφρονας·
57 ἥ τε μουσικὴ θεραπείας ἕνεκα τοῖς ἀνθρώποις[3]
εὑρῆσθαι δοκεῖ τῶν παθῶν καὶ μάλιστα δὴ τοῦ[4]
μεταστρέφειν ψυχὰς ἀπηνῶς καὶ ἀγρίως διακειμένας.
διὰ τοῦτο καὶ τῶν φιλοσόφων ἔνιοι πρὸς λύραν

---

[1] θυμιωμένων] θυμιαμάτων Schwartz and Wilamowitz,
θυωμένων B.
[2] καὶ κάκιον Crosby : κάκιον καί. Arnim deletes κάκιον.
[3] τοῖς ἀνθρώποις Reiske : τῶν ἀνθρώπων.
[4] τοῦ added by Capps.

serve one's self-control, but on the contrary forcing those who use it stupidly and in excess to commit many distasteful acts, yet men intoxicated by song and in far worse condition than those who are crazed by wine—and what is more, at the very start and not by easy stages as at a drinking party—such men, I say, are to be found nowhere but in Alexandria. Among certain barbarians, it is true, we are told that a mild kind of intoxication is produced by the fumes of certain incense when burned.[1] After inhaling it they are joyful and get up and laugh, and behave in all respects like men who have been drinking, and yet without doing injury to one another; but of the Greeks you alone reach that state through ears and voice, and you talk more foolishly than do those barbarians, and you stagger worse and are more like men suffering the after-effects of a debauch.

And yet the arts of the Muses and Apollo are kindly gifts and pleasing. For Apollo is addressed as Healer and as Averter-of-Evil, in the belief that he turns men aside from misfortune and implants health in soul and body, not sickness or madness; and the Muses are called maidens, implying their modesty and their chastity. Furthermore, music is believed to have been invented by men for the healing of their emotions, and especially for transforming souls which are in a harsh and savage state. That is why even some philosophers attune themselves

---

[1] Dio is here recording the practice in such vague terms that one cannot tell whether he had more exact knowledge or not. The effects which he mentions might have been produced by hasheesh. Pliny, *Hist. Nat.* 24. 164, speaks of an herb called gelotophyllis which, when mingled with wine and myrrh, produced great mental excitement and immoderate laughter.

αὐτοὺς ἡρμόσαντο ἔωθεν, ἀποπαύοντες τῆς διὰ
τῶν ὀνειράτων ταραχῆς. καὶ θεοῖς μετὰ μέλους
θύομεν, ἵνα εὔτακτοι καὶ καθεστηκότες ὦμεν.
ἕτερος δὲ αὖ τρόπος αὐλοῦ τε καὶ ᾠδῆς ἐν πέν-
θεσιν, ἰωμένων, οἶμαι, τὸ σκληρὸν καὶ ἄτεγκτον
τοῦ πάθους, θηλυτέραν δὲ τὴν λύπην ἐργαζο-
μένων δι᾽ ᾠδῆς λανθανούσης μετὰ γόων, ὥσπερ οἱ
ἰατροὶ τὰ φλεγμαίνοντα τῶν ἑλκῶν ὑγραίνοντες
καὶ μαλακοποιοῦντες ἀνώδυνα ἔθηκαν.

58   Οὐχ ἧττον δὲ καὶ περὶ συνουσίας ἔδοξε πρέπειν
ἡ μουσικῆς δύναμις, ἁρμονίαν καὶ τάξιν αὐτόματον ταῖς ψυχαῖς ἐπεισάγουσα καὶ τὸ σφα-
λερὸν τῆς ἐν οἴνῳ τέρψεως παραμυθουμένη μετὰ
ξυγγενοῦς δυνάμεως, ᾗπερ αὐτὸ[1] συγκεραννύ-
μενον ἐμμελὲς γίγνεται καὶ μέτριον. ταῦτα
δὴ πάντα ἀνέστραπται νῦν καὶ μεθέστηκεν εἰς
τοὐναντίον. οὐ γὰρ ἐκ Μουσῶν, ἀλλ᾽ ἐκ Κορυ-
βάντων τινῶν κατέχεσθε, καὶ πιστὰ ποιεῖτε τὰ
τῶν ποιητῶν μυθολογήματα· ὡς ἐκεῖνοί γε
παρεισάγουσι[2] Βάκχας τινὰς μαινομένας ὑπὸ μέλους
καὶ Σατύρους· οὐκοῦν ὑμῖν τὰ τῶν νεβρίδων τε
καὶ θύρσων ἐνδεῖ καὶ τὸ λέοντας φέρειν ἐν ταῖς
ἀγκάλαις· τὰ δὲ ἄλλα καὶ πάνυ μοι δοκεῖτε
59   ἐοικέναι Νύμφαις καὶ Σατύροις. ἱλαροί τε γὰρ
ἀεὶ καὶ φιλογέλωτες καὶ φιλορχησταί· πλὴν οὐκ
αὐτόματος ὑμῖν ἀναβλύει διψήσασιν ὁ οἶνος ἐκ

---

[1] ᾗπερ αὐτὸ Emperius: ὥσπερ αὐτῷ.
[2] ἐκεῖνοί γε παρεισάγουσι Emperius: ἐκεῖνοί τε γὰρ εἰσάγουσι.

---

[1] The Greeks took their music seriously. Its effect upon
morals is a familiar topic in Plato.
[2] More than one Greek dramatist dealt with the Bacchants,
but Dio seems to have in mind the *Bacchae* of Euripides.

to the lyre at dawn, thereby striving to quell the confusion caused by their dreams. And it is with song that we sacrifice to the gods, for the purpose of insuring order and stability in ourselves. And there is, moreover, a different type of song, accompanied by the flute, that is employed at time of mourning, as men attempt, no doubt, to heal the harshness and the relentlessness of their grief and to mitigate the pain by means of song, song that operates scarce noticed amid lament, just as physicians, by bathing and softening wounds that are inflamed, remove the pain.

And the spell of music has been deemed no less appropriate also in social gatherings, because it brings harmony and order spontaneously into the soul and along with a kindred influence abates the unsteadiness that comes from delight in wine—I mean that very influence blended with which the unsteadiness itself is brought into tune and tempered to moderation.[1] All this, of course, in the present instance has been reversed and changed to its opposite. For it is not by the Muses but by a kind of Corybantes that you are possessed, and you lend credibility to the mythologizings of the poets, since they do indeed bring upon the scene creatures called Bacchants,[2] who have been maddened by song, and Satyrs too. No doubt in your case the fawn-skin and the thyrsus are lacking, nor do you, like the Bacchants, bear lions in your arms;[3] yet in all else you do appear to me to be quite comparable to Nymphs and Satyrs. For you are always in merry mood, fond of laughter, fond of dancing; only in your case when you are thirsty wine does not bubble up of its own

[3] Euripides, *Bacchae* 699–700, says 'wolf-cubs,' not 'lions'; Dio may be thinking of Agavê (1278–9).

πέτρας ποθέν τινος ἢ νάπης, οὐδὲ γάλα καὶ
μέλι δύνασθε εὐχερῶς οὕτως ἔχειν ἄκροις δακτύ-
λοις διαμῶντες χθόνα· ἀλλ' οὐδὲ[1] τὸ ὕδωρ ὑμῖν
ἀφικνεῖται δεῦρο αὐτόματον οὐδὲ τὴν μᾶζαν
ἔχετε ἐν ἐξουσίᾳ δήπουθεν, ἀλλὰ καὶ ταύτην ἐκ
τῆς τῶν κρειττόνων χειρὸς λαμβάνετε· ὥστε
ἴσως καιρὸς ἦν ὑμᾶς παύσασθαι βακχειῶν καὶ
προσέχειν μᾶλλον αὐτοῖς. νυνὶ δὲ ἂν μόνον
ἀκούσητε χορδῆς, ὥσπερ σάλπιγγος ἀκηκοότες,
οὐκέτι δύνασθε εἰρήνην ἄγειν.

60   Ἆρά γε μὴ Λακεδαιμονίους μιμεῖσθε; φασὶ
γοῦν αὐτοὺς τὸ ἀρχαῖον πρὸς αὐλὸν πολεμεῖν·
ὑμεῖς δὲ πρὸς κιθάραν αὐτὸ δρᾶτε. ἢ βούλεσθε,
ἐπειδὴ τοῖς βασιλεῦσι τοὺς δήμους κἀγὼ παρ-
έβαλον, Νέρωνι φαίνεσθαι τὴν αὐτὴν ἔχοντες
νόσον; ἀλλ' οὐδ' ἐκεῖνον ὤνησεν ἡ λίαν ἐμπειρία
περὶ τοῦτο καὶ σπουδή. καὶ πόσῳ κρεῖττον
μιμεῖσθαι τὸν νῦν ἄρχοντα παιδείᾳ καὶ λόγῳ
προσέχοντα; οὐκ ἀποθήσεσθε τὴν αἰσχρὰν ταύτην
καὶ ἄμετρον φιλοτιμίαν; οὐ φυλάξεσθε τοὺς
ἄλλους σκώπτοντες, καὶ ταῦτα ἐν ἀνθρώποις, εἰ
θεμιτὸν εἰπεῖν, οὐδὲν μέγα οὐδὲ θαυμαστὸν
61 ἔχουσιν; εἰ γὰρ Ἰσμηνίας ηὔλει παρ' ὑμῖν ἢ
Τιμόθεος ᾖδεν ὁ παλαιὸς ἢ Ἀρίων, ὑφ' οὗ

----

[1] οὐδὲ Geel: οὔτε.

----

[1] *Bacchae* 708–10.
[2] Cf. §§ 25–8.
[3] Nero's infatuation for music and poetry and the stage is
well known. Tacitus refers to it briefly in his *Annals*; but
see especially Suetonius, *Nero*, 20–23, 38. 2, 41. 1, 49. 3.
Suetonius reports, among other things, that Nero recited

accord from some chance rock or glen, nor can you so
readily get milk and honey by scratching the ground
with the tips of your fingers; [1] on the contrary, not
even water comes to you in Alexandria of its own
accord, nor is bread yours to command, I fancy, but
that too you receive from the hand of those who are
above you; and so perhaps it is high time for you to
cease your Bacchic revels and instead to turn your
attention to yourselves. But at present, if you merely
hear the twang of the harp-string, as if you had heard
the call of a bugle, you can no longer keep the peace.

Surely it is not the Spartans you are imitating, is
it? It is said, you know, that in olden days they
made war to the accompaniment of the pipe; but
your warfare is to the accompaniment of the harp.
Or do you desire—for I myself have compared king
with commons [2]—do you, I ask, desire to be thought
afflicted with the same disease as Nero? Why, not
even he profited by his intimate acquaintance with
music and his devotion to it. [3] And how much better
it would be to imitate the present ruler in his devotion
to culture and reason! [4] Will you not discard that disgraceful and immoderate craving for notoriety? Will
you not be cautious about poking fun at everybody
else, and, what is more, before persons who, if I may
say so, have nothing great or wonderful to boast of? [5]
For if an Ismenias were piping in your presence or a
Timotheus [6] of early times were singing or an Arion,

the *Sack of Ilium* while Rome burned, and that just before
killing himself to escape his pursuers he repeated a line from
Homer.

[4] Trajan; though the scholiast says Vespasian.

[5] The musicians of Alexandria.

[6] Famous poet and musician, about 450–360 B.C. Dio
seems to allude to him in § 67, with which compare Or. 33. 57.

λέγουσιν ᾄδοντος ἐν τῷ πελάγει τοὺς δελφῖνας
ἀφικέσθαι πρὸς τὴν ναῦν, καὶ μετὰ ταῦτα ἐκπεσόν-
τα αὐτὸν κατὰ τύχην τινὰ ἀναλαβεῖν καὶ σῶσαι,
πῶς ἂν διέκεισθε; τούτων μὲν γάρ ἐστιν οὐδεὶς
Ἀμφίων οὐδὲ Ὀρφεύς· ὁ μὲν γὰρ υἱὸς ἦν
Μούσης, οἱ δὲ ἐκ τῆς Ἀμουσίας αὐτῆς[1] γεγόνασι,
διαστρέψαντες[2] καὶ κατάξαντες τὸ σεμνὸν τοῦ
μέλους καὶ πάντα τρόπον λωβησάμενοι τὴν
ἀρχαίαν μουσικήν.

62   Τίς γὰρ αὐτῶν ᾠδὴν τέλειον ἢ γενναῖον ῥυθμὸν οἷός τε εἰπεῖν; ἀλλὰ ᾄσματα γυναικῶν καὶ
κρούματα ὀρχηστῶν καὶ παροινίας τερατισμάτων,[3]
ὥσπερ κακοὶ καὶ περίεργοι μάγειροι, συντρίψαντες,
εἰς τοὺς νόμους[4] ἰδιώτας καὶ λίχνους ἀκροατὰς
κινοῦσιν. τοιγαροῦν οὐκ ἀπὸ κύκνων οὐδὲ ἀηδό-
νων ὁ ζῆλος αὐτῶν ὠνόμασται παρ' ὑμῖν αὐτοῖς
ἀλλ', ὡς ἔοικε, κνυζηθμοῖς[5] καὶ ὑλαγμοῖς εἰκά-
ζετε· καίτοι φιλοσόφους μὲν ᾔδειν οὕτως καλουμένους, κιθαρῳδοὶ δὲ Κυνικοὶ παρὰ μόνοις ὑμῖν
γεγόνασιν. ὁ μὲν οὖν Ἀμφίων πρὸς τὸ μέλος,
ὥς φασιν, ἤγειρε καὶ ἐπύργου τὴν πόλιν, οὗτοι
δὲ ἀνατρέπουσι καὶ καταλύουσιν. καὶ μὴν ὅ
γε Ὀρφεὺς τὰ θηρία ἥμερου καὶ μουσικὰ ἐποίει
διὰ τῆς ᾠδῆς· οὗτοι δὲ ὑμᾶς, ἀνθρώπους ὄντας,
ἀγρίους πεποιήκασι καὶ ἀπαιδεύτους.

---

[1] αὐτῆς Emperius : αὐτοί.
[2] διαστρέψαντες Casaubon, διαθρύψαντες Reiske : διατρέψαντες
UB, διὸ τρέψαντες M.
[3] παροινίας τερατισμάτων Crosby, παροινίων τερετίσματα
Arnim : παροινίας τερετισμάτων.
[4] εἰς τοὺς νόμους Emperius : τοὺς νόμους, which Arnim deletes.
[5] κνυζηθμοῖς Casaubon : κυζηθμοῖς UB, σκυζηθμοῖς M.

---

[1] See Herodotus 1. 24.

at whose song, according to tradition, the dolphins in the deep flocked to his ship and afterwards, when he had plunged overboard, rescued him by lucky chance and brought him safe ashore [1]—if those artists were performing for you, what would be your state of mind? For among these performers here there is no Amphion [2] and no Orpheus either; for Orpheus was the son of a Muse,[3] but these are unmusical offspring of Disharmony herself, having perverted and shattered the majesty of song and in every way outraged the grand old art of the Muses.

For who of the lot can produce a finished song or a noble rhythm? Nay, it is a potpourri of effeminate ditties and music-hall strummings of the lyre and the drunken excesses of monsters which, like villainous cooks with an itch for novelty, they mash together to form their arias and thus excite an ignorant and avid audience. Accordingly not from swans or nightingales has their passion got its name with you, but rather, as it seems, you liken it to the whining and howling of dogs; and yet, while I knew that there are philosophers called Cynics, harpists of that canine breed have been produced in Alexandria alone. So while Amphion to the accompaniment of his melody, according to the tale, built the walls and towers of his city, these creatures are engaged in the work of overturning and destroying. And as for Orpheus, by his song he tamed the savage beasts and made them sensitive to harmony; yet these performers here have turned you human beings into savages and made you insensible to culture.

[2] At the music of Amphion the stones of their own accord moved into place to form the walls of Thebes.

[3] Calliopê.

233

63 Ἔχω δὲ καὶ ἄλλον εἰπεῖν λόγον ἀνθρώπου
Φρυγὸς ἀκούσας, Αἰσώπου συγγενοῦς, δεῦρο
ἐπιδημήσαντος, ὃν εἰς Ὀρφέα καὶ ὑμᾶς ἔλεγεν.
ἔστι δὲ τῶν ὑμετέρων σκωμμάτων ἀτοπώτερος
καὶ μακρότερος. σκοπεῖτε οὖν, εἰ βούλεσθε
ἀκοῦσαι, καὶ μὴ δυσχεράνητε. ἔφη τοίνυν ἐκεῖνος
περί τε Θράκην καὶ Μακεδονίαν τὸν Ὀρφέα
μελῳδεῖν, καθάπερ εἴρηται, κἀκεῖ τὰ ζῷα προσιέναι αὐτῷ, πολύ τι πλῆθος, οἶμαι, πάντων τῶν [1]
θηρίων. πλεῖστα δὲ ἐν αὐτοῖς εἶναι τούς τε
ὄρνιθας καὶ τὰ πρόβατα. τοὺς μὲν γὰρ
64 λέοντας καὶ τὰ τοιαῦτα διὰ τὴν ἀλκὴν καὶ
τὴν ἀγριότητα δυσπιστότερα εἶναι, καὶ τὰ μὲν
οὐδ᾽ ὅλως πελάζειν, τὰ δ᾽ εὐθὺς ἀποχωρεῖν,
οὐχ ἡδόμενα τῷ μέλει. τὰ δὲ πτηνὰ καὶ τὰ
πρόβατα μᾶλλόν τε προσιέναι καὶ μηκέτ᾽ ἀπαλ-
λάττεσθαι· τὰ μέν, οἶμαι, διὰ τὸ εὔηθες καὶ
τὴν φιλανθρωπίαν, τῶν δὲ ὀρνίθων μουσικὸν
δήπου τὸ γένος αὐτὸ καὶ φιλῳδόν. ζῶντος μὲν
οὖν Ὀρφέως συνέπεσθαι αὐτῷ πανταχόθεν ἀκούοντα [2] ὁμοῦ καὶ νεμόμενα· καὶ γὰρ ἐκεῖνον ἔν
τε τοῖς ὄρεσι καὶ περὶ τὰς νάπας τὰ πολλὰ διατρί-
βειν· ἀποθανόντος δὲ ἐρημωθέντα ὀδύρεσθαι καὶ
χαλεπῶς φέρειν· ὥστε τὴν μητέρα αὐτοῦ Καλλιό-
πην διὰ τὴν πρὸς τὸν υἱὸν εὔνοιαν καὶ φιλίαν
αἰτησαμένην παρὰ Διὸς τὰ σώματα αὐτῶν
μεταβαλεῖν εἰς ἀνθρώπων τύπον, τὰς μέντοι
ψυχὰς διαμένειν, οἷαι πρότερον ἦσαν.
65 Χαλεπὸν οὖν ἤδη ἐστὶ τὸ λειπόμενον τοῦ

---

[1] πάντων τῶν Capps, παντοίων Arnim: τῶν πάντων.
[2] After ἀκούοντα Arnim deletes αὐτοῦ.

And I have, furthermore, a story to tell that I heard from a Phrygian, a kinsman of Aesop's, who paid a visit here, a story that he told about Orpheus and yourselves. However, that story is more weird and lengthier than your jokes. Consider, therefore, if you wish to hear it, and don't be vexed if I tell it. Well then, the man from Phrygia said that Orpheus sang his songs throughout Thrace and Macedonia, as we have been told,[1] and that the creatures there came up to him—a great company, I imagine, of all the animals. " And," he continued, " most numerous among them were the birds and the sheep. For the lions and other animals of that sort were more distrustful because of their strength and savage nature, and some would not even come near him, while others immediately withdrew, not being pleased with the music; but the feathered creatures and the sheep not only came to him more readily but also did not leave him afterwards—the sheep, no doubt, because of their guilelessness and fondness for human society, while the birds, of course, are a musical tribe themselves and fond of song. So then, as long as Orpheus was alive they followed him from every quarter, listening as they fed—for indeed he spent his time for the most part on the mountains and about the glens; but when he died, in their desolation they wailed and were distressed; and so it came about that the mother of Orpheus, Calliopê, because of her goodwill and affection toward her son, begged Zeus to change their bodies into human form; yet their souls remained as they had been before."

Well, the remainder of the tale from this point on is

---

[1] The phrase seems to refer to the preceding section, which, however, does not name Thrace and Macedonia.

DIO CHRYSOSTOM

λόγου, καὶ δέδοικα πρὸς ¹ ὑμᾶς σαφῶς αὐτὸ εἰπεῖν.
ἔλεγε γὰρ ἐξ ἐκείνων γένος τι φῦναι Μακεδόνων,
καὶ τοῦτο αὖθις ² ὕστερον μετὰ 'Αλεξάνδρου
διαβὰν ἐνθάδε οἰκῆσαι. καὶ διὰ τοῦτο δὴ τὸν
τῶν 'Αλεξανδρέων δῆμον ἄγεσθαι μὲν ὑπὸ ᾠδῆς,
ὡς οὐδένας ἄλλους, κἂν ἀκούσωσι κιθάρας
ὁποιασοῦν, ἐξεστάναι καὶ φρίττειν κατὰ μνήμην
τὴν 'Ορφέως. εἶναι δὲ τῷ τρόπῳ κοῦφον καὶ
ἀνόητον, ὡς ἐκ τοιούτου σπέρματος· ἐπεὶ τούς
γε ἄλλους Μακεδόνας ἀνδρείους καὶ πολεμικοὺς
γενέσθαι καὶ τὸ ἦθος βεβαίους.

66 Ἔλεγε δὲ καὶ περὶ τῶν κιθαρῳδῶν τῶν παρ'
ὑμῖν ἕτερον ³ τοιοῦτόν τινα λόγον. τὰ γὰρ
ζῷα ἐν τῇ συνουσίᾳ τῇ πρὸς τὸν 'Ορφέα τὰ μὲν
ἄλλα ἥδεσθαι μόνον καὶ ἐκπεπλῆχθαι, μιμεῖσθαι
δὲ μηδὲν ἐπιχειρεῖν· τῶν κυνῶν δὲ ἐνίους, οἷα δὴ
γένος ἀναιδὲς καὶ περίεργον, ἐπιθέσθαι τῇ μουσικῇ,
καὶ μελετᾶν τότ' εὐθὺς ἀπιόντας καθ' αὑτοὺς
καὶ τὰ εἴδη μεταβαλόντας ⁴ εἰς ἀνθρώπους
διαφυλάττειν τὴν ἐπιμέλειαν. εἶναι δὲ τοῦτο
αὐτὸ τὸ γένος τῶν κιθαρῳδῶν· διὸ μὴ δύνασθαι
παντάπασιν ἐκβῆναι τὴν αὑτῶν φύσιν, ἀλλὰ
μικρὸν μέν τι διασώζειν τῆς 'Ορφέως διδασκαλίας,
τὸ πολὺ δ' αὐτοῖς ἐμμένειν κύνειον τοῦ μέλους.

67 Ταῦτα μὲν ἐκεῖνος ἔπαιζεν ὁ Φρύξ. ἐγὼ δ'
ὑμῖν βούλομαι Λακεδαιμονίων ἔργον εἰπεῖν, ὡς
ἐκεῖνοι προσηνέχθησαν ἀνδρὶ κιθαρῳδῷ θαυμα-

¹ πρὸς added by Reiske.
² αὖθις Emperius : εὐθὺς.
³ ἕτερον Reiske : ὕστερον.
⁴ μεταβαλόντας Reiske : μεταβαλόντα UB, μεταβάλλοντα M.

236

painful and I am reluctant to tell it to you in plain language. For the Phrygian went on to say that from those wild creatures whom Zeus transformed a tribe of Macedonians was born, and that it was this tribe which at a later time crossed over with Alexander and settled here. He added that this is the reason why the people of Alexandria are carried away by song as no other people are, and that if they hear music of the lyre, however bad, they lose their senses and are all aquiver in memory of Orpheus. And he said that they are giddy and foolish in behaviour, coming as they do from such a stock, since the other Macedonians certainly have shown themselves to be manly and martial and steadfast of character.

The Phrygian also spoke regarding the harpists of your city about as follows : He said that in their association with Orpheus the other animals merely experienced pleasure and wonder but made no attempt at imitation ; but that some of the dogs, being of course a shameless and inquisitive breed, applied themselves to music and then and there began to practice it, going off by themselves, and that after they had been changed to human form they maintained their addiction to the art. And he declared that this very breed is the stock from which the harpists sprang ; therefore they have been unable wholly to slough off their own nature, but, while retaining some small part of the instruction derived from Orpheus, for the most part their music has remained canine in character.

All this the Phrygian spoke in jest. But I want to tell you something that happened at Sparta, how the people of that land behaved toward a harpist who was

ζομένῳ τότε ἐν τοῖς Ἕλλησιν. ὅτι γὰρ λίαν
ἡδὺς ἐδόκει καὶ περιττὸς εἶναι, μὰ Δί᾽ οὐκ ἐτί-
μησαν αὐτόν, ἀλλ᾽ ἀφείλοντο τὴν κιθάραν καὶ
τὰς χορδὰς ἐξέτεμον, ἀπιέναι προειπόντες[1] ἐκ
τῆς πόλεως. ἐκεῖνοι μὲν οὖν τὸ πρᾶγμα οὕτως
ὑφεωρῶντο καὶ ἐφύλαττον τὰ ὦτα, ὡς ἂν μὴ
διαφθαρῶσιν αἱ ἀκοαὶ μηδὲ τρυφερώτεραι γένωνται τοῦ δέοντος· ὑμεῖς δὲ οὕτως ἀγεννῶς δεδού-
λωσθε ὑπὸ τῆς τοιαύτης ἡδονῆς.

68   Δι᾽ ὑμᾶς δὲ ἤδη μοι δοκεῖ τὸ πρᾶγμα καὶ τῶν
ῥητόρων ἅπτεσθαι καὶ φιλοσόφων ἐνίων· μᾶλλον
δὲ τοὺς ῥήτορας οὐδὲ γνῶναι ῥᾴδιον. ὡς γὰρ
ὁρῶσι τὴν σπουδὴν ὑμῶν τὴν περὶ τοῦτο καὶ
τὴν ἐπιθυμίαν, πάντες δὴ ᾄδουσι καὶ ῥήτορες καὶ
σοφισταί, καὶ πάντα περαίνεται δι᾽ ᾠδῆς· ὥστ᾽,
εἴ τις παρίοι δικαστήριον, οὐκ ἂν γνοίη ῥᾳδίως
πότερον ἔνδον πίνουσιν ἢ δικάζονται· κἂν σοφισ-
τοῦ δὲ οἴκημα πλησίον ᾖ, οὐκ ἔσται γνῶναι τὴν
διατριβήν. δοκεῖ δέ μοι, καὶ ἐν τῷ γυμνασίῳ
προϊόντες ἤδη γυμνάσονται[2] πρὸς μέλος καὶ
τοὺς κάμνοντας ἰάσονται. περὶ γὰρ τῆς τέχνης
καὶ νῦν ὑμῖν[3] διαλέγονται ᾄδοντες.

69   Κινδυνεύει δ᾽ ὁ βίος σχεδὸν ἅπας γεγονέναι
κῶμος εἷς, οὐχ ἡδὺς οὐδὲ πρᾷος, ἀλλ᾽ ἄγριος

---

[1] ἀπιέναι προειπόντες Reiske: ἀπεῖναι προσειπόντες.
[2] καὶ after γυμνάσονται deleted by Emperius.
[3] ὑμῖν Capps as in T: ἡμῖν.

---

much in vogue among the Greeks in those days. Just because this harpist had the reputation of being very charming and unusual, they did not, by Zeus, honour him, but instead they took his harp from him, cut away the strings, and ordered him to leave their city.[1] Such, you see, were the misgivings the Spartans entertained regarding his calling and such the care they took of their ears, lest their hearing be corrupted or become more fastidious than was fitting; but you have been thus ignominiously enslaved by that kind of pleasure.

And through your influence, it would seem, the disease is already affecting, not only public speakers, but some philosophers as well—though it would be more correct to say that public speakers are no longer easy to recognize. For since they observe your interest in singing and your passion for it, they all sing now, public speakers as well as sophists,[2] and everything is done to music; if you were to pass a courtroom, you could not easily decide whether a drinking-party was in progress or a trial; and if there is in your neighbourhood a sophist's lecture-room, you will be unable to distinguish the lecture. And in my opinion people will presently go so far as to use song to accompany their exercise in the gymnasium, yes, even to heal the sick. For even now, when physicians discourse to you on their art, they chant.

But in all likelihood life with you has become, one may almost say, just one continuous revel, not a sweet or gentle revel either, but savage and harsh, a revel

---

[2] 'Public speakers' ($\dot{\rho}\acute{\eta}\tau o\rho\epsilon\varsigma$) would include teachers of rhetoric, politicians, and lawyers; the sophists lectured on a variety of topics, including philosophy.

καὶ χαλεπός, ἅμα ὀρχουμένων, τερετιζόντων,
μιαιφονούντων. οἱ δ' οὖν Λακεδαιμόνιοι πλεῖστον
ὅσον ὑμῶν διέφερον, περὶ ταῦτα, ὡς ἔφην, εὐλαβῶς
ἔχοντες. οἱ μὲν γὰρ ἄρχειν ἦσαν ἱκανοί, καὶ
τῶν μὲν Ἑλλήνων προέστησαν πολλὰ ἔτη, τοὺς
δὲ βαρβάρους ἐνίκων ἀεὶ πάντας, ὑμεῖς δὲ οὐδὲ
ἄρχεσθαι καλῶς ἐπίστασθε. τοιγαροῦν εἰ μὴ
τῶν προεστηκότων ἐτύχετε, χαλεπῶς ἄν, οἶμαι,
70 καὶ ἐσῴζεσθε. τεκμήριον δὲ τὰ τελευταῖα συμ-
βάντα περὶ ὑμᾶς. ὅτε γὰρ καθ' αὑτοὺς ἦτε,
οὐχ ὁ μὲν βασιλεὺς ὑμῶν περὶ αὔλησιν ἠσχολεῖτο
καὶ μόνῳ τούτῳ προσεῖχεν, ὑμεῖς δὲ πρὸς ἐκεῖνον
μὲν ἀπεχθῶς, πρὸς ἀλλήλους δὲ στασιαστικῶς
διέκεισθε, χωρὶς ἕκαστοι καὶ καθ' αὑτοὺς δια-
φθείροντες τὰ πράγματα, Σιμάριστοι καὶ τοιαῦθ'
ἕτερα ἑταιρειῶν ὀνόματα· ὥστε φυγεῖν αὐτὸν ἠναγ-
κάσατε καὶ μετὰ ταῦτα κατιέναι πολέμῳ καὶ διὰ
Ῥωμαίων· καὶ τέλος ἐκεῖνος μὲν αὐλῶν, ὑμεῖς δὲ
71 ὀρχούμενοι τὴν πόλιν ἀπωλέσατε. καὶ νῦν οὕτως
ἐπιεικεῖς ἔχοντες ἡγεμόνας εἰς ὑποψίαν αὐτοὺς καθ'
ὑμῶν αὐτῶν ἠγάγετε, ὥστε ἐπιμελεστέρας[1] χρῆναι
φυλακῆς ᾠήθησαν ἢ πρότερον· καὶ τοῦτο εἴργυσθε
δι' ἀγερωχίαν, οὐκ ἐπιβουλεύοντες. ὑμεῖς γὰρ
ἂν ἀποσταίητέ τινος; πολεμήσαιτε δ' ἂν ὑμεῖς
μίαν ἡμέραν; οὐκ ἐν τῇ γενομένῃ ταραχῇ μέχρι
σκωμμάτων ἐθρασύνοντο οἱ πολλοί, τινὲς δὲ

---

[1] ἐπιμελεστέρας Casaubon : ἐπιεικεστέρας.

---

[1] Thermopylae was at least a ' moral victory.'
[2] The Romans.
[3] Ptolemy XI (80–51 B.C.), nicknamed 'The Piper,' was
driven into exile in 58 B.C. and restored by Aulus Gabinius,
proconsul of Syria, three years later.

of dancers, whistlers, and murderers all combined. But the Spartans were vastly different from you Alexandrians, for they were cautious in these matters, as I have said. For while they showed capacity to rule, having held the leadership in Greece for many years and being always victorious over the barbarians without exception,[1] you do not understand even how to be good subjects. Therefore, if you had not been fortunate in your present leaders,[2] hardly, I fancy, would your existence be secure. As evidence I cite the most recent chapters in your history. For instance, when you were still independent, did not your king busy himself with piping and concentrate on that alone; and were you not on hostile terms with him and torn with faction among yourselves, each faction separately and independently working the ruin of the state—Simaristoi and other parties of like names—in consequence of which you forced your king to flee, and later on to obtain his return by means of war, and with the aid of Romans, too?[3] And finally he with his piping and you with your dancing destroyed the state.[4] And though you now have such reasonable men as governors, you have brought them to a feeling of suspicion toward yourselves, and so they have come to believe that there is need of more careful watchfulness than formerly; and this you have brought about through arrogance and not through plotting. For would *you* revolt from anybody? Would *you* wage war a single day? Is it not true that in the disturbance which took place the majority went only as far as jeering in their show of

[4] By having invoked the aid of Rome? Dio seems to say that independence was lost under 'The Piper,' which is manifestly false.

ὀλίγοι βάλλοντες ὅ τι ἔτυχον ἅπαξ ἢ δίς, ὥσπερ
οἱ καταχέοντες τῶν παριόντων, κατέκειντο εὐθὺς
ᾄδοντες, οἱ δ᾽ ἐπὶ τοὺς ὅρμους ᾖεσαν, ὥσπερ ἐν
ἑορτῇ πιούμενοι; [1]

72 Καὶ μὴν ἐκεῖνο μέμνησθε τὸ γελοῖον ὡς ὁ
βέλτιστος ὑμῖν Κόνων ἐχρήσατο προελθών, οὗ
μάλιστα τὸ πλῆθος ὑμῶν συνειστήκει, καὶ δείξας
τινὰ τόπον βραχὺν προηγόρευεν ὡς εἰ μὲν αὐτὸς
ἐκεῖ προέλθοι, νενικηκὼς εἴη καὶ δέοι [2] ὑμᾶς
ἀπαλλάττεσθαι καθ᾽ αὑτοὺς καὶ παραχωρεῖν·
εἰ δ᾽ ὑμεῖς, ἔφη, τέτταρα ἢ πέντε βήματα
νικᾶτε, κἀγὼ βαδιοῦμαι· ταῦτα δὲ ἔλεγε,
φειδόμενος ὑμῶν καὶ καταγελῶν καὶ καθάπερ
παισὶ προσπαίζων. ἐπεὶ [3] τὸ στράτευμα
ἐφειστήκει κἀκεῖνος οὐδένα εἴα ἅπτεσθαι, γυμ-
νοὺς ἅπαντας ὁρῶν καὶ ἑτοίμους ἀπόλλυσθαι.
τί οὖν; ἐβιάσαντο μετὰ ταῦτα οἱ προπετεῖς καὶ
ἀκόλαστοι καὶ ἐπίτηδες ἀνατρέψαι [4] καὶ συγχέαι
πάντα ἐπιβουλεύσαντες, καὶ οὐ πρότερον ὑμᾶς
ἀνῆκαν ἕως ἐγεύσασθε πολέμου καὶ τὸ δεινὸν
ἄχρι πείρας προῆλθεν.

73 Τί δὴ καὶ τούτων ἐπεμνήσθην; ὅπως εἰδῆτε
τὰ φυόμενα ἐκ τῆς περὶ τὸν βίον ταύτης ἀταξίας.
οὐ γὰρ ἔστι τοὺς οὕτως ἐπτοημένους περὶ τὰ
μικρὰ καὶ μηδενὸς ἄξια, φαύλως καὶ ἀκρατῶς
ἔχοντας ἐν τούτοις ἃ πράττουσι καθ᾽ ἡμέραν,

---

[1] πιούμενοι Casaubon : ποιούμενοι.
[2] δέοι Selden : δέον.   [3] ἐπεὶ Valesius : ἐπί.
[4] ἀνατρέψαι Reiske : ἀναστρέψαι.

---

[1] Cf. Aristophanes, *Acharnians* 616–17: ὥσπερ ἀπονίπτρον
ἐκχέοντες ἑσπέρας, ἅπαντες ᾽ἐξίστω᾽ παρήνουν οἱ φίλοι.
[2] Dio is our only authority for this disturbance.

courage, while only a few, after one or two shots with anything at hand, like people drenching passers-by with slops,[1] quickly lay down and began to sing, and some went to fetch garlands, as if on their way to a drinking party at some festival?[2]

And surely you recall that comical incident—how the excellent Conon[3] treated you when, advancing to the place where your forces were most concentrated and pointing out a little stretch of ground, he declared: " If I can get there by myself, I am the victor, and you must depart by yourselves and leave the field; but if you," said he, " can win your way as much as four or five steps, I will take a walk myself." This he said out of a desire to spare you, laughing at you and playing with you as if you were children; since the army had halted and he would not permit a single soldier to lay hands on you, seeing, as he did, that you all were unarmed and faced with destruction. What then? Force was next employed by the headstrong and unruly spirits, who purposely aimed at a complete overthrow and utter chaos, and they did not let you go until you had had a taste of warfare, and what you formerly had dreaded had become a matter of bitter experience.

Why, then, have I mentioned these events also? Because I wanted you to understand the natural outcome of this disorderliness that rules your lives. For it is not possible that those who get so excited over trifles and things of no importance, those who behave so thoughtlessly and with such lack of self-control in these matters of daily life, should be temperate in other matters and competent to plan

[3] Unknown. Apparently the commander of the Roman troops in Alexandria.

τἄλλα σωφρονεῖν καὶ περὶ τῶν μειζόνων ὀρθῶς
βουλεύεσθαι. ἡ γὰρ τῶν τρόπων κουφότης καὶ
τὸ ἀλόγιστον οὐκ ἐᾷ μένειν ἐπὶ τοῖς ἐλάττοσιν,
οὐδ' ἔχει μέτρον οὐδὲν ἡ ἄνοια τῶν ἁμαρτημάτων, ἀλλ' ἐπὶ πᾶν ὁμοίως πρόεισι καὶ παντὸς
74 ἅπτεται μετὰ τῆς ἴσης εὐχερείας. μὴ οὖν οἴεσθε
περὶ μικρῶν εἶναι τὸν λόγον, ὅταν τις ὑμῖν διαλέγηται περὶ τῶν ἐν τοῖς θεάτροις θορύβων. οὐ
γὰρ οὕτως ἡ πενία ταχὺ πέφυκε συμβαίνειν διὰ
τὰς κατ' ὀλίγον ζημίας, ὡς ἡ κακία πρόεισιν
ἐκ τῶν κατὰ μέρος τούτων ἁμαρτημάτων καὶ
τελευταῖον ἐπ' αὐτὸ τὸ πέρας καὶ τὸν ὄλεθρον
αὐξηθεῖσα ἤγαγεν.

Καὶ ταῦτα μὲν δὴ [1] τὰ περὶ τὸ θέατρον. ἀλλ'
ὅταν εἰς τὸ στάδιον ἔλθητε, τίς ἂν εἰπεῖν δύναιτο
τὰς ἐκεῖ κραυγὰς καὶ θόρυβον καὶ ἀγωνίαν καὶ
σχημάτων μεταβολὰς καὶ χρωμάτων καὶ βλασφημίας οἵας καὶ ὅσας ἀφίετε; εἰ γὰρ μὴ τοὺς
ἵππους ἑωρᾶτε ἁμιλλωμένους καὶ τούτους συνήθεις, αὐτοὶ δ' ὑπὸ μαστίγων ἠλαύνεσθε τῶν ἐν
ταῖς τραγῳδίαις, οὐκ ἂν οὕτως χαλεπῶς δι-
75 έκεισθε. αὐτὸν γάρ, οἶμαι, τὸν Ἰξίονα λῆρον
ἀποφαίνετε τὸν ἐν τῷ τροχῷ παρὰ τοῖς ποιηταῖς
ἐνδεδεμένον καὶ κολαζόμενον διὰ τοιαύτην τινὰ
ἀσέβειαν. φέρε οὖν, εἰ μεταξὺ θεῶν τις ὑμῖν
ἐπιστὰς εἴποι διατεινάμενος,

δαιμόνιοι, μαίνεσθε καὶ οὐκέτι κεύθετε θυμῷ
βρωτὺν οὐδὲ ποτῆτα.

---

[1] δὴ Emperius: ἤδη.

---

[1] Apparently the whips wielded by the Furies.

wisely regarding things of greater moment. For the frivolity of your conduct and your lack of reason do not permit you to call a halt at things of minor importance, and the folly of your misconduct knows no bounds, but instead goes right on to any length without discrimination, and touches everything with equal recklessness. So do not think that a man is dealing with trifles when he speaks to you about your disorders in the theatre. For poverty follows quickly enough from gradual losses, but not as quickly as wickedness progresses from these successive errors, until finally, having attained its growth, it brings men to the very end—destruction.

So much, then, on the subject of the theatre. However, when you enter the stadium, who could describe the shouts you utter there, and your hubbub and anguish and bodily contortions and change of colour, and the many awful curses that you emit? For if you were not merely watching the horses race —and horses, too, that are used to racing—but were yourselves being driven by the whips of tragedy,[1] you would not exhibit the agony you do. Why even Ixion himself, methinks, you show to have been a second-rater, the Ixion who is represented by the poets as bound on the wheel and punished for some such impiety as yours.[2] Well then, if in the midst of it all some god should take his stand beside you and in a loud voice should say:

" Fools, you are mad; no more your spirit hides
Your food and drink.[3]

[2] Arnim views this clause as an interpolation, but the reference may be to the degree of impiety rather than the kind.

[3] *Odyssey* 18. 406–7. Telemachus upbraids the suitors at their final banquet before the slaughter.

τί σφόδρα οὕτω κυκᾶσθε; τίς ἡ σπουδή; τίς
ὁ ἀγών; οὐ γὰρ Πέλοψ ἐστὶν ὁ διώκων, οὐδ᾽
Οἰνόμαος οὐδὲ Μυρτίλος,[1] οὐδὲ περὶ βασιλείας
οὐδὲ γυναικὸς οὐδὲ θανάτου πρόκειται κρίσις,
ἀλλ᾽ ἔστιν ὁ ἀγὼν ἀνδραπόδων ὑπὲρ τοῦ τυχόντος
ἀργυρίου, νῦν μὲν ἡττωμένων νῦν δὲ νικώντων, ἀεὶ
76 τῶν αὐτῶν· εἰ λέγοι ταῦτα, τί ἐρεῖτε; ἢ δῆλον
ὅτι οὐδ᾽ ἀκούσεσθε παρ᾽ ἐκείνου τὸν καιρόν, οὐδὲ
ἂν αὐτὸς ὑμῖν ὁ τοῦ Πέλοπος διαλέγηται
πρόγονος;

Τίνα οὖν εὕρῃ τις ἐπικουρίαν ἢ τίνα ἐξιλάσασθαι
δεῖ δαιμόνων; ἔστιν Ὀλυμπίασι κατὰ μέσον τὸν
ἱππόδρομον Ταραξίππου Ποσειδῶνος βωμός, ἔνθα
μάλιστα συνέβαινε τοὺς ἵππους πτοεῖσθαι καὶ
πλεῖστα διαφθείρεσθαι τῶν ἁρμάτων. ἔδοξεν
οὖν τοῖς Ἠλείοις ὡς δαιμονίου τινὸς ὄντος
ἱδρύσασθαι βωμόν. καὶ τὸ λοιπόν φασιν ἀπ᾽
77 ἐκείνου γεγονέναι τὸν τόπον ἀσφαλῆ. πολὺ δὴ
μᾶλλον ἔγωγε ὑμῖν συμβουλεύω τὸν θεὸν τοῦτον
ἐξιλάσασθαι καὶ βωμὸν ἱδρύσασθαι τὸν αὐτόν,
μὰ Δί᾽ οὐχ ὑπὲρ τῶν ἵππων, ἀλλ᾽ ὑπὲρ ὑμῶν αὐτῶν,
ὅπως μὴ ταράττησθε μηδὲ ἐκπίπτητε τῆς τάξεως.
μὴ γὰρ δαιμόνια πάντ᾽ ἢ[2] τὰ τοιαῦτα καὶ μείζονος
δεόμενα ἀποτροπῆς. φασὶν ἀρχαίαν βασιλίδα
ἐν Κρήτῃ τῶν Ἡλιαδῶν ἐρασθῆναι ταύρου, καὶ
συγγενομένην χαλεπόν τι καὶ μέγα τεκεῖν τέρας.

[1] After Μυρτίλος Crosby deletes as a gloss ὁ μὲν δεύτερος
ἀπὸ Διὸς γεγονώς, ὁ δὲ Ἑρμοῦ παῖς: "the second sprung from
Zeus, the other Hermes' son."
[2] πάντ᾽ ἢ Pflugk: πάντῃ.

---

[1] Myrtilus is famed as the charioteer of Oenomaüs, whom
he betrayed in his well-known race with Pelops.

THE THIRTY-SECOND DISCOURSE

Why are you so violently disturbed? What is the excitement? What the contest? For it is not Pelops who is driving, or Oenomaüs, or Myrtilus,[1] nor is it a question of a kingship or a wife or a death that hangs in the balance, nay, it is only a contest of slaves for a paltry bit of silver, slaves who sometimes are defeated and sometimes victorious, but slaves in any case." If the god should speak thus, what would your reply be? Or is it clear that you would not even listen at such a moment as that, not even if the grandsire[2] of Pelops were himself the speaker?

What succour, then, can one find, or what divine power must one propitiate? There is at Olympia, at the centre of the race-course, an altar to Poseidon Taraxippos, or Terror of Horses, on the spot where it happened that the horses most frequently became frightened and where many chariots were smashed.[3] So the Eleans decided to erect an altar on the spot, believing that some deity was there. And from that time forward, they say, the place has been safe. Well then, much more earnestly do I advise *you* to propitiate this god and raise an altar of the same kind, not, by Zeus, for the sake of the horses, but rather for the sake of yourselves, so that you may not be terrorized yourselves or be pitched headlong from your proper station. For perhaps all such disasters are the work of a deity, requiring unusual efforts to avert. It is said that an ancient Cretan queen, one of the daughters of Helius, became enamoured of a bull, and that after union with him she brought forth a savage, mighty monster.[4] So I myself am appre-

[2] Zeus.
[3] See Pausanias 6. 20. 15–19.
[4] The familiar tale of Pasiphaê and the Minotaur.

δέδοικα δὴ κἀγὼ τὸν ἱππικὸν τοῦτον ἔρωτα τῆς
πόλεως, μή τι δυσχερὲς ὑμῖν καὶ ξένον ἐνέγκῃ τῷ
78 χρόνῳ.¹ Ἀθήνησι δὲ αὐτὸ τοῦτο τὸ ζῷον ἀγαπη-
θῆναι τὸ καὶ παρ' ὑμῖν εὐδοκιμοῦν· καὶ νῦν
ἔστιν ἐν τῇ πόλει τόπος οὕτω καλούμενος Ἵππου
καὶ Κόρης ἄβατον. ὁ γὰρ πατὴρ συγκαθεῖρξε
τὴν παῖδα τῷ ἵππῳ, καί φασιν οὕτω διαφθαρῆ-
79 ναι τὴν κόρην. σκοπεῖτε δὲ μὴ καὶ ὑμεῖς ὑπὸ τῆς
τοιαύτης ἐπιθυμίας ἀπόλησθε.

Ποῖος γὰρ Ὅμηρος ἢ τίς ἀνθρώπων δύναται
τὰ συμβαίνοντα εἰπεῖν; οὐ γὰρ οὕτως ἐκεῖνός
φησι τὰ ἅρματα ταπεινὰ γίγνεσθαι μεταξὺ καὶ
σφόδρα ὑψηλὰ κατὰ τὸν δρόμον, ὡς τὰς ὑμετέρας
ψυχὰς ἰδεῖν ἔστι πασχούσας. φησὶ δ' οὕτως,
ἵν' ὑμῖν καὶ χαρίσωμαί τι μικρόν·

ἅρματα δ' ἄλλοτε μὲν χθονὶ πίλνατο πουλυ-
    βοτείρῃ,
ἄλλοτε δ' ἀΐξασκε μετήορα· τοὶ δ' ἐλατῆρες
ἕστασαν ἐν δίφροισι, πάτασσε ·δὲ θυμὸς ἑκάστου
νίκης ἱεμένων, κέκλοντο δὲ οἷσιν ἕκαστος
ἵπποις.

80 ἐνταῦθα τοὺς μὲν ἡνιόχους πεποίηκεν ἀγωνιστὰς
καὶ φιλοτιμουμένους, τοὺς δὲ θεατὰς καθ' ἡσυχίαν
θεωροῦντας, ὥσπερ καὶ προσῆκε. μόνον δ'

¹ After χρόνῳ Selden and editors delete as an interpolation
πάλιν δὲ ἑτέραν παρθένον ποταμοῦ τινος ἐρασθεῖσαν κ.τ.λ.: "And
again, that another virgin, having become enamoured of a
certain river, paid daily visits to the stream, and took the
foam in her arms and received the water in her bosom."

THE THIRTY-SECOND DISCOURSE

hensive lest this passion for horses that infects the
city may in time bring forth some strange and
distressing offspring for you. They say also that
at Athens this very species that you so much admire
became the object of infatuation, and today there is
in that city a site that bears the name, Sanctuary of
Horse and Maiden.[1] For the maiden's father confined his daughter along with the horse, and thus,
they say, she was ruined. And do you beware lest
you also through a passion like that be destroyed.

For what Homer or what mortal man at all
can describe the things that happen here ? For
example, in Homer's narrative the chariots do not
sink so low at times and then rise so high on the
course as your spirits may be seen to rise and fall.
And this is the way he puts it, if I may favour you
with a short passage :

> At times the cars clung close to bounteous earth,
> At times they bounded high ; the drivers still
> Stood firm, though hearts did pound as each man
>   strove
> To win the goal, and each called to his team.[2]

In this passage it is the charioteers who are represented as contestants and rivals, while the spectators
look on in silence,[3] as indeed was fitting. And only

---

[1] Pausanias does not mention this sanctuary. He does,
however, record that Poseidon and Athena share with
Demeter and her daughter a shrine on the road to Eleusis
(1. 37. 2); he also reports that Poseidon and Demeter once
held intercourse as horse and mare (8. 25. 5). Dio's allusion
may be the outgrowth of some such traditions.
[2] *Iliad* 23. 368–72. Taken from the account of the chariot
race at the funeral games held in honour of Patroclus.
[3] *Iliad* 23. 448.

ἐπὶ τῷ τέλει φησὶν Αἴαντα τὸν Λοκρὸν ὁρᾶν[1]
ἀπρεπέστερον καὶ λοιδορεῖσθαι Ἰδομενεῖ περὶ
τῶν ἵππων τῶν Εὐμήλου. οὗτος μέντοι ἐστὶν
ὁ περὶ τὴν Ἀθηνᾶν αὖθις ἀσεβήσας ἁλισκομένης
τῆς Τροίας, καὶ αὐτός τε[2] διὰ τοῦτο κεραυνωθεὶς
καὶ τοῦ χειμῶνος καὶ τῆς ναυαγίας τοῖς πᾶσιν
αἴτιος γενόμενος. ὁ γὰρ ἐν τοιούτοις θρασὺς καὶ
προπετὴς οὐδὲ τἆλλα εἶναι δύναται σώφρων,
ὥσπερ καὶ εἶπον ἤδη.

81 Τοῦτο μὲν οὖν τοιοῦτο παράδειγμα κακίας
καὶ ἀνοίας[3] ὁμοίως κἀκ τῶν τοιούτων ἀνθρώπων
οἵπερ[4] παρ᾽ ὑμῖν, πλὴν ὅτι μάχεσθαί γε οὐδεὶς
ἱκανός ἐστιν οὐδὲ ἀριστεύειν οὐδὲ αἱρεῖν πόλεις,
ὡς ἐκεῖνος. ὑμῶν δὲ οὐδεὶς ἐν τῇ θέᾳ καθέστη-
κεν, ἀλλὰ πολὺ μᾶλλον πέτεσθε τῶν ἵππων καὶ
τῶν ἡνιόχων, καὶ γελοίως ἐλαύνετε καὶ ἡνιοχεῖτε
καὶ διώκετε καὶ ἡγεῖσθε καὶ πίπτετε. τοιγαροῦν οὐ κακῶς τις παρεποίησε τῶν σαπρῶν
τούτων ποιητῶν·

82   ἅρματα δ᾽ ἄλλοτε μὲν χθονὶ πίλνατο πουλυ-
            βοτείρῃ,
        ἄλλοτε δ᾽ ἀΐξασκε μετήορα· τοὶ δὲ θεαταὶ
        θώκοις ἐν σφετέροις οὔθ᾽ ἔστασαν οὔτε κάθηντο,
        χλωροὶ ὑπαὶ δείους πεφοβημένοι, ἠδ᾽ ὑπὸ
            νείκης

---

[1] ὁρᾶν] ὀργᾶν Unger, ὁρμᾶν Geel, δρᾶν Cobet, βοᾶν, Post.
[2] αὐτός τε Emperius: αὐτὸς δὲ.
[3] ἀνοίας] ἀνὴρ εἰς Arnim.
[4] ὁμοίως κἀκ τῶν τοιούτων ἀνθρώπων οἵπερ Crosby, ὅμοιος ἐκ
τῶν τοιούτων ἄνθρωπος τοῖς Emperius, ὅμοιος ἐκ τῶν τοσούτων
ἀνθρώπων τοῖς Arnim, ὅμως δ᾽ οὐ τῶν τοιούτων ἀνθρώπων τοῖς
Casaubon, ὅμως οὐκ ἐκ τούτων ἀνθρώπων, οἷοι Selden: ὁμοίως
ἐκ τῶν τοιούτων ἀνθρώπων τοῖς.

at the end does the poet say that Ajax the Locrian behaved in rather unseemly fashion as a spectator by abusing Idomeneus with reference to the horses of Eumelus.[1] It was Ajax, moreover, who also was guilty of impiety toward Athena at the capture of Troy [2] and on that account was himself smitten with a thunderbolt and thereby caused the storm and shipwreck that befell them all.[3] For the man who in such matters as those is brazen and forward cannot act sanely in other matters, as I have said before.[4]

Here, then, you have an instance of wickedness and folly alike, and from men also such as are at Alexandria, except that in fighting, in deeds of valour, and in capturing cities no man here is the equal of Ajax. But among you not a man keeps his seat at the games; on the contrary you fly faster than the horses and their drivers, and it is comical to see the way you drive and play the charioteer, urging the horses on and taking the lead and—getting spilled.[5] And so it is no bad parody that has been composed by one of your feeble versifiers:

At times the cars clung close to bounteous earth,
At times they bounded high; but in their seats
The gaping crowd did neither stand nor sit,
Pallid with fear and fright, and in their zeal

---

[1] *Iliad* 23. 473–98.

[2] The allusion may be either to the seizure of Athena's image or—the later version—to the violation of Cassandra at Athena's altar.

[3] *Odyssey* 4. 499–510; *Aeneid* I. 39–45.

[4] § 73.

[5] Manifestly the sort of conduct on the part of the spectators that may be paralleled at football matches when the crowd unconsciously pushes in the effort to advance the ball.

ἀλλήλοισί τε κεκλόμενοι καὶ πᾶσι θεοῖσι
χεῖρας ἀνίσχοντες μεγάλ᾽ εὐχετόωντο ἕκαστοι.
ἠΰτε περ κλαγγὴ γεράνων πέλει ἠὲ κολοιῶν,
αἵτ᾽ ἐπεὶ οὖν ζῦθόν[1] τ᾽ ἔπιον καὶ ἀθέσφατον
οἶνον,
κλαγγῇ καί γε πέτονται ἐπὶ σταδίοιο κελεύθου.
οἱ δ᾽ ὥστε ψαρῶν νέφος ἔρχεται ἠὲ κολοιῶν

83   οὖλον κεκλήγοντες, ὅτε προΐδωσιν ἰόντα
ἵππον, ὃς ἀνθρώποισι φόνον φέρει ἠλιθίοισιν·
ὣς οἱ κεκλήγοντες ἐπ᾽ ἀλλήλοισιν ἔπιπτον.
ὡς δ᾽ ἄνεμος ἄχνας φορέει ἱερὰς κατ᾽ ἀλωάς,
ὡς δ᾽ ἀναμαιμάει βαθέ᾽ ἄγκεα θεσπιδαὲς πῦρ,
πάντῃ δ᾽ εἰλυφόων ἄνεμος φέρει, οἱ δέ τε θάμνοι
πρόρριζοι πίπτουσιν ἐπειγόμενοι πυρὸς ὁρμῇ·
ὣς οἱ μὲν μάρναντο πυρὸς δέμας· οὐδέ κε φαίης
οὔτε ποτ᾽ ἠέλιον σόον ἔμμεναι οὔτε σελήνην.

84   οἵηπερ φύλλων γενεή, τοίη δὲ καὶ ἀνδρῶν,
ἀνδρῶν κουφονόων, φιλαοιδοτάτων, ἀγερώχων,
ἠχὴ δ᾽ ἀμφοτέρων ἵκετ᾽ αἰθέρα καὶ Διὸς αὐλάς.[2]
ὧδε δέ τις εἴπεσκεν ἰδὼν ἐς πλησίον ἄλλον·
οἰνοβαρές, κυνὸς ὄμματ᾽ ἔχων, κραδίην δ᾽
ἐλάφοιο,
τί πτώσσεις; τί δ᾽ ὀπιπεύεις κατὰ ἄρμ᾽ ἐν
ἀγῶνι;
εἰ δ᾽ ἄγε νυν πείρησαι, ἵνα κναφθεὶς[3] ἀποτίνῃς.[4]
τὸν δ᾽ αὖθ᾽ Ἱπποκόων ἀπαμειβόμενος προσέ-
ειπε·
τέττα, σιωπῇ ἦσο, ἐμῷ δ᾽ ἐπιπείθεο μύθῳ·
ἠπεδανὸς δέ νύ τοι θεράπων, βραδέες δέ τοι
ἵπποι.

---

[1] ζῦθόν Morel : ζοῖθόν.
[2] αὐλάς Reiske : αὐγάς.

THE THIRTY-SECOND DISCOURSE

To win they shouted each to each, and, hands
Upraised, they vowed great offerings to all the gods.
Just as the scream of cranes or cry of daws
Doth rise, when they have drunk of beer and
    wine
O'ermuch, and clamourous they fly to reach
The course; as daws or starlings in a cloud
With baleful screaming swoop, when they behold
A horse onrushing, bearing death to fools;
So these with yells upon each other fell.
Just as the wind o'er sacred floor doth bear
The chaff, as flaming fire doth sweep deep glens,
Whirled by the wind now here now there, and
    'neath
Its onslaught thickets shrivel, root and branch;
So these did strive like fire; nor couldst thou say
That either sun or moon was safe from them.
Just like the growth of leaves, so that of men,
Shallow of mind, devoted to song, and proud,
And from both sides the noise pierced heaven's
    vault,
The courts of Zeus. And thus one turned and
    spake
Unto his neighbour: " Heavy with wine art thou;
Thou hast the eyes of a dog, the heart of a hind.
Why dost thou quake and stare at a car in the
    race?
Just try me, then, if thou wouldst mangled lie."
Hippocoön to him made this reply:
" Kind sir, in silence sit and heed my word:
A weak thing is thy driver, slow thy team."

---

85 τὸν δ' ἄρ' ὑπὸ ζυγόφιν προσέφη πόδας αἰόλος
    ἵππος·
οὐχ ὁράᾳς οἷος κἀγὼ καλός τε μέγας τε;
ἀλλ' ἔπι τοι κἀμοὶ θάνατος καὶ μοῖρα κραταιή.
αἳ γάρ πως ὑμᾶς γε καὶ αὐτοὺς ἐνθάδε πάντας
ὁπλήεντας ἔθηκε θεὰ λευκώλενος Ἥρη,
ὡς μή μοι τρύζητε καθήμενοι ἄλλοθεν ἄλλος.
ὣς ἔφαθ'. οἱ δ' εὔχοντο Διὶ Κρονίωνι ἄνακτι.

86 Ταῦτα μὲν ὑμῖν ἀπὸ πολλῶν καὶ φαύλων ὀλίγα,
ὅπως μὴ μόνοι δοκῆτε εἶναι γελοῖοι. καὶ μὴν
αἰσχρόν ἐστιν, ἄνδρες Ἀλεξανδρεῖς, τοὺς πυνθανο-
μένους περὶ τῆς πόλεως τὰ μὲν ἄλλ' ἀκούειν
θαυμαστὰ οἷα, περὶ δὲ ὑμῶν αὐτῶν μηδὲν σεμνὸν
λέγεσθαι μηδ' ἄξιον ζήλου, τοὐναντίον δὲ ὡς
φαύλους τοὺς ἀνθρώπους διαβεβλῆσθαι, μίμους
καὶ γελωτοποιοὺς μᾶλλον, οὐκ ἄνδρας ἐρρωμένους,
ὡς τῶν κωμικῶν ἔφη τις ἐπὶ τοῖς τοιούτοις·

    ἀκόλαστος ὄχλος ναυτική τ' ἀταξία.

87 ἔστι γὰρ ὅμοιον ὥσπερ εἰ οἰκίαν μέν τις ἴδοι πάνυ
καλήν, τὸν δὲ δεσπότην αὐτὸν ἀνδράποδον μηδὲ
θυρωρεῖν ἄξιον. τῷ παντὶ γὰρ κρεῖττον ἐρημίαν
καθορᾶν ἢ [1] δεκαπέντε ἀνθρώπους εὐπόρους καὶ [1]
πλῆθος ἀνήριθμον ἀνθρώπων ἀθλίων καὶ μαινομένων,

---

[1] ἢ and καὶ Wilamowitz: καὶ and ἢ.

---

[1] This ' parody ' is a cento in the making of which the author
—doubtless Dio himself—has levied upon virtually the whole
of the *Iliad*. It contains scarcely a phrase that may not be
traced to that poem, but the combination is intentionally
ludicrous.

[2] Euripides, *Hecuba* 607. Spoken by Hecuba with reference to the Greek forces. Either Dio's memory failed him

THE THIRTY-SECOND DISCOURSE

To him then spake the charger fleet from 'neath
The yoke: " See'st not how fine a steed am I,
How handsome and stalwart? Still for even me
Doth wait grim death and stubborn-hearted fate.
I would that you yourselves had all received
From white-armed Hera just such hooves as mine ;
No more would you sit and murmur each to
     each."
He spake. But they made vows to Zeus the
     King.[1]

There you have just a few out of many sorry
verses, to prove that you are not the only ones to
seem ridiculous. And certainly it is disgraceful,
men of Alexandria, that those who inquire about your
city are told how wonderful everything else is here,
but that with respect to yourselves nothing is mentioned of which to be proud or fit to emulate, but that,
on the contrary, you are given a bad name as being
worthless fellows, mere mimes and buffoons instead of
men of real valour, as one of the comic poets said of
people like yourselves,

An unbridled mob, a disorderly gang of tars.[2]

In fact it is just as if you should see a house that is
very beautiful, but should discover that the master
himself is a slave and not fit to be even the porter.
For on the whole it is better to face empty benches [3]
than to behold no more than fifteen substantial
citizens in the midst of an innumerable horde of
wretched, raving creatures, a sort of concentrated

or some comic poet did use the line, wilfully substituting
ἀταξία for ἀναρχία. Arnim would save Dio's reputation by
deleting the quotation.
[3] Perhaps ἐρημίαν means wilderness.

ὥσπερ τινὰ κόπρον βαθεῖαν ἐν ταὐτῷ νενημένην
ἐκ παντοδαπῶν λυμάτων. οὐδὲ γὰρ πόλιν εἴποι
τις ἂν [1] ὀρθῶς τὴν ἐκ τοιούτων, οὐδέ γε χορὸν
τοὺς ὁποίους δήποτε συνελθόντας, οὐδὲ στρατό-
πεδον πάντα ὄχλον.

88 Οὐδὲ γὰρ τὸ τοῦ Ξέρξου στράτευμα λαμπρὸν
ἦν, πλὴν εἰ μή τι διορύττειν ἢ διασκάπτειν ἢ
τοιοῦτον ἕτερον ἔργον πράττειν· οὐδὲ ἡ τῶν
Τρώων πόλις εὐδαίμων, ὅτι πονηρῶν καὶ ἀκολάστων
ὑπῆρξε πολιτῶν. καίτοι μεγάλη τε καὶ ἔνδοξος
ἦν· ἀλλ᾽ ὅμως ὁ τῆς Ἰθάκης πολίτης ἐπόρθησεν
αὐτήν, ὁ τῆς μικρᾶς καὶ ἀδόξου σφόδρα οὖσαν
εὐρύχωρον. φοβοῦμαι δὴ μὴ καὶ ὑμεῖς ἀπόλησθε
ἐκείνοις παραπλησίως, εἰ καὶ ψυχρότερόν ἐστιν
εἰπεῖν ὅτι κἀκείνην ὑπὸ ἵππου τινὸς φθαρῆναι
λέγεται· πλὴν οἱ μὲν ἴσως ὑφ᾽ ἑνός, ὑμεῖς δὲ
89 ὑπὸ πλειόνων ἑαλώκατε. μὴ γὰρ τοῦτο μόνον
ἡγεῖσθε ἅλωσιν εἶναι πόλεως, ἄν τινες τὸ τεῖχος
καταβαλόντες ἀποσφάττωσι τοὺς ἀνθρώπους καὶ
τὰς γυναῖκας ἀπάγωσιν καὶ τὰς οἰκίας κατακάωσιν.
αὕτη μὲν ἴσως τελευταία καὶ πρὸς ὀλίγον γιγνο-
μένη καὶ μᾶλλον ἐλεεῖσθαι τοὺς παθόντας ἢ
καταγελᾶσθαι παρασκευάζουσα· παρ᾽ οἷς δ᾽
ἂν ᾖ πάντων ἀμέλεια τῶν καλῶν, ἑνὸς δὲ πράγματος ἀγεννοῦς ἔρως, καὶ πρὸς μόνον τοῦτο ἀπο-
βλέπωσι καὶ περὶ τοῦτο διατρίβωσιν ἀεὶ [2] πηδῶντες καὶ μαινόμενοι καὶ παίοντες ἀλλήλους καὶ
ἀπόρρητα λέγοντες καὶ τοὺς θεοὺς αὐτοὺς πολλάκις

---

[1] ἂν added by Pflugk.
[2] διατρίβωσιν ἀεὶ Reiske: διατρίβωσιν ἢ M, διατρίβουσιν ἢ
UB.

dunghill piled high with the sweepings of every kind. Why, the word ' city ' could not justly be applied to a community composed of men like that,[1] any more than ' chorus ' befits a chance company of nondescripts or ' army ' just any mob!

For example, even the host of Xerxes was not brilliant, except at breaching a wall or digging a canal or some other manual labour[2]; nor was the city of the Trojans fortunate, since it consisted of depraved, licentious citizens. And yet it was both large and famous; but still the man from Ithaca[3] sacked it, yes, the man from that tiny, inglorious island sacked a city of exceeding wide domain. Therefore I fear that you also may perish like those Trojans—if I may be permitted the trite observation that Troy also is said to have been destroyed by a certain horse; however, while the Trojans perhaps were taken captive by a single horse, your capture is the work of many horses. For you must not think that the taking of a city consists alone in levelling its ramparts, slaughtering its men, leading its women into captivity, and burning its dwellings; nay, those happenings may mark the final stage, a stage of short duration and one that makes the victims more deserving of pity than of ridicule; but in the case of people who disregard all that is noble and are passionately enamoured of one thing that is ignoble, who centre their attention upon that alone and spend their time on that, constantly leaping and raving and beating one another and using abominable language and often reviling even the

---

[1] Dio gives a definition of ' city ' in Or. 36. 20.
[2] Cf. Herodotus 7. 22–24.
[3] Odysseus.

λοιδοροῦντες καὶ τὰ ὄντα ῥιπτοῦντες καὶ γυμνοὶ
βαδίζοντες ἀπὸ τῆς θέας ἐνίοτε, τοῦτ' ἔστιν
αἰσχρὰ πόλεως καὶ ἐπονείδιστος ἅλωσις.

90 Καὶ γὰρ ἀνθρώπους ἑαλωκέναι φαμὲν οὐχ
ὑπὸ λῃστῶν μόνον ἢ ἑτέρων,[1] ἀλλὰ καὶ ἑταίρας καὶ
γαστρὸς καὶ ἄλλης τινὸς φαύλης ἐπιθυμίας. αἰχμά-
λωτος οὖν γενέσθαι καλῶς ἂν λέγοιτο καὶ ἀνὴρ καὶ
πόλις, ἥτις ἂν τῶν κρειττόνων ἐπιτηδευμάτων
ἀφεμένη καὶ μήτε ὁρῶσα μηδὲν μήτε ἀκούουσα
τῶν φερόντων εἰς σωτηρίαν, ἀλλ' αἱρεθεῖσα ὑπὸ
μέθης ἢ ᾠδῆς γυναικῶν ἢ ἁρμάτων ἄγηται καὶ
φέρηται καὶ πᾶσα δι' ὅλης θορυβῆται περὶ τοῦτο
καὶ ἐκφρονῇ·[2] καὶ νὴ Δία ἑαλωκέναι λέγοιτ' ἂν καὶ
κατὰ κράτος ὃς οὕτως[3] ἑάλωκεν,[4] καὶ περιηγκωνί-
σθαι. οὐ γὰρ ἂν μὲν τὸ σῶμά τινος κρατῆται
καὶ περιέχηται δεσμοῖς τισιν ἢ φρουροῖς, τὰ δυσχερῆ δεῖ ταῦτα νομίζειν αἰχμαλωσίαν καὶ δουλείαν καὶ ἀπαγωγήν,[5] τῆς δὲ ψυχῆς ἠνδραποδισμέ-
νης καὶ ἀπολωλυίας εἰρωνεύεσθαι καὶ ὑποτιμᾶσθαι.

91 Καίτοι δεινὰ μέν που καὶ ἐφ' ἑκάστων[6] τὰ
τοιαῦτα, τῷ παντὶ δὲ αἰσχίω δημοσίᾳ φαινόμενα.
καὶ γὰρ αἱ λοιπαὶ νόσοι μέχρι μὲν τῶν καθ'
ἕνα εἰσὶν οὐ μεγάλης οὐδὲ φοβερᾶς προσηγορίας
τυγχάνουσιν· ὅταν δὲ κοινὸν γένηται τὸ πρᾶγμα,

---

[1] ἢ ἑτέρων U, ἢ ἑταίρων TM, ἢ ἑταιρῶν B; deleted by Reiske.
[2] ἐκφρονῇ Emperius: ἐκφρονεῖ or ἐκφρονῇ.
[3] ὃς οὕτως Emperius: ὡς οὔθ'.
[4] ἑάλωκεν Geel: ἑαλωκέναι.
[5] ἀπαγωγὴν Emperius: ἀπάτην.
[6] ἑκάστων Emperius: ἑκάστῳ.

gods themselves and flinging away their own belongings [1] and sometimes departing naked from the show—that is a disgraceful, an ignominious capture for a city.

For I assert that men have been taken captive, not by pirates only or other persons, but also by a courtesan or gluttony or by any other low desire. The term ' captive,' then, may well be used, not only of a person, but of a city too, provided that city, abandoning the nobler pursuits and having neither eyes nor ears for anything conducive to salvation, but yielding instead to the clutches of drink or singing girls or racing chariots, is made the prize of conquest and thrown into utter confusion thereby and bereft of its senses. Yes, by Zeus, the man who has experienced such a capture might well be said to have been taken by storm and manacled to boot. For if when a man's body has been overpowered and confined by chains or guards, we consider that these disagreeable happenings constitute captivity and slavery and violent seizure, when the soul has been taken captive and ruined, we should not dissimulate or underrate it. [2]

And yet, while such experiences are doubtless terrible even in the case of individuals, they are altogether more disgraceful when they happen to a people. For indeed all other afflictions, as long as they affect a single person, receive no great or awful label; but when the visitation becomes

[1] Dio seems to be referring to such exuberance of conduct as the tossing away of hats and caps at a modern football match.

[2] The contrast between soul and body bears general resemblance to that which pervades the attitude of Socrates at his trial. See, for example, Plato, *Apology* 28 b.

τότε λοιμὸς καλεῖται. καθόλου γὰρ πάντα ἁμαρτήματα εὕροι[1] τις ἂν πανταχοῦ, καὶ οἰνόφλυγες καὶ πόρνοι καὶ γυναιμανεῖς ἐν πάσαις εἰσὶ ταῖς πόλεσιν· ἀλλ' οὐδὲ[2] τοῦτο χαλεπὸν οὐδὲ ὑπερβάλλον· ὅταν δὲ ἐπικρατῇ τὸ πάθος καὶ βλέπηται κοινόν, τότε ἐπίσημον καὶ μέγα καὶ δημοσίᾳ γίγνεται.

92 Ποία γὰρ πόλις ἐστὶ τῶν μὴ σφόδρα ἐρήμων καὶ μικρῶν, ἐν ᾗ μὴ καθ' ἡμέραν τις πυρέττει πάντως; ἀλλὰ Καυνίους μόνον οὐ[3] παρείληφε κἀκείνων κοινόν[4] ἐστι τὸ ὄνειδος, ὅτι πάντες αὐτὸ πάσχουσιν· ὥσπερ καὶ ἀπὸ τῶν βελτιόνων τινὲς ἐθαυμάσθησαν καὶ δόξαν ἔσχον. πόσους γὰρ οἴεσθε Ἀθηναίων ἢ Μεγαρέων ἢ Κορινθίων τὰ σώματα ἀσκεῖν καὶ ζῆν φιλοπόνως; πολλοὺς δῆλον ὅτι, καὶ ταῦθ' ὅτ' ἀναγκαῖον ἦν αὐτοῖς ἄνδρας ἀγαθοὺς ὑπὲρ τῶν πατρίδων γίγνεσθαι.

93 τί οὖν μόνοι[5] Λακεδαιμόνιοι τοῦτ' ἔσχον τὸ ὄνομα καὶ τῆς δόξης ἀπολαύουσιν ἔτι καὶ νῦν; ὅτι κοινῇ[6] ἐκτήσαντο τὴν φιλοτιμίαν. τοὺς δὲ Ἀθηναίους τὰ περὶ τοὺς λόγους μᾶλλον ἐπιτηδεύοντας καὶ ποίησιν καὶ χοροὺς ἐπὶ τούτοις αὖ τοῦτ'[7] ἐποίησε θαυμάζεσθαι διὰ τὴν αὐτὴν αἰτίαν. σκοπεῖτε δὲ μὴ ὑμεῖς οὐχ ὁμοίας μεταλάβητε δόξης τοῖς Ἀθηναίοις καὶ Λακεδαιμονίοις, ἀλλὰ μᾶλλον ἑτέροις τισίν· οὐ βούλομαι γὰρ ὀνομάσαι.

---

[1] εὕροι Reiske: εἴποι.
[2] οὐδὲ Emperius: οὐδὲν.
[3] οὐ added by Crosby.
[4] κοινόν added by Weil.
[5] μόνοι Reiske: μόνον.
[6] κοινῇ Casaubon, κοινὴν Post: καὶ ὦν,
[7] αὖ τοῦτ' Emperius: αὐτούς.

general, then it is called a plague. For, on the whole, all varieties of human weakness might be discovered anywhere at all, and drunkards, perverts, and woman-crazed wretches are present in every city; and yet not even that condition is disturbing or beyond endurance; but when the malady becomes prevalent and a common spectacle, then it becomes noteworthy and serious and a civic issue.

For example, what city is there, unless it be one very sparsely populated and small, in which day by day there is not at least one person ill with fever? However, fever has all but taken possession of the Caunians, and in their case it is a reproach to the community, because they all suffer from it [1]; just as also certain peoples have won admiration and esteem for traits that are better. For instance, how many Athenians or Megarians or Corinthians, do you suppose, used to cultivate their bodies and live laborious lives? Many, obviously, and especially in the days when they had to be valiant in defence of their countries. Why is it, then, that the Spartans alone among them got a name for that and have enjoyed the reputation ever since? It is because as a people they acquired the love of honour. And as to the Athenians, because they were more devoted to the cultivation of the arts of speech and poetry and choral song and dance, that devotion, for the same reason, caused them in their turn to be admired in these fields. But take care lest the reputation that *you* gain resemble, not that of the Athenians and the Spartans, but rather that of certain others—for I do

---

[1] Caunus was a Carian city near the coast and in the neighbourhood of swampy land. Strabo (14. 2. 3) bears eloquent testimony to the truth of Dio's words.

ὅπερ γὰρ ἤδη πολλάκις εἶπον, αἰσχίω τὰ αἰσχρὰ
καὶ καταγέλαστα μᾶλλον, ὅταν ᾖ περὶ τὰς πόλεις.
94 ὥσπερ ἐν ταῖς κωμῳδίαις καὶ διασκευαῖς Καρίωνα
μὲν εἰσάγοντες μεθύοντα καὶ Δᾶον οὐ σφόδρα
κινοῦσι γέλωτα, τὸν δὲ Ἡρακλέα τοιοῦτον
ὁρῶσι γελοῖον δοκεῖ, παραφερόμενον, καὶ καθάπερ
εἰώθασιν, ἐν κροκωτῷ, παραπλησίως καὶ δῆμος
οὕτως μέγας[1] μινυρίζων διὰ βίου καὶ πάλιν
ἡνιοχῶν χωρὶς ἵππων αἰσχρὸν γίγνεται καὶ κατα-
γέλαστον. αὐτὸ γὰρ τοῦτο Εὐριπίδης τὸν
Ἡρακλέα φησὶ παθεῖν μαινόμενον·

> ἐκ τοῦδε[2] βαίνων ἅρματ' οὐκ ἔχων ἔχειν
> ἔφασκε, δίφρου δ' εἰσέβαινεν ἄντυγας
> κἄθεινε[3] κέντρον δῆθεν ὡς ἔχων χερί.

95 μὴ οὖν καὶ ὑμεῖς[4] κατὰ ζῆλον τὸν ἐπ' Ἀλεξάνδρῳ·
καὶ γὰρ αὐτὸς ἔλεγε Διὸς υἱὸς εἶναι. μᾶλλον δ'
ἴσως οὐχ Ἡρακλεῖ προσέοικεν ὑμῶν ὁ δῆμος,
ἀλλὰ Κενταύρῳ τινὶ ἢ Κύκλωπι πεπωκότι[5]
καὶ ἐρῶντι, τὸ μὲν σῶμα ἰσχυρῷ καὶ μεγάλῳ,
τὴν δὲ διάνοιαν ἀμαθεῖ.

---

[1] μέγας Selden : μέγα.
[2] ἐκ τοῦδε Euripides : αὐτοῦ δὲ.
[3] κἄθεινε Euripides : καὶ ἔτεινε.
[4] ὑμεῖς Casaubon : ὑμᾶς.
[5] πεπωκότι Reiske : πεπτωκότι.

---

[1] See especially § 91.
[2] 'Revues' is an attempt to harmonize διασκευαῖς with
the context. The word commonly means 'revisions' of
scholarly nature. Suidas, *s.v.* Timotheus, lists eight *diaskeuai*
among the works of that well known poet, but we do not know
their nature. The term is not recognized as a label for a
particular dramatic genre.

not care to name them. For, as I have often said,[1] shameful conduct is more shameful and ridiculous when it involves whole cities. Just as in the case of comedies and revues [2] when the poets bring upon the scene a drunken Carion or a Davus,[3] they do not arouse much laughter, yet the sight of a Heracles in that condition does seem comical,[4] a Heracles who staggers and, as usually portrayed, is clad in woman-ish saffron; in much the same way also, if a populace of such size as yours warbles all through life or, it may be, plays charioteer without the horses,[5] it becomes a disgrace and a laughing stock. Indeed this is precisely what Euripides says befell Heracles in his madness:

> Then striding to a car he thought was there,
> He stepped within its rails and dealt a blow,
> As if he held the goad within his hand.[6]

Maybe, then, like so many others, you are only following the example set by Alexander, for he, like Heracles, claimed to be a son of Zeus.[7] Nay rather, it may be that it is not Heracles whom your populace resembles, but some Centaur or Cyclops in his cups and amorous, in body strong and huge but mentally a fool.

[3] Slave names familiar in comedy, symbolizing slaves as a class.

[4] Heracles plays a comic rôle in comedy (e.g., Aristophanes, *Wasps* 60, *Peace* 741) and also in satyr-drama and tragedy (e.g., Euripides, *Alcestis* 747–66) as glutton and heavy drinker. His womanish masquerade at the court of Omphalê, to which Dio alludes, also lent itself to travesty.

[5] Cf. § 81.

[6] Euripides, *Heracles* 947–9. Dio's reading differs slightly from the text of Euripides.

[7] Cf. Or. 1. 7 and 4. 19.

DIO CHRYSOSTOM

Πρὸς τοῦ Διὸς οὐχ ὁρᾶτε ὅσην ὁ αὐτοκράτωρ
ὑμῶν πεποίηται τῆς πόλεως ἐπιμέλειαν; οὐκοῦν
χρὴ καὶ ὑμᾶς ἀντιφιλοτιμεῖσθαι καὶ τὴν πατρίδα
κρείττω ποιεῖν, μὰ Δί' οὐ κρήναις οὐδὲ προπυλαί-
οις· εἰς[1] ταῦτα μὲν γὰρ οὐ δύνασθε ὑμεῖς ἀναλίσκειν, οὐδ' ἂν ὑπερβάλοισθέ ποτε, οἶμαι, τὴν
ἐκείνου μεγαλοψυχίαν· ἀλλ' εὐταξίᾳ, κόσμῳ,
τῷ δεικνύειν ὑμᾶς αὐτοὺς σώφρονας καὶ βεβαίους.
οὕτως γὰρ ἂν οὔτ' ἐπὶ τοῖς γεγονόσι μετανοήσειε[2]
καὶ πλείονα ὑμᾶς ἀγαθὰ ἐργάσεται. καὶ ἴσως
ἂν αὐτῷ καὶ τῆς ἐνθάδε ἀφίξεως παράσχοιτε
96 πόθον. οὐ γὰρ οὕτως τὸ κάλλος τῶν οἰκοδομημάτων προσάγειν αὐτὸν δύναται· πάντα γὰρ
κρείττω καὶ πολυτελέστερα ἔχει τῶν ὅπου
δήποτε·[3] ἀλλ' ὅταν ἀκούσῃ τοὺς ὑποδεξομέ-
νους αὐτὸν εὐνοίας καὶ πίστεως ἀξίους καὶ τῶν
πεμπομένων ἕκαστος καὶ διοικούντων ὑμᾶς προτιμήσῃ.[4] μὴ γὰρ οἴεσθε ὑμᾶς μὲν πυνθάνεσθαι
περὶ τῶν καταπλεόντων, ὁποῖοί τινες τυγχάνουσιν
ὄντες, καὶ τοιαύτην ἔχειν γνώμην εὐθὺς πρὸς
αὐτοὺς οἵας[5] ἂν μετάσχητε τῆς φήμης, ἐκείνους
δὲ περὶ ὑμῶν μὴ πολυπραγμονεῖν, ὁποῖος ὁ τῶν
Ἀλεξανδρέων δῆμος. οὐκοῦν ἂν ἀκούσωσιν ὅτι
φρόνιμος, ἀλλ' οὐχ οἷα τὰ νῦν λεγόμενα, ὡς ἐπτοη-
μένος, ὡς εὐχερής, τὰ μικρὰ θαυμάζων, ἥττων[6]

---

[1] εἰς added by Casaubon.
[2] μετανοήσειε Pflugk: μετανοήσει.
[3] ὅπου δήποτε Dindorf: ὁποιδήποτε.
[4] προτιμήσῃ Emperius: προτιμήσει.
[5] οἵας Emperius: ἧς B, οἷς UM.
[6] ἥττων Reiske: ἢ τῶν.

THE THIRTY-SECOND DISCOURSE

In heaven's name, do you not see how great is the consideration that your emperor has displayed toward your city?[1] Well then, you also must match the zeal he shows and make your country better, not, by Zeus, through constructing fountains or stately portals—for you have not the wealth to squander on things like that, nor could you ever, methinks, surpass the emperor's magnificence [2]—but rather by means of good behaviour, by decorum, by showing yourselves to be sane and steady. For in that case not only would he not regret his generosity because of what has happened,[3] but he might even confer on you still further benefactions. And perhaps you might even make him long to visit you. For it is not so much the beauty of your buildings that might attract him, for he has buildings of every kind finer and more costly than anywhere; but he may be attracted when he hears that the people to receive him are worthy of his favour and his trust, and when each of his emissaries and ministers speaks highly of you. For you must not imagine, that, although you yourselves inquire about those who enter your harbour, what kind of people they may chance to be, and your judgement concerning them at once corresponds to their reputation, yet the emperor's agents are not curious to learn what kind of people the Alexandrians are. Therefore, if they hear that you are sensible, and not, as is now the common report, flighty, easy-going, inclined to admire petty things,

[1] Arnim, *Dio von Prusa*, p. 426, refers this to some recent gift from Trajan to be employed on public works. The next sentence ·ends plausibility to this interpretation.

[2] For Trajan's activity in public works at Rome, see *Cambridge Ancient History* 11. 205–7.

[3] Doubtless the riot referred to in §§ 71 and 72.

τοῦ τυχόντος,[1] ἐραστὴς ἡνιόχων καὶ κιθαρῳδῶν,
οὐκ ἄδηλον ὅπως ἕξουσιν.

97   Θεόφιλόν φασι παρ' ὑμῖν γενόμενον ἄνδρα σο-
φὸν σιωπᾶν πρὸς ὑμᾶς καὶ μηδὲν ἐθέλειν διαλέγεσθαι. καίτοι τίνα γνώμην νομίζετε αὐτὸν
ἔχειν; πότερον ὡς σοφοὺς ὑμᾶς καὶ μὴ δεομένους θεραπείας; ἢ μᾶλλον ὡς ἀνιάτων ἀπεγνω-
κέναι; παραπλήσιον γάρ, ὥσπερ εἴ τις τῶν
ἐμπόρων πολλὰ καὶ τίμια ἔχων καταπλεύσειεν εἰς
πόλιν, ἔπειθ' ὑπ' ἀνέμων τινῶν ἢ τύχης ἄλλης
κρατούμενος καὶ διατρίβων ἐκεῖ χρόνον συχνὸν
μήτε προθείη τῶν ὠνίων μηδὲν μήτε δείξειε
μηδέποτε· δῆλον γὰρ ὡς ἐσχάτην τινὰ αὐτῶν
πενίαν κατεγνωκὼς ἢ ἀπειρίαν οὐκ ἂν θέλοι μάτην
ἐνοχλεῖσθαι, σαφῶς εἰδὼς ὅτι οὔτ' ἂν ὠνήσαιτο
τῶν ἀνθρώπων τούτων οὐθεὶς οὔτ' ἂν ἴσως
προσέλθοι.[2] καὶ Θεόφιλος τοίνυν πολλὰ ἔχων καὶ
μεγάλα ἔνδον ὤνια κατεῖχε[3] παρ' αὑτῷ ταῦτα,
συνειδὼς ὑμῖν τὴν ἐσχάτην ἀπορίαν, οὐ χρημάτων,
ἀλλὰ νοῦ καὶ συνέσεως. τοιγαροῦν τέθνηκε κατα-
σιωπήσας ὑμῶν τὴν πόλιν,[4] καὶ ὑμεῖς τοῦ δεῖνος
μὲν πολλάκις ἀκηκόατε καὶ διαμέμνησθε τῶν
σκωμμάτων αὐτοῦ καὶ τῶν τοῦ δεῖνος ᾀσμάτων,
Θεοφίλου δὲ οὐκ οἶδα εἴ ποτε ἠκούσατε· ὥσπερ
ἔφη τις τοὺς ἐν τῇ Ἀττικῇ κανθάρους, τοῦ
καθαρωτάτου μέλιτος ὄντος, τοῦ μὲν μηδέποτε γεύσασθαι, μηδ' ἂν ἐκχέηται, τῆς δὲ ἑτέρας
τροφῆς.

---

[1] πραγμάτων after τυχόντος deleted by Arnim.
[2] προσέλθοι Hemsterhuis: προέλθοι.
[3] κατεῖχε added by Reiske.
[4] τοῦτ' ἔστι καταδικάσας αὐτήν after πόλιν deleted by Reiske.

with a weakness for trivialities, passionately devoted to jockeys and harpists, there is no doubt how they will feel.

Theophilus,[1] they say, who proved himself a man of wisdom here in Alexandria, preserved silence toward you and would hold no converse with you. And yet what do you think was his purpose? Was it because he thought you to be wise yourselves and in no need of treatment: or rather had he despaired of you as being incurable? For it is very much as if a trader with many precious wares should land at a city, and then, constrained by certain winds or by some mischance, should spend a long time there without either setting out any of his wares or displaying them at all; for evidently it would be because he was convinced either that the inhabitants were in extreme poverty, or else that they were ignorant, and so he would be unwilling to go to useless trouble, feeling certain that no one of the inhabitants would either make a purchase or, perhaps, come to see him. Theophilus too, we conclude, though he had many notable wares inside of him, kept them to himself, being aware that you were extremely poor, not in money, but in judgement and understanding. Well, then, he is dead, having by his silence passed adverse judgement on your city, and, though you have often heard so-and-so speak and can well recall his jokes, and also the songs of what's-his-name, I am not sure that you have ever heard Theophilus; just as someone has said of the beetles in Attica, that, though Attica has the purest honey, the beetles never taste of it, not even if it is poured out for them, but only of the other kind of food.[2]

[1] Unknown. [2] I.e., dung; cf. Aristophanes, *Pax*, 1–18.

99   'Αλλ' ἐστὲ ἱλαροὶ καὶ σκῶψαι πάντων δεινότατοι.
οὐ δήμου τὸ ἐπιτήδευμα· πόθεν; οὐδὲ πόλεως,
ἀλλὰ Θερσίτου τινός· αὐτὸν γοῦν ἐκεῖνον εἴρηκεν
Ὅμηρος ἐν τοῖς πᾶσιν Ἕλλησιν ἀφικέσθαι
γελωτοποιόν, οὐ κατὰ κόσμον λέγοντα,[1]

> ἀλλ' ὅ τί οἱ εἴσαιτο γελοῖον Ἀργείοισιν
> ἔμμεναι.

ἀλλ' οὐ τὸ γελοῖον ἀγαθόν ἐστιν οὐδὲ τίμιον, ἀλλὰ
τὸ χαίρειν· ἀπορίᾳ δὲ καὶ ἀγνοίᾳ χαρᾶς[2] ἄνθρωποι
διώκουσι[3] γέλωτα. τὴν γοῦν βοτάνην ἀκηκόατε
τὴν σαρδόνιον καλουμένην, ἣ γέλωτα μὲν ποιεῖ,
100 χαλεπὸν δὲ τοῦτον καὶ ἐπ' ὀλέθρῳ. μὴ οὖν
σφόδρα οὕτως περιέχεσθε τούτου, μηδὲ ἀμούσους
καὶ φορτικὰς καὶ ἀμαθεῖς ποιεῖτε τὰς Χάριτας,
ἀλλὰ μᾶλλον Εὐριπίδην μιμεῖσθε οὕτω λέγοντα·

> μὴ παυσαίμην τὰς Χάριτας
> Μούσαις ἀναμιγνύς, ἁδίσταν συζυγίαν,

ἵνα μὴ τὸ Μουσεῖον ὑμῖν ἄλλως εἶναι δοκῇ τόπος
ἐν τῇ πόλει, καθάπερ, οἶμαι, καὶ ἄλλοι τόποι
μάτην προσαγορεύονται, τὸ πρᾶγμα μὴ ἔχοντες
μετὰ τοῦ ὀνόματος.
101   Ἀλλὰ γὰρ δέδοικα μὴ κἀμοὶ συμβέβηκεν ὃ
φασιν Αἰγυπτίων τινὶ τῶν σφόδρα ἀρχαίων μουσι-

---

[1] οὐ κατὰ κόσμον λέγοντα added by Arnim out of Homer.
[2] χαρᾶς Pflugk: καὶ χαρᾷ.   [3] διώκουσι Reiske: διοικοῦσι.

---

[1] Iliad 2. 214–6.
[2] The 'sardonic grin' of pain. Cf. Odyssey 20. 302 and
Virgil, Eclogues 7. 41. Pausanias 10. 17. 13 gives a typical
explanation in harmony with Dio. Popular etymology seems
to have transformed Homer's σαρδάνιον into σαρδόνιον, thus
placing the plant in Sardinia.

But, someone will say, you are a jolly folk and the best jesters in the world. That is no calling for a people—how could it be?—nor for a city, but rather for a Thersites. At least Homer says that Thersites himself came among all the Greeks as a jester, not speaking with decorum,

> But what he thought would make the Argives laugh.[1]

Yet not what makes men laugh is good or honourable, but rather what makes them joyful; and for lack of joy and for ignorance thereof men seek laughter. You must have heard of the plant called Sardonian, which produces laughter, to be sure, but a laughter which is distressing and disastrous.[2] Therefore be not so devoted to that laughter, nor cause the Graces to be unmusical and vulgar and boorish, but rather imitate Euripides in these lines of his:

> May I ne'er cease to join in one
> The Muses and the Graces;
> Such union is surpassing sweet,[3]

and thus will your Mouseion[4] be regarded, not just as a place in the city, as indeed, I fancy, there are other places with labels devoid of meaning, not possessing a character to match the name.

But enough of this, for I fear that I too have had the experience that they say befell a certain Egyptian, a musician of the very early school. For

---

[3] Euripides, *Heracles* 673-5. Dio's reading differs slightly from the text of the poet.

[4] The famous Alexandrian centre for intellectual interests of all sorts. Dio, of course, like a good Greek, is toying with etymology.

κῷ. ἐκείνῳ γὰρ τὸ δαιμόνιόν ποτε προειπεῖν καθ᾽ ὕπνον ὡς εἰς ὄνου ὦτα ᾄσεται. καὶ δὴ τὸν μὲν ἄλλον [1] χρόνον οὐ προσεῖχεν οὐδὲ ἐφρόντιζε τοῦ ὀνείρατος, ὡς οὐδενὸς ὄντος. ἐπεὶ δὲ ὁ τύραννος τῶν Σύρων ἧκεν εἰς Μέμφιν, ἐκπληττομένων αὐτὸν τῶν Αἰγυπτίων ἐκάλεσεν. ἐπεδείκνυτο οὖν πάσῃ προθυμίᾳ καὶ τἀκριβέστερα τῆς τέχνης· ὁ δέ, οὐ γὰρ ἦν οἱ σύνεσις μουσικῆς, ἐκέλευε παύσασθαι αὐτὸν ἀτιμάσας. ὁ δὲ ἀναμνησθεὶς ἐκείνου τοῦ ὀνείρατος, Τοῦτ᾽ ἦν ἄρα, ἔφη, τὸ εἰς ὄνου ὦτα ᾄδειν. ὁ δὲ τύραννος ἀκούσας τῶν ἑρμηνέων οἷα ἔλεγεν ἔδει καὶ ἐμαστίγου τὸν ἄνδρα, καὶ τοῦτο [2] πολέμου λέγουσιν αἴτιον γενέσθαι.

---

[1] μὲν ἄλλον Reiske : μέλλοντα.
[2] τοῦτο Reiske : τοῦ.

the story goes that the deity once told that musician in a dream that he was destined to sing into an ass's ears. And for a while he paid no heed and gave no thought to the dream, as being a matter of no consequence. But when the tyrant of Syria came to Memphis, since the Egyptians admired the artist greatly, he summoned him. So the musician gave a performance with all zest and displayed the more intricate phases of his art; but the tyrant—for he had no appreciation of music—bade him cease and treated him with disdain. And the musician, recalling that forgotten dream, exclaimed, "So that was the meaning of the saying, 'to sing into an ass's ears'". And the tyrant, having heard from his interpreters what the musician had said, bound and flogged the man, and this incident, they say, was the occasion of a war.[1]

[1] This story may have been of Dio's own manufacture, since it occurs nowhere else and resembles other tales of his that are thought to be apocryphal. Both the period and the people alike are unknown.

THE THIRTY-THIRD, OR FIRST
TARSIC, DISCOURSE

In this Discourse Dio appears to be addressing a public gathering of the people of Tarsus upon invitation. Like the comic poets to whom he refers, he treats his audience to λοιδορία, inveighing against their wantonness and moral decay. Fully half of what he has to say is concerned with what he calls ῥέγκειν. Though his treatment of that topic is manifestly humorous, it is designed to make palatable the serious charges that he desires to make.

The word ῥέγκειν is said to mean now 'snort,' now 'snore.' For lack of an English word of like flexibility, the translator has elected to use consistently that one of the two conventional meanings that seemed the better adapted to the majority of occurrences. 'Snort,' however, is doubtless inadequate as an interpretation of Dio's meaning. He himself appears to be perplexed as to the proper label for the sound to which he has applied the term (55). He does give some clues. It is a sound made by some persons when asleep (33), by small boys, and by some mature men of good standing (33–34). It might be taken to denote the presence of a brothel (36). It is made by persons of uncertain sex (36). It is more suitable for the elderly (45). It is produced by the nose (50). It is a symptom of bad morals (50–51). It is not clucking or smacking of the lips or whistling, nor is it employed by shepherds, plowmen, huntsmen, or sailors (55). It is a sound peculiar to neither man nor woman, not even to a harlot, but rather to a male of the most debased sort (60). If, then, Dio himself, in spite of elaborate efforts to define the sound, has found no better term to symbolize his meaning, perhaps indulgence may be shown the translator.

To the modern reader Tarsus inevitably suggests the name of Paul. The picture of that ancient city, half Greek and half oriental, to be found in this Discourse and in the one to follow, awakens the keener interest for that reason. Sir William Ramsay holds that the Athenodorus of whom we hear exerted an influence upon the thought of Paul. Arnim assigns the present Discourse to Dio's latest period.

33. ΤΑΡΣΙΚΟΣ ΠΡΩΤΟΣ

1 Ἐγὼ θαυμάζω τί ποτ᾽ ἐστὶ τὸ ὑμέτερον καὶ τί προσδοκῶντες ἢ βουλόμενοι τοὺς τοιούτους ἀνθρώπους διαλέγεσθαι ὑμῖν ζητεῖτε, πότερον εὐφώνους οἴεσθε εἶναι καὶ φθέγγεσθαι ἥδιον τῶν ἄλλων, ἔπειτα ὥσπερ ὀρνέων ποθεῖτε ἀκούειν μελῳδούντων ὑμῖν, ἢ δύναμιν ἄλλην ἔχειν ἔν τε ὀνόμασι καὶ διανοήμασι δριμυτέρας τινὸς πειθοῦς καὶ τῷ ὄντι δεινῆς, ἣν καλεῖτε ῥητορικήν, ἔν τε ἀγοραῖς καὶ περὶ τὸ βῆμα δυναστεύουσαν, ἤ τινα ἔπαινον καθ᾽ αὑτῶν ἀκούσεσθαι οἰόμενοι καὶ δημόσιον ὕμνον τῆς πόλεως, περί τε Περσέως καὶ Ἡρακλέους καὶ τοῦ τῆς τριαίνης[1] καὶ περὶ χρησμῶν τῶν γενομένων, καὶ ὥς ἐστε Ἕλληνες καὶ Ἀργεῖοι καὶ ἔτι βελτίους καὶ ἀρχηγοὺς ἔχετε ἥρωας καὶ ἡμιθέους, μᾶλλον δὲ Τιτᾶνας· 2 ἔτι δέ, οἶμαι, περί τε τῆς χώρας καὶ τῶν ὀρῶν τῶν κατ᾽ αὐτὴν καὶ τοῦδε τοῦ Κύδνου, ὡς δεξιώτατος[2] ἁπάντων ποταμῶν καὶ κάλλιστος, οἵ τε ἀπ᾽ αὐτοῦ πίνοντες ἀφνειοὶ καὶ μακάριοι καθ᾽

---

[1] τοῦ τῆς τριαίνης Capps, τοῦ Ἀπόλλωνος τῆς τε τριαίνης Valesius: τοῦ Ἀπόλλωνος τῆς τριαίνης.

[2] δεξιώτατος] λειότατος Naber.

---

[1] Tarsus, as a semi-oriental city, may well have been touchy regarding its claim to Hellenic origin. There does not seem to have been agreement as to the founder. Dio himself is not consistent on that topic: here he speaks of

274

THE THIRTY-THIRD, OR FIRST
TARSIC, DISCOURSE

I wonder what on earth is your purpose, and what your expectation or desire, in seeking to have such persons as myself discourse for you. Do you think us to be sweet-voiced and more pleasant of utterance than the rest, so that, as if we were song-birds, you long to hear us make melody for you; or do you believe that we possess a different power in word and thought alike, a power of persuasion that is keener and truly formidable, which you call rhetoric, a power that holds sway both in the forum and on the rostrum; or is it because you expect to hear some laudation directed at yourselves, some patriotic hymn in praise of your city, all about Perseus and Heracles and the Lord of the Trident and the oracles that you have received, and how you are Hellenes, yes, Argives or even better, and how you have as founders heroes and demigods—or, I should say, Titans? [1] You may even, methinks, expect to hear a eulogy of your land and of the mountains it contains and of yonder Cydnus, how it is the most kindly of all rivers and the most beautiful and how those who drink its waters are 'affluent and blessed,' to use the words

[1] ' founders ' but in section 47 he calls Heracles ' the founder.' Other deities especially honoured by the Tarsians were Perseus, Apollo, and Athenê. According to Strabo (14. 5. 12) the city was founded by Triptolemus and a band of Argives. To this list of possible founders Capps by his plausible emendation adds Poseidon. See critical note.

Ὅμηρον. ταῦτα γὰρ ἐστὶ μὲν ἀληθῆ, καὶ συνεχῶς αὐτὰ ἀκούετε τῶν τε ποιητῶν ἐν μέτροις καὶ ἄλλων ἀνδρῶν αὐτὸ τοῦτο ἔργον πεποιημένων ἐγκωμιάζειν, δεῖται δὲ μεγάλης τινὸς παρασκευῆς 3 καὶ δυνάμεως. τί οὖν ἡμᾶς ἐλπίζετε ἐρεῖν; ἢ τί μάλιστα ἀκοῦσαι σπεύδετε παρὰ ἀνδρῶν οὐκ εὐτραπέλων οὐδὲ πρὸς χάριν ὁμιλεῖν εἰδότων οὐδὲ αἱμύλων οὐδὲ ὑπὸ τρυφῆς ἰόντων ἐπὶ τοὺς λόγους; ὅτι μὲν γὰρ οὐ χρήματα ἐλπίζοντες παρ' ἡμῶν[1] οὐδὲ ἄλλο τι δῶρον καὶ πάνυ ἐπίσταμαι.

Φέρε οὖν ἔγωγε εἴπω τὴν ἐμαυτοῦ ὑπόνοιαν. 4 δοκεῖτέ μοι πολλάκις ἀκηκοέναι θείων ἀνθρώπων, οἳ πάντα εἰδέναι φασὶ καὶ περὶ πάντων ἐρεῖν ᾗ διατέτακται καὶ τίνα ἔχει φύσιν, περί τε ἀνθρώπων καὶ δαιμονίων[2] καὶ περὶ θεῶν, ἔτι δὲ γῆς καὶ οὐρανοῦ καὶ θαλάττης, καὶ περὶ ἡλίου καὶ σελήνης καὶ τῶν ἄλλων ἄστρων, καὶ περὶ τοῦ σύμπαντος κόσμου, καὶ περὶ φθορᾶς καὶ γενέσεως καὶ μυρίων ἄλλων. ἔπειτ', οἶμαι, προσελθόντες ὑμῶν πυνθάνονται τί βούλεσθε αὐτοὺς εἰπεῖν καὶ περὶ τίνος, κατὰ τὸν Πίνδαρον,

Ἰσμηνὸν ἢ χρυσηλάκατον Μελίαν ἢ Κάδμον·

ὅ τι δ' ἂν ἀξιώσητε ὑμεῖς, ἔνθεν ἑλὼν[3] ἄθρουν καὶ

---

[1] ἡμῶν T: ὑμῶν UBM.
[2] δαιμονίων] δαιμόνων Emperius.
[3] ἑλὼν Reiske: ἐλθών.

---

[1] Iliad 2. 525 : ἀφνειοί, πίνοντες ὕδωρ μέλαν Αἰσήποιο.
[2] Aristotle has left us a work entitled περὶ γενέσεως καὶ φθορᾶς. Plato too dealt with this topic. Cf. Phaedo, 95 E.
[3] Lucian, Demosthenis Encomium 19, quotes the entire sentence, which contains a remarkable list of alternatives proposed by the poet. See Sandys, Odes of Pindar (L.C.L.), p. 512.

of Homer.[1] For such praise is true indeed and you are constantly hearing it both from the poets in their verse and from other men also who have made it their business to pronounce encomia; but that sort of performance requires ample preparation and the gift of eloquence. What, then, do you expect *us* to say? Or what above all are you eager to hear from men who are not of nimble wit and know not how to make gratification the aim of their discourse, who are not flatterers nor moved by insolence to mount the platform? For that you are not expecting money from us nor any other contribution, I am well aware.

Well then, let me state my own suspicions. You seem to me to have listened frequently to marvellous men, who claim to know all things, and regarding all things to be able to tell how they have been appointed and what their nature is, their repertoire including, not only human beings and demigods, but gods, yes, and even the earth, the sky, the sea, the sun and moon and other stars—in fact the entire universe— and also the processes of corruption and generation [2] and ten thousand other things. And then, methinks, they come to you and ask you what you want them to say and upon what topic—as Pindar puts it,

Ismenus or Melia of the golden distaff or noble
    Cadmus; [3]

and whatsoever you may deem suitable, the speaker starts from there [4] and pours forth a steady and copious

---

[4] Reiske's attractive emendation, ἔνθεν ἑλὼν, is seemingly an epic phrase—cf. *Odyssey* 8. 500—employed with humorous intent.

πολὺν ἀφήσει τὸν λόγον, ὥσπερ τι ῥεῦμα ἄφθονον
5 ἐν αὐτῷ κατακεκλειμένον. ἔπειθ᾽ ὑμεῖς ἀκούοντες
τὸ μὲν ἐξετάζειν καθ᾽ ἕκαστον ἢ ἀπιστεῖν ἀνδρὶ
σοφῷ φαῦλον ἡγεῖσθε καὶ ἄκαιρον, ἄλλως δὲ
τῇ ῥώμῃ καὶ τῇ ταχυτῆτι τῶν λόγων ἐπαίρεσθε
καὶ πάνυ χαίρετε ἀπνευστὶ ξυνείροντος [1] τοσοῦτον
ὄχλον ῥημάτων, καὶ πεπόνθατε ὅμοιον τοῖς
ὁρῶσι τοὺς ἵππους τοὺς ἀπὸ ῥυτῆρος θέοντας·
οὐδὲν ὠφελούμενοι θαυμάζετε [2] ὅμως καὶ μακάριόν
φατε κτῆμα. καίτοι [3] τοῖς ἵπποις ἰδεῖν ἔστιν
οὐ τοὺς δεσπότας χρωμένους πολλάκις, ἀλλὰ
φαῦλον ἀνδράποδον.

6 Ἡ μὲν οὖν τοιάδε ἀκρόασις θεωρία τις οὖσα
καὶ πομπὴ παραπλήσιον ἔχει τι ταῖς ἐπιδείξεσι
τῶν καλουμένων ἰατρῶν,[4] οἳ προκαθίζοντες ἐν τῷ
μέσῳ ξυμβολὰς ἄρθρων καὶ ὀστέων συνθέσεις καὶ
παραθέσεις καὶ τοιαῦθ᾽ ἕτερα ἐπεξίασι, πόρους
καὶ πνεύματα καὶ διηθήσεις. οἱ δὲ πολλοὶ
κεχήνασι καὶ κεκήληνται τῶν παιδίων μᾶλλον.
ὁ δ᾽ ἀληθὴς ἰατρὸς οὐκ ἔστι τοιοῦτος οὐδὲ οὕτως
διαλέγεται τοῖς ὄντως δεομένοις· πόθεν; ἀλλὰ
προσέταξε τί δεῖ ποιεῖν, καὶ φαγεῖν βουλόμενον ἢ
πιεῖν ἐκώλυσε, καὶ λαβὼν ἔτεμεν ἀφεστηκός τι
7 τοῦ σώματος. ὥσπερ οὖν εἰ συνελθόντες οἱ κάμνον-
τες εἶτ᾽ ἐπὶ τὸν ἰατρὸν ἐπεκώμαζον καὶ κωθω-

---

[1] ξυνείροντος Casaubon: ξυνείροντες.
[2] After θαυμάζετε Schwartz deletes δὲ.
[3] καίτοι Reiske, καίτοι καὶ Wilamawitz: καὶ.
[4] ἰατρῶν] ἰατροσοφιστῶν or λογιάτρων Arnim.

---

[1] Strabo (14. 5. 13) stresses the enthusiasm for education
displayed by Tarsus in his day. He ranks it above Athens

flood of speech, like some abundant river that has been dammed up within him. Then, as you listen, the thought of testing his several statements or of distrusting such a learned man seems to you to be shabby treatment and inopportune, nay, you are heedlessly elated by the power and the speed of his delivery and are very happy, as, without a pause for breath, he strings together such a multitude of phrases, and you are affected very much as are those who gaze at horses running at a gallop—though not at all benefited by the experience, still you are full of admiration and exclaim, "What a marvellous thing to own!" And yet in the case of the horses it is frequently not the owners who may be seen handling the reins, but rather some worthless slave.

Well then, the sort of recitation of which I speak, being a kind of spectacle or parade, has some resemblance to the exhibitions of the so-called physicians, who seat themselves conspicuously before us and give a detailed account of the union of joints, the combination and juxtaposition of bones, and other topics of that sort, such as pores and respirations and excretions. And the crowd is all agape with admiration and more enchanted than a swarm of children.[1] But the genuine physician is not like that, nor does he discourse in that fashion for the benefit of those who actually need medical attention—of course not—but instead he prescribes what should be done, and if a man wants to eat or drink, he stops him, or he takes his scalpel and lances some abscess of the body. Just as, therefore, in case the sick were to assemble and then proceed to serenade the physician and call

and Alexandria in that regard, but adds that Tarsus did not attract foreign scholars as they did.

νίζεσθαι ἠξίουν, οὐκ ἂν αὐτοῖς κατ᾽ ἐλπίδα τὸ
πρᾶγμα ἀπήντησεν, ἀλλ᾽ ἴσως ἠγανάκτουν πρὸς
τὴν ὑποδοχήν, τοῦτο[1] μοι πεπονθέναι δοκοῦσιν οἱ
πολλοὶ ξυνιόντες ἐπὶ τὸν τοιοῦτον καὶ λέγειν
κελεύοντες, ἄγευστοι δῆλον ὅτι τῶν τῆς ἀληθείας
ὄντες λόγων, ἔπειθ᾽ ἡδύ τι καὶ προσηνὲς ἀκούσεσθαι προσδοκῶντες.

Φέρε δὴ πρὸς τῶν θεῶν, ἆρα ἀνέξεσθε, εἰ[2] μὴ
πάνυ τις τῇ παρρησίᾳ χρῷτο μηδὲ ἐπὶ πάντα
ἔρχοιτο τὰ προσόντα ὑμῖν, ἀλλ᾽ ἕν εἴποι τι μόνον
8 ἢ δεύτερον; σκοπεῖτε δὴ μὴ ταὐτὸ πάσχητε[3]
Ἰλιεῦσιν ἐκείνοις, οἳ τραγῳδόν τινα ἐπιδημή-
σαντα ἠνώχλουν, ἐπιδείξασθαι κελεύοντες· ὁ δὲ
ἐᾶν αὐτοὺς ἠξίου καὶ τὴν ἡσυχίαν ἄγειν. ὅσῳ
γὰρ ἄν, ἔφη, κρεῖττον ἀγωνίσωμαι, τοσούτῳ
φανήσεσθε ὑμεῖς ἀτυχέστεροι. τὸν οὖν φιλόσοφον
κρεῖττόν ἐστι τοῖς πολλοῖς σιωπῶντα ἐᾶν.

9 Σκοπεῖτε δὲ τὸ πρᾶγμα οἷόν ἐστιν. Ἀθηναῖοι γὰρ εἰωθότες ἀκούειν κακῶς, καὶ νὴ Δία
ἐπ᾽ αὐτὸ τοῦτο συνιόντες εἰς τὸ θέατρον ὡς
λοιδορηθησόμενοι, καὶ προτεθεικότες ἀγῶνα καὶ
νίκην τοῖς ἄμεινον αὐτὸ πράττουσιν, οὐκ αὐτοὶ
τοῦτο εὑρόντες, ἀλλὰ τοῦ θεοῦ συμβουλεύσαντος,
Ἀριστοφάνους μὲν ἤκουον καὶ Κρατίνου καὶ
Πλάτωνος, καὶ τούτους οὐδὲν κακὸν ἐποίησαν.
ἐπεὶ δὲ Σωκράτης ἄνευ σκηνῆς καὶ ἰκρίων ἐποίει

---

[1] τοῦτό] ταὐτό Emperius.   [2] εἰ Emperius : ἦν.
[3] πάσχητε Emperius : πάσχοιτε.

---

[1] Apparently he would have acted the Fall of Troy.
[2] Presumably the god Dionysus. We have no record that
he gave such advice, but Dio might well assume it, since
the drama was an element in his worship.

for a drinking-bout, the outcome would not meet their expectation, nay, they might well be annoyed at their reception, such it seems to me, is the situation of the masses when they gather before a man like me and bid him make a speech, obviously never having sampled the words of truth and consequently expecting to hear something sweet and pleasant.

Come then, tell me, in heaven's name, will you be indulgent toward a speaker, provided he is not wholly outspoken and does not touch upon all the ailments that afflict you, but rather confines himself to just one item or maybe two? Take care, I warn you, lest you meet with the same experience as those people of Ilium, who, when a certain tragic actor paid them a visit, annoyed him by demanding an exhibition of his skill, until he finally bade them to let him alone and keep quiet. " For," said he, " the better my performance, so much the more hapless will you appear." [1] So, then, with the philosopher, it is better for the masses to let him hold his tongue.

But consider what the situation is. The Athenians, for example, being accustomed to hearing themselves abused, and, on my word, frequenting the theatre for the express purpose of hearing themselves abused, and, having established a contest with a prize for the most proficient in that sort of thing—not having hit upon the idea by themselves but acting upon the advice of the god [2]—used to listen to Aristophanes and Cratinus and Plato [3] and inflicted no punishment on them. But when Socrates without the protection of stage and benches undertook to carry out the

---

[3] The comic poet, not the philosopher—contemporary with Aristophanes and Cratinus.

τὸ τοῦ θεοῦ πρόσταγμα, οὐ κορδακίζων οὐδὲ
10 τερετίζων, οὐχ ὑπέμειναν. ἐκεῖνοι μὲν γὰρ ὑφορώμενοι καὶ δεδιότες τὸν δῆμον ὡς δεσπότην
ἐθώπευον, ἠρέμα δάκνοντες καὶ μετὰ γέλωτος,
ὥσπερ αἱ τίτθαι τοῖς παιδίοις, ὅταν δέῃ τι τῶν
ἀηδεστέρων πιεῖν, αὐταὶ[1] προσφέρουσι μέλιτι
χρίσασαι τὴν κύλικα. τοιγαροῦν ἔβλαπτον οὐχ
ἧττον ἤπερ ὠφέλουν, ἀγερωχίας καὶ σκωμμάτων
καὶ βωμολοχίας ἀναπιμπλάντες τὴν πόλιν. ὁ δὲ
φιλόσοφος ἤλεγχε καὶ ἐνουθέτει.

11   Καὶ μὴν ὅσῳ τὸ λοιδορεῖν καὶ τὴν ἀβελτερίαν
τὴν ἑκάστου καὶ τὴν πονηρίαν φανερὰν ποιεῖν
κρεῖττόν ἐστι τοῦ χαρίζεσθαι διὰ τῶν λόγων καὶ
τοῖς ἐγκωμίοις θρύπτειν τοὺς ἀκούοντας, οὐχ
ἥκιστα ἐκεῖθεν εἴσεσθε. δύο γὰρ ποιητῶν γεγονότων ἐξ ἅπαντος τοῦ αἰῶνος, οἷς οὐδένα τῶν
ἄλλων ξυμβάλλειν ἄξιον, Ὁμήρου τε καὶ Ἀρχιλό-
χου, τούτων Ὅμηρος μὲν σχεδὸν πάντα ἐνεκω-
μίασε, καὶ θηρία καὶ φυτὰ καὶ ὕδωρ καὶ γῆν καὶ
ὅπλα καὶ ἵππους, καὶ οὐδὲν ἔσθ' ὅτου μνησθεὶς
χωρὶς ἐπαίνου τε καὶ τιμῆς, ὡς ἂν εἴποι τις,
παρῆλθεν. ἕνα[2] γοῦν μόνον ἐξ ἁπάντων ἔβλασ-

---

[1] αὐταὶ Crosby, αὐτά Geel : αὗται.
[2] ἕνα Crosby, ὃν Reiske : ἐν or ἐν.

---

[1] Socrates interpreted the well-known oracle of Apollo as
equivalent to an order to devote his life to the examination
and correction of his fellow-citizens, a procedure which, as
Socrates himself perceived, they found most irritating. See,
for example, Plato, *Apology* 21 e–23 b.
[2] Whatever timidity Aristophanes displayed was of the
ironic sort.

instructions of his god,[1] indulging in no vulgar dances or idiotic piping, they would not endure it. Those comic poets, you see, being distrustful and timid,[2] flattered the assembled multitude as one flatters a master, tempering their mild snapping with a laugh, just as nurses, whenever it is necessary for their charges to drink something rather unpleasant, themselves smear the cup with honey before they hold it out to the children.[3] So it happens that the comic poets did no less harm than good, by infecting the city with effrontery and gibes and ribald jests. On the other hand, the philosopher censured and rebuked his auditors.

And, indeed, how much better it is to abuse people and to hold up to the light each man's stupidity and wickedness than to court favour by what is said and by compliments debauch one's auditors, you will discover best from what I am about to tell you. For while there have been since the world began two poets with whom no other poet deserves to be compared, namely, Homer and Archilochus,[4] one of them, Homer, praised practically everything—animals, plants, water, earth, armour, and horses; in fact it may be said that there is nothing which he failed to mention with praise and honour. At any rate, there is only one out of all the characters in his poems about whom he said harsh things, namely, Thersites, and

---

[3] Cf. Lucretius 1. 936–8 :

sed veluti pueris absinthia taetra medentes
cum dare conantur, prius oras pocula circum
contingunt mellis dulci flavoque liquore.

[4] Cf. Velleius 1. 5 : *neque quemquam alium cuius operis primus fuerit auctor, in eo perfectissimum praeter Homerum et Archilochum reperiemus.*

283

12 φήμησε Θερσίτην, καὶ τοῦτον λιγὺν εἶναί φησιν
ἀγορητήν. Ἀρχίλοχος δὲ ἐπὶ τὴν ἐναντίαν ἧκε,
τὸ[1] ψέγειν, ὁρῶν, οἶμαι, τούτου μᾶλλον δεομένους
τοὺς ἀνθρώπους, καὶ πρῶτον αὐτὸν ψέγει. τοιγαροῦν μόνος καὶ μετὰ τὴν τελευτὴν καὶ πρὶν ἢ
γενέσθαι τῆς μεγίστης ἔτυχε μαρτυρίας παρὰ τοῦ
δαιμονίου. τὸν μέν γε ἀποκτείναντα αὐτὸν ὁ
Ἀπόλλων ἐξελαύνων ἐκ τοῦ νεὼ Μουσῶν αὐτὸν
ἀνεῖπε θεράποντα ἀνῃρηκέναι. καὶ τὸ δεύτερον,
ὡς ἀπελογεῖτο ἐν πολέμῳ λέγων ἀποκτεῖναι,
πάλιν Μουσῶν θεράποντα ἔφη τὸν Ἀρχίλοχον.
τῷ πατρὶ δὲ αὐτοῦ χρωμένῳ πρὸ τῆς γενέσεως
ἀθάνατόν οἱ παῖδα γενήσεσθαι προεῖπεν.

13 Ὥσθ' ὁ λοιδορεῖν ἱκανὸς καὶ καθάπτεσθαι
καὶ φανερὰ τῷ λόγῳ ποιεῖν τὰ ἁμαρτήματα
δῆλον ὅτι κρείττων ἐστὶ καὶ προκέκριται τῶν
ἐπαινούντων. εἰ δ' ἄρα ὑμεῖς ἐπαινούμενοι
μᾶλλον ἤδεσθε, ἐπ' ἄλλους ὑμῖν ἰτέον. ὅταν οὖν
πρῶτον αὐτόν τινα ἴδητε κολακεύοντα ἐν ἅπασιν
οἷς ποιεῖ καὶ χαριζόμενον ἐν τροφαῖς, ἐν ἐσθῆσι,
καὶ περιόντα ἀκόλαστον, τοῦτον οἴεσθε κολακεύ-
σειν καὶ ὑμᾶς καὶ παρὰ τούτου προσδοκᾶτε
λόγον ἡδύν, ὃν ὑμεῖς ἔπαινον ὀνομάζετε, τρυφῶντα

14 δὴ παρὰ τρυφῶντος. ὅταν δὲ αὐχμηρόν τινα
καὶ συνεσταλμένον ἴδητε καὶ μόνον βαδίζοντα,
πρῶτον αὐτὸν ἐξετάζοντα καὶ λοιδοροῦντα, μὴ

[1] ἧκε, τὸ Selden : ἤκετο.

---

[1] Iliad 2. 246.
[2] Cf. Heraclides Ponticus (F.H.G. 2. 214): Ἀρχίλοχον τὸν
ποιητὴν Κόραξ ὄνομα ἔκτεινε, πρὸς ὃν φασιν εἰπεῖν τὴν Πυθίαν,
Ἔξιθι νηοῦ. τοῦτον δ' εἰπεῖν, Ἀλλὰ καθαρός εἰμι, ἄναξ· ἐν
χειρῶν γὰρ νόμῳ ἔκτεινα. Galen, Protrepticus 9, preserves a

even Thersites is called a ' clear-voiced speaker.' [1]
But Archilochus went to the other extreme, toward
censure—seeing, I imagine, that men have greater
need of that—and first of all he censures himself.
That is why he alone, not only after his death, but
before his birth, obtained the highest tribute from the
deity. Certainly Apollo drove his slayer from the
temple, declaring that he had slain a servant of the
Muses. And again, when the man stated in self-
defence that he had slain him in war, once more
Apollo called Archilochus a servant of the Muses.[2]
And when the father of Archilochus was consulting
the oracle prior to the birth of his son, Apollo pro-
phesied that he was destined to have a son who would
be immortal.

So, you see, he who is good at rebuking and up-
braiding, and at revealing by his words the sins of
men, is evidently superior and preferred above those
who praise. If, then, it is praise that gives you more
delight, you must betake yourselves to other men
than me. Therefore, whenever you see someone
flattering himself first and foremost in everything he
does, and courting favour by his table and his dress,
and moving about in licentious fashion, you may be
sure that man will flatter you as well, and you may
expect from him sweet words, which you call praise—
dainty language from a dainty man. But whenever
you see someone who is unkempt and wears his garments closely wrapped about him and has no companions on his walks, a man who makes himself the
first target for examination and reproof,[3] do not

fuller form of the Pythia's words : Μουσάων θεράποντα κατ-
έκτανες· ἔξιθι νηοῦ.
[3] A manifest description of the speaker.

ζητεῖτε παρὰ τοῦ τοιούτου μηδεμίαν θωπείαν
μηδὲ ἀπάτην, μηδὲ τὸν δεξιὸν ἐκεῖνον καὶ προσηνῆ
λόγον, ὃς δὴ μάλιστα διατρίβει περὶ δήμους καὶ
σατράπας καὶ τυράννους.

οὗτοι τοιοίδ᾽[1] εἰσὶν ὑποδρηστῆρες ἐκείνων,
ἀλλὰ νέοι, χλαίνας εὖ εἱμένοι ἠδὲ χιτῶνας,
αἰεὶ δὲ λιπαροὶ κεφαλὰς καὶ καλὰ πρόσωπα.

οἶδε μὲν γὰρ ὥσπερ ἐπίκωμοί τινες ἥκουσιν εἰς
τὸν βίον αὐλούμενοι καὶ ᾀδόμενοι καὶ μεθύοντες
εἰς ἑορτήν τινα καὶ πανήγυριν ἀσώτων εἰσβεβλη-
κέναι νομίζοντες.

15   Ἀλλ᾽ ὅστις[2] ἰδὼν ὅσα δεινὰ καὶ δυσχερῆ καὶ
ὅτι μεστὰ πάντα πολεμίων καὶ ἐχθρῶν, ὅπου
τρυφὴ καὶ ἀπάτη δυναστεύουσιν,

αὐτόν μιν πληγῇσιν ἀεικελίῃσι δαμάσσας,
σπεῖρα κάκ᾽ ἀμφ᾽ ὤμοισι βαλών, οἰκῆι ἐοικώς,
ἀνδρῶν θρυπτομένων κατέδυ πόλιν εὐρυ-
    άγυιαν·

ἐπ᾽ οὐδενὶ κακῷ τῶν πέλας, ὥσπερ Ὀδυσσεὺς ἐπὶ
κακῷ τῶν μνηστήρων ἧκε τοιοῦτος, ἀλλὰ τοὐναντίον ζητῶν ἂν ἄρα τι δύνηται λαθὼν ἀγαθὸν
ἐργάσασθαι· τί δὴ κινεῖτε τὸν τοιοῦτον ἢ τί προ-
καλεῖσθε δύσκολόν τινα καὶ ἄγριον ὑμῖν φανού-
μενον δημηγόρον; οὐ γὰρ ὑμῶν παρεσκεύασται
τὰ ὦτα δέξασθαι τραχεῖς τε καὶ στερεοὺς λόγους·

---

[1] οὗτοι τοιοίδ᾽ Homer: οὗτοι τοιοῦτοι.
[2] ἀλλ᾽ ὅστις Emperius: ἄλλος δέ τις.

---

[1] Odyssey 15. 330-2.

expect from such a man any flattery or deception, or that clever and seductive language which is most in use in dealing with democracies and satraps and dictators.

> Not so are they who wait upon such men,
> But rather youths with handsome cloaks and
> frocks,
> Whose locks are ever sleek, whose faces fair.[1]

Aye, for these men enter upon life as if they were going to some revel, piping and singing and drinking on the supposition that it is a kind of festival or conclave of wastrels into which they have burst.

But if a man, having seen how much there is that is dreadful and hateful in the world, and that everywhere are countless enemies, both public and private, with whom wantonness and deceit hold sway,

> Subdues his body with injurious blows,
> Casts round his shoulders sorry rags, in guise
> A slave, steals into the wide-wayed town of those
> Who hold debauch,[2]

meaning no harm to his neighbours—such as Odysseus meant to the suitors when he came in that guise—but on the contrary seeking if perchance he may unobtrusively do them some good—if, I say, such a man comes among you, why do you stir him up, or why do you call upon one who will appear to you to be a churlish and savage person as a speaker ? For your ears have not been prepared for the reception of

---

[2] *Odyssey* 4. 244-6. In Dio's text θρυπτομένων has displaced δυσμενέων of Homer. The words immediately following the quotation suggest that Dio was quoting from memory and thus confused the visit of Odysseus to Ilium, of which Homer was speaking, with his return to Ithaca.

ἀλλ' ὥσπερ ἀσθενεῖς ὁπλαὶ κτηνῶν τῶν ἐν
μαλακοῖς τε καὶ λείοις τραφέντων χωρίοις,
ὁμοίως ὦτα τρυφερὰ ἐν κολακείᾳ τραφέντα καὶ
λόγοις ψευδέσι.

16 Τί οὖν προθυμεῖσθε ἀκούειν ὧν οὐκ ἀνέξεσθε;
ἀλλὰ μὴν τοιοῦτον πεπόνθατε οἷον Αἴσωπος ἔφη
τοὺς ὀφθαλμοὺς παθεῖν, ἐπειδὴ ἑαυτοὺς[1] μὲν
ἐνόμιζον πλείστου εἶναι ἀξίους, τὸ στόμα δὲ
ἑώρων ἀπολαῦον τῶν τε ἄλλων καὶ δὴ τοῦ
μέλιτος ἡδίστου ὄντος. οὐκοῦν ἠγανάκτουν τε
καὶ ἐμέμφοντο τῷ ἀνθρώπῳ. ἐπεὶ δὲ αὐτοῖς
ἐνῆκε τοῦ[2] μέλιτος, οἱ δὲ ἐδάκνοντό τε[3] καὶ
ἐδάκρυον καὶ δριμὺ καὶ ἀηδὲς αὐτὸ ἡγοῦντο. μὴ
οὖν καὶ ὑμεῖς ἐπιζητεῖτε γεύσασθαι τῶν ἐκ
φιλοσοφίας λόγων, ὥσπερ ὀφθαλμοὶ μέλιτος·
ἔπειτα, οἶμαι, καὶ δακνόμενοι δυσχερανεῖτε καὶ
φήσετε ἴσως οὐδαμῶς φιλοσοφίαν εἶναι τὸ τοιοῦτον,
ἀλλὰ λοιδορίαν καὶ βλάβην.

17 Ἡγεῖσθε μὲν γάρ, ὦ ἄνδρες, εὐδαίμονας
ἑαυτοὺς καὶ μακαρίους, ἐπειδὴ πόλιν τε μεγάλην
οἰκεῖτε καὶ χώραν ἀγαθὴν νέμεσθε καὶ πλεῖστα
δὴ καὶ ἀφθονώτατα παρ' αὑτοῖς ὁρᾶτε τὰ ἐπιτήδεια,
καὶ ποταμὸς ὑμῖν οὗτος διὰ μέσης διαρρεῖ τῆς
πόλεως, πρὸς τούτοις δὲ μητρόπολις ἡ Ταρσὸς
τῶν κατὰ Κιλικίαν. ὁ δὲ Ἀρχίλοχος, ὅν φημι

---

[1] ἑαυτοὺς Casaubon : τούτους.
[2] ἐνῆκε τοῦ Reiske : ἐνήκετο τοῦ or ἐνίκετο τοῦ.
[3] ἐδάκνοντό τε Selden : ἐδάκνοντο (or δάκνοντο) τότε.

harsh and stubborn words; nay, as the hooves of cattle are tender when they are reared in soft, smooth country, so men's ears are dainty when reared in the midst of flattery and lying speech.

Why, then, are you eager to hear what you will not endure? Something must have happened to you like what Aesop says happened to the eyes. They believed themselves to be the most important organs of the body, and yet they observed that it was the mouth that got the benefit of most things and in particular of honey, the sweetest thing of all. So they were angry and even found fault with their owner. But when he placed in them some of the honey, they smarted and wept and thought it a stinging, unpleasant substance.[1] Therefore, do not you yourselves seek to taste the words that philosophy has to offer, as the eyes tasted honey; if you do, methinks, not only will you be vexed when they cause a smart, but perhaps you will even say that such a thing cannot possibly be philosophy, but rather abuse and mischief.

The fact is, my friends, that you consider yourselves fortunate and blessed because your home is in a great city and you occupy a fertile land, because you find the needs of life supplied for you in greatest abundance and profusion, because you have this river flowing through the heart of your city, and because, moreover, Tarsus is the capital of all the people of Cilicia.[2] But Archilochus, who, as I have

---

[1] This fable seems to be recorded by no one but Dio.

[2] Xenophon, *Anabasis* 1. 2. 22–3, bears witness to the natural advantages of Tarsus. When Cilicia became a Roman province, Tarsus was made its capital.

τῷ Ἀπόλλωνι ἀρέσαι, περὶ στρατηγοῦ λέγων
οὕτω φησίν·

οὐ φιλέω μέγαν στρατηγὸν οὐδὲ διαπεπλιγμένον [1]
οὐδὲ βοστρύχοισι γαῦρον οὐδ' ὑπεξυρημένον·

ἀλλά μοι, φησίν, εἴη ῥαιβός, ἀσφαλῶς βεβηκὼς
18 καὶ ἐπὶ κνήμαισιν δασύς. μὴ οὖν αὐτὸν οἴεσθε
στρατηγὸν μὲν μὴ ἀγαπᾶν οἷον εἴρηκε, μηδ' ἐν
σώματος μεγέθει καὶ κόμῃ τίθεσθαι τὸ τοῦ
στρατηγοῦ ὄφελος, πόλιν δ' ἂν ἐπαινέσαι ποτὲ
εἰς ταῦτα ὁρῶντα, ποταμοὺς καὶ βαλανεῖα καὶ
κρήνας καὶ στοὰς καὶ πλῆθος οἰκιῶν καὶ μέγε-
θος· κόμῃ γὰρ ἀτεχνῶς καὶ βοστρύχοις ταῦτα
ἔοικεν· ἀλλ' ἔμοιγε δοκεῖ μᾶλλον ἂν τούτων [2]
προκρῖναι σμικράν τε καὶ ὀλίγην σωφρόνως
οἰκουμένην κἂν ἐπὶ πέτρας.

19 Ἀλλὰ Ἀρχίλοχος μὲν οὕτως εἶπεν, Ὅμηρος
δὲ πῶς; οὐχ ὁ μὲν Ὀδυσσεὺς νησιώτης ἦν οὐδὲ
τῶν συμμέτρων νήσων· πόθεν; οὐδὲ τῶν
ἐγκάρπων, ἀλλ' ἦν [3] μόνον ἐπαινέσαι θέλων
αἰγίβοτον εἴρηκεν. ἀλλ' ὅμως φησὶ τῇ τούτου βουλῇ τε καὶ γνώμῃ καὶ τὴν Τροίαν αἱρεθῆναι,
τηλικαύτην πόλιν καὶ τοσούτων ἄρχουσαν,

ὅσσον Λέσβος ἄνω μακάρων ἕδος ἐντὸς ἐέργει
καὶ Φρυγίη καθύπερθε καὶ Ἑλλήσποντος ἀπείρων·

---

[1] διαπεπλιγμένον Hemsterhuis : διαπεπλεγμένον.
[2] ἂν τούτων Geel : ἐν τούτῳ.
[3] ἀλλ' ἦν Casaubon : ἀλλ' ἢ or ἀλλή.

---

[1] Dio's paraphrase of lines 3 and 4 of the Archilochus
fragment does not agree with the accepted text : ἀλλά μοι
σμικρός τις εἴη καὶ περὶ κνήμας ἰδεῖν ῥοικός, ἀσφαλῶς βεβηκὼς
ποσσί, καρδίης πλέως. See Edmonds, Elegy and Iambus,
L.C.L., vol. 2, p. 126.

said, found favour in the eyes of Apollo, in speaking of a general thus expresses his opinion:

> A general who is tall doth please me not,
> Who walks with legs apart, delights in curls,
> And shaves the hair that grows upon his calves.

'Nay,' says he, 'let me rather have one who is bandy-legged, stands firmly, and has hairy shins.'[1] Therefore you must not think that if Archilochus had no love for the sort of general he has described and did not gauge the value of a general by his height or hair, he would ever have praised a city because he found in it such things as rivers and baths and fountains and porticoes and a multitude of houses and a wide extent of space, for such things are simply like hair and ringlets on a man; to me at least it appears that in place of these things he would have preferred a city that is both small and weak, even if perched upon a rock, provided it is wisely managed.[2]

Well, there you have what Archilochus has to say, but how about Homer? Did not Odysseus come from an island, and not even from one of medium size—of course not—nor yet from a fertile one, but rather from one of which the poet could only say by way of praise that it 'pastured goats'?[3] But still Homer says that it was by that man's counsel and judgement that even Troy was taken, a city that was so great, and held sway over so many peoples,

> Seaward as far as Lesbos, the abode
> Of gods, and, landward, Phrygia and the stream
> Of boundless Hellespont;[4]

---

[2] This sentiment is contained in a couplet from Phocylides cited by Dio 36. 13.

[3] *Odyssey* 4. 606.   [4] *Iliad* 24. 544-5.

ἣν πάντας φησὶ μυθεῖσθαι πολύχρυσον, πολύχαλκον.
20 μή τι οὖν ὤνησεν αὐτοὺς ἢ τοῦ πλούτου τὸ μέγεθος
ἢ τῶν ὑπηκόων ἢ τῶν συμμάχων τὸ πλῆθος ἢ
τῶν πεδίων ἢ τῆς Ἴδης τὸ κάλλος ἢ τοῦ Σιμό-
εντος ἢ τοῦ Ξάνθου τοῦ δινήεντος,

ὃν ἀθάνατος τέκετο Ζεύς;

καίτοι φησὶ καὶ πηγάς τινας πάνυ καλὰς ἐν τῷ
προαστείῳ, τὴν μὲν ἀλεεινὴν[1] καὶ σφόδρα προση-
νοῦς ὕδατος, ὥστε καὶ καπνὸν ἀπ’ αὐτῆς ἐγεί-
ρεσθαι, τὴν δ’ ἐοικυῖαν τῇ ψυχρότητι κρυστάλλῳ
τοῦ θέρους, ὥστε καὶ θέρους καὶ χειμῶνος μὴ
δυσχερῶς πλύνειν τὰς καλὰς Τρώων θυγατέρας.
21 οὐ μόνον δὲ πλούτῳ καὶ χώρας ἀρετῇ καὶ πλήθει
διέφερον, ἀλλὰ καὶ ἄνθρωποι κάλλιστοι παρ’
αὐτοῖς ἐγίγνοντο, καὶ ἄνδρες καὶ γυναῖκες, καὶ
ἵπποι τάχιστοι, καὶ θεοφιλεῖς ἐδόκουν εἶναι,
καὶ τείχει καρτερωτάτῳ περιπεφραγμένοι ἦσαν.
τὸ μέν γε τεῖχος αὐτοῖς Ποσειδῶνος ἔργον ἦν
καὶ Ἀπόλλωνος. ὁ δὲ Ζεὺς τῶν ὑπὸ τὸν ἥλιον
πόλεων ἐκείνην ἔφη μάλιστα ἀγαπῆσαι. τάχος
δ’ ἵππων, ὥστε ἐπ’ ἄκρων θεῖν τῶν σταχύων.
ἐπὶ κάλλει δὲ Γανυμήδην ὁ Ζεὺς ἐποιήσατο
οἰνοχόον. Ἀλεξάνδρῳ δὲ ἐκ τῆς Ἑλλάδος ἐπη-
κολούθησεν ἡ ἀρίστη τῶν ἐκεῖθεν γυναικῶν.
τὴν δὲ Κασσάνδραν Ὅμηρος οὔ φησι λείπεσθαι
τῆς Ἀφροδίτης τὸ εἶδος.

---

[1] ἀλεεινὴν Geel: ἀνειμένην.

---

[1] *Iliad* 18. 288–9. [2] *Iliad* 14. 434.
[3] *Iliad* 22. 147–55. [4] *Iliad* 5. 263–73.
[5] *Iliad* 21. 441–9. Homer, however, states that Poseidon
alone built the wall, while Apollo was tending the herd of
Laomedon.

a city which he declares all men call ' rich-in-gold, rich-in-copper '.[1] Did Troy receive any benefit from either the magnitude of its wealth, or the number of its subjects or allies, or the beauty of its fields, or of Mt. Ida or Simoïs or ' eddying Xanthus ',

> whom Zeus the immortal created ? [2]

And yet the poet says that there were also certain springs of rare beauty in the suburbs, one that was warm and whose waters were most pleasant, such that steam actually rose from it, and the other as cold as ice, even in summer, so that both in summer and in winter the lovely daughters of the Trojans could do their washing without discomfort.[3] And not only were the Trojans distinguished for wealth and richness of soil and number of inhabitants, but also human beings born at Troy were very beautiful, both men and women, horses were very fleet,[4] the people were held to be dear to the gods, and they were fenced about with a circuit-wall most strong—in fact that wall of theirs was the work of Poseidon and Apollo.[5] Moreover, Zeus declared that of all the cities beneath the sun he loved that city most.[6] Such was the fleetness of their steeds that they could run upon the tips of the heads of grain,[7] such the beauty of Ganymede that he was made the cupbearer of Zeus[8]; and Alexander lured away from Greece the noblest woman of that land; as for Cassandra, Homer declares that she was not inferior to Aphroditê in beauty.[9]

[6] *Iliad* 4. 44–7.
[7] This striking phrase is not found in Homer.
[8] *Iliad* 20. 232–5.
[9] *Iliad* 24. 699.

22 Ἀλλ᾽ ὅμως, ἐπειδὴ τρυφὴ καὶ ὕβρις εἰσῆλθεν αὐτοὺς καὶ παιδείας καὶ σωφροσύνης οὐδὲν ᾤοντο δεῖσθαι, πολὺ πάντων ἀτυχέστατοι[1] γεγόνασιν. οὐχ ἡ σύμπασα χθὼν ταῖς συμφοραῖς αὐτῶν διατεθρύληται; καὶ οὐδὲν ὤνησεν αὐτοὺς οὔτε τῶν ἵππων τὸ τάχος οὔτε ὁ Ζεὺς οὔτε ὁ Γανυμήδης, ἀλλ᾽ ὑπ᾽ ἀνδρὸς ἐξ οὕτω λυπρᾶς[2] καὶ ἀδόξου πόλεως ἀπώλοντο, καὶ ἴσχυσεν ὁ τῆς Ἰθάκης πολίτης περιγενέσθαι τῶν ἐκ τοῦ Ἰλίου πάντων, καὶ τὴν εὐρυάγυιαν ἅπασαν πορθῆσαι καὶ ἀνελεῖν;

23 Οὐδὲ γὰρ οὐδ᾽ οἱ θεοὶ φιλοῦσιν ἔτι τοὺς ἀσελγεῖς καὶ ἄφρονας καὶ ἀκολάστους καὶ πρὸς ὕβριν ἐγκλίνοντας καὶ ῥαθυμίαν καὶ τρυφήν. ὥστε μὴ τούτοις θαρρεῖτε μηδὲ ἀποδέχεσθε τὸν συνηδόμενον ὑμῖν καὶ θαυμάζοντα λόγον μηδὲ τοὺς δεινοὺς ἐγκωμιάζειν· οὗτοι μὲν γὰρ ἐξαπατῶσιν ὑμᾶς καὶ μάτην ἐπαίρουσιν, ὥσπερ νηπίους παῖδας· ἀλλὰ μᾶλλον, ὃς ὑμῖν δείξει τι τῶν ἁμαρτημάτων, καὶ πρῶτον ἁπάντων, ἂν δύνηται, παρασκευάσει φρονεῖν ὑμᾶς, ὅτι τούτων ἕνεκεν, ὧν εἶπον, οὐκ ἐστὲ εὐδαίμονες, οὐδ᾽ ἂν ὁ Νεῖλος ὑμῶν διέρχηται τὴν πόλιν τῆς Κασταλίας γενόμενος διαυγέστερος, οὐδ᾽ ἂν ὁ Πακτωλὸς ἐνθάδε φανεὶς μὴ κατὰ ψῆγμα τὸ χρυσίον ὑμῖν φέρῃ, καθάπερ φασὶ Λυδοῖς πρότερον, ἀλλ᾽ ἄθρουν ὥσπερ ἰλύν, μηδ᾽ ἂν Αἴγυπτον ἢ Βαβυλῶνα τῇ πολυτελείᾳ τῶν οἰκοδομημάτων ὑπερβάλλησθε·

24 εἰ γὰρ ταῦτα δύναται ποιεῖν ἀνθρώπους μακαρίους, ποταμὸς ἢ κρᾶσις ἀέρος ἢ τόπος γῆς ἢ καὶ θαλάτ-

---

[1] ἀτυχέστατοι Reiske: ἀτυχέστεροι.
[2] λυπρᾶς] μικρᾶς Arnim, cf. Or. 32, 88.

THE THIRTY-THIRD DISCOURSE

But despite all that, because luxury and insolence came among them and they thought they had no need of culture and sobriety, they have become by far the most unfortunate of all men. Has not the whole earth been filled with the tale of their disasters? Yea, neither the speed of their horses nor Zeus nor Ganymede availed them aught, but a man from a city so wretched and obscure destroyed them, and that citizen of Ithaca was able to overcome the men of Ilium one and all and to pillage utterly and destroy the 'wide-wayed land.'[1]

Aye, the gods no longer love men who are wanton and senseless and unrestrained and inclined toward insolence and laziness and luxury. Therefore, rely not on these speakers of yours and do not accept their words of congratulation and admiration or the men themselves who are so clever at singing praises; for they only deceive and vainly excite you like foolish children; but rather welcome the man who will point out to you some of your faults, and will first of all, if he can, enable you to think, because such things as I have named do not make you blessed, not even if the mighty Nile itself should flow through your city with waters clearer than Castalia; not even if Pactolus,[2] appearing here, should bear to you its gold, not grain by grain, as they say it used to do for the Lydians in days gone by, but in a mass like mud; not even if you should surpass Egypt and Babylon in the costliness of your buildings. For if these are the things which can make men blessed—rivers or climate or situation or even harbours opening on the

---

[1] Dio expresses this thought in similar language in 32. 88.
[2] A tributary of the Hermus and famous in antiquity for the wealth of gold it brought to Lydian Sardis.

της λιμένες[1] ἢ ναὸς ἢ τεῖχος, οὐκ ἔστιν εἰπεῖν ὅσων λείπεσθε.

Βυζαντίους ἐκείνους ἀκούετε παρ' αὐτὸν οἰκοῦντας τὸν Πόντον, μικρὸν ἔξω τοῦ στόματος,[2] αὐτομάτων ἰχθύων αὐτοῖς ἐπὶ τὴν γῆν ἐκπιπτόντων ἐνίοτε· ἀλλ' ὅμως οὐδεὶς ἂν εἴποι διὰ τὸν ἰχθῦν εὐδαίμονας Βυζαντίους, εἰ μὴ καὶ τοὺς λάρους, οὐδὲ Αἰγυπτίους διὰ τὸν Νεῖλον οὐδὲ Βαβυλωνίους

25 διὰ τὸ τεῖχος. οὐχ ὁ Πηνειὸς δι' ἐρήμου ῥεῖ Θετταλίας; οὐχ ὁ Λάδων διὰ τῆς Ἀρκαδίας ἀναστάτου γενομένης; οὐκ αὐτὸς ὁ Κύδνος ἄνω καθαρώτερος; διὰ τοῦτο βελτίους φήσετε ἐκείνους ἑαυτῶν; ἴσως μὲν ἀληθεύετε, ἐὰν λέγητε· οὐ μὴν ἐρεῖτε.[3] τοὺς γὰρ ἀπείρους τρυφῆς καὶ πανουργίας, τούτους ἐγώ φημι πράττειν ἄμεινον. τί δ' αὐτῆς τῆς Ἰταλίας; οὐ Σύβαρις μὲν ὅσῳ μάλιστα ἐτρύφησεν, τοσούτῳ θᾶττον ἀπώλετο; Κρότων δὲ καὶ Θούριοι καὶ Μεταπόντιον[4] καὶ Τάρας, ἐπὶ τοσοῦτον ἀκμάσασαι καὶ τηλικαύτην ποτὲ σχοῦσαι δύναμιν, ποίας πόλεως οὐκ εἰσὶ νῦν ἐρημότεραι;

---

[1] λιμένες] ἢ λιμένος Reiske.
[2] Assuming a lacuna Arnim supplies after στόματος, *exempli gratia*, καὶ πλεῖστον ἀπὸ τοῦ τόπου κερδαίνοντας.
[3] ἐρεῖτε Reiske : εἴρηται.
[4] Μεταπόντιον Schwartz : Μεταπόντιοι or Μεταποντῖνοι.

---

[1] Aristotle, *Politics* 1291 b. 23, notes the importance of the fishing industry at Byzantium but fails to record the phenomenon here mentioned by Dio.
[2] Thessaly no doubt had little political importance in Dio's day, but the adjective which he applies to it seems overdrawn. He may have depended on hearsay.
[3] Cf. Strabo 8. 8. 388 : διὰ δὲ τὴν τῆς χώρας παντελῆ κάκωσιν

sea or temples or fortifications—it is impossible to list the cities that surpass you.

You are told that the people of Byzantium yonder, who dwell close beside the Pontus itself but a short distance outside its entrance [reap much profit from their situation], since from time to time fish are thrown out upon their shores without man's intervention[1]; but still no one would call Byzantines blessed because of the fish—unless he would say the same of cormorants—nor would he call Egyptians blessed because of the Nile, or Babylonians because of their wall. Does not the Peneus flow through a Thessaly that is desolate?[2] Does not the Ladon flow through an Arcadia whose people have been driven from their homes?[3] Is not the Cydnus itself purer higher up? What then? Will you say that on that account the people in that region are superior to yourselves? You might be speaking the truth if you said they were—though you will not say it—for those who are unacquainted with luxury and rascality are in my opinion better off. What of Italy itself? Take Sybaris, for example; is it not true that the more luxurious it became the more speedily it perished?[4] And as for Croton, Thurii, Metapontum, and Tarentum, in spite of the high level of prosperity to which they each attained and the great power that once was theirs, what city is there that they do not now surpass in desolation?[5]

οὐκ ἂν προσήκοι μακρολογεῖν περὶ αὐτῶν (the Arcadians)· αἵ τε γὰρ πόλεις ὑπὸ τῶν συνεχῶν πολέμων ἠφανίσθησαν . . . τήν τε χώραν οἱ γεωργήσαντες ἐκλελοίπασιν, κ.τ λ.

[4] Sybaris, proverbial for luxury, was destroyed in 510 B.C.

[5] These four cities of southern Italy at the close of the second Punic war fell permanently into the hands of the Romans and rapidly decayed.

26 Πολὺ δ' ἂν ἔργον εἴη πάντας ἐπεξιέναι τοὺς
διὰ τρυφὴν ἀπολωλότας, Λυδοὺς πάλαι, Μήδους,
Ἀσσυρίους πρότερον, τὰ τελευταῖα Μακεδόνας·
οἳ νεωστὶ μὲν τὰ ῥάκη[1] περιηρημένοι καὶ ποιμένες
ἀκούοντες, τοῖς Θραξὶ περὶ τῶν μελινῶν μαχόμενοι,
τοὺς Ἕλληνας ἐκράτησαν, εἰς τὴν Ἀσίαν διέβησαν,
ἄχρις Ἰνδῶν ἦρξαν. ἐπεὶ δὲ τὰ ἀγαθὰ τὰ Περσῶν
ἔλαβον, τούτοις ἐπηκολούθησε καὶ τὰ κακά.
27 τοιγαροῦν ἅμα σκῆπτρα καὶ ἁλουργίδες καὶ
Μηδικὴ τράπεζα καὶ τὸ γένος αὐτῶν ἐξέλιπεν·
ὥστε νῦν εἴ τις διέρχοιτο Πέλλαν, οὐδὲ σημεῖον
ὄψεται πόλεως οὐδέν, δίχα τοῦ πολὺν κέραμον
εἶναι συντετριμμένον ἐν τῷ τόπῳ. καίτοι μένει
τὰ χωρία τῶν πόλεων, ὧν εἶπον, καὶ τῶν ἐθνῶν,
οἷα καὶ πρότερον ἦν, καὶ τοὺς ποταμοὺς οὐδεὶς
ἄλλοσε[2] ἔτρεψεν, οὐδέ τι[3] τοιοῦτον ἦν ἕτερον·
ἀλλ' ὅμως[4] ὧν ἂν πολυτέλεια καὶ τρυφὴ ἅψηται,
τούτοις οὐκ ἔστι πλείω χρόνον διαγενέσθαι.
28 Μὴ γὰρ οἴεσθε τοὺς κριοὺς μηδὲ τὰς ἑλεπόλεις
καὶ τὰς ἄλλας μηχανὰς οὕτως ἀνατρέπειν ὡς
τρυφήν, εἴτε ἄνδρα βούλεταί τις πεπτωκότα ἰδεῖν
εἴτε πόλιν. οὐ ποταμός ἐστιν οὐδὲ πεδίον οὐδὲ
λιμὴν ὁ ποιῶν εὐδαίμονα πόλιν οὐδὲ χρημάτων
πλῆθος οὐδὲ οἰκοδομημάτων οὐδὲ θησαυροὶ θεῶν,
οἷς οὐδὲν προσέχει τὸ δαιμόνιον· οὐδ' ἂν εἰς

---

[1] ῥάκη] νάκη Emperius.   [2] ἄλλοσε Reiske: ἄλλος.
[3] οὐδέ τι Crosby: οὐδ' εἴ τι.   [4] ὅμως] ὅλως Geel.

---

[1] Pella was the ancient capital of Macedonia. Dio again
exaggerates, for Lucian, *Alexander* 6, states that Pella still
(*ca.* A.D. 150) had some inhabitants.
[2] Diodorus 20. 48. and 91 tells of these siege-towers. They

THE THIRTY-THIRD DISCOURSE

But it would be a vast undertaking to attempt to catalogue all who through luxury have suffered ruin: the Lydians long ago, the Medes, the Assyrians who preceded them, and lastly the Macedonians. For the Macedonians, although they had but lately shed their rags and were known as shepherds, men who used to fight the Thracians for possession of the millet-fields, vanquished the Greeks, crossed over into Asia and gained an empire reaching to the Indians; yet when the good things of the Persians came into their possession, the bad things also followed in their train. Accordingly both sceptre and royal purple and Median cookery and the very race itself came to an end, so that to-day, if you should pass through Pella, you would see no sign of a city at all, apart from the presence of a mass of shattered pottery on the site.[1] And yet the districts belonging to the cities and peoples I have named still remain just as they used to be, and no one has diverted the rivers into other channels, nor was anything else of that sort different once from what it is today; but in spite of that, whatever is touched by extravagance and luxury cannot long endure.

For think not that rams and siege-towers [2] and the other engines of war are as ruinous as luxury, whether it is a man whom one wishes to see prostrate or a city. No, it is not river or plain or harbour that makes a city prosperous, nor quantity of riches or multitude of houses or treasuries of the gods—objects to which deity pays no heed—nay, not even if some people do

may have been the invention of Demetrius Poliorcetes, who used them effectively against Rhodes. Ammianus, who has no Latin term for the device, describes it at some length (23. 4. 10–13).

τὰς πόλεις τινὲς μεταφέρωσι τὰ ὄρη καὶ τὰς
πέτρας ξὺν πολλῇ ταλαιπωρίᾳ καὶ πόνοις καὶ
μυρίοις ἀναλώμασιν· ἀλλὰ σωφροσύνη καὶ νοῦς
ἐστι τὰ σῴζοντα. ταῦτα ποιεῖ τοὺς χρωμένους
μακαρίους, ταῦτα τοῖς θεοῖς προσφιλεῖς, οὐχὶ
λιβανωτὸς οὐδὲ σμύρνα· πόθεν; οὐδὲ ῥίζαι
καὶ δάκρυα δένδρων οὐδὲ τὰ Ἰνδῶν καὶ Ἀράβων
29 φρύγανα. ὑμεῖς δέ, ἂν μὲν ἐκ τύχης ὁ ποταμὸς
μεταβάλῃ καὶ ῥυῇ θολερώτερος, ἄχθεσθε καὶ πρὸς
τοὺς πρῶτον ἐπιδημήσαντας αἰτίαν λέγετε· τὸν
δὲ τρόπον τῆς πόλεως μεταβάλλοντα ὁρῶντες καὶ
χείρω γιγνόμενον καὶ τεταραγμένον ἀεὶ μᾶλλον
οὐ φροντίζετε. ἀλλὰ ὕδωρ μὲν οὐ μόνον πίνειν
βούλεσθε καθαρόν, ἀλλὰ καὶ ὁρᾶν· ἦθος δὲ καθα-
30 ρὸν καὶ μέτριον οὐ ζητεῖτε. καίτοι πολλάκις
ἀκοῦσαί τινων ἔστι· μὴ γὰρ ἡμεῖς μόνοι μετα-
βεβλήκαμεν, ἀλλὰ σχεδὸν ἅπαντες. ἔστι δὲ τοῦτο
καθάπερ εἴ τις ἐν λοιμῷ διὰ τὸ πάντας ἢ τοὺς
πλείστους νοσεῖν μηδεμίαν ἐθέλοι ποιεῖσθαι πρό-
νοιαν, ὥστε αὐτὸς ὑγιαίνειν, ἢ νὴ Δία ἐν θαλάττῃ
χειμαζόμενος, ἔπειτα πάντας ὁρῶν[1] τοὺς ἐν
τῇ νηὶ κινδυνεύοντας ἀμελοῖ τῆς σωτηρίας.
τί δέ; ἂν ὅλος καταδύηται στόλος, διὰ τοῦτο
ἧττόν ἐστιν ἄτοπον τὸ ξυμβαῖνον;
31   Τί οὖν ἁμαρτάνομεν ἡμεῖς; τὰ μὲν ἄλλα ἐῶ.
γελοῖον γάρ, εἴ τις πρὸς τὸν ὅλως οὐκ ἐπιστάμενον
κιθαρίζειν, ἔπειτα ὡς ἔτυχε κρούοντα, ἐπιχειροῖ

[1] ὁρῶν Geel: ὁρᾷ.

[1] For building purposes.

transport to their cities the mountains and rocks [1] at the cost of great physical pain and labour and untold expense, does that bring happiness; instead it is sobriety and common sense that save. These make blessed those who employ them; these make men dear to the gods, not frankincense or myrrh, God knows, nor roots and gum of trees or the fragrant herbs of India and Arabia.[2] But as for you, if by chance the river shifts its course and flows with more turbid stream than usual, you are annoyed and feel that you must offer an explanation to people who have come to Tarsus for the first time; on the other hand, though you see the manners of the city shifting and growing worse and ever more and more disordered, you pay no heed. Yet, though you want water to be pure, not only for drinking but also for sightliness, you fail to seek a character that is pure and free from excess. Indeed one may often hear men say: "Yet perhaps it is not we alone who have changed, but practically everybody." But that is just as if in time of epidemic someone, because all, or nearly all, were ill, should not care to take any precautions for his own health, or, by Zeus, as if a man storm-tossed at sea, perceiving that all on board were in peril, should therefore neglect his own safety. What! If an entire fleet goes down, does that make the disaster any the less portentous!

"Well, what is the fault we are guilty of?" Your other faults I shall refrain from mentioning. For it would be ludicrous if one should try to tell a man who has absolutely no knowledge of the harp, and yet goes on to strike its strings at random, what

[2] For the aromatic plants and trees of India and Arabia see Diodorus 2. 49, 3. 46; Strabo 15. 1. 22, 16. 4. 25.

λέγειν ὅ τι ἥμαρτεν ἢ τίνα φθόγγον παρέβη.
τοσοῦτον δὲ μόνον εἰπεῖν ἄξιον, ὃ μηδεὶς ἂν ἀρνή-
σαιτο· φημὶ δὴ θαυμαστόν τι πάθος ἐν τῇ πόλει
ταύτῃ πεπονθέναι πολλούς, ὃ παρ' ἄλλοις τισὶ
πρότερον ἤκουον μᾶλλον ἢ παρ' ὑμῖν γιγνόμενον.
32 τί δὲ τοῦτ' ἔστιν ἂν μὴ δύνωμαι δηλῶσαι σαφῶς,
ἀλλὰ ὑμεῖς γε πειρᾶσθε ὑπονοεῖν· καὶ μηδέν με
νομίσητε τῶν ἀπορρήτων λέγειν μηδ' ὃ κρύπτουσιν
οἱ ποιοῦντες, εἰ καὶ σφόδρα δόξει θαυμαστόν.
μεταξὺ γοῦν ὀρθοὶ βαδίζοντες, λαλοῦντες οἱ πλείους
καθεύδουσιν· εἰ δ' ἐγρηγορέναι τοῖς πλείοσι
δοκοῦσιν, οὐδὲν ἂν εἴη τοῦτο. καὶ γὰρ τοὺς λαγὼς
φήσει τις ἐγρηγορέναι τῶν ἀπείρων ἐὰν ἴδῃ
κοιμωμένους. πόθεν οὖν ἐγνώσθη τοῦτο ; ἐξ ἑτέρων
τινῶν, ἃ σημεῖά ἐστι τοῦ καθεύδειν· ἐπεὶ τά γε
ὄμματα αὐτῶν ἀναπέπταται.

33   Τί οὖν οὗτοι ποιοῦσι κοιμωμένων ; πολλὰ μὲν δὴ
τά γε ἄλλα· σχεδὸν γὰρ πάντα ὀνείρασιν ἔοικεν
αὐτῶν τὰ ἔργα. καὶ γὰρ χαίρουσι μάτην καὶ λυποῦν-
ται καὶ θρασύνονται καὶ δεδοίκασι, μηδενὸς ὄντος,
καὶ σπουδάζουσι, καὶ τῶν ἀδυνάτων ἐπιθυμοῦσιν,
καὶ τὰ μὴ ὄντα νομίζουσιν εἶναι, καὶ τῶν ὄντων
οὐκ αἰσθάνονται. πλὴν ταῦτα μὲν ἴσως κοινὰ
καὶ ἡμῶν ἐστιν. ἐκεῖνο δέ, οἶμαι, φανερώτατον
ὕπνου τεκμήριον ποιοῦσι, ῥέγκουσιν. οὐ γὰρ ἔχω

---

¹ This peculiarity of the rabbit was so widely known that
it passed into a proverb. Cf. Suidas, s.v. λαγὼς καθεύδων:
ἐπὶ τῶν προσποιουμένων καθεύδειν. It is noted also by Pliny,
Naturalis Historia 11. 147 : *Quin et patentibus (oculis) dormiunt
lepores multique hominum, quos κορυβαντιᾶν Graeci dicunt.*
² In the preceding section Dio attempts to prepare his
audience for this troublesome word by stating that they

particular mistake he has made or what note he has misplayed. But so much at least is worth mentioning, and nobody could deny it: I assert that an amazing thing has happened in this city to many people, something that I used to hear occurred formerly in other cities rather than at Tarsus. However, if I prove unable to explain clearly what that thing is, at least you may try to guess my meaning; and, furthermore, do not think that I am telling any secret or something that the guilty ones attempt to disguise, no matter if their conduct does appear most amazing. At any rate, however amazing it may be, while on your feet, walking or talking, most of you all the while are fast asleep; and even if you seem to most men to be awake, that would mean nothing at all. For instance, anyone unacquainted with rabbits will say they are awake, even if he sees them sleeping.[1] How, then, has this state been recognized? From certain other signs which indicate their sleeping, since their eyes at least are wide open.

What, then, do these people do that marks persons who are asleep? Many indeed are the other symptoms; for practically all their actions bear a resemblance to the dream state. For example, they experience joy and sorrow, and courage and timidity, for no reason at all, they are enthusiastic, they desire the impossible, and what is unreal they regard as real, while what is real they fail to perceive. However, these traits, perhaps, they share in common with ourselves. But this, in my opinion, is the clearest mark of slumber—they snort.[2] For, by heaven, I have

must guess at his meaning if he fails to make it plain. For a summary of his usage of the term consult the Introduction to the Discourse.

μὰ τοὺς θεοὺς εἰπεῖν εὐπρεπέστερον. καίτοι
καὶ τῶν κοιμωμένων ὀλίγοι μέν, οἳ τοῦτο πάσ-
χουσι· τῶν δὲ ἄλλων τοῖς μεθύουσι ξυμβαίνει καὶ
τοῖς ἐμπλησθεῖσι καὶ τοῖς μὴ καλῶς κατα-
κειμένοις.

34 Ἐγὼ δέ φημι τοῦτο τὸ ἔργον αἰσχρὰν τὴν
πόλιν ποιεῖν καὶ δημοσίᾳ καταισχύνειν, καὶ τὴν
μεγίστην ὕβριν εἰς τὴν πατρίδα ὑβρίζειν τοὺς
μεθ᾽ ἡμέραν τούτους κοιμωμένους, καὶ δικαίως
ἂν αὐτοὺς ἐξορισθῆναι καὶ παρ᾽ ὑμῶν καὶ πανταχόθεν. οὐδὲ γὰρ μέτριόν ἐστι τὸ γιγνόμενον
οὐδὲ σπανίως συμβαῖνον, ἀλλ᾽ ἀεὶ καὶ πανταχοῦ
τῆς πόλεως, κἂν ἀπειλῇ τις κἂν παίζῃ κἂν
καταγελᾷ. καὶ τὸ λοιπὸν ἤδη ξύνηθές ἐστι καὶ
τοῖς πάνυ σμικροῖς παισί, καὶ τῶν τελείων ὅσοι
δοκοῦσιν αἰδεῖσθαι, προάγονται πολλάκις ὥσπερ
ἐπιχωρίῳ [1] τινὶ χρῆσθαι, κἂν ἐπιστήσαντες διατρα-
πῶσιν, ἀνέπνευσαν γοῦν ὅμοιον.

35 Εἰ δή τις ὑπῆρχε τοιαύτη πόλις, ὥστε ἀεὶ
θρηνούντων ἐν αὐτῇ ἀκούειν καὶ μηδένα δύνασθαι
δίχα τῆς δυσφημίας ταύτης προελθεῖν μηδὲ ἐπ᾽
ὀλίγον, πρὸς τοῦ Διὸς ἔστιν ὅστις ἂν ἡδέως
ἐπεδήμησεν; καίτοι τὸ μὲν θρηνεῖν, ὡς ἂν εἴποι
τις, ἀτυχίας ἐστὶ σημεῖον, τὸ δὲ τοιοῦτον ἀναισχυντίας, ἀσελγείας τῆς ἐσχάτης. οὐκοῦν εἰκὸς
ἐν δυστυχέσι μᾶλλον ἀνθρώποις ἐθέλειν διατρίβειν ἢ ἀκολάστοις. ἐγὼ μὲν γὰρ οὐκ ἂν ἑλοίμην
ἀκούειν οὐδὲ αὐλούντων διηνεκῶς· ἀλλ᾽ εἴ τις
ἔστι τοιοῦτος τόπος, ἐν ᾧ συνεχής ἐστιν ἦχος
εἴτε αὐλῶν εἴτε ᾠδῆς εἴτε κιθάρας, οἷον δή φασι

---

[1] ἐπιχωρίῳ Arnim, ἔπει ἀώρῳ Emperius: ἐπὶ δώρῳ.

no more becoming name to give it. And yet even among sleepers few suffer from that affliction, while with everybody else it occurs only when men are drunk, or have gorged themselves with food, or are reclining in an uncomfortable position.

But I claim that such conduct shames the city and disgraces it as a state, and that the greatest outrage is dealt to their country by these daytime slumberers, and that they would deservedly be banished, not only by you, but by all men everywhere. For indeed this habit is no trifling matter nor of rare occurrence either; nay, it occurs all the time and everywhere in the city, despite all threats and jests and ridicule. And what is more, the sound is by now habitual even with the very small boys, and such adults as have a reputation for good form are often led to indulge in it as a kind of local usage, and even though they may check it in embarrassment, at any rate they have given vent to a sound quite similar.

Now, if there existed any city in which you were continually hearing persons making lament, and in which no one could walk even a short distance without encountering that ill-omened sound, is there anyone, by Zeus, who would like to visit such a place? And yet lamentation, one might say, is a sign of misfortune, whereas the sound of which I am speaking is a sign of shamelessness and of extreme licentiousness. Surely it is reasonable that men should prefer to spend their time among those who are unfortunate rather than among those who are licentious. I for my part would not choose to hear even the pipes constantly; nay, if there exists a place in which there is a constant sound of pipes or song or lyres, as indeed they say is the case with the

τὸν τῶν Σειρήνων εἶναι σκόπελον ἀεὶ μελω-
δούμενον, οὐκ ἂν δυναίμην ἐκεῖσε ἐλθὼν διάγειν. τὸν
36 δέ γε ἄγριον τοῦτον καὶ χαλεπὸν ἦχον τίς ἂν μέτριος
ἄνθρωπος ὑπομείνειεν; ἀλλ' ἐὰν μέν τις οἴκημα
παριὼν ἀκούσῃ τοῦ τοιούτου, δῆλον ὅτι φήσει
χαμαιτυπεῖον αὐτὸ εἶναι. τὴν δὲ πόλιν τί φήσουσιν, ἐν ᾗ πανταχοῦ σχεδὸν εἷς ἐπικρατεῖ
φθόγγος, καὶ οὔτε καιρὸν οὔτε ἡμέραν οὔτε
τόπον ἐξαίρετον οὐδένα ποιοῦνται, ἀλλ' ἐν στενωποῖς, ἐν οἰκίαις, ἐν ἀγοραῖς, παρὰ τὸ θέατρον,
ἐν τῷ γυμνασίῳ δυναστεύει τὸ πρᾶγμα; καὶ
αὐλοῦντος μὲν ἕωθεν οὐδενὸς ἀκήκοα ἐγὼ μέχρι
νῦν ἐν τῇ πόλει, τοῦτο δὲ τὸ θαυμαστὸν μέλος
εὐθὺς ἅμα τῇ ἡμέρᾳ κινεῖται.

37   Καίτοι με οὐ λέληθεν ὅτι ἴσως τινὲς ληρεῖν
με νομίζουσι τὰ τοιαῦτα ἐξετάζοντα, καὶ μηδὲν
εἶναι παρὰ τοῦτο, μόνον ἂν τὰ λάχανα ἁμάξαις
εἰσφέρητε καὶ πολλοὺς ἄρτους θεωρῆτε ἐν τῷ
μέσῳ καὶ τὸ τάριχος ἢ[1] καὶ τὰ κρέα. σκοπούντων δὲ ὅμως αὐτοὶ τὸ πρᾶγμα οὕτως. εἴ τις
αὐτῶν παραγένοιτο εἰς πόλιν, ἐν ᾗ πάντες ὅ τι
ἂν δεικνύωσι τῷ μέσῳ δακτύλῳ δεικνύουσι,
κἂν δεξιὰν ἐμβάλῃ τις,[2] οὕτως ἐνέβαλε, κἂν προ-
τείνῃ τὴν χεῖρα ὅλως,[3] κἂν ὁ δῆμος χειροτονῶσι,
κἂν οἱ δικασταὶ τὴν ψῆφον φέρωσι, ποίαν τινὰ
ἡγήσονται τὴν πόλιν ταύτην; ἐὰν δὲ ἀνασυρά-
38 μενοι πάντες βαδίζωσιν, ὥσπερ ἐν λίμνῃ; ἆρα

---

[1] ἢ Crosby, ἄξιον ἢ Reiske: ἢ.
[2] ἐμβάλῃ τις] ἐμβάλλῃ τις Reiske: ἐμβαλεῖν M.
[3] ὅλως] οὕτως Reiske.

---

[1] See note on Or. 32. 47.

Sirens' crag,[1] which ever resounds with melody, I could not bring myself to go and live there. But as for that boorish and distressing sound you make, what ordinary mortal could endure it? Why, if a man in passing by a house hears a sound like that, of course he will say it's a brothel. But what will men say of the city in which almost everywhere just one note prevails, and whose inhabitants make no exception of season or day or place, but, on the contrary, in alley-ways, in private houses, at market, at the theatre, in the gymnasium this snorting is dominant? Besides, while I have never up to the present moment heard anybody play the pipes at sunrise in the city, this amazing tune of yours starts going at break of day.

However, I am not unaware that some may believe that I am talking nonsense when I inquire into matters such as this, and think that this snorting makes no difference, provided only that you continue to bring in your vegetables by the wagon-load and to find bread in abundance for all to buy, and your salt fish and meats as well. But still let them consider the matter for themselves in this way: Supposing one of them came to a city in which everybody always uses his middle finger in pointing to anything,[2] and, if he offers his right hand, offers it in that fashion, and, if he extends his hand for any purpose, either for voting in assembly or in the casting of his ballot as a juryman, extends it so, what sort of place would the newcomer think that city to be? And suppose everybody walked with his clothes pulled up, as if wading in a pool? Are you not aware

---

[2] An indecent gesture. See scholium to Aristophanes, *Clouds* 653: δείκνυσι τὸν μέσον δάκτυλον αἰσχρῶς, and also Juvenal 10.53: *mediumque ostenderet unguem.*

ἀγνοεῖτε ὅτι ταῦτ' ἐστὶ τὰ καθ' ὑμῶν ἀφορμὴν
δεδωκότα βλασφημίας, ὥστε δημοσίᾳ κατὰ τῆς
πόλεως ἔχειν ὅ τι λέγωσι τοὺς ἀπεχθῶς ὑμῖν
διακειμένους; ἀλλὰ πόθεν τοὺς Κέρκωπας[1]
ὑμῖν ἐπιβοῶσιν; καίτοι[2] οὔ φασι δεῖν διαφέρειν
οὔθ' ὑμῖν οὔτε τοῖς ἄλλοις ὑπὲρ ὧν ἕτεροι λέγουσιν,
ἀλλ' ὑπὲρ ὧν αὐτοὶ ποιεῖτε.[3] φέρε, ἂν καταλάβῃ
τοιοῦτο πάθος δημοσίᾳ τινάς, ὥστε γυναικῶν
λαβεῖν φωνὴν ἅπαντας καὶ μηδένα δύνασθαι μήτε
νέον μήτε πρεσβύτερον ἀνδριστὶ[4] μηδὲν εἰπεῖν,
οὐ δόξει χαλεπὸν εἶναι καὶ παντός, οἶμαι, λοιμοῦ
βαρύτερον,[5] ὥστε πέμποιεν ἂν εἰς θεοῦ καὶ τὸ
δαιμόνιον πολλὰ ἱλάσκοιντο; καίτοι τὸ μὲν
γυναικῶν ἀφιέναι φωνὴν ἀνθρώπων ἐστὶ φωνὴν
ἀφιέναι, καὶ οὐδεὶς ἂν ἀκούων γυναικὸς δυσχε-
39 ράνειεν. ὁ δὲ τοιοῦτος ἦχος τίνων ἐστίν; οὐχὶ
τῶν ἀνδρογύνων; οὐχὶ τῶν τὰ αἰδοῖα ἀποκεκομ-
μένων; οὐδὲ τούτων ἀεὶ καὶ πρὸς ἅπαντας, ἀλλὰ
ἴδιον αὐτῶν ὥσπερ ξύμβολον.

Φέρε δ' εἰ κατεζωσμένοι πάντες ἐβαδίζετε ἢ
τυμπανίζοντες, καὶ μηδὲν ὑμῖν ἐδόκει τοῦτ' εἶναι
χαλεπόν; εἰ συνέβαινεν ὑμᾶς ὑψηλήν τινα ἔχειν

---

[1] τοὺς Κέρκωπας Selden, τὰς Κερκνίδας Reiske: τὰς Κερκίδας.
[2] καίτοι Reiske: καὶ.
[3] ἆρα ἀγνοεῖτε . . . αὐτοὶ ποιεῖτε rejected by Arnim as a
revised version of καίτοι με οὐ λέληθεν . . . τὰ κρέα in § 37.
[4] ἀνδριστὶ Emperius, ἀνδρείως Reiske: ἄνδρα.
[5] After βαρύτερον the MSS. read οὐ γὰρ τὸ πυρέττειν αἰσχρὸν
οὐδὲ τὸ ἀποθνήσκειν, which Arnim deletes.

---

[1] A mythical pair of ape-like men closely associated with
Heracles and a natural subject for comic treatment. The
intimate connection between Tarsus and Heracles lends plausibility to Selden's conjecture.

THE THIRTY-THIRD DISCOURSE

that such conduct has provided occasion for slander against you, with the result that those who are ill-disposed toward you are supplied with material wherewith to defame you as a people? Well, how comes it that people shout at you the name Cercopes?[1] And yet men say that it should make no difference either to you or to anybody else what others say, but only what you yourselves do. Well then, supposing certain people should as a community be so afflicted that all the males got female voices and that no male, whether young or old, could say anything man-fashion, would that not seem a grievous experience and harder to bear, I'll warrant, than any pestilence, and as a result would they not send to the sanctuary of the god and try by many gifts to propitiate the divine power? And yet to speak with female voice is to speak with human voice, and nobody would be vexed at hearing a woman speak. But who are they who make that sort of sound? Are they not the creatures of mixed sex?[2] Are they not men who have had their testicles lopped off? Nay, even they do not always make that sound, nor to all persons, but it is reserved for themselves, a sort of password of their own.

Come, suppose you all were accustomed to walk with clothes girt tight, or playing the tambourine,[3] and that this practice did not seem to you at all vexatious. Suppose you happened to possess a lofty rock,

---

[2] The word ἀνδρογύνων had several meanings, none of them complimentary. See Suidas *s.v.* Cf. Plato, *Symposium* 189E: ἀνδρόγυνον γὰρ ἓν τότε μὲν ἦν καὶ εἶδος καὶ ὄνομα ἐξ ἀμφοτέρων κοινὸν τοῦ τε ἄρρενος καὶ θήλεος, νῦν δ' οὐκ ἔστιν ἀλλ' ἢ ἐν ὀνείδει ὄνομα κείμενον.

[3] Both traits characteristic of women.

ἄκραν ἢ νὴ Δία ὄρος[1] ὑπερκείμενον, ὥσπερ ἕτεραι
πόλεις, ὅπου τις ἀνελθὼν ἕκαστον μὲν σαφῶς
ἀκούειν μὴ δύναιτο, τὸν δὲ ξύμπαντα θροῦν, ποῖος
ἦχος ὑμῖν ἂν[2] ἀνενεχθῆναι δοκεῖ[3]; ἢ δῆλον ὅτι ὁ[4]
40 τοῦ πλείονος ὥσπερ ἐν ἁρμονίᾳ κρατοῦντος; εἰ
δὲ ἐκ τῆς ἀκοῆς δέοι, τεκμαίρεσθαι περὶ τῶν
ἀνθρώπων, ὥσπερ Ὅμηρός φησι προσιόντα[5] τὸν
Ὀδυσσέα τῇ αὑτοῦ οἰκίᾳ μὴ περιμεῖναι θεάσασθαι
τοὺς μνηστῆρας ἐστιωμένους, ἀλλ᾿ εὐθὺς εἰπεῖν
πρὸς τὸν Εὔμαιον, ὡς αὐτὸν ἡ κιθάρα περιήνεγκε,

γιγνώσκειν δὴ ὅτι πολλοὶ ἐν αὐτῇ δαῖτα τίθενται·

καὶ πάλιν ἐκ τῆς νήσου τῶν Κυκλώπων ἀκούοντα
τῶν τε προβάτων βληχωμένων καὶ αὐτῶν τῆς
φωνῆς, ὡς ἄν, οἶμαι, νεμόντων, νοεῖν ὅτι ποιμένων
41 τινῶν ἐστιν ἡ χώρα. φέρε καὶ ὑμᾶς εἴ τις ἐκ τοῦ
φερομένου ἤχου πόρρωθεν εἰκάζοι, ποίους ἂν[6]
ἀνθρώπους ὑπολάβοι εἶναι καὶ τί πράττειν; οὐ
γὰρ ἱκανοί ἐστε οὔτε βουκολεῖν οὔτε ποιμαίνειν·
καὶ πότερον ὑμᾶς Ἀργείων ἀποίκους, ὡς λέγετε,
φήσει τις, ἢ μᾶλλον ἐκείνων Ἀραδίων; καὶ πότερον Ἕλληνας ἢ Φοινίκων τοὺς ἀσελγεστάτους;
Ἐγὼ μὲν γὰρ ἡγοῦμαι μᾶλλον προσήκειν
ἀνδρὶ σώφρονι ἐν τοιαύτῃ πόλει κηρὸν ἐπαλεῖψαι[7]

---

[1] ὄρος Reiske: ἀέρος.   [2] ἂν added by Reiske.
[3] δοκεῖ] ἐδόκει Arnim.   [4] ὁ added by Reiske.
[5] προσιόντα Reiske: προϊόντα.
[6] ποίους ἂν Crosby, οἴους ἂν Reiske: οἴους.
[7] ἐπαλεῖψαι Reiske: ὑπαλίψαι or ἀλεῖψαι.

---

[1] *Odyssey* 17. 269. Dio has adapted the line somewhat
to serve his purpose. He might well have included in his
quotation the next two verses, had not the poet introduced
also κνίση, which does not suit our passage.

or, by Zeus, an overhanging mountain such as other cities have, and that a man who made the ascent could not hear distinctly individual voices but only the general murmur, what kind of sound do you think would have been borne aloft to him? Would it not, evidently, be the sound made by the majority, prevailing as if by harmony of tone? And suppose one had to guess from what was heard who made the sound, as Homer says about Odysseus when he approached his own home, that he did not have to wait to see the suitors at their feast but straightway said to Eumaeus, as the note of the harp smote his ear, that he

Knew well that many were feasting in his hall; [1]

and again, when from the island of the Cyclopes he heard both the bleating of sheep and the voices of men (as he would, methinks, if they were pasturing their sheep), that he perceived that it was the country of shepherds [2]—well then, suppose that a man were to judge you too by the sound that came to him from a distance, what kind of men would he guess you were and what your occupation? For you haven't the capacity for tending either cattle or sheep! And would any one call you colonists from Argos,[3] as you claim to be, or more likely colonists rather of those abominable Aradians?[4] Would he call you Greeks, or the most licentious of Phoenicians?

I believe it is more appropriate for a man of sense to plug his ears with wax in a city like yours

---

[2] *Odyssey* 9. 167. Homer does not make Odysseus draw the inference with which Dio credits him.

[3] See § 1.

[4] Aradus was a tiny island off the coast of Phoenicia.

τοῖς ὠσὶν ἢ εἰ τὰς Σειρῆνας παραπλέων ἔτυχεν.
ὅπου μὲν γὰρ ὑπῆρχε θανάτου κίνδυνος, ὅπου δὲ
42 ἀσελγείας, ὕβρεως, τῆς ἐσχάτης διαφθορᾶς. καὶ
πρόσεστιν οὐδεμία τέρψις οὐδ' ἱστορία δήπου.
πρότερον μὲν οὖν ἡ παραίνεσις τῶν ἀμεινόνων
ἐκράτει, νῦν δ', ὡς ἔοικε, τῶν χειρόνων. θαυμάσαι
δ' ἄν τις τὴν αἰτίαν τοῦ ζηλοῦν αὐτὸ τοὺς πλείους
ἐνθάδε [1] καὶ συνηθέστερον ἀεὶ γίγνεσθαι προβαῖνον.
ὥσπερ Ἰωνική τις ἐκράτησεν ἁρμονία καὶ Δώριος
καὶ Φρύγιος ἄλλη καὶ Λύδιος· οὕτως νῦν ἡ τῶν
Ἀραδίων κρατεῖ μουσική, καὶ τὰ Φοινίκων ὑμῖν
κρούματα ἀρέσκει, καὶ τὸν ῥυθμὸν τοῦτον ἐξαι-
ρέτως ἠγαπήκατε, ὥσπερ ἕτεροι τὸν σπονδεῖον.
43 ἢ καὶ γένος τι πέφηνεν ἀνθρώπων ταῖς ῥισὶν
εὔμουσον, ὥσπερ τοὺς κύκνους φασὶ τοῖς πτεροῖς,
ἔπειτα τῶν λιγυφώνων τρόπον ὀρνέων τέρπουσιν
ἀλλήλους ἔν τε ταῖς ὁδοῖς καὶ παρὰ τὰ ξυμπόσια,
μηδὲν δεόμενοι λύρας μηδὲ αὐλῶν; ἀρχαῖα δὴ
ταῦτα καὶ σκληρᾶς τε [2] καὶ ἀγροίκου τινὸς
μουσικῆς ὄργανα. νῦν δὲ τρόπος ἄλλος ἀνθεῖ,
βαρβίτων κρείττων καὶ προσηνέστερος. οὐκοῦν
μετὰ χρόνον καὶ χοροὺς ὑπὸ τῷ μέλει τούτῳ
στησόμεθα παίδων καὶ παρθένων ἐπιμελῶς ἐκδιδά-
ξαντες.
44   Ἀλλ' ὅτι μὲν ἄχθεσθε ἀκούοντες σαφῶς οἶδα,

[1] ἐνθάδε Reiske: ἔνθα δή.   [2] τε Crosby: ἔτι.

[1] Strabo (14. 5. 13–15) paints an interesting picture of
intellectual life at Tarsus and lists a number of philosophers,

than if he chanced to be sailing past the Sirens. For there one faced the risk of death, but here it is licentiousness, insolence, the most extreme corruption that threatens. And here we find no real enjoyment and no love of learning either, I imagine. At any rate in days gone by it was the counsel of the better citizens that had its way,[1] whereas now, it seems, it is the counsel of the worse. And one might wonder why the majority here in Tarsus follow that baser counsel so eagerly, and why that tendency is constantly growing more general as time goes on. Just as formerly an Ionian mode became dominant in music, and a Dorian, and then a Phrygian also, and a Lydian, so now the Aradian mode is dominant and now it is Phoenician airs that suit your fancy and the Phoenician rhythm that you admire most, just as some others do the spondaic. Or can it be that a race of men has been created with the gift of music in their noses (as swans are said to have the gift of music in their wings [2]), so that like shrill-voiced birds these men delight one another in the streets and at symposia without any need of lyre and pipes? No doubt the lyre and pipes are antiquated and, furthermore, instruments that produce a harsh and rustic kind of music. Ah well, another style now is flourishing, superior to lyres and more agreeable. Therefore, in course of time, we shall even institute choruses to accompany that variety of tune, choruses of boys and girls, most carefully instructed.

Well, I understand perfectly that you are vexed

---

poets, and grammarians there in residence. Those days had passed.

[2] Aristotle, *Historia Animalium* 535b, 31, ὁ γινόμενος ταῖς πτέρυξι ψόφος οὐ φωνή ἐστι.

καὶ προεῖπον ὅτι τοὺς λόγους ἀποδέξεσθε οὐχ
ἡδέως. ὑμεῖς δ᾽ ἴσως με περὶ ἄστρων καὶ γῆς
ἐδοκεῖτε διαλέξεσθαι. καὶ τινὲς μὲν ὑμῶν ὀργίζον-
ται καί φασί με ὑβρίζειν τὴν πόλιν, τοὺς δὲ ταῦτα
ποιοῦντας οὐκ αἰτιῶνται· τινὲς δὲ ἴσως καταγελῶ-
σιν, εἰ περὶ μηδενὸς κρείττονος εὗρον εἰπεῖν·
ἐγὼ δὲ ὁρῶ καὶ τοὺς ἰατροὺς ἔσθ᾽ ὅτε ἁπτομένους
ὧν οὐκ ἂν ἤθελον, οὐχὶ τῶν καλλίστων τοῦ σώματος, καὶ πολλοὺς οἶδα τῶν θεραπευομένων ἀγανακ-
τοῦντας, ὅταν ἅπτηται τοῦ πεπονθότος. ὁ δὲ
πολλάκις ἀμύττει τοῦτο καὶ τέμνει βοῶντος.
οὔκουν ἀνήσω περὶ τούτου λέγων, πρὶν ἂν σφόδρα
δηχθῆτε. καίτοι πάνυ ἀσθενοῦς φαρμάκου τυγχά-
νετε τοῦ λόγου τούτου καὶ πολὺ ἐλάττονος ἢ κατὰ
τὴν ἀξίαν.

45 Ἄγε δὴ πρὸς τοῦ Ἡρακλέους καὶ τοῦ Περσέως
καὶ τοῦ Ἀπόλλωνος καὶ τῆς Ἀθηνᾶς καὶ τῶν
ἄλλων θεῶν, οὓς τιμᾶτε, ἀποκρίνασθέ μοι προθύμως, εἴ τις ὑμῶν ἐβούλετο γυναῖκα τοιαύτην
ἔχειν, λέγω δέ, ὥσπερ κιθαρίστρια καλεῖται γυνὴ
καὶ νὴ Δία αὐλητρὶς ἢ ποιήτρια καὶ τἆλλα ὁμοίως
ἀπὸ τῶν ἄλλων ἐπιτηδευμάτων, οὕτως ἦν ἄν τις
συνήθως ὀνομάσειεν ἀπὸ τούτου τοῦ ἔργου. καὶ
μὴ δυσχεραίνετε μηδὲ ἄχθεσθε· τοὺς γὰρ λόγους
τούτους αὐτὸ παρέχει τὸ πρᾶγμα τῷ βουλομένῳ
περὶ αὐτοῦ λέγειν, οὐκ ἐγώ ποθεν ἀνευρίσκω.

---

[1] § 15.

with me for what I have been saying, and indeed I told you beforehand [1] that you would not receive my words with any pleasure. However, you may have supposed that I was going to discourse on astronomy and geology. And though some of you are angry and claim that I am insulting your city, still they do not blame those who are guilty of the things I mention; on the other hand, others may be laughing at me because I could find nothing better to talk about. However, I find that physicians too sometimes handle things they would rather not, parts of the body that are not the most beautiful, and many of their patients, I know, are irritated when the physician touches the sore spot. But he often scarifies and lances it despite the outcry. I, therefore, shall not cease to talk upon this theme until I make you smart indeed. And yet, after all, it is a very mild medicine you are getting in this speech of mine, much less severe than your case calls for.

Come now, in the name of Heracles and Perseus and Apollo and Athenê and the other deities whom you honour, tell me freely whether any one of you would want to have a wife like that—I mean a wife whom men would habitually call by a name derived from the practice of which I speak,[2] just as a woman receives the name of harpist or flautist or poetess, and so forth, each in keeping with its own activity. And pray do not be displeased or vexed; for these words of mine are words that the situation itself supplies to any man who chooses to deal with the subject, rather than some invention of my own.

---

[2] That is, the practice of " snorting." Arnim believes that after the word ἔργου the text has lost a noun descriptive of that particular activity, e.g., ῥεγκητρίδα.

γυναικὶ μὲν δὴ τοιαύτῃ ξυνοικεῖν οὐδεὶς ἂν
ἐθελήσειεν ὑμῶν οὐδὲ ἐπὶ πεντακοσίοις ταλάντοις,
οἶμαι, θυγατέρα δὲ σχεῖν ἕλοιτο ἄν; ἀλλὰ νὴ Δία
μητέρα πως οὐ[1] χαλεπὸν τοιαύτην ἔχειν καὶ
γηροβοσκεῖν· σεμνὸν γὰρ δῆλον ὅτι καὶ πρεσβυ-
46 τέροις πρέπον μᾶλλον. εἶεν· οὐκοῦν ἐπὶ μὲν
γυναικὸς ἢ θυγατρὸς οὐδ᾽ ἀκούοντες ἀνέχεσθε,
πόλιν δὲ τοιαύτην καὶ πατρίδα οἰκεῖν οὐ δεινὸν
ὑμῖν δοκεῖ; καὶ ταῦθ᾽, ὃ τῷ[2] παντὶ χαλεπώτερον,
οὐ τοιαύτην οὖσαν ἐξ ἀρχῆς, ἀλλ᾽ ἣν αὐτοὶ
ποιεῖτε; καίτοι μητρόπολις ὑμῶν ἐστιν ἡ πόλις,
ὥστε καὶ τὴν σεμνότητα καὶ τὸ ἀξίωμα ἔχει τὸ
τῆς μητροπόλεως· ἀλλ᾽ ὅμως οὔτε τοῦ ὀνόματος
οὔτε τῆς ἀρχαιότητος οὔτε τῆς δόξης φείδεσθε.
47 τί ἂν οἴεσθε, εἰ καθάπερ εἰκός ἐστι καὶ φασι τοὺς
οἰκιστὰς ἥρωας ἢ θεοὺς πολλάκις ἐπιστρέφεσθαι
τὰς αὐτῶν πόλεις τοῖς ἄλλοις ὄντας ἀφανεῖς ἔν τε
θυσίαις καί τισιν ἑορταῖς δημοτελέσιν, ἔπειθ᾽ ὁ
ἀρχηγὸς ὑμῶν Ἡρακλῆς παραγένοιτο, ἤτοι πυρᾶς
οὔσης, ἣν πάνυ καλὴν αὐτῷ ποιεῖτε, σφόδρα γε
ἂν αὐτὸν ἡσθῆναι τοιαύτης ἀκούσαντα φωνῆς·
οὐκ ἂν εἰς Θράκην ἀπελθεῖν μᾶλλον ἢ Λιβύην καὶ
τοῖς Βουσίριδος ἢ τοῖς Διομήδους ἀπογόνοις
θύουσι[3] παρεῖναι; τί δέ; ὁ Περσεὺς οὐκ ἂν
ὄντως ὑπερπτῆναι δοκεῖ τὴν πόλιν;

---

[1] μητέρα πως οὐ Schwartz and Wilamowitz, μητέρα πῶς;
οὐ Geel: μητέρα; πῶς οὐ.
[2] ταῦθ᾽, ὃ τῷ Reiske: ταῦθ᾽ οὕτω or ταῦτ᾽ οὐ τῷ or ταῦτα
οὐ τῷ.
[3] θύουσι Reiske: θύσομαι.

---

[1] In memory of his death and deification.
[2] Busiris, mythical king of Egypt, and Diomedes the
Thracian were both slain by Heracles.

Well then, no one among you would be willing to live with a wife like that, not even, methinks, for five hundred talents; then would he choose a daughter of her kind? I grant you that perhaps, by Zeus, it may not be so distressing to have a mother of that sort and to support her in old age; for evidently snorting is a solemn performance and rather suited to the elderly! Very well, then if, when it is a question of wife or daughter, you cannot endure even to hear of such a thing, does it not seem to you an awful calamity to reside in a city or a country of that kind? And furthermore—a thought which makes it altogether more distressing—a city or a country which was not like that to begin with, but which you yourselves are making so? And yet the city in question is your mother-city, and so it has the dignity and the esteem belonging to a mother-city; but still neither its name nor its antiquity nor its renown are spared by you. What would you think, if, just as you might reasonably expect (and as men report) that founding heroes or deities would often visit the cities they have founded, invisible to everybody else (both at sacrificial rites and at certain other public festivals)—if, I ask you, your own founder, Heracles, should visit you (attracted, let us say, by a funeral pyre such as you construct with special magnificence in his honour[1]), do you think he would be extremely pleased to hear such a sound? Would he not depart for Thrace instead, or for Libya, and honour with his presence the descendants of Busiris or of Diomedes[2] when they sacrifice? What! Do you not think that Perseus[3] himself would really pass over your city in his flight?

[3] For the prominence of Perseus at Tarsus see also §§ 1 and 45.

48 Καίτοι¹ τί δεῖ μεμνῆσθαι θεῶν; ἀλλὰ Ἀθηνό-
δωρος ὁ πρύτανις² γενόμενος, ὃν ᾐδεῖτο ὁ Σεβαστός,
ἆρα οἴεσθε, εἴπερ ἔγνω τοιαύτην οὖσαν τὴν πόλιν,
προύκρινεν ἂν τῆς μετ᾽ ἐκείνου διατριβῆς τὴν
ἐνθάδε; πρότερον μὲν οὖν ἐπ᾽ εὐταξίᾳ καὶ
σωφροσύνῃ διαβόητος ἦν ὑμῶν ἡ πόλις καὶ
τοιούτους ἀνέφερεν ἄνδρας· νῦν δὲ ἐγὼ δέδοικα
μὴ τὴν ἐναντίαν λάβῃ τάξιν, ὥστε μετὰ τῶνδε καὶ
τῶνδε ὀνομάζεσθαι. καίτοι πολλὰ τῶν νῦν ἔτι
μενόντων ὅπως δήποτε ἐμφαίνει τὸ σῶφρον καὶ
τὸ αὐστηρὸν τῆς τότε ἀγωγῆς, ὧν ἐστι τὸ περὶ
τὴν ἐσθῆτα τῶν γυναικῶν, τὸ τοῦτον τὸν τρόπον
κατεστάλθαι καὶ βαδίζειν ὥστε μηδένα³ μηδὲ ἐν
αὐτῶν μέρος ἰδεῖν μήτε τοῦ προσώπου μήτε τοῦ
λοιποῦ σώματος, μηδὲ αὐτὰς ὁρᾶν ἔξω τῆς ὁδοῦ
49 μηδέν. καίτοι τί δύνανται τοιοῦτον ἰδεῖν οἷον
ἀκούουσιν; τοιγαροῦν ἀπὸ τῶν ὤτων ἀρξάμεναι
τῆς διαφθορᾶς ἀπολώλασιν αἱ πλείους. ἡ γὰρ
ἀσέλγεια καὶ δι᾽ ὤτων καὶ δι᾽ ὀφθαλμῶν πανταχόθεν εἰσδύεται. ὥστε τὰ μὲν πρόσωπα κεκαλυμ-
μέναι⁴ βαδίζουσι, τῇ ψυχῇ δὲ ἀκαλύπτῳ καὶ
σφόδρα ἀναπεπταμένῃ. τοιγαροῦν ὀξύτερον βλέ-
πουσιν ἑνὶ τῶν ὀφθαλμῶν, ὥσπερ οἱ γεωμέτραι.
50 Καὶ τουτὶ μὲν ἔκδηλόν ἐστι τὸ τῶν ῥινῶν,

¹ καίτοι Capps: καὶ.
² πρύτανις Crosby: πρῴην. Cf. Or. 34. 36 and 42 for the
πρύτανις at Tarsus.
³ μηδένα added by Cobet.
⁴ κεκαλυμμέναι Reiske: κεκαλυμμένα.

¹ Athenodorus, Stoic philosopher and former tutor of
Augustus, came to Tarsus in his old age and with the backing
of the Roman emperor reformed the government, of which
he became the head. He was respected not only by Augustus

And yet what need have we to mention deities?
Take Athenodorus,[1] who became governor of Tarsus,
whom Augustus held in honour—had he known
your city to be what it is to-day, would he, do you
suppose, have preferred being here to living with the
emperor? In days gone by, therefore, your city
was renowned for orderliness and sobriety, and the
men it produced were of like character; but now I
fear that it may be rated just the opposite and so be
classed with this or that other city I might name.
And yet many of the customs still in force reveal in
one way or another the sobriety and severity of
deportment of those earlier days. Among these is
the convention regarding feminine attire, a convention which prescribes that women should be so
arrayed and should so deport themselves when in the
street that nobody could see any part of them,
neither of the face nor of the rest of the body, and
that they themselves might not see anything off the
road.[2] And yet what could they see as shocking as
what they hear? Consequently, beginning the process of corruption with the ears, most of them have
come to utter ruin. For wantonness slips in from
every quarter, through ears and eyes alike. Therefore, while they have their faces covered as they walk,
they have their soul uncovered and its doors thrown
wide open. For that reason they, like surveyors,
can see more keenly with but one of their eyes.[3]
And while this nasal affliction[4] is wholly manifest,

but also by Cicero, whom he aided in the composition of the
De Officiis. His friend Strabo has much to say of him.

[2] This prescription may have been due to the oriental
element at Tarsus.

[3] That is, peeping through the veil.

[4] That is, 'snorting.'

319

ἀνάγκη δὲ καὶ τὰ ἄλλα ἀκολουθεῖν τῷ τοιούτῳ
ῥυθμῷ. μὴ γὰρ οἴεσθε, ὥσπερ ἑτέρων ἕτερα[1]
πολλάκις εἴς τινα μέρη κατασκήπτει, χεῖρας ἢ
πόδας ἢ πρόσωπον, οὕτω καὶ παρ' ὑμῖν ἐπιχώριόν
τι νόσημα ταῖς ῥισὶν ἐμπεπτωκέναι, μηδ' ὥσπερ
Λημνίων ταῖς γυναιξὶ τὴν Ἀφροδίτην ὀργισθεῖσαν
λέγουσι διαφθεῖραι τὰς μασχάλας, κἀνθάδε νομίζετε
τῶν πλειόνων διεφθάρθαι τὰς ῥῖνας ὑπὸ δαιμονίου
χόλου, κἄπειτα τοιαύτην φωνὴν ἀφιέναι· πόθεν;
ἀλλ' ἔστι σημεῖον τῆς ἐσχάτης ὕβρεως καὶ
ἀπονοίας καὶ τοῦ καταφρονεῖν τῶν καλῶν ἁπάντων
51 καὶ μηδὲν αἰσχρὸν ἡγεῖσθαι. φημὶ δὴ διαλέγεσθαι ταύτας[2] ὁμοίως καὶ βαδίζειν καὶ βλέπειν.
εἰ δὲ μηδὲν ἔκδηλον οὕτω ποιεῖν διὰ τῶν ὀμμάτων
δύνανται, ὥστε ἐπιστρέφειν ἅπαντας, ἢ μηδέπω
τὴν τέχνην ἐπὶ τοσοῦτο προαγήοχασιν, οὐδὲν
ἐπιεικέστερον τἆλλα ἔχουσιν.

Εἶτ' ἄχθεσθε τοῖς Αἰγεῦσι καὶ τοῖς Ἀδανεῦσιν,
ὅταν ὑμᾶς λοιδορῶσι, τοὺς δὲ ἐκείνοις μαρτυροῦν-
τας ὡς ἀληθῆ λέγουσι τῶν ὑμετέρων πολιτῶν οὐκ
52 ἐξελαύνετε τῆς πόλεως; οὐκ ἴστε ὅτι τὸ μὲν
ποιεῖν τι τῶν ἀπορρήτων καὶ τῶν παρὰ φύσιν
ὑποψίαν ἐπὶ τῶν πλείστων μόνον ἔχει, καὶ οὐδεὶς
ἑόρακεν οὐδὲν τῶν πολλῶν, ἀλλ' ἐν τῷ σκότει
που καὶ κρύφα λανθάνοντες ἀσεβοῦσιν οἱ κακο-

---

[1] ἕτερα added by Capps.
[2] ταύτας Koehler, τούτους Arnim: τούτοις.

---

[1] See Apollodorus, *Bibliotheca* 1. 17 (Frazer, L.C.L.):
The Lemnian women did not honour Aphroditê, and she
visited them with a noisome smell . . ., αἱ Λήμνιαι τὴν
Ἀφροδίτην οὐκ ἐτίμων· ἡ δὲ αὐταῖς ἐμβάλλει δυσοσμίαν.
[2] Aegae and Adana were Cilician towns not far east of

it is inevitable that everything else also must be a fit accompaniment for a condition such as that. For you must not suppose that, just as other disorders often attack certain particular parts of other people, such as hands or feet or face, so also here among you a local disorder has assailed your noses; nor that, just as Aphroditê, angered at the women of Lemnos, is said to have polluted their armpits,[1] so also here in Tarsus the noses of the majority have been polluted because of divine anger, in consequence of which they emit that dreadful noise. Rubbish! No, that noise is a symptom of their utter wantonness and madness, and of their scorn for all that is honourable, and their belief that nothing is dishonourable. So I assert that the talk of these women is quite in keeping with their gait and the glance of their eye. And if they cannot make anything so manifest by means of their eyes as to cause everyone to turn and gaze at them, or if they have not yet carried their art so far, still they are by no means the more respectable in other ways.

In view of that are you irritated at the people of Aegae and of Adana [2] when they revile you, while on the other hand you fail to banish from Tarsus those of your own people who testify to the truth of what your neighbours declare? Do you not know that, while the charge of doing some forbidden thing, something in violation of Nature's laws, in most cases rests only on suspicion, and no one of the masses has really seen anything at all, but, on the contrary, it is in some dark and secret retreat that the wretched culprits commit their heinous deeds all unobserved;

Tarsus and envious of its power and authority. See Or. 34. 10, 14, and 47.

δαίμονες· τὰ δὲ τοιαῦτα ξύμβολα τῆς ἀκρασίας
μηνύει τὸ ἦθος καὶ τὴν διάθεσιν, ἡ φωνή, τὸ
βλέμμα, τὸ σχῆμα, καὶ δὴ[1] καὶ ταῦτα[2] δοκοῦντα
σμικρὰ καὶ ἐν μηδενὶ λόγῳ, κουρά, περίπατος,
τὸ τὰ ὄμματα ἀναστρέφειν, τὸ ἐγκλίνειν τὸν
τράχηλον, τὸ ταῖς χερσὶν ὑπτίαις διαλέγεσθαι.
μὴ γὰρ οἴεσθε αὐλήματα μὲν καὶ κρούματα καὶ
μέλη τὰ μὲν ἐμφαίνειν τὸ ἀνδρεῖον, τὰ δὲ τὸ
θῆλυ, κινήσεις δὲ καὶ πράξεις μὴ διαφέρειν μηδ'
εἶναι μηδένα ἐν τούτοις ἔλεγχον.

53 Ἀλλ' ἐγὼ βούλομαί τινα λόγον ὑμῖν εἰπεῖν, ὃν
ἴσως καὶ ἄλλοτε ἀκηκόατε. τῶν γὰρ ἐνθάδε
δεινῶν τινα λέγουσιν εἴς τινα πόλιν ἐλθεῖν[3] τῶν
αὐτὸ τοῦτο ἔργον πεποιημένων, ὥστε εὐθὺς
εἰδέναι τὸν τρόπον ἑκάστου καὶ διηγεῖσθαι τὰ
προσόντα, καὶ μηδενὸς ὅλως ἀποτυγχάνειν· ἀλλ'
ὥσπερ ἡμεῖς τὰ ζῷα γιγνώσκομεν ὁρῶντες, ὅτι
τοῦτο μέν ἐστι πρόβατον, εἰ τύχοι, τοῦτο δὲ
κύων, τοῦτο δὲ ἵππος ἢ βοῦς· οὕτως ἐκεῖνος τοὺς
ἀνθρώπους ἠπίστατο ὁρῶν καὶ λέγειν ἠδύνατο ὅτι
οὗτος μὲν ἀνδρεῖος, οὗτος δὲ δειλός, οὗτος δὲ
ἀλαζών, οὗτος δὲ ὑβριστὴς ἢ κίναιδος ἢ μοιχός.

54 ὡς οὖν θαυμαστὸς ἦν ἐπιδεικνύμενος καὶ οὐδαμῇ
διημάρτανε, προσάγουσιν αὐτῷ σκληρόν τινα τὸ
σῶμα καὶ σύνοφρυν ἄνθρωπον, αὐχμῶντα καὶ
φαύλως διακείμενον καὶ ἐν ταῖς χερσὶ τύλους
ἔχοντα, φαιόν τι καὶ τραχὺ περιβεβλημένον ἱμάτιον,

---

[1] καὶ δὴ Wilamowitz : ἤδη.   [2] ταῦτα] ταῦτα τὰ Reiske.
[3] ἐλθεῖν added by Koehler.

yet such symptoms of their incontinence as the following reveal their true character and disposition: voice, glance, posture; yes, and the following also, which are thought to be petty and insignificant details: style of haircut, mode of walking, elevation of the eye, inclination of the neck, the trick of conversing with upturned palms.[1] For you must not think that the notes of pipes and lyre or songs reveal sometimes manliness and sometimes femininity, but that movements and actions do not vary according to sex and afford no clue to it.

But I should like to tell you a story, one that you may possibly have heard before.[2] It seems that one of the clever people of Tarsus—so the story runs—once went to a certain city. He was a man who had made it his special business to recognize instantly the character of each individual and to be able to describe his qualities, and he had never failed with any person; but just as we recognize animals when we see them and know that this, for instance, is a sheep, if such is the case, and this a dog and this a horse or ox, so that man understood human beings when he saw them and could say that this one was brave and this one a coward and this one an impostor and this man wanton or a catamite or an adulterer. Because, therefore, he was noted for his display of power and never made a mistake, the people brought before him a person of rugged frame and knitted brows, squalid and in sorry state and with callouses on his hands, wrapped in a sort of coarse, gray mantle,

---

[1] Dio leaves us in the dark regarding the precise form of most of the things here criticized. What was the significance of the upturned palm? Merely an oriental gesture?

[2] Diogenes Laertius, 7. 173, tells this story of Cleanthes.

δασὺν ἕως τῶν σφυρῶν καὶ φαύλως κεκαρμένον·
καὶ τοῦτον ἠξίουν εἰπεῖν ὅστις ἦν. ὁ δὲ ὡς
πολὺν χρόνον ἑώρα, τελευταῖον ὀκνῶν μοι δοκεῖ
τὸ παριστάμενον λέγειν οὐκ ἔφη ξυνιέναι, καὶ
βαδίζειν αὐτὸν ἐκέλευσεν. ἤδη δὲ ἀποχωρῶν
πτάρνυται· κἀκεῖνος εὐθὺς ἀνεβόησεν ὡς εἴη
κίναιδος.

55   Εἶτα ἐπ᾽ ἀνθρώπου μὲν ὁ πταρμὸς ἐξήλεγξε
τὸν τρόπον καὶ πρὸς τὰ ἄλλα πάντα ἴσχυσε τὸ μὴ
λαθεῖν· πόλιν δὲ οὐκ ἂν ἕν τι τούτων διαβάλοι
καὶ δόξης ἀναπλήσειε πονηρᾶς, καὶ ταῦθ᾽ ὅπου
μὴ δεῖται δεινοῦ τοῦ συνήσοντος τίνος ἐστὶ
σημεῖον; ἀλλ᾽ ἔγωγε πυθοίμην ἂν[1] ἡδέως τῶν
ἐμπείρων τίνι τοῦτο ἔοικεν ἢ τί βούλεται δηλοῦν.
οὔτε γὰρ κλωσμὸς οὔτε ποππυσμὸς οὔτε συριγμός
ἐστιν· ἢ τίνος ἐστὶν οἰκεῖον ἔργου καὶ πότε
μάλιστα γιγνόμενον· οὔτε γὰρ νέμουσιν οὕτως
οὔτε ἀροῦσιν οὔτε κυνηγετοῦσιν, ἀλλ᾽ οὐδὲ
56   ναυτῶν[2] ἐστιν ἡ φωνή. πότερον οὖν ἀσπαζομέ-
νων ἀλλήλους ἢ καλούντων ἢ φιλοφρονουμένων;[3]
ἀλλ᾽ ὥσπερ ὑμέναιος ἴδιόν τι μέλος ἐστὶν ἀρχαῖον
ἐπὶ τῶν γαμούντων, οὕτως καινὸς οὗτος εὕρηται
ῥυθμὸς ἄλλης τινὸς ἑορτῆς.

       Ἀλλ᾽ ἀπελεύσεσθε ἀγανακτοῦντες καὶ λελερη-
κέναι με φάσκοντες, εἰ τοσούτους λόγους μάτην

---

[1] ἂν added by Dindorf.
[2] οὐδὲ ναυτῶν Selden: οὐδὲν (οὐδὲ) αὐτῶν.
[3] After φιλοφρονουμένων Vahlen conjectured οὐμενοῦν.

his body shaggy as far as the ankles and his locks wretchedly shingled; and our friend was asked to tell what this man was. But after he had observed the man for a long while, the expert finally, with seeming reluctance to say what was in his mind, professed that he did not understand the case and bade the man move along. But just as the fellow was leaving, he sneezed, whereupon our friend immediately cried out that the man was a catamite.[1]

You see, then, that the sneeze revealed the character of a man, and in the face of all his other traits was sufficient to prevent his eluding detection; and might not some such thing subject a city to false accusations and infect it with an evil reputation, and that too in a matter requiring no expert to determine what disorder the trait betokens? However, I for my part should like to ask the experts what this snorting resembles or what it means—for it is neither a clucking sound nor a smacking of the lips nor yet an explosive whistling—or to what line of work it is related and when it is most likely to be made; for neither shepherds nor plowmen nor huntsmen employ that sound, nor does it belong to sailors. Is it, then, a sound made by men when they greet one another or call to one another or display affection? On the contrary, just as the hymeneal is a special song of early origin and used at weddings, so this must be a rhythm of recent origin, no doubt, and used at a different kind of festival.

However, you will depart in high dudgeon, declaring that I have talked nonsense, if I have uttered

---

[1] The sneeze is a well-known omen and doubtless capable of varied meanings in keeping with varied conditions; but it is not clear why so specialized a meaning should have been given in the present instance.

DIO CHRYSOSTOM

διεθέμην καὶ πρὸς οὐδὲν τῶν χρησίμων. μηδεμίαν γὰρ ἐκ τούτου βλάβην ἀπαντᾶν μηδὲ[1] χεῖρον
57 οἰκεῖσθαι τὴν πόλιν. παρὰ δὲ τοῖς Ἕλλησι πρότερον δεινὸν ἐδόκει τὸ μετακινεῖν τὴν μουσικήν, καὶ κατεβόων πάντες τῶν ῥυθμὸν εἰσαγόντων ἕτερον καὶ τὰ μέλη ποικιλώτερα ποιούντων, ὡς διαφθειρομένης ἐν τοῖς θεάτροις τῆς Ἑλλάδος. οὕτω σφόδρα τὰ ὦτα ἐφύλαττον, καὶ τηλικαύτην ἡγοῦντο δύναμιν τὴν ἀκοὴν ἔχειν, ὥστε θηλύνειν τὴν διάνοιαν, καὶ ἀδικεῖσθαι τὰ τῆς σωφροσύνης, εἰ παρὰ μικρὸν ἐνδοίη τὰ τῆς ἁρμονίας. τοιγαροῦν φασι Λακεδαιμονίους, ἐπειδὴ Τιμόθεος ἧκε παρ' αὐτούς, λαμπρὸς ὢν ἤδη καὶ δυναστεύων ἐν τῇ μουσικῇ, τήν τε κιθάραν αὐτὸν ἀφελέσθαι καὶ τῶν χορδῶν τὰς περιττὰς ἐκτεμεῖν. καὶ ὑμεῖς, ἄνδρες Ταρσεῖς, μιμήσασθε τοὺς Λακεδαιμονίους, ἐκτέμετε τὸν περιττὸν φθόγγον.

58 Ὁ παλαιὸς μῦθός φησι τὴν Κίρκην μεταβάλλειν τοῖς φαρμάκοις, ὥστε σῦς καὶ λύκους ἐξ ἀνθρώπων γίγνεσθαι· καὶ ταῦτα ἀπιστοῦμεν Ὁμήρου λέγοντος,

οἱ δὲ συῶν μὲν ἔχον κεφαλὰς φωνήν τε τρίχας τε

καὶ δέμας.

---

[1] μηδὲ Selden : μηδέν.

---

[1] The important position assigned to music in Greek education is a notable phenomenon. Plato devotes much space to the subject in books 3 and 4 of his *Republic*. Especially apposite is *Republic* 424 C. See also Aristophanes, *Clouds*, 968–72.

so many words in vain and to no useful purpose. For you will assert that no harm is encountered in consequence of this snorting and that the city is none the worse in its administration because of it. But among the Greeks in times gone by it used to be regarded as an awful thing to tamper with the art of music, and they all cried out against those who tried to introduce a different rhythm or to complicate the melody, holding that Greece was being corrupted in the theatre. So carefully did they safeguard their ears; and they attributed to what was heard such power as to effeminate the mind and violate the virtue of self-control if the principles of harmony should give way ever so little.[1] For instance, they say that the Spartans, on an occasion when Timotheus was visiting their city, he being already an artist of distinction and an authority in music, not only took away from him his lyre but even cut out the superfluous strings.[2] Do you likewise, men of Tarsus, in imitation of the Spartans, cut out the superfluous sound.

The ancient story relates that Circê worked transformations by means of her drugs, so that swine and wolves were produced from men; and we are incredulous when Homer says:

Both heads and voice and hair of swine had they,
And e'en the shape. [3]

---

[2] Dio tells the same story in 32. 67 but without specifying the victim. The " superfluous strings " presumably were strings 8 to 11, the lyre usually having no more than seven. Timotheus himself (*Persae* 215–43) refers to his quarrel with the Spartans with reference to his innovations and boasts that he had added an eleventh string to the ten of Terpander.

[3] *Odyssey* 10. 239–40.

ἀλλ' ἐκείνοις[1] μὲν τὸν νοῦν μένειν φησὶν ἔμπεδον,
τούτων δὲ ὁ νοῦς πρῶτος ἀπόλωλε καὶ διέφθαρται.
καὶ μὴν οὐχ οὕτω δεινόν ἐστιν, εἰ ἄνθρωποι
μεταξὺ προβάτων φωνὴν λάβοιεν οὐδ' εἰ βοῶν,[2]
οὐδ' ἂν χρεμετίζωσιν οὐδ' ἂν ὑλακτῶσιν, ὥσπερ
τὴν Ἑκάβην οἱ ποιηταὶ λέγουσιν ἐπὶ πᾶσι τοῖς
δεινοῖς τελευταῖον ποιῆσαι τὰς Ἐρινύας

> χαροπὰν κύνα·
> χάλκεον δέ οἱ γνάθων ἐκ πολιᾶν φθεγγομένας
> ὑπάκουε μὲν Ἴδα Τένεδός τε περίρρυτα
> Θρηίκιοί τε φιλήνεμοι πέτραι.[3]

60 οὐχ οὕτω φημὶ τοῦτ' εἶναι τὸ τέρας δεινὸν οὐδ'
ἀποτρόπαιον, ὡς ὅταν ἀνήρ τις ὢν καὶ τὸν
χαρακτῆρα ἔχων τὸν αὐτὸν καὶ τὴν φωνὴν τὴν
ἑαυτοῦ, καὶ τὰ σημεῖα τῆς φύσεως μὴ δυνάμενος
ἀνελεῖν, μηδ' ἂν ἅπαντα ποιῆται περιστέλλων,
καθάπερ φώρια κλέπτης, ὑπ' Ἐρινύων τινῶν
τυπτόμενος καὶ διαστρεφόμενος καὶ πάντα τρόπον
διακλώμενος πάντα βούληται ποιεῖν καὶ μηδὲν
ὡς πέφυκε·[4] κἄπειτα Πρωτέως τινὸς δίκην
ἀλλάττων καὶ μετατιθεὶς αὑτὸν ἐξεύρῃ φωνὴν
ἀφιέναι μήτε ἀνδρὸς μήτε γυναικὸς μήτε ἄλλου
τινὸς ζῴου,[5] μιμούμενος μηδὲ χαμαιτύπην αὐτὸ
τοῦτο χαμαιτυποῦσαν, ἀλλὰ[6] τοῦ αἰσχίστου[7] ἔργου
καὶ τῆς ἀσελγεστάτης πράξεως ὥσπερ ἂν φθεγ-

---

[1] ἐκείνοις Reiske: ἐκείνος.
[2] βοῶν Reiske: βοῶσιν.
[3] φιλήνεμοι πέτραι Jacobs, φιλάνεμοί γε πέτραι Geel, φιλήνεμοι
γύαι Wilamowitz: φιλίην ἔμοιγε.
[4] Emperius regards πάντα βούληται . . . ὡς πέφυκε as
trochaic tetrameter.
[5] After ζῴου the MSS. read μιαρὰν καὶ ἀνδρόγυνον, which
Emperius deletes.

THE THIRTY-THIRD DISCOURSE

Their minds, however, remained steadfast, he says, whereas the mind of the men of Tarsus has been the very first thing to be ruined and utterly corrupted. And really it is not so terrible that human beings should for a time take on the voice of sheep or kine or that they should neigh or howl—as indeed the poets say of Hecuba, that, as a climax to all her terrible misfortunes, the Furies made her

> Like to a hound with flashing eyes; and when
> She poured her brazen cry from hoary jaws,
> Ida gave ear and sea-girt Tenedos
> And all the wind-swept crags of Thrace.[1]

Not so terrible, in my opinion, nor so abominable was that portent as when someone who is a male and retains a male's distinctive marks and his proper speech—being incapable of eradicating also the marks of Nature, even though he makes every effort to hide them from the world, just as the thief hides stolen goods—being smitten by Furies and perverted and in every way made effeminate, is ready to do anything at all, but nothing in accord with his own nature. And then, 'some Proteus like,' in the course of his changes and bodily transformations he discovers how to emit a sound belonging to neither man nor woman nor to any other creature, not even patterning after a harlot in the practice of her calling but rather, it would seem, producing such a sound as he would make if engaged in the most shameful action, the most licentious conduct, and, what is

[1] From an unknown poet.   See Bergk, *Poetae Lyrici Graeci*, Vol. 3, pp. 721-2.

---

[6] After ἀλλά Wilamowitz adds τό.
[7] τοῦ αἰσχίστου Jacobs : τοῦ λαχίστου or τούλαχίστου.

γόμενος, καὶ ταῦτα μεθ᾽ ἡμέραν ἐκφανοῦς ὄντος
61 ἡλίου πολλῶν παρόντων. οὐχ οὕτω δεινὸν ἦν τὸ
τὰς βύρσας τῶν βοῶν ἕρπειν οὐδὲ τὸ μυκᾶσθαι τὰ
κρέα.

Ποῖος οὖν Ὅμηρος ἢ τίς Ἀρχίλοχος ἰσχύει τὰ
κακὰ ταῦτα ἐξᾶσαι; δοκεῖ γὰρ ἔμοιγε νὴ τὸν
Ἡρακλέα γενναίου τινὸς καὶ τραγικοῦ δεῖσθαι
ποιητοῦ τὸ τούτων ¹ τῶν ἀνθρώπων, ὅστις δυνή-
σεται κατασχεῖν καὶ ἀνακόψαι τοσαύτην φοράν· ²
ὡς ἤδη μανίᾳ τὸ γιγνόμενον ἔοικεν αἰσχρᾷ καὶ
62 ἀπρεπεῖ. καὶ τοῦτο τὸ νόσημα τῆς ἀπρεπείας
καὶ ἀναισχυντίας κύκλῳ περιὸν ὑμᾶς ἐπὶ πάντα
ἄγει τὸ λοιπὸν καὶ ἔργα καὶ φωνὰς καὶ σχήματα,
καὶ παντὸς ἅπτεται καὶ καθικνεῖται μέρους,
ποδῶν, χειρῶν, ὀμμάτων, γλώττης. οὔκουν ἡμῶν
ὄφελος οὐδὲν οὐδὲ τῆς ἀνειμένης ταύτης καὶ
ἀσθενοῦς παραμυθίας, ἀλλὰ μᾶλλον Στέντορός
τινος χρεία φθεγγομένου χάλκεον ἢ σιδήρεον, ὃς
ἐμοῦ βοήσεται ³ μεῖζον καὶ σαφέστερον. ὁρᾶτε
63 γὰρ οἷ πρόεισιν. γενείων τὸ πρῶτον εὑρέθη
κουρά, καὶ τοῦτο ἐδόκει μέτριον, τὸ μὴ σφόδρα
καθεικέναι, μηδ᾽ ἐπὶ πλέον, ἀλλὰ πρᾴως ἐπανορθοῦν τὴν φύσιν. οὐκοῦν ὁ τοιοῦτος ἐδόκει
πολλοῖς ἐπιδέξιος. εἶτα ἐξύρων μέχρι τῶν

¹ τούτων added by Reiske.
² φθοράν Geel.   ³ ἐμοῦ βοήσεται Koehler : ἐμβοήσεται.

more, in the light of day, under the rays of the sun, and in the presence of many. Not so terrible a portent was it when the hides of cattle crawled and their flesh bellowed.[1]

What Homer, then, or what Archilochus has the power to exorcize these evil doings? For it seems to me, by Heracles, that a noble and tragic kind of poet is needed by the conduct of these men, one who will be able to check and repel so mighty a surge of evil; since what is taking place already is like a madness that is disgraceful and unseemly. And this plague of impropriety and shamelessness, as it goes on its rounds among you, is already leading to every sort of deed and cry and posture, and attacking and invading every portion of your bodies—feet, hands, eyes, and tongue. Therefore, I can do no good at all, nor can this easy-going, feeble exhortation to which you have listened; no, a Stentor is required with throat of bronze or iron,[2] who will be able to shout more loudly and more clearly than I can. For consider the progress of the malady. The first innovation consisted in trimming the beard; and this was looked upon as moderate enough, merely not to let it grow too long, and nothing more, but just to make a slight improvement upon Nature. Well then, the man so trimmed was thought by many to look smart. The next step was to shave as far as

---

[1] An allusion to the portent that attended the eating of the kine of Helius by the comrades of Odysseus (*Odyssey* 12. 394–6).

[2] Considering the later fame of Stentor, it is surprising to discover that Homer refers to him but once, *Iliad* 5. 785–6:

Στέντορι εἰσαμένη μεγαλήτορι χαλκεοφώνῳ,
ὃς τόσον αὐδήσασχ᾽ ὅσον ἄλλοι πεντήκοντα.

παρειῶν· οὐδὲ τοῦτό πω [1] δεινόν·· ἀλλ' ὅμως ὁ
κωμικὸς καὶ τοῦτον ἐκέλευσε κατακάειν

ἐπὶ φαλήτων συκίνων ἑκκαίδεκα.

πλὴν εἶχον εὐειδῆ τὰ πρόσωπα καὶ παιδικὰ παρ'
ἡλικίαν [2] τῆς λάχνης [3] ταύτης ἀπηλλαγμένα. εἶτα,
τοῦτο λοιπὸν ἔτι, τὰ [4] σκέλη καὶ τὸ στέρνον,
ἵνα καὶ τἆλλα ὅμοιοι [5] παισὶν ὦσιν. [6] εἶτα μέχρι
τῶν βραχιόνων, εἶτα ἐπὶ τὰ αἰδοῖα μετέβαινον, [7]
ᾖ καὶ τὸ ἡβᾶν δοκεῖν [8] περιττόν. σκώπτεται δὴ
καὶ καταγελᾶται παρὰ τοῖς σοφοῖς καὶ νέοις ἡ
τῆς φύσεως τέχνη, καθάπερ ἀρχαία τις οὖσα καὶ
σφόδρα εὐήθης, ἀχρεία καὶ [9] περιττὰ προσθεῖσα
64 τῷ σώματι. τί γὰρ ὑμῖν ὀνύχων ἔδει, τί δὲ
τριχῶν; ἀλλ' οὐδὲ χειρῶν ἴσως οὐδὲ ποδῶν.
αἰδοῖα μόνον ὑμῖν [10] ἔδει ποιῆσαι καὶ γαστέρας
καὶ τροφὴν παραθεῖναι καὶ τἆλλα ὧν ἔστιν
ἀπολαύειν. τοιγαροῦν αὐτοὶ περικόπτομεν ἑαυτούς, καὶ τὰ μὲν γένεια καὶ τὴν ἥβην ἀφαιροῦμεν,
ἃ τῶν ἀνδρῶν ἴδιά ἐστιν· εἰ δὲ ἦν δυνατὸν παρὰ
τῶν γυναικῶν προσλαβεῖν ἕτερα, δῆλον ὅτι
παντελῶς τότ' ἂν ἦμεν εὐδαίμονες, οὐ καθάπερ
νῦν ἐνδεεῖς ὄντες, ἀλλ' ὁλόκληροί τινες καὶ κατὰ
φύσιν ἀνδρόγυνοι.

---

[1] τοῦτό πω Emperius : τοῦτό πῶς or τω τοπω.
[2] καὶ after ἡλικίαν deleted by Emperius.
[3] λάχνης Casaubon : ἄχνης.
[4] λοιπὸν ἔτι, τὰ Jacobs : λοιπὸν ἐπὶ τὰ.
[5] ὅμοιοι Koehler : ὅμοια.   [6] ὦσιν Crosby : ὦμεν.
[7] μετέβαινον Arnim : μεταβάν.
[8] δοκεῖν Capps : δοκεῖ.
[9] ἀχρεῖα καὶ Reiske : καὶ ἀχρεῖα.
[10] ὑμῖν Crosby : ὑμᾶς.

the cheeks[1]; and even that was nothing terrible; and yet the comic poet did bid that even such a man be burned

> Upon a heap of sixteen fig-wood phalluses.[2]

However, they did have faces that were comely and boyish beyond their years when rid of that down. Next—since this was still to try—they shaved the legs and chest, to insure that in all other respects as well they might resemble boys. Then they progressed as far as the arms; then shifted to the genitals, where evidence of youthful vigour is indeed superfluous. Thus ridicule and scorn are being showered by the clever younger set upon the artistry of Nature as being something out of date and extremely foolish, seeing that she has attached to the body things that are useless and superfluous. For instance, what need had you of nails and hair? No, not even of hands, perhaps, or feet. All that Nature had to do for you was to create genitals and bellies and to supply food and the other things from which one may derive enjoyment. That is why we trim ourselves and remove from our chins and private parts the hair which is distinctive of the full-grown male. And, if it were possible to borrow from the female certain other attributes, clearly then we should be supremely happy, not defective as at present, but whole beings and natural—epicenes!

---

[1] "As far as the cheeks" in this context seems to mean the whole face, the previous stage involving merely trimming, not shaving, and the next stage involves the legs and chest.

[2] Kock, *Com. Att. Frag.*, Aristophanes, frag. 577.

THE THIRTY-FOURTH, OR SECOND TARSIC, DISCOURSE

This Discourse, like the one preceding, was evidently delivered before a public gathering of the citizens of Tarsus. Which of the two was the earlier we have no means of knowing. Both seem to belong to Dio's later years. Yet the tone of each is so distinct as to proclaim two separate visits. In the one the speaker has much to say regarding the decadence of the times, but he still feels at liberty to treat that theme in lighter vein, laughing both at and with his audience and interlarding his remarks with quotations from the ancient poets and with literary criticism, and in general showing himself quite at ease, as indeed would befit one who spoke on invitation. In the other there seems to be no question of an invitation: Dio comes as a messenger from God in time of need. He gives not a single line of verse, and his only reference to classic times consists in the citation of Sparta and Athens as horrible examples of the fate reserved for arrogance and selfishness. The few touches of humour only serve to emphasize the speaker's earnestness.

Thus the two speeches serve to complement each other and to reveal a proud city of ancient origin, thoroughly alive, though suffering from the natural results of too great prosperity. Despite the oriental element in the population, Tarsus could be relied upon to understand allusions to Greek poetry and myth and history, and the gymnasium and the sports connected with it might well explain Paul's fondness for athletic phrase and imagery.

335

34. ΤΑΡΣΙΚΟΣ ΔΕΥΤΕΡΟΣ

1 Οὐκ ἀγνοῶ μέν, ὦ ἄνδρες Ταρσεῖς, ὅτι νομίζεται καὶ παρ' ὑμῖν καὶ παρὰ τοῖς ἄλλοις τοὺς πολίτας παριέναι καὶ συμβουλεύειν, οὐ τοὺς τυχόντας, ἀλλὰ τοὺς γνωρίμους καὶ τοὺς πλουσίους, ἔτι δὲ τοὺς καλῶς λελειτουργηκότας. οὐ γὰρ εὔλογον ἴσως τῆς μὲν οὐσίας τῆς τῶν πλουσίων μετέχειν ὑμᾶς τὸ μέρος, τῆς δὲ διανοίας μὴ ἀπολαύειν, ὁποία ποτ' ἂν ᾖ. καίτοι κιθαρῳδῶν γε ὁπόταν ἀκούειν ἐθελήσητε ἢ αὐλητῶν ἢ ἀθλητὰς θεωρεῖν, οὐ καλεῖτε τοὺς πλουσίους οὐδὲ τοὺς πολίτας, ἀλλὰ τοὺς ἐπισταμένους καὶ δυναμένους, οὐχ ὑμεῖς μόνον, ἀλλὰ πάντες οἱ τοιοῦτοι.

2 Οὐ μὴν οὐδὲ ἐκεῖνο λανθάνει με,[1] ὅτι τοὺς ἐν τούτῳ τῷ σχήματι σύνηθες μέν ἐστι τοῖς πολλοῖς Κυνικοὺς καλεῖν· οὐ μόνον δὲ οὐδὲν οἴονται διαφέρειν αὐτῶν οὐδ' ἱκανοὺς εἶναι περὶ πραγμάτων,[2] ἀλλὰ τὴν ἀρχὴν οὐδὲ σωφρονεῖν ἡγοῦνται, μαινομένους δέ τινας ἀνθρώπους καὶ ταλαιπώρους εἶναι.

---

[1] λανθάνει με Geel: λανθάνειν.
[2] Reiske would add διαλέγεσθαι after πραγμάτων, Wilamowitz σπουδαίων διαλέγεσθαι.

---

[1] These special services, called liturgies, were a form of tax imposed upon the wealthier citizens and involved the outlay of money for such public needs as the equipping and training of a chorus or the maintenance of a trireme. Some-

THE THIRTY-FOURTH, OR SECOND TARSIC, DISCOURSE

I AM well aware, men of Tarsus, that it is customary both here and elsewhere for citizens to mount the platform and give advice; not just any citizens, but those who are prominent and men of wealth, and particularly those who have honourably performed their special services toward the state.[1] For it is not reasonable, if I may say so, that you should have your share in the possessions of the wealthy but fail to profit by their intelligence, whatever that may be. And yet, whenever you wish to listen to harpists or pipers or to enjoy the sight of athletes, you do not call upon only men of wealth or your fellow citizens, but rather upon those who have expert knowledge and capacity, and this is true not only of you but of everybody like you.[2]

However, I am well aware also that it is customary for most people to give the name of Cynic to men who dress as I do;[3] and not only do they think Cynics to be no better than themselves and incompetent in practical affairs, but they consider them to be not even of sound mind to begin with, but a crazy,

times the liturgy was performed in niggardly fashion; *cf.* Aristophanes, *Acharnians* 1150–5.

[2] That is, citizens of all Greek states.

[3] For the conventional appearance of the philosopher and the popular attitude toward it see Or. 33. 14 and 72. 2.

337

σκώπτειν δὲ καὶ καταγελᾶν ἔνιοι τούτων ἑτοίμως
ἔχουσι καὶ πολλάκις μηδὲ σιγῶσιν ἐπιτρέπειν,
οὐχ ὅπως λεγόντων ἀνέχεσθαι.

3   Ἔτι δέ φασιν ὑμᾶς ἐν τῷ παρόντι καὶ λίαν
παρωξύνθαι πρὸς τοὺς φιλοσόφους καὶ καταρᾶσθαί
γε, οὐ πᾶσιν, ἀλλὰ ἐνίοις[1] αὐτῶν, πάνυ μὲν
εὐλαβῶς καὶ μετρίως τοῦτο ποιοῦντας, ὅτι μὴ
κοινῇ κατὰ[2] πάντων ἐβλασφημεῖτε, εἴ τι οἱ
ἐνθάδε ἡμάρτανον, ἐκεῖνο δὲ ἴσως ἀγνοοῦντας,
ὅτι, εἴπερ κατηρᾶσθε, οὐ τοῖς φιλοσόφοις. οὐ
γάρ ἐστιν οὐδεὶς φιλόσοφος τῶν ἀδίκων καὶ
πονηρῶν, οὐδ' ἂν τῶν ἀνδριάντων περίῃ[3] γυμνό-
τερος. οἱ δὲ δὴ τὴν πατρίδα βλάπτοντες καὶ
συνιστάμενοι κατὰ τῶν πολιτῶν πόρρω που
δοκοῦσιν εἶναί μοι τούτου τοῦ ὀνόματος.

4   Τί[4] ποτ' οὖν[5] ἐλπίσας καὶ τί βουληθεὶς παρελήλυθα
τοιοῦτος ὢν ἐν καιρῷ τοιούτῳ; μανίας γὰρ τοῦτο
ἀληθινῆς. ὅτι μηδενὸς αὐτὸς δέομαι παρ' ὑμῶν,
ἀλλὰ τῆς ὑμετέρας ὠφελείας ἕνεκα ἐσπούδακα.
ἐὰν οὖν μὴ ἀνάσχησθέ μου, δῆλον ὅτι ὑμᾶς
αὐτούς, οὐκ ἐμέ, ζημιώσετε. καίτοι οὐ[6] προσήκει

---

[1] ἐνίοις Geel: οἷς.   [2] κατὰ Reiske: μετὰ.
[3] περίῃ Emperius: περ ᾖ or ἄνπερ ᾖ.
[4] τί Pflugk: ὅτι.   [5] οὖν Emperius: ἂν.
[6] οὐ deleted by Reiske.

---

[1] The special grievance to which he refers—like so many of
the allusions in this Discourse—has escaped our knowledge.
We do know that, for a time at least, philosophers played a

wretched lot. And some are prone to mock and ridicule such people, and all too often not even to endure their silence, much less listen patiently when they speak.

And furthermore, I hear that at the present moment you have a special grievance [1] against philosophers, and indeed that you uttered curses against them—not as a class, to be sure, but in a few instances, displaying great reserve and moderation in so doing, inasmuch as you refrained from cursing philosophers in general if merely the philosophers in Tarsus were guilty of some blunder, but possibly failing to note that, though you cursed indeed, it was not really at philosophers. For no one is a philosopher [2] who belongs among the unjust and wicked, not even if he goes about more naked than statues are.[3] But those, in truth, who seek to harm their fatherland and band together against their fellow-citizens seem to me somewhat far removed from that classification.

Then in what expectation and with what purpose has a man of my stamp come before you at such a crisis? For such a step savours of real madness. I am here because there is nothing which I myself require of you, while on the contrary I have been much concerned to be of service to you. If, then, you refuse to bear with me, clearly it will be your loss and not my own. Yet is it not fitting, if you believe

prominent part in the affairs of Tarsus. Cf. Or. 33. 48 and Strabo 14. 14.

[2] Here and in the sentence to follow Dio dwells on the literal meaning of philosopher : lover of wisdom.

[3] Cf. Or. 35. 3. Possibly Dio has in mind the Gymnosophists of India (Brachmanes) ; cf. Lucian, *Fugitivi* 6 and 7.

DIO CHRYSOSTOM

γε ὑμῖν, εἴ[1] με ἡγεῖσθε καὶ τῷ ὄντι μαίνεσθαι,
δι' αὐτὸ τοῦτο ἀκοῦσαι; μὴ γὰρ οἴεσθε ἀετοὺς
μὲν καὶ ἱέρακας προσημαίνειν ἀνθρώποις τὸ δέον,
καὶ τὴν παρὰ τῶν[2] τοιούτων συμβουλὴν πιστὴν
εἶναι διὰ τὸ αὐτόματον καὶ τὸ θεῖον, ἄνδρα δὲ
ἀφιγμένον οὕτως καὶ μηδαμόθεν ὑμῖν προσήκοντα
μὴ κατὰ τὸ δαιμόνιον ἥκειν ἐροῦντα καὶ συμβουλεύ-
5 σοντα. καίτοι τὰ μὲν τῶν οἰωνῶν εἰκάζειν δεῖ,
τῶν δὲ ὑπ' ἐμοῦ λεγομένων ἔστιν ἀκούσασι
συνιέναι καὶ σκέψασθαι, ἐὰν ἄρα σαφῶς ᾖ τι
χρήσιμον.

Βούλομαι δέ, ἐπεὶ τῶν τοιούτων ἐμνήσθην, ἐν
Φρυγίᾳ τι συμβὰν εἰπεῖν, ἵν' εὐθὺς ἐνθένδε μου
καταγελᾶν ἔχητε.[3] ἀνὴρ Φρὺξ ἐπὶ κτήνους ἐβά-
διζεν. ὡς δ' ἐθεάσατό τινα κορώνην, οἰωνισά-
μενος, οἱ γὰρ Φρύγες τὰ τοιαῦτα δεινοί, λίθῳ
βάλλει καί πως τυγχάνει αὐτῆς. πάνυ οὖν ἥσθω,
καὶ νομίσας εἰς ἐκείνην τετράφθαι τὸ χαλεπὸν
ἀναιρεῖται καὶ ἀναβὰς ἤλαυνεν. ἡ δὲ μικρὸν
διαλιποῦσα ἀνέσφηλε· τὸ δὲ κτῆνος πτοηθὲν
ἀποβάλλει τὸν ἄνδρα, καὶ ὃς πεσὼν κατάγνυσι
τὸ σκέλος. ἐκεῖνος μὲν οὖν οὕτως ἀπήλλαξεν,
6 ἀχάριστος γενόμενος περὶ τὸ σύμβολον. ἐγὼ
δὲ πολύ μοι δοκῶ τῆς κορώνης ἀσφαλέστερον
βεβουλεῦσθαι καὶ πρὸς εὐγνωμονεστέρους ἄνδρας

---

[1] εἴ Jacobs: ἕνα.   [2] τῶν Jacobs: αὐτῶν.
[3] ἔχητε Emperius: ἔχοιτε.

---

[1] Madness was early associated with divine inspiration and
guidance.
[2] The subject of omens and their interpretation.
[3] Dio is making a frank appeal for the good-humoured

340

that I am really mad,[1] that you should for that very reason listen to me? For you must not think that eagles and falcons foretell to mankind what is required of them and that the counsel derived from such creatures is trustworthy because of its spontaneity and its divine inspiration, while refusing to believe that a man who has come, as I have come, having no connection with you from any point of view, has come by divine guidance to address and counsel you. Moreover, the messages of birds of omen require conjecture for their interpretation, whereas, as soon as one has heard my message one can understand its meaning and can take it under consideration, if in fact it clearly is something useful.

But now that I am on the subject,[2] I want to tell you something that happened in Phrygia, in order that at the very outset you may have an opportunity to laugh at my expense.[3] A man of Phrygia was riding on an ox. And when he spied a crow, having made the proper observation of the omen (for Phrygians are clever at that sort of thing), he hurled a stone at it and, by good luck, struck the bird. Accordingly he was much pleased, and, thinking that his own ill-fortune had thus been diverted to the crow, he picked up the bird, remounted the ox, and rode along. But the crow after a brief interval recovered; and the ox, taking fright, threw the man, and he broke his leg in the fall. So that is the way he fared for having shown ingratitude for the sign.[4] But I, methinks, have planned much more safely than the crow, and have come to men who are more

sympathy of his audience, a purpose which he successfully achieves.
    [4] This sounds very like a fable of Aesop.

ἥκειν τοῦ Φρυγός. ἐὰν γὰρ ὑμῖν δοκῶ φλυαρεῖν,
οὐ δήπου λίθοις βαλεῖτέ με, ἀλλὰ θορυβήσετε.

Φέρε οὖν, ἐπεὶ σιωπᾶτε καὶ ὑπομένετε, πρῶτον
μὲν ἐκεῖνο, εἰ μὴ σαφῶς ἴστε, ἐπιδείξω, ὅτι δεῖσθε
γνώμης ἐν τῷ παρόντι, καὶ τοιαῦτα ὑμῶν τὰ
πράγματά ἐστιν ὥστε βουλῆς ἄξια εἶναι καὶ
πολλῆς προνοίας· ἔπειθ᾿, ὅτι μηδεὶς ὑμῖν δύναται
ῥᾳδίως τούτων τὸ δέον παραινέσαι, οἱ μὲν ἀγνοίᾳ
τοῦ συμφέροντος, οἱ δέ τινες καὶ δειλίᾳ τῇ πρὸς
ὑμᾶς [1] ἢ τῇ πρὸς ἑτέρους καὶ τὸ αὑτῶν ἴσως μᾶλλον
7 ἔνιοι σκοποῦντες· ἔπειτα, ἣν αὐτὸς ἔχω γνώμην
περὶ τούτων, καὶ τί πράξασιν [2] ὑμῖν ἐπὶ τοῦ
παρόντος καὶ πῶς καθόλου προϊσταμένοις [3] τῆς
πόλεως εἰς ἅπαντα καὶ τὸν αὖθις οἴομαι συνοίσειν
χρόνον.

Ὑμῖν γάρ, ἄνδρες Ταρσεῖς, συμβέβηκε μὲν
πρώτοις εἶναι τοῦ ἔθνους, οὐ μόνον τῷ μεγίστην
ὑπάρχειν τὴν πόλιν τῶν ἐν τῇ Κιλικίᾳ καὶ μητρό-
πολιν ἐξ ἀρχῆς, ἀλλ᾿ ὅτι καὶ τὸν δεύτερον Καίσαρα
ὑπὲρ πάντας ἔσχετε οἰκείως ὑμῖν διακείμενον.
τὸ γὰρ δι᾿ ἐκεῖνον ἀτύχημα τῇ πόλει συμβὰν
εἰκότως αὐτὸν εὔνουν ὑμῖν ἐποίει καὶ σπουδάζειν,
ὅπως μείζονες ὑμῖν φανήσονται τῶν δι᾿ αὐτὸν
8 συμφορῶν αἱ παρ᾿ αὐτοῦ χάριτες. τοιγαροῦν ἃ

[1] ὑμᾶς Morel : ἡμᾶς.
[2] πράξασιν Emperius : πράξας ἄν.
[3] προϊσταμένοις Reiske : προϊστάμενος.

---

[1] Cf. Or. 33. 17. Note that the word " metropolis " no
longer bears the ancient meaning, " mother-city," but has
come to mean very much what it means today. " From the
start " refers, not to the founding of Tarsus, but presumably
to the creation of Cilicia as a Roman province in 66 B.C., from
which time Tarsus seems to have played a leading rôle.

considerate than the Phrygian. For if I seem to you to be talking rubbish, you will surely not pelt me with stones but will merely raise a hubbub.

Well then, since you are silent and indulgent toward me, first of all I wish to point out to you one thing, in case you are not fully aware of it—that you need good judgement in the present emergency, and that your problems are such as to merit counsel and much foresight; secondly, that no man in this company can readily advise you as to the proper course of action, some being really ignorant of your true advantage and some being swayed by fear of you or of others, and in certain instances, I dare say, looking rather to their own interests. Next I shall indicate my own opinion with reference to these affairs and suggest by what course of action on your part at the moment and by what general policy in your leadership of the city, things will, as I believe, work out in all respects to your advantage for the future also.

For, men of Tarsus, it has come to pass that you are foremost among your people, not merely because your city is the greatest of all the cities of Cilicia and a metropolis from the start,[1] but also because you beyond all others gained the friendly support of the second Caesar.[2] For the misfortune that befell the city on his account naturally made him well disposed toward you, and eager that the favours received at his hands should appear in your eyes of greater importance than the misfortunes he had occasioned.[3] Accordingly everything a man might

[2] That is, Augustus.
[3] Loyal to the Caesars, Tarsus had opposed Cassius and his associates; but in 42 B.C. Cassius entered the city and levied a contribution of 1500 talents. Cf. Cassius Dio 47. 30–31.

τις ἂν φίλοις ὄντως καὶ συμμάχοις καὶ τηλικαύτην
προθυμίαν ἐπιδειξαμένοις κἀκεῖνος ὑμῖν παρέσχε,
χώραν, νόμους, τιμήν, ἐξουσίαν τοῦ ποταμοῦ,
τῆς θαλάττης τῆς καθ᾽ αὑτούς.[1] ὅθεν ταχὺ μείζων
ἐγένετο ἡ πόλις καὶ διὰ τὸ μὴ πολύν τινα χρόνον
διελθεῖν τὸν ἀπὸ τῆς ἁλώσεως, καθάπερ οἱ μεγάλῃ
μὲν νόσῳ χρησάμενοι, ταχὺ δ᾽ ἀνασφήλαντες,
ἐπειδὰν τύχωσιν[2] ἱκανῆς τῆς μετὰ ταῦτα ἐπιμελείας, πολλάκις μᾶλλον εὐέκτησαν.

9   Καὶ μὴν τά γε ἐφεξῆς, οὐχ ὡς[3] οἴεταί τις,
ὤνησε τὴν πόλιν τὸ γενέσθαι τινὰς τῶν ἡγεμόνων
βιαίους καὶ τούτοις ἐπεξελθεῖν ὑμᾶς. πρὸς μέν
γε τὸ φανῆναί τινας ὄντας[4] καὶ μὴ μόνον ἑαυτοῖς,
ἀλλὰ καὶ τοῖς ἄλλοις[5] βοηθῆσαι, καὶ νὴ Δία ὥστε
τοὺς αὖθις ὀκνηρότερον ἐξαμαρτάνειν, συνήνεγ-
κε τὸ δίκην ἐκείνους ὑποσχεῖν· ἄλλως δὲ τὴν
πόλιν ἐπίφθονον ἐποίησε καὶ δυσχερεστέρους ὑμᾶς
δοκεῖν φύσει καὶ ῥᾳδίως αἰτιᾶσθαι. τὸ γὰρ πολλάκις ἐγκαλεῖν ἤδη ποτὲ ἔδοξε τοῦ συκοφαντεῖν
σημεῖον, ἄλλως τε ὁπόταν περὶ ἡγεμόνων ὁ λόγος
ᾖ πρὸς ἡγεμόνας. οὐ γὰρ τῷ πλέον τι πάσχειν,
ἀλλὰ τῷ μὴ ἐθέλειν ἄρχεσθαι τὴν ἀπέχθειαν
ὑπονοοῦσι γίγνεσθαι.

[1] αὑτούς Reiske: αὑτήν.
[2] ἐπειδὰν τύχωσιν Reiske: ἐπιτύχωσιν.
[3] οὐχ ὡς Emperius: ὡς οὐκ.
[4] After ὄντας Reiske adds ὑμᾶς.
[5] After ἄλλοις Arnim adds ἱκανούς.

[1] After Philippi both Augustus and Antony showed special
favour to Tarsus. Among other things, independence and
exemption from taxation were granted the city. Cf. Cassius
Dio 47. 31 and Appian, *Bellum Civile* 5. 7.

bestow upon those who were truly friends and allies and had displayed such eagerness in his behalf he has bestowed upon you:[1] land, laws, honour, control of the river and of the sea in your quarter of the world. And this is why your city grew rapidly, and also because not much time had elapsed since its capture;[2] just as with men who have experienced serious illness but have speedily recovered: when they receive adequate care thereafter, they are frequently in better health than before.

Furthermore, as to subsequent events at least, contrary to popular belief it benefited your city when some of your superior officers proved to be men of violence and you proceeded to prosecute them.[3] Certainly in order to show that you amounted to something, and could aid yourselves and others too—and also, by Zeus, to make their successors not quite so ready to do wrong—it was really beneficial for those men of violence to pay the penalty for their misdeeds; and yet, in another way, it made the city an object of hatred, and gave you the reputation of being naturally captious and prone to bring accusations rashly. For to make many accusations has ere this been held to be a sign of malicious prosecution, especially when the accusation involves men in authority, and is brought before men in authority. For people suspect that the hostility arose, not because you were treated too severely, but because you were unwilling to submit to authority.

[2] That is, by Cassius.
[3] Cf. § 42. Dio appears to use the term ἡγεμόνες repeatedly in this Discourse with reference to 'leaders' who owed their authority, not to election, but to appointment.

10 Πάλιν τοίνυν ἕτερον πρᾶγμα συμβὰν ὑπὲρ
ὑμῶν τρόπον τινὰ ὅμοιον τούτῳ γέγονεν. οἱ
γὰρ Αἰγαῖοι φιλοτιμίαν ἀνόητον ἐπανελόμενοι
πρὸς ὑμᾶς, τὸ περὶ τὰς ἀπογραφὰς ἐξαμαρτάνοντες, αὐτοὶ μὲν ἔπταισαν, ἔτι δὲ μᾶλλον τὸν
καθ᾿ ὑμῶν φθόνον καὶ τοιαύτην τινὰ ἡσυχῇ δια-
βολὴν εἰργάσαντο πρὸς τὴν πόλιν ὡς ἐπαχθῆ
11 καὶ βαρεῖαν ταῖς ἄλλαις. καὶ ταῦτα μὲν ἐκ τοῦ
πρότερον χρόνου· τὰ δὲ νῦν οἵ γε[1] Μαλλῶται
διαφέρονται πρὸς ὑμᾶς, αὐτοὶ μὲν ἅπαντα ἀδικοῦντες
καὶ θρασυνόμενοι, τῷ δὲ ἀσθενεῖς εἶναι καὶ πολὺ
ἥττους[2] μᾶλλον τὴν τῶν ἀδικουμένων τάξιν ἀεὶ
λαμβάνοντες. οὐ γὰρ ἃ ποιοῦσιν ἔνιοι σκοποῦσιν,
ἀλλὰ τίνες ὄντες, οὐδὲ τοὺς ἀδικοῦντας ἢ βιαζο-
μένους ἐθέλουσιν ἐξετάζειν πολλάκις, ἀλλ᾿ οὓς
εἰκὸς βιάζεσθαι τῷ δύνασθαι πλέον. εἰ γοῦν
ὑφ᾿ ὑμῶν ἐπράχθη τι τοιοῦτον οἷον ὑπ᾿ ἐκείνων
νῦν γέγονε, πορθεῖν ἂν ἐδοκεῖτε τὰς πόλεις καὶ
ἀποστάσεως ἄρχειν[3] καὶ πολέμου, καὶ στρατο-
πέδου δεῖν ἐφ᾿ ὑμᾶς.

12 Οὐκοῦν δεινὰ πάσχομεν, ἐρεῖ τις, εἰ τούτοις μὲν
ἐξέσται ποιεῖν ὅ τι ἂν ἐθέλωσι καὶ τοῦτο ἀπολαύ-

---

[1] γε Reiske : τε.
[2] ἀεὶ after ἥττους deleted by Emperius.
[3] ἄρχειν Casaubon : ἀρχὴν.

---

[1] A Cilician city some miles east of Tarsus, on the gulf
of Issus, now Ayas Kalê. Cf. also §§ 14, 47, 48.
[2] The precise nature of the " registers " is unknown; but
the incident is typical of the general resentment in Cilicia at
the overlordship of Tarsus. Cf. especially § 14.

THE THIRTY-FOURTH DISCOURSE

To continue then, another happening in which you were concerned has, in a measure, turned out like that just mentioned. For the people of Aegae,[1] having resumed a foolish quarrel with you, being at fault in the matter of the registers,[2] did indeed fail in that enterprise, but they made the dislike against you still greater, and they stealthily developed a prejudice against your city as being obnoxious and oppressive toward the other cities. And these instances, it is true, are drawn from times gone by; but at this present moment the people of Mallus[3] certainly are at odds with you and, although wholly in the wrong themselves and guilty of insolence, yet because of their weakness and their great inferiority as compared with you, they always assume the air of being the injured party. For it is not what men do that some persons consider but who they are; nor is it the wrong-doers or those who actually resort to force whom they often wish to criticize, but rather those who may be expected to resort to force because they have the greater power. At any rate, if anything had been done by you such as has been done by Mallus in the present instance,[4] people would think that you were sacking their cities and starting a revolution and war, and that an army must take the field against you.

" Well, it is a shame, then," someone will say, " if they are to be at liberty to do whatever they

---

[3] On the river Pyramus, a short distance east of Tarsus. The quarrel involved certain territorial claims as well as the requirement that Cilicians come to Tarsus for certain religious and judicial purposes. Cf. §§ 43–47.

[4] Presumably Mallus had seized the territory in dispute, territory which Dio calls worthless (§§ 45–6).

σουσι¹ τῆς ἐρημίας τῆς ἑαυτῶν, ἡμεῖς δὲ κινδυνεύ-
σομεν, ἐὰν μόνον κινηθῶμεν. ἔστω δεινὸν καὶ
ἄδικον· ἀλλ' οὐκ, εἴ τι μὴ δίκαιον πέφυκε γίγνεσθαι, δεῖ πρὸς τοῦτο φιλονικοῦντας αὐτοὺς περι-
βάλλειν ἀτόπῳ τινί, μᾶλλον δὲ προορᾶν καὶ
φυλάττεσθαι. τὸ γὰρ συμβαῖνον ὅμοιόν ἐστι τῷ
περὶ τοὺς ἀθλητάς, ὅταν ἐλάττων πρὸς πολὺ μείζω
13 μάχηται. τῷ μὲν γὰρ οὐδὲν ἔξεστι παρὰ τὸν
νόμον, ἀλλὰ κἂν ἄκων ἁμάρτῃ τι, μαστιγοῦται·
τὸν δ' οὐδεὶς ὁρᾷ πάνθ' ἃ δύναται ποιοῦντα.
τοιγαροῦν κἀκεῖ σωφρονοῦντος ἀνδρός ἐστι καὶ
ταῖς ἀληθείαις κρείττονος τῇ δυνάμει περιεῖναι,
τὰς δὲ πλεονεξίας ταύτας ἐᾶν, καὶ ὑμεῖς ἂν²
ἔχητε νοῦν, τοῖς δικαίοις περιέσεσθε καὶ τῷ
μεγέθει τῆς πόλεως τῶν φθονούντων, πρὸς ὀργὴν
δὲ οὐδὲν οὐδὲ ἀγανακτοῦντες δράσετε. καὶ περὶ
μὲν τούτων αὖθις, ὥσπερ, οἶμαι, καὶ προεθέμην.

14 Νῦν δὲ καὶ τὰ λοιπὰ ἐπέξειμι διὰ πλείονος
σκέψεως, ἧς φημι δεῖσθαι τὸν ἐνεστῶτα καιρόν.
ἡ μέν γε τῶν Μαλλωτῶν ἀπέχθεια καὶ στάσις
ἧττον ὀφείλει λυπεῖν ὑμᾶς. τὸ δὲ Σολεῖς τούτους
καὶ Ἀδανεῖς καί τινας ἴσως ἄλλους ὁμοίως ἔχειν
καὶ μηδὲν ἐπιεικέστερον, ἀλλὰ καὶ βαρύνεσθαι
καὶ βλασφημεῖν καὶ μᾶλλον ἑτέρων ὑπακούειν
ἐθέλειν, ὑποψίαν ποιεῖ τοῦ μηδὲ τοὺς Αἰγαίους

---

¹ ἀπολαύσουσι Reiske: ἀπολαύουσι.
² ἐάν, καὶ ὑμεῖς ἂν Reiske: ἐὰν ὑμεῖς.

---

¹ Athletic scenes on Greek vases depict an official with arm
upraised to administer punishment for infraction of the rules.
On scourging athletes cf. Or. 31. 119.
² § 7.
³ Soli and Adana were near neighbours of Tarsus, to west
and east respectively.

please and to derive that advantage from their very helplessness, while we are to be in danger if we make a single move." Granted that it is a shame and unfair, still, if some unfairness is the natural consequence, you should not through obstinacy on that point cause yourselves to be involved in an absurd situation, but should rather look to the future and be on your guard. For what is happening to you resembles what happens in the case of athletes when a smaller man contends against one much larger. For the larger man is not allowed to do anything contrary to the rules, but even if unwittingly he is guilty of a foul, he gets the lash;[1] whereas nobody observes the smaller, though he does anything within his power. Accordingly not only in athletics is it the part of a man of discretion and one who is really the better man to win by his strength and overlook these unfair advantages, but also in your case, if you are sensible, you will by justice and by the greatness of your city overcome those who bear you malice, and you will do nothing in anger or vexation. And on that subject more later, as indeed, methinks, I promised in the beginning.[2]

But at the moment I shall treat the other items that still remain, giving to them that fuller consideration which I claim is required by the present crisis. At any rate the hatred and rebellion of Mallus ought to disturb you less than it does. But the fact that your neighbours in Soli and in Adana,[3] and possibly some others, are in a similar frame of mind and are not a whit more reasonable, but chafe under your domination and speak ill of you and prefer to be subject to others than yourselves—all this creates the suspicion that possibly the people of Aegae and

τάχα μηδὲ τοὺς Μαλλώτας παντάπασιν ἀδίκως
ἄχθεσθαι, μηδὲ τοὺς μὲν φθόνῳ, τοὺς δὲ πλεονεκ-
τεῖν βουλομένους ἠλλοτριῶσθαι πρὸς ὑμᾶς, ἀλλ᾽
ἴσως εἶναί τι [1] τοιοῦτον περὶ τὴν πόλιν καὶ ὑβρίζειν
15 πως καὶ ἐνοχλεῖν τοὺς ἐλάττονας. ταῦτα γὰρ ἔστι
μὲν οὐκ ἀληθῆ, ταὐτὰ δ᾽ ἂν [2] ὑμᾶς ὡς ἀληθῆ
βλάψειεν.

Φέρε δὴ καὶ τὰ [3] πρὸς τὸν στρατηγὸν ὑμῖν ὡς
ἔχει λογίσασθε.   πρότερον μὲν ὑποψία μόνον
ὑπῆρχεν ὡς οὐχ ἡδέως ὑμῶν διακειμένων, ἀλλ᾽
ὅμως ἐκεῖνός τε ἐπολιτεύετο πρὸς ὑμᾶς καὶ ὑμεῖς
πρὸς ἐκεῖνον καὶ φανερὸν οὐδὲν ἦν· ἄρτι δὲ ὑμεῖς
τε τῷ δοκεῖν ἐλαττοῦσθαι παροξυνθέντες εἴπατέ
τι κἀκεῖνος προήχθη καὶ γράψαι πρὸς ὀργὴν καὶ
ποιῆσαι τοῦθ᾽, ὅπερ μὴ πρότερον.

16   Νὴ Δία, ἀλλά γε τὰ τῆς πόλεως αὐτῆς [4] καὶ
τὰ πρὸς ἀλλήλους ἡμῖν [5] ὡς δεῖ πρόεισιν. οὐ χθὲς
καὶ [6] πρῴην χωρὶς ἦν ὁ δῆμος καὶ χωρὶς ἡ βουλὴ
καὶ νῦν ἔτι καθ᾽ αὑτοὺς οἱ γέροντες, ἰδίᾳ [7]
τὸ συμφέρον ἑκάστων [8] δῆλον ὅτι σκοπούντων;
ὥσπερ εἰ καταπλεόντων [9] ἰδίᾳ μὲν οἱ ναῦται τὸ

[1] τι Casaubon: τό.
[2] ταὐτὰ δ᾽ ἂν Emperius and Koehler: ταῦτα δ᾽.
[3] τὰ added by Reiske.
[4] νὴ Δία, ἀλλά γε τὰ τῆς πόλεως αὐτῆς Casaubon: νὴ δία
ἀλλά γε νὴ δία τῆς πόλεως αὐτῆς M; νὴ δία ἀλλά γε νὴ δία διὰ
τῆς πόλεως ὑμῖν αὐτῆς UB.
[5] ἡμῖν Capps: ὑμῖν.
[6] οὐ χθὲς καὶ Wilamowitz: οὐχ ὡς.
[7] ἰδίᾳ Valesius: διὰ.   [8] ἑκάστων Reiske: ἑκάστῳ.
[9] καταπλεόντων] καὶ τὰ πλεόντων M, κοινῇ (or ἅμα) πλεόντων
Emperius, πλεόντων Arnim.

---

[1] The term στρατηγός occurs in the records of many cities
of that day. His functions and authority were not always

of Mallus also are not wholly unwarranted in their vexation, and that their estrangement has not been due in the one instance to envy and in the other to a determination to get unfair advantage, but that possibly there is an element of truth in what they say about your city, namely, that it does somehow bully and annoy peoples who are weaker. For although these charges are not actually true, still they might do you the same harm as if they were.

Well then, consider also the nature of your relations with the general.[1] At first there was merely distrust, on the assumption that you were not agreeably disposed toward him; but still he performed his civic duties toward you and you toward him, and there was nothing visible on the surface; but recently you, irritated by the thought that you were getting the worst of it, made a statement, and he on his part was moved to write angrily and to put that anger into operation, a thing he had never done before.

'Yes, by Zeus,' some one may retort, 'but at least the business of the city itself and our dealings with one another are proceeding as they should.' Is it not true that but a day or two ago the Assembly took one course and the Council another and that the Elders [2] still maintain a position of independence, each body clearly consulting its own self-interest? It was just as if, when a ship is putting in for shore,

---

the same. Cf. Mitteis und Wilcken, *Grundzüge und Chrestomathie der Papyruskunde*, s.v. στρατηγός. The precise status of the general at Tarsus is unknown. Was he chosen by the citizens or appointed by Rome? Was it to Rome that he wrote? Possibly he was at odds with the *prytanis* (§ 42).

[2] Poland, *Geschichte des griechischen Vereinswesens*, p. 99, maintains that the Elders formed a distinct political organization both in Tarsus and in many other cities of that time.

DIO CHRYSOSTOM

συμφέρον αὐτοῖς ζητοῖεν, ἰδίᾳ[1] δὲ ὁ κυβερνήτης
ἰδίᾳ δὲ ὁ ναύκληρος. καὶ γὰρ εἰ πολλάκις ταῦτα
λέγεται, ἀλλ' οὖν προσήκει μὴ[2] διὰ τοῦτο παραπέμπειν. οὐ γὰρ τὸ πρώτως ῥηθὲν οὐδ' ὃ μὴ
πρότερόν τις ἤκουσε δεῖ προθύμως ἀποδέχεσθαι,
τὸ δὲ οἰκεῖον τῷ πράγματι καὶ τὸ χρείαν τινὰ
ἔχον.

17 Νὴ Δία, ἀλλὰ νῦν ὡμολογήκαμεν καὶ κοινῇ
βουλευόμεθα. καὶ τίς ἂν ἀσφαλῆ καὶ βέβαιον
ἡγήσαιτο τὴν τοιαύτην ὁμόνοιαν, τὴν ὑπ' ὀργῆς
μὲν γενομένην, τριῶν δὲ οὖσαν ἢ τεττάρων ἡμερῶν; οὐδὲ γὰρ ὑγιαίνειν ἀσφαλῶς εἴποι τις
ἂν[3] τὸν πρὸ μικροῦ πυρέττοντα. μὴ τοίνυν μηδὲ
ὑμεῖς αὐτοὺς ὁμονοεῖν λέγετε, πρὶν ἂν ὑμῖν
μάλιστα μὲν πολλαπλάσιος διέλθῃ χρόνος· εἰ
δ' οὖν, τοσοῦτος[4] ὅσον δὴ διεφέρεσθε·[5] μηδ' εἰ
ταὐτό ποτ' ἐφθέγξασθε[6] καὶ τὴν αὐτὴν ἔσχετε[7]
ὁρμήν, καὶ δὴ νομίζετε ἐξῃρῆσθαι τὸ νόσημα τῆς
18 πόλεως. καὶ γὰρ ἐν τοῖς ἀναρμόστοις ὀργάνοις
ἐνίοτε οἱ φθόγγοι συνεφώνησαν πρὸς ὀλίγον,
εἶτα εὐθὺς ἀπάδουσιν. ὥσπερ οὖν τὸ μὲν τρῶσαί
τι καὶ διελεῖν ταχὺ γίγνεται καὶ πάνυ ῥᾳδίως, τὸ

---

[1] ἰδίᾳ Valesius: διὰ.
[2] ἀλλ' οὖν προσήκει μὴ] προσήκει μὴ M, ἀλλ' οὐ προσήκει
Reiske, ἀλλ' οὐ προσήκει με Wendland.
[3] ἂν added by Dindorf.
[4] τοσοῦτος Casaubon: τοιοῦτον.
[5] δὴ διεφέρεσθε Reiske, δὴ διαφέρεσθε Emperius: μὴ διαφέρεσθαι.
[6] εἰ . . . ἐφθέγξασθε Pflugk: ἐπ' αὐτόποτε φθέγξασθαι.
[7] ἔσχετε Pflugk: ἔχετε.

---

[1] Dio seems to be apologizing for comparing Tarsus to
a ship and warning against treating the comparison lightly

the sailors should seek their own advantage, the pilot his, and the owner his. For even if this comparison[1] is made repeatedly, still it is your duty not on that account to disregard it. For it is not that which is told for the first time nor that which one has never heard before which one should eagerly accept as true,[2] but rather that which is germane to the situation and may be put to some practical use.

" Oh yes," you may reply, " but now we have reached an agreement and are united in our counsel." Nay, who could regard as safe and sure that sort of concord, a concord achieved in anger and of no more than three or four days' standing? Why, you would not say a man was in assured good health who a short time back was burning with fever. Well then, neither must you say you are in concord until, if possible, you have enjoyed a period of concord many times as long as that—at any rate as long as your discord—and just because perhaps on some occasion you all have voiced the same sentiment and experienced the same impulse, you must not for that reason assume that now at last the disease has been eradicated from the city. For the fact is that with discordant instruments of music sometimes the notes do sound in unison for a brief moment, only straightway to clash again. Or again, just as the act of wounding and dismembering takes place quickly and quite easily, but the process

as a figure that is trite. The passage has caused some trouble, but the text seems sound.

[2] Dio may have in mind the saying of Homer, *Odyssey* 1. 351-2 : " for men praise that song the most which comes the newest to their ears " (Murray, L.C.L.).

δὲ συμφῦσαι καὶ συναγαγεῖν χρόνου δεῖται καὶ προσοχῆς, οὕτω καὶ ἐπὶ τῶν πόλεων ἔχει· τὸ μὲν διενεχθῆναι καὶ στασιάσαι πρόχειρον καὶ διὰ μικρὰ συμβαίνει πολλάκις, τὸ δὲ καταστῆναι καὶ τὴν προσήκουσαν λαβεῖν διάθεσιν καὶ πίστιν μὰ Δί᾽ οὐκ ἔστιν εἰπόντας οὐδὲ δόξαντας μετανοεῖν εὐθὺς ἔχειν.

19   "Ἴσως μὲν γὰρ οὐ παρὰ μόνοις [1] ὑμῖν, ἀλλὰ καὶ παρὰ τοῖς ἄλλοις ἅπασι μεγάλης τινὸς τοῦτο δεῖται θεραπείας, μᾶλλον δὲ εὐχῆς. οὐ γὰρ ἔστιν ἄλλως ἢ τῶν κινούντων κακῶν καὶ ταρασσόντων ἀπολυθέντας, φθόνου,[2] πλεονεξίας, φιλονεικίας, τοῦ ζητεῖν ἕκαστον αὔξειν ἑαυτόν, καὶ τὴν πατρίδα καὶ τὸ κοινῇ συμφέρον ἐάσαντα,[3] συμπνεῦσαί ποτε ἰσχυρῶς καὶ ταὐτὰ προελέσθαι. ὡς παρ᾽ οἷς ἂν ἰσχύῃ ταῦτα καὶ τοιαῦθ᾽ ἕτερα, τούτους ἀνάγκη τὸν ἀεὶ χρόνον ἐπισφαλεῖς εἶναι καὶ διὰ μικρὰ συμπίπτειν καὶ θορυβεῖσθαι, καθάπερ ἐν θαλάττῃ πνευμάτων ἐναντίων [4] ἰσχυόν-
20   των. ἐπεί τοι μηδὲ τὴν βουλὴν αὐτὴν ἡγεῖσθ᾽ ὁμονοεῖν μηδ᾽ ὑμᾶς τὸν δῆμον. εἰ γοῦν τις ἐπεξίοι πάντας, δοκεῖ μοι μηδ᾽ ἂν δύο ἄνδρας εὑρεῖν [5] ἐν τῇ πόλει τὸ αὐτὸ φρονοῦντας, ἀλλ᾽ ὥσπερ ἔνια τῶν ἀνιάτων καὶ χαλεπῶν νοσημάτων, ἃ δι᾽ ὅλων εἴωθεν ἔρχεσθαι τῶν σωμάτων καὶ οὐδέν ἐστι μέρος εἰς ὃ μὴ κάτεισιν, οὕτως ἡ

---

[1] οὐ παρὰ μόνοις Casaubon : συνταραττομένοις or συμπραττο-
μένοις.
[2] φθόνου Reiske : φόνου.   [3] ἐάσαντα Reiske : ἐάσαντας.
[4] ἐναντίων Reiske : ἐναντίως.

of healing and knitting together requires time and serious attention, so it is also in the case of cities: quarrelling and party strife are within easy reach and frequently occur for paltry reasons, whereas men may not, by Zeus, immediately arrive at a real settlement of their difficulties and acquire the mental state and the confidence of their neighbours befitting such a settlement merely by claiming to be repentant, nor yet by being thought to be repentant.

For not among you alone, I dare say, but also among all other peoples, such a consummation requires a great deal of attentive care—or, shall I say, prayer? For only by getting rid of the vices that excite and disturb men, the vices of envy, greed, contentiousness, the striving in each case to promote one's own welfare at the expense of both one's native land and the common weal—only so, I repeat, is it possible ever to breathe the breath of harmony in full strength and vigour and to unite upon a common policy. Since those in whom these and similar vices are prevalent must necessarily be in a constant state of instability, and liable for paltry reasons to clash and be thrown into confusion, just as happens at sea when contrary winds prevail. For, let me tell you, you must not think that there is harmony in the Council itself, nor yet among yourselves, the Assembly. At any rate, if one were to run through the entire list of citizens, I believe he would not discover even two men in Tarsus who think alike, but on the contrary, just as with certain incurable and distressing diseases which are accustomed to pervade the whole body, exempting no member of it from their inroads,

---

⁵ εὑρεῖν Reiske: ἔχειν.

τραχύτης αὕτη καὶ τὸ μικροῦ δεῖν ἅπαντας
ἀλλήλων ἀπεστράφθαι διαπεφοίτηκε τῆς πόλεως.

21 Ἵνα γὰρ τὴν βουλὴν ἀφῶ καὶ τὸν δῆμον τούς
τε[1] νέους καὶ τοὺς γέροντας, ἔστι πλῆθος οὐκ
ὀλίγον ὥσπερ ἔξωθεν τῆς πολιτείας· τούτους δὲ
εἰώθασιν ἔνιοι λινουργοὺς καλεῖν· καί ποτε μὲν
βαρύνονται καί φασιν ὄχλον εἶναι περισσὸν καὶ
τοῦ θορύβου καὶ τῆς ἀταξίας αἴτιον, ποτὲ[2] δὲ
μέρος ἡγοῦνται τῆς πόλεως καὶ πάλιν[3] ἀξιοῦσιν.
οὓς εἰ μὲν οἴεσθε βλάπτειν ὑμᾶς καὶ στάσεως
ἄρχειν καὶ ταραχῆς, ὅλως ἐχρῆν ἀπελάσαι καὶ μὴ
παραδέχεσθαι ταῖς ἐκκλησίαις· εἰ δὲ τρόπον
τινὰ πολίτας[4] εἶναι τῷ[5] μὴ μόνον οἰκεῖν, ἀλλὰ
καὶ γεγονέναι τοὺς πλείους ἐνθάδε καὶ μηδεμίαν
ἄλλην ἐπίστασθαι πόλιν, οὐδὲ ἀτιμάζειν δήπου

22 προσήκει[6] οὐδὲ ἀπορρηγνύειν αὐτῶν. νυνὶ δὲ ἐξ
ἀνάγκης ἀφεστᾶσι τὴν γνώμην τοῦ κοινῇ[7] συμφέροντος, ὀνειδιζόμενοι καὶ δοκοῦντες ἀλλότριοι.
τούτου δὲ οὐθέν ἐστι βλαβερώτερον ταῖς πόλεσιν
οὐδὲ ὃ μᾶλλον στάσιν ἐγείρει καὶ διαφοράν,[8]
ὥσπερ ἐπὶ τῶν σωμάτων ὁ προσγενόμενος ὄγκος,
ἂν μὲν οἰκεῖος ᾖ τῷ λοιπῷ σώματι καὶ συμφυής,

---

[1] τούς τε Emperius : τε τούς.
[2] ποτὲ UB] πᾶν M, πάλιν Emperius.
[3] πάλιν] πολλοῦ Reiske.
[4] πολίτας Reiske : πολιτίας or πολιτείας.
[5] τῷ Reiske : τό.
[6] προσήκει Casaubon : προσήκειν.
[7] κοινῇ Reiske : κοινοῦ.
[8] διαφοράν Emperius : διαφθοράν.

---

[1] The phrase τούς τε νέους καὶ τοὺς γέροντας seems natural
enough in such a connection, but see § 16 and Poland, *Geschichte*

so this state of discord, this almost complete estrangement of one from another, has invaded your entire body politic.

For instance, to leave now the discord of Council and Assembly, of the Youth and the Elders,[1] there is a group of no small size which is, as it were, outside the constitution. And some are accustomed to call them 'linen-workers,'[2] and at times the citizens are irritated by them and assert that they are a useless rabble and responsible for the tumult and disorder in Tarsus, while at other times they regard them as a part of the city and hold the opposite opinion of them. Well, if you believe them to be detrimental to you and instigators of insurrection and confusion, you should expel them altogether and not admit them to your popular assemblies; but if on the other hand you regard them as being in some measure citizens, not only because they are resident in Tarsus, but also because in most instances they were born here and know no other city, then surely it is not fitting to disfranchise them or to cut them off from association with you. But as it is, they necessarily stand aloof in sentiment from the common interest, reviled as they are and viewed as outsiders. But there is nothing more harmful to a city than such conditions, nothing more conducive to strife and disagreement. Take for example the human body: the bulk that comes with the passing years, if it is in keeping with the rest of the person and natural to it, produces

des griechischen Vereinswesens, p. 95. Poland cites evidence to show that both groups formed political organizations.

[2] Poland, *op. cit.*, p. 117, views the " linen-workers " as a gild. It may be remarked that weavers are said to be in relatively low repute in the Orient to-day.

εὐεξίαν ποιεῖ καὶ μέγεθος· εἰ δὲ μή, νόσου καὶ
διαφθορᾶς αἴτιος γίγνεται.

23 Τί οὖν σὺ κελεύεις ἡμᾶς; τοὺς ἅπαντας
ἀναγράψαι πολίτας, ναί φημι,[1] καὶ τῶν αὐτῶν
ἀξίους,[2] ἀλλὰ μηδὲ[3] ὀνειδίζειν μηδὲ ἀπορρίπτειν,
ἀλλὰ μέρος αὐτῶν,[4] ὥσπερ εἰσί, νομίζειν. οὐ μὲν
γάρ, ἄν τις καταβάλῃ πεντακοσίας δραχμάς, δύναται φιλεῖν ὑμᾶς καὶ τῆς πόλεως εὐθὺς ἄξιος
γεγονέναι· εἰ δέ τις ἢ πένης ὢν[5] ἢ πολιτογραφοῦν-
τός τινος οὐ μετείληφε τοῦ ὀνόματος, οὐ μόνον
αὐτὸς παρ' ὑμῖν γεγονώς, ἀλλὰ καὶ τοῦ πατρὸς
αὐτοῦ καὶ τῶν προγόνων, οὐχ οἷός ἐστιν ἀγαπᾶν
τὴν πόλιν οὐδ' ἡγεῖσθαι πατρίδα, καὶ λίνον[6] μὲν
εἴ τις ἐργάζεται, χείρων ἐστὶν ἑτέρου καὶ δεῖ
τοῦτο προφέρειν αὐτῷ καὶ λοιδορεῖσθαι· βαφεὺς
δὲ ἢ σκυτοτόμος ἢ τέκτων ἐὰν ᾖ,[7] οὐδὲν προσήκει
ταῦτα[8] ὀνειδίζειν.

24 Καθόλου δὲ οὐ[9] τοῦτο μάλιστα τῶν ἐν τῇ
πόλει βουλόμενος εἰπεῖν οὐδὲ οἷόν ἐστι δεῖξαι
προῆλθον ἴσως, ἀλλ' ἐκεῖνο σαφὲς ὑμῖν ποιήσων,[10]
ὅπως διάκεισθε πρὸς ἀλλήλους, καὶ νὴ Δία εἰ[11]
πιστεύειν ὑμᾶς ἄξιον τῇ παρούσῃ καταστάσει καὶ
κατ' ἀλήθειαν οἴεσθαι νῦν[12] συμπεπνευκέναι.

---

[1] ναί φημι] omitted by M, deleted by Arnim.
[2] ἀξίους Wilamowitz, ἀξιοῦν Casaubon : αἰτίους.
[3] ἀλλὰ μηδὲ] ἀλλὰ μὴ Reiske, ἅμα μηδὲ Wilamowitz.
[4] αὐτῶν Emperius : αὐτῶν.
[5] ἢ πένης ὢν] πένης ὢν B, εἴη πένης ὢν M, ἢ πένης ἐστὶν
Emperius.
[6] λίνον Arnim : δεινόν.   [7] ᾖ added by Casaubon.
[8] ταῦτα Casaubon : αὐτά.
[9] οὐ added by Casaubon.
[10] ποιήσων Reiske : ποιῶν.
[11] εἰ added by Emperius.

well-being and a desirable stature, but otherwise it is a cause of disease and death.

" Well then, what do *you* bid us do? " I bid you enroll them all as citizens— yes, I do—and just as deserving as yourselves, and not to reproach them or cast them off, but rather to regard them as members of your body politic, as in fact they are. For it cannot be that by the mere payment of five hundred drachmas a man can come to love you and immediately be found worthy of citizenship;[1] and, at the same time, that a man who through poverty or through the decision of some keeper-of-the-rolls has failed to get the rating of a citizen—although not only he himself had been born in Tarsus, but also his father and his forefathers as well—is therefore incapable of affection for the city or of considering it to be his fatherland; it cannot be that, if a man is a linen-worker, he is inferior to his neighbour and deserves to have his occupation cast in his teeth and to be reviled for it, whereas, if he is a dyer or a cobbler or a carpenter, it is unbecoming to make those occupations a reproach.[2]

But, speaking generally, it was not, perhaps, with the purpose of treating this special one among the problems of your city nor of pointing out its seriousness that I came before you, but rather that I might make plain to you how you stand with regard to one another, and, by Zeus, to make plain also whether it is expedient that you should rely upon the present system and believe that now you are really

---

[1] Tarsus was evidently a timocracy.

[2] St. Paul was a tent-maker (*Acts* 18. 3), yet he claimed to be a ' citizen ' of Tarsus (*Acts* 21. 39).

---

12 οἴεσθαι νῦν Casaubon: οἴεσθε οὖν.

DIO CHRYSOSTOM

οἰκίαν γὰρ ἔγωγε καὶ ναῦν καὶ τἄλλα οὕτως ἀξιῶ
δοκιμάζειν, οὐ τὸ παρὸν[1] σκοποῦντας, εἰ σκέπει
νῦν καὶ μὴ δέχεται τὴν θάλατταν, ἀλλὰ καθόλου
πῶς παρεσκεύασται καὶ πέπηγεν, εἰ μηδέν ἐστι
25 διεστηκὸς μηδὲ σαθρόν.   καὶ μὴν ὅ γε ἔφην τὸ
πρότερον αὐξῆσαι τὴν πόλιν, τοῦτο οὐχ ὁρῶ νῦν
ὑμῖν ὑπάρχον, τὸ ἐξαίρετον εὐεργεσίαν καὶ χάριν
καταθέσθαι τῷ κρατοῦντι, δῆλον ὅτι τῷ μὴ
δεηθῆναι μηδενὸς αὐτὸν τοιούτου· πλὴν ὅτι γε[2]
μηδὲν τῶν ἄλλων ἔχετε πλεῖον πρὸς αὐτόν· ὥστε
ὧν παρ' ἐκείνου[3] τότε δι' εὔνοιαν καὶ φιλίαν
ἐτύχετε, ταῦτα ὀφείλετε φυλάττειν τὸν λοιπὸν
χρόνον δι' εὐταξίαν καὶ τὸ μηδεμίαν αἰτίαν διδόναι
καθ' αὑτῶν.

26   Καὶ μηδείς με νομίσῃ ταῦτα λέγειν ἁπλῶς
ἁπάντων ἀνέχεσθαι παραινοῦντα ὑμῖν καὶ πάντα
πάσχειν, ἀλλ' ὅπως ἔμπειροι τῶν καθ' αὑτοὺς
ὄντες καὶ νῦν ἄμεινον βουλεύησθε[4] καὶ τὸ λοιπὸν
οὕτως ἀπαιτῆτε[5] τὸν παριόντα μὴ ῥᾳδίως[6] ὑμῖν
μηδ' ὡς ἂν ἐπέλθῃ μηδὲν εἰσηγεῖσθαι, πάντα δὲ
εἰδότα καὶ περὶ πάντων ἐσκεμμένον. καὶ γὰρ
ἰατρόν, ὅστις ἐξήτακεν ἀκριβῶς τὰ τοῦ κάμνοντος,
ὡς μηδὲν αὐτὸν λανθάνειν, τοῦτον εἰκὸς ἄριστα
θεραπεύειν.

---

[1] τὸ παρὸν Casaubon : τόπον.
[2] εἰ after γε deleted by Emperius.
[3] ἐκείνου Reiske : ἐκείνῳ.
[4] βουλεύησθε Casaubon : βουλεύεσθε.
[5] ἀπαιτῆτε Casaubon : ἀπαιτεῖτε or ἀπαιτεῖται.
[6] μὴ ῥᾳδίως Emperius : μὴ δὲ ῥαδίως.

---

[1] See § 7.

united. Take, for example, a house or a ship or other things like that; this is the way in which I expect men to make appraisal. They should not consider merely present conditions, to see if the structure affords shelter *now* or does not let in the sea, but they should consider how as a whole it has been constructed and put together, to see that there are no open seams or rotten planks. And I must add that I do not find existing in your favour now that asset which I said [1] had in the past increased the prestige of Tarsus—your having placed to your credit with the Emperor exceptional service and kindness—evidently because he has no further need of such assistance. However, the fact remains that you have no advantage with him over the other dominions; consequently what you obtained from Caesar on that former occasion through your loyalty and friendship you should safeguard for the future through good behaviour and through giving no occasion for criticism.

And let no one suppose that in saying this I am advising you to put up with absolutely anybody and to endure any and every thing; nay, my purpose is rather that you, being acquainted with your own situation, may not only take better counsel in the present instance, but may also in the future demand that the man who comes forward to speak shall make his proposals to you, not in an off-hand manner nor on the inspiration of the moment, but with full knowledge and after careful examination of every detail. For the physician who has investigated minutely the symptoms of his patient, so that nothing can escape him, is the one who is likely to administer the best treatment.

27 Ὅτι μὲν οὖν δεῖται τὰ παρόντα προσοχῆς καὶ
βελτίονος συμβούλου[1] τῶν ἀπὸ τῆς τύχης καὶ δι᾽
ἀργύριον ἢ διὰ γένος παριόντων, ἐνθένδε ὁρᾶτέ
πως. ὅταν γὰρ μήτε αὐτοὶ βεβαίως ὁμονοῆτε
μήθ᾽ αἱ[2] πλείους τῶν πέριξ πόλεων οἰκείως ὑμῖν
ἔχωσιν, ἀλλ᾽ οἱ μὲν φθονῶσιν ἐκ πολλοῦ ἀντιφιλο-
τιμούμενοι πρὸς ὑμᾶς, οἱ δὲ ἀπεχθάνωνται διὰ τὸ
ὑπὲρ τῆς χώρας ἀμφισβητεῖν, οἱ δὲ οὐκ οἶδα
ὅπως γε ἐνοχλεῖσθαι λέγωσιν, ὁ δὲ στρατηγὸς
οἴηται μὲν τὰ βελτίω φρονεῖν περὶ αὑτοῦ[3] ὑμᾶς,
ἠναγκασμένοι δὲ ἦτε[4] προσκροῦσαι καὶ πρότερον
ἀλλήλοις, ἔτι δὲ ἐπίφθονοι τῷ τε μεγέθει τῆς
πόλεως νομίζησθε καὶ τῷ πολλὰ τῶν ὄντων
ἀπολαβεῖν δυνήσεσθαι· πῶς οὐχὶ διὰ ταῦτα
ἐπιμελοῦς καὶ περιεσκεμμένης γνώμης δεῖσθε;

28 Τί οὖν; οὐχ ἱκανοὶ ταῦτα οἱ πολῖται συνιδεῖν
καὶ παραινέσαι; πόθεν; εἰ γὰρ ἦσαν ἱκανοὶ τὸ
δέον εὑρίσκειν ἐν ταῖς πόλεσιν οἱ προεστῶτες
καὶ πολιτευόμενοι, πάντες ἂν ἀεὶ καλῶς ἀπήλλατ-
τον καὶ ἀπαθεῖς ἦσαν κακῶν, εἰ μή τις αὐτόματος
ἄλλως ἐπέλθοι τισὶ συμφορά. ἀλλ᾽, οἶμαι, καὶ πάλαι
καὶ νῦν πλείονα εὕροι τις ἂν συμβεβηκότα δεινὰ
ταῖς πόλεσι δι᾽ ἄγνοιαν τοῦ συμφέροντος καὶ
τὰ τῶν προεστώτων ἁμαρτήματα τῶν ἐκ τοῦ
δαιμονίου καὶ παρὰ τῆς τύχης.

---

[1] οὐ after συμβούλου deleted by Arnim, with M.
[2] μήθ᾽ αἱ Emperius : μηδ᾽ αἱ or μηδὲ.
[3] αὑτοῦ Casaubon : αὐτούς.
[4] ἦτε Reiske : ἐστέ.

THE THIRTY-FOURTH DISCOURSE

That your present situation, then, demands careful attention, and a better adviser than those who ascend the rostrum by chance or for mercenary reasons or because of family position, you can perceive in some measure from what follows. For at a time when your own harmony is not assured, and when most of the cities that surround you are not on friendly terms with you, but some are envious through long rivalry with you, while others are actively hostile because of disputes over territory, and still others claim to be subject to annoyance in one form or another, and when the general supposes, to be sure, that your feeling toward him is improving, although you and he have been compelled to clash with one another even previously, and when, furthermore, you are viewed with jealousy because of the very magnitude of your city and the ability you will have to rob your neighbours of many of their possessions—at a time like this, how can you for these reasons fail to require careful and well-considered judgement?

" Well then," you interject, " are not the citizens competent to appraise this situation and to give advice regarding it ? " Absurd! For if the leaders and statesmen in the cities were competent to hit upon the proper course, all men would always fare handsomely and be free from harm—unless of course some chance misfortune should perversely befall one city or another. But on the contrary, in my opinion, both in former days and at the present time you would find that more dreadful things have happened to cities through ignorance of what is to their interest and through the mistakes of their leaders than the disasters that happen by divine will or through mere chance.

363

29   Οἱ μὲν γὰρ οὐδὲν δυνάμενοι τῶν δεόντων
ἰδεῖν οὐδ' ἐπιμεληθέντες αὐτῶν πρότερον, μηδὲ
κώμην ὄντες ἱκανοὶ διοικῆσαι κατὰ τρόπον,
ἄλλως δὲ ὑπὸ χρημάτων ἢ γένους συνιστάμενοι
προσέρχονται τῷ πολιτεύεσθαι· τινὲς δὲ ταύτην
ἐπιμέλειαν εἶναι νομίζοντες, ἂν ῥήματα συμφορῶσι
καὶ ταῦτα τῶν πολλῶν ὁπωσδὴ [1] θᾶττον συνείρωσι,
μηδενὸς τἄλλα ἀμείνους ὄντες. τὸ δὲ μέγιστον,
διὰ μὲν τὸ βέλτιστον καὶ τῆς πατρίδος αὐτῆς
ἔνεκεν οὔ, λοιπὸν δὲ διὰ δόξας καὶ τιμὰς καὶ
τὸ δύνασθαι πλέον ἑτέρου καὶ στεφάνους καὶ
προεδρίας καὶ πορφύρας διώκοντες, πρὸς ταῦτα
ἀποβλέποντες καὶ τούτων ἐξηρτημένοι τοιαῦτα
πράττουσι καὶ λέγουσιν, ἐξ ὧν αὐτοί τινες εἶναι
30 δόξουσιν.[2] τοιγαροῦν ἐστεφανωμένους πολλοὺς
ἰδεῖν ἔστι καθ' ἑκάστην πόλιν καὶ θύοντας ἐν
κοινῷ καὶ προϊόντας ἐν πορφύρᾳ· γενναῖον δὲ
καὶ φρόνιμον ἄνδρα καὶ κηδεμόνα ὄντως τῆς
ἑαυτοῦ πατρίδος καὶ φρονοῦντα καὶ λέγοντα
τἀληθῆ [3] καὶ δι' ὃν ἄμεινον οἰκεῖται καὶ μετ-
έσχηκεν ἀγαθοῦ τινος ἡ πειθομένη πόλις, σπάνιον
εὑρεῖν.

31   Καὶ τοῦτο ἀναγκαῖον συμβαίνειν τρόπον τινά.
ὅταν γὰρ οἴωνται τοὺς λελειτουργηκότας ἢ
τοὺς μέλλοντας [4] ἑαυτοῖς δεῖν συμβουλεύειν,

---

[1] ὁπωσδὴ Geel : ὅπως δὴ.
[2] δόξουσιν Arnim : δόξωσιν or δόξωσι.
[3] τἀληθῆ Reiske : ἀληθῆ.
[4] τοὺς λελειτουργηκότας ἢ τοὺς μέλλοντας Reiske : τοὺς
μέλλοντας ἢ τοὺς λελειτουργηκότας.

---

[1] Greeks had long awarded crowns as a mark of distinction
for public service.

For sometimes men without any ability to perceive what is needful, men who have never given heed to their own welfare in the past, incompetent to manage even a village as it should be managed, but recommended only by wealth or family, undertake the task of government; still others undertake that task in the belief that they are displaying diligence if they merely heap up phrases and string them together in any way at all with greater speed than most men can, although in all else they are in no way superior to anybody else. And what is most serious is that these men, not for the sake of what is truly best and in the interest of their country itself, but for the sake of reputation and honours and the possession of greater power than their neighbours, in the pursuit of crowns [1] and precedence [2] and purple robes,[3] fixing their gaze upon these things and staking all upon their attainment, do and say such things as will enhance their own reputations. Consequently one may see in every city many who have been awarded crowns, who sacrifice in public, who come forth arrayed in purple; but a man of probity and wisdom, who is really devoted to his own country, and thinks and speaks the truth, whose influence with the city that follows his advice insures better management and the attainment of some blessing—such a man is hard to find.

Yes, this is bound to happen, one might say. For when men think it is those who have performed liturgies or will some day do so [4] who should counsel

[2] Literally, the privilege of a front seat.

[3] An innovation of Roman times.

[4] Cf. § 1. Since the liturgies were assigned to men of wealth, it was easy to know in advance who were likely to be called upon for such service.

κἂν ᾖ τις γυμνασίαρχος ἢ δημιουργός τις,[1]
τῷ τοιούτῳ μόνῳ λέγειν ἐπιτρέπωσιν ἢ νὴ
Δία τοῖς καλουμένοις ῥήτορσιν, ὅμοιόν ἐστιν
ὥσπερ ἂν εἰ τοὺς κήρυκας ἐκάλουν μόνους ἢ
τοὺς κιθαρῳδοὺς ἢ τοὺς τραπεζίτας. τοιγαροῦν
ἄνθρωποι παρίασι[2] καὶ ἀνόητοι καὶ δοξοκόποι
καὶ πρὸς τὸν ἀπὸ τοῦ πλήθους θόρυβον κεχηνότες,
οὐδὲν ἀπὸ γνώμης ἀσφαλοῦς οὐδὲ συνέντες[3]
λέγουσιν, ἀλλ᾽ ὥσπερ ἐν σκότει βαδίζοντες
κατὰ τὸν κρότον ἀεὶ καὶ τὴν βοὴν φέρονται.

32   Καίτοι κυβερνήταις εἴ τις λέγοι αὐτοῖς ὡς
δεῖ[4] ζητεῖν ἐξ ἅπαντος ἀρέσκειν τοῖς ἐπιβάταις,
καὶ κροτουμένοις ὑπ᾽ αὐτῶν, ὅπως ἂν ἐκεῖνοι
θέλωσιν, οὕτως κυβερνᾶν, οὐ μεγάλου τινὸς
αὐτοῖς δεήσει χειμῶνος, ὥστε ἀνατρέψαι. πολλάκις γοῦν ἄγροικος ἄνθρωπος ναυτιῶν ἢ γύναιον,
ἐὰν ἴδῃ πέτρας, γῆν ἑωρακέναι δοκεῖ καὶ λιμένα,[5]
33 καὶ δεῖται προσσχεῖν. ἐγὼ δὲ τὸν σύμβουλον
τὸν ἀγαθὸν καὶ τὸν ἄξιον προεστάναι πόλεώς φημι
δεῖν πρὸς ἅπαντα μὲν ἁπλῶς παρεσκευάσθαι τὰ
δοκοῦντα δυσχερῆ, μάλιστα δὲ πρὸς τὰς λοιδορίας
καὶ τὴν τοῦ πλήθους ὀργήν, καὶ ταῖς ἄκραις
ὅμοιον εἶναι ταῖς ποιούσαις τοὺς λιμένας, αἵτινες
ἅπασαν ἐκδέχονται τὴν βίαν τῆς θαλάττης, τὸ
δὲ ἐντὸς ἀκίνητον καὶ γαληνὸν φυλάττουσι, κἀκεῖνον

---

[1] καὶ after τις deleted by Arnim.
[2] παρίασι Casaubon : χαίρουσι.
[3] συνέντες Casaubon : συνθέντες.
[4] ὡς δεῖ Geel : ὥστε.
[5] λιμένα Reiske : λιμένας.

---

[1] An important liturgy at Tarsus. Antony gave the city
a gymnasium and appointed Boethus gymnasiarch.

them, and when, provided a man is gymnasiarch [1] or demiourgos,[2] he is the only one whom they allow to make a speech—or, by Zeus, the so-called orators [3]—it is very much as if they were to call upon only the heralds or the harpists or the bankers. Accordingly men come forward to address you who are both empty-headed and notoriety-hunters to boot, and it is with mouth agape for the clamour of the crowd, and not at all from sound judgement or understanding, that they speak, but just as if walking in the dark they are always swept along according to the clapping and the shouting.

And yet if someone should tell pilots that they should seek in every way to please their passengers, and that when applauded by them they should steer the ship in whatever way those passengers desired, it would take no great storm to overturn their ship. Frequently, you know, a seasick land-lubber or some nervous female at the sight of rocks fancies that land and harbour are in view and implores the skipper to steer for shore. But I say that the counsellor who is a good counsellor and fit to be leader of a city should be prepared to withstand absolutely all those things which are considered difficult or vexatious, and especially the vilifications and the anger of the mob. Like the promontories that form our harbours, which receive the full violence of the sea but keep the inner waters calm and peaceful,

---

[2] Thucydides (5. 49. 9), Demosthenes (18. 157), and Polybius (23. 5. 16) testify to the existence of such an official in the Peloponnese. At Tarsus he seems to have stood first in authority.

[3] The phrase οἱ ῥήτορες seems to signify a definite standing at Tarsus. It is frequent in Greek literature.

δὲ ἐκκεῖσθαι τῷ δήμῳ, κἂν ὀργισθῆναί ποτε
θέλῃ κἂν κακῶς εἰπεῖν κἂν ὁτιοῦν ποιῆσαι,
πάσχειν δὲ μηδὲν ὑπὸ τῶν τοιούτων θορύβων,
μήτε ἂν ἐπαινῆται, διὰ τοῦτο ἐπαίρεσθαι, μήτε
ἂν ὑβρίζεσθαι δοκῇ, ταπεινοῦσθαι.

34 Τὸ μέντοι γε παρ' ὑμῖν γιγνόμενον οὐ [1] τοιοῦτόν ἐστι. οὐδείς, ὡς [2] ἐγὼ πυνθάνομαι, τῶν πο-
λιτευομένων τοῦτο ἔχει [3] προκείμενον οὐδ' ἐστὶν
ἔτι τῶν κοινῶν· ἀλλ' οἱ μὲν ὅλως ἀφεστᾶσιν, οἱ
δ' ἐκ παρέργου προσίασιν ἁπτόμενοι μόνον [4] τοῦ
πράγματος, ὥσπερ οἱ σπονδῆς θιγγάνοντες, οὐκ
ἀσφαλὲς εἶναι λέγοντες ἀναθεῖναι αὑτοὺς [5] πολιτείᾳ.
καίτοι ναυκληρεῖν μὲν ἢ δανείζειν ἢ γεωργεῖν
οὐδεὶς ἂν ἱκανῶς δύναιτο πάρεργον αὐτὸ ποιούμενος,
πολιτεύεσθαι δὲ ἐπιχειροῦσιν ἐκ περιουσίας καὶ
35 πάντα ἔμπροσθεν τούτου τιθέντες. ἔνιοι δ'
ἂν εἰς ἀρχήν τινα καταστῶσιν, ἐν ἐκείνῃ μόνον
ζητοῦσιν ἅψασθαί τινος πράξεως, ὅπως ἀπέλθωσιν
ἐνδοξότεροι, τοῦτο μόνον σκοποῦντες. τοιγαροῦν
πρὸς ἓξ μῆνάς εἰσιν ὑμῖν ἀνδρεῖοι, πολλάκις
οὐδὲ ἐπὶ τῷ συμφέροντι τῆς πόλεως. ὥστε
νῦν μέν ἐστιν οὗτος ὁ λέγων, κἀπ' ἐκείνῳ [6] ἔτι
εὐθὺς ἄλλος, εἶθ' ἕτερος· καὶ τὸν [7] πρὸ τριάκοντα

---

[1] οὐ added by Reiske.
[2] οὐδείς, ὡς Emperius, οὐδ' εἰς, ὡς Reiske: οὐδ' ἴσως or
οὐδὲ ἴσως.
[3] ἔχει Reiske: ἔχειν.
[4] μόνον Casaubon: μόνου.
[5] αὑτοὺς Emperius: αὐτούς.
[6] κἀπ' ἐκείνῳ Weil (who omits ἔτι): κἀκείνῳ.
[7] τὸν added by Wilamowitz.

---

[1] That is, the stalwart leadership advocated in the preceding paragraph.

o he too should stand out against the violence of the
people, whether they are inclined to burst into a
rage or abuse him or take any measures whatever,
and he should be wholly unaffected by such outbursts,
and neither if they applaud him, should he on that
account be elated, nor, if he feels he is being insulted,
should he be depressed.

However, what happens at Tarsus is not like that.
No one of your statesmen, as I am told, holds that [1]
to be his function, nor is it so any longer with
the commons; but, on the contrary, some persons
stand absolutely aloof, and some come forward to
speak quite casually, barely touching on the issue—
as people touch the libation with their lips—claiming
that it is not safe for them to dedicate their lives to
government. And yet, though no one could be
successful as a ship-owner or money-lender or farmer
if he made those occupations a side-issue, still men
try to run the government out of their spare time
and put everything else ahead of statecraft. And
some, in case they do accept office, seek therein
only to engage in some enterprise out of which they
may emerge with added glory for themselves, making
that their sole aim. Accordingly for six months [2]
they are your ' men of valour,' frequently not to the
advantage of the city either. And so at one moment
it is So-and-so who makes the motions, and hard upon
his heels comes someone else in quick succession,
and then a third; and he who but one brief month

---

[2] Apparently the regular term of office at Tarsus and not
restricted to the *prytanis* (§ 36). No wonder the administration of affairs was chaotic! On the *prytanis*, see also § 42.
Aristotle, *Politics* 1305 a, states that Miletus too had a single
prytanis.

ἡμερῶν λαμπρὸν καὶ μόνον φάσκοντα κήδεσθαι
τῆς πόλεως οὐδ' ἰδεῖν ἔστι προσιόντα τῇ ἐκκλησίᾳ,
36 καθάπερ, οἶμαι, τῶν πομπευόντων αὐτὸς ἕκαστος
ὀφθῆναι ἐπιθυμῶν κατὰ τοῦτ' [1] ἐσπούδακεν,
ἕως ἂν παρέλθῃ, μικρὸν δὲ ἀποστὰς ἔλυσε τὸ
σχῆμα καὶ τῶν ἄλλων εἷς ἐστι καὶ ὅπως δήποτε
ἄπεισιν. ἐχρῆν μέντοι τὸν μὲν [2] πρυτανεύοντα
τῆς ἀρχῆς τοὺς ἓξ μῆνας ἡγεῖσθαι μέτρον·
τοῦτο γὰρ ὁ νόμος κελεύει· τὸν μέντοι γε πολιτευό-
μενον τῆς εὐνοίας τῆς πρὸς ὑμᾶς καὶ τῆς ὑπὲρ
τῶν κοινῶν ἐπιμελείας καὶ σπουδῆς μὴ μὰ
Δία καιρόν τινα ἐξαίρετον ἔχειν, καὶ ταῦτα
βραχὺν οὕτως, ἀλλ' εἰς αὐτὸ τοῦτο ἀποδύεσθαι
37 καὶ ἀεὶ παραμένειν. νῦν δὲ ὥσπερ οἱ τοῖς
ἀπογείοις, μᾶλλον δὲ τοῖς ἀπὸ τῶν γνόφων
πνεύμασι πλέοντες, οὕτως φέρεσθε, ἄνδρες Ταρσεῖς,
οὔτε τῆς τοιαύτης πολιτείας, οὔτ' ἐκείνου τοῦ πλοῦ
βέβαιον οὐδ' ἀσφαλὲς ἔχοντος οὐδέν. διαρκέσαι
μὲν γὰρ ἄχρι παντὸς ἢ διαστήματος δίχα [3] οὐχ
οἷαί τέ εἰσιν αἱ τοιαῦται προσβολαί, πολλάκις δὲ
κατέδυσαν ἀκεραίως [4] προσπεσοῦσαι. ἔδει δὲ
πόλιν οὕτως μεγάλην καὶ λαμπρὰν ἔχειν τοὺς
ἀληθῶς προνοοῦντας. ταύτῃ [5] δὲ ἴσως ὑπὸ τῶν
ἐφημέρων τούτων καὶ πρὸς ὀλίγον δημαγωγῶν
οὐδέν ἐστιν ἀγαθὸν παθεῖν.
38   Περὶ μὲν οὖν τούτων καὶ μυρίων ἄλλων πολλὰ
ἂν ἔχοι τις λέγειν. ἐπεὶ δὲ καὶ αὐτὸς ἀφ' ἧς
ἐπεδήμησα ἡμέρας ὑμῖν γέγονα δημαγωγός, καὶ

---

[1] κατὰ τοῦτ' Emperius: καὶ τοῦτ'.
[2] μὲν added by Emperius.
[3] δίχα added by Capps; Casaubon deleted ἢ διαστήματος.
[4] ἀκεραίως] ἀκαίρως Reiske.

ago was resplendent and claimed to be the only one who cared for the city cannot be seen even coming to the assembly. It reminds me of a parade, in which each participant, eager to catch the public eye, exerts himself to that end until he has passed beyond the spectators, but when he gets a short distance away, he relaxes his pose and is just one of the many and goes home in happy-go-lucky style. However, while your president should regard his six months as the limit to his term of office—for so the law prescribes— still the statesman should not, by heaven, observe any set term for the exercise of benevolence toward you and of care and concern for the commonwealth— and that too a term so brief—nay, he should strip for action for that very purpose and hold himself in readiness for service constantly. But at present, just like men who sail with offshore breezes—or rather with gusts from the storm-clouds—so are you swept along, men of Tarsus, though neither such statecraft nor such voyaging has aught of certainty or of safety in it. For such blasts are not the kind to last for ever or to blow devoid of interruption, but they often sink a ship by falling upon it with undiminished violence. And a city of such size and splendour as your own should have men who truly take thought on its behalf. But as things go now, I dare say, under these transitory, short-lived demagogues no good can come to you.

Well then, on these topics, as well as on countless others too, there is a great deal one might say. But since I myself also from the very day of my arrival here have played the demagogue for you,

---

[5] ταύτῃ Emperius: αὐτῇ or αὐτῇ.

ταῦτα ἐπιτιμῶν τοῖς τοιούτοις, ὅμως δεῖ εἰπεῖν [1]
ἅπερ ὑπεσχόμην, ἃ γιγνώσκω περὶ τῶν παρόντων.
καὶ πρῶτον μὲν τὰ πρὸς τὸν στρατηγόν. ἔσται
δέ μοι περὶ πάντων ὁ λόγος. φημὶ δὴ τοίνυν τοὺς ἐν τοιαύτῃ καταστάσει τυγχάνοντας,
ὁποία δὴ τὰ νῦν ἐστι παρὰ πᾶσιν, οὕτω προσήκειν
φρονεῖν, ὡς μήτε πάντα ἀνεξομένους καὶ παρ-
έξοντας αὐτούς [2] ἁπλῶς χρῆσθαι τοῖς ἐπὶ τῆς
ἐξουσίας, ὅπως ἂν [3] αὐτοὶ θέλωσι, κἂν εἰς
ὁτιοῦν προΐωσιν ὕβρεως καὶ πλεονεξίας, μήτε ὡς
ὅλως μηδὲν οἴσοντας διακεῖσθαι, μηδὲ προσδοκᾶν
ὅτι Μίνως τις ὑμῶν ἀφίξεται νῦν ἢ Περσεὺς
39 ἐπιμελησόμενος. τὸ μὲν γὰρ ἐφ᾽ ἅπαν ἀποστῆναι [4]
τοῦ βοηθεῖν αὐτοῖς ἀνδραπόδων ἐστί, καὶ δυσχερές,
εἰ μηδεὶς ὄκνος μηδὲ ὑποψία καταλειφθήσεται
τοῖς ἀγνωμονοῦσιν. τὸ δὲ πλῆθος ἀπεχθάνεσθαι
καὶ πάντα ἐξετάζειν οὐχ ὑπὲρ ὑμῶν ἐστιν.
ἐὰν γὰρ ἀλόγως ἐνίοτε ἐγκαλεῖν δόξητε [5] καί
τις ὑμῶν περιγένηται· διὰ πολλὰς δ᾽ ἂν αἰτίας
τοῦτο συμβαίη· δέδοικα μὴ τελέως ἀποβάλητε
τὴν παρρησίαν. ὁρᾶτε δὲ τοὺς περὶ τὴν Ἰωνίαν,
ὅτι μηδενὸς ἁπλῶς [6] κατηγορεῖν ἐψηφίσαντο

---

[1] ὅμως δεῖ εἰπεῖν Crosby, ὅμως εἴποιμ᾽ ἂν Emperius: ὅμως
εἰπεῖν.
[2] αὐτοὺς Emperius : αὐτούς.
[3] ἂν added by Emperius.
[4] ἀποστῆναι Wyttenbach : ἄπιστον εἶναι.
[5] δόξητε Reiske : δόξετε.
[6] ἁπλῶς Arnim : αὐτοὺς or αὐτούς.

---

[1] Cf. §§ 7 and 24. The logical nexus may not be apparent
on the surface. In the first sentence of the paragraph Dio
seems to be dismissing the topic just treated; but then he
recalls that he has not wholly fulfilled his promise. His

and that too though I find fault with men of that sort, I must notwithstanding express my opinion regarding your present situation, as indeed I promised to do.[1] And first of all, your dealings with the general—but what I have to say will cover everything. Very well then, I say that men who find themselves in such a situation as yours,[2] which of course is the common situation everywhere today, should be so minded as not, on the one hand, to submit to any and every thing and allow those in authority to treat them simply as they please, no matter to what lengths of insolence and greed they may proceed; nor, on the other hand, to be disposed to put up with nothing disagreeable whatever, or to expect, as you might, that some Minos or Perseus[3] will arrive in these days to take care of them. For to refrain entirely from coming to one's own assistance is the conduct of slaves, and it is a serious matter if no remnant of hesitancy or distrust is to be left in the minds of those who deal unfairly. And yet for the populace to incur hatred and be constantly prying into everything is not to your advantage either. For if you get the reputation of making complaints now and then without good reason, and someone gets the better of you—and there are many reasons why this might happen—I fear that you may lose the right of free speech altogether. Pray consider what the people of Ionia have done. They have passed a decree prohibiting accusations against anyone at all.

calling himself a demagogue resembles the device employed in § 5 to win the crowd to his side by a touch of humour.

[2] Apparently he refers to the situation of control by officials sent from Rome.

[3] Minos is selected as typifying wisdom and justice, Perseus as having a special interest in Tarsus.

δεῖ δὴ τοὺς νοῦν ἔχοντας ἅπαντα ταῦτα προορᾶ-
σθαι, καὶ μὴ καθάπερ τοὺς ἀπείρους ἐν τῷ μάχεσθαι ῥᾳδίως ἀφέντας τὸ παρὸν αὐτοῖς [1] ἀνόπλους
εἶναι τὸ λοιπὸν καὶ μηδὲν ἔχειν ποιῆσαι, μηδ'
ἂν ἀποσφάττῃ τις.

40   Ἐκεῖνο μέντοι καθόλου λέγω, τὴν τοιαύτην
ἀνάτασιν [2] μηδαμῶς συμφέρειν, καθ' ἣν οὐδὲν
ποιῆσαι διεγνωκότες εἰς ὑποψίαν ἔρχεσθε τοῖς
ἡγεμόσιν· ἀλλ' ὃν μὲν ἂν κρίνητε ἐξαιρήσεσθαι
καὶ δοκῇ τοιαῦτα ἀδικεῖν, ὥστε παραπέμψαι [3]
μὴ συμφέρειν, τοῦτον ὡς ἐξελέγχοντες παρα-
σκευάζεσθε, καὶ τὴν γνώμην εὐθὺς ἔχετε ὡς
πρὸς ἐχθρὸν καὶ ἐπιβουλεύοντα ὑμῖν. περὶ οὗ δ'
ἂν ἄλλως [4] προνοῆτε, ἐὰν [5] μηδὲν ἢ μὴ μεγάλα
ἁμαρτάνειν ἢ [6] δι' ἣν δήποτε αἰτίαν μὴ νομίζητε [7]
ἐπιτήδειον εἶναι, τοῦτον μηδὲ ἐρεθίζετε μηδὲ
41   εἰς ὀργὴν κατὰ τῆς πόλεως ἄγετε· ὥσπερ,
οἶμαι, τὰ βάρη ταῦτ', ἂν μὲν σφόδρα πιέζῃ καὶ
ἀνέχεσθαι μὴ δυνώμεθα, ζητοῦμεν ὡς τάχιστα
ἀπορρῖψαι, μετρίως δὲ ἐνοχλούμενοι καὶ ὁρῶντες
ἀνάγκην οὖσαν φέρειν ἢ τοῦτο ἢ μεῖζον ἕτερον,
σκοποῦμεν ὡς κουφότατα ἐπέσται.

Ταῦτά ἐστι σωφρονούσης πόλεως. οὕτως καὶ
ἀγαπήσουσιν ὑμᾶς οἱ πλείους καὶ φοβήσεταί
τις ἀδικεῖν, καὶ οὐ [8] μὴ πλῆθος ἄδικον μηδὲ

---

[1] τὸ παρὸν αὐτοῖς] τὸ παρὸν αὐτοῖς ⟨ὅπλον⟩ Reiske, τὸ
παλτὸν Wilamowitz.
[2] ἀνάτασιν Valesius : ἀνάστασιν.
[3] παραπέμψαι Reiske : παραπέμψειν.
[4] περὶ οὗ δ' ἂν ἄλλως Selden : περὶ οὐδὲν ἀλλ' ὡς.
[5] ἐὰν added by Crosby : Arnim notes lacuna.
[6] ἢ added by Reiske.   [7] νομίζητε Reiske : νομίζειν.
[8] οὐ added by Dindorf.

So men of sense should foresee all these contingencies and not, like men inexperienced in fighting, rashly abandoning the equipment they have, be defenceless from then on and unable to act at all, not even if an enemy threatens them with slaughter.

This, however, I declare as a general principle: that so uncompromising a policy on your part is in no way beneficial, a policy which, although you have no intention to proceed to active measures, nevertheless makes you incur the distrust of your superior officers; but on the contrary, when you decide that you are going to remove some one, and it is thought that he is guilty of such misdeeds that it is not expedient to ignore them, make yourselves ready to convict him and immediately behave toward him as toward a personal enemy, and one who is plotting against you. But regarding a man concerning whom you foresee a different outcome, if you believe him to be guilty of no misdeeds—or none of any importance—or if for whatever reason you do not believe him to deserve such treatment, do not irritate him or move him to anger against the city. In very much the same way, I fancy, if those burdens that we bear are very oppressive and we cannot endure them, we seek to cast them off as speedily as possible, whereas if we are only moderately inconvenienced by them and see that we must carry either the load we have or another that is greater, we consider how they may rest upon our shoulders as lightly as possible.

That is the policy of a prudent state. Under such a policy not only will most people be fond of you, but a man will fear to do you wrong, and men in general will not think you to be a wicked populace or an

ἀλόγιστον ὄχλον ὑμᾶς νομίσωσιν,[1] ὁρμῇ τινι
42 καὶ φορᾷ χρώμενον. τουτὶ μὲν γὰρ ὃ ποιεῖ
νῦν ὁ πρύτανις καὶ παντελῶς ἀνόητον ἦν ἄν, εἰ καὶ
διεγνώκειτε κατηγορεῖν· μηδέπω μέντοι καιρὸς
ᾖ φανερῶς οὕτως διαφέρεσθαι καὶ προλέγειν·
ἀλλ' ἐπειδή τις τῶν ὑμετέρων πολιτῶν ἐν καιροῖς
ἀναγκαίοις τῇ πόλει παρέσχεν αὑτὸν καὶ λαμπρὸς[2]
ἔδοξε δυοῖν[3] ἡγεμόνων κατηγορήσας ἐφεξῆς,
οἱ πολλοὶ νομίζουσι τοιούτου τινὸς ἔργου δεῖν
αὑτοῖς. τοῦτο δὲ ὅμοιόν ἐστιν, ὥσπερ εἴ τις
ἰατρὸν ἰδὼν εἴς τι τῶν ὠφελίμων φαρμάκων[4]
ἐκ μέρους τι μιγνύντα καὶ θανάσιμον, μηδὲν
ἄλλο εἰδώς, μήτε ὅπως συνετέθη μήτε ὁπόσον
δεῖ[5] λαβεῖν, μιμεῖσθαι βούλοιτο. τὸ μέντοι[6] αὐτο-
σχεδιάζειν τὰ μέγιστα καὶ προεστάναι πόλεως
ἡγεῖσθαι παντὸς εἶναι τοῦ ἐλπίσαντος οὐ πολὺ
τῶν τοιούτων ἀφέστηκεν.

43 Ἐγὼ δ' ὑπὲρ τῶν πρὸς τοὺς Μαλλώτας καὶ τὰς
ἄλλας πόλεις εἰπὼν ἔτι παύσομαι· καὶ γὰρ
ἱκανῶς ἀνέχεσθαι δοκεῖτέ μοι. πρὸς μὲν οὖν
τούτους, λέγω δὲ Μαλλώτας, εἴ τι πεποιήκασιν
ἀγνωμόνως, ὥσπερ πεποιήκασι, τὴν ὀργὴν καταβαλόντες καὶ τὴν τιμωρίαν, ἣν ἐνομίζετε ὀφείλεσθαι ὑμῖν, αὐτοῖς χαρισάμενοι, περὶ τοῦ πράγματος διακρίθητε τοῦ περὶ τῆς χώρας,[7] τὸ φέρειν τὰ

---

[1] νομίσωσιν Dindorf : νομίζωσιν.
[2] λαμπρὸς Casaubon : λαμπρόν.
[3] δυοῖν Arnim, δύο δὴ Emperius : δύο δ'.
[4] φαρμάκων Reiske : φάρμακον.
[5] δεῖ added by Emperius.
[6] τὸ μέντοι Capps, τὸ μὲν οὖν Emperius : μὲν.
[7] τοῦ περὶ τῆς χώρας Capps : καὶ τὸ περὶ τῆς χώρας, which
Selden deletes.

unreasoning mob, a mob that acts on a kind of impulse and in headless fashion. For this thing that your president is now doing [1] would truly be altogether foolish, even if you were of a mind to bring accusations—though perhaps it may not yet be the proper moment to quarrel so openly and to make pronouncements; but remember that as soon as one of your fellow-citizens has in a moment of urgent need placed himself at the disposal of the state and gained a brilliant reputation by accusing two officials in quick succession, the masses think that they too must try some such exploit. But that is very much as if a man, on seeing a physician mix with some beneficent drug a small portion also of one that is deadly, and without any further knowledge as to how the medicine was compounded or how much to take, should wish to follow his example. Yet surely the belief that impromptu action in matters of highest moment and political leadership are within the competence of any one who has aspired to undertake it is not far removed from such behaviour.

However, when I have made a few more remarks regarding your dealings with the people of Mallus and with the other cities, I shall cease; for you seem to me to have displayed sufficient patience. Well then, with reference to the first—I mean the people of Mallus—if they have behaved at all senselessly, as indeed they have, lay aside your anger, graciously forgive them the revenge that you thought to be your due, and come to terms regarding your boundary dispute, believing that to endure such

[1] We cannot be sure what Dio has in mind. Perhaps in the crisis to which he refers so often the *prytanis* has taken sides with the people against the general. There may have been talk of removing the general from office.

τοιαῦτα καὶ μὴ [1] φιλονεικεῖν, τοῦθ', ὥσπερ ἐστίν,
ἡγησάμενοι μέγα καὶ τῷ παντὶ κρειττόνων ἀνδρῶν,
44 ἄλλως τε [2] πρὸς τοσούτῳ καταδεεστέρους. οὐ γάρ
ἐστι κίνδυνος μὴ Μαλλωτῶν ἐσομένων [3] ἀσθενέστεροι
δόξετε. μηδὲ τοὺς παροξυνοῦντας ὑμᾶς ἀποδέξασθε, [4] ἀλλὰ μάλιστα μὲν αὐτοὶ δικασταὶ γενόμενοι
καὶ τὸ πρᾶγμα ἐπιμελῶς ἐξετάσαντες ἄνευ πάσης
ἀπεχθείας καὶ τῆς πρὸς αὐτοὺς [5] χάριτος κατά-
θεσθε, μὴ μόνον ἀποστάντες τῆς ἔριδος καὶ τοῦ
ζητεῖν ἐξ ἅπαντος πλέον ἔχειν, ἀλλὰ συγχωροῦντές
τε καὶ παριέντες αὐτοῖς ὅ τι ἂν ᾖ μέτριον. ὥσπερ
γὰρ καὶ τῶν ἰδιωτῶν ἐπαινεῖτε τοὺς εὐγνώμονας
καὶ βλαβῆναί τινα [6] μᾶλλον αἱρουμένους ἢ διαφέρεσθαι πρός τινας, οὕτω καὶ κοινῇ συμβαίνει
τὰς τοιαύτας πόλεις εὐδοκιμεῖν.

45 Αἱ μὲν οὖν θῖνες καὶ τὸ πρὸς τῇ λίμνῃ χωρίον
οὐδενὸς ἄξια· τίς γάρ ἐστιν ἡ τούτων πρόσοδος ἢ
λυσιτέλεια; τὸ μέντοι χρηστοὺς φαίνεσθαι καὶ
μεγαλόφρονας οὐκ ἔστιν εἰπεῖν ὅσου [7] νομίζεται
δικαίως ἄξια. τὸ μὲν γὰρ ἁμιλλᾶσθαι πρὸς
ἅπαντας ἀνθρώπους ὑπὲρ δικαιοσύνης καὶ ἀρετῆς,
καὶ τὸ [8] φιλίας καὶ ὁμονοίας ἄρχειν, καὶ τούτοις
περιεῖναι τῶν ἄλλων καὶ κρατεῖν ἡ καλλίστη
πασῶν νίκη καὶ ἀσφαλεστάτη. τὸ δ' ἐξ ἅπαντος
τρόπου ζητεῖν μαχομένους ὑπερέχειν ἀλεκτρυόνων
46 ἐστὶ μᾶλλον γενναίων ἤπερ ἀνδρῶν. εἰ μὲν οὖν
παρὰ τὰς θῖνας ἔμελλε Μαλλὸς [9] μείζων ἔσεσθαι

---

[1] μὴ added by Reiske.
[2] ἄλλως τε Casaubon : ὥς γε ἄλλως or ὥστε ἄλλως.
[3] ἐσομένων] ἡσσώμενοι Selden.
[4] ἀποδέξασθε added by Crosby, ἀκούετε by Casaubon.
[5] αὐτοὺς Reiske : αὐτούς.

treatment and not to court a quarrel is, as in fact it is, a great achievement and one befitting men who are altogether superior, especially in relation to men so vastly inferior. For there is no danger that you will be thought weaker than any men of Mallus that the future may produce. And do not listen to those who try to stir you up, but, if at all possible, act as your own judges, and, examining the matter with care, apart from all malice or partiality for your own interests, make a settlement of the trouble; do not merely refrain from strife and from seeking to gain the advantage by any and every means, but concede and yield to them anything within reason. For just as you have words of praise for those in private life who are reasonable and prefer occasionally to submit to wrong rather than to quarrel with people, so also in public relations we find that cities of that sort are in good repute.

No, sand-dunes and swamp-land are of no value— for what revenue is derived from them or what advantage?—yet to show one's self to be honourable and magnanimous is rightly regarded as inexpressibly valuable. For to vie with the whole world in behalf of justice and virtue, and to take the initiative in friendship and harmony, and in these respects to surpass and prevail over all others, is the noblest of all victories and the safest too. But to seek by any and every means to maintain ascendancy in a conflict befits blooded game-cocks rather than men. It may be true that, if Mallus because of the dunes and the

---

6 τινα Capps : τινας, which Wilamowitz deletes.

7 ὅσου Reiske : ὡς οὐ.

8 τὸ added by Arnim.

9 ἔμελλε Μαλλὸς Casaubon : ἔμελλε μάλως or ἔμελλεν ἄλλως.

τῆς Ταρσοῦ καὶ παρὰ τὴν ἐπὶ τῆς ψάμμου νομήν,
τάχα ἔδει [1] σπουδάζειν ὑμᾶς ἐπὶ τοσοῦτον· νυνὶ
δὲ αἰσχύνη καὶ γέλως ἐστὶν ὑπὲρ ὧν διαφέρεσθε.
τί οὖν οὐκ ἐκεῖνοι κατεφρόνησαν; ὅτι οὐκ εἰσὶ
βελτίους ὑμῶν. ὑμεῖς δέ γε βούλεσθε πρὸς τοῦ
Διός.[2] ἀλλ' ἔγωγε ἠξίουν ἐπιτιμῆσαι λόγῳ πέμ-
ψαντας αὐτοῖς [3]—τοῦτο γὰρ ἦν ὑπερεχόντων καὶ
φρονούντων—τὸ δὲ μᾶλλον τοῦ δέοντος κεκινῆ-
σθαι καὶ καταφεύγειν ἐπὶ τὴν ἐξουσίαν εὐθὺς
καὶ νομίζειν ὑβρίζεσθαι μικροπολιτῶν μᾶλλον
ἀνθρώπων ἐστίν.

47 Ὁμοίως δὲ καὶ πρὸς τὰς ἄλλας πόλεις ὑμᾶς
ἀξιῶ προσφέρεσθαι πρᾴως καὶ κηδεμονικῶς καὶ
φιλοτίμως καὶ μὴ ἀπεχθῶς. οὕτω γὰρ ἑκόντες
ἀκολουθήσουσιν ὑμῖν ἅπαντες θαυμάζοντες καὶ
ἀγαπῶντες· ὃ μεῖζόν ἐστι τοῦ θύειν [4] παρ' ὑμῖν
καὶ δικάζεσθαι Μᾶλλον.[5] ταῦτα μὲν γὰρ οὐδ'
ἡντινοῦν ἔχει ὠφέλειαν, ἐπελθεῖν ἐπὶ θυσίαν
δεῦρο ἢ τοὺς Ἀδανεῖς ἢ τοὺς Αἰγαίους, ἀλλὰ
τῦφον καὶ ἀπάτην καὶ φιλοτιμίαν ἄλλως ἀνόητον·
48 ἡ δὲ εὔνοια καὶ τὸ φαίνεσθαι διαφέροντας ἀρετῇ
καὶ φιλανθρωπίᾳ, ταῦτά ἐστιν ὄντως ἀγαθά,
ταῦτά ἐστιν ἄξια ζήλου καὶ σπουδῆς. ἃ καὶ
σκοπεῖτε· ὡς τά γε νῦν γέλως ἐστίν. καὶ εἴτε

---

[1] ἔδει Selden : δεῖ.
[2] Arnim marks a lacuna at this point.
[3] αὐτοῖς Arnim : αὐτούς.
[4] θύειν Valckenaer : εἶναι.
[5] Μᾶλλόν Casaubon, ἄλλους Valesius : μᾶλλον.

---

[1] That is, " better than you are." Dio taunts his audience
with expecting from their foes a higher moral standard than
they themselves maintained.

pasturage on the sand were likely to become greater than Tarsus, you ought possibly to show so much concern; but as it is, disgrace and mockery are all you stand to gain from the objects of your quarrel. "Why, then," you may ask, "did not the people of Mallus scorn those things?" Because they are no better than you are. But, by heaven, it is you who want them to be so.[1] However, what *I* thought fitting was that you should send them messengers and file an oral protest—for that would have been the procedure of superior and sensible men—but to be unduly excited and to have recourse immediately to the assertion of your authority and to feel insulted is rather to be expected of small-town folk.

So also with reference to the other cities, I ask that you behave mildly, considerately, with regard to your honour, and not in a spirit of hostility and hatred. For if you do, all men will follow your leadership willingly, with admiration and affection; and that is of more importance than to have Mallus sacrifice in Tarsus and there conduct its litigation.[2] For it is of no advantage to you at all to have the people of either Adana or Aegae come to Tarsus to offer sacrifice; it is merely vanity and self-deception and empty, foolish pride. On the other hand, goodwill and a reputation for superiority in virtue and kindliness—those are your true blessings, those are the objects worthy of emulation and serious regard. And you should pay heed to them, since your present behaviour is ridiculous. And whether it is a question of

[2] The 'allies' of Athens in the fifth century B.C. had to settle inter-state disputes in Athenian courts. They were not, however, compelled to worship in Athens. For the quarrel between Aegae and Adana and Tarsus, see also Or. 33. 51, and 34. 10 and 14.

Αἰγαῖοι πρὸς ὑμᾶς εἴτε Ἀπαμεῖς πρὸς Ἀντιοχεῖς
εἴτε ἐπὶ τῶν πορρωτέρω Σμυρναῖοι πρὸς Ἐφεσίους
ἐρίζουσι, περὶ ὄνου σκιᾶς, φασί, διαφέρονται. τὸ
γὰρ προεστάναι τε καὶ κρατεῖν ἄλλων ἐστίν.

49 Ἀλλὰ καὶ πρότερον ἦν ποτε Ἀθηναίοις πρὸς
Λακεδαιμονίους ζηλοτυπία, καὶ τό γε[1] πρῶτον
ἡγοῦντο οἱ Λάκωνες, εἶτα συνέβη πρὸς τοὺς
Ἀθηναίους μᾶλλον ἀποκλῖναι τοὺς Ἕλληνας μετὰ
τὰ Μηδικά. τί οὖν ὁ Σπαρτιάτης; καὶ τὸν
νησιώτην καὶ τὸν Ἴωνα καὶ τὸν Ἑλλησπόντιον
ἀφεὶς αὐτὸν ἐσωφρόνιζε, καὶ τὰ τῆς Σπάρτης
ἑώρα, σαφῶς εἰδὼς ὅτι καὶ τῶν νόμων καὶ τῆς
εὐταξίας οὐδὲν δεῖ περὶ πλείονος ποιεῖσθαι. τοιγαροῦν μάλιστα εὐδαιμόνησαν ἐκεῖνον τὸν χρόνον.
50 τοῖς δὲ Ἀθηναίοις συνέβη, μέχρι μὲν οἰκείως
πρὸς αὐτοὺς αἱ πόλεις εἶχον[2] καὶ[3] κατ᾽ εὔνοιαν
ἡγοῦντο, εὐδαιμονεῖν,[4] μετὰ ταῦτα δέ, ὡς ἐγκλή-
ματα καὶ φθόνος αὐτοῖς συνελέγη καὶ μὴ βουλο-
μένων ἄρχειν ἠξίουν, πολλὰ καὶ δυσχερῆ παθεῖν·
καὶ πρῶτον μὲν ἁπάντων ἀπολέσαι τὸν ἔπαινον
καὶ τὴν εὐφημίαν, ἔπειτα καὶ τὴν ἰσχὺν καὶ τὰ
χρήματα, καὶ τελευταῖον ὑπὸ τοῖς ἐχθροῖς γενέσθαι·
καὶ τοῖς Λακεδαιμονίοις[5] ὁμοίως, ἐπειδὴ κἀκεῖνοι

---

[1] γε Casaubon : τε.
[2] εἶχον Emperius : ἔσχον.
[3] καὶ added by Selden.
[4] εὐδαιμονεῖν added by Crosby ; Selden noted the lacuna.
[5] τοῖς Λακεδαιμονίοις Reiske : τοὺς Λακεδαιμονίους.

---

[1] Dio seems to mean the Apamea and Antioch of Comma-
genê, north-east of Tarsus. The precise nature of their
dispute is unknown ; the same holds good regarding Smyrna
and Ephesus.

THE THIRTY-FOURTH DISCOURSE

Aegaeans quarrelling with you, or Apameans with men of Antioch,[1] or, to go farther afield, Smyrnaeans with Ephesians, it is an ass's shadow, as the saying goes, over which they squabble;[2] for the right to lead and to wield authority belongs to others.[3]

Yes, there was a time in days gone by when jealous rivalry existed also between Athens and Sparta; and, at first, Sparta held the ascendancy, and then it came to pass that the Greeks inclined rather toward Athens, after the Persian wars. What, then, did the Spartan do? Abandoning his claims upon the islander, the Ionian, and the Greek of Hellespont, he proceeded to teach himself self-control and confined his attention to the affairs of Sparta, understanding clearly that nothing should be held more dear than law and order. Accordingly Sparta achieved its greatest prosperity during that period. And as for the Athenians, it so happened that, as long as the cities were on friendly terms with them, and the Athenians behaved kindly as their leaders, they too prospered; but afterwards, when accusations and ill-will toward them accumulated and they saw fit to rule unwilling subjects, they suffered many disagreeable things. And the first thing of all to happen was to lose their commendation and good repute, and next to lose their power and wealth, and finally to become subject to their foes. And the Spartans had a similar experience: when they too

[2] A proverbial saying used by Sophocles, Plato, Aristophanes and others. The proverb seems to have originated in an amusing tale recorded by pseudo-Plutarch (*Vitae X. Oratorum*, p. 401) and included among the fables of Aesop. *Vid.* Halm, *Fabulae Aesopicae*, 339.

[3] Rome, after all, was supreme.

πάλιν εἶχον τὰ ¹ τῆς ἀρχῆς, ἀποστάντες τῆς προτέρον ² γνώμης, ἐν τοῖς αὐτοῖς γενέσθαι.

51 καίτοι τὰ μὲν ἐκείνων εἶχεν ἀληθῆ δύναμιν καὶ μεγάλας ὠφελείας, εἰ δεῖ τὰς πλεονεξίας οὕτως καλεῖν· τὰ δὲ τῶν νῦν ἀμφισβητήματα καὶ τὰ αἴτια τῆς ἀπεχθείας κἂν αἰσχυνθῆναί μοι δοκεῖ τις ἂν ἰδών· ἔστι γὰρ ὁμοδούλων πρὸς ἀλλήλους ἐριζόντων περὶ δόξης καὶ πρωτείων.

Τί οὖν; οὐδὲν ἀγαθόν ἐστιν ἐν τῷ χρόνῳ τούτῳ, περὶ οὗ χρὴ σπουδάζειν; ἔστι τὰ μέγιστα καὶ μόνα σπουδῆς ἄξια καὶ τότε ὄντα καὶ νῦν καὶ ἀεὶ ἐσόμενα· ὧν οὐκ ἔχει δήπουθέν τις ἐξουσίαν οὔτ' ³ ἄλλῳ παρασχεῖν οὔτε ⁴ ἀφελέσθαι ⁵ τὸν κτησάμενον,⁶ ἀλλ' ἀεί ἐστιν ἐπ' αὐτῷ, κἂν ἰδιώτης ᾖ κἂν πόλις.⁷ ὑπὲρ ὧν ἴσως μακρότερον

52 λέγειν πρὸς ὑμᾶς. καίτοι με οὐ λέληθεν ὅτι τοὺς φιλοσόφους πολλοὶ νομίζουσιν ἐκλύειν ἅπαντα καὶ ἀνιέναι τὰς ὑπὲρ τῶν πραγμάτων σπουδάς, καὶ διὰ τοῦτο βλάπτειν μᾶλλον· ὥσπερ εἴ τις τὸν μουσικὸν σκοπεῖν ⁸ βούλοιτο ⁹ ἁρμοζόμενον, κἄπειτ' ¹⁰ ἀνιέντα ὁρῶν ¹¹ τῶν φθόγγων τινὰς καὶ πάλιν ἑτέρους

---

¹ εἶχον τὰ] εἴχοντο Reiske.
² αὐτοῖς after πρότερον deleted by Dindorf.
³ οὔτ' Emperius : οὐδ'.   ⁴ οὔτε Emperius : οὐδὲ.
⁵ δύναται after ἀφελέσθαι deleted by Cobet.
⁶ κτησάμενον Emperius : χρησάμενον.
⁷ πόλις Dindorf : πολίτης.
⁸ σκοπεῖν added by Crosby, ἰδεῖν by Reiske.
⁹ After βούλοιτο Reiske conjectures λύραν.
¹⁰ κἄπειτ' Crosby : ἔπειτ'.
¹¹ ὁρῶν added by Reiske.

---

¹ A fair summary of the course of Greek affairs during the century following the Persian wars.

once more held the reins of empire, departing from
their own former principle, they found themselves in
the same position as the Athenians.[1] And yet those
states of old possessed real power and great utility,
if it be correct to call self-seeking by that name;
whereas anyone seeing the disputes and occasions
for hostility of the present time would, methinks,
blush for shame, for in reality they make one think
of fellow-slaves quarrelling with one another over
glory and pre-eminence.

What then? Is there nothing noble in this our
day to merit one's serious pursuit? The greatest
things, yes the only things worthy of serious
pursuit, were present then, are present now, and
always will be; and over these no man, surely,
has control, whether to confer them on another or to
take them away from him who has them, but, on the
contrary, they are always at one's disposal, whether
it be a private citizen or the body politic. But the
discussion of these matters perhaps would take too
long. And yet I am not unaware that the philosophers
are believed by many to be engaged in relaxing
everything and in slackening the serious pursuit
of practical affairs and on that account in working
more harm than good.[2] It is just as if one should
wish to watch a musician tuning his instrument, and
then, seeing the same man slacken some strings[3]

[2] This criticism of the philosopher is as old as Plato, who
devotes much space in his *Republic* to the defence of real
philosophers as practical men. See especially *Republic* 473 D,
487 B–489 D. Cf. Plutarch, *Moralia* 776 C, for a vigorous
refutation of the charge of impracticality.

[3] For this unusual meaning of φθόγγων, cf. Or. 10. 19.
Philostratus, *Apollonius* 5. 21, uses that word of the 'stops'
of a pipe.

53 ἐπιτείνοντα σκώψειε[1] τὸν αὐτόν.[2] ἔχει δὴ καὶ τὰ
τῶν πόλεων πράγματα οὕτως. αἱ μὲν γὰρ
πονηραὶ καὶ ἀνωφελεῖς σπουδαὶ καὶ φιλοτιμίαι
μᾶλλόν εἰσι τοῦ προσήκοντος ἐντεταμέναι καὶ
τρόπον τινὰ αὐτοὶ[3] δι᾿ αὐτοὺς ἀπορρήγνυνται
πάντες· αἱ δὲ ὑπὲρ τῶν καλλίστων ὅλως ἐκλύονται.
θεάσασθε δ᾿ εὐθέως, εἰ βούλεσθε, τὴν τῆς φιλαργυ-
ρίας ἐπίτασιν, τὴν τῆς ἀκρασίας.

   Ἀλλ᾿ ἔοικα γὰρ πόρρω προάγειν, καὶ καθάπερ
οἱ ἐν ταῖς γαλήναις μακρότερον νηχόμενοι, τὸ
μέλλον οὐ προορᾶν.

---

[1] ἐπιτείνοντα σκώψειε Crosby, ἐπιτείνοντα σκῶψαι Arnim,
ἐντείνοντα σκώψει Selden : ἐντείνοντας ὄψει.

[2] τὸν αὐτόν] τὸν τόνον Capps, ὡς τοὐναντίον αὐτῷ πράττοντα
Arnim.

[3] αὐτοὶ added by Capps.

and tighten others again, should scoff at him. That in fact is precisely the situation in civic matters. For the base and unprofitable pursuits and ambitions have become more tense than is fitting, and all who are swayed by them, through no one's fault but their own, become broken men, as one may say; but those pursuits and ambitions which aim at what is noblest are wholly relaxed. And consider, for example, if you will, the tension that marks covetousness, that marks incontinence!

But I seem to be going too far afield, and, like those who in calm weather swim too far, I seem not to foresee what lies ahead.[1]

---

[1] This sudden termination of the theme is a bit perplexing. The figure contained in Dio's concluding sentence suggests the fear of 'stormy weather.' Possibly he sensed that his hearers were getting restless.

THE THIRTY-FIFTH DISCOURSE, DELIVERED IN CELAENAE IN PHRYGIA

Celaenae, as Dio himself tells us, was situated at the head-waters of the Maeander in the heart of Phrygia, on the main highway between East and West and was the focus of five other well-marked natural routes (Ramsay, *Cities and Bishoprics of Phrygia*). From Herodotus (7. 26) we learn that Xerxes paused there on his way to Greece; and there too the younger Cyrus tarried thirty days in 401 B.C. while assembling his forces (Xenophon, *Anabasis* 1. 2. 5–8). Despite its manifest importance, Celaenae does not appear again in literature until Roman times. In fact Strabo, who devotes considerable space to the site (12. 8. 15–18), uses the name Apamea rather than Celaenae. He explains that Antiochus Soter (280–261 B.C.), on moving the inhabitants a short distance away, renamed the settlement in honour of his mother. According to Ramsay, the old name was revived in the second century of our era, presumably in consequence of a ' re-invigorated national sentiment.'

Arnim locates this Discourse in the same general period of Dio's career as the three that precede it. We are in the dark regarding the occasion of its delivery. Dio seems to be quite at his ease and enjoys the opportunity to introduce himself and to flatter and amuse his audience. Much of what he says was doubtless uttered with a twinkle of the eye.

35. ΕΝ ΚΕΛΑΙΝΑΙΣ ΤΗΣ ΦΡΥΓΙΑΣ

1 Οὐκ ἐπιδειξόμενος ὑμῖν, ὦ ἄνδρες, παρῆλθον
οὐδὲ ἀργυρίου παρ' ὑμῶν δεόμενος οὐδ' ἔπαινον
προσδεχόμενος. ἐπίσταμαι γὰρ οὔτε αὐτὸς ἱκανῶς
παρεσκευασμένος, ὥστε ὑμῖν ἀρέσαι λέγων, οὔτε
ὑμᾶς οὕτως ἔχοντας, ὥστε προσδεῖσθαι τῶν ἐμῶν
λόγων. πλεῖστον δὲ τὸ μεταξὺ τῆς ὑμετέρας
βουλήσεως καὶ τῆς ἐμῆς δυνάμεως. ἐγὼ μὲν
γὰρ ἁπλῶς πέφυκα καὶ φαύλως διαλέγεσθαι καὶ
οὐδενὸς ἄμεινον τῶν τυχόντων· ὑμεῖς δὲ θαυμασ-
τῶς καὶ περιττῶς ἐπιθυμεῖτε ἀκούειν καὶ μόνων
ἀνέχεσθε τῶν πάνυ δεινῶν.

2 Οὐ δὴ[1] τούτου χάριν προῆλθον, ἵνα με θαυμά-
σητε· οὐ γὰρ ἔστιν ὅπως ἂν ἐγὼ θαυμασθείην
ὑφ' ὑμῶν, οὐδ' ἂν ἀληθέστερα λέγω τῶν Σιβύλλης
ἢ Βάκιδος· ἀλλὰ ἵνα μηδεὶς ὑποβλέπῃ με μηδὲ
πυνθάνηται παρ' ἑτέρων ὅστις εἰμὶ καὶ ὁπόθεν
ἔλθοιμι. νῦν γὰρ ἴσως ὑπονοοῦσιν εἶναί με τῶν
σοφῶν ἀνθρώπων καὶ πάντα εἰδότων, γελοίῳ
καὶ ἀτόπῳ τεκμηρίῳ χρώμενοι, τῷ κομᾶν. εἰ
γὰρ τοῦτο αἴτιον ὑπῆρχεν ἀρετῆς καὶ σωφροσύνης,
οὐδεμιᾶς ἂν ἐδεῖτο μεγάλης οὐδὲ χαλεπῆς δυνάμεως
τὰ τῶν ἀνθρώπων.

[1] οὐ δὴ Selden : οὐδὲ.

---

[1] The Sibyl and Bacis occur together also in Or. 13. 36.
[2] Regarding his long hair, cf. also 12. 15 and 72. 2.

THE THIRTY-FIFTH DISCOURSE, DE-LIVERED IN CELAENAE IN PHRYGIA

GENTLEMEN, I have come before you not to display my talents as a speaker nor because I want money from you, or expect your praise. For I know not only that I myself am not sufficiently well equipped to satisfy you by my eloquence, but also that your circumstances are not such as to need my message. Furthermore, the disparity between what you demand of a speaker and my own powers is very great. For it is my nature to talk quite simply and unaffectedly and in a manner in no wise better than that of any ordinary person; whereas you are devoted to oratory to a degree that is remarkable, I may even say excessive, and you tolerate as speakers only those who are very clever.

Nay, my purpose in coming forward is not to gain your admiration—for I could not gain that from *you* even were I to utter words more truthful than those of the Sibyl or of Bacis [1]—but rather that no one may look askance at me or ask others who I am and whence I came. For at present quite possibly people suspect that I am one of your wiseacres, one of your know-it-alls, basing their suspicion upon a ludicrous and absurd bit of evidence, namely, that I wear my hair long. [2] For if long hair were accountable for virtue and sobriety, mankind would need no great power nor one difficult of attainment.

3 Ἀλλ᾽ ἐγὼ δέδοικα μὴ οὐδὲν ᾖ τοῖς ἀνοήτοις ὄφελος τοῦ κομᾶν,[1] οὐδ᾽ ἂν τὴν καρδίαν αὐτὴν γένωνται δασεῖς, καθάπερ Ἀριστομένη τὸν Μεσσήνιόν φασιν, ὃς πλεῖστα Λακεδαιμονίοις πράγματα παρέσχε, καὶ πολλάκις ἁλοὺς ἀπέδρα παρ᾽ αὐτῶν,[2] τοῦτον, ἐπεὶ δή ποτε ἀπέθανεν, οὕτως ἔχοντα εὑρεθῆναι. φημὶ τοίνυν οὐδὲν ὄφελος εἶναι τοῖς γυμνῆσι τούτοις, οὐδ᾽ ἂν πελτασταὶ γένωνται,[3] πρός γε τὸ δίκαιον καὶ σωφροσύνην ἀληθῆ καὶ φρόνησιν, οὐδ᾽ ἂν ἔτι μᾶλλον ἀποδύσωνται καὶ γυμνοὶ περιτρέχωσι τοῦ χειμῶνος ἢ τὴν Μήδων καὶ Ἀράβων στολὴν λάβωσιν, ὥσπερ οὐδὲ αὐλεῖν ἱκανοὶ ἔσονται τὰ τῶν αὐλητῶν ἐνδεδυκότες. οὐδὲ γὰρ τοὺς ὄνους ἵππους γενέσθαι δυνατόν, οὐδ᾽ ἂν ἔτι πλέον τὰς ῥῖνας ἀνατμηθῶσιν, οὐδ᾽ ἂν τὰς γνάθους τρήσαντες αὐτῶν ψάλιον[4] ἐμβάλωσιν, οὐδὲ ἂν ἀφέλῃ τις τὰ σάγματα·[5] ἀλλὰ ὀγκήσονται πρὸ τῶν τειχῶν πάνυ μέγα καὶ τἆλλα ποιήσουσι τὰ πρέποντα αὐτοῖς.

4 Ὥστε μηδεὶς ἕνεκα τοῦ σχήματος νομισάτω

---

[1] ὥσπερ οὐκ ἔστιν (just as in fact they don't) after κομᾶν deleted by Emperius.

[2] παρ᾽ αὐτῶν] deleted by Cobet.

[3] οὐδ᾽ ἂν πελτασταὶ γένωνται suspected by Emperius, deleted by Arnim and Bude.

[4] ψάλιον Valesius : ψέλιον.

[5] σάγματα Casaubon : ἀγάλματα.

---

[1] A romantic hero commonly associated with the second Messenian war. Pausanias tells his exploits at much length (4. 14. 7 to 4. 24. 3). For the portent of the shaggy heart, see Pliny, Nat. Hist. 11. 184-5.

THE THIRTY-FIFTH DISCOURSE

However, I fear that fools get no good from their long hair, not even if they get shaggy to the very heart —as in the case of Aristomenes,[1] the Messenian, who caused a deal of trouble for the Spartans, and who, though taken captive many times, always managed to escape from them—he, we are told, when at last he met his death, was found to be in that condition. I claim, therefore, that these nude philosophers[2] get no good from their shagginess— not even if they should join the light infantry— at least with regard to justice and true sobriety and wisdom, nay, not even if they should strip off still more clothing and run about stark naked in winter time, or else adopt the garb of Medes and Arabs;[3] just as they will not acquire proficiency with the flute by merely donning the costume of flautists.[4] Neither can asses[5] become horses even if they have their nostrils slit still more, or even if they have their jaws bored and a curb-chain placed between their teeth, or even if their pack-saddles are taken from them; nay, they will still bray before the walls right lustily and perform the other acts that befit their nature.

Therefore, let no one suppose that my guise

---

[2] Cf. Or. 34.3, where reference is made to the scanty clothing of certain would-be philosophers. In the present passage he seems to be toying with the double meaning inherent in γυμνῆτες : 'naked' (or lightly clad) and 'light-armed soldiers.' This accounts for the following clause, which contains the term πελτασταί, its synonym. The word-play is aimed to make his victims still more ludicrous. Emperius, however, was suspicious of that second clause.

[3] That is, go to the other extreme and muffle up.

[4] Phrygia was the home of the flute.

[5] Asses would be familiar objects at such a trading centre as Celaenae.

διαφέρειν με μηδενὸς μηδὲ τούτῳ πεποιθότα
λέγειν, ἀλλὰ τοὐναντίον ὁρᾶν,[1] ἂν μὲν ἡσυχίαν
ἄγω καθάπαξ καὶ διαλέγωμαι μηδενί, πολλῷ
μᾶλλον ὑπονοεῖν τοὺς ἀνθρώπους, ὡς[2] ἄν, οἶμαι,
σεμνυνόμενον, ὡς σπουδαῖον κρύπτοντα· πολλοὶ
γὰρ δὴ δι' αὐτὸ τοῦτο ἐθαυμάσθησαν, τὸ σιγᾶν·
ἐὰν δὲ ἐν τῷ μέσῳ καταστὰς μηδενὸς ἄμεινον
λέγων φαίνωμαι τῶν καπήλων καὶ τῶν ὀρεοκόμων,
οὐκ ἐνοχλήσειν, σαφῶς αὐτοὺς ἑωρακότας ὁποῖός
εἰμι.

5   Σχεδὸν δὲ τοῦτο καὶ ἐπ' ἄλλων ἰδεῖν ἔστι
γιγνόμενον· οἷον ἐπειδάν τινες ὑπονοήσωσιν ἔχειν
τινὰ[3] τοῦτο αὐτό, ὃ τυγχάνουσι ζητοῦντες,
προσίασι καὶ ἀνερευνῶσιν· ἐὰν οὖν περιστείλῃ[4]
καὶ μὴ ἐθέλῃ δεικνύειν, ἔτι μᾶλλον ὑπονοοῦσιν·
ἐὰν δὲ παραχρῆμα ἀποκαλύψῃ καὶ γένηται φα-
νερὸς οὐκ ἔχων οὐδέν, ἀπίασι, διημαρτηκέναι
νομίσαντες. πολὺ δὴ κρεῖττον τοῖς οὐ δεομένοις
δόξης ἀποκαλύπτεσθαι πρὸς τοὺς πολλοὺς καὶ
φανερὸν τῷ λόγῳ ποιεῖν[5] αὐτὸν τοῖς δυναμένοις
ξυνεῖναι τὸν ἄνθρωπον ὁποῖός ἐστιν. οἶμαι γὰρ
αὐτοὺς καταφρονήσειν σαφῶς, ὡς ἔγωγε νῦν
πέπονθα, καὶ[6] οὐ ξυνήσειν ἀλλήλων ἡμᾶς, οὔτε
ἐμὲ τῶν ἀκουόντων οὔτε ἐκείνους τοῦ λέγοντος.

---

[1] ὁρᾶν] ὁρῶντα Arnim, ἅπαν Pflugk.
[2] ὡς Reiske : ὧν.   [3] τινὰ Reiske : τινὰς.
[4] περιστείλῃ] περιστέλλῃ Reiske.
[5] After ποιεῖν Arnim suspects a lacuna.
[6] πέπονθα, καὶ] πέποιθα Emperius.

---

[1] Cf. Shakespeare, *Merchant of Venice*, Act. 1, Scene 1,
where the same idea is ably put by Gratiano.

makes me different from any other man, or that it is this that gives me confidence to speak. On the contrary, let it be understood by all that I can see that, if I keep absolutely silent and do not talk with anyone at all, people are much more likely to distrust me, I fancy, as giving myself airs, as concealing something of importance—for, in fact, in many instances men have won admiration merely by reason of their silence ; [1] whereas, if I take my stand in your midst and show myself to be no better as a speaker than any huckster or muleteer, I see that none will be vexed with me, once they have seen for themselves what sort of man I am.

This is virtually what you may see occurring with other men also. For example, when certain people suspect a man of having the very thing for which they happen to be searching, they go up to him and put him through a close questioning. If, then, he draws his cloak about him and declines to uncover, they are all the more suspicious, but if he immediately unwraps and it becomes evident that he is concealing nothing, they go away convinced that they have been in error. You see, it is far better for those who are not seeking notoriety to disclose themselves to the people, and for a person by speaking to reveal himself for the benefit of those who can understand what sort of man he is. For I fancy that they will clearly show contempt for me, to judge by the treatment I have been receiving,[2] and that we shall *not* understand one another, neither I my audience nor they

---

[2] Dio seems to indicate that his audience has been displaying either restlessness or amusement. Or possibly his words refer to some gossip of which he had been the subject upon coming to Celaenae.

τούτου δὲ αἴτιον ἔγωγε θείην ἂν ἐμαυτὸν μᾶλλον ἢ ὑμᾶς.

6 Μιὰ μὲν οὖν αὕτη πρόφασις τοῦ προελθεῖν. ἑτέρα δὲ τὸ φοβεῖσθαι μὴ διαφθαρῶ αὐτὸς διὰ τὴν ὑμετέραν ὑποψίαν καὶ τῷ ὄντι νομίσω προσεῖναί σπουδαῖόν τι ἐμαυτῷ. μεγάλης γὰρ διανοίας καὶ δυνάμεως ἔοικε δεῖν, ὅταν θαυμάσωσιν ἕνα πολλοὶ καὶ διαφέρειν ἡγῶνται τῶν ἄλλων, εἰ μέλλει σωφρονεῖν οὗτος ὁ ἀνὴρ καὶ μηδὲν ἀνόητον πάσχειν μηδὲ ἐπαίρεσθαι τοῖς τῶν [1] πολλῶν λόγοις, ὥσπερ πτεροῖς· καθάπερ τὸν Ἀχιλλέα πεποίηκεν Ὅμηρος διὰ τὴν ἀλαζονείαν ὑπὸ τῶν ὅπλων ἐπαιρόμενον καὶ φερόμενον·

τῷ δ' αὖτε πτερὰ γίνετ', ἄειρε δὲ ποιμένα λαῶν.

7 Ἡλίκη δέ ἐστιν ἡ τῶν πολλῶν δύναμις τοῦ πείθειν ὅ τι ἂν αὐτοὶ θέλωσιν, οὐχ ἥκιστα ἀπὸ τῶν παίδων μάθοι τις ἄν· ὅταν ἀνθρώπῳ σωφρονοῦντι παιδάρια ἀκολουθῇ, φάσκοντα μαίνεσθαι. τὸ μὲν γὰρ πρῶτον ἄπεισιν ἀγανακτῶν καθ' αὐτόν, ἔπειτα προσκρούων ἀεὶ καὶ λοιδορούμενος ἑκάστῳ καὶ διώκων αὐτὸ τοῦτο ἔπαθεν, ἐξέστη τελευτῶν, καὶ τὴν φήμην ὑπέλαβε θεῖον [2] εἶναι, οὐ μόνον τὴν τῶν ἀνδρῶν, ἀλλὰ καὶ τὴν τῶν παίδων.

8 Δοκεῖ δέ μοι καὶ τὸ τῶν σοφιστῶν γένος ἐντεῦθεν αὔξεσθαί ποθεν. ἐπειδὰν πολλοὶ νεανί-

---

[1] τῶν added by Geel.
[2] θεῖον Capps : θεὸν.

---

[1] *Iliad* 19. 386.

their speaker. And the blame for this misunderstanding I would set down to my account rather than to yours.

This, then, is one reason for my coming forward. But there is another reason—my fear that I myself may become spoiled through your suspicions of me and come to believe that there is actually something of importance in my make-up. For when many people display admiration for one man and consider him superior to the rest, great wisdom and strength of character are seemingly needed if he is to preserve his common sense and not be made a fool or be uplifted, as by wings, by the words of the crowd—as Homer has portrayed Achilles,[1] through vainglory because of his new armour, being uplifted and in full career:

> To him they were as wings and raised aloft
> The shepherd of the host.[1]

And how great the power of the populace is to make men believe anything they please may perhaps best be learned from children: when a sane man is followed by urchins who keep calling him crazy. For at first the man goes away inwardly annoyed, and then, from constantly falling foul of them and reviling and chasing them one by one, he gets into that very state and ends by going mad, and the spoken word he took to be a manifestation of deity,[2] not merely the utterance of men, but even that of boys.

And, methinks, the tribe of sophists also owes its development to some such cause as this. When a lot

[2] Cf. Aristophanes, *Birds* 720, on φήμη as the voice of God. Cf. also *Odyssey* 20. 100–21.

σκοι σχολὴν ἄγοντες ἕνα θαυμάζωσι πηδῶντες, καθάπερ αἱ Βάκχαι περὶ τὸν Διόνυσον, πᾶσα ἀνάγκη τοῦτον τὸν ἄνθρωπον οὐ πολλῷ τινι χρόνῳ πολλοῖς τῶν ἄλλων [1] δόξαι τι λέγειν. σχεδὸν γὰρ ὥσπερ οἱ γονεῖς διαλέγεσθαι τὰ παιδία διδάσκουσιν, ἐπὶ παντὶ χαίροντες ὅ τι ἂν εἴπωσιν· οὐκοῦν ἐκ τούτων θαρρεῖ καὶ μᾶλλον πρόεισι [2] καὶ σαφέστερον ἀεὶ διαλέγεται καὶ τέλος ἐξέμαθε τὴν φωνὴν τῶν ξυνόντων, ἐάν τε Ἕλληνες ὦσιν ἐάν τε βάρβαροι· καὶ τοὺς σοφιστὰς ἀνάγκη τὴν διάνοιαν τῶν ἀκροατῶν ἀναλαβεῖν, τοιαῦτα καὶ λέγοντας καὶ διανοουμένους, ὁποῖοί ποτ' ἂν οὗτοι τυγχάνωσιν ὄντες· εἰσὶ δὲ οἱ πλείους ἐπιεικῶς ἠλίθιοι καὶ δυστυχεῖς.

9 Οὗτος μὲν οὖν ἴσως οὐ μέγας κίνδυνος, εἴ τις αὑτῷ [3] καὶ ἑτέροις [4] δοκεῖ δεινὸς εἶναι καὶ περιάξει πλῆθος ἀνθρώπων ἀνοήτων· ὥσπερ τὸν Ὀρφέα φασὶ τὰς δρῦς καὶ τὰς πέτρας καὶ τοὺς λίθους· τὸ δ' αὐτὸν ἀνόητον ὄντα καὶ δειλὸν καὶ ἀκόλαστον καὶ μηδὲν διαφέροντα τῶν βοσκημάτων ἀρετῆς τι νομίσαι [5] προσήκειν αὑτῷ καὶ καλοκἀγαθίας, τοῦτο δὴ παντελῶς δεινὸν καὶ τῆς χαλεπωτάτης πασῶν ἀνοίας καὶ μανίας. ἀλλ' ὅταν φήμη καταλαμβάνῃ τινὰ καὶ τοιοῦτος ἄρξηται λόγος ὑποτύφεσθαι, δεῖ περιρρηξάμενον ἐκπηδᾶν γυμνὸν εἰς τὰς ὁδούς, ἐπιδεικνύντα πᾶσιν ὅτι μηδενὸς 10 ἐστι βελτίων. ἐὰν δὲ ἐπακολουθῇ τις φάσκων

---

[1] πολλοῖς τῶν ἄλλων] πολλοῖς τε τῶν ἄλλων καὶ ἑαυτῷ Emperius, καὶ αὐτῷ καὶ πολλοῖς τῶν ἄλλων Herwerden.
[2] πρόεισι Reiske: πρόσεισι.
[3] αὑτῷ Casaubon: αὐτῷ or αὐτό.
[4] ἑτέροις Casaubon: ἕτερος.

of young men with nothing to do go leaping about a man with cries of admiration, as the Bacchants leap about Dionysus, inevitably that man after no great lapse of time will gain a reputation with many others for talking sensibly. Why, that is very much the way in which parents teach their children how to talk, expressing keen delight over anything the children may utter. Accordingly, in consequence of that applause, the children take courage and make further progress and keep speaking more and more distinctly, until finally they have mastered the language of their associates, be they Greeks or barbarians. The sophists also can't help adopting the thought of their listeners, saying and thinking such things as fit the nature of those listeners, whatever it happens to be ; but the majority of these are pretty much simpletons, victims of an unkind fate.

Well then, conceivably there is no great risk involved if a man appears to himself and others to be clever, and draws in his train a crowd of fools—just as it is said of Orpheus, that he drew to himself trees and rocks and stones—but that, while himself a fool, a coward, intemperate, in no wise superior to dumb cattle, a man should believe that he has any claim to virtue and gentility—that indeed is utterly preposterous and a mark of the most grievous folly and madness. Nay, whenever fame lays hold upon a man and that sort of talk starts to smoulder, he should tear off his garments and leap forth naked upon the public highways, proving to all the world that he is no better than any other man. And if someone follows at his heels claiming to be his

---

⁵ νομίσαι Reiske : νομίσας.

εἶναι μαθητής, ἀπελαύνειν παίοντα καὶ βάλλοντα
ταῖς βώλοις καὶ τοῖς λίθοις, ὡς ἀνόητον ἢ πονηρόν.

Λέγω δὲ οὐ πρὸς ἅπαντας· εἰσὶ γὰρ οἱ καλῶς
καὶ συμφερόντως τὸ πρᾶγμα πράττοντες, οἷς
ἔδει σπένδειν καὶ θυμιᾶν· ἀλλ' οὓς [1] σοφοὺς
ὑμῖν ἀποδεικνύουσι, τρεῖς ἢ τέτταρας κομήτας,[2]
καθάπερ τοὺς ἱερέας τῶν παρ' ὑμῖν· τοὺς μακαρίους
λέγω, τοὺς ἁπάντων ἄρχοντας τῶν ἱερέων, τοὺς
ἐπωνύμους τῶν δύο ἠπείρων τῆς ἑτέρας [3] ὅλης.
ταῦτα γάρ ἐστι τὰ ποιοῦντα καὶ τούτους εὐδαίμονας,
στέφανος καὶ πορφύρα καὶ παιδάρια κομῶντα
λιβανωτὸν φέροντα.

11 Ταῦτα μὲν οὖν ὅπως ποτὲ ἔχει, λελέχθω·
τὸ δὲ κομᾶν οὐ χρὴ πάντως ὑπολαμβάνειν ὡς
ἀρετῆς σημεῖον. πολλοὶ γὰρ δὴ [4] διὰ θεόν τινα
κομῶσιν ἄνθρωποι· καὶ [5] γεωργοὶ κομῆται, μηδὲ
τοὔνομα ἀκούσαντές ποτε τὸ φιλοσοφίας, καὶ
νὴ Δία οἱ πλείους τῶν βαρβάρων, οἱ μὲν σκέπης
ἕνεκεν, οἱ δὲ καὶ πρέπειν αὑτοῖς νομίζοντες.
τούτων [6] οὐκ ἔστιν ἐπίφθονος οὐδεὶς οὐδὲ κατα-
12 γέλαστος. ἴσως γὰρ ὀρθῶς αὐτὸ πράττουσιν·
ἐπεὶ καὶ τοὺς λαγὼς ὁρᾶτε τοὺς πάνυ ἀσθενεῖς
ὑπὸ τῆς δασύτητος σωζομένους, καὶ τῶν ὀρνέων

---

[1] ἀλλ' οὓς Casaubon : ἄλλους.
[2] ἢ τέτταρας κομήτας B] ἢ τέτταρας κοσμήτας M, ἢ τέ γαρ
ἀσκομήτας U, ἤτε γὰρ ἀσκομήτας T, ἢ τέτταρες κομῆται Arnim.
[3] ἑτέρας Mommsen : ἑσπέρας.
[4] δὴ Arnim : ἤδη.
[5] καὶ added by Emperius.
[6] After τούτων Reiske adds δ'.

---

[1] Cf. Or. 32. 61-6.

pupil, he must try to drive him away, striking him with his fists and pelting him with clods of earth and stones,[1] knowing that the fellow is either fool or knave.

However, my remarks are not levelled at all sophists, for there are some who follow that calling honourably and for the good of others, men to whom we should pour libation and offer incense; nay, I mean rather those whom they appoint to serve you as experts in wisdom, three or four long-haired persons like the high-priests of your local rites. I refer to the ' blessed ones,' who exercise authority over all your priests, whose title represents one of the two continents in its entirety.[2] For these men too owe their ' blessedness ' to crowns and purple[3] and a throng of long-haired lads bearing frankincense.

Well then, whatever be the truth in these matters, let this suffice. However, I still maintain that long hair must not by any means be taken as a mark of virtue. For many human beings wear it long because of some deity; and farmers wear long hair, without ever having even heard the word philosophy; and, by Zeus, most barbarians also wear long hair, some for a covering and some because they believe it to be becoming. In none of these cases is a man subjected to odium or ridicule. The reason may well be because their practice is correct. For instance, you observe that rabbits,[4] weak creatures that they are, are protected by their shaggy coats,

[2] Ramsay, *Cities and Bishoprics of Phrygia*, pp. 436–7, refers this to the Asiarchos, or Highpriest of Asia, as he is called in two inscriptions. The two continents were manifestly Asia and Europe.

[3] Cf. Or. 34. 29–30.

[4] Dio is familiar with rabbits. Cf. 33. 32.

τοῖς ἀσθενεστάτοις ἐξαρκεῖ τὰ πτερὰ εἴργειν
τὸν ἄνεμον καὶ τὸ ὕδωρ.¹ ἡμεῖς δὲ τὴν μὲν
κόμην ἀφαιροῦμεν, ὥσπερ οἱ νομεῖς τῶν ἵππων,
ἃς ἂν ἐθέλωσι παραβαλεῖν² τοῖς ὄνοις, καὶ τὰ
γένεια ἀποκείρομεν, τὰς δὲ κεφαλὰς σκέπομεν.³
τοὺς δὲ ἀλεκτρυόνας ὁρῶμεν οὐδενὸς τοιούτου προσδεομένους, ὧν ἄνθρωποι,⁴ σισύρας καὶ
πίλους καὶ τοιαῦθ' ἕτερα ξυρράπτοντες. καίτοι⁵
ποῖος ἂν γένοιτο πῖλος Ἀρκαδικὸς ἢ Λακωνικὸς
μᾶλλον ἁρμόττων τῆς αὑτοῦ κόμης ἑκάστῳ;
καὶ τί δεῖ, φησί, τοσούτων τῶν⁶ σκεπασμάτων;
οὐδὲν τοῖς γε πλουσίοις· ἐκείνοις μὲν οὐδὲ
χειρῶν οὐδὲ ποδῶν.⁷

13 Ἐγὼ δὲ ὁρῶ καὶ ταύτην τὴν πόλιν οὐδεμιᾶς
ἐνδεεστέραν τῶν πρώτων, καὶ ξυνήδομαι καὶ
ἀγαπῶ. τῆς γὰρ ἠπείρου τὸ καρτερώτατον
νέμεσθε καὶ πιότατον, πεδίων δὲ⁸ καὶ ὀρῶν
μεταξὺ καλλίστων ἵδρυσθε, καὶ πηγὰς ἀφθο-
νωτάτας ἔχετε καὶ χώραν εὐκαρποτάτην ξύμπαντα
μυρία φέρουσαν,

πυρούς τε ζειάς τ' ἠδ'⁹ εὐρυφυὲς κρῖ λευκόν,

---

¹ διότι ἐξ αὐτῶν πέφυκεν after ὕδωρ deleted by Sonny as
the gloss of some Christian writer who had in mind
Genesis 1. 20.
² παραβαλεῖν] ὑποβαλεῖν Cobet.
³ σκέπομεν Jacobs : πλέκομεν.
⁴ τοὺς δὲ ἀλεκτρυόνας . . . ἄνθρωποι deleted by Emperius.
⁵ καίτοι UB : καὶ other MSS.
⁶ τῶν Crosby : ὄντων.
⁷ After ποδῶν Reiske suspects a lacuna. Arnim brackets
§§ 11 and 12 as having been misplaced; see note 4,
page 403.
⁸ δὲ Reiske : τε.
⁹ τ' ἠδ' Homer : τε εἰδ' M, τε ἠδ' UB.

and that among the birds even the weakest find
their feathers a sufficient protection against wind
and rain. But as for us human beings, while we
shear off our locks (just as horse-breeders shear the
manes of mares [1] that they plan to mate with asses)
and also shave our beards,[2] we make coverings for
our heads. Yet we observe that cocks require
nothing extra as human beings do, goat-skin coats
and caps of felt and other similar coverings which
we stitch together. And yet what cap of Arcadian
or Laconian make could be more suitable than a
man's own hair? "Besides," someone will ask,
"what need is there for so many coverings for the
body?" No need, at least for men of wealth;
indeed they do not need hands or feet either.[3]

But [speaking of protection],[4] I perceive that this
city of yours also is inferior to none of the first rank,
and I rejoice with you and am content that it is so.
For example, you occupy the strongest site and the
richest on the continent; you are settled in the
midst of plains and mountains of rare beauty; you
have most abundant springs and a soil of greatest
fertility, bearing, all told, unnumbered products,

Both wheat and spelt and broad-eared barley
    white; [5]

---

[1] Pliny, *Nat. Hist.*, 10. 180, in reporting the practice, adds
that it was intended to make the mare properly humble. See
also Aelian, *De Natura Animalium*, 2. 10 and 12. 16.

[2] Dio criticizes shaving also in 33. 63.   [3] Cf. Dio 33. 64.

[4] Possibly this phrase may represent the transition, which is
none too clear on the surface. Arnim regards §§ 11 and 12
as an intrusion from another passage; but that supposition
does not provide any better connection, and the extended
treatment of the topic of long hair is quite in keeping with
Dio's habits.   [5] *Odyssey*, 4. 604.

καὶ πολλὰς μὲν ἀγέλας, πολλὰς δὲ ποίμνας ποιμαί-
νετε καὶ βουκολεῖτε. τῶν τε ποταμῶν οἱ μέγιστοι
καὶ πολυωφελέστατοι τὴν ἀρχὴν ἐνθένδε ἔχουσιν,
ὅ τε Μαρσύας οὗτος, διὰ μέσης τῆς πόλεως
ὑμῶν ῥέων, ὅ τε Ὀργᾶς,[1] ὅ τε Μαίανδρος, πολὺ
πάντων τῶν ποταμῶν θειότατος καὶ σοφώτατος,
ὃς[2] ἑλίττων μυρίας καμπὰς σχεδόν τι τὴν
14 ἀρίστην τῆς Ἀσίας ἔπεισιν. τῆς τε Φρυγίας
προκάθησθε καὶ Λυδίας, ἔτι δὲ Καρίας, ἄλλα τε
ἔθνη περιοικεῖ πολυανδρότατα, Καππάδοκές τε
καὶ Πάμφυλοι καὶ Πισίδαι, καὶ τούτοις ἅπασιν
ἀγορὰν ὑμεῖς καὶ ξύνοδον παρέχεσθε τὴν αὐτῶν
πόλιν. καὶ τοῦτο μὲν πολλὰς τῶν ἀνωνύμων
πόλεων, τοῦτο δὲ πολλὰς εὐδαίμονας κώμας
ὑπηκόους ἔχετε. σημεῖον δὲ μέγιστον τῆς δυνάμεως
ὑμῶν τὸ πλῆθος τῶν φόρων. ὥσπερ γάρ,[3]
οἶμαι, τῶν ὑποζυγίων κράτιστα δοκεῖ τὰ
πλεῖστον[4] ἕλκοντα, οὕτω καὶ τῶν πόλεων εἰκὸς
ἀρίστας εἶναι τὰς πλεῖστον ἀργύριον ὑποτελούσας.
15 Πρὸς δὲ τούτοις αἱ δίκαι παρ᾽ ἔτος ἄγονται
παρ᾽ ὑμῖν καὶ ξυνάγεται πλῆθος ἀνθρώπων
ἄπειρον δικαζομένων, δικαζόντων, ῥητόρων, ἡγεμόνων, ὑπηρετῶν, οἰκετῶν, μαστροπῶν, ὀρεοκόμων,
καπήλων, ἑταιρῶν[5] τε καὶ βαναύσων. ὥστε
τά τε ὤνια τοὺς ἔχοντας πλείστης ἀποδίδοσθαι
τιμῆς καὶ μηδὲν ἀργὸν εἶναι τῆς πόλεως, μήτε

---

[1] Ὀργᾶς Casaubon : Ὄρβας or νόρβας.
[2] ὃς added by Casaubon.
[3] ὥσπερ γάρ Crosby, ὡς γὰρ Arnim : ὥσπερ.
[4] πλεῖστον Arnim : πλεῖον or πλέον.
[5] ἑταιρῶν Jacobs, ἑτέρων τε Emperius : ἑταίρων.

---

[1] Greeks commonly deified rivers.

and many are the droves of cattle and many the
flocks of sheep you tend and pasture. And as
for rivers, the largest and most serviceable have
their source here—the Marsyas yonder, bearing its
waters through the midst of your city, and the
Orgas, and the Maeander, by far the most godlike [1]
and the wisest of all rivers, a river which with its
countless windings visits, one may almost say, all
that is best in Asia.[2] Furthermore, you stand as a
bulwark in front of Phrygia and Lydia and Caria
besides;[3] and there are other tribes around you
whose members are most numerous, Cappadocians
and Pamphylians and Pisidians, and for them all your
city constitutes a market and a place of meeting.[4]
And also many cities unknown to fame and many
prosperous villages are subject to your sway. And
a very great index of your power is found in the
magnitude of the contributions with which you are
assessed. For, in my opinion, just as those beasts of
burden are judged to be most powerful which carry
the greatest loads, so also it is reasonable to suppose
that those cities are the most considerable which
pay the largest assessments.

And what is more, the courts are in session every
other year in Celaenae, and they bring together an
unnumbered throng of people—litigants, jurymen,
orators, princes, attendants, slaves, pimps, mule-
teers, hucksters, harlots, and artisans. Consequently
not only can those who have goods to sell obtain the
highest prices, but also nothing in the city is out of

[2] Cf. Strabo 12. 8. 15–18 for the geography of the district.
[3] This is true, for Celaenae was near the eastern border of
Phrygia, astride the main highway between the East and
West. Cf. Introduction.
[4] Strabo (12. 8. 15) confirms this.

τὰ ζεύγη μήτε τὰς οἰκίας μήτε τὰς γυναῖκας.
16 τοῦτο δὲ οὐ σμικρόν ἐστι πρὸς εὐδαιμονίαν·
ὅπου γὰρ ἂν πλεῖστος ὄχλος ἀνθρώπων ξυνῇ,
πλεῖστον ἀργύριον ἐξ ἀνάγκης ἐκεῖ γίγνεται,
καὶ τὸν τόπον εἰκὸς εὐθηνεῖν· ὥσπερ, οἶμαί,
φασι τὴν χώραν, οὗ ἂν πρόβατα πλεῖστα αὐλισθῇ,
κρατίστην γίγνεσθαι τοῖς γεωργοῖς διὰ τὴν
κόπρον, καὶ πολλοὶ δέονται τῶν ποιμένων παρ'
17 αὑτοῖς αὐλίζειν τὰ πρόβατα. τοιγαροῦν μέγιστον
νομίζεται πρὸς ἰσχὺν πόλεως τὸ τῶν δικῶν
καὶ πάντες ἐσπουδάκασιν ὑπὲρ οὐδενὸς οὕτω.
μέτεστι δὲ αὐτοῦ ταῖς πρώταις πόλεσιν ἐν μέρει
παρ' ἔτος. φασὶ δὲ νῦν ἔσεσθαι διὰ πλείονος
χρόνου, τοὺς γὰρ ἀνθρώπους οὐχ ὑπομένειν
ξυνεχῶς ἐλαύνεσθαι πανταχοῦ. καὶ μὴν τῶν
ἱερῶν τῆς Ἀσίας μέτεστιν ὑμῖν τῆς τε δαπάνης
τοσοῦτον ὅσον ἐκείναις ταῖς πόλεσιν, ἐν αἷς
ἐστι τὰ ἱερά.

Οὔκουν ἔγωγε ταύτης εὐποτμοτέραν ἐπίσταμαι
πόλιν οὐδὲ ἀνθρώπους ἄμεινον ζῶντας, χωρὶς
18 Ἰνδῶν. ἐκεῖ γάρ, ὥς φασι, ποταμοὶ ῥέουσιν
οὐχ ὥσπερ παρ' ὑμῖν ὕδατος, ἀλλ' ὁ μὲν γάλακτος,
ὁ δὲ οἴνου διαυγοῦς, ἄλλος δὲ μέλιτος, ἄλλος
δὲ ἐλαίου. ῥέουσι δ' ἐγγύθεν ἐκ λόφων, ὥσπερ ἐκ
μαστῶν τῆς γῆς. πάντα δὲ ταῦτα τῶν παρ'
ἡμῖν ἄπειρον διαφέρει πρός τε ἡδονὴν καὶ δύναμιν.

---

[1] See also § 15. Ramsay, *Cities and Bishoprics of Phrygia*,
p. 428, note 5, names Apamea (Celaenae) and Eumenea as
the foremost cities thus to share in the court business; but he
would interpret παρ' ἔτος in such a way as to include also
Acmonia.

[2] Ramsay, *op. cit.*, p. 429, note 2, refers this to the emperor
worship, for which the cities were assessed.

work, neither the teams nor the houses nor the women. And this contributes not a little to prosperity; for wherever the greatest throng of people comes together, there necessarily we find money in greatest abundance, and it stands to reason that the place should thrive. For example, it is said, I believe, that the district in which the most flocks are quartered proves to be the best for the farmer because of the dung, and indeed many farmers entreat the shepherds to quarter their sheep on their land. So it is, you see, that the business of the courts is deemed of highest importance toward a city's strength and all men are interested in that as in nothing else. And the foremost cities share this business each in its turn in alternate years.[1] However, it is said that now the interval is going to be longer, for they claim that the people resent being constantly driven here and there. Yes, and you share also in the sanctuaries of Asia and in the expenditures they entail, quite as much as do those cities in which the sanctuaries are.[2]

Accordingly I know of no city that is more favoured by fortune than Celaenae and no people that leads a better existence—save only the people of India. For in India,[3] according to report, there are rivers, not of water as in your land, but one of milk, one of translucent wine, another of honey, and another of olive oil. And these streams spring from hills near by, as if from the breasts of Mother Earth. And all these products are immeasurably superior to those we have both in flavour and in potency.

[3] Dio could have found material for this idyllic story in many writers from Herodotus on. Lucian, *Vera Historia*, 2. 6–16, outdoes Dio in the marvels listed, though the resemblance to our passage is striking.

τὰ μὲν γὰρ ἐνθάδε γλίσχρως καὶ μόλις ἀπὸ
ζῴων τινῶν καὶ φυτῶν συλλέγομεν,[1] καρποὺς
ξύλων βρίζοντες [2] καὶ τροφὴν ζῴων βδάλλοντες
καὶ βλίττοντες, τὰ δὲ ἐκεῖ τῷ παντὶ καθαρώτερα,
χωρίς, οἶμαι, βίας καὶ πανουργίας. οἱ δὲ
ποταμοὶ ῥέουσιν ἕνα μῆνα τῷ βασιλεῖ, καὶ
φόρος οὗτός ἐστιν αὐτῷ, τὸν δὲ λοιπὸν χρόνον
τοῖς δημόταις.

19   Ξυνίασιν [3] οὖν καθ᾽ ἑκάστην ἡμέραν μετὰ
παίδων καὶ γυναικῶν εἴς τε τὰς πηγὰς καὶ πρὸς
τὰ ῥεύματα τῶν ποταμῶν παίζοντες καὶ γελῶντες,
ὡς ἂν ἐπ᾽ εὐωχίαν. φύεται δὲ παρὰ ταῖς ὄχθαις
ὅ τε λωτὸς ἰσχυρὸς καὶ σχεδὸν ἁπάντων σιτίων
ἥδιστος, οὐχ ὥσπερ ὁ παρ᾽ ἡμῖν τετράποσι
τροφή, καὶ πολλὰ σήσαμα καὶ σέλινα, ὡς ἂν
εἰκάσειέ τις ἐκ τῆς ὁμοιότητος· τὴν δὲ ἀρετὴν
οὐκ ἄξιον συμβάλλειν. γίγνεται δὲ αὐτόθι ἕτερον
σπέρμα, τῶν πυρῶν καὶ τῶν κριθῶν ἀμείνων
τροφὴ καὶ μᾶλλον ξυμφέρουσα. φύεται δὲ ἐν
κάλυξι μεγάλαις, οἷον ῥόδων, εὐοσμοτέραις δὲ
καὶ μείζοσιν. ταύτας τὰς ῥίζας καὶ τὸν καρπὸν
ἐσθίουσιν, οὐδὲν πονήσαντες.

20   Εἰσὶ δὲ ὀχετοὶ πολλοὶ ῥέοντες ἐκ τῶν ναμάτων,
οἱ μὲν μείζους, οἱ δὲ ἐλάττους, ξυμμιγνύντες
ἀλλήλοις, τῶν ἀνθρώπων πεποιηκότων, ὅπως ἂν
αὐτοῖς δοκῇ. μετοχετεύουσι δὲ ῥᾳδίως, ὥσπερ
ἡμεῖς τὸ ἐν τοῖς κήποις ὕδωρ. ἔστι δὲ καὶ λουτρὰ

----

[1] συλλέγομεν added by Wilamowitz.
[2] βρίζοντες] Scholiast to B: ἔσθοντες, πιέζοντες· λαμβάνεται
δὲ καὶ ἐπὶ τοῦ κυοῦντες. Emperius deleted καρποὺς . . .
βλίττοντες.
[3] ξυνίασιν Morel: ξύνεισιν.

For what we have in our country we gather in scanty measure and with difficulty from certain animals and plants, crushing the fruits of trees and plants [1] and extracting the food of living creatures by milking and by robbing the hive; while the products of India are altogether purer, untainted, methinks, by violence and ruthlessness. Moreover, the rivers flow during one month for the king, and that constitutes his tribute, while for the rest of the year they flow for the people.

So every day the Indians assemble with their children and their wives at the springs and river-banks, sporting and laughing as if in expectation of a feast. And by the banks there grows the lotus—a sturdy plant and, one might say, the sweetest of all foods, not, as the lotus in our land, mere fodder for quadrupeds—and also much sesame and parsley, at least as one might judge from the outward similarity of those plants, although for quality they are not to be compared. And that country produces also another seed, a better food than wheat and barley and more wholesome. And it grows in huge calyxes, like those of roses but more fragrant and larger. This plant they eat, both root and fruit, at no expense of labour.[2]

And there are many canals which issue from the rivers, some large and some small, mingling with one another and made by man to suit his fancy. And by their aid the Indians convey with ease the fluids I have named, just as we convey the water of our gardens. And there are baths also close by at their

---

[1] That is, of the olive tree and the grape-vine.

[2] This account of the lotus and of the 'other seed' may be due to Herodotus 2. 93.

πλησίον αὐτοῖς ὕδατος, τὸ μὲν θερμὸν λευκότερον
ἀργύρου, τὸ δὲ ὑπὸ τοῦ βάθους καὶ τῆς ψυχ-
ρότητος κυανοῦν. ἐνταῦθα νήχονται γυναῖκες
ἅμα καὶ παῖδες, καλοὶ πάντες. ἔπειτα, οἶμαι,
κατακλινέντες ἐν τοῖς λειμῶσιν ᾄδουσι καὶ μινυρί-
ζουσιν.

21 Εἰσὶ δὲ λειμῶνες αὐτόθι πάγκαλοι καὶ φύσις
ἀνθῶν τε καὶ δένδρων παρεχόντων τὴν μὲν σκιὰν
ἄνωθεν ἐξ ὕψους, τὸν δὲ καρπὸν ἐν ἐφικτῷ τοῖς
βουλομένοις λαβεῖν νευόντων τῶν κλάδων. οἵ
τε ὄρνιθες κατάδουσιν, οἱ μὲν ἐν ταῖς ὀργάσιν [1]
ἐγκαθήμενοι, πολύ τι πλῆθος, οἱ δὲ ἄνωθεν ἀπὸ
ἀκρεμόνων, εὐφωνότεροι τῶν παρ' ἡμῖν ὀργάνων.
πνεῦμά τε ἀεὶ μέτριον διαρρεῖ, καὶ τῶν ἀέρων ἡ
κρᾶσις ὁμοία διὰ παντός, μάλιστα δὲ ἔοικεν
ἀρχομένῳ θέρει. πρὸς δὲ τούτοις ὅ τε οὐρανὸς
ἐκεῖ καθαρώτερος καὶ τὰ ἄστρα πλείω καὶ λαμ-
πρότερα. ζῶσι δὲ [2] πλεῖον τετρακοσίων ἐτῶν,
πάντα τὸν χρόνον τοῦτον ὡραῖοι καὶ νέοι καὶ οὔτε
γῆράς ἐστι παρ' ἐκείνοις οὔτε νόσος οὔτε πενία.

22 Τούτων δὲ τοιούτων ὄντων καὶ τοσούτων ὑπαρχόντων ἀγαθῶν, ὅμως εἰσὶν ἄνθρωποι καλούμενοι
Βραχμᾶνες, οἳ χαίρειν ἐάσαντες τούς τε ποταμοὺς
ἐκείνους καὶ τοὺς παρ' αὐτοῖς ἐρριμμένους ἐκτρα-
πέντες ἰδίᾳ τι ξυλλογίζονται καὶ φροντίζουσι,
πόνους τε θαυμαστοὺς ἀναλαβόμενοι τοῖς σώμασιν οὐδενὸς ἀναγκάζοντος καὶ καρτερήσεις
δεινὰς ὑπομένοντες. φασὶ δὲ ἐξαίρετον αὐτοῖς
εἶναι μίαν πηγὴν τὴν τῆς ἀληθείας, πολὺ πασῶν

---

[1] ταῖς ὀργάσιν Herwerden: τοῖς ὄρεσιν.
[2] οὐ after δὲ deleted by Emperius.

disposal, the water of which in the one case is warm and whiter than silver and in the other it is blue from its depth and coldness. In these they swim, women and children together, all of them beautiful. And after the bath, I dare say, reclining in the meadows they sing and hum.

And there are in that land meadows of utter beauty and a variety of flowering trees that provide shade from high above, though they bring their fruit within reach of all who wish to pluck it as the branches nod. And the birds charm them by their song, some seated in the meadows, a great flock of them, and some high up among the topmost branches, their notes more tuneful than those of our musical instruments. And a gentle breeze is ever blowing, and the climate is nearly constant throughout the year, and it resembles most closely that of early summer. And what is more, not only is their sky clearer, but also the stars are more numerous and more brilliant. And these people live more than four hundred years, and during all that time they are beautiful and youthful and neither old age nor disease nor poverty is found among them.

So wonderful and so numerous are these blessings, and yet there are people called Brachmanes [1] who, abandoning those rivers and the people scattered along their banks, turn aside and devote themselves to private speculation and meditation, undertaking amazing physical labours without compulsion and enduring fearful tests of endurance. And it is said that they have one special fountain, the Fountain

[1] On the Brachmanes, see also Or. 49. 7. Strabo (15. 59-71) assembles further details drawn from many sources.

ἀρίστην καὶ θειοτάτην, ἧς οὐδέποτε ψεύσασθαι
τοὺς ἐμπιμπλαμένους.¹ τὰ μὲν οὖν ἐκεῖθεν λόγος
ἐστὶν ἀψευδής. ἤδη γάρ τινες τῶν ἀφικνουμένων
ἔφασαν· ἀφικνοῦνται δὲ οὐ πολλοί τινες ἐμπορίας
ἕνεκεν· οὗτοι δὲ ἐπιμίγνυνται τοῖς πρὸς θαλάττῃ.
23 τοῦτο δὲ ἄτιμόν ἐστιν Ἰνδῶν τὸ γένος, οἵ τε ἄλλοι
ψέγουσιν² αὐτούς.

Τούτους ἀνάγκη ὁμολογεῖν ὑμῶν εὐδαιμονεστέ-
ρους, τῶν δὲ ἄλλων ὑμᾶς, πλὴν ἑνὸς ἀνθρώπων ἔτι
γένους, τῶν πολυχρυσοτάτων. τὸ δὲ χρυσίον
λαμβάνουσι παρὰ μυρμήκων, οὗτοι δέ· εἰσιν
ἀλωπέκων μείζονες, τἆλλα δὲ ὅμοιοι τοῖς παρ'
ἡμῖν. ὀρύττουσι δὲ κατὰ γῆς, ὥσπερ οἱ λοιποὶ
μύρμηκες. ὁ δὲ χοῦς αὐτοῖς ἐστι χρυσίον καθαρώ-
τατον πάντων χρυσίων καὶ στιλπνότατον. εἰσὶν οὖν
πλησίον ἐφεξῆς, ὥσπερ κολωνοὶ τοῦ ψήγματος,
καὶ τὸ πεδίον ἅπαν ἀστράπτει. χαλεπὸν οὖν
ἰδεῖν ἐστι πρὸς τὸν ἥλιον, καὶ πολλοὶ τῶν ἐπιχει-
24 ρούντων ἰδεῖν τὰς ὄψεις διεφθάρησαν. οἱ δὲ
προσοικοῦντες ἄνθρωποι τὴν μεταξὺ χώραν δι-
ελθόντες, ἔρημον οὖσαν οὐ πολλήν, ἐφ' ἁρμάτων,
ὑποζεύξαντες ἵππους ταχίστους, ἀφικνοῦνται τῆς
μεσημβρίας, ἡνίκα δεδύκασι κατὰ γῆς· ἔπειτα
φεύγουσι τὸν χοῦν ἁρπάσαντες. οἱ δὲ αἰσθανό-

---

¹ ψεύσασθαι τοὺς ἐμπιμπλαμένους Cobet, τοὺς γευσαμένους
ἐμπίμπλασθαι Reiske: γεύσασθαι τοὺς ἐμπιμπλαμένους.
² ψέγουσιν] φεύγουσιν Lobeck.

---

¹ Strabo (15. 2–4) speaks of the dearth of trustworthy
information regarding India. By Dio's time many Greeks
were sailing to India, and the mercantile class knew a great
deal about the land.
² Dio seems to mean 'these people of the coast' when
he says that they were in ill repute. It looks like a tardy

of Truth, by far the best and most godlike of all, and that those who drink their fill thereof have never been known to lie. Regarding conditions in that land, then, it is a true story that you have heard. For some of those who have been there have vouched for it; though only a few do go there, in pursuit of trade, and they mingle only with the people of the coast.[1] And that branch of the Indian race is in low repute, and all the others say harsh things of them.[2]

It must be admitted that the people of India are more fortunate than you are, but that you are more fortunate than all others—with the exception of just one more race of mortals, namely, those most rich in gold. And their gold is obtained from ants. These ants are larger than foxes, though in other respects similar to the ants we have. And they burrow in the earth, just as do all other ants. And that which is thrown out by their burrowing is gold, the purest of all gold and the most resplendent. Now there are close to one another a series of what might be called hills of gold dust, and the whole plain is agleam. Therefore it is difficult to look thereon in the sunlight, and many of those who have made the attempt have lost their sight. But the people who live near that land, having traversed the intervening territory (desert land of no great extent) in chariots drawn by horses of greatest speed, arrive at midday, at which time the ants have gone underground; and then these men seize the gold that has been cast forth and flee. And the ants, becoming

admission that perhaps his tale may not be trustworthy. The tall stories with which he closes his Discourse, while doubtless intended to amuse, may also have been aimed as a sly thrust at his audience.

μενοι διώκουσι καὶ μάχονται καταλαβόντες, ἕως
ἂν ἀποθάνωσιν ἢ ἀποκτείνωσιν· ἀλκιμώτατοι
γάρ εἰσι θηρίων ἁπάντων. ὥστε οὗτοί γε
ἐπίστανται τὸ χρυσίον ὁπόσου ἐστὶν ἄξιον, καὶ
οὐδὲ προΐενται πρότερον ἢ ἀποθανεῖν.

25 Φέρε δή, τίνας ἄλλους τῶν καθ᾽ ἡμᾶς εὐδαίμονας ἀκούομεν; Βυζαντίους, χώραν τε ἀρίστην
νεμομένους καὶ θάλατταν εὐκαρποτάτην. τῆς
δὲ γῆς ἠμελήκασι διὰ τὴν ἀρετὴν τῆς θαλάττης.
ἡ μὲν γὰρ διὰ μακροῦ φέρει τὸν καρπὸν αὐτοῖς
καὶ δεῖ λαβεῖν ἐργασαμένους, ἡ δὲ αὐτόθεν μηδὲν
πονήσασιν.

---

[1] This story of the ants seems to have been taken out
of Herodotus 3. 102–5, where the scene is laid in India.
Herodotus names the Persians as his informants.

aware of what has happened, give chase, and, having overtaken their quarry, fight until they either meet their death or kill the foe—for they are the most valiant of all creatures.[1]   And so these at any rate know what their gold is worth, and they even die sooner than give it up.

Well then, what other people among the nations of our time are said to be fortunate?   The people of Byzantium, who enjoy a most fertile land and a sea abounding in fruits.   But they have neglected the land because of the excellence of the sea.   For whereas the land produces its fruits for them only after a long interval of time and toil is required to secure them, the sea yields up its treasures at once without any labour on their part.[2]

[2] Cf. Or. 33. 24, where Dio refuses to call the people of Byzantium ' fortunate ' because of the abundance of fish and the ease with which they are taken.   Our passage is in lighter vein and contains no question as to the propriety of the adjective.   The Discourse stops very abruptly at this point. It seems likely that the original ending has been lost.

THE THIRTY-SIXTH, OR BORYS-THENITIC, DISCOURSE, WHICH DIO DELIVERED IN HIS NATIVE LAND

In this Discourse Dio recounts for the benefit of his fellow-townsmen a conversation which took place between himself and certain citizens of Borysthenes in Pontus. Borysthenes was an ancient Greek trading-centre near the mouth of the Hypanis (Bug), and Dio states that he had gone there in the hope of pushing into the interior for the purpose of visiting the Getae, whose culture he was to describe in Τὰ Γετικά, a work no longer extant.

Arnim holds that Dio was in Borysthenes in A.D. 95 and suggests that his failure to reach the land of the Getae at that time may have been due to trouble between Rome and Dacia. It is plain that he had met with disappointment and that people knew of his purpose to leave Borysthenes by ship. If Arnim's date is correct, his destination could hardly have been Prusa—despite the word οἴκαδε used by Hieroson in section 25—for in A.D. 95 he was still an exile. However, he seems to have been at home as early as A.D. 97, and Arnim supplies arguments in favour of A.D. 101 as the year in which he made this report to the people of Prusa.

The narrative opens in leisurely manner and with a natural charm somewhat reminiscent of the opening of Plato's *Phaedrus*, to which, indeed, Dio may have owed also some of the ideas to which he gives expression, although for the most part he seems to be employing Stoic doctrine. In the course of his account he introduces a myth which he ascribes to the Zoroastrian lore of the Magi. That myth is responsible for not a little of the fame enjoyed by this Discourse. Dio, like Plato, was fond of myths and used them to good advantage. Some

418

of them at least are believed to have been his own invention; what shall we say of this one ?

It would not be surprising if the Greek world of that day had some acquaintance with Zoroastrianism. The name Zoroaster occurs in Greek as early as the pseudo-Platonic *Alcibiades,* and Herodotus, Xenophon, Strabo, and other Greeks who antedate Dio have not a little to tell of the Magi, some of the information being demonstrably authentic. Hirzel (*Der Dialog*) is of the opinion that, whatever may be true of other myths in Dio, this one at least emanates from Zoroastrian sources, and Jackson (*Zoroastrian Studies*) shares that belief, though admitting that ' the conception may have received some Greek colouring in its transmission.' Whatever Dio's indebtedness to the Magi, resemblances between their extant records and this myth are so slight as to warrant the belief that in its present form it is Dio's own creation, in the formation of which he may have drawn upon more than one source of inspiration, among which it seems safe to suggest the *Phaedrus* and the *Timaeus* of Plato, as well as familiar Stoic concepts on related subjects.

19. ΒΟΡΥΣΘΕΝΙΤΙΚΟΣ ΟΝ ΑΝΕΓΝΩ ΕΝ ΤΗΙ ΠΑΤΡΙΔΙ

1 Ἐτύγχανον μὲν ἐπιδημῶν ἐν Βορυσθένει τὸ θέρος, ὡς τότε εἰσέπλευσα μετὰ τὴν φυγήν, βουλόμενος ἐλθεῖν, ἐὰν δύνωμαι, διὰ Σκυθῶν εἰς Γέτας, ὅπως θεάσωμαι τἀκεῖ πράγματα ὁποῖά ἐστι. καὶ δὴ καὶ περιεπάτουν περὶ πλήθουσαν ἀγορὰν παρὰ τὸν Ὕπανιν. ἡ γὰρ πόλις τὸ μὲν ὄνομα εἴληφεν ἀπὸ τοῦ Βορυσθένους διὰ τὸ κάλλος καὶ τὸ μέγεθος τοῦ ποταμοῦ, κεῖται δὲ πρὸς τῷ Ὑπάνιδι, ἥ τε νῦν καὶ ἡ πρότερον οὕτως ᾠκεῖτο, οὐ πολὺ ἄνωθεν τῆς Ἱππολάου καλου-
2 μένης ἄκρας ἐν τῷ κατ' ἀντικρύ. τοῦτο δέ ἐστι τῆς χώρας ὀξὺ καὶ στερεὸν ὥσπερ ἔμβολον, περὶ ὃ συμπίπτουσιν οἱ ποταμοί. τὸ δὲ ἐντεῦθεν ἤδη λιμνάζουσι μέχρι θαλάττης ἐπὶ σταδίους σχεδόν τι διακοσίους· καὶ τὸ εὖρος οὐχ ἧττον ταύτῃ τῶν ποταμῶν. ἔστι δὲ αὐτοῦ τὸ μὲν πλέον τέναγος

---

[1] Also called Olbia (Herodotus 4. 18, Strabo 7. 3. 17), an important trading-centre on the right bank of the Hypanis (Bug), about four miles above the junction with the Borysthenes (Dnieper).

THE THIRTY-SIXTH, OR BORYS-THENITIC, DISCOURSE, WHICH DIO DELIVERED IN HIS NATIVE LAND

I happened to be visiting in Borysthenes[1] during the summer, for I had sailed there then,[2] after my exile, with the purpose of making my way, if possible, through Scythia to the Getan country, in order to observe conditions there. Well, one day toward noon I was strolling along the Hypanis. I should explain that, although the city has taken its name from the Borysthenes because of the beauty and the size of that river, the actual position, not only of the present city, but also of its predecessor, is on the bank of the Hypanis, not far above what is called Cape Hippolaüs,[3] on the opposite shore. This part of the land, near where the two rivers meet, is as sharp and firm as the beak of a ship. But from there on these rivers form a marshy lake down to the sea for a distance of approximately two hundred stades; and the breadth of the two rivers in that district is not less than that. The fact is that most of that stretch

---

[2] The word τότε presumably refers to τὸ θέρος; unfortunately we are not told which summer. Of course summer was the season best adapted to travel, and that may be the sole reason why Dio uses the phrase.

[3] Herodotus (4. 53) is the only other Greek to mention this cape.

καὶ γαλήνη ταῖς εὐδίαις ὥσπερ ἐν λίμνῃ γίγνεται
σταθερά.[1] ἐν δὲ τοῖς δεξιοῖς φαίνεται ποταμός,
καὶ τεκμαίρονται οἱ εἰσπλέοντες ἀπὸ τοῦ ῥεύ-
ματος τὸ βάθος. ὅθενπερ καὶ ἐξίησι, διὰ τὴν
ἰσχὺν τοῦ ῥοῦ· εἰ δὲ μή, ῥᾳδίως ἂν ἐφράττετο[2]
3 τοῦ νότου πολλοῦ κατὰ στόμα εἰσπνέοντος. τὸ
δὲ λοιπὸν ᾐών ἐστιν ἑλώδης[3] καὶ δασεῖα καλάμῳ
καὶ δένδροις. φαίνεται δὲ τῶν δένδρων πολλὰ
καὶ ἐν μέσῃ τῇ λίμνῃ, ὡς ἱστοῖς προσεοικέναι,
καὶ ἤδη τινὲς τῶν ἀπειροτέρων διήμαρτον, ὡς
ἐπὶ πλοῖα ἐπέχοντες. ταύτῃ δὲ καὶ τῶν ἁλῶν
ἐστι τὸ πλῆθος, ὅθεν οἱ πλείους τῶν βαρβάρων
λαμβάνουσιν ὠνούμενοι τοὺς ἅλας καὶ τῶν Ἑλλήνων καὶ Σκυθῶν οἱ Χερρόνησον οἰκοῦντες τὴν
Ταυρικήν. ἐκδιδόασι[4] δὲ οἱ ποταμοὶ εἰς θάλασσαν
παρὰ φρούριον Ἀλέκτορος, ὃ λέγεται τῆς γυναικὸς
εἶναι τοῦ Σαυρομάτων βασιλέως.

4 Ἡ δὲ πόλις ἡ τῶν Βορυσθενιτῶν τὸ μέγεθός
ἐστιν οὐ πρὸς τὴν παλαιὰν δόξαν διὰ τὰς συνεχεῖς
ἁλώσεις καὶ τοὺς πολέμους. ἅτε γὰρ ἐν μέσοις
οἰκοῦσα τοῖς βαρβάροις τοσοῦτον ἤδη χρόνον,
καὶ τούτοις σχεδόν τι τοῖς πολεμικωτάτοις, ἀεὶ
μὲν πολεμεῖται, πολλάκις δὲ καὶ ἑάλωκε· τὴν
δὲ[5] τελευταίαν καὶ μεγίστην ἅλωσιν οὐ πρὸ

---

[1] σταθερά] σταθερᾷ Reiske.
[2] ἂν ἐφράττετο Arnim : ἀνεφράττετο UB, ἐνεφράττετο M.
[3] ἑλώδης Emperius : ὑλώδης.
[4] ἐκδιδόασι Emperius : ἐκδιδοῦσι UB, ἐκδίδοσιν M.
[5] δὲ added by Reiske.

consists of shoals, and in fair weather unruffled calm prevails as in a swamp. But on the right there are signs of a river, and sailors inward bound judge its depth by the current.[1] And this explains why the water does make its way out to sea, because of the strength of the current; but for that it would easily be held in check when the south wind blows strongly dead against it. As for the rest, we have only muddy shore overgrown with reeds and trees. And many of the trees are to be seen even in the midst of the marsh, so as to resemble masts of ships; and at times some who were less familiar with those waters have lost their way, supposing that they were approaching ships. And it is here also that we find the vast number of salt-works from which most of the barbarians buy their salt,[2] as do also those Greeks and Scythians who occupy the Tauric Chersonese.[3] The rivers empty into the sea near the Castle of Alector,[4] which is said to belong to the wife of the Sauromatian[5] king.

The city of Borysthenes, as to its size, does not correspond to its ancient fame, because of its ever-repeated seizure and its wars. For since the city has lain in the midst of barbarians now for so long a time—barbarians, too, who are virtually the most warlike of all—it is always in a state of war and has often been captured, the last and most disastrous capture occurring not more than one hundred and

---

[1] The depth in summer is said to be no more than six feet. Therefore the pilot had to watch the current carefully in order to keep in the channel.

[2] For these salt-works, cf. Herodotus 4. 53.

[3] The Crimea.   [4] Unknown.

[5] The Sauromatians (Sarmatians) were an Iranian people. Cf. Rostovtzeff, *Iranians and Greeks in South Russia.*

πλειόνων ἢ πεντήκοντα καὶ ἑκατὸν ἐτῶν. εἷλον δὲ καὶ ταύτην Γέται καὶ τὰς ἄλλας τὰς ἐν τοῖς ἀριστεροῖς τοῦ Πόντου πόλεις μέχρι ᾿Απολλωνίας.
5 ὅθεν δὴ καὶ σφόδρα ταπεινὰ τὰ πράγματα κατέστη τῶν ταύτῃ ῾Ελλήνων, τῶν μὲν οὐκέτι συνοικισθεισῶν πόλεων, τῶν δὲ φαύλως, καὶ τῶν πλείστων βαρβάρων εἰς αὐτὰς συρρυέντων.¹ πολλαὶ γὰρ δή τινες ἁλώσεις κατὰ πολλὰ μέρη γεγόνασι τῆς ῾Ελλάδος, ἅτε ἐν πολλοῖς τόποις διεσπαρμένης. ἁλόντες δὲ τότε οἱ Βορυσθενῖται πάλιν συνῴκησαν, ἐθελόντων ἐμοὶ δοκεῖν τῶν Σκυθῶν διὰ τὸ δεῖσθαι τῆς ἐμπορίας καὶ τοῦ κατάπλου τῶν ῾Ελλήνων. ἐπαύσαντο γὰρ εἰσπλέοντες ἀναστάτου τῆς πόλεως γενομένης, ἅτε οὐκ ἔχοντες ὁμοφώνους τοὺς ὑποδεχομένους οὐδὲ αὐτῶν Σκυθῶν ἀξιούντων οὐδὲ ἐπισταμένων ἐμπόριον αὐτῶν κατασκευάσασθαι τὸν ῾Ελληνικὸν τρόπον.
6 Σημεῖον δὲ τῆς ἀναστάσεως ἥ τε φαυλότης τῶν οἰκοδομημάτων καὶ τὸ συνεστάλθαι τὴν πόλιν ἐς βραχύ. μέρει γάρ τινι προσῳκοδόμηται τοῦ παλαιοῦ περιβόλου, καθ᾿ ὃ πύργοι τινὲς οὐ πολλοὶ διαμένουσιν οὐ πρὸς τὸ μέγεθος οὐδὲ πρὸς τὴν ἰσχὺν τῆς πόλεως. τὸ δὲ μεταξὺ συμπέφρακται κατ᾿ ἐκεῖνο ταῖς οἰκίαις οὐκ

¹ συρρυέντων Emperius : συρρεόντων UB, συνρυέντων M.

fifty years ago. And the Getae on that occasion seized not only Borysthenes but also the other cities along the left shore of Pontus as far as Apollonia.[1] For that reason the fortunes of the Greeks in that region reached a very low ebb indeed, some of them being no longer united to form cities, while others enjoyed but a wretched existence as communities, and it was mostly barbarians who flocked to them. Indeed many cities have been captured in many parts of Greece, inasmuch as Greece lies scattered in many regions. But after Borysthenes had been taken on the occasion mentioned, its people once more formed a community, with the consent of the Scythians,[2] I imagine, because of their need for traffic with the Greeks who might use that port. For the Greeks had stopped sailing to Borysthenes when the city was laid waste, inasmuch as they had no people of common speech to receive them, and the Scythians themselves had neither the ambition nor the knowledge to equip a trading-centre of their own after the Greek manner.

Evidence of the destruction of Borysthenes is visible both in the sorry nature of its buildings and in the contraction of the city within narrow bounds. For it has been built adjacent to one section of the ancient circuit-wall where a few towers, but only a few, yet remain, not at all in keeping with the original size or power of the city. The intervening space in that quarter has been blocked off by means

[1] On the Thracian coast of Pontus, about 125 miles north-west of Byzantium.

[2] Coins of that period are said to support Dio's conjecture (Diehl, in Pauly-Wissowa XVII. 2422).

ἐχούσαις ὁποῖα¹ διαλείπει. τειχίον δὲ παρα-
βέβληται πάνυ ταπεινὸν καὶ ἀσθενές. τῶν δὲ
πύργων εἰσί τινες πολὺ ἀφεστῶτες τοῦ νῦν
οἰκουμένου, ὥστε μηδ' εἰκάσαι ὅτι μιᾶς ἦσαν
πόλεως. ταῦτά τε δὴ οὖν σημεῖα ἐναργῆ τῆς
ἁλώσεως καὶ τὸ μηδὲν τῶν ἀγαλμάτων διαμένειν
ὑγιὲς τῶν ἐν τοῖς ἱεροῖς, ἀλλὰ ξύμπαντα λελωβη-
μένα εἶναι, ὥσπερ καὶ² τὰ ἐπὶ τῶν μνημάτων.

7 Ὅπερ οὖν ἔφην, ἔτυχον περιπατῶν πρὸ τῆς
πόλεως, καί τινες ἐξῄεσαν ἔνδοθεν τῶν Βορυσθενιτῶν πρὸς ἐμέ, ὥσπερ εἰώθεσαν· ἔπειτα Καλλίστρατος ἐφ' ἵππου τὸ μὲν πρῶτον παρίππευσεν ἡμᾶς
ἔξωθεν προσελαύνων, παρελθὼν δὲ ὀλίγον κατέβη,
καὶ τὸν ἵππον τῷ ἀκολούθῳ παραδοὺς αὐτὸς πάνυ
κοσμίως προσῆλθεν ὑπὸ τὸ ἱμάτιον τὴν χεῖρα
ὑποστείλας. παρέζωστο δὲ μάχαιραν μεγάλην
τῶν ἱππικῶν καὶ ἀναξυρίδας εἶχε καὶ τὴν ἄλλην
στολὴν Σκυθικήν, ἄνωθεν δὲ τῶν ὤμων ἱμάτιον
μικρὸν μέλαν, λεπτόν, ὥσπερ εἰώθασιν οἱ Βορυσθενῖται. χρῶνται δὲ καὶ τῇ ἄλλῃ ἐσθῆτι μελαίνῃ
ὡς τὸ πολὺ ἀπὸ γένους τινὸς Σκυθῶν τῶν

¹ οὐκ ἐχούσαις ὁποῖα] συνεχούσαις ὅπου τι Casaubon.
² καὶ added by Herwerden.

---

¹ Dio seems to say that in the reconstruction of the city
that portion of the old circuit-wall which was best preserved
was retained, the ends being joined together by a continuous
line of dwellings with party-walls, so as themselves to serve
as a defence. The same plan may be observed in many
Aegean islands. The result for Borysthenes was a narrowing
of its former limits. Cf. Diehl, *ibid.*, 2412 and 2416.

of the houses, built so as to form a continuous whole.[1] However, a bit of wall has been constructed parallel to this line of houses, quite low and weak. As for the towers, there are some which stand quite apart from the portion of the city that is now inhabited, so that you would not surmise that they once belonged to a single city. These, then, are clear tokens of the city's capture, as well as the fact that not a single statue remains undamaged among those that are in the sanctuaries, one and all having suffered mutilation, as is true also of the funeral monuments.

Well, as I was saying,[2] I chanced to be strolling outside the city, and there came to meet me from within the walls some of the people of Borysthenes, as was their custom. Thereupon Callistratus at first came riding by us on horseback on his way from somewhere outside of town, but when he had gone a short distance beyond us, he dismounted, and, entrusting his horse to his attendant, he himself drew near in very proper fashion, having drawn his arm beneath his mantle.[3] Suspended from his girdle he had a great cavalry sabre, and he was wearing trousers[4] and all the rest of the Scythian costume, and from his shoulders there hung a small black cape of thin material, as is usual with the people of Borysthenes. In fact the rest of their apparel in general is regularly black, through the influence of a

---

[2] In § 1. The length of the digression is surprising in view of the seeming prominence of Borysthenes. Was it merely the enthusiasm of the traveller?

[3] It was not good form for a Greek gentleman to appear in public with bare arms. Cf. Aeschines, *in Timarchum* 52, Plutarch, *Phocion* 4.

[4] To a Greek, trousers appeared especially foreign.

Μελαγχλαίνων, ὡς ἐμοὶ δοκοῦσι, κατὰ τοῦτο
ὀνομασθέντων ὑπὸ τῶν Ἑλλήνων.

8 Ἦν δὲ ὡς ὀκτωκαίδεκα ἐτῶν ὁ Καλλίστρατος,
πάνυ καλὸς καὶ μέγας, πολὺ ἔχων Ἰωνικὸν τοῦ
εἴδους. ἐλέγετο δὲ καὶ τὰ πρὸς τὸν πόλεμον
ἀνδρεῖος εἶναι, καὶ πολλοὺς Σαυρομάτων τοὺς
μὲν ἀνῃρηκέναι, τοὺς δὲ αἰχμαλώτους εἰληφέναι.
ἐσπουδάκει δὲ καὶ περὶ λόγους καὶ. φιλοσοφίαν,
ὥστε καὶ ἐκπλεῦσαι σὺν ἐμοὶ ἐπεθύμει. διὰ
πάντα δὴ ταῦτα εὐδοκίμει παρὰ τοῖς πολίταις,
οὐχ ἥκιστα δὲ ἀπὸ τοῦ κάλλους, καὶ εἶχε πολλοὺς
ἐραστάς. πάνυ γὰρ δὴ τοῦτο ἐμμεμένηκεν αὐτοῖς
ἀπὸ τῆς μητροπόλεως, τὸ περὶ τοὺς ἔρωτας τοὺς
τῶν ἀρρένων· ὥστε κινδυνεύουσιν ἀναπείθειν καὶ
τῶν βαρβάρων ἐνίους οὐκ ἐπ᾽ ἀγαθῷ σχεδόν, ἀλλ᾽
ὡς ἂν ἐκεῖνοι τὸ τοιοῦτον ἀποδέξαιντο, βαρβαρικῶς
καὶ οὐκ ἄνευ ὕβρεως.

9 Εἰδὼς οὖν αὐτὸν φιλόμηρον ὄντα περὶ τούτου
εὐθὺς ἐπυνθανόμην. σχεδὸν δὲ καὶ πάντες οἱ
Βορυσθενῖται περὶ τὸν ποιητὴν ἐσπουδάκασιν
ἴσως διὰ τὸ πολεμικοὶ εἶναι ἔτι νῦν, εἰ μὴ ἄρα καὶ
διὰ[1] τὴν πρὸς τὸν Ἀχιλλέα εὔνοιαν· τοῦτον μὲν
γὰρ ὑπερφυῶς τιμῶσι, καὶ νεὼν τὸν μὲν ἐν τῇ
νήσῳ τῇ Ἀχιλλέως καλουμένῃ ἵδρυνται, τὸν δὲ
ἐν τῇ πόλει· ὥστε οὐδὲ ἀκούειν ὑπὲρ οὐδενὸς
ἄλλου θέλουσιν ἢ Ὁμήρου. καὶ τἆλλα οὐκέτι

---

[1] διὰ added by Arnim.

---

[1] Herodotus (4. 20) says that the Blackcloaks were not
Scythians. He is less cautious than Dio in explaining the
name (4. 107).
[2] Miletus.

certain tribe of Scythians,[1] the Blackcloaks, so named by the Greeks doubtless for that very reason.

Callistratus was about eighteen years of age, very tall and handsome, having much of the Ionian in his appearance. And it was said also that in matters pertaining to warfare he was a man of courage, and that many of the Sauromatians he had either slain or taken captive. He had become interested also in oratory and philosophy, so that he had his heart set on sailing away in my company. For all these reasons, then, he was in high repute with his fellow-townsmen, and not least of all because of his beauty, and he had many lovers. For this practice has continued on among them as a heritage from the city of their origin [2]—I refer to the love of man for man—so much so that they are likely to make converts of some of the barbarians, for no good end, I dare say, but rather as those people would adopt such a practice, that is to say, like barbarians and not without licentiousness.

Knowing, then, that Callistratus was fond of Homer, I immediately began to question him about the poet. And practically all the people of Borysthenes also have cultivated an interest in Homer, possibly because of their still being a warlike people, although it may also be due to their regard for Achilles, for they honour him exceedingly, and they have actually established two temples for his worship, one on the island that bears his name [3] and one in their city; and so they do not wish even to hear about any other poet than Homer. And although in

[3] Presumably an island at the mouth of the Dnieper, though the evidence is confused. Strabo (7. 3. 16–17) and Maximus Tyrius (9. 7) refer to worship of Achilles on an island at the mouth of the Danube.

σαφῶς ἑλληνίζοντες διὰ τὸ ἐν μέσοις οἰκεῖν τοῖς
βαρβάροις ὅμως τήν γε Ἰλιάδα ὀλίγου πάντες
ἴσασιν ἀπὸ στόματος.

10 Εἶπον οὖν προσπαίζων πρὸς αὐτόν, Πότερόν σοι
δοκεῖ, ὦ Καλλίστρατε, ἀμείνων ποιητὴς Ὅμηρος
ἢ Φωκυλίδης; καὶ ὃς γελάσας ἔφη, Ἀλλ᾽ οὐδὲ
ἐπίσταμαι ἔγωγε τοῦ ἑτέρου ποιητοῦ τὸ ὄνομα,
οἶμαι δὲ μηδὲ τούτων μηδένα. οὐδὲ γὰρ ἡγούμεθα
ἡμεῖς ἄλλον τινὰ ποιητὴν ἢ Ὅμηρον. τοῦτον δὲ
σχεδόν τι οὐδὲ ἄλλος οὐδεὶς ἀγνοεῖ. μόνου[1] γὰρ
Ὁμήρου μνημονεύουσιν οἱ ποιηταὶ αὐτῶν ἐν τοῖς
ποιήμασιν, καὶ ἄλλως μὲν εἰώθασι λέγειν, ἀεὶ δὲ
ὁπόταν μέλλωσι μάχεσθαι παρακελεύονται τοῖς
αὑτῶν ὥσπερ τὰ Τυρταίου ἐν Λακεδαίμονι ἐλέγετο.
εἰσὶ δὲ πάντες οὗτοι τυφλοὶ καὶ οὐχ ἡγοῦνται
δυνατὸν εἶναι ἄλλως τινὰ ποιητὴν γενέσθαι.

11 Τοῦτο μέν, ἔφην, ἀπολελαύκασιν οἱ ποιηταὶ
αὐτῶν ἀπὸ Ὁμήρου ὥσπερ ἀπὸ ὀφθαλμίας. τὸν
δὲ Φωκυλίδην ὑμεῖς μὲν οὐκ ἐπίστασθε, ὡς
λέγεις· πάνυ δὲ τῶν ἐνδόξων γέγονε ποιητῶν.
ὥσπερ οὖν ἐπειδάν τις τῶν ἐμπόρων καταπλεύσῃ
πρὸς ὑμᾶς οὐ πρότερον παραγεγονώς,[2] οὐκ εὐθὺς
ἠτιμάσατε αὐτόν, ἀλλὰ πρότερον γευσάμενοι τοῦ
οἴνου, κἂν ἄλλο τι φορτίον ἄγῃ, δεῖγμα λαβόντες,

[1] μόνου Casaubon : μόνοι.
[2] παραγεγονώς Emperius : γεγονώς.

---

[1] A gnomic poet of the sixth century B.C. For the scanty
remains of his verse, mostly couplets, see Edmonds, *Elegy
and Iambus*, vol. I, pp. 168 ff. (*L.C.L.*).

[2] Unless αὐτῶν should be read αὑτῶν and construed (as
also αὑτῶν two lines later) as a pronoun of the first person,
Callistratus is guilty of exaggeration, a fault that might be
ascribed to provincialism and the enthusiasm of youth.

general they no longer speak Greek distinctly, because they live in the midst of barbarians, still almost all at least know the *Iliad* by heart.

Accordingly I said to him by way of jest, " Callistratus, which do you think is the better poet, Homer or Phocylides ? " [1] And he laughed and said, " Why, as for myself, I do not even know the other poet's name, and I suppose that none of these men does, either. For we do not believe in any other poet than Homer. But as for Homer, you might say that no man alive is ignorant of him. For Homer is the only one whom their poets recall in their compositions, [2] and it is their habit to recite his verses on many an occasion, but invariably they employ his poetry to inspire their troops when about to enter battle, just as the songs of Tyrtaeus [3] used to be employed in Lacedaemon. Moreover, all these poets are blind, and they do not believe it possible for any one to become a poet otherwise."

" That at any rate," said I, " their poets caught from Homer, [4] as it were from a case of sore eyes. But as for Phocylides, while you people do not know him, as you state, for all that he is certainly rated among the famous poets. Therefore, just as, when a merchant sails into your port who has never been there before, you do not immediately scorn him but, on the contrary, having first tasted his wine and sampled any other merchandise in his cargo, you

[3] Thought to have lived at Sparta about 640 B.C. For the extant fragments of his verse, see Edmonds, *op. cit.*, vol. I, pp. 50 ff.
[4] The tradition regarding Homer's blindness may be due to the " Homeric " *Hymn to Apollo*, verse 172 ; but Homer himself portrays his bard Demodocus as being blind.

ἐὰν μὲν ἀρέσῃ ὑμᾶς, ὠνεῖσθε, εἰ δὲ μή, ἐᾶτε·
οὕτως, ἔφην, καὶ τῆς τοῦ Φωκυλίδου ποιήσεως
12 ἔξεστί σοι λαβεῖν δεῖγμα ἐν βραχεῖ. καὶ γάρ
ἐστιν οὐ τῶν μακράν τινα καὶ συνεχῆ ποίησιν
εἰρόντων, ὥσπερ ὁ ὑμέτερος μίαν ἐξῆς διέξεισι
μάχην ἐν πλείοσιν ἢ πεντακισχιλίοις ἔπεσιν, ἀλλὰ
κατὰ δύο καὶ τρία ἔπη αὐτῷ καὶ ἀρχὴν ἡ ποίησις
καὶ πέρας λαμβάνει. ὥστε καὶ προστίθησι τὸ
ὄνομα αὐτοῦ καθ᾽ ἕκαστον διανόημα, ἅτε σπουδαῖον καὶ πολλοῦ ἄξιον ἡγούμενος, οὐχ ὥσπερ
Ὅμηρος οὐδαμοῦ τῆς ποιήσεως ὠνόμασεν αὐτόν.
13 ἢ οὐ δοκεῖ σοι εἰκότως προσθεῖναι Φωκυλίδης
τῇ τοιαύτῃ γνώμῃ καὶ ἀποφάσει,

καὶ τόδε Φωκυλίδου· πόλις ἐν σκοπέλῳ κατὰ
  κόσμον
οἰκεῦσα σμικρὴ[1] κρέσσων Νίνου ἀφραινούσης;

ἀλλ᾽ οὐ πρὸς ὅλην Ἰλιάδα καὶ Ὀδύσσειαν ταῦτα
τὰ ἔπη ἐσθλά[2] ἐστι τοῖς μὴ παρέργως ἀκροωμένοις;
ἢ μᾶλλον ὑμῖν ἀκούειν συνέφερε περὶ τῶν τοῦ
Ἀχιλλέως πηδήσεών τε καὶ ὀρούσεων καὶ τῆς
φωνῆς, ὅτι μόνον φθεγξάμενος ἔτρεπε τοὺς
Τρῶας; ταῦτα μᾶλλον ὠφελεῖ ὑμᾶς ἐκμανθάνον-
τας ἢ ἐκεῖνο, ὅτι ἡ σμικρὰ πόλις ἐν τραχεῖ σκοπέλῳ κειμένη κρείττων ἐστὶ καὶ εὐτυχεστέρα κατὰ
κόσμον οἰκοῦσα ἢ μεγάλη ἐν λείῳ καὶ πλατεῖ
πεδίῳ, ἐάνπερ ἀκόσμως καὶ ἀνόμως ὑπὸ ἀνθρώπων
ἀφρόνων οἰκῆται;

---

[1] οἰκεῦσα σμικρὴ Morel : οἰκεῦσα (or οἰκεῦσαι) μικρὴ.
[2] ἐσθλά added by Capps.

---

[1] Dio may have had in mind books 11 to 17 of the *Iliad*.

buy it if it suits your taste, otherwise you pass it by; just so," said I, " with the poetry of Phocylides you may take a sample of small compass. For he is not one of those who string together a long and continuous poem, as your Homer does, who uses more than five thousand verses of continuous narration in describing a single battle;[1] on the contrary, the poems of Phocylides have both beginning and end in two or three verses. And so he adds his name to each sentiment, in the belief that it is a matter of interest and great importance, in so doing behaving quite differently from Homer, who nowhere in his poetry names himself. Or don't you think Phocylides had good reason for attaching his name to a maxim and declaration such as this?

This too the saying of Phocylides:
The law-abiding town, though small and set
On a lofty rock, outranks mad Nineveh.[2]

Why, in comparison with the entire *Iliad* and *Odyssey* are not these verses noble to those who pay heed as they listen? Or was it more to your advantage to hear of the impetuous leaping and charging of Achilles, and about his voice, how by his shouts alone he routed the Trojans?[3] Are those things more useful for you to learn by heart than what you just have heard, that a small city on a rugged headland is better and more fortunate, if orderly, than a great city in a smooth and level plain, that is to say, if that city is conducted in disorderly and lawless fashion by men of folly?"

[2] Edmonds, *op. cit.*, vol. 1, p. 174.
[3] *Iliad* 18. 228–9.

14 Καὶ ὃς οὐ μάλα ἡδέως ἀποδεξάμενος, Ὦ ξένε, εἶπεν ὅτι, ἡμεῖς σε ἀγαπῶμεν καὶ σφόδρα αἰδούμεθα· ὡς ἄλλως [1] γε οὐδεὶς ἂν ἠνέσχετο Βορυσθενιτῶν εἰς Ὅμηρον καὶ Ἀχιλλέα τοιαῦτα εἰπόντος. ὁ μὲν γὰρ θεὸς ἡμῶν ἐστιν, ὡς ὁρᾷς, ὁ δὲ καὶ σχεδόν τι μετὰ τοὺς θεοὺς τιμᾶται. κἀγὼ πραῦναι βουλόμενος αὐτόν, ἅμα δὲ ἐπί τι χρήσιμον ἀγαγεῖν, Παραιτοῦμαί σε, εἶπον, καθ᾽ Ὅμηρον συγγνώμην ἔχειν μοι,

εἴ τι κακὸν νῦν
εἴρηται.

αὖθις γάρ ποτε ἐπαινεσόμεθα Ἀχιλλέα τε καὶ
15 Ὅμηρον ὅσα δοκεῖ ἡμῖν ὀρθῶς λέγειν. τὸ δὲ παρὸν σκεπτέον ἂν εἴη τὸ τοῦ Φωκυλίδου· ὡς ἐμοὶ δοκεῖ σφόδρα καλῶς λέγειν ὑπὲρ τῆς πόλεως. Σκόπει, ἔφη, ἐπεὶ καὶ τούσδε ὁρᾷς πάντας ἐπιθυμοῦντας ἀκοῦσαί σου καὶ διὰ τοῦτο συνερρυηκότας δεῦρο πρὸς τὸν ποταμόν, καίτοι οὐ σφόδρα ἀθορύβως ἔχοντας. οἶσθα γὰρ δήπου ὅτι χθὲς οἱ Σκύθαι προσελάσαντες μεσημβρίας τοὺς μέν τινας ἀπέκτειναν τῶν σκοπῶν οὐ προσέχοντας, τοὺς δὲ ἐζωγρήκασιν ἴσως· οὐ γάρ πω ἐπιστάμεθα διὰ τὸ μακροτέραν αὐτοῖς γενέσθαι τὴν φυγήν, ἅτε οὐ πρὸς τὴν πόλιν φεύγουσιν.
16 Ἦν δὲ τῷ ὄντι ταῦτα οὕτως, καὶ αἵ τε πύλαι συγκέκλειντο καὶ τὸ σημεῖον ἦρτο ἐπὶ τοῦ τείχους τὸ πολεμικόν. ἀλλ᾽ ὅμως οὕτως ἦσαν φιλήκοοι

---

[1] ἄλλως Casaubon : ἄλλος.

---

[1] *Iliad* 4. 362–3.

And Callistratus, receiving my remarks with no great pleasure, replied, " My friend, we admire and respect you greatly; for otherwise no man in Borysthenes would have tolerated your saying such things of Homer and Achilles. For Achilles is our god, as you observe, and Homer ranks almost next to the gods in honour." And I in turn, wishing to appease him and at the same time to guide him in the direction of his own advantage, said, " I beg you to forgive me, to use the Homeric phrase,

' if aught of harm hath now been spoken.' [1]

For some other time we shall praise both Achilles and Homer in so far as the poet seems to us to speak correctly. But now we might well consider the case of Phocylides, since in my opinion he speaks very nobly regarding the city." " Pray do so," said he, " since you can see that all these men now present are just as eager as I am to listen to you, and that for that very reason they have streamed together here beside the river, although in no very tranquil state of mind. For of course you know that yesterday the Scythians made a raid at noon and put to death some of the outposts who were not on their guard, and in all likelihood took others captive; for we do not yet know definitely about that, because their rout took them some distance away; for their flight was not *toward* the city." [2]

And in truth it was precisely as he had said, and not only were the city gates fast shut but also there had been hoisted on the ramparts the standard that betokens war. Yet they were such ardent listeners,

---

[2] Seemingly a touch of humour.

καὶ τῷ τρόπῳ Ἕλληνες, ὥστε μικροῦ δεῖν
ἅπαντες παρῆσαν ἐν τοῖς ὅπλοις, βουλόμενοι
ἀκούειν. κἀγὼ ἀγάμενος αὐτῶν τὴν προθυμίαν,
Βούλεσθε, ἔφην, καθιζώμεθα ἰόντες ποι τῆς
πόλεως; τυχὸν γὰρ νῦν οὐ πάντες ὁμοίως
ἀκούουσιν ἐν τῷ βαδίζειν, ἀλλ' οἱ ὄπισθεν πράγματα ἔχουσι καὶ παρέχουσι τοῖς πρὸ αὐτῶν,
17 σπεύδοντες ἐγγυτέρω προσελθεῖν. ὡς δὲ τοῦτο
εἶπον, εὐθὺς ὥρμησαν ἅπαντες εἰς τὸ τοῦ Διὸς
ἱερόν, οὗπερ εἰώθασι βουλεύεσθαι. καὶ οἱ μὲν
πρεσβύτατοι καὶ οἱ γνωριμώτατοι καὶ οἱ ἐν ταῖς
ἀρχαῖς κύκλῳ καθίζοντο ἐπὶ βάθρων· τὸ δὲ
λοιπὸν πλῆθος ἐφεστήκεσαν. ἦν γὰρ εὐρυχωρία
πολλὴ πρὸ τοῦ νεώ. πάνυ οὖν ἄν τις ἥσθη τῇ
ὄψει φιλόσοφος ἀνήρ, ὅτι ἅπαντες ἦσαν τὸν
ἀρχαῖον τρόπον, ὥς φησιν Ὅμηρος τοὺς Ἕλληνας,
κομῶντες καὶ τὰ γένεια ἀφεικότες, εἷς δὲ ἐν
αὐτοῖς μόνος ἐξυρημένος, καὶ τοῦτον ἐλοιδόρουν τε
καὶ ἐμίσουν ἅπαντες. ἐλέγετο δὲ οὐκ ἄλλως
τοῦτο ἐπιτηδεύειν, ἀλλὰ κολακεύων Ῥωμαίους
καὶ τὴν πρὸς αὐτοὺς φιλίαν ἐπιδεικνύμενος·
ὥστε εἶδεν ἄν τις ἐπ' ἐκείνου τὸ αἰσχρὸν τοῦ
πράγματος καὶ οὐδαμῇ πρέπον ἀνδράσιν.
18 Ἐπεὶ δὲ ἡσυχία ἐγένετο, εἶπον ὅτι δοκοῦσί μοι
ὀρθῶς ποιεῖν, πόλιν οἰκοῦντες ἀρχαίαν καὶ
Ἑλληνίδα, βουλόμενοι ἀκοῦσαι περὶ πόλεως.
καὶ πρῶτόν γε, ἔφην, ὅ τι ἐστὶν αὐτὸ τοῦτο
ὑπὲρ οὗ ὁ λόγος γνῶναι σαφῶς· οὕτω γὰρ ἂν

---

[1] The phrase κάρη κομόωντες Ἀχαιοί is frequent in
Homer. He is silent regarding the beard, though beards
may have been usual. Though the Greeks had long known
of the razor, Alexander the Great is said to have made shaving

so truly Greek in character, that almost all the inhabitants were present, under arms, eager to hear me. And I, admiring their earnestness, said, " If it please you, shall we go and sit down somewhere in the city ? For perchance at present not all can hear equally well what is said as we stroll; on the contrary, those in the rear find it difficult themselves and also make it difficult for those ahead through their eagerness to get closer." And no sooner had I made this suggestion than they all set out together for the temple of Zeus, where they are wont to meet in council. And while the eldest and the most distinguished and the officials sat on benches in a circle, the rest of the company stood close by, for there was a large open space before the temple. A philosopher would have been vastly pleased at the sight, because all were like the ancient Greeks described by Homer, long-haired and with flowing beards,[1] and only one among them was shaven, and he was subjected to the ridicule and resentment of them all. And it was said that he practised shaving, not as an idle fancy, but out of flattery of the Romans and to show his friendship toward them. And so one could have seen illustrated in his case how disgraceful the practice is and how unseemly for real men.

But when quiet had been secured, I said that in my opinion they did well, seeing that they dwelt in a city that was ancient and Greek, in wishing to hear about a city. " And," said I, " surely the first essential is that we should know precisely the true nature of the thing about which we are to speak;

really popular. Scipio Africanus seems to have been the first Roman to shave regularly. Our passage suggests that even in Dio's day some Greeks wore beards.

εἴητε ἅμα ἠσθημένοι καὶ ὁποῖόν τί ἐστιν. οἱ
γὰρ πολλοί, ἔφην, ἄνθρωποι τὸ ὄνομα αὐτὸ
ἴσασι καὶ φθέγγονται τοῦ πράγματος ἑκάστου,
19 τὸ δὲ πρᾶγμ᾽ ἀγνοοῦσιν. οἱ δὲ πεπαιδευμένοι
τοῦτο φροντίζουσιν, ὅπως καὶ τὴν δύναμιν
εἴσονται ἑκάστου οὗ λέγουσιν· οἷον τὸ τοῦ
ἀνθρώπου ὄνομα πάντες οὕτω λέγουσιν οἱ ἑλληνίζοντες, ἐὰν δὲ πύθῃ τινὸς αὐτῶν ὅ τι
ἐστὶ τοῦτο, λέγω δὲ ὁποῖόν τι καὶ καθ᾽ ὃ μηδενὶ
τῶν ἄλλων ταὐτόν, οὐκ ἂν ἔχοι εἰπεῖν ἀλλ᾽ ἢ
δεῖξαι μόνον αὐτὸν ἢ ἄλλον, ὥσπερ οἱ βάρβαροι.
ὁ δὲ ἔμπειρος τῷ πυνθανομένῳ τί ἐστιν ἄνθρωπος
ἀποκρίνεται ὅτι ζῷον λογικὸν θνητόν. τὸ γὰρ
τοῦτο εἶναι μόνῳ ἀνθρώπῳ συμβέβηκε καὶ
20 οὐδενὶ ἄλλῳ. οὕτως οὖν καὶ τὴν πόλιν φασὶν
εἶναι πλῆθος ἀνθρώπων ἐν ταὐτῷ κατοικούντων
ὑπὸ νόμου διοικούμενον. ἤδη οὖν δῆλον ὅτι
τῆς προσηγορίας ταύτης οὐδεμιᾷ προσήκει τῶν
καλουμένων πόλεων τῶν ἀφρόνων καὶ ἀνόμων.
οὔκουν οὐδὲ περὶ Νίνου εἴη ἂν ὁ ποιητὴς ὡς περὶ
πόλεως εἰρηκώς, ἀφραινούσης[1] γε αὐτῆς. ὥσπερ
γὰρ οὐδὲ ἄνθρωπος ἐκεῖνός ἐστιν ᾧ μὴ πρόσεστι
τὸ λογικόν, οὕτως οὐδὲ πόλις, ᾗ μὴ συμβέβηκε
νομίμῳ εἶναι. νόμιμος δὲ οὐκ ἂν εἴη ποτὲ
ἄφρων καὶ ἄκοσμος οὖσα.
21 Ἴσως οὖν ζητῆσαι ἄν τις, εἰ ἐπειδὰν οἱ ἄρχοντες
καὶ προεστῶτες ὦσι φρόνιμοι καὶ σοφοί, τὸ δὲ
λοιπὸν πλῆθος διοικῆται[2] κατὰ τὴν τούτων
γνώμην νομίμως καὶ σωφρόνως, τὴν τοιαύτην
χρὴ καλεῖν σώφρονα καὶ νόμιμον καὶ τῷ ὄντι

---

[1] ἀφραινούσης Emperius: ἀφρενούσης M, ἀφρονούσης B.
[2] διοικῆται Reiske: διοικεῖται.

for in that way you would at the same time have perceived what its attributes are. For most men," said I, " know and employ merely the names of things, but are ignorant of the things themselves. On the other hand, men who are educated make it their business to know also the meaning of everything of which they speak. For example, *anthropos* is a term used by all who speak Greek, but if you should ask any one of them what *anthropos* really is—I mean what its attributes are and wherein it differs from any other thing—he could not say, but could only point to himself or to someone else in true barbarian fashion. But the man who has expert knowledge, when asked what *anthropos* is, replies that it is a mortal animal endowed with reason. For that happens to be true of *anthropos* alone and of nothing else. Well, in that way also the term ' city ' is said to mean a group of *anthropoi* dwelling in the same place and governed by law.[1] It is immediately evident, therefore, that that term belongs to none of those communities which are called cities but are without wisdom and without law. Consequently not even in referring to Nineveh could the poet use the term ' city,' since Nineveh is given over to folly. For just as that person is not even an *anthropos* who does not also possess the attribute of reason, so that community is not even a city which lacks obedience to law. And it could never be obedient to law if it is foolish and disorderly.

Perhaps, then, someone might inquire whether, when the rulers and leaders of a community are men of prudence and wisdom, and it is in accordance with their judgement that the rest are governed, lawfully and sanely, such a community may be called sane and

[1] A Stoic definition, more succinctly stated in § 29.

439

πόλιν ἀπὸ τῶν διοικούντων· ὥσπερ χορὸν ἴσως
φαίημεν ἂν μουσικόν, τοῦ κορυφαίου μουσικοῦ
ὄντος, τῶν δὲ ἄλλων ἐκείνῳ συνεπομένων καὶ
μηδὲν παρὰ μέλος φθεγγομένων ἢ σμικρὰ καὶ
22 ἀδήλως. ἀγαθὴν μὲν γὰρ ἐξ ἁπάντων ἀγαθῶν
πόλιν οὔτε τις γενομένην πρότερον οἶδε θνητὴν
οὔτε ποτὲ ὡς ἐσομένην ὕστερον ἄξιον διανοη-
θῆναι, πλὴν εἰ μὴ θεῶν μακάρων κατ᾽ οὐρανόν,
οὐδαμῶς ἀκίνητον οὐδὲ ἀργήν, ἀλλὰ σφοδρὰ
οὖσαν καὶ πορευομένην, τῶν μὲν ἡγουμένων
τε καὶ πρώτων θεῶν χωρὶς ἔριδος καὶ ἥττης·
οὔτε γὰρ ἐρίζειν θεοὺς οὔτε ἡττᾶσθαι θέμις
οὔτε ὑπ᾽ ἀλλήλων ἅτε φίλων οὔτε ὑπὸ ἄλλων
κρειττόνων, ἀλλὰ πράττειν ἀκωλύτως τὰ σφέτερα
ἔργα μετὰ πάσης φιλίας ἀεὶ πάντων κοινῆς·
τῶν μὲν φανερωτάτων πορευομένων ἑκάστου καθ᾽
ἑαυτόν, οὐ πλανωμένων ἄλλως ἀνόητον πλάνην,
ἀλλὰ χορείαν εὐδαίμονα χορευόντων μετά τε
νοῦ καὶ φρονήσεως τῆς ἄκρας· τοῦ δὲ λοιποῦ
πλήθους ὑπὸ τῆς κοινῆς φορᾶς ἀγομένου μιᾷ
γνώμῃ καὶ ὁρμῇ τοῦ ξύμπαντος οὐρανοῦ.
23 Μίαν γὰρ δὴ ταύτην καθαρῶς εὐδαίμονα
πολιτείαν εἴτε καὶ πόλιν χρὴ καλεῖν, τὴν θεῶν
πρὸς ἀλλήλους κοινωνίαν, ἐάν τε καὶ ξύμπαν
τὸ [1] λογικὸν περιλάβῃ τις, ἀνθρώπων σὺν θεοῖς
ἀριθμουμένων, ὡς παῖδες σὺν ἀνδράσι λέγονται

---

[1] ξύμπαν τὸ Casaubon : ξύμπαντα.

---

[1] Dio is evidently identifying the gods with the stars.
The dancing of the stars is an idea contained in more than one
ancient Greek writing, but cf. especially Plato, *Epinomis* 982 E,
Timaeus 40 C. Beginning with § 39, Dio presents the same
general theme in an altered form in what he is pleased to call

law-abiding and really a city because of those who govern it; just as a chorus might possibly be termed musical provided its leader were musical and provided further that the other members followed his lead and uttered no sound contrary to the melody that he set—or only slight sounds and indistinctly uttered. For no one knows of a good city made wholly of good elements as having existed in the past, that is, a city of mortal men, nor is it worth while to conceive of such a city as possibly arising in the future, unless it be a city of the blessed gods in heaven, by no means motionless or inactive, but vigorous and progressive, its guides and leaders being gods, exempt from strife and defeat. For it is impious to suppose that gods indulge in strife or are subject to defeat, either by one another, friends as they are, or by more powerful beings; on the contrary, we must think of them as performing their several functions without let or hindrance and with unvarying friendship of all toward all in common, the most conspicuous among them each pursuing an independent course—I don't mean wandering aimlessly and senselessly, but rather dancing a dance [1] of happiness coupled with wisdom and supreme intelligence— while the rest of the celestial host are swept along by the general movement, the entire heaven having one single purpose and impulse.

For that, indeed, is the only constitution or city that may be called genuinely happy—the partnership of god with god; even if you include with the gods also everything that has the faculty of reason, mankind being thus included as boys are said to share

a myth of the Magi, according to which the universe constitutes a four-horse team yoked to the chariot of Zeus.

μετέχειν πόλεως, φύσει πολῖται ὄντες, οὐ τῷ
φρονεῖν τε καὶ πράττειν τὰ τῶν πολιτῶν οὐδὲ τῷ
κοινωνεῖν τοῦ νόμου, ἀξύνετοι ὄντες αὐτοῦ. ἐκ δὲ
τῶν ἄλλων πανταχοῦ πασῶν σχεδὸν ἁπλῶς ἡμαρτη-
μένων τε καὶ φαύλων πρὸς τὴν ἄκραν εὐθύτητα
τοῦ θείου καὶ μακαρίου νόμου καὶ τῆς ὀρθῆς
διοικήσεως, ὅμως δὲ πρὸς τὸ παρὸν εὐπορήσομεν [1]
παραδειγμάτων τῆς ἐπιεικέστερον ἐχούσης πρὸς
τὴν παντελῶς διεφθαρμένην, ὡς ἐν πᾶσι νοσοῦσι
τόν γ' [2] ἐλαφρότατα διάγοντα τῷ κάκιστα
διακειμένῳ παραβάλλοντες.

24   Ἐγὼ μὲν οὖν πρός τι τοιοῦτον ὥρμων τῷ
λόγῳ. μεταξὺ δὲ τῶν παρόντων εἷς ἐφθέγξατο
εἰς τὸ μέσον, ὅσπερ ἦν πρεσβύτατος αὐτῶν καὶ
μέγιστον ἀξίωμα ἔχων, εἶπε δὲ πάνυ εὐλαβούμενος,
Μηδαμῶς, ὦ ξένε, ἄγροικον μηδὲ βαρβαρικὸν
ἡγήσῃ τὸ τοιοῦτον, ὅτι μεταξὺ λέγοντί σοι
ἐμποδὼν ἐγενόμην. παρ' ὑμῖν μὲν γὰρ οὐκ
ἔθος ἐστὶ τὸ τοιοῦτο διὰ τὸ πολλὴν ἀφθονίαν
εἶναι τῶν ἐκ [3] φιλοσοφίας λόγων καὶ περὶ παντὸς
ὅτου ἂν ἐπιθυμῇ τις ἐξεῖναι παρὰ πολλῶν ἀκοῦσαι·
παρ' ἡμῖν δὲ ὥσπερ τέρας τι τοῦτο πέφηνε τὸ
25   σὲ ἡμῖν ἀφικέσθαι. τὸ δὲ λοιπὸν σχεδόν τι
δεῦρο ἀφικνοῦνται ὀνόματι Ἕλληνες, τῇ δὲ
ἀληθείᾳ βαρβαρώτεροι ἡμῶν, ἔμποροι καὶ ἀγοραῖοι,
ῥάκη φαῦλα καὶ οἶνον πονηρὸν εἰσκομίζοντες
καὶ τά γε παρ' ἡμῶν οὐδὲν βελτίω τούτων
ἐξαγόμενοι. σὲ δὲ αὐτὸς ἡμῖν ὁ Ἀχιλλεὺς
ἔοικε δεῦρο ἀπὸ τῆς νήσου διαπέμψαι, καί σε
πάνυ μὲν ἡδέως ὁρῶμεν, πάνυ δὲ ἡδέως ἀκούομεν

---

[1] εὐπορήσομεν Reiske : εὐπορήσωμεν.
[2] τόν γ' Emperius : τὸν δ'.   [3] ἐκ added by Emperius.

in citizenship with men, being citizens by birth though not by reason of conceiving and performing the tasks of citizens or sharing in the law, of which they have no comprehension. However, if we take communities of a different kind, though everywhere and in every instance, we may almost say, they are absolutely faulty and worthless as compared with the supreme righteousness of the divine and blessed law and its proper administration, still for our present purpose we shall be supplied with examples of the type that is fairly equitable when compared with that which is utterly corrupt, just as among persons who are all ill we compare the man who had the lightest case with the one who is in worst condition."

Well then, I was launching forth upon that general line in my discussion, when one of those who were present, the eldest in the company and held in high esteem, spoke up, interrupting me, and in a very guarded manner said, " Stranger, pray do not think it boorish or barbarous of me to intervene in the midst of your discourse. For while in your country such conduct is not good manners, because of the great abundance of philosophical discussions and because one may listen to many men upon any topic he may desire, in ours this visit of yours to our city seems almost a miraculous event. As a usual thing those who come here are nominally Greeks but actually more barbarous than ourselves, traders and market-men, fellows who import cheap rags and vile wine and export in exchange products of no better quality. But you would appear to have been sent to us by Achilles himself from his holy isle,[1] and we are very glad to see you and very glad also to listen to what-

[1] Cf. § 9.

ὅ τι ἂν λέγῃς.[1] οὐ μέντοι πολύν τινα χρόνον
ἡγούμεθα ἔσεσθαι τοῦτον οὐδὲ βουλόμεθα, ἀλλά
σε εὖ πράξαντα οἴκαδε κατελθεῖν τὴν ταχίστην.
26 νῦν οὖν ἐπεὶ ἧψω τῷ λόγῳ τῆς θείας διοικήσεως,
αὐτός τε ἀνεπτέρωμαι δαιμονίως καὶ τούσδε
ὁρῶ πάντας ὀργῶντας πρὸς ἐκεῖνον τὸν λόγον·
καὶ γὰρ ἡμῖν ἔδοξας μεγαλοπρεπῶς καὶ τοῦ
πράγματος οὐκ ἀναξίως ὅσα εἶπες εἰρηκέναι καὶ
ὡς ἂν μάλιστα ἡμεῖς βουλοίμεθα ἀκοῦσαι. τῆς
μὲν γὰρ ἀκριβεστέρας ταύτης φιλοσοφίας ἄπειροί
ἐσμεν, Ὁμήρου δέ, ὡς οἶσθα, ἐρασταὶ καί τινες
οὐ πολλοὶ Πλάτωνος· ὧν δὴ κἀμὲ ὁρᾷς ὄντα,
ἀεί ποτε ἐντυγχάνοντα τοῖς ἐκείνου ὅπως ἂν δύ-
νωμαι· καίτοι ἴσως ἄτοπον βαρβαρίζοντα τῶν
πολιτῶν μάλιστα τῷ ἑλληνικωτάτῳ καὶ σοφωτάτῳ
χαίρειν καὶ ξυνεῖναι, καθάπερ εἴ τις μικροῦ
τυφλὸς τὸ μὲν ἄλλο φῶς ἀποστρέφοιτο, πρὸς
αὐτὸν δὲ τὸν ἥλιον ἀναβλέποι.

27 Ἔχει μὲν δὴ τὰ ἡμέτερα οὕτως. σὺ δὲ εἰ
θέλεις πᾶσιν ἡμῖν χαρίσασθαι, τὸν μὲν ὑπὲρ τῆς
θνητῆς πόλεως ἀναβαλοῦ λόγον, ἐὰν ἄρα σχολὴν
ἡμῖν οἱ γείτονες παράσχωσιν εἰς αὔριον καὶ μὴ
δέῃ προσγυμνάζεσθαι αὐτοῖς, ὥσπερ ἔθος ἡμῖν
τὸ πολύ· περὶ δὲ τῆς θείας εἴτε πόλεως εἴτε δια-
κοσμήσεως φίλον σοι καλεῖν, εἰπὲ ὅπῃ τε καὶ
ὅπως ἔχει, ὡς δύνασαι ἐγγύτατα τείνων τῆς τοῦ

_____

[1] λέγῃς Emperius : λέγῃ τις.

ever you have to say. However, we do not believe that this visit of yours is to be of very long duration, nor do we desire it to be, but rather that you may have a prosperous voyage home as speedily as possible.[1] Now therefore, since in your remarks you have touched upon the divine form of government, I myself am tremendously excited, and I see that my friends here also are all worked up in anticipation of that theme. The fact is that in our opinion everything you have said has been magnificently expressed, in a manner not unworthy of your theme, and precisely as we should most desire to hear. For although we are unacquainted with this more refined form of philosophy, yet we are, as you know, lovers of Homer, and some, not many, lovers of Plato too. To this latter group I myself belong, for I always read his writings as best I can; and yet it may perhaps seem odd that one who speaks the poorest Greek of all the people of Borysthenes should delight in the man who is most Greek and most wise and should cultivate that man's society, quite as if a person almost wholly blind were to shun every other light but turn his gaze upward to the sun itself.

" This, then, is our situation; and if you wish to do us all a favour, postpone your discussion of the mortal city—possibly our neighbours may after all grant us leisure tomorrow, and not compel us to exert ourselves against them as is generally our wont—and tell us instead about that divine city or government, whichever you prefer to call it, stating where it is and what it is like, aiming as closely as possible

[1] The speaker clearly has heard of Dio's frustrated plans and of his present purpose to sail away (cf. § 8) and is merely being polite.

DIO CHRYSOSTOM

Πλάτωνος ἐλευθερίας περὶ τὴν φράσιν, οἷον δὴ
καὶ ἄρτι ποιεῖν ἡμῖν ἔδοξας. εἰ γὰρ μηδενὸς
ἄλλου, τῆς γε φωνῆς ξυνίεμεν ὑπὸ συνηθείας ὅτι
οὐ σμικρὸν οὐδὲ πόρρω τοῦ Ὁμήρου φθέγγεται.

28 Κἀγὼ σφόδρα γε ἤσθην τῇ ἁπλότητι τοῦ
πρεσβύτου, καὶ γελάσας εἶπον, Ὦ φίλε Ἱεροσῶν,[1]
εἴ με[2] ἐκέλευες χθὲς εἰσβεβληκότων ὑμῖν τῶν
πολεμίων λαβόντα ὅπλα ὥσπερ τὸν Ἀχιλλέα
μάχεσθαι, τὸ μὲν ἕτερον ἐπείσθην ἄν, πειρώμενος
ἀμύνεσθαι ὑπὲρ ἀνδρῶν φίλων, τὸ δὲ ἕτερον οὐκ
ἄν, οἶμαι, ἐδυνάμην, καίτοι σφόδρα βουλόμενος,
ὁμοίως τῷ Ἀχιλλεῖ ἀγωνίζεσθαι. καὶ νῦν ὧν
κελεύεις ποιήσω τὸ ἕτερον, προθυμήσομαι εἰπεῖν
τὸν λόγον, ὡς ἂν ἐγὼ δύνωμαι κατ᾽ ἐμαυτόν·

ἀνδράσι δὲ προτέροισιν ἐριζέμεν οὐκ ἐθελήσω,

οὔτε Πλάτωνι οὔτε Ὁμήρῳ. οὐ γάρ τοι οὐδὲ
τῷ Εὐρύτῳ φησὶ συνενεγκεῖν ὁ ποιητής, ὅτι
ἤριζε πρὸς τοὺς κρείττονας. οὐ μέντοι σπουδῆς
29 γε, ἔφην, οὐδὲν ἀπολείψομεν. ταῦτα δὲ εἰπὼν
πρὸς ἐκεῖνον οὐδὲν ἧττον ὑπεκίνουν[3] καὶ ἀνεφερό-
μην τρόπον τινὰ ἀναμνησθεὶς Πλάτωνός τε καὶ
Ὁμήρου.

[1] Ἱεροσῶν Boeckh : Ῥόσων UB, ῥοσῶν M.
[2] εἴ με Selden : εἰ μὲν.
[3] ὑπεκίνουν Cobet : ὑπ᾽ ἐκείνων M, ὑπ᾽ ἐκείνου UB.

[1] Perhaps a reference to § 22, which in a way foreshadows
the myth of §§ 39 ff.

at Plato's nobility of expression, just as but now you seemed to us to do.[1] For if we understand nothing else, we do understand at least his language because of our long familiarity with it, for it has a lofty sound, not far removed from the voice of Homer."

I in turn was exceedingly pleased with the simple frankness of the old gentleman, and with a laugh I said, " My dear Hieroson,[2] if yesterday when the enemy made their attack you had bidden me to take up arms and give battle like Achilles, I should have obeyed one part of your injunction, endeavouring to come to the aid of men who are my friends ; but the other part, I fancy, I could not have managed, however much I should have wished to do so, to fight as your Achilles did. Similarly in the present instance also I will do part of what you bid—I will strive to tell my story as best I can in my own way ;

Though ancient heroes I'll not try to match,[3]

whether it be Plato or Homer. For, you remember, the poet says that in the case of Eurytus himself such rivalry worked not to his advantage, since it was aimed at his superiors.[4] However, I shall not lack for devotion," I added. Yet, despite my brave words to Hieroson, I was moved and heaved a sigh, as it were, when I bethought me of Homer and Plato.

[2] Although we know nothing of this Hieroson apart from what Dio tells us, the name, which is quite unusual, is found in an inscription relating to Borysthenes and to its worship of Achilles (*C.I.G.* 2. 2077).

[3] *Odyssey* 8. 223.

[4] Dio is still thinking of the passage just quoted, verses 224–8 of which allude to the slaying of Eurytus by Apollo for having dared to challenge the god to a trial of skill in archery. It was the bow of Eurytus with which Odysseus slew the suitors.

Τὸ μὲν δὴ τῆς πόλεως οὕτως, ἔφην, δεῖ[1]
ἀκούειν ὡς οὐκ ἄντικρυς τῶν ἡμετέρων[2] τὸν
κόσμον ἀποφαινομένων πόλιν· ἐναντίον γὰρ ἂν[3]
ὑπῆρχε τοῦτο[4] τῷ λόγῳ τῷ περὶ τῆς πόλεως, ἥν,[5]
ὥσπερ οὖν εἶπον, σύστημα ἀνθρώπων ὡρίσαντο·
ἅμα τε οὐκ ἦν ἴσως πρέπον οὐδὲ πιθανὸν κυρίως
εἰπόντας εἶναι τὸν κόσμον ζῷον ἔπειτα φάσκειν
30 ὡς ἔστι πόλις· τὸ γὰρ αὐτὸ πόλιν τε καὶ ζῷον
οὐκ ἄν, οἶμαι, ῥᾳδίως ὑπομένοι τις ὑπολαβεῖν.
ἀλλὰ τὴν νῦν διακόσμησιν, ὁπηνίκα διῄρηται καὶ
μεμέρισται τὸ πᾶν εἰς πολλάς τινας μορφὰς
φυτῶν τε καὶ ζῴων θνητῶν καὶ ἀθανάτων, ἔτι δὲ
ἀέρος καὶ γῆς καὶ ὕδατος καὶ πυρός, ἓν[6] οὐδὲν
ἧττον πεφυκὸς ἐν ἅπασι τούτοις καὶ μιᾷ ψυχῇ
καὶ δυνάμει διεπόμενον,[7] ἀμηγέπη[8] πόλει προσ-
εικάζουσι διὰ τὸ πλῆθος τῶν ἐν αὐτῇ γιγνομένων
τε καὶ ἀπογιγνομένων, ἔτι δὲ τὴν τάξιν καὶ τὴν
εὐκοσμίαν τῆς διοικήσεως.

31   Ὁ δὲ λόγος οὗτος ἔμβραχυ ἐσπούδακε ξυν-
αρμόσαι τῷ θείῳ[9] τὸ ἀνθρώπειον γένος καὶ ἑνὶ
λόγῳ περιλαβεῖν πᾶν τὸ λογικόν, κοινωνίας
ἀρχὴν καὶ δικαιοσύνης[10] μόνην ταύτην ἰσχυρὰν
καὶ ἄλυτον εὑρίσκων. πόλις μὲν γὰρ δὴ κατὰ

---

[1] δεῖ Reiske : δὴ M, δεῖν UB.
[2] τῶν ἡμετέρων Emperius : τῶν ἡμερῶν M, τῶν ἥμερον ζῴων UB.
[3] ἂν added by Emperius.
[4] τοῦτο Selden : τούτῳ.
[5] ἥν added by Emperius.
[6] ἓν Arnim : ἐν.
[7] διεπόμενον Emperius : διεπομένων.
[8] ἀμηγέπη Emperius : ἃ μήτε τῇ.
[9] θείῳ Geel : θεῷ.
[10] δικαιοσύνης Reiske : δικαιοσύνην.

" Well then," said I, " the term ' city ' must be taken on the understanding that our sect[1] is not literally defining the universe as a city; for that would be in direct conflict with our doctrine of the city, which, as I have said, the Stoics define as an organization of human beings;[2] and at the same time it would possibly not be suitable or convincing, if, after stating in the strict sense of the term that the universe is a living creature,[3] they should then call it a city, for that the same thing is both a city and a living being is a proposition that, I imagine, no one would readily consent to entertain. Yet the present orderly constitution of the universe ever since the whole has been separated and divided into a considerable number of forms of plants and animals, mortal and immortal, yes, and into air and earth and water and fire,[4] being nevertheless by nature in all these forms one thing and governed by one spirit and force—this orderly constitution, I say, the Stoics do in one way or another liken to a city because of the multitude of the creatures that are constantly either being born or else ending their existence in it, and, furthermore, because of the arrangement and orderliness of its administration.

" This doctrine, in brief, aims to harmonize the human race with the divine, and to embrace in a single term everything endowed with reason, finding in reason the only sure and indissoluble foundation for fellowship and justice. For in keeping with that

---

[1] The Stoics.
[2] Cf. § 20.
[3] Cf. Plato, *Timaeus* 30 B.
[4] Cf. §§ 43-6, where Dio treats these four as horses.

τοῦτο ἂν εἴη λεγομένη μὰ Δι' οὐ φαύλων οὐδὲ
μικρῶν τυχοῦσα ἡγεμόνων οὐδὲ ὑπὸ τυράννων τε
καὶ δήμων καὶ δεκαρχιῶν δὴ καὶ ὀλιγαρχιῶν καί
τινων ἄλλων τοιούτων ἀρρωστημάτων διαφορου-
μένη καὶ στασιάζουσα τὸν ἅπαντα χρόνον,
ἀλλὰ τῇ σωφρονεστάτῃ καὶ ἀρίστῃ βασιλείᾳ
κεκοσμημένη, τῷ ὄντι βασιλευομένη κατὰ νόμον
32 μετὰ πάσης φιλίας καὶ ὁμονοίας· ὅπερ δὴ ὁ
σοφώτατος καὶ [1] πρεσβύτατος ἄρχων καὶ νομοθέτης
ἅπασι προστάττει θνητοῖς καὶ ἀθανάτοις, ὁ τοῦ
ξύμπαντος ἡγεμὼν οὐρανοῦ καὶ τῆς ὅλης δεσπότης
οὐσίας, αὐτὸς οὕτως ἐξηγούμενος καὶ παράδειγμα
παρέχων τὴν αὐτοῦ διοίκησιν [2] τῆς εὐδαίμονος καὶ
μακαρίας καταστάσεως· ὃν οἱ θεῖοι ποιηταὶ
μαθόντες ἐκ Μουσῶν ὑμνοῦσιν ἅμα καὶ ὀνομάζουσι
πατέρα θεῶν καὶ ἀνθρώπων.

33   Κινδυνεύει γὰρ οὖν δὴ τὸ ποιητικὸν γένος οὐ
πάνυ ἄστοχον εἶναι τῶν ἱερῶν λόγων οὐδὲ ἀπὸ
στόχου φθέγγεσθαι τὰ τοιαῦτα πολλάκις, οὐ
μέντοι [3] οὐδὲ μεμυῆσθαι καθαρῶς κατὰ θεσμὸν
καὶ νόμον τῶν μυουμένων οὐδὲ εἰδέναι τοῦ
ξύμπαντος πέρι τῆς ἀληθείας σαφὲς οὐδέν, ὡς
ἔπος εἰπεῖν· ἀτεχνῶς δὲ ἔοικεν ὅμοιον εἶναι τοῖς
ἔξω περὶ θύρας ὑπηρέταις τῶν τελετῶν, πρόθυρα
κοσμοῦσι καὶ βωμοὺς τοὺς ἐν τῷ φανερῷ καὶ τὰ
ἄλλα τὰ τοιαῦτα παρασκευάζουσιν, οὐδέ ποτ'
ἔνδον παριοῦσιν. ὅθεν δὴ καὶ θεράποντας Μουσῶν
αὐτοὺς ὀνομάζουσιν, οὐ μύστας οὐδὲ ἄλλο σεμνὸν

---

[1] After καὶ Wilamowitz deletes ὁ.
[2] τὴν αὐτοῦ διοίκησιν Emperius: τῆς αὐτοῦ διοικήσεως.
[3] μέντοι Emperius: τοίνυν.

---

[1] Cf. Hesiod, *Theogony* 99–101.

concept the term ' city ' would be applied, not, of
course, to an organization that has chanced to get mean
or petty leaders nor to one which through tyranny or
democracy or, in fact, through decarchy or oligarchy
or any other similar product of imperfection, is being
torn to pieces and made the victim of constant party
faction. Nay, the term would be applied rather to
an organization that is governed by the sanest and
noblest form of kingship, to one that is actually under
royal governance in accordance with law, in complete
friendship and concord. And this, indeed, is precisely what the wisest and eldest ruler and law-giver
ordains for all, both mortals and immortals, he who is
the leader of all the heaven and lord of all being,
himself thus expounding the term and offering his own
administration as a pattern of the happy and blessed
condition, he whom the divine bards, instructed by
the Muses, praise in song and call the ' father of
gods and men.'

" For the chances are, indeed, that poets as a class
are not utterly bad marksmen when they speak of
sacred things and that they are not missing the mark
when they use such expressions as that repeatedly ; on
the other hand, it is not likely that they have received
a real initiation according to the rites and regulations
of true initiates, or that with reference to the
universe they know anything, if I may say so, which
is true and clear. But we may think of them as
merely like the attendants at the rites, who stand
outside at the doors, decking portals and the altars
which are in full view and attending to the other
preparations of that kind but never passing within.
Indeed that is the very reason why the poets call
themselves ' attendants of the Muses,'[1] not initiates

451

34 ὄνομα. οὐκοῦν, ὡς ἔφην, τούς τε[1] πλησίον
ἀναστρεφομένους τελετῆς τινος πρὸς ταῖς εἰσόδοις
εἰκὸς τό γε τοσοῦτον τῶν[2] ἔνδοθεν αἰσθάνεσθαί
τινος, ἤτοι ῥήματος ἐκβοηθέντος ἑνὸς μυστικοῦ
ἢ πυρὸς ὑπερφανέντος, καὶ τοῖς ποιηταῖς ἐνίοτε,
λέγω δὲ τοῖς πάνυ ἀρχαίοις, φωνή τις ἐκ Μουσῶν
ἀφίκετο βραχεῖα καί πού τις ἐπίπνοια θείας
φύσεώς τε καὶ ἀληθείας, καθάπερ αὐγὴ πυρὸς
ἐξ ἀφανοῦς λάμψαντος· ἃ ἔπασχον ἐκ Μουσῶν
35 καὶ κατείχοντο Ὅμηρός τε καὶ Ἡσίοδος. οἱ δὲ
μετ᾽ ἐκείνους ὕστερον ἐπὶ σκηνὰς καὶ θέατρα τὴν
αὑτῶν σοφίαν ἀγαγόντες ἀμύητοι ἀμυήτοις πολλάκις ἐξέφερον ἀτελῆ παραδείγματα ὀργίων·
θαυμαζόμενοι δὲ ὑπὸ τῶν πολλῶν ἐπεχείρουν
αὐτοὶ τελεῖν τὸν ὄχλον, τῷ ὄντι βακχείων τινὰς
σκηνὰς ἀκαλύπτους πηξάμενοι ἔν τισι τραγικαῖς
τριόδοις.

Οὗτοι δ᾽ οὖν πάντες οἱ ποιηταὶ κατὰ ταὐτὰ[3]
τὸν πρῶτον καὶ μέγιστον θεὸν πατέρα καλοῦσι
συλλήβδην ἅπαντος τοῦ λογικοῦ γένους καὶ δὴ
36 καὶ βασιλέα. οἷς πειθόμενοι οἱ ἄνθρωποι Διὸς
βασιλέως ἱδρύονται βωμούς, καὶ δὴ καὶ πατέρα
αὐτὸν οὐκ ὀκνοῦσι προσαγορεύειν τινὲς ἐν ταῖς
εὐχαῖς, ὡς τοιαύτης τινὸς ἀρχῆς καὶ συστάσεως
οὔσης τοῦ παντός. ὥστε ταύτῃ γε οὐδὲ οἶκον
δοκοῦσί μοι ὀκνῆσαι ἂν ἀποφήνασθαι τοῦ Διὸς

---

[1] τούς τε Emperius: τοὺς.   [2] τῶν added by Emperius.
[3] ταὐτὰ Selden: ταῦτα.

---

[1] Cf. Hesiod, *Theogony* 22–34.
[2] Dio is contrasting with the privacy and secrecy of the
mysteries (§§ 33, 34) the openness and profane character of
dramatic productions. Hence ἀκαλύπτους and τριόδοις are

or any other august name. So, as I was saying, it is reasonable to suppose that not only do those who busy themselves near some ritual, hard by the entrance to the sanctuary, gain some inkling of what is going on within, when either a lone mystic phrase rings out loudly, or fire appears above the enclosure, but also that there comes sometimes to the poets—I mean the very ancient poets—some utterance from the Muses, however brief, some inspiration of divine nature and of divine truth, like a flash of fire from the invisible. This is what happened to Homer and Hesiod when they were possessed by the Muses.[1] But the poets who came after them in later days, bringing to stage and theatre naught but their own wisdom, uninitiate addressing uninitiate, have ofttimes disclosed imperfect patterns of holy rites; but, being applauded by the multitude, they tried in their own right to initiate the mob, actually, as we might say, building open booths for Bacchic rites at tragic crossroads.[2]

" Yet all these poets in precisely the same fashion call the first and greatest god Father of the whole rational family collectively, yes, and King besides. And trusting to these poets men erect altars to Zeus the King and, what is more, some do not hesitate even to call him Father in their prayers, believing that there exists some such government and organization of the universe as that. Therefore, from that standpoint at least, it seems to me, they would not hesitate to apply the term ' home of Zeus '[3] to the

the significant words. For ' building booths ' = presenting plays, see Plato, *Laws* 817 c.

[3] Euripides called the aether the οἴκησις of Zeus, for which the malicious wit of Aristophanes (*Frogs* 100) substituted the word δωμάτιον.

τὸν ἅπαντα κόσμον, εἴπερ ἐστὶ πατὴρ τῶν [1] ἐν
αὑτῷ, καὶ νὴ Δία πόλιν, ὥσπερ ἡμεῖς προσεικά-
37 ζομεν κατὰ τὴν μείζονα ἀρχήν. βασιλεία γὰρ
πόλει μᾶλλον ἢ οἴκῳ πρεπόντως ἂν λέγοιτο. οὐ
γὰρ δὴ βασιλέα εἰπόντες τὸν ἐπὶ τῶν ὅλων οὐκ
ἂν βασιλεύεσθαι τὸ ὅλον ὁμολογοῖεν οὐδὲ βασιλεύεσθαι φήσαντες οὐκ ἂν πολιτεύεσθαι φαῖεν οὐδὲ
εἶναι πολιτείαν βασιλικὴν τοῦ παντός. πολιτείαν
δ' αὖ συγχωροῦντες πόλιν οὐκ ἂν ἀποτρέποιντο
ὁμολογεῖν ἤ τι τούτῳ παραπλήσιον τὸ πολιτευό-
μενον.

38 Ὅδε μὲν οὖν ὁ τῶν φιλοσόφων λόγος, ἀγαθὴν
καὶ φιλάνθρωπον ἀποδεικνὺς κοινωνίαν δαιμόνων
καὶ ἀνθρώπων, μεταδιδοὺς νόμου καὶ πολιτείας οὐ
τοῖς τυχοῦσι τῶν ζῴων, ἀλλ' ὅσοις μέτεστι λόγου
καὶ φρονήσεως, πολὺ κρείττω καὶ δικαιοτέραν τῆς
Λακωνικῆς νομοθεσίας εἰσηγούμενος, καθ' ἣν
οὐδὲ ὑπάρχει τοῖς Εἵλωσι γενέσθαι Σπαρτιάταις,
ὅθεν δὴ καὶ διατελοῦσιν ἐπιβουλεύοντες τῇ
Σπάρτῃ.

39 Ἕτερος δὲ μῦθος ἐν ἀπορρήτοις τελεταῖς ὑπὸ
μάγων ἀνδρῶν ᾄδεται θαυμαζόμενος, οἳ τὸν
θεὸν τοῦτον ὑμνοῦσιν ὡς τέλειόν τε καὶ πρῶτον
ἡνίοχον τοῦ τελειοτάτου ἅρματος. τὸ γὰρ Ἡλίου
ἅρμα νεώτερόν φασιν εἶναι πρὸς ἐκεῖνο κρινόμενον,
φανερὸν δὲ τοῖς πολλοῖς, ἅτε προδήλου γιγνομένης
τῆς φορᾶς. ὅθεν κοινῆς φήμης [2] τυγχάνειν, ὡς
ἔοικεν ἀπὸ [3] πρώτων σχεδόν τι τῶν ποιητῶν
ἀνατολὰς καὶ δύσεις ἑκάστοτε λεγόντων κατὰ

___

[1] τῶν Jacobs: αὐτῶν.
[2] κοινῆς φήμης Reiske: κοιναῖς φήμαις.
[3] ἀπὸ Emperius: ὑπό.

entire universe—if indeed he is father of all who live in it—yes, by Zeus, and his ' city ' too, our Stoic similitude, to suggest the greater office of the god. For kingship is a word more appropriate to a city than to a home. For surely men would not apply the term King to him who is over all and then refuse to admit that the whole is governed by a king, nor would they admit that they are governed by a king and then deny that they are members of a state or that there is a kingly administration of the universe. And again, conceding ' administration,' they would not balk at accepting ' city,' or something very like it, as descriptive of that which is administered.

" This, then, is the theory of the philosophers, a theory which sets up a noble and benevolent fellow-ship of gods and men which gives a share in law and citizenship, not to all living beings whatsoever, but only to such as have a share in reason and intellect, intro-ducing a far better and more righteous code than that of Sparta, in accordance with which the Helots have no prospect of ever becoming Spartans, and con-sequently are constantly plotting against Sparta.

" Moreover, there is besides a myth which arouses admiration as sung in secret rites by the Magi, who extol this god of ours as being the perfect and original driver of the most perfect chariot. For the chariot of Helius, they claim, is relatively recent when compared with that of Zeus, though visible to the many because its course is run in full view. Therefore, they say, the chariot of Helius has enjoyed a reputation with all mankind, since the poets, beginning practically with the earliest times, so it would seem, are always telling of its rising and

ταὐτὰ¹ πάντων ἐξηγουμένων ζευγνυμένους τε
τοὺς ἵππους καὶ τὸν Ἥλιον αὐτὸν ἐπιβαίνοντα
τοῦ δίφρου.

40 Τὸ δὲ ἰσχυρὸν καὶ τέλειον ἅρμα τὸ Διὸς
οὐδεὶς ἄρα ὕμνησεν ἀξίως τῶν τῇδε οὔτε Ὅμηρος
οὔτε Ἡσίοδος, ἀλλὰ Ζωροάστρης καὶ μάγων
παῖδες ᾄδουσι παρ' ἐκείνου² μαθόντες· ὃν
Πέρσαι λέγουσιν ἔρωτι σοφίας καὶ δικαιοσύνης
ἀποχωρήσαντα τῶν ἄλλων καθ' αὑτὸν ἐν ὄρει
τινὶ ζῆν· ἔπειτα ἀφθῆναι τὸ ὄρος πυρὸς ἄνωθεν
πολλοῦ κατασκήψαντος συνεχῶς τε κάεσθαι.
τὸν οὖν βασιλέα σὺν τοῖς ἐλλογιμωτάτοις Περσῶν
ἀφικνεῖσθαι πλησίον, βουλόμενον εὔξασθαι τῷ
θεῷ· καὶ τὸν ἄνδρα ἐξελθεῖν ἐκ τοῦ πυρὸς
ἀπαθῆ, φανέντα δὲ αὐτοῖς ἵλεων θαρρεῖν κελεῦσαι
καὶ θῦσαι θυσίας τινάς, ὡς ἥκοντος εἰς τὸν τόπον
41 τοῦ θεοῦ. συγγίγνεσθαί τε μετὰ ταῦτα οὐχ
ἅπασιν, ἀλλὰ τοῖς ἄριστα πρὸς ἀλήθειαν πεφυκόσι
καὶ θεοῦ ξυνιέναι δυναμένοις, οὓς Πέρσαι μάγους
ἐκάλεσαν, ἐπισταμένους θεραπεύειν τὸ δαιμόνιον,
οὐχ ὡς Ἕλληνες ἀγνοίᾳ τοῦ ὀνόματος οὕτως
ὀνομάζουσιν ἀνθρώπους γόητας. ἐκεῖνοι δὲ τά
τε ἄλλα δρῶσι κατὰ λόγους ἱεροὺς καὶ δὴ τῷ
Διὶ τρέφουσιν ἅρμα Νισαίων ἵππων· οἱ δέ

¹ κατὰ ταὐτὰ Reiske : κατὰ ταῦτα M, καὶ κατὰ ταῦτα UB.
² ἐκείνου Morel : ἐκείνων.

¹ Hesiod, *Theogony* 760–1, speaks of the rising and the
setting of Helius, though not expressly of his chariot. The
earliest reference to his chariot may be *Hymn to Hermes* 68–9.
² Dio, like Herodotus (2. 53), regards Homer and Hesiod
as creators of the orthodox views about Greek gods.
³ Cf. Or. 49. 7. Greeks did, not infrequently, associate
Magi and magic as related terms.

its setting, all in the same manner describing the yoking of the horses and Helius himself mounting his car.[1]

"But the mighty, perfect chariot of Zeus has never been praised as it deserves by any of the poets of our land, either by Homer or by Hesiod;[2] and yet Zoroaster sings of it, as do the children of the Magi, who learned the song from him. For the Persians say that Zoroaster, because of a passion for wisdom and justice, deserted his fellows and dwelt by himself on a certain mountain; and they say that thereupon the mountain caught fire, a mighty flame descending from the sky above, and that it burned unceasingly. So then the king and the most distinguished of his Persians drew near for the purpose of praying to the god; and Zoroaster came forth from the fire unscathed, and, showing himself gracious toward them, bade them to be of good cheer and to offer certain sacrifices in recognition of the god's having come to that place. And thereafter, so they say, Zoroaster has associated, not with them all, but only with such as are best endowed with regard to truth, and are best able to understand the god, men whom the Persians have named Magi, that is to say, people who know how to cultivate the divine power, not like the Greeks, who in their ignorance use the term to denote wizards.[3] And all else that those Magi do is in accordance with sacred sayings, and in particular they maintain for Zeus a team of Nisaean horses [4]—

---

[4] Herodotus (7. 40), describing the march of Xerxes' army, mentions 'ten sacred Nisaean horses, most beautifully adorned,' which went before a chariot drawn by eight white horses, and sacred to Zeus. There is no evidence to substantiate Dio's claim that the Magi sang of the team of Zeus.

DIO CHRYSOSTOM

εἰσὶ κάλλιστοι καὶ μέγιστοι τῶν κατὰ τὴν Ἀσίαν·
τῷ δέ γε Ἡλίῳ ἕνα ἵππον.

42 Ἐξηγοῦνται δὲ τὸν μῦθον οὐχ ὥσπερ οἱ
παρ' ἡμῖν προφῆται τῶν Μουσῶν ἕκαστα φράζουσι
μετὰ πολλῆς πειθοῦς, ἀλλὰ μάλα αὐθαδῶς.
εἶναι γὰρ δὴ τοῦ ξύμπαντος μίαν ἀγωγήν τε
καὶ ἡνιόχησιν ὑπὸ τῆς ἄκρας ἐμπειρίας τε καὶ
ῥώμης γιγνομένην ἀεί, καὶ ταύτην ἄπαυστον
ἐν ἀπαύστοις αἰῶνος περιόδοις. τοὺς δὲ Ἡλίου
καὶ Σελήνης δρόμους, καθάπερ εἶπον, μερῶν
εἶναι κινήσεις, ὅθεν ὑπ' ἀνθρώπων[1] ὁρᾶσθαι
σαφέστερον. τῆς δὲ τοῦ ξύμπαντος κινήσεως
καὶ φορᾶς μὴ ξυνιέναι[2] τοὺς πολλούς, ἀλλ'
ἀγνοεῖν τὸ μέγεθος τοῦδε τοῦ ἀγῶνος.

43 Τὸ δὴ μετὰ τοῦτο αἰσχύνομαι φράζειν τῶν
ἵππων πέρι καὶ τῆς ἡνιοχήσεως, ὅπως ἐξηγούμενοι
λέγουσιν, οὐ πάνυ τι φροντίζοντες ὅμοιόν σφισι
γίγνεσθαι πανταχῇ τὸ τῆς εἰκόνος. ἴσως γὰρ
ἂν φαινοίμην ἄτοπος παρὰ Ἑλληνικά τε καὶ
χαρίεντα ᾄσματα βαρβαρικὸν ᾆσμα ἐπᾴδων·[3]
ὅμως δὲ τολμητέον.

Φασὶ τῶν ἵππων τὸν πρῶτον ἄνωθεν ἀπείρῳ

---

[1] ἀνθρώπων Arnim : αὐτῶν.
[2] ξυνιέναι Reiske : ξυνεῖναι.
[3] ἐπᾴδων Emperius : παίδων.

---

[1] I.e., ' spokesmen.'
[2] Figurative usage of the term.
[3] The ' barbarian lay ' finds no counterpart in Zoroastrian
literature; though the Avesta does refer to the team of
Mithra, god of light, as crossing the firmament. Gomperz,
Griechische Denker, vol. I, p. 65, maintains that the Greeks did
not know the Avestan Zoroaster or the teaching of the

458

and these horses are the finest and largest to be found in Asia—but for Helius they maintain only a single horse.

" These Magi narrate their myth, not in the manner of our prophets [1] of the Muses, who merely present each detail with much plausibility, but rather with stubborn insistence upon its truthfulness. For they assert that the universe is constantly being propelled and driven along a single path, as by a charioteer endowed with highest skill and power, and that this movement goes on unceasingly in unceasing cycles of time. And the coursing of Helius and Selenê, according to their account, is the movement of portions of the whole, and for that reason it is more clearly perceived by mankind. And they add that the movement and revolution of the universe as a whole is not perceptible to the majority of mankind, but that, on the contrary, they are ignorant of the magnitude of this contest.[2]

" What follows regarding the horses and their driving I really am ashamed to tell in the manner in which the Magi set it forth in their narrative, since they are not very much concerned to secure consistency at all points in their presentation of the picture. In fact, quite possibly I may appear absurd when, in contrast with Greek lays of grace and charm, I chant one that is barbarian; [3] but still I must make the venture.

" According to the Magi, that one of the horses

Gathas. Dio's myth may be, at least in large measure, his own fanciful treatment of familiar Stoic doctrine, that the universe consisted of four concentric spheres : earth, water, air, and fire (aether). These four can readily be identified with Dio's ' horses.' Cf. Zeller, *Philosophie der Griechen*, vol. III, pt. 1, p. 172.

DIO CHRYSOSTOM

διαφέρειν κάλλει τε καὶ μεγέθει καὶ ταχυτῆτι,
ἅτε[1] ἔξωθεν περιτρέχοντα τὸ μήκιστον τοῦ
δρόμου, αὐτοῦ Ζηνὸς ἱερόν· πτηνὸν δὲ εἶναι·
τὴν δὲ χρόαν λαμπρόν, αὐγῆς τῆς καθαρωτάτης·
τὸν δὲ Ἥλιον ἐν αὐτῷ καὶ τὴν Σελήνην σημεῖα
προφανῆ ὁρᾶσθαι, ὥσπερ, οἶμαι, καὶ τῶνδε τῶν
ἵππων ἐστὶ σημεῖα, τὰ μὲν μηνοειδῆ, τὰ δὲ
44 ἀλλοῖα. ταῦτα δὲ ὑφ᾽ ἡμῶν ὁρᾶσθαι συνεστραμ-
μένα, καθάπερ ἐν[2] αὐγῇ λαμπρᾷ φλογὸς σπινθῆρας
ἰσχυροὺς διαθέοντας, ἰδίαν δὲ κίνησιν ἔχειν καθ᾽
αὐτά. καὶ τἆλλα ἄστρα δι᾽ ἐκείνου φαινόμενα
καὶ ξύμπαντα ἐκείνου πεφυκότα μέρη τὰ μὲν
περιφέρεσθαι σὺν αὐτῷ μίαν ταύτην ἔχοντα
κίνησιν, τὰ δὲ ἄλλους θεῖν δρόμους. τυγχάνειν δὲ παρὰ τοῖς ἀνθρώποις ταῦτα μὲν ἰδίου
ἕκαστον ὀνόματος, τὰ δὲ ἄλλα κατὰ πλῆθος
ἀθρόα, διανενεμημένα εἴς τινα σχήματα καὶ
μορφάς.

45 Ὁ μὲν δὴ λαμπρότατος ἵππος καὶ ποικιλώτατος
αὐτῷ τε Διὶ προσφιλέστατος, ὧδέ πως ὑμνούμενος
ὑπ᾽ αὐτῶν, θυσίας τε καὶ τιμὰς ἅτε πρῶτος
εἰκότως πρώτας ἔλαχεν· δεύτερος δὲ μετ᾽ ἐκεῖνον ἁπτόμενος αὐτοῦ καὶ πλησιώτατος Ἥρας
ἐπώνυμος, εὐήνιος καὶ μαλακός, πολὺ δὲ ἥττων
κατά τε ῥώμην καὶ τάχος. χροιὰν[3] δὲ τῇ μὲν
αὐτοῦ φύσει μέλας, φαιδρύνεται δὲ ἀεὶ τὸ κατα-
λαμπόμενον Ἡλίῳ· τὸ δὲ σκιασθὲν ἐν τῇ περιφορᾷ

---

[1] ἅτε Emperius : τά τε.
[2] ἐν added by Reiske.
[3] χροιὰν Emperius : χροιᾶι U, χροιὰ BM.

---

[1] Aether, abode of the fixed stars and the planets.

which is the highest in the heavens [1] is immeasurably superior in beauty, size, and speed, since it has the outside track and runs the longest course, a horse sacred to Zeus himself. Furthermore, it is a winged creature, brilliant in colour with the brilliance of the purest flame; and in it Helius and Selenê are to be seen as conspicuous signs or marks—like, I fancy, the marks which horses bear here on earth, some crescent-shaped and some of other patterns. And they say that these ' marks ' appear to us to be in close array, as it were great sparks of fire darting about in the midst of brilliant light, and yet that each has its own independent motion. Furthermore, the other stars also which are visible through that Horse of Zeus, one and all being natural parts of it, in some instances revolve along with it and have the same motion, and in others follow different tracks. And they add that among men these stars which are associated with the Horse of Zeus have each its own particular name; [2] whereas the rest are treated collectively in groups, distributed so as to form certain figures or patterns.[3]

"Well then, the horse that is most brilliant and most spangled with stars and dearest to Zeus himself, being praised by the Magi in their hymns for some such attributes as these, quite properly stands first in sacrifice and worship as being truly first. Next in order after that, in closest contact with the Horse of Zeus, comes one that bears the name of Hera,[4] a horse obedient to the rein and gentle, but far inferior in strength and speed. In colour this horse is of its own nature black, but that portion which receives the light of Helius is regularly bright, whereas where it is

[2] The planets.   [3] Constellations.
[4] Air.

46 τὴν αὐτοῦ μεταλαμβάνει τῆς χρόας ἰδέαν. τρί-
τος Ποσειδῶνος ἱερός, τοῦ δευτέρου βραδύτερος.
τούτου δὲ μυθολογοῦσιν εἴδωλον οἱ ποιηταὶ
γενέσθαι παρ' ἀνθρώποις, ἐμοὶ δοκεῖν, ὅντινα
ὀνομάζουσι Πήγασον, καί φασιν ἀνεῖναι κρήνην ἐν
Κορίνθῳ χαράξαντα τῇ ὁπλῇ. ὁ δὲ δὴ τέταρτος
εἰκάσαι πάντων ἀτοπώτατος, στερεός τε καὶ
ἀκίνητος, οὐχ ὅπως πτερωτός, ἐπώνυμος Ἑστίας.
ὅμως δὲ οὐκ ἀποτρέπονται τῆς εἰκόνος, ἀλλὰ
ἐνεζεῦχθαί φασι καὶ τοῦτον τῷ ἅρματι, μένειν
δὲ κατὰ χώραν χαλινὸν ἀδάμαντος ἐνδακόντα.
47 συνερείδειν δὲ πανταχόθεν αὐτῷ [1] τοῖς μέρεσι,
καὶ τὼ δύο τὼ πλησίον ὁμοίως πρὸς αὐτὸν
ἐγκλίνειν, ἀτεχνῶς ἐπιπίπτοντε καὶ ὠθουμένω·
τὸν δὲ ἐξωτάτω πρῶτον ἀεὶ περὶ τὸν ἑστῶτα
ὡς νύσσαν φέρεσθαι.

Τὸ μὲν οὖν πολὺ μετ' εἰρήνης καὶ φιλίας
διατελοῦσιν ἀβλαβεῖς ὑπ' ἀλλήλων. ἤδη δέ ποτε
ἐν μήκει χρόνου καὶ πολλαῖς περιόδοις ἰσχυρὸν
ἆσθμα τοῦ πρώτου προσπεσὸν ἄνωθεν, οἷα δὴ

[1] αὐτῷ] αὐτῷ Arnim.

---

[1] This notion seems to have been borrowed from the
behaviour of the moon.   [2] Water.

[3] Cf. especially Statius, *Thebais* 4. 60. The most familiar
version of the myth is associated with Hippocrenê on Helicon.
However, Pegasus is connected also with other fountains,
probably because of the meaning attached to his name.
According to Pindar and others, Peirenê at Corinth is linked
with the capture of Pegasus by Bellerophon. It is probably
the Peirenê on Acrocorinth which Dio has in mind—an
excellent spot from which to take off—for in Roman times
that spring became more prominent in the Pegasus story than
the more sumptuous spring of the lower city. *Vid.* Broneer,
Corinth III, pt. i, pp. 59–60.

in shadow in its revolution it has its own proper colour.[1] Third comes a horse that is sacred to Poseidon,[2] still slower than the second. Regarding this steed the poets have a myth to the effect that its counterpart appeared among men—he whom they call Pegasus, methinks—and they claim that he caused a fountain to burst forth at Corinth by pawing with his hoof.[3] But the fourth is the strangest conception of them all, a horse both firm and immovable, to say nothing of its having no wings, and it is named after Hestia.[4] However, the Magi do not shrink from its portrayal; on the contrary, they state that this steed also is harnessed to the chariot, and yet it remains immovable, champing its adamantine curb. And from all sides the other horses press close to him with their bodies and the pair that are his neighbours[5] swerve toward him abreast, falling upon him, as it were, and crowding him, yet the horse that is farthest off[6] is ever first to round that stationary steed as horses round the turn in the hippodrome.[7]

"Now for the most part the horses continue in peace and friendship, unharmed by one another. But on one occasion in the past, in the course of a long space of time and many revolutions of the universe, a mighty blast from the first horse fell from on high,

---

[4] Here to be interpreted as the earth. See note to § 43.

[5] Water and air.   [6] Aether.

[7] In § 43 Dio warns us that the Magi are not much concerned regarding consistency. The translator assumes that all four horses are harnessed to one car—their varying speed would allow of that interpretation, since three of them move about the fourth; but how could the outermost (Aether) obtain a lead? Perhaps the spectator in the hippodrome might receive that impression.

θυμοειδοῦς, ἐθέρμηνε τοὺς ἄλλους, σφοδρότερόν
γε μὴν τὸν τελευταῖον· τήν τε [1] δὴ χαίτην
περιέφλεξεν αὐτοῦ, ᾗ μάλιστα ἠγάλλετο, καὶ
48 τὸν ἅπαντα κόσμον. τοῦτο δὲ τὸ πάθος ἅπαξ
Ἕλληνας μνημονεύοντάς φασι Φαέθοντι προσάπτειν, οὐ δυναμένους μέμφεσθαι τὴν Διὸς ἡνιόχησιν,
τούς τε Ἡλίου δρόμους οὐκ ἐθέλοντας ψέγειν.
διό φασι νεώτερον ἡνίοχον, Ἡλίου παῖδα θνητόν,
ἐπιθυμήσαντα χαλεπῆς καὶ ἀξυμφόρου πᾶσι τοῖς
θνητοῖς παιδιᾶς, αἰτησάμενον παρὰ τοῦ πατρὸς
ἐπιστῆναι τῷ δίφρῳ, φερόμενόν τε ἀτάκτως
πάντα καταφλέξαι ζῷα καὶ φυτά, καὶ τέλος αὐτὸν
διαφθαρῆναι πληγέντα ὑπὸ κρείττονος πυρός.

49　Πάλιν δὲ ὅταν διὰ πλειόνων ἐτῶν ὁ Νυμφῶν
καὶ Ποσειδῶνος ἱερὸς πῶλος ἐπαναστῇ, παρὰ
τὸ σύνηθες ἀγωνιάσας καὶ ταραχθείς, ἱδρῶτι
πολλῷ κατέκλυσε τὸν αὐτὸν τοῦτον ἅτε
ὁμόζυγα· πειρᾶται δὴ τῆς ἐναντίας τῇ πρότερον
φθορᾷ, ὕδατι πολλῷ χειμαζόμενος. καὶ τοῦτον
ἕνα χειμῶνα διηγεῖσθαι τοὺς Ἕλληνας ὑπὸ
νεότητός τε καὶ μνήμης ἀσθενοῦς, καὶ [2] Δευκα-
λίωνα βασιλεύοντα τότε σφίσιν ἀρκέσαι πρὸ τῆς
παντελοῦς φθορᾶς.

---

[1] τήν τε Emperius : τὴν δὲ.
[2] After καὶ Reiske deletes λέγουσι.

---

[1] Earth.
[2] The Stoics believed in periodic conflagrations by which the
universe was consumed, to be made anew.
[3] Cf. Ovid, *Metamorphoses* 1. 750 to 2. 400.

and, as might have been expected from such a fiery-tempered steed, inflamed the others, and more especially the last in order;[1] and the fire encompassed not alone its mane, which formed its special pride, but the whole universe as well.[2] And the Magi say that the Greeks, recording this experience as an isolated occurrence, connect it with the name of Phaethon, since they are unable to criticize the driving of Zeus and are loath to find fault with the coursings of Helius. And so they relate that a younger driver, a mortal son of Helius, desiring a sport that was to prove grievous and disastrous for all mankind, besought his father to let him mount his car and, plunging along in disorderly fashion, consumed with fire everything, both animals and plants, and finally was himself destroyed, being smitten by too powerful a flame.[3]

" Again, when at intervals of several years the horse that is sacred to Poseidon and the Nymphs rebels, having become panic-stricken and agitated beyond his wont, he overwhelms with copious sweat that same steed, since they two are yoke-mates. Accordingly it meets with a fate which is the opposite of the disaster previously mentioned, this time being deluged with a mighty flood. And the Magi state that here again the Greeks, through youthful ignorance and faulty memory, record this flood as a single occurrence and claim that Deucalion, who then was king, saved them from complete destruction.[4]

[4] According to Ovid, *ibid.*, 1. 318–29, only Pyrrha and Deucalion were saved. Apollodorus 1. 7. 2 says a few others escaped by fleeing to the highest mountains. Lucian, *De Dea Syria* 12, gives a version quite similar to the story of Noah.

50   Ταῦτα δὲ σπανίως ξυμβαίνοντα δοκεῖν[1] μὲν
ἀνθρώποις διὰ τὸν αὐτῶν ὄλεθρον γίγνεσθαι μὴ
κατὰ λόγον μηδὲ μετέχειν τῆς τοῦ παντὸς τάξεως,
λανθάνειν δὲ αὐτοὺς ὀρθῶς γιγνόμενα καὶ κατὰ
γνώμην τοῦ σῴζοντος καὶ κυβερνῶντος τὸ πᾶν.
εἶναι γὰρ ὅμοιον ὥσπερ ὅταν ἅρματος ἡνίοχος
τῶν ἵππων τινὰ κολάζῃ χαλινῷ σπάσας ἢ κέντρῳ
ἁψάμενος· ὁ δ' ἐσκίρτησε καὶ ἐταράχθη, παραχρῆμα εἰς δέον καθιστάμενος.

Μίαν μὲν οὖν λέγουσι[2] ταύτην ἡνιόχησιν
ἰσχυράν, οὐχ ὅλου φθειρομένου τοῦ παντός.
51 πάλιν δὲ ἑτέραν τῆς τῶν τεττάρων κινήσεως καὶ
μεταβολῆς, ἐν ἀλλήλοις μεταβαλλομένων καὶ δι-
αλλαττόντων τὰ εἴδη, μέχρις ἂν εἰς μίαν ἅπαντα
συνέλθῃ φύσιν, ἡττηθέντα τοῦ κρείττονος. ὅμως
δὲ καὶ ταύτην τὴν κίνησιν ἡνιοχήσει προσεικάζειν
τολμῶσιν ἐλάσει τε ἅρματος, ἀτοπωτέρας δεόμενοι
τῆς εἰκόνος· οἷον εἴ τις θαυματοποιὸς ἐκ κηροῦ
πλάσας ἵππους, ἔπειτα ἀφαιρῶν καὶ περιξύων
ἀφ' ἑκάστου προστιθεὶς ἄλλοτε ἄλλῳ, τέλος δὲ
ἅπαντας εἰς ἕνα τῶν τεττάρων ἀναλώσας μίαν
52 μορφὴν ἐξ ἁπάσης τῆς ὕλης ἐργάσαιτο.[3] εἶναί
γε μὴν τὸ τοιοῦτο μὴ καθάπερ ἀψύχων πλασμά-
των ἔξωθεν τοῦ δημιουργοῦ πραγματευομένου
καὶ μεθιστάντος τὴν ὕλην, αὐτῶν δὲ ἐκείνων
γίγνεσθαι τὸ πάθος, ὥσπερ ἐν ἀγῶνι μεγάλῳ τε

---

[1] δοκεῖν Geel : δοκεῖ.   [2] λέγουσι added by Reiske.
[3] ἐργάσαιτο Emperius : ἐργάσοιτο.

" According to the Magi, these rare occurrences are viewed by mankind as taking place for their destruction, and not in accord with reason or as a part of the order of the universe, being unaware that they occur quite properly and in keeping with the plan of the preserver and governor of the world. For in reality it is comparable with what happens when a charioteer punishes one of his horses, pulling hard upon the rein or pricking with the goad; and then the horse prances and is thrown into a panic but straightway settles down to its proper gait.

" Well then, this is one kind of driving of which they tell, attended by violence but not involving the complete destruction of the universe. On the other hand, they tell also of a different kind that involves the movement and change of all four horses, one in which they shift among themselves and interchange their forms until all come together into one being, having been overcome by that one which is superior in power. And yet this movement also the Magi dare to liken to the guidance and driving of a chariot, though to do so they need even stranger imagery. For instance, it is as if some magician were to mould horses out of wax, and then, subtracting and scraping off the wax from each, should add a little now to this one and now to that, until finally, having used up all the horses in constructing one from the four, he should fashion a single horse out of all his material. They state, however, that in reality the process to which they refer is not like that of such inanimate images, in which the craftsman operates and shifts the material from without, but that instead the transformation is the work of these creatures themselves, just as if they were striving for victory in a

καὶ ἀληθινῷ περὶ νίκης ἐριζόντων· γίγνεσθαι δὲ
τὴν νίκην καὶ τὸν στέφανον ἐξ ἀνάγκης τοῦ
πρώτου καὶ κρατίστου τάχει τε καὶ ἀλκῇ καὶ τῇ
ξυμπάσῃ ἀρετῇ, ὃν εἴπομεν ἐν ἀρχῇ τῶν λόγων
53 ἐξαίρετον εἶναι Διός. τούτου γάρ, ἅτε πάντων
ἀλκιμώτατον καὶ φύσει διάπυρον, ταχὺ ἀναλώ-
σαντα τοὺς ἄλλους, καθάπερ, οἶμαι, τῷ ὄντι
κηρίνους, ἐν οὐ πολλῷ τινι χρόνῳ, δοκοῦντι δὲ
ἡμῖν ἀπείρῳ πρὸς τὸν ἡμέτερον αὐτῶν λογισμόν,
καὶ τὴν οὐσίαν πάντων πᾶσαν εἰς αὑτὸν ἀναλα-
βόντα, πολὺ κρείττω καὶ λαμπρότερον ὀφθῆναι
τοῦ πρότερον, ὑπ' οὐδενὸς ἄλλου θνητῶν οὐδὲ
ἀθανάτων, ἀλλ' αὐτὸν ὑφ' αὑτοῦ νικηφόρον
γενόμενον τοῦ μεγίστου ἀγῶνος. στάντα δὲ
ὑψηλὸν καὶ γαῦρον, χαρέντα τῇ νίκῃ, τόπον τε ὡς
πλεῖστον καταλαβεῖν καὶ μείζονος χώρας δεηθῆναι
τότε ὑπὸ ῥώμης καὶ μένους.

54   Κατὰ τοῦτο δὴ γενόμενοι τοῦ λόγου δυσωποῦν-
ται τὴν αὐτῶν[1] ἐπονομάζειν τοῦ ζῴου φύσιν.
εἶναι γὰρ αὐτὸν ἤδη τηνικάδε ἁπλῶς τὴν τοῦ
ἡνιόχου καὶ δεσπότου ψυχήν, μᾶλλον δὲ αὐτὸ τὸ
φρονοῦν καὶ τὸ ἡγούμενον αὐτῆς. οὕτως δὴ
λέγομεν καὶ ἡμεῖς τιμῶντες καὶ σεβόμενοι τὸν
μέγιστον θεὸν ἔργοις τε ἀγαθοῖς καὶ ῥήμασιν
55 εὐφήμοις.[2] λειφθεὶς γὰρ δὴ μόνος ὁ νοῦς καὶ
τόπον ἀμήχανον ἐμπλήσας αὑτοῦ, ἅτε γ' ἐπ'
ἴσης[3] πανταχῇ κεχυμένος, οὐδενὸς ἐν αὐτῷ

────────
[1] αὑτῶν Capps : αὐτῶν or αὑτὴν.

contest that is great and real. And they add that the victory and its crown belong of necessity to that horse which is first and best in speed and prowess and general excellence, I mean to that one which we named in the beginning of our account as the special steed of Zeus. For that one, being most valiant of all and fiery by nature, having speedily used up the others—as if, methinks, they were truly made of wax—in no great span of time (though to us it seems endless according to our reckoning) and having appropriated to itself all the substance of them all, appeared much greater and more brilliant than formerly; not through the aid of any other creature, either mortal or immortal, but by itself and its own efforts proving victor in the greatest contest. And, standing tall and proud, rejoicing in its victory, it not only seized the largest possible region but also needed larger space at that time, so great was its strength and its spirit.

"Having arrived at that stage in their myth, the Magi are embarrassed in search of a name to describe the nature of the creature of their own invention. For they say that now by this time it is simply the soul of the charioteer and master; or, let us say, merely the intellect and leadership of that soul. (Those, in fact, are the terms we ourselves employ when we honour and reverence the greatest god by noble deeds and pious words). For indeed, when the mind alone had been left and had filled with itself immeasurable space, since it had poured itself evenly in all directions and nothing in it remained dense but

---

[2] οὕτως . . . εὐφήμοις suspected by Casaubon.

[3] αὐτοῦ . . . ἴσης Von der Muehll: αὐτοῦ γε πίθως M, αὐτοῦ γ' ἔπειθ' ὡς B, αὐτοῦ ἅτε γε πίθος U.

πυκνοῦ λειφθέντος, ἀλλὰ πάσης ἐπικρατούσης
μανότητος, ὅτε κάλλιστος γίγνεται, τὴν καθαρω-
τάτην λαβὼν αὐγῆς [1] ἀκηράτου φύσιν, εὐθὺς
ἐπόθησε τὸν ἐξ ἀρχῆς βίον. ἔρωτα δὴ λαβὼν
τῆς [2] ἡνιοχήσεως ἐκείνης καὶ ἀρχῆς καὶ ὁμονοίας
τῆς τε τῶν τριῶν φύσεων καὶ ἡλίου καὶ σελήνης
καὶ τῶν ἄλλων ἄστρων, ἁπάντων τε ἁπλῶς
ζῴων καὶ φυτῶν, ὥρμησεν ἐπὶ τὸ γεννᾶν καὶ
διανέμειν ἕκαστα καὶ δημιουργεῖν τὸν ὄντα νῦν
κόσμον ἐξ ἀρχῆς πολὺ κρείττω καὶ λαμπρότερον
56 ἅτε νεώτερον. ἀστράψας δὲ ὅλον οὐκ ἄτακτον
οὐδὲ ῥυπαρὰν ἀστραπήν, οἷα ἐν χειμερίοις [3]
ἐλαυνομένων βιαιότερον πολλάκις τῶν νεφῶν
διῆξεν, ἀλλὰ καθαρὸν καὶ ἀμιγῆ παντὸς σκοτεινοῦ,
μετέβαλε ῥᾳδίως ἅμα τῇ νοήσει. μνησθεὶς δὲ
Ἀφροδίτης καὶ γενέσεως ἐπράϋνε καὶ ἀνῆκεν
αὑτόν, καὶ πολὺ τοῦ φωτὸς ἀποσβέσας εἰς ἀέρα
πυρώδη τρέπεται πυρὸς ἠπίου. μιχθεὶς δὲ τότε
Ἥρᾳ καὶ μεταλαβὼν τοῦ τελειοτάτου λέχους,
ἀναπαυσάμενος ἀφίησι τὴν πᾶσαν αὖ τοῦ παντὸς
γονήν. τοῦτον ὑμνοῦσι παῖδες σοφῶν ἐν ἀρρήτοις
τελεταῖς Ἥρας καὶ Διὸς εὐδαίμονα γάμον.
57 ὑγρὰν δὲ ποιήσας τὴν ὅλην οὐσίαν, ἓν σπέρμα τοῦ
παντός, αὐτὸς ἐν τούτῳ διαθέων, καθάπερ ἐν
γονῇ πνεῦμα τὸ πλάττον καὶ δημιουργοῦν, τότε
δὴ μάλιστα προσεοικὼς τῇ τῶν ἄλλων συστάσει
ζῴων, καθ' ὅσον ἐκ ψυχῆς καὶ σώματος συν-
εστάναι λέγοιτ' ἂν οὐκ ἀπὸ τρόπου, τὰ λοιπὰ ἤδη

---

[1] αὐγῆς Emperius: αὐτός.
[2] τῆς Geel: τήν.
[3] οἷα ἐν χειμερίοις Casaubon: οἷαν χειμερίος BM, οἷαν
χειμερίοις U.

complete porosity prevailed—at which time it becomes most beautiful—having obtained the purest nature of unadulterated light, it immediately longed for the existence that it had at first. Accordingly, becoming enamoured of that control and governance and concord which it once maintained not only over the three natures of sun and moon and the other stars, but also over absolutely all animals and plants, it became eager to generate and distribute everything and to make the orderly universe then existent once more far better and more resplendent because newer. And emitting a full flash of lightning, not a disorderly or foul one such as in stormy weather often darts forth, when the clouds drive more violently than usual, but rather pure and unmixed with any murk, it worked a transformation easily, with the speed of thought. But recalling Aphroditê and the process of generation, it tamed and relaxed itself and, quenching much of its light, it turned into fiery air of gentle warmth, and uniting with Hera and enjoying the most perfect wedlock, in sweet repose it emitted anew the full supply of seed for the universe. Such is the blessed marriage of Zeus and Hera [1] of which the sons of sages sing in secret rites. And having made fluid all his essence, one seed for the entire world, he himself moving about in it like a spirit that moulds and fashions in generation, then indeed most closely resembling the composition of the other creatures, inasmuch as he might with reason be said to consist of soul and body, he now

---

[1] An apparent allusion to what was commonly called the Hieros Gamos or Holy Wedding, the earliest reference to which seems to be *Iliad* 14. 294–6. Theocritus 15. 64 asserts that women generally knew all the details. Hera presided over the rites of marriage.

ῥᾳδίως πλάττει καὶ τυποῖ, λείαν καὶ μαλακὴν
αὑτῷ περιχέας τὴν οὐσίαν καὶ πᾶσαν εἴκουσαν
εὐπετῶς.

58 Ἐργασάμενος δὲ καὶ τελεώσας ἀπέδειξεν ἐξ
ἀρχῆς τὸν ὄντα κόσμον εὐειδῆ καὶ καλὸν ἀμηχάνως,
πολὺ δὴ λαμπρότερον ἢ οἷος ὁρᾶται νῦν. πάντα
γάρ που καὶ τἄλλα ἔργα τῶν δημιουργῶν καινὰ [1]
ἀπὸ τῆς τέχνης καὶ τῶν χειρῶν παραχρῆμα τοῦ
ποιήσαντος κρείττω καὶ στιλπνότερα, καὶ τῶν
φυτῶν τὰ νεώτερα εὐθαλέστερα τῶν παλαιῶν
ὅλα τε βλαστοῖς ἐοικότα. καὶ μὴν τά γε ζῷα εὐ-
χάριτα καὶ προσηνῆ ἰδεῖν μετὰ τὴν γένεσιν, οὐ
μόνον τὰ κάλλιστα αὐτῶν, πῶλοί τε καὶ μόσχοι
καὶ σκύλακες, ἀλλὰ καὶ θηρίων σκύμνοι τῶν
59 ἀγριωτάτων. ἡ μὲν γὰρ ἀνθρώπου φύσις νηπία
τε καὶ ὑδαρὴς ὁμοία Δήμητρος ἀτελεῖ χλόη,
προελθοῦσα δὲ εἰς τὸ μέτρον ὥρας καὶ νεότητος
παντὸς ἀτεχνῶς φυτοῦ κρεῖττον καὶ ἐπιφανέσ-
τερον βλάστημα. ὁ δὴ ξύμπας οὐρανός τε καὶ
κόσμος, ὅτε πρῶτον συνετελέσθη, κοσμηθεὶς
ὑπὸ τῆς σοφωτάτης τε καὶ ἀρίστης τέχνης,
ἄρτι τῶν τοῦ δημιουργοῦ χειρῶν ἀπηλλαγμένος,
λαμπρὸς καὶ διαυγὴς καὶ πᾶσι τοῖς μέρεσι
παμφαίνων, νήπιος μὲν οὐδένα χρόνον ἐγένετο
οὐδὲ ἀσθενὴς κατὰ τὴν ἀνθρωπίνην τε καὶ θνητὴν
τῆς φύσεως ἀσθένειαν, νέος δὲ καὶ ἀκμάζων
60 εὐθὺς ἀπὸ τῆς ἀρχῆς. ὅτε δὴ καὶ ὁ δημιουργὸς
αὐτοῦ καὶ πατὴρ ἰδὼν ἥσθη μὲν οὐδαμῶς·

with ease moulds and fashions all the rest, pouring about him his essence smooth and soft and easily yielding in every part.

" And having performed his task and brought it to completion, he revealed the existent universe as once more a thing of beauty and inconceivable loveliness, much more resplendent, indeed, than it appears to-day. For not only, I ween, are all other works of craftsmen better and brighter when fresh from the artistic hand of their maker, but also the younger specimens of plants are more vigorous than the old and altogether like young shoots. And indeed animals, too, are charming and attractive to behold right after their birth, not merely the most beautiful among them—colts and calves and puppies—but even the whelps of wild animals of most savage kind. For, on the one hand, the nature of man is helpless and feeble like Demeter's tender grain, but when it has progressed to the full measure of its prime, it is a stronger and more conspicuous creation than any plant at all. However, the entire heaven and universe when first it was completed, having been put in order by the wisest and noblest craft, just released from the hand of the creator, brilliant and translucent and brightly beaming in all its parts, remained helpless for no time at all, nor weak with the weakness that nature ordains for man and other mortal beings, but, on the contrary, was fresh and vigorous from the very beginning. At that time, therefore, the Creator and Father of the World, beholding the work of his hands, was not by any means merely pleased, for that is a lowly

---

[1] καινὰ Reiske : καὶ τὰ.

ταπεινὸν γὰρ ἐν ταπεινοῖς πάθος· ἐχάρη δὲ καὶ
ἐτέρφθη διαφερόντως

ἥμενος Οὐλύμπῳ, ἐγέλασσε δέ οἱ φίλον ἦτορ
γηθοσύνῃ, ὅθ' ὁρᾶτο θεοὺς

τοὺς ἅπαντας ἤδη γεγονότας καὶ παρόντας.

Τὴν δὲ τότε μορφὴν τοῦ κόσμου, λέγω δὲ
τήν τε ὥραν καὶ τὸ κάλλος ἀεὶ καλοῦ ὄντος
ἀμηχάνως, οὐδεὶς δύναιτ' ἂν ἀνθρώπων διανοη-
θῆναι καὶ εἰπεῖν ἀξίως οὔτε τῶν νῦν οὔτε
τῶν πρότερον, εἰ μὴ Μοῦσαί τε καὶ 'Απόλλων
ἐν θείῳ ῥυθμῷ τῆς εἰλικρινοῦς τε καὶ ἄκρας
61 ἁρμονίας. ὅθεν δὴ καὶ ἡμεῖς ἐάσωμεν τὰ νῦν,
ὅσον ἡμῖν δυνατὸν ἐπᾶραι τὸν λόγον οὐκ ὀκνήσαντες.
εἰ δὲ ἀτεχνῶς ὑψηλόν τε καὶ ἐξίτηλον ἀπέβη τὸ
τοῦ λόγου σχῆμα, ὥσπερ οἱ δεινοὶ περὶ τοὺς
ὄρνιθάς φασι τὸν σφόδρα ἄνω χωρήσαντα καὶ
τοῖς νέφεσιν ἐγκρύψαντα αὐτὸν ἀτελῆ τὴν μαντείαν
ποιεῖν, οὐκ ἐμὲ ἄξιον αἰτιᾶσθαι, τὴν δὲ Βορυσθενιτῶν ἀξίωσιν, ὡς τότε ἐκεῖνοι λέγειν προσ-
έταξαν.

experience of lowly beings; nay, he rejoiced and was delighted exceedingly,

> As on Olympus he sat, and his heart did laugh
> For joy, beholding the gods [1]

who were now all created and present before him."

But the form of the universe at that moment—I mean both the bloom and the beauty of that which is for ever ineffably beauteous—no man could conceive and fitly express, neither among men of our time nor among those of former days, but only the Muses and Apollo with the divine rhythm of their pure and consummate harmony. For that reason let us also refrain for the present, now that we have not shirked exalting the myth to the best of our power. And if the form of that myth has turned out to be utterly lofty and indistinct, just as those who are expert in augury declare that the bird which ascends too high into the heavens and hides itself in the clouds makes divination incomplete, still it is not I whom you should blame, but rather the insistence of those men of Borysthenes, because it was they who bade me speak that day.

[1] *Iliad* 21. 389-90.

INDEX

477

INDEX

Athenians, have uninscribed statue of boy, 96.92; pay court to Romans, 108.105; not wealthy, 110.106; careless in conferring honours, 118.116; unworthy of ancient glory, 120.117; example of baseness, 124.119; devoted to gladiatorial shows, 124.121; respect their statues, 128.123; compared with Rhodians, 132.126; 134.129; exalted in the past, 160.157; grant comic licence, 176.6; lived laborious lives, 260.92; devoted to oratory and poetry, 260.93; establish prize for comedy, 280.9; rivalry with Sparta, 382.49; decline in power, 382.50

Athenodorus, governor of Tarsus, 318.48

Athens, erases names of condemned criminals, 88.84; grants exemption from public burdens, 134.130; has sanctuary of Horse and Maiden, 248.78

Attica, has purest honey, 266.97

Augustus, honoured Athenodorus, 318.48

Babylon, 294.23; its walls, 296.24

Bacchants, 228.58; leap about Dionysus, 398.8

Bacis, the oracles of, 390.2

Bactrians, at Alexandria, 210.40; good horsemen, 212.43

Bellerophon, 198.28

Black Sea, visited by Rhodian warships, 106.103

Borysthenes (the city), on the Black Sea, 420.1; suffered decay, 422.4; captured by Getae, *ibid.*; resettled with consent of Scythians, 424.5; its destruction, 424.6; 426.7; devoted to Homer, 428.9; 444.26; 474.61

Borysthenes (the river), 420.1

Brachmanes, are ascetics, 410.22

Busiris, his descendants, 316.47

Byzantium, pays court to Romans, 108.105; its fishing industry, 296.24; has fertile land and a sea teeming with fish, 414.25

Cadmus, 276.4

Caesar ('the second'), 342.7; (Augustus), 360.25

Calliopê, mother of Orpheus, 234.64

Callistratus, young warrior of Borysthenes, 426.7; described, 428.8; fond of Homer, 428.9; 434.14

Calymnians, 54.50

Calypso, visited by Hermes, 192.21

Cappadocians, are numerous, 404.14

Caria, owned by Rhodians, 50.47; yields revenue to Rhodes, 104.101; protected by Celaenae, 404.14

Carion, drunken slave, 262.44

Carpathus, owned by Rhodians, 52.48

Cassandra, not inferior to Aphroditê, 292.21

Castalia, 294.23

Caunians, are foolish, 54.50; compared with Rhodians, 130.124; in slavery to both Rhodes and Rome, 130.125; suffer from fever, 261.92

Celaenae, its law-courts, 404.15; favoured by fortune, 406.17

Centaurs, invented by poets and artists, 198.28; their famous party, 224.53; 262.95

Cercopes, a name applied to Tarsians, 308.38

Chimaeras, invented by poets and artists, 198.28

Cilicia, visited by Rhodian warships, 106.103; compared with Rhodes, 166.163; its citizens in Alexandria, 210.40; 342.7

Circê, transforms men, 326.58

Conon, taunts Alexandrians, 242.72

Corinth, visited by few Rhodian vessels, 106.103; has fountain created by Pegasus, 274.2

Corinthians, watch gladiatorial shows outside the city, 126.121; exalted for a while, 160.157; lived laborious lives, 260.92

Corybantes, 228.58

Cratinus, enjoyed comic licence, 280.9

Crete, its queen enamoured of a bull, 246.77

Croton, desolate, 296.25

Cyclopes, island of, 310.40

Cyclops, a drunken, 262.95

Cydnus, praised, 274.2; 296.25

Cymê, a man of, 94.89

Cynics, have bad influence, 180.9; 232.62; incompetent in practical affairs, 336.2

Cyprus, visited by Rhodian warships, 106.103

478

INDEX

Davus, a slave in comedy, 262.94
Delphi, plundered by Nero, 150.148
Demeter, her "tender grain," 472.59
Deucalion, saved the Greeks, 464.49
Diomedes, his descendants, 316.47
Dionysus, believed identical with Apollo and Helius, 16.11; his theatre the scene of gladiatorial shows, 126.121; the Bacchants leap about him, 398.8
Dorian, a musical mode, 312.42
Dorieus, victor at Olympia, 132.126

Egypt, has colossal statue of Memnon, 96.92; visited by Rhodian warships, 106.103; its slaves fare better than the Rhodians, 116.113; the framework of Alexandria, 204.36; its buildings, 294.23
Egyptian, musician, 268.101
Eleans, their festival, 114.110; impartial administrators, 114.111; have self-respect, 114.112; erect altar to Poseidon Taraxippos, 246.76
Eleusis, its mysteries, 96.92
Ephesians, in charge of great wealth, 58.54; not as wealthy as Rhodians, 60.55; would not mishandle wealth in their keeping, 68.65; quarrel with Smyrna, 382.48
Epidaurus, its statues removed to Rome, 154.151
Ethiopia, source of Nile, 208.38; its people visit Alexandria, 210.40
Eumaeus, accompanies Odysseus, 310.40
Eumelus, his horses, 250.80
Euripides, his Heracles quoted, 262.94; 268.100

Furies, madden Hecuba, 328.59; 328.60

Ganymede, cupbearer of Zeus, 292.21
Getae, border on Scythia, 420.1; captured Borysthenes, 424.4
Graces, believed to be goddesses, 40.37; joined with the Muses, 268.100

Harmodius, his descendants, 134.128; 136.132
Hector, alone defends Troy, 22.17
Hecuba, maddened by Furies, 328.59
Helius, his statue, 16.10; believed identical with Apollo and Dionysus, 16.11; his children, 96.93; father of Pasiphaë, 246.77; his chariot, 454.39; his sacred horse, 458.41; his coursing, 458.42; seen in the horse of Zeus, 460.43; sheds light on horse of Hera, 460.45
Hellas, blotted out, 22.18; exalted by many peoples in the past, 160.157; its grandeur dependant on stones and ruins, 162.160
Hellenes, their honour upheld by Rhodes, 22.18; 22.20; 44.40; 60.55; conservative regarding music, 326.57; misunderstand the term Magi, 456.41; connect cosmic phenomenon with Phaëthon, 464.48; their account of Deucalion, 464.49
Hellespont, 290.19
Helots, can never become Spartans, 454.38; plot against Sparta, ibid.
Hera, "white-armed," 254.85; her horse, 460.45; her wedding with Zeus, 470.56
Heracles, his labours, 20.16; his statue at Thebes, 96.92; his statue at Athens, ibid.; 96.93; on the stage, 262.94; honoured at Tarsus, 316.47
Hermes, visits Calypso, 192.21; a winged god, 192.22
Hesiod, possessed by the Muses, 452.34; did not fitly praise chariot of Zeus, 456.40
Hestia, her horse, 462.46
Hieroson, elderly citizen of Borysthenes, 446.28; 446.29
Hippocoön, 252.84
Hippolatis, Cape, 420.1
Homer, calls the mob cruel, 192.22; a simile of his, 200.30; 208.38; his Thersites, 268.99; praised everything, 282.11; his charm, 380.61; favourite poet in Borysthenes, 428.9; compared with Phocylides, 430.10; devoted more than 5000 lines to a single battle, 432.12; nowhere named himself, ibid.; ranked close to gods, 434.14; 436.17; 444.26; 446.28; 446.29; possessed by the Muses, 452.34; did not do justice to chariot of Zeus, 456.40; quoted: 248.79; 326.58; 396.6
Hypanis (the river Bug), 420.1

479

INDEX

Ida, 292.20; 328.59

Idomeneus, insulted by Ajax, 250.80

Iliad, known by heart in Borysthenes, 430.9; compared with lines from Phocylides, 432.13

Ilium, overcome by citizen of Ithaca, 294.22

India, its fragrant herbs, 300.28; its marvels, 406.18; its products purer, *ibid.*

Indian Ocean, rarely heard of formerly, 296.25

Indians, in Alexandria, 210.40; form limit of Alexander's conquest, 298.26; live happy life, 408.19 to 410.21; more fortunate than people of Celaenae, 412.23

Ionian, musical mode, 312.42

Ismenias, famous piper, 230.61

Ismenus, 276.4

Italians, in Alexandria, 210.40

Italy, 296.25

Ithaca, the man from, 256.88; citizen of, 294.22

Ixion, bound on the wheel, 244.75

Ladon, flows through Arcadia, 296.25

Lemnos, the women of, 320.50

Leonidas, Olympic victor, 132.126

Leptines, the law of, 134.128

Lesbos, 290.19

Libya, its slaves fare better than the Rhodians, 116.113; its people visit Alexandria, 210.40; home of descendants of Busiris, 316.47.

Lyceum, 166.163

Lycia, tributary to Rhodes, 104.101

Lydia, protected by Celaenae, 404.14

Lydians, their sons wear earrings, 174.3; 294.23; 298.26

Macedonia, scene of activity of Orpheus, 234.63

Macedonians, their statues assigned to others, 46.43; sprung from beasts charmed by Orpheus, 236.65; most are manly, *ibid.*; 298.26

Maeander, rises near Celaenae, 404.13

Magi, their secret rites, 454.39; 456.40; meaning of the term, 456.41; maintain for Zeus Nisaean horses, *ibid.*; 458.42; 458.43; 460.45; 462.46; 464.48; accuse Greeks of ignorance, 464.49

Mallus, quarrels with Tarsus, 346.11;

348.14; 350.14; 376.43; claims coast-land, 378.46; resists coming to Tarsus, 380.47

Marsyas, flows through Celaenae, 404.13

Medes, 298.26; 392.3

Megara, its statues removed to Rome, 154.151

Megarians, lived laborious lives, 260.92

Melia, 276.4

Memnon, his colossal statue, 96.92

Memphis, seat of worship of Apis, 184.13; visited by tyrant of Syria, 270.101

Menander, has statue at Athens, 120.116

Metapontum, desolate, 296.25

Minos, wise protector, 372.38

Mithridates, his subjugation, 116.113

Muses, daughters of Zeus, 204.34; called maidens, 226.56; 284.12; instruct the poets, 450.32; 450.33; 452.34; possess Homer and Hesiod, 458.42; 474.60

Myconos, its statues removed to Rome, 154.151

Myndians, compared with Rhodians, 130.124

Myrtilus, 246.75

Mysians, scorned, 162.160

Mytilenê, pays court to Romans, 108.105

Nero, plundered Olympia, Delphi, the Acropolis, Pergamum, but not Rhodes, 150.148; spared treasures of Rhodes, 152.150; not benefited by love of music, 230.60

Nicanor, his statue, 120.116

Nile, praised, 208.38; 210.41; 294.23; 296.24

Nineveh, 432.13; 438.20

Nisaean, horses sacred to Zeus, 456.41

Nymphs, 228.58; associated with Poseidon, 464.49

Ocean, 106.103; 116.113

Odysseus, comes as beggar, 286.15; takes Troy, 290.19; speaks to Eumaeus, 310.40

Odyssey, quoted, 192.21; compared with lines from Phocylides, 432.13

Oenomaüs, 246.75

Olympia, 24.21; Theagenes victorious, 100.95; its crown of olive prized,

INDEX

128.123; compared with Rhodians, 132.126; exalted in the past, 160.157; go to war to sound of the pipe, 230.60; rebuke famous harpist, 236.67; compared with Alexandrians, 240.69; hardy and vigorous, 260.93; cut away strings of lyre, 326.57; compete with Athens, 382.49; have trouble with Aristomenes, 392.3; do not allow Helots to become citizens, 454.38; plotted against by Helots, *ibid.*

Sphinxes, invented by poets and artists, 198.28

Stoics, their definition of the cosmos, 448.30

Sybaris, perished because of luxury, 296.25

Syria, compared with Rhodes, 166.163; its people in Alexandria, 210.40; its tyrant visits Memphis, 270.101

Tarentum, desolate, 296.25

Tarsus, capital of Cilicia, 288.17; 300.29; 302.31; 312.42; 320.50; 320.51; 322.53; its philosophers, 338.3; greatest city in Cilicia, 342.7; 354.20; 356.21–22; its franchise, 358.23; favoured by Augustus, 360.25; tries to compel attendance of people of Mallus, Adana, Aegae for sacrifice and trials, 380.47

Tauric Chersonese, 422.3

Tenedos, 328.59

Thasian, Theagenes the, 100.95; Thasians consult oracle, 100.97

Theagenes, Thasian athlete, 100.95; his statue mistreated, 100.96; 102.97; victim of political jealousy, 102.99

Thebes, has statue by Alcaeus, 96.92; exalted in the past, 160.157

Theophilus, a wise man at Alexandria, 266.97

Thersites, 268.99; "clear-voiced," 284.12

Theseus, his labours, 20.16; his statues, 96.92

Thessaly, desolate, 296.25

Thrace, 234.63; 316.47

Thracians, despised, 160.158; fought Macedonians, 298.26

Thurii, desolate, 296.25

Timotheus, 230.61; his encounter with Spartans, 326.57

Titans, 274.1

Tlepolemus, 96.93

Trojans, their city unfortunate, 256.88; ruined by a horse, *ibid.*; routed by voice of Achilles, 432.13

Troy, captured by Odysseus, 290.19; praised, 292.21

Tyre, 120.116

Tyrtaeus, his songs used by Spartans, 430.10

Xanthus, 292.20

Xerxes, 256.88

Zeus, 16.10; 116.113; aegis-bearing, 204.34; besought by Calliopê, 234.64; preference for Troy, 292.21; his temple at Borysthenes, 436.17; "King," 452.36; "Father," *ibid.*; his home, *ibid.*, his chariot, 454.39; 456.40; his special horse, 460.43; 460.44; 460.45; 468.52; his wedding with Hera, 470.56

Zoroaster, sings of chariot of Zeus, 456.40; goes into the wilderness, *ibid.*; unharmed by sacred fire, *ibid.*; associates with Magi, 456.41